5th
EDITION

The Complete
Blackpowder
Handbook

by Sam Fadala

The Latest Guns and Gear

©2006 Krause Publications

Published by

krause publications
An Imprint of F+W Publications

700 East State Street • Iola, WI 54990-0001
715-445-2214 • 888-457-2873

Our toll-free number to place an order or obtain a free catalog is (800) 258-0929.

Library of Congress Catalog Number: 2006930831

ISBN 13-digit: 978-0-89689-390-0
ISBN 10-digit: 0-89689-390-1

Designed by Donna Mummery
Edited by Ken Ramage

Printed in the United States of America

v

Dedication

For a Few of My Best Friends

Judy
Mom
Nick
Pat
Bob Hodgdon
John Kane

About the Cover

The centerpiece of our cover is Thompson/Center's Pro Hunter 209x50 muzzleloading rifle. Based on the proven Encore action, this 50-caliber stainless steel muzzleloader is fitted with a fluted 28-inch barrel rifled for conical bullets. It uses the #209 primer for ignition and incorporates T/C's new quick-release breech plug that is easily removed by turning it only 90 degrees. Another new feature is the adjustable hammer spur that T/C calls the "swing hammer." Simple yet practical, the hammer spur can be adjusted to the left, right or center position to improve scope clearance and suit the shooter's preference.

The Pro Hunter is fitted with a synthetic buttstock and forend, and is equipped with a synthetic ramrod that incorporates a handy pivoting T-handle; T/C calls it the Power Rod. The buttstock includes a buffering system designed to reduce felt recoil by 43 percent, according to Thompson/Center.

A number of T/C accessories accompany the rifle. These are (top, clockwise): Number 13 Bore Cleaner is an all-natural bore cleaner that cleans quickly. Moving along, we come to the Rip-Cord Speed Loader, an unique item that carries a second propellant charge and up to two #209 primers. Clip the carabiner to something sturdy—belt, suspenders etc.—and your reload is only a quick pull away.

Next is a handy device that fits over the end of your ramrod, providing a better grip and a more comfortable way to seat a tight projectile. Called the Flex Priming Palm Saver, this device carries up to four #209 primers and fits nicely in pouch or pocket.

A modern in-line ignition muzzleloader needs a modern projectile system, and T/C has it. Named the Shock Wave and designed for the matching sabot, the bullet has a tapered copper jacket and lead core as well as a polymer spire tip for a flatter trajectory and accelerated expansion upon impact. Available in three bullet weights in 50-caliber, and one bullet weight in 45-caliber, the Shock Wave system includes both the bullet and mating sabot.

Finally, T/C's cleaning and seasoning patches, saturated with Natural Lube Bore Butter and compatible with the company's other cleaning products, are good to use after a thorough cleaning to protect your muzzleloader and 'season' the bore. They work great for field use, too.

Thompson/Center has been at the forefront of America's modern muzzleloading pursuit from the very beginning. In fact, T/C's Hawken Rifle, introduced in 1970 and still produced today, has been a major influence in developing our broad muzzleloading market.

Today the T/C line of muzzleloaders and accessories is very different from those early years. In-line ignition, new propellants and primers, specialized conical bullets and delivery sabot systems, an array of accessories—all are found in Thompson/Center's product lineup.

For more information, contact Thompson/Center Arms, P.O. Box 5002, Rochester, NH 03866; call 603-332-2394 or visit their Web site: www.tcarms.com

Contents

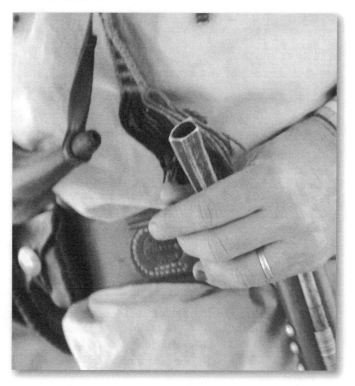

Introduction to the Fifth Edition

Figuring out exactly why blackpowder shooting thrives into the 21st century is a little bit like trying to lasso a whirlwind. After all, we now have the most accurate modern firearms ever developed and sold to shooters anywhere, any time, along with factory ammo that puts previous fodder in the shade, plus all those plump short and supershort rounds. Scope sights eclipse those of the past. And super-modern shooting tools abound. So why blackpowder? My take on the reason for the continued success of the sport is the fact that a

In spite of the finest cartridge ammunition in the world fired from the most accurate guns ever, blackpowder guns continue to soar in popularity.

hunter has to own a muzzleloader before he or she is allowed to take part in one of the many special blackpowder-only hunts offered each year just about everywhere. But that does not account for silhouette excitement as enthusiasts launch heavy lead bullets downrange at metallic cutouts representing *gallina, javelina, guajolote, and borrego*—chicken, peccary, turkey, and ram to English-speaking readers. Nor does it explain the interest in Cowboy Action Shooting, where arms from the blackpowder era are fired upon targets by modern day gunslingers. Likewise the continu-

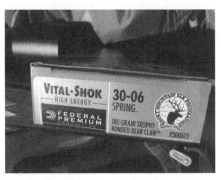

Federal found a way to reach original 300 H&H Magnum ballistics from 30-06 ammunition, perhaps with a new triple-base powder. The 21st century shooter/hunter has the option of both smokeless powder and blackpowder. Thousands do just that—enjoying both.

ing interest in the rendezvous, where men, women, and children emulate the gear, clothing, guns, and ways of the 19th century mountain man.

The Fifth Edition continues to put the emphasis on shooting. That's where the action is, and no doubt about it. Factually, the modern muzzleloader has taken over, to the chagrin of purists and delight of a few million hunters who go for big game with the smokepole. At the same time, I was surprised to learn of recent brisk sales in non-replicas and

even replicas. While there is good reason to continue relying on sidelocks, because they have worked for centuries and still do, shooter ingenuity and Yankee enterprise have created a mad run to the high-tech muzzleloader. The race will not cross the finish line for a long time because the garden of invention is continually watered with new ideas. And so we have carloads of muzzleloaders that don't look anything like the long guns carried by Dan'l Boone and Davy Crockett, nor the half-stock plains rifles of Jim Bridger and Kit Carson. These (mostly) rifles look nothing like the originals. Furthermore, and perhaps more importantly, they don't behave the same. The modern shooter has wide choice. He or she can look for guns that range from replicas, as well as originals that remain available in surprisingly good numbers. But most will go for the in-line charcoal-burner that loads from the muzzle, one shot at a time, qualifying the hunter and the rifle (despite resembling a bolt-action cartridge rifle) for those special blackpowder hunts. In short, there is room for everyone in the 21st century world of blackpowder shooting, be it accomplished with

Special blackpowder-only hunts, especially for whitetail deer, bring thousands of hunters into the field annually. This fine buck was taken with a Knight modern muzzleloader.

The blackpowder silhouette game retains its popularity. Here, a younger shooter introduces moisture to the bore of his silhouette rifle, which happens to be an original Remington Rolling Block.

guns that great grandfather would find familiar, to space age models that are easily mistaken for 270s and 30-06s, except for the ramrod hanging beneath the barrel.

The goal of the Fifth remains the same as the Fourth, Third, Second, and First—to provide the reader/shooter with solid information based on testing, not reading monkey bones, Nordic runes, or tea leaves. To that end, the Fifth is crammed with more hard data than

previous editions. The text is a bit longer than past editions because it has to be. The author plied his modest writing skill in attempting to trim superfluous words here and there to render the reading faster and smoother. But for every word cut another had to be added for clarity and to present more information about the ever-changing muzzleloader and blackpowder cartridge-shooting scene.

Old-time colors remain bright on this canvas. The guns of yesteryear are neither forgotten nor left out. A friend with artistic ways says that a lovely woman possesses the most beautiful form on earth. I won't argue with that, but second has to be my custom ball-shooting muzzleloading rifle I call Number 47, the 47th built by Dennis Mulford. Meanwhile, I have come to appreciate the tremendously interesting development called the modern muzzleloader. I have shot many of them and have yet to come up with a failure. They are accurate, powerful, and deadly, these in-lines, and also the Markesbery Outer Line, so called because it angles fire from nipple to powder charge in the breech on a 45-degree angle.

He goes by "Chucky" and he happens to be the editor of Shoot! magazine, the handsome and informative periodical on Cowboy Action Shooting. Here, he demonstrates good shooting form with a blackpowder handgun.

I took a little time out from muzzleloader hunting to go with a 30-06. Any gunwriter on the continent who didn't grasp the fact that the world's most popular big game cartridge turned a hundred in 2006 was asleep in the hay. That being over, including

Trader Row at Rendezvous, a place where many fine guns and gear can be found, along with myriad implements for the blackpowder shooting game.

The emphasis for the Fifth Edition is shooting, shooting, and more shooting. Here, a marksman takes aim with a Knight modern muzzleloader.

a run to Africa and a Cape buffalo by special permission, along with a huge Livingstone eland and other trophies, all with a 30-06 rifle, I'm back in the blackpowder saddle. Every tag I put in for this coming season will be smokepole only. I'm loading up No. 47 with prospects of putting a few 54-caliber round balls out of the muzzle, but in deference to the fact that most blackpowder hunting (by far) will be carried out with modern-type guns, I'll go that way as well. I've learned to appreciate the looks of some of these rifles and shotguns, even a pistol or two, while never forsaking my true and first love: a Pennsylvania-Kentucky style long arm. The Fifth delves into the cracks and corners of development—all kinds—in the world of charcoal burning. This includes the hot new rifles capable of terrific big game authority, as well as new propellants and even a few new accouterments (tools) that match the blackpowder shooting game.

The chronograph remains my favorite tool for testing blackpowder shooting theories. However, I have taken advantage of other resources in coming up with what I hope can be called *facts*. Special thanks goes to the Hodgdon Powder Company for running pressure tests that I could not otherwise accomplish. I do have access to a pressure gauge that attaches to the barrel, a device any shooter can apply to his or her rifle to learn about pressure. But I felt more comfortable relying on ballistics engineers who not only have the savvy to gather accurate data, but also the high-tech tools on hand to get the best information in the shortest amount of time. Also, I referred to modern guns by way of comparison to clarify points to shooters who have spent their lifetimes, literally, firing smokeless powder cartridges. As a brief example, check out Chapter 3, where describing how more mass in front of a powder charge produces greater pressure. In using this crossover, the 30-06 was selected with IMR-4064 powder, showing how the charges of that specific propellant were reduced as cartridge weight escalated. And why? Because as the bullet got heavier, pressure per powder charge rose, and so the powder charge was consequently reduced to maintain safe pressures in those 30-06 loads.

While paying proper attention to the modern muzzleloader, in-line or Outer Line, the sidelock is far from ignored. There is a full chapter on non-replicas, another on custom front-loaders. The topics of rifling twist, facts about the cloth ball patch, blackpowder pistol, cap 'n' ball revolver, shotgun, squirrel rifle, how to load for success and safety—it's all here. Blackpowder ballistics, how to use the chronograph to promote best loads, and data on the latest blackpowder from GOEX are included. Notes on Triple Seven are presented describing its unique clean-up feature with nothing more than water on a patch. Not left out are those important perennial topics on chemicals for shooting, maintenance, smoothbore management, and troubleshooting the muzzleloader. The rendezvous is not forgotten, in spite of the modern muzzleloader takeover, nor is rendezvous shooting, blackpowder knives and tomahawks, running the best possible cast bullets, rifled musket range and power, along with hunting talk and tips. The old-time gunmaker is honored, as are those who build muzzleloaders today. Snipers of the Civil War receive mention, as well as ivory hunters of 19th century Africa.

The replica blackpowder firearm remains healthy in the 21st century. Here, Sam shoots one of his favorite replicas, a Pedersoli Remington Rolling Block in 38-55 Winchester.

The modern muzzleloader has evolved into an excellent firearm in its own right without respect for personal preference. This Austin & Halleck rifle is a solid representation of the finest among the breed.

All phases of blackpowder shooting remain popular with the front-loader leading the pack primarily due to the special hunts allowed across North America. Here, a hunter takes a shot with a Knight modern muzzleloader.

The modern muzzleloader of bolt-action design closely resembles its smokeless powder brother, but resemblance is where the comparison ends. The modern muzzleloader "loads from up front" one shot at a time. This is the Ultimate, an extremely powerful bolt-action design muzzleloader.

The guns of yesteryear are far from forgotten. Fadala holds an original Martini-Henry from Atlanta Cutlery.

Meanwhile, the reader is treated to a good-sized Directory so that he or she does not have to go through dozens of catalogs or on-line searches to find companies catering to the needs and wants of a charcoal-burning fan. Blackpowder shooting associations earn a place in the Fifth, along with a host of useful data presented in tables on shot sizes, and choke dimensions for shotguns, plus ballistic data, and a listing of books related to shooting old-time as well as modern-style blackpowder guns, be they loaded from the front or with a shotshell or cartridge. The beginner should pick out first those chapters pertaining to the basics of shooting blackpowder guns: choosing the right ones, learning how they function, the all-important topic of safety, accouterments (tools) and how to use them, how to load properly for optimum results, as well as sights and sighting in, with tips on working with "the rainbow" of blackpowder trajectory. The veteran will continue to find topics to enlarge his or her knowledge—about the pyrotechnics of powders and other subjects common to advanced interests. There is much new data in the Fifth, including information on the latest blackpowder cartridges that have found their way into those fine breech-loading rifles,

along with notes on the big thumpers that have crept back onto the shooting range and into the hunting field—true big bores noted in bore size, not caliber (how about a 4-bore firing a 1,750-grain bullet at 1,500 feet-per-second? – Ouch!)

There remains a great deal of enthusiasm expressed by those in the business of making and/or selling blackpowder guns and gear to a growing number of smokepole addicts. Val Forgett, whose father took the Big 5 in Africa with a 58-caliber, and who is now the new captain at the Navy Arms Company, pointed out that replica muzzleloaders have actually gained considerable impetus in the past half-decade to the point that dealers have taken keen notice. "Dealers who choose brands that respect lines of distribution

Like them. Hate them. Or remain neutral. The modern muzzleloader is here to stay and it's better than ever from various companies. This is a Remington Omega, absolutely unique in design, as are its contemporaries from Lyman, CVA, Thompson/Center, and other companies.

Arguably the most beautiful rifle design of any era, the Pennsylvania-Kentucky long rifle is not forgotten today. This is the Pedersoli Flintlock Kentucky Rifle.

are sure to be profitable," Forgett promises. Brian Herrick of Savage Arms explained what his company had in mind with the development of the only muzzleloader, which, at the time of the Fifth, is approved safe with judicious amounts of specific smokeless powders. He said, "Savage sees a bright future in the muzzleloading market. Our muzzleloader sales are strong and continue to rise dramatically."

Eric Brooker of Thompson/Center pointed out that, "Last year (2005) was the best in the history of T/C," adding that, "Today we see a shift towards premium products within the muzzleloading arena. A lot of entry-level hunters are learning that muzzleloading is not complicated. Therefore, it is no longer intimidating. It's actually fun. So why not start shooting a muzzleloader this year?" Principals at Hodgdon Powder Company add that the advent of Pyrodex Pellets and Triple Seven Pellets has made shooting muzzleloaders even easier. Figures show that a full 40 percent of U.S. deer hunters have hunted with a muzzleloader. Significantly, 70 percent of these hunters hail from 15 states. The reason that these 15 states prevail in numbers of blackpowder-shooting deer hunters is glaringly evident. These states offer more and better blackpowder-only hunting seasons than other states. As more game departments get on board with special muzzleloader big-game hunts, that 40 percent figure is bound to rise. I like what Eric Brooker came up with when

Although the author's first love is the smokepole, Sam took some time out to hunt Africa with a 30-06, including a Cape buffalo (by special permission), normally requiring a 375-caliber and larger. Enjoying blackpowder shooting does not mean that modern firearms must be put away.

Any game can be taken with the proper muzzleloader, although backup is required on animals that "shoot back," such as this Cape buffalo taken by Jim Gefroh with a big-bore muzzleloader of his own make. Professional hunter Johan Wolvaardt, who specializes in blackpowder hunts as well as hunts with modern arms, backed Jim up.

The custom blackpowder firearm, mainly in rifle form, continues to thrive in many different forms. Jim Gefroh builds custom blackpowder rifles for big game—really big game—including elephants. Here he displays one of his big-bore muzzleloaders.

States that offer special blackpowder-only seasons attract many hunters of all ages and both genders. Every deer taken with a muzzleloader is a trophy. This one was dropped with a Parker Productions bullet.

he said, "The proliferation of deer in some states is so great that it's no longer a challenge to many hunters. Converting to muzzleloaders picks up that challenge." This is true, but the user-friendly modern muzzleloader, along with pelletized powder and easy-to-use tools, makes the challenge welcome, not formidable.

The wishes of author and publisher of the Fifth are simply that the reader finds an empty notch on the bookshelf for this book, with our hope that the covers will become tattered and the pages worn from use.

Sam Fadala, Wyoming

BLACKPOWDER TRUE AND FALSE

Can You Pass the Test?

Colorful myths and near superstition thrived in pre-science days when blackpowder was the only powder in town, and simply known as "gunpowder." That many of these falsehoods survived into the 20th and even 21st century run along the border of amazing. And yet, we're still hearing—and reading—sworn statements about the reality of blackpowder shooting that make *Alice in Wonderland* read like a scientific documentary. On the other hand, by far the vast majority of data from yesteryear stands solid as a boulder. Furthermore, there are blackpowder truths that sound fictional, but they are factual. See how will you do on this short blackpowder true and false. You probably know a lot more about the realities of shooting the smokepole, be it an original 19th-century fowler or the latest in-line boomer, than most shooters of the golden era of the sport knew so long ago.

THE QUESTIONS

1. At last, we have true non-corrosive blackpowder substitutes that clean up like smokeless powder.

2. The New Triple Seven powder from the Hodgdon Powder Company wipes away perfectly with nothing more than a little water and a few patches.

3. The powerful Ultimate in-line muzzleloaders that are allowed four Pyrodex Pellets for an equivalent 200 grains volume can be sighted in for a flat 150 yards with no holdover on deer-sized and larger big game at over 200 yards.

4. Blackpowder cannot develop over 25,000 psi (pounds per square inch) pressure, the excess powder in the bore simply blows harmlessly out of the muzzle.

5. We're certain that separated powder and bullet charges where bullet or shot does not rest firmly upon the powder charge—known as a short-start—can cause a walnut (bulge) in a barrel, or even a rupture.

6. One perfectly legitimate method of determining an ideal hunting load in a blackpowder rifle is shooting over snow, because unburned granules of powder will be seen in contrast against the white carpet on the ground.

7. The round ball shooting patch is important because one of its main functions is to seal expanding powder gases behind the projectile.

8. Since blackpowder is essentially the same formulation, different *brands* have no effect upon how a firearm behaves in terms accuracy and power.

9. FFFg blows shotgun patterns.

10. Old-time, 19th-century blackpowder guns had just as much power potential as modern in-line rifles, sometimes a lot more power than we're getting today.

11. The amazing one-mile shot during the American Civil War is just a colorful story, but it never happened.

12. Up close, a round lead ball is just as efficient in dropping big game as a modern bullet.

13. The in-line muzzleloader has taken over at the expense of replicas, as well as long rifles and other 19th-century and early firearms. It is predicted that soon only in-line muzzleloaders will be sold.

14. Compression upon the blackpowder charge can affect how a muzzleloader shoots, especially in terms of accuracy.

15. A blackpowder shotgun can be loaded volume-for-volume with shot and powder using the same measure at the same setting.

THE ANSWERS

1. *FALSE*. There is no truly non-corrosive replica blackpowder on the market today. Many formulas have been tested and some muzzleloader powders have been called non-corrosive, but they were not. A truly non-corrosive powder allows the shooter to put his gun away for a day or two, or under low humidity conditions much longer, with no harm. Consider that many 22-rimfire guns are fired and left uncleaned for quite some time without harm. Don't do this with any muzzleloader or blackpowder cartridge firearm using any powder that we have today. These powders are hygroscopic—with a g not a d—which means they attract moisture, which in turn can promote rust.

2. *TRUE*. After extensive testing on my own I concluded that after shooting Hodgdon's Triple Seven powder a gun could be cleaned satisfactorily with nothing but water. Make it hot water (hot from the tap is OK) to heat the metal, thereby encouraging evaporation of any moisture that may remain in the bore or inside the blackpowder cartridge case.

3. *TRUE*. Yes, some of the new in-line rifles that are allowed a full 150 grains volume of blackpowder or blackpowder substitute, such as Pyrodex and Triple Seven, can be sighted in for 150 yards on the button, especially with racy bullets such as the SSB (Special Saboted Bullet) from the Buffalo Bullet Company with its spitzer profile and high ballistic coefficient.

4. *FALSE*. This unfortunate tale survived into modern times. One otherwise astute blackpowder shooter argued that he knew blackpowder loads could never harm a gun because pressures could not exceed 25,000 psi. "The excess just blows out of the muzzle," he assured. No way. Back in 19th century England, two scientists got 100,000 psi with blackpowder. The U.S. Navy repeated this pressure level in tests, also in the 19th century. Furthermore, muzzleloaders today have failed because of excessive blackpowder charges. Abide by the maximum rating the manufacturer puts on his gun and do not go over that powder charge.

5. *TRUE*. We are certain that the short-started load, also known as the separated charge, can bulge a barrel or even cause fragmentation. But no one has proved exactly why this happens, although it was known many years ago with warnings to always drive the bullet or shot charge fully down upon the powder resting in the breech of the gun. We're also told to leave no air space in the blackpowder cartridge between the base of the bullet and the top of the powder charge in the case.

6. *FALSE*. This old wives' tale has been around for a very long time. It lasts because it sounds good. Unfortunately, it's not correct practice. That's because half and even more than half of a blackpowder charge does *not* go from solid to gas during combustion. Shooting over snow will show dark flecks that represent solids. A chronograph, on the other hand, does show the law of diminishing returns, where adding more powder creates more smoke and recoil, but not much more velocity.

7. *FALSE*. The round ball shooting patch is extremely important because it serves many useful functions including the safety factor of holding the round bullet down upon the powder charge where it belongs. However, it does not function as a true gasket, sealing hot gases behind the projectile. After all, it is only a bit of cloth. High-speed movie cameras have captured the patched bullet emerging from the muzzle of a rifle *following* an expulsion of smoke. In other words, smoke from burning powder went past the patched ball in the bore and got ahead of the ball. If the patch were a true gasket that would not happen.

8. *FALSE*. Yes, blackpowder is basically the same formulation of 75/15/10: 75 percent saltpeter, 15 percent charcoal, and 10 percent sulfur. But there are numerous factors involved in creating blackpowder that cause significant differences in performance. Just looking at a sample of blackpowder on a white sheet of paper reveals a lot about its nature, including uniformity of granulation, shape of kernel, coating, and other factors.

9. *FALSE*. This one is false because of the reason given for FFFg blowing shotgun patterns. I have gotten blown patterns with "holes" from FFFg loads. Supposedly, FFFg blows patterns because it drives the wad system and powder charge too fast. Quite unlikely. It may be, however, that a hot charge of FFFg burns through or otherwise damages the over-powder wad, perhaps to the extent that the base wad supporting the shot charge is disrupted, which would cause a problem with

patterns. Stick to Fg or FFg in the muzzleloading shotgun. These granulations work fine.

10. *TRUE*. While our modern muzzleloaders are allowed a great deal of powder with heavy bullets, the front-loader remains basically a barrel with an avenue for ignition. Old-style round ball-shooting muzzleloaders from October Country, including a 4-bore (each round ball weighing 1,750 grains) have immense power. The 19th-century William Moore 2-bore rifle fired a 3,500-grain round ball at 1,500 fps for an energy rating just short of 17,500 foot-pounds. Compare that to the 458 Winchester "elephant" rifle at 5,000 foot-pounds.

11. *FALSE*. The story has its flaws. It goes that a Northern captain kills a Southern general at a range of one mile, 187 feet—calculated (somehow) at the time the shot was made. Names are given. The Yankee captain was John Metcalf III. The unfortunate victim was General Lainhart. The captain practices the shot elsewhere at the exact calculated distance to the general's tent. Now he knows just how to aim. A lieutenant stands by with a stopwatch to call elapsed time from rifle going off to bullet arrival. And wham! The poor general is dropped like a sack of wheat. But when Norris K. Maxwell ran the tale down he could find no military record of a Captain John Metcalf, nor did the Military Academy show a General Lainhart. Proof is lacking. But never say never. Right?

12. *TRUE*. This may sound ridiculous because the round ball is so inefficient compared to the conical, easily losing 50 percent of its initial velocity after going only 100 yards. On the other hand, get that ball big enough and it's deadly. Up close a large-sized round ball will drop any animal on earth, as proved by 19th-century ivory hunters. A tip—aim the round ball for the "boiler room" (chest region). It will flatten out and impart its energy in that area. Meanwhile, direct big lead conical bullets more into the shoulder region, because sometimes these heavyweight lead missiles don't open up all that well in softer tissue.

13. *FALSE*. This is one of those gray areas where facts weave themselves into a flawed fabric. The in-line muzzleloader has taken over in sales, but there are numerous replicas on the market. If blackpowder cartridge guns are included, the numbers soar with Remington Rolling Blocks, Sharps, and a boat-load of revolvers, most of them of Colt derivation. As for fine long guns, there are few like the Austin & Halleck 50-caliber rifle—a handsome and accurate long rifle with a timeworn pedigree.

14. *TRUE*. I don't worry about precisely repeated pressure on the loading rod or ramrod for hunting. But consistent ramrod or loading rod pressure has to deliver consistent pressure upon bullet or shot charge, which in turn applies consistent pressure on the powder charge underneath the bullet or shot. For precise shooting and testing, I do insist upon maintained pressure upon the powder charge. The Kadooty is a loading rod built to supply the same pressure on the powder charge for every shot. I have compiled data with the chronograph that shows more consistency with consistent (lower standard deviations) with consistent load pressure.

15. *TRUE*. This one sounds like a tale told by an idiot, but it is not. The very same measure can be used for both powder and shot when creating blackpowder shotgun loads. For example, a measure can be set at 100 to deliver 100-grains volume Fg or FFg powder down the bore of a 12-gauge shotgun. Then the same measure at the same unchanged setting is used to provide the shot charge. This method of loading the shotgun creates a good balance between powder and shot, although it does not excuse overloading either shot or powder.

How did you do? Think about it. Muzzleloaders and blackpowder cartridge guns require more knowledge and experience than demanded of cartridge/shotshell guns. Buy a box of factory ammo and insert the proper cartridge or shell into the gun and fire away. Meanwhile, the muzzleloader insists upon hands-on attention with every load prepared on the spot, while putting good blackpowder cartridges together demands plenty of know-how, not only in preparing the round, but also in managing the gun, especially for long-range silhouette shooting.

YOUR BLACKPOWER GUNS

All kinds of game, big and small, can be hunted with blackpowder firearms, including the feral hog.

Reasons were given in the Introduction for joining the several million shooters who have discovered the intense interest created by shooting blackpowder muzzleloaders and cartridge guns, along with the distinct advantage of belonging to that group of hunters eligible for "primitive" hunts. Now comes an additional thrill—along with small and big game hunting, waterfowl, wild turkey, plus rendezvous adventure shooting, comes Cowboy Action Shooting, in which old-time guns come to life again in a shooting game of speed and accuracy under "Old West" conditions. While smoke-less powder is allowed for these games, there are special blackpowder-only events, as well as myriad Cowboy Action shooters who prefer the true old way of the west with a proper plume of smoke spewing from the muzzles of their guns. Because of the different blackpowder applications now available to the 21st century shooter, various firearm types are necessary. Big-game hunting comes first in our list because, after all, despite all of the other wonderful applications of guns of old, it is the lure of taking deer, elk, antelope—any big game—with a muzzleloader that leads all others.

Cowboy Action Shooting has captured the imagination of thousands, including those who prefer "doing it with blackpowder."

Big Game Blackpowder Guns
The Modern Muzzleloader

The modern muzzleloader is now the number one choice of big-game hunters in North America. These are the in-lines, as described in their own Chapter 8, along with the Outer-Line, which marches to its own drummer with a 45-degree angle from flame of ignition to a waiting powder charge in the breech. Among these rifles there are two major branches. For lack of a better description, I separate the two branches as modern and ultra-modern, the modern muzzleloader having all of the major appointments of the family: in-line or direct ignition, familiar style, removable breech plug for "back-end" cleaning, scope-ready, contemporary trigger, sling-friendly, recoil pad—and so forth. The ultra-modern example carries each of these, plus a slightly greater resemblance and sometimes even handling of the most advanced cartridge-shooting rifle. Examples of this clan are rifles built essentially on the plan of the company's cartridge rifle, such as the Savage 110ML-II, Rem-

There are modern muzzleloaders and ultra-modern muzzleloaders that so closely resemble cartridge-shooting firearms that it's difficult to tell them apart at first glance. This Knight rifle might be considered an ultra-modern muzzleloader.

ington's 700ML, and Ruger's 77/50. See Chapter 8 for a more in-depth look at the modern muzzleloader.

The major advantage of the modern muzzleloader is ease of use, due to familiarity. Except for loading from the "front end," these rifles carry most of the appointments normally found on the familiar smokeless powder rifle. Consider the Remington Model 700ML. Except for the ramrod in its under-barrel pipes (thimbles) the blackpowder version of this rifle is difficult to distinguish from its parent, the Model 700. The only disadvantage of the modern muzzleloader is the fact that if a hunter wants to emulate old-time shooters, this is not the rifle type of choice.

The Non-Replica Big Game Muzzleloading Rifle

This rifle type also enjoys its own chapter (6) and so the goal here is relating the simple fact that the non-replica is often chosen because it is usually not as expensive to purchase as some, certainly not all, modern front-loaders. While the non-replica does not include all of the familiar features of the modern muzzleloader, on the other hand, it is generally easier to carry in the field than an original or replica, often with integral sling swivel eyes ready to go, and it is readily scoped. Another good feature of the non-replica is ruggedness. Not that the modern or replica muzzleloader is a pansy. Each is field-tough. But non-

The modern muzzleloader rules in blackpowder big game hunting, as with this lever-action rifle from Austin & Halleck employed to take a fine whitetail buck. Only the ramrod resting below the barrel gives this rifle away as a muzzleloader.

The major difference between the modern muzzleloader and all other types is total familiarity. These guns look like and handle like cartridge firearms. These Austin & Halleck rifles are prime examples of the clan.

The rifle used here to dispatch the hyena is two things in one—it is a custom rifle built by Jim Gefroh (holding the rifle), but it is also a non-replica that does not exactly copy any rifle from the past.

This Pedersoli Hawken rifle is close enough to the original lines and overall function of the 19th century plains rifle to qualify as a replica.

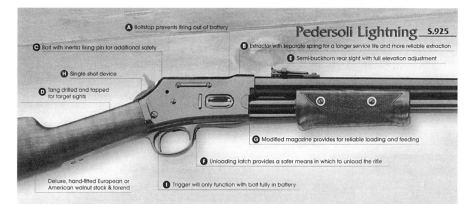

Another fine replica becomes available to the 21st century blackpowder shooter. It's the Colt Lightning offered by several companies. This one is from Pedersoli. While a replica in all major respects, the Pedersoli Colt rifle also embodies several important improvements not only in function, but also in safety.

replicas have a plainness that renders them especially field-worthy.

Replica and Original Muzzleloader

Lumping these together works because a true replica is, after all, a fairly decent copy of an original from the past. The disadvantage of the replica/original big game rifle is its general style. Most are not scope-happy. Mounting a scope means tapping and drilling. Furthermore, a glass sight is almost out of place on many of these rifles, although a few shooters of the 19th century and earlier did affix scopes to their rifles.

The original in the Pennsylvania/ Kentucky long rifle style is just that— long—generally with a barrel a lot longer than modern or non-replica muzzleloaders. The plains rifle of Hawken fame has a shorter barrel, but still over 30 inches in most cases. Weight-wise, not all, but most originals, caliber-for-caliber, were heavier than modern or non-replica rifles.

The grand advantage to the replica or original big-game muzzleloader is the joy of truly taking a step back in time, shooting the way our forebears actually shot. Viewed as either plus or negative, the replica/original is also more challenging than the modern or non-replica, especially where weatherproofing and after-shooting cleaning are concerned. Add to this list what I call in-the-spirit guns, especially rifles that are not true replicas of anything from the past, but embody the same general handling and style. See Chapter 7.

The Big Game Pistol

The late Al Georg was a gifted handgunner-hunter. He got away with, and I use that term advisedly, taking big game with a cap 'n' ball revolver that carried no more authority than a well-loaded 38 Special. All in all, however, the blackpowder revolver, even in the big 44-caliber Walker, is more at home on smaller game and especially for the great enjoyment it offers in any type of target shooting, from plinking to high-

The Lyman Plains Pistol, available in 54-caliber, can take big game in the hands of a patient, practiced, big game hunter. While the energy rating is comparatively low, at close range the large-caliber ball is capable of good penetration.

and 50-caliber bore. The Harper's Ferry Pistol drives a 570-grain Lyman bullet at about 700 fps. The Lyman 54-caliber Plains Pistol pushes a round ball at over 900 fps, while the Encore drives a 350-grain bullet at almost 1,500 fps for a muzzle energy over 1,350 foot-pounds at 50 yards.

The Rifled Musket

Overlooked for the most part, the rifled musket is extremely big-game worthy. While it falls into the replica lineup, I have given this rifle its own place because it deserves it due to uniqueness. My Navy Arms Whitworth rifled musket can send a 490-grain missile away at 1,300 fps. For reasons unknown to me, Navy Arms allowed a stronger blackpowder charge in its very similar Volunteer Rifle, also 45-calber, but with a 490-grain Lyman bullet leaving the muzzle at close to 1,475 fps. Bullets of 45-caliber

grade competition. On the other hand, there are blackpowder pistols suited to big-game hunting. These are big bores shooting heavy bullets. From the old days, there is the 58-caliber Harper's Ferry 1855 pistol. While velocity is low, this handgun propels a bullet in the 500-grain class that carries close-range deep penetration capability. The Lyman Plains Pistol is also big-game worthy, especially in 54-caliber. Another pistol of big game authority is Thompson/Center's Encore 209/50, the numbers signifying a No. 209 shotgun primer

The rifled musket replica is a good big-game rifle—rugged and dependable with accuracy and power. It makes a good choice for forest and brush big game hunting where a rifle has to be tough, but it is also of historical interest and just plain fun to shoot. This one is from the Navy Arms Company.

The flintlock big-game rifle escalates the challenge a notch, but is also entirely field-worthy when properly loaded. This one from Pedersoli is in the Jaeger style (early German origin). Notice the sling swivels for ease of carrying in the hunting field.

The double-barrel blackpowder shotgun is essentially a replica of shotguns past. This one from Pedersoli is 12-gauge percussion and capable of firing a heavy payload of shot in front of a stout powder charge. It is also a good choice for blackpowder shotgun competition.

in the 500-grain realm "carry up" well and the two rifled muskets noted here are worthy of big game at 200 yards and even beyond for well-practiced big-game hunters. After all, these rifles develop the same, and even a bit more, downrange energy than the Winchester 45-90, which was considered "big medicine" for big game in its era.

Flintlock Big Game Rifles

The method of ignition has almost nothing to do with big game authority, and there are many flinters entirely capable of dropping any form of wild animal, including the massive elephant.

Shotguns and Smoothbores

Each has its own chapter in the book, 12 and 36 respectively, and each is big game worthy due to large bore and big bullet, not higher velocity. Big bore is too small a term to describe some of the smoothbores of the distant past. These were elephant guns capable of driving bullets as heavy as one-half pound at velocities not too far off the speed of sound. They were big thumpers, as Chapter 37 of the same title explains. Meanwhile, the common 12-gauge blackpowder shotgun can throw a round ball in the 500-grain class at about 900 fps, depending of course on allowable powder charge.

Not a lot of muzzle energy, you say, and you're right. But one fat ball in the boiler room of even a moose at close range spells meat in the pot. I tested a Pedersoli side-by-side slug shotgun that put a 494-grain round ball into the atmosphere at over 1,200 fps—bang, bang—two shots faster than you can say Jack Robinson. At 100 yards, this shotgun produced right at the 1,000 foot-pound mark so often gauged as adequate for deer-size game.

The Blackpowder Cartridge Rifle

Leaving out the blackpowder cartridge pistol or revolver, we go directly to the rifle. Two breeds are evident: single-shots and lever-actions; the first type in Chapter 31, the second in Chapter 32.

The blackpowder cartridge rifle has earned a prominent place in 21st century shooting. Many are replicas from the 19th century, such as this Winchester 44-40 rifle.

While Chapter 31 deals with the Remington Rolling Block and the Sharps, there were other fine rifles cut from the same fabric, such as the Ballard. The thrust of the single-shot blackpowder cartridge was, as with muzzleloaders, big bullets from big bores. As one example only, consider the 45-120 Sharps, which punched a long 45-caliber bullet downrange well enough to win target matches out to 1,000 yards, even with a less-than 120-grain powder charge (45-100-550). The lever guns were big game-worthy on two counts—big bullets again, but also repeat firing. The latter made rifles of comparatively puny power capable of taking big game, the 44-40 Winchester being a good example. Normally driving a 200-grain 43-caliber bullet below the 1,000 foot-per-second mark, the low-power cartridge managed to put down considerable big game, sometimes with second and third bullets striking home. A par-

The Sharps rifle could never be left out of the picture. Today's rifle shooters have the same love affair with the Sharps, as did 19th century hunters.

The Remington Rolling Block is another excellent choice for the blackpowder silhouette shooter, but also for the hunter as well as modern marksman who simply wants to enjoy shooting a rifle style from the past. This is Sam's Pedersoli 38-55 Rolling Block.

Marlin's lever-action rifles have never moved entirely away from the original design, the original design was that good. Today, Marlin rifles are available in a multitude of models including the 336-type action capable of handling any blackpowder cartridge, including the 38-55 and 45-70.

ticular favorite of my own in this niche is the 38-55 Winchester chambered in my Marlin 336 Cowboy. The 255-grain bullet doesn't seem to know that it isn't all that strong. It just keeps on bowling the deer over.

All Others

I know from experience that trying to include each and every type of firearm in any specific category is difficult at best. What about matchlocks, for example? Can't a matchlock rifle take big game? I suppose so, but then we might have to include the firestick.

The sun shines brightly on this Wyoming cottontail rabbit. The rabbit is huntable with a multitude of blackpowder guns: pistol, revolver, shotgun, rifle—with smallbores being most desirable, but not necessary with the meat-saving head shot.

Small Game Blackpowder Guns

The hunter lacking one or more of these wonderful sub-bore blackpowder guns is missing out on a great deal of inexpensive shooting—plus highly interesting and rewarding hunting of upland game, such as the No. 1 cottontail rabbit and No. 2 tree squirrel. This clan includes muzzleloading pistols and rifles running 32- to 40-caliber. There are smaller ones, including caliber 22, but 32s and 36s are far more popular and available, while 40s and especially 38s are far fewer in number. I've come to prefer the little 32-caliber in the rifle because it does everything in the smallbore hunting arena I could possibly ask for, but the 36 is just as good. The only advantage of the 32 is less lead required to cast ball, and 22 Long Rifle velocity with only 10 grains volume FFFg blackpowder or equivalent. I have enjoyed many happy hours after rabbits with a Dixie Tennessee Squirrel Rifle, 32-caliber with a long 41 1/2-inch barrel—a flintlock. The same rifle with 30-grains FFFg pushes the 45-grain lead pill close to 2,100 fps. Up to 50 yards this load is on par with the fine 22 Winchester Magnum rimfire cartridge. All of the blackpowder pistols I have shot are also small game-worthy, as are the cap 'n' ball revolvers.

The Wild Turkey

Almost in the big game category, the wild turkey enjoys more attention today than ever before in history. It even has its own Wild Turkey Federation. In some areas, only shotguns are allowed. That's OK, because the blackpowder shotgun is capable of dropping the biggest tom that ever gobbled with a single dose of pellets. The advent of the modern in-line blackpowder shotgun puts an exclamation point at the end of that last sentence. I don't know of a 12-gauge shotgun incapable of turkey taking at close range. On the other hand, there is the magnum in-line gun. The Knight in this category is allowed two full ounces of shot with 110-grains volume FFg blackpowder or equivalent. Velocity is not high, a little under 1,000 fps, but the payload is large. The White Tominator offers similar ballistics. Where rifles are allowed for wild turkey, give me a good-shooting 32 or 36, and one well-placed ball will do the job every time. I prefer the slightly heavier powder charges with consequently higher muzzle velocity for Ben's Bird, so-called because Franklin voted for the wild turkey as our national symbol. Luckily, his wish fell fruitless or we could not hunt this fine bird. A 32-caliber round chunk of lead starting at 1,800 and higher velocity according to barrel length is sufficient. Aim for the pinion area—where wing joins body.

Waterfowl

Not all that long ago regarding the history of shooting, the blackpowder shotgun was the only game in town for waterfowl. The shotguns noted above for wild turkey are also good for ducks and geese. There was a monkey wrench tossed in the works for a while when the law demanded only non-toxic shot for waterfowl. Steel was the first non-toxic shot to come along. Even though made of "soft iron," the new steel shot was not proper in blackpowder guns with barrels of standard steel. First move on the part of manufacturers and importers was creating steel-capable barrels

Target Shooting

Below, plinking is separated from target shooting, although most target shooting is more plinking than a quest for a medal. On the other hand, there are very serious target shooting events accomplished with blackpowder guns, including international as well as national meets. This work is accomplished with pistols, revolvers and rifles. The blackpowder shotgun slips in here, too, with its own events. Bench guns of the past are not yet driven into extinction. I attended a match where these huge rifles were loaded in their own specific manner to make groups that any shooter would be proud of, even at longer ranges. But most target shooting with blackpowder guns will fall into the realm of enjoying the range for a simple shoot-fest that can be accomplished with just about any gun type. That said, it's somewhat pointless to pick from the entire range of blackpowder guns, muzzleloader or cartridge persuasion, as target shooters.

Silueta

Born in Mexico with the Spanish title, *Silueta*, this game has blossomed into a first-class shooting event in North America. I watched in wonder as a shooter with an original Sharps 45-120 rifle managed to hit repeatedly a target at over 1,000 yards. Of course, this fellow was talented. However, if his old blackpowder cartridge rifle was incapable of producing target-grade results at long range, his effort would

The wild turkey is a prime game bird for pursuit with shotgun or, where legal, rifle. Sam prefers a smallbore rifle, but admits that the blackpowder shotgun in replica, non-replica, or modern muzzleloader form is also ideal for bagging Ben's Bird.

for muzzleloaders. Then bismuth came along. Now we can shoot non-toxic shot in shotguns that are not built for steel. Dan Flaherty of the Bismuth Cartridge Company said, "On the Vickers scale of hardness lead is 13, bismuth is 18, steel is 136 and tungsten alloys are about 270. Bismuth is safe for use in the old blackpowder guns since it is almost as soft as lead." Imagine a full two ounces of bismuth shot, even if starting at only a grand velocity. Lead properly and the blackpowder shotgun becomes a fine taker of waterfowl. Patterns with bismuth are excellent, especially in properly choked guns.

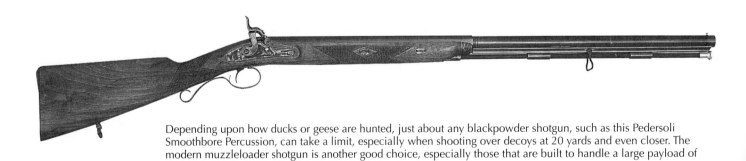

Depending upon how ducks or geese are hunted, just about any blackpowder shotgun, such as this Pedersoli Smoothbore Percussion, can take a limit, especially when shooting over decoys at 20 yards and even closer. The modern muzzleloader shotgun is another good choice, especially those that are built to handle a large payload of shot in front of a heavy powder charge.

Any blackpowder firearm is prime for plinking, while for serious target shooting the gun must match the competition. Here, the game is plinking.

The silhouette game was born in Mexico, but lives a happy healthy life in the USA as well.

Jerry Meyer demonstrates his ability in Cowboy Action Shooting with a blackpowder revolver. Jerry is one of the best at the game.

have been futile. The game calls for specific rifles. A cursory examination of the guns is included in Chapter 38, for blackpowder silhouette shooting enjoys its own unique and individual place. Those who participate seriously pay particular attention to every detail, right down to the blow tube used to introduce moist breath to the bore to keep powder fouling softer.

The targets are very far away, very far, and that is why every detail must be attended to. No sloppy work here. The rifles are single-shot blackpowder cartridge guns of yesteryear, for the most part Remington rolling blocks, and Sharps—but not to exclude the wonderful Ballards and similar rifles capable of high-grade accuracy "way out yonder" with big-bore blackpowder cartridges. See Chapter 33 for a review of blackpowder rounds, including those capable of long-range shooting, such as the venerable 45-70 Government, as well as many others.

Cowboy Action Shooting

Now a big-time shooting event of its own, this sport began with the discovery that those blackpowder cartridge revolvers, shotguns and rifles—aside from the single-shot "buffalo rifles" of the 19th century—were a great deal of fun. Add competition designed by imaginative minds, and the B western movie comes to life, real life, oftentimes with plenty of smoke in the air. Special names are required for members of the national organization that overlooks cowboy action shooting. Chapter 38 serves as a jumping off place for both the cowboy and silhouette events. Jump off only; because both require intense study and dedication for best results, not merely in winning a competition, but in enjoying what each has to offer. In keeping with the era, the cowboy game requires specific guns only. But the rules are not stringent. The pump-action shotgun, mainly Winchester's model of 1897, prevails. Handguns bearing the Colt name rule, but are not exclusive. Ruger has its own cowboy

six-gun, for example, that is entirely welcome to the sport. Rifles fall into the old-time lever-action domain, especially the Marlins and Winchesters. You don't even have to shoot cowboy to enjoy the spectacle. The dress-up and funny "handles," that is, special names, such as The Jersey Kid, Penelope Jane, and Billy Boots, lend color to an already rainbow time.

The Rendezvous

During the Fur Trade era and conquest of the Far West, the rendezvous came to light. This was a grand time for the mountain men who had been trapping beaver in the frigid waters of the Rocky Mountains. Now was a time of relaxation and enjoyment of their fruits of labor. Games of all kinds prevailed, many of them shooting contests. The rendezvous carries into

modern times with old-time camping in basic tents and teepees, trading goods of 19th century times, cooking over open fires, wearing period clothing, often made by the wearer himself or herself, blacksmithing, tomahawk and knife throwing, and of course the shooting, most definitely the shooting. Rendezvous of 19th century strictly forbid modern clothing and most modern implements (many of the lads and ladies, however, are seen wearing their Timex watches). In keeping with the times represented, replicas are the rule. There remain a number of acceptable replicas offered today; some, but not all, of plains rifle style. Certain gatherings are far less demanding of 19th century kit and gun, and here we may find non-replicas. I have not, to date, spotted a modern muzzleloader at a rendezvous.

Rendezvous can mean setting up a handsome tipi like this one, but it is also a place of blackpowder shooting with many different types of guns from smoothbore pistol to chunk gun and slug gun benchrest competition.

Just plain plinking away—President Abraham Lincoln, we're told, considered plinking an honorable and useful pastime. Here, Val Forgett III, president of the Navy Arms Company, plinks away with a Winchester lever-action copy.

Just Plain Plinking

Noted elsewhere in the book, a gun company spokesman noted that more bullets are fired into dirt banks than anywhere else. How right that is. And talk about a good time. I have never heard a single discouraging word from the lips of anyone shooting just for the fun of shooting, be the target nothing more than a beverage can in front of that dirt bank. I especially like plinking games; my favorite being a circle inscribed in the sand in front of that dirt bank, cans placed in the circle, and he or she who knocks the most cans out of the circle wins. The usual prize is a malt or similar. Many prominent figures in history enjoyed the game of plinking, shooting guns in the most informal way. Abraham Lincoln was known to fire shots at in-animate objects of little consequent, and certainly Teddy Roosevelt did the same in his routine of practice. Joseph Smith, leader of the Mormons in the 19th century, was known to enjoy the pastime of "shooting at a mark," an entirely informal target. While the 22-rimfire cartridge is king of plinking, any blackpowder gun also serves the purpose, with the added attraction of smoke on the air and a bit more deliberate time of enjoyment.

Not for Shooting at All

Collecting can be as serious as seeking out originals rare and interesting, or as down-to-earth as gathering replicas, especially replicas from a specific time frame. Originals are not out of the question price-wise. I was treated to viewing a collection of long rifles from the 18th and 19th centuries, all hanging on the walls of a separate building behind the owner's main house on his farm. My companion at the time, Dr. Lou Palmisano, purchased a plain but entirely functional and downright handsome percussion rifle for 300 dollars. Naturally, rifles bearing the names of well-known makers demand much more. I saw a collection of revolvers, all of them replicas, that was very interesting. The fellow had gathered up a couple dozen, and was seeking more to add to his holdings. One way to go about this search is studying originals first from a good source, such as The Gun List. There, the reader will see a multitude of originals that have been brought out in modern times as replicas. Then take a look at catalogs from Pedersoli, Navy

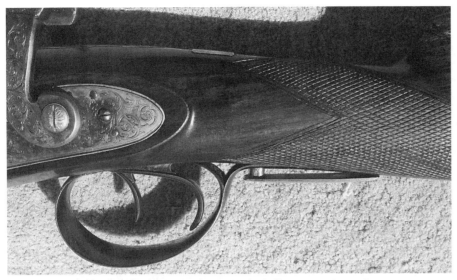

Some guns are best appreciated for collecting, although this very unique and expensive shotgun was seen in the hands of its owner as he competed at Skeet during a rendezvous. This 19th century shotgun has a unique feature—the small piece just behind the trigger guard is removable. Remove it and the gun will not fire.

This shows the 19th century collectible shotgun (costing several thousand dollars). Here, the small piece referred to has been removed, making the shotgun entirely safe. It will not fire until the piece is reinstalled.

Arms, Cimarron, Uberti, and others and check out the offerings. While the 1860 Colt and 1858 Remington 44-caliber revolvers dominate, they do not take away from the many other handguns now offered in replica form. Just to name three examples of revolvers from the many: Navy Arms 1836 Paterson, Euroarms Rogers and Spencer Revolver, 1st U.S. Model Dragoon from Dixie Gun Works.

In this 21st century, the blackpowder firearm has come of age—again—and in a variety of descriptions. The ultra-modern muzzleloader is widely available in models such as the Austin & Halleck 420, which could pass for something Mr. Weatherby might offer. Cabela's Blue Ridge Rifle is in-the-spirit, replicating nothing exactly, but embodying the appointments found on the original Pennsylvania-Kentucky long rifle. There are smoothbore and rifled muskets. Handguns of all descriptions. Shotguns both old-time and modern. Sharps, Remingtons and Ballards from buffalo days. The cup indeed runneth over.

How They Work

There were endless inventions in bygone days, including this interesting American Superimposed Repeating Rifle dated 1825 to 1845, probably in the New York area, maker unknown. It is a 50-caliber smoothbore in the collection at the Cody Firearms Museum in Cody, Wyoming.

Would you believe that there were in-line flintlock rifles a couple hundred years before Bell came along with his telephone? Well, it's true. This minor fact rests upon the tip of a huge iceberg of blackpowder gun types, from ancient to today's modern muzzleloader. There are far too many different individual types to include in our book. However, several deserve, if not demand, at least a nodding acquaintance with their principles of design. A shooting friend, in justifying the advancement of today's front-loader, commented, "It's a simple matter of blackpowder rifles and shotguns, as well as a few pistols, coming of age. It had to happen." His point is well taken. It was inevitable for designers of firearms to continue development

of old-time guns. However, no matter how modern the blackpowder firearm becomes, interest in the very old, the truly obsolete, continues. And why not? Without these old-time firearms, gunmakers would not have had history to build upon. And that's important. Consider aviation. The modern airplane of commerce or warfare has come a long way from the World War I fighter with its comparative tortoise speed and popcorn power, let alone the pitiful little Flyer of Wright Brothers fame.

The Muzzleloader Simplified

In effect, the most up-to-date muzzleloader is in reality a tube (call it a barrel) blocked on one end, open on the other, with a source of ignition. This

is so true that for test purposes (only), and under **strict rules of safety**, I built a few "blackpowder guns" with nothing more than copper pipe, sealing one end via hardened cement in a small can. A hole drilled in the pipe served to hold a fuse. The closed breech end of this device of experimentation (only) held a powder charge in what served as a breech. The tiny hole for the fuse did not split out (but sometimes the entire device did) because of the rule that insists upon expanding gases seeking a larger hole rather than a smaller one. In other words, the gas from the powder charge worked mainly to push the bullet out of the pipe's open end, rather than a blowtorch effect through the hole created to contain the fuse. When

The cannon of old was nothing more than a muzzleloader—it loaded powder and ball straight down the barrel from the muzzle and it was fired through a passageway that can be termed a touchhole or vent.

The most modern muzzleloader in the world, such as this fine Austin & Halleck scoped rifle, continues to be a tube (barrel) with one open end and one blocked end with a means of ignition at the blocked end.

this tube (barrel) becomes a legitimate firearm, it grows in sophistication to include a stock if rifle or shotgun, and some sort of grip for a pistol or revolver. But the basic function remains the same—a barrel with a hole in it (bore), a means of ignition, and the capability of installing powder and missile in some form of breech. From this simple platform—a mere tube—a significant structure was built—a structure of firearms that came to include considerable high-grade art at times, along with myriad additions to make shooting safer and more enjoyable, along with upgraded accuracy and a power band suited to many applications.

They Don't All Agree

No surprise that collectors and students of firearms do not hold a consensus across the board concerning the advent of specific old-time firearms. It's a story that belongs to guns in general. The clouds of passing time cover facts, and so detectives of firearm development must sometimes burn off the haze to gain a credible view of the truth. There were literally,

not figuratively, hundreds of different gun designs from the first firestick to the cartridge-shooter of today. It's safe to add that, at least where aggression and defense are concerned, there will be advances that put powder and bullets into the annals of history. Sporting guns, I think, will remain quite as they are for a very long time to come in spite of advances. Surely, this is true of the blackpowder rifle, shotgun, pistol, or revolver, partly because replication, in spite of modern muzzleloader popularity, continues to lure thousands of us to the shooting game. There is room for all types. I can be found immersed in shooting a replica of a gun created

hundreds of years ago. Or you might see me toting a modern muzzleloader. Every person who has a basic interest in firearms finds this to be true.

Firestick/Hand Gun

The *baston-a-feu*, or firestick, was essentially a hand-held cannon, little more than a metal tube containing powder in its base followed by a projectile. Firesticks were common in the Netherlands in the 15th and 16th centuries, some functioning as clubs or battleaxes as well as guns. The soldier fires his weapon, and then turns the unloaded tube into a club to whack his enemy. Certain firesticks or handguns

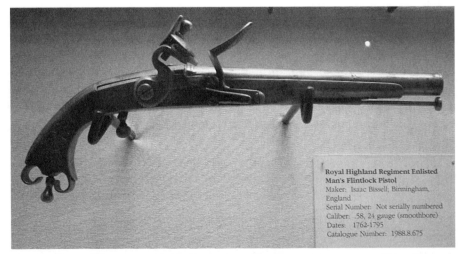

Royal Highland Regiment Enlisted Man's Flintlock Pistol
Maker: Isaac Bissell; Birmingham, England
Serial Number: Not serially numbered
Caliber: .58, 24 gauge (smoothbore)
Dates: 1762-1795
Catalogue Number: 1988.8.675

There never was full agreement on the beginning of firearms and there never will be. Progression is somewhat certain, however, and so the flintlock, as shown here in a Royal Highland Regiment Enlisted flintlock seen at the Cody Firearms Museum, predated percussion guns, while postdating the snaphaunce.

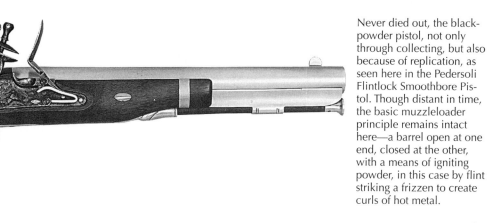

Never died out, the black-powder pistol, not only through collecting, but also because of replication, as seen here in the Pedersoli Flintlock Smoothbore Pistol. Though distant in time, the basic muzzleloader principle remains intact here—a barrel open at one end, closed at the other, with a means of igniting powder, in this case by flint striking a frizzen to create curls of hot metal.

had attached hatchets that prevented an empty one from becoming entirely useless on the battlefield. The Buffalo Bill Historical Society located in Cody, Wyoming, (home of both the Winchester and Remington collections) has many examples of truly ancient shooting devices. Along with considerable Indian artifacts and high-grade art depicting times past, the gun collections at this museum draw strong attention, even from those who never fired one and probably never will. One gun of particular interest to me was a two-foot long firearm with a hole at the *top* of the breech.

This touchhole was very little different from the drilled avenue I used for my pipe tests. The importance of its location signifies that ignition was accomplished with a handheld "slow-match," a sort of smoking rope. This gun functioned in a very simplistic manner. The tube or barrel was closed on one end with a small orifice to admit fire for ignition. Thereby, the vast majority of expanding gases sought the larger hole, rather than trying to exit through the smaller one. Most likely, the firestick had minor battle advantage as a projectile-shooter. But flame, smoke, and noise no doubt had a negative psychological effect on the opposing army. Close your eyes and imagine aiming the firestick as it is held under your arm or perhaps on the shoulder like a bazooka. Ready? I almost said "aim," but you didn't with the hand-gun. Fire! by placing that smoldering rope against the touchhole.

Aren't we fortunate arms development continued through time?

The Firestick Evolves

The firestick or handgun eventually evolved into a tool capable of encompassing not only powder and projectile, but also a source of ignition. A stock was added with a mortise or channel into which the metalwork, especially barrel, fit. Barrel and stock could be joined in various ways, as with a flat metal key, or more than one key, going all the way through the forestock. There was a tennon (metal piece attached to the underside of the barrel) that anchored the barrel in place. Where the key or keys entered and exited the stock, there were metal plates called *escutcheons* on either side. (See illustration.) Some stocks used pins to join wood and metal. (See illus-

tration.) Keys were prominent on half-stock plains rifles, while pins were found on long rifles of many different descriptions. A mortise in the rear of the stock contained the lock. Some sort of guard to prevent accidental discharge usually surrounded a trigger on the underside of the stock. No more firestick. Now we have a rifle.

Matchlock

The matchlock probably followed the firestick. The progression seems logical, since the major difference between firestick and matchlock is the addition of a device that secures the match, rather than the match (smoldering rope) being hand-held. Precise date of invention falls into the twilight zone of history. A German manuscript from the 1500s describes a matchlock, but that

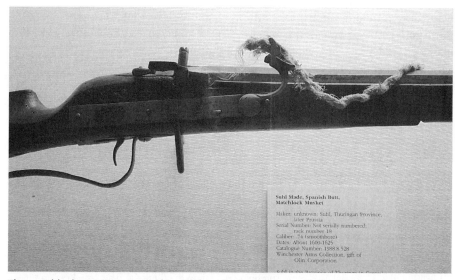

The matchlock ignition system, this one from Spain now in the Cody Firearms Museum collection, employed a smoldering piece of rope that made contact with ignition powder.

One manner of attaching barrel to stock was pinning. This original smoothbore has a pinned stock. Pins are sometimes tapered, which means they must be driven out from the "fat" to "thin" end to avoid splitting the stock.

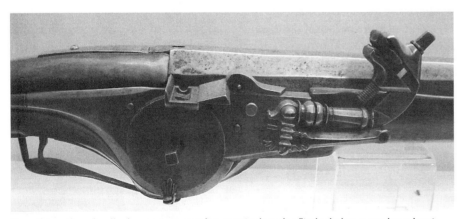

Another means of marrying stock to barrel was with tennon and escutcheon, as shown on this Austin & Halleck Mountain Rifle.

does not prove origin. Functionally, the slow match was held in a serpentine, so-called because it was built in a snake-like backward S-shape. The serpentine, also categorized as a cock, pivoted on an axis, its most forward part delivering flame from the burning match, while its lower portion served as a trigger. When the lower section of the serpentine was pulled rearward, the upper section pivoted forward, delivering fire to a touchhole. There were many variations of the matchlock, including one that foretold of the future flintlock, because it had a sort of flash pan to deliver flame into the touchhole. Lock time is that period elapsed from pulling the trigger to the gun "going off." Obviously, the match-lock had a very slow lock time. The shooter of a matchlock had to master follow-through: Pull the "trigger." Hold very still until the gun fires, maintaining the muzzle in the general direction you want the projectile to take.

Wheellock

The wheellock follows the match-lock with one significant advantage—it was the first gun to contain both load and ignition in a single unit, rather than a separate "slow-match" for ignition. That great inventor, Leonardo da Vinci (1452-1519) is credited with its invention. Naturally, experts disagree. Some believe that Germany, not Italy, was home to the first wheellock. But the time frame is the same—the 16th century, give or take a few decades. Regardless of who invented the system or in which country, it lasted for a couple hundred years (we think). And no wonder. Imagine trying to keep a slow-match burning in wet weather, as well as wielding the matchlock in any sort of deliberate aiming fashion. The caveman had the original idea that would become a wheellock when he (or she?) created sparks from flint. One example of a wheellock is the spark-ignited Monk's Gun, dating back to the very early 1500s. It had a serpentine, which in itself disqualifies it as a true wheellock, but instead of holding a slow-match by hand, the Monk's Gun had jaws that gripped a piece of flint or pyrite for spark ignition. The gun had a sort of plunger connected to the ser-pentine. By drawing the plunger with a thumb or forefinger ring, a roughened steel bar scraped against the pyrite or flint, creating sparks that in turn flew into a touchhole located immediately in front of the serpentine's jaws.

Leonardo was gone by 1519. His idea, however, may have found its way to Nuremberg. Or, as with so many other great inventions, the wheellock may have surfaced through another inventor independent of any information about

If anything, the wheellock was more surefire certain than the flintlock that came later, but it cost more to make and it was slower to reload. This wheellock is available for anyone to see at the Cody Firearms Museum in Cody, Wyoming.

da Vinci's model. The year 1515 is given as the date when a true gun had a wheel without a serpentine. The wheel was an integral part of the lock system, functioning much like a clock mechanism. A key or spanner wound a spring, just like a clock. Firing the wheellock required first opening the flash pan lid to expose ignition powder. The cock or hammer, securing pyrites in its jaws, when activated, fell forward to make contact with the wheel. Whir! Sparks were flying, because pulling the trigger uncoiled a spring that powered the whirling wheel round and round rapidly against the pyrites. Rather than "a spark," a shower of sparks encouraged ignition. Numerous improvements turned the wheellock into an ignition system of high merit and reliability. Instead of a slow-match or a few sparks from a modified matchlock, multiple sparks rained down upon the powder in the pan, almost certain to ignite that fuel.

Snaphaunce

The snaphaunce, also snaphance, is treated here as a flintlock. The name is derived from a Dutch or Flemish word, *snaphaan*, meaning "snapping hen." Dedicated historians require much greater depth. But we don't. This particular lock style is close enough to the flintlock in function that we won't belabor its finer points. Howard Blackmore, respected firearms historian, put the snaphance in the same chapter as the flintlock, which is good enough for me.

The Flintlock

Good as it was, the wheellock had its faults: intricate design, difficult production, and high cost. Surely, it was not fast loading. Sometimes true inventive genius stems from simplicity. There is no doubt that the flintlock was simpler than the wheellock, while not going back to the primitive nature of the matchlock. The cock or hammer of wheellock design was retained. But now the tang or *comb* section of the hammer had jaws designed to grip a well-beveled

This Mortimer-style flintlock has a unique pan arrangement. Pedersoli offers this lock for custom guns. The high quality is obvious at a glance.

flint as if that flint were in a little vise. The two jaws pinched together via a screw running from top to bottom jaw. Thin sheets of lead were used in certain flintlock muskets to improve jaw grip on the flint. But soft tanned leather made a "flint pad" for most flintlock rifles, pistols, and fowlers. There were numerous variations, but each observed the same function, even though some flintlocks were breechloaders, such as the British Ferguson. To make the flintlock work: cock the hammer, which pivots on the lock plate. Bring it all the way to full cock. Now pull the trigger, causing the spring-powered hammer to travel in an arc, bringing the carefully sharpened beveled edge of the flint into full contact with the "spark maker". This spark maker was called a frizzen, also known as a frizzle, battery, steel, or hen. See Chapter 14 for details on locating the flint to meet squarely with the frizzen. This chapter also reveals proper loading procedure. The falling flint, under the power of the hammer, scrapes tiny bits of hot metal from the face of the frizzen. A frizzen spring, also known as a *feather spring*, located on the exterior of the lock plate, provided the energy to fully force the frizzen forward, uncovering the pan cover (also called *flash pan*) so sparks could enter. The fine-grain powder in the pan flames up instantly from curls of hot metal scraped from the face of the frizzen by the flint. Flame from ignited pan powder now darts through the touchhole and into the powder charge in the breech. Boom!

Function of the flintlock becomes clear upon simple observation. This fine lock from Pedersoli boasts a good strong frizzen spring, frizzen of proper metal, plus a correct angle on the jaws of the hammer to deliver the sparks directly into the pan for ignition of the FFFFg powder.

The In-Line Flintlock Rifle

Doc Carlson, in his fine article "The In-Line Muzzle-Loader in History," *Gun Digest*, described the function of the Paczelt rifle with its trapdoor frizzen, an ingenious flintlock system that "could be used to build a modern percussion in-line rifle." It is, however, a flintlock, whose jaws, holding a flint, dart forward under spring tension to strike a frizzen, which in turn pivots upward to expose the pan. The touchhole, however, lies in line with the bore, not in a side barrel flat. Therefore, by definition, this flintlock is an in-line.

The Breech-Loading Flintlock Rifle

The best example of this type is the aforementioned British Ferguson. The trick was accomplished with a breech that opened so the gun could be loaded from "the back" rather than through the muzzle only. The section of barrel was locked back in place and the gun was primed for firing. To work the Furguson, turn the trigger guard, which drops the breech screw. Pop the ball into the breech section. Pour in the powder charge. Close the breech. There may be a few particles of powder remaining on top of the breech section. Sweep these into the priming pan. Pull the cock (hammer) back into battery. The Ferguson is now loaded and when the trigger is pulled it functions like any other flintlock.

The Lock of the Flintlock

The flintlock's lock contains a *lock plate*, as seen from the outside. This plate covers the interior workings of the lock. A *tumbler* in the lock is a metal piece that in function "tumbles" or rotates when the hammer is activated. The tumbler has built-in notches. These notches are engaged by a *sear*, which operates with a *sear spring*. When the sear spring is depressed, the nose of the sear disengages from the notches in the tumbler. The nose of the sear falls into a deep half-cock notch. This is the position the firearm is placed in during inactivity. It is not a safety, as we might find today with cross-bolts and other devices. Nor is it like the safety transfer bar on a revolver which, when functioning properly, will not allow the gun to go off should it be dropped. However, the half-cock notch, when fully engaged by the nose of the sear, will prevent the hammer from falling forward. The *full-cock notch* is entirely different. Now the hammer is in its most rearward position, and when the trigger is pulled, the nose of the sear disengages from the full-cock notch in the tumbler so the hammer can fly forward to bring the flint in the hammer's jaws into contact with the frizzen. A *mainspring* powers the hammer. The lock may also have a *bridle*, which is a piece that spans over both the tumbler and the sear, providing solid pivot points for both tumbler and sear.

There may also be a *fly* in the tumbler, also known as a detent. The

The half-cock notch, as on this Austin & Halleck lever-action type muzzleloader, is an important device. Regardless, the muzzle of the firearm must always be pointed in a safe direction, even when the half-cock notch is engaged.

fly serves an important function with double-set triggers by preventing the sear nose from falling into the half-cock notch when the gun is fired. In effect, the fly is an override device—causing the nose of the sear to override the half-cock notch in the tumbler. The fly also allows the firearm to be brought into battery (firing) position without the sear hanging up in the half-cock notch. It also allows the falling hammer to avoid the half-cock notch. The workings of the lock may also contain a *stirrup* that rests between the tumbler and spring tip, reducing friction at this contact point. While the interior workings of the lock sound intricate, they're actually extremely functional. The flintlock was reliable, not to the extent of later percussion models, but far

more trustworthy than often credited, or should that be discredited? Naturally, lock quality made a big difference in surefire ignition. But think about it—if the flintlock failed to go off at that moment of truth when a pioneer took aim at game or foe, this country never would have been settled.

Drum and Nipple

Converting flintlock to caplock was most often accomplished with a drum and nipple setup. The drum and nipple system also stands on its own as another percussion system. A cylindrical metal piece with a channel running through it is screwed into a side barrel flat, its outfacing end sealed off with a cleanout screw. Tapped into this metal cylinder is a nipple seat, which

The interior of the flintlock reveals the workings, including the tumbler and other essentials required for function.

Sam's No. 47 ball-shooting 54-caliber rifle has a drum and nipple ignition system, whereby a drum (metal cylinder) is screwed into a side barrel flat, and then a nipple is screwed into the drum.

in turn takes a regular percussion nipple. Fire from the percussion cap flies downward into the drum, making a left-hand turn (for a right-hand lock) into the breech. In spite of percussion cap flame diversion into the breech, the drum and nipple system provides excellent ignition. My own No. 47 54-caliber ball-shooter is of the drum and nipple design. In dry weather it is essentially infallible.

Front-Action Percussion Lock

This is the standard lock of the day, called a *sidehammer*, because the hammer is mounted on the side of the lock. The name front-action applies because the mainspring is in front of the hammer, rather than behind it.

Back-Action Percussion Lock

This lock has the mainspring behind the hammer. It's easy to identify because the hammer, mounted on the side, is forward of the lock plate.

Back-Action Sidehammer Percussion Lock

In this system, the hammer cocks out to the side of the firearm. Sometimes it's called a "mule ear" lock because the spur of the hammer resembles an ear sticking out sideways. A nipple is seated in the side barrel flat for *direct ignition* into the breech. While not an in-line, having the nipple screwed directly into the barrel produces a direct avenue for ignition.

Underhammer Percussion System

There were many wonderful under-hammer rifles with proper mechanisms in days gone by; but also simple rifles and pistols whereby the trigger guard served as the mainspring. The nipple on the underhammer is seated into a lower barrel flat for direct ignition into the breech, just as on the mule ear lock. The Bennet & Haviland Rifle, an under-hammer design, was a repeater with a magazine composed of 12 chambers.

In-Line Percussion System

The distinguishing feature here is exactly what the name describes—fire from the source of ignition is introduced on the same plane as the bore of the gun. An in-line muzzleloader may have a plunger that strikes a percussion cap or modern primer, or it may have an exposed hammer. Bolt-action models are widespread. Typically, there is a screw-in breech plug with a channel running through it. A standard percussion cap, musket cap, small rifle primer, small pistol primer, or No. 209 shotgun primer rests on the "back end" of the breech plug. When the igniter is set off with a thump from a plunger, hammer nose, whatever, fire darts through the channel and directly into the waiting powder charge in front of it. Many different designs can be incorporated into the in-line niche. One type is the break-open rifle, somewhat resembling a single-shot break-open shotgun. When this rifle is in the open position, a primer or cap (usually a No. 209 shotgun primer) is fitted into what amounts to the rear of the breech plug. Closed, the break-open muzzleloader is ready to fire. After shooting, the barrel is broken open again, which allows removal of the spent primer. Now the rifle can be loaded once again, from the muzzle, of course, because it is a true muzzleloader with a solid breech plug at the back.

The Markesbery Outer-Line Rifle

This uniquely designed rifle has interchangeable barrels and an exposed hammer. It is not an in-line system, because fire from a No. 11 percussion cap or a small rifle/small pistol primer does not enter the powder charge on the same plane as the powder charge. Instead, flame arrives from above the powder charge on a 45-degree angle. While not an in-line, the Outer-Line is direct ignition because fire from the igniter goes *directly* into the main charge in the breech, albeit not on the same plane as the bore of the rifle. My own Markesbery rifle has not to date

This sidehammer lock is a front-action design because the mainspring is in front of the hammer.

The back-action lock has the mainspring behind the hammer.

The sidehammer lock is just that—the hammer strikes from the side.

In-line ignition means that fire goes directly from cap or primer into the main charge waiting in the breech, as seen here on the Remington Genesis modern muzzleloader. Note that the primer holder swings outward on the Genesis.

misfired once with a No. 11 percussion cap.

The Savage Model 10ML and 10ML-II

To date, I know of no other muzzle-loader on the market that allows the use of smokeless powder. *Smokeless powder in any other muzzleloader could cause the firearm to explode.* Initially, Savage retained the locking lugs of this bolt-action rifle as functional. This is why the Model 10ML could handle smokeless powder. The heart of the system was a "percussion module" with a slightly acorn shape. The back of the module was built very much like the head of a rimless cartridge case with an integral groove gripped by the rifle's extractor. The module was loaded into the chamber just like a cartridge. It is also extracted after firing like a cartridge case. The back end of the module accepted a No. 209 shotgun primer. Continued development followed. The Model 10ML-II current as this was written does not retain the locking lugs of the parent Model 110 cartridge rifle, as did the original. Rather, the Model 10ML-II locks up at the rear of the bolt. The Savage 10ML-II remains smokeless powder capable with total safety when the rules are followed, especially to carefully *weighed* powder charges as recommended by Savage and no other powders in any amount. Ignition is now simplified in the 10ML-II. Load powder. Load bullet (via the muzzle—this is still a muzzleloader). Insert a primer into the recess of the bolt face for retention. No capping tool required.

The Shotgun

Flintlock shotguns are called fowlers or fowling pieces, while the caplock muzzle-loading shotgun is essentially one or two barrels with breech plugs and locks, quite similar to the caplock rifle with respect to function. Now we also have modern in-line blackpowder shotguns. The break-open design described above is also a candidate for a blackpowder shotgun.

This original percussion shotgun from the 19th century is a double barrel with a high "fence," the fence being a plate that goes between the shooter and the nipples of the gun.

The Pistol

The muzzle-loading pistol, for present purposes, is treated as a "short rifle," its workings being the same as the muzzle-loading caplock or flintlock long gun.

The Caplock Revolver

There were flintlock revolvers in days gone by, but they are of historical interest only. The works of the blackpowder cap 'n' ball revolver are more involved than the percussion or flintlock rifle. Essentially, this gun is a frame with barrel, grips, loading lever, cylinder, and internal moving parts that revolve the cylinder into battery position. The frame is the body. There is, of course, a barrel attached to the forepart of the frame. The frame may or may not have a top strap, a piece between the rearmost of the barrel and the hammer. The famous 1860 Colt blackpowder revolver had no top strap. The equally famous Remington Model of 1858 did. Sometimes revolvers are called "wheel guns" because of the revolving cylinder containing chambers that align, one at a time, with the bore of the barrel. The word "revolver" says it all. The cylinder revolves on a *pin* at its center. The cylinder rotates when the hammer is pulled back via a *hand*. A *cylinder* bolt locks the cylinder in place aligned so that one chamber is "looking" right out of the barrel. There are springs and many other parts that allow the single-action blackpowder revolver to function. Chapter 11 explains how the caplock revolver is loaded, which in turn describes its function, from loading powder into the cylinder chambers to forcing bullets into the same chambers with the use of the loading lever, to placing caps on nipples that are screwed into the back of the cylinder. Sights vary.

The Cartridge Revolver

The major difference between the cap 'n' ball revolver and the cartridge revolver is the cylinder, which holds cartridges instead of powder and ball, and, of course, there are no percussion caps, since primers installed into the heads of the cartridges provide ignition. The hammer falls on a firing pin instead of a percussion cap.

The Single-Shot Cartridge Rifle

The Remington Rolling Block and the Sharps were two of the most famous single-shot blackpowder cartridge rifles of all time, and both continue manufacture to this day. (See Chapter 31.) Essentially, these rifles lock up with a block system, a very strong metal piece that slides into position behind the cartridge. On the Sharps, the operation of a lever slides the block up or down. When the block is down, a cartridge can be inserted into the waiting chamber. When the block is in the up position, the chamber is locked off and the rifle is ready to fire. The Remington has a block, too, but it rolls into position, rather than "falling" down and rising back up, hence "rolling block." These two actions are both strong in principle and, and when made of modern steel, can hold quite a bit of pressure. Original Remington Rolling Blocks were chambered for smokeless powder cartridges, such as the 7x57mm Mauser, while various modern falling block actions have been used to chamber many modern rounds, including magnums.

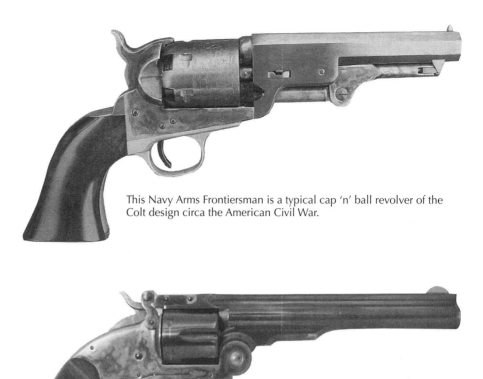

This Navy Arms Frontiersman is a typical cap 'n' ball revolver of the Colt design circa the American Civil War.

The Navy Arms Schofield comes in 45 Colt chambering. It's one of the earlier blackpowder cartridge revolvers and a good one.

The Lever-Action Blackpowder Cartridge Rifle

Lever-action rifles, along with slide-action models, were developed for rapid fire of blackpowder cartridges. It was not until 1895 that these rifles were offered with smokeless powder ammunition. That year saw the advent of what we call today the 30-30 and the 25-35 Winchester rounds. Although various magazines can be employed, most lever-actions, such as the Model 1894 Winchester, Marlins, and others, carried a tube beneath the barrel with cartridges fitting one behind the other. Working the lever downward expelled a fired round, with the comeback of the bolt re-cocking the hammer. A follower lifted another cartridge into line with the chamber and the upward thrust of the lever slammed the bolt forward, locking a new cartridge into the chamber ready for firing.

Muzzleloader Triggers

Depression of the muzzleloader trigger sets the wheels of motion into action, tripping the sear, which in turn activates a hammer, which in turn raps a percussion cap (or primer), or causes flint and frizzen to produce a shower of sparks. An exception is the modern muzzleloader with modern-type trigger, which is a release-type mechanism instead of a trip-type mechanism. The following touches only on some of the more widespread trigger styles. As with all other aspects of firearms history, noting each trigger design would require a book of its own. After all, there were not only air guns in days of yore, but models of electric firearms as well. Lewis and Clark had a large-caliber air gun on their march across America. Leonardo da Vinci, the amazing inventor credited above, laid out a plan for a gun working with steam.

Single Trigger

Simplest is the single trigger pinned directly into the stock without a trigger plate, as found on old-time fowlers. There is no trigger adjustment in this design, and today it is seldom seen.

Single Trigger with Metal Trigger Plate

Simple, effective and popular, this type of trigger is mounted on a metal trigger plate, rather than pinned directly to the stock. The trigger plate acts as an anchor for a tang screw, also serving as a solid base for the trigger to pivot upon. The single trigger does have some travel before engaging the sear, which is bothersome, but be corrected by installing a weak mousetrap-type spring on the trigger plate to hold the trigger against the sear.

Single-Set Trigger

The single-set trigger offers a very light trigger pull with only one trigger, instead of two, and comes in various

Many different types of triggers have been employed in muzzleloaders over the years, including the double-trigger, whereby one trigger "sets" the other to make it into a "hair" trigger with a light pull. This Pedersoli Caplock Kentucky shows an example of the two-trigger system.

The lever-action blackpowder cartridge rifle gained impetus because of repeat shots, but not necessarily due to greater power than the muzzleloader. The Winchester Model 1886, shown here as seen at the Cody Firearms Museum, was a John Browning design. Its design was foolproof, and the rifle handled some powerful blackpowder cartridges, such as the 45-90. Note the workings of the action.

sub-styles. It demands precise adjustment for full benefit and it must be set before the lock can be cocked. The more advanced single-set *multiple-function* trigger also has but one trigger. However, the gun can be fired in two modes. The trigger can be set by moving it forward until it clicks, or pulled without setting and the gun will still fire. Setting the trigger provides a very light let-off, while for fast-action, the trigger need not be set.

The Single-Lever Double-Set Trigger

There are two triggers in this system: the rear trigger is the set; the front trigger is the hair. Incidentally, this can be reversed, as seen on the now discontinued (and still worthy) Thompson/Center Patriot pistol. Unset, the gun will not fire. When the trigger is set, trigger pull is very light. An adjustment screw between the triggers alters let-off. The deeper the screw is threaded upward, the lighter the trigger pull, sometimes measured in mere ounces. **Caution:** this type of trigger can be set too light for safety.

The Double-Lever Double-Set Trigger

Similar to the single-lever double-set, the double-lever double-set can be fired either in the set or unset position. It is the most common type of trigger found on today's muzzleloaders that have two triggers, as well as on numerous originals. **Caution:** the adjustment screw can be set too light, making the gun dangerous. Double-set triggers are also found on some modern rifles. My own Mannlicher 9x56mm carbine is an example, as are many other rifles. Double-set triggers can be mounted on lever-action, single-shot, break-open, and just about any other type of firearm.

The Modern Muzzleloader Trigger

Little to be said here, this is the same trigger found on modern cartridge guns. It is normally adjustable, and as with any trigger, can be set too light for full safety. My take on trigger manipulation is that alterations should be left to a competent gunsmith.

The majority of modern muzzleloaders, such as this Remington Genesis, employ the single trigger, which is most familiar to the majority of today's shooters.

Common Action Types

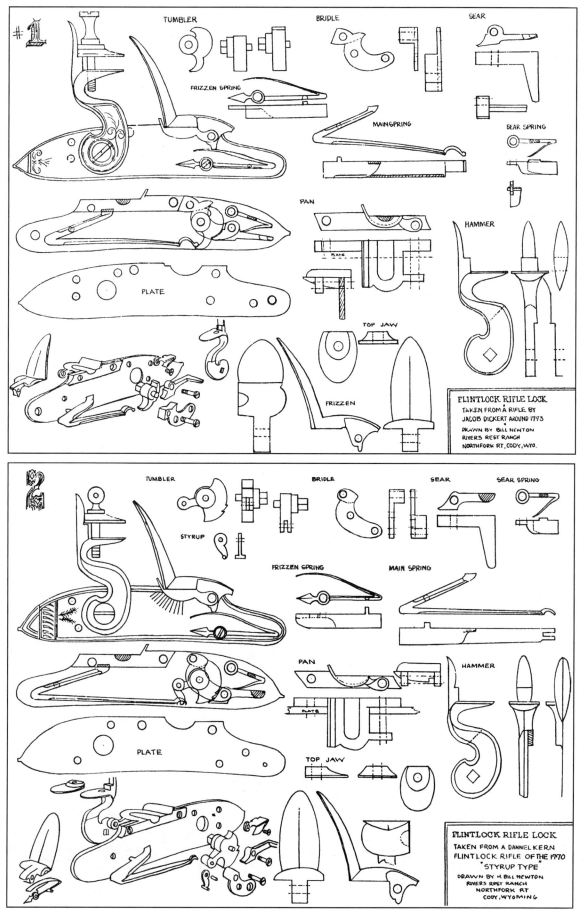

#1

TUMBLER BRIDLE SEAR

FRIZZEN SPRING

MAINSPRING

SEAR SPRING

PAN

HAMMER

PLATE

TOP JAW

FRIZZEN

FLINTLOCK RIFLE LOCK
TAKEN FROM A RIFLE BY
JACOB DICKERT AROUND 1773
DRAWN BY BILL NEWTON
RIVERS REST RANCH
NORTHFORK RT, CODY, WYO.

TUMBLER BRIDLE SEAR SEAR SPRING

STYRUP

FRIZZEN SPRING MAIN SPRING

PAN HAMMER

PLATE

TOP JAW

FLINTLOCK RIFLE LOCK
TAKEN FROM A DANNEL KERN
FLINTLOCK RIFLE OF THE 1770
"STYRUP TYPE"
DRAWN BY H. BILL NEWTON
RIVERS REST RANCH
NORTHFORK RT
CODY, WYOMING

Common Action Types

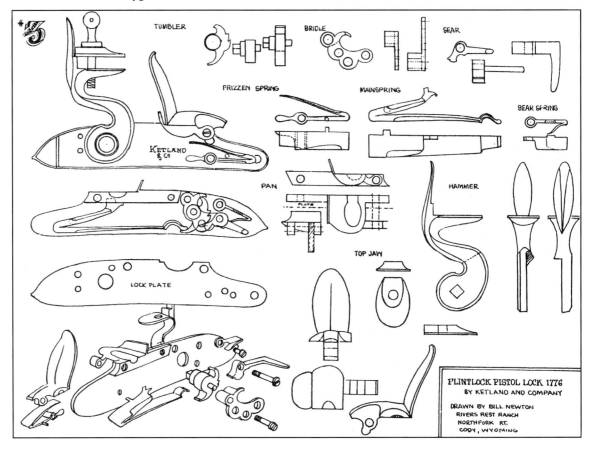

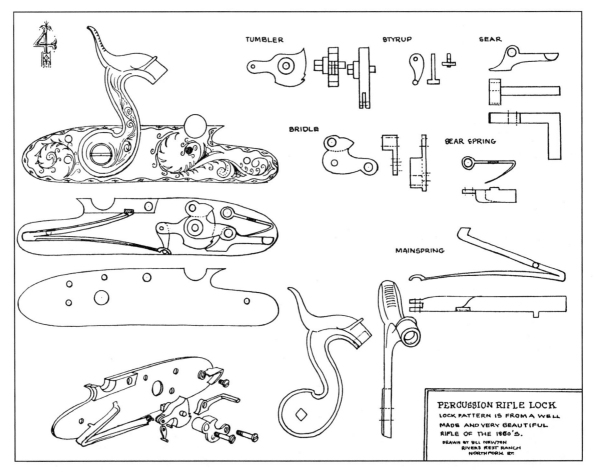

Common Action Types

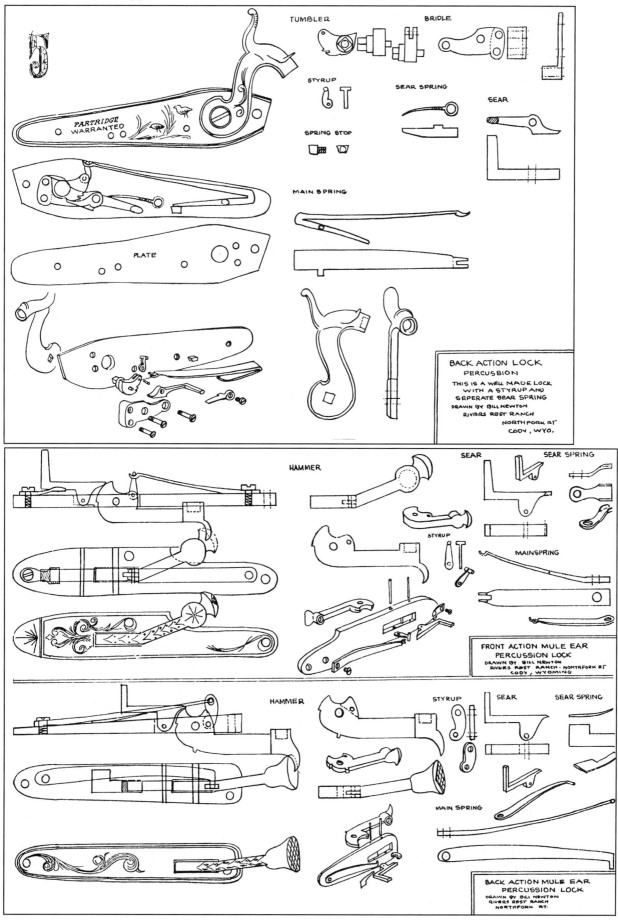

TUMBLER

BRIDLE

STYRUP

SEAR SPRING

SEAR

SPRING STOP

MAIN SPRING

PARTRIDGE WARRANTED

PLATE

BACK ACTION LOCK
PERCUSSION
THIS IS A WELL MADE LOCK
WITH A STYRUP AND
SEPERATE SEAR SPRING
DRAWN BY BILL NEWTON
RIVERS REST RANCH
NORTHFORK RT
CODY, WYO.

HAMMER

SEAR

SEAR SPRING

STYRUP

MAINSPRING

FRONT ACTION MULE EAR
PERCUSSION LOCK
DRAWN BY BILL NEWTON
RIVERS REST RANCH · NORTHFORK RT
CODY, WYOMING

HAMMER

STYRUP

SEAR

SEAR SPRING

MAIN SPRING

BACK ACTION MULE EAR
PERCUSSION LOCK
DRAWN BY BILL NEWTON
RIVERS REST RANCH
NORTHFORK RT.

3 STAYING SAFE

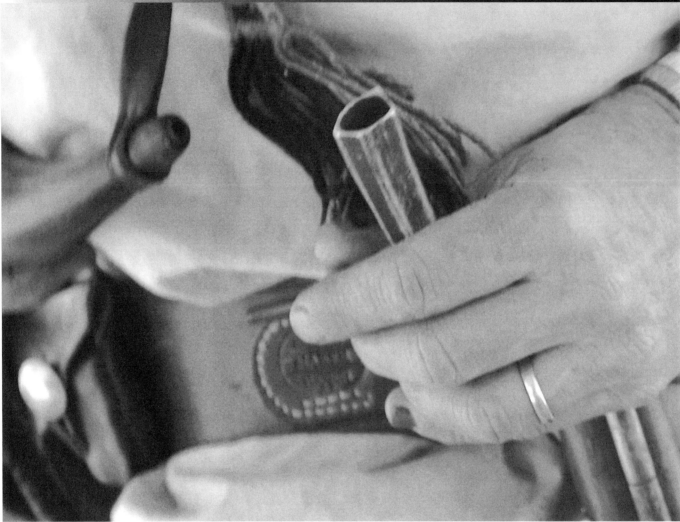

A safe powder measure is any measure that meters out a proper quantity of propellant. This bit of cut-off antler, drilled out, is a safe volumetric powder measure that holds the right amount of powder for a specific firearm.

Accidents happen. That's why they're called accidents. And I can think of no one who has never had one, be it slipping on a banana peel or suffering a mishap on the shooting range or in the hunting field. Some accidents are unavoidable. In the courtroom, where I serve as an expert witness on shooting claims, this is called "an act of God." But most accidents can be prevented. Shooting is a safe sport. It must be. For the many thousands of shooters who fire millions of rounds each year, there are but a comparative handful of misadventures. Not often, but sometimes, the hardware failed. That is, a gun

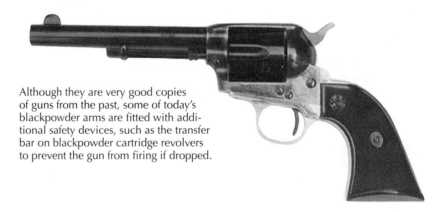

Although they are very good copies of guns from the past, some of today's blackpowder arms are fitted with additional safety devices, such as the transfer bar on blackpowder cartridge revolvers to prevent the gun from firing if dropped.

"went off" or broke at an inopportune time. That is why product liability exists. There is no excuse nowadays for unsafe firearms, such as handguns that

"go off" if dropped. My Navy Arms replica Bisley Colt 45, for example, has a transfer bar to prevent accidental discharge. The original did not enjoy this

A typical example of a replica firearm with additional modern safety features is the Colt Lightning, the one shown here from Pedersoli in the standard model. There is an unloading latch for safety in removing live rounds from the rifle as well as the trigger working only when the hammer is on full-cock.

important, even necessary, advantage. However, its inclusion does not in any way reduce the spirit or pure enjoyment of shooting this fine six-gun.

Truth is, the shooter himself causes the vast majority of range and field accidents. Following the rules of safety can prevent these. That is the thrust of this chapter, presented early on in the book, because the only good shooting is safe shooting. We do not fear guns. We respect them. They are tools. And like so many other tools, such as hammers, picks, knives, and toenail clippers, misuse can bring disaster. Huckleberry Finn's papa, our old friend Mark Twain, said that, "Never meddle with old unloaded firearms, they are the most deadly and unerring things that have ever been created by man. You don't have to have a rest; you don't have to have any sights on the gun; you don't have to take aim, even. You just pick out a relative and bang away at him. A youth, who can't hit a cathedral at thirty yards with a cannon in three-quarters of an hour, can take up an old empty musket and bag his grandmother every time, at a hundred." Safety factors are repeated in other chapters, such as Chapter 12 on the blackpowder shotgun. That's on purpose because reminders are important.

One sure way to blow up a muzzleloader is with smokeless powder, the single exception being the Savage Model 10MLII, which has an entirely different design from other muzzleloaders. There are many smokeless powders that are black in color but they are not blackpowder!

Blackpowder and Black Powder

The reader may wonder why the word is misspelled throughout this book. It's because written as blackpowder there can be no mistaking this specific propellant for powder that is simply black. Many smokeless powders are black. As this is written, there is one, and only one, muzzleloader specifically designed to shoot smokeless powder. That is the Savage Model 10ML-II. I know of no other. **Smokeless powder can destroy a muzzleloader with the possibility of serious bodily injury.** This means—**never use smokeless powder** in your muzzleloader, emphasis on the word "never." Duplex loads of mixed black and a little smokeless powder to "touch off the charge" are no exception. Blackpowder and safe replica propellants, such as Triple Seven, ignite quite successfully without help of any kind from any other type of fuel. My tests with small amounts of bulk shotgun powder, supposedly used to kick off a charge of blackpowder, *proved* that not one foot-per-second velocity was gained (so said the Oehler 35P Proof chronograph). Nor was after-shooting cleanup easier. A smear of blackpowder is found on some pellets, but it is only a fine coating used to encourage the compacted powder to ignite. A muzzleloader with stubborn ignition probably benefits from this almost microscopic coating. However, I can reverse these pellets in my rifles with blackpowder side facing the muzzle, not ignition, with no apparent change.

Pyrodex and Triple Seven

The proper management of these two replica propellants is so simple that

Load blackpowder and allowable blackpowder substitutes, such as Pyrodex and Triple Seven, by volume, as this shooter is doing. Note also that the muzzle of the rifle is pointed away from both shooter and his partner.

it defies any problems. Pyrodex and Triple Seven are loaded **by volume** just like blackpowder, not weighed out. If the muzzleloader normally takes 100-grains volume blackpowder for a given load, the same powder measure used to produce that load is employed with Pyrodex and Triple Seven *at the same setting*. That's all there is to it.

Powder Measure and Charger Safety

Adjustable powder measures, as well as their non-adjustable charger cousins, are not only important for creating proper loads. They are also safety tools. While providing correct volumetric amounts of powder, each of these accouterments also destroys any excuse for pouring powder down a muzzleloader's bore directly from a horn or any other dispenser, which could cause a blowup should a spark linger down in that bore, be it rifle, pistol, or shotgun.

Extreme Range

Muzzleloaders, on the whole, have a much shorter extreme range than cartridge guns. That is why they are often allowed for hunting in areas closed to the modern big game cartridge. A standard velocity 22 Long Rifle cartridge shoots farther than a 32-caliber squirrel rifle. I find this warning on a box of 22-rimfire ammo: "Range 1-1/4 Miles." Another box admonishes: "Range One Mile-Be Careful!" A 30-'06 with 180-grain boat-tail bullet starting at 2,875 fps, which is what current Federal Vital*Shok ammo in the High Energy mode gains, travels over three miles when the muzzle is pointed upward at about a 45 degree angle. I know of no definitive extreme range tests with 50-caliber muzzleloaders, the most popular bore size used by blackpowder hunters.

Observing extreme range includes having a backstop to prevent a projectile from traveling its full potential distance. In hunting, the terrain, as well as the target, normally captures a bullet. In some hunting instances, however, such as a skylined animal, shooting is unwarranted.

Firearms properly stowed, as in a rack, and with a watchful eye in attendance, prevents guns from getting into the wrong hands—a good safety precaution.

However, whereas a 30-06 bullet might go a full three miles, I'll give half that distance to higher profile blackpowder bullets, much shorter for the low ballistic coefficient round ball. Regardless of comparative extreme range limitations, the front-loader marksman must never send a missile away without first being certain of backstop, be it target range butts, hillside, or forest of trees.

In the Wrong Hands

"Keep out of Reach of Children." That is what safety-minded experts tell us. And they are right. Guns in the hands of unsupervised kids can spell trouble. Add powder and percussion caps to this warning.

The Short-Start Load

Not only was his rifle extremely overloaded, but the young man had also short-started the load, which means *failing to seat the bullet*, be it a patched round ball or conical, *firmly upon the powder charge*. This condition can destroy a barrel. In the case of the above short-start a serious injury was sustained when the barrel ruptured. No one has proved beyond a doubt why short-started loads can cause trouble. There are several theories grounded mainly in speculation. One theory suggests that a short-start load allows the powder charge to lie in a "trough" in the barrel, in other words the granules are laid out along the bottom of the bore. Now rather than a compacted charge in the form of a column burning somewhat progressively with a normal curve, the charge *detonates*, going off all at once. Maybe this is right. Maybe not.

Another theory is related to the fact that blackpowder and its substitutes do not transform from solid to gas nearly as completely as smokeless powder. Following combustion, about half of the charge remains as solids (See Chapter 24). These solids are only partially expelled from the bore. A simple way to look at this one is imagining a dirty bore that retards the full seating of a round or conical bullet. That unseated bullet becomes a *bore obstruction* very much like a barrel clogged with mud. Furthermore, a significant caking in the fired bore actually reduces its volume, which in turn raises pressures. Now add an unseated bullet to this condition and trouble is the result. These possible causes for short-start problems are based on pure speculation.

Yet another theory is the secondary explosion effect, abbreviated SEE. Simplifying greatly, SEE occurs when a projectile is thrust *partway* down the bore and then it *stops*, followed by a second powder burn. The stopped bullet becomes a bore obstruction. If it does not move forward again with dispatch, the barrel may break or bulge. Or a depressed ring may occur within the bore. The difficulty in arriving at a good answer for the short-start lies in the fact that results do not repeat in tests, at least not in the many tests I have conducted. A barrel may remain intact without bulge, ring, or rupture following several

Using a loading rod or ramrod properly is one way to prevent a short-start condition, although bouncing the ramrod upon a correctly seated projectile does nothing except possibly disfigure the nose of that bullet. Keeping the bore clean also helps proper seating of bullets on the powder charge.

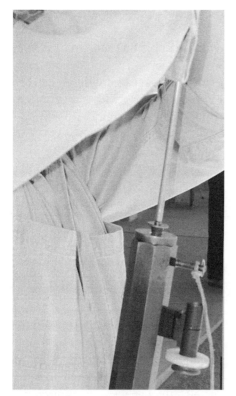

The best idea is to seat one and only one bullet fully downbore upon the powder charge. Putting one projectile upon another is not a good practice, lest the one on top become a bore obstruction.

short-starts, only to come apart suddenly with the tenth shot. In one test, a barrel of good reputation blew apart from a short-start following tortuous overloads that the barrel held up to. In another test, several short-starts with excessive charges of the wrong powder (Elephant FFFFFg—5F) caused no *apparent* damage, although it is impossible to know if there was hidden damage that could promote a rupture later.

Regardless of the absence of exact scientific proof for short-start load problems, and while we have no answer as to why short-start loads sometimes damage barrel, sometimes not, **short starting must be avoided!** This fact was known many years ago. Here is what Ezekiel Baker said in *Remarks on Rifle Guns*, first published in 1835:

> Every rifleman should mark his ramrod at the muzzle end of the barrel, when loaded, which will shew him when the ball is close [firmly down] on the powder. After firing a few rounds, the filth from the powder will clog the bottom of the barrel, and prevent the ball from going close on the powder: in this case, a little pressing with the rammer will be required to get the ball into the right place. More accidents happen from a neglect of this precaution than can be imagined: if the ball be not rammed close on the powder, the intervening air will frequently cause the barrel to burst.

Copper Pipe Tests and Short-Start Loads

The following tests are not to be attempted by the reader under any conditions. They could prove extremely dangerous. These tests were conducted under strict safety conditions with a substantial barrier between shooter and copper pipe instruments. Copper pipes sized to accept 54-caliber patched round balls and conicals were seated in cans of molten lead, the lead hardening to form a breech. A drilled hole where pipe closely met "breech" served as a

touchhole, into which fuses were installed for ignition. The goal was testing for specific ruptures or bulges when using specific loads. Amazingly, the thin copper pipes withstood modest loads of blackpowder with single projectiles. However, when short-started with what would be normal loads for a 54-caliber muzzleloader, every pipe was destroyed or damaged. In all cases, a bulge or rupture occurred where the base of the short-started projectile rested within the pipe. Light loads produced a "walnut" in these copper devices, a term from old-time literature that simply means a bulge. Heavier loads split the pipes open. No wonder Elisha Lewis, in his 1885 book *The American Sportsman*, warned: "We are consequently forced to adhere to the ancient doctrine of explosion, and still believe that a fowling-piece is more apt to burst with a wad or a ball far up the barrel than if pushed home upon the shot or powder." Lewis concluded, "This phenomenon we cannot account for." We cannot account for it either, in provable scientific terms. We just know that short-starts can cause a disaster.

Multiple Bullets

I have not run across it lately. However, suggestions for putting down more than one patched round ball on top of a powder charge have seen print. The idea was delivering two projectiles instead of one to dispatch a big game animal. It's a bad notion that can cause serious trouble. Should the second ball not be seated firmly on top of the first one, this condition is surely a barrel obstruction. In one test a firearm loaded with two patched balls, one seated off of the other, suffered a ruptured barrel where the base of the off-seated bullet rested. Furthermore, accuracy goes south with multiple projectiles. Simply stated: *don't do it!*

Bore Obstructions

As with any other firearm, the bore of the muzzleloader or blackpowder cartridge gun must be clear of any obstruction. An obstruction can cause the barrel to burst, resulting in serious injury or worse.

Dirty Bores and Pressure

Pressures rise with a very dirty bore for at least three reasons. First, a caked-up bore has a reduced volume from when it was clean. The smaller the area for expanding powder gases to work in, the higher the pressure. This is why we see higher pressures with small-bore muzzleloaders opposed to big-bore muzzleloaders using the same powder and charge. For example, Lyman's tests with a 32-caliber rifle and 70-grains volume Elephant Brand FFg blackpowder produced 17,700 psi (pounds per square inch) pressure, while the exact same powder and 70-grain volume charge in a 54- caliber rifle showed only 6,200 psi, both guns shooting patched round balls sized respectively to fit their bores. Another negative with a dirty bore is friction or drag. Built up

Keeping any firearm clean shows shooting wisdom. Keeping blackpowder guns clean is even more important. A fouled bore may not raise pressures enough to cause a problem. But a fouled bore could prevent the proper seating of a projectile, including a shot charge, upon the powder for a short-start.

fouling creates greater friction and drag in the bore, which can raise pressures. But the biggest problem concerning a dirty bore is short-starting. A dirty bore can retard the full seating of a projectile firmly upon the powder charge in the breech section of the barrel where it belongs.

Overloading

This is the era of the magnum muzzleloader gulping big powder charges to boost velocity and trajectory for greater downrange authority. For example, the Ultimate 50-caliber muzzleloader is allowed four Pyrodex or Triple Seven pellets for an equivalent 200-grains volume. However, each firearm, even the well-made Ultimate, has a maximum load imperative set by the manufacturer. This limit is never to be exceeded for any reason. Too much powder can also violate the law of diminishing returns, which means there will be more smoke and recoil with *insignificant* velocity/ energy increase. Sometimes an overload can actually result in lower velocity because blackpowder does not transform from solid to gaseous state with the efficiency of smokeless powder. So the superfluous extra powder spends part of its energy pushing unburned powder from the bore. This entire discharge from the muzzle is known as the *ejecta*. Ejecta is the total mass fired from the bore: including bullet, patch or sabot, and also unburned powder, as well as fouling. The rule is: *do not let fouling build up.* This rule changes, however, with different powders and even lubrications. For example, several shots can be fired in a row without undue powder buildup with Pyrodex, while regular blackpowder normally requires more frequent in-betweens-shot-string bore cleaning.

Managing the Short Starter, Loading Rod, and Ramrod

Don't hurry when shooting blackpowder guns, except in the game field when a second shot is required. Calm enjoyment is what the sport is all

Short starters can vary greatly. This short starter is intended to start a bore-size projectile. A wooden mallet is used to encourage the bullet downbore a few inches before full seating with a loading rod at the range.

about—taking time out from a busy world to do something in a more deliberate and slow-paced fashion. Patched round balls, along with most conicals, require the use of a short starter to introduce these bullets into the bore a short distance, followed by ramrod or loading rod to seat the bullet fully upon the powder charge. Even with undersized conicals that can be pushed partway down into the muzzle of the bore without a thumb, the loading rod or ramrod must once again be put into service for full seating. Short starters, loading rods, and ramrods are not merely tools. They are also safety devices. Meanwhile, instructions about pinching the ramrod between forefinger and thumb sound good and are often repeated in blackpowder stories. Should the gun "go off," the tale goes, the ramrod will slide between the fingers harmlessly. This is simply a spoonful of pabulum. Think about it. A mere moment earlier, the short starter was just used with palm pressure and the hand directly over the muzzle. True safety with short starter, loading rod, and ramrod means full certainty that the gun is *not capped or pan-charged* during the loading procedure. That is how to be safe.

Ramrod/Loading Rod Pressure

Consistent pressure on the loading rod or ramrod produces low standard deviations in velocity, which is good. That is why we have tools such as the Kadooty. But blackpowder is percussion sensitive, which means a charge could be set off with a blow. It is also conceivable that very high pressure placed upon a charge down in the breech might do the same thing. Firm seating of projectiles is necessary. Leaning full body weight on the rod, however, is unwise, uncalled for, and could be dangerous.

Half-cock Notch When Loading

It's a good idea, with muzzleloaders that have exposed hammers, to place the hammer in the half-cock position when loading. A hammer fully down upon the cone of the nipple can impede the escape of air from the bore during the bullet seating process. With the hammer on half-cock, air in the bore is more easily expelled through the powder charge and out of the nipple vent. When air is trapped in the bore, it may force the seated bullet back up the bore a short distance, producing a short-start condition.

Extending the ramrod by adding a T-handle to this Markesbery ramrod promotes ease of bullet seating. This in turn promotes safety by ensuring that the shot charge or bullet is seated fully upon the powder charge.

The Power Rod has a built-in T-handle to promote good bullet seating. The T-handle folds in when not in use, and a well-seated bullet is the safety goal.

Blackpowder Pressures

Old wives' tales persist in the world of muzzleloading. One of these fictional stories suggests that overloads of blackpowder are not a problem, because excess propellant "just blows out of the muzzle." This is absolutely false. Another untrue tale goes: blackpowder can never achieve over 25,000 psi. In the late 19th century, two Englishman, Captain Noble and his partner Mr. Abel, generated 100,000 psi with blackpowder under laboratory conditions. The United States Navy repeated these findings in a similar time frame. Under proper load conditions, blackpowder generates perfectly safe working pressure levels. But it can be overloaded.

Pressure and Conicals

Proof is extremely difficult to come by in blackpowder tests, even with careful chronographing. In general, the more mass in front of a powder charge, the greater the pressure generated. Check loading manuals for modern ammo and you see that as bullet weight goes up, the powder charge goes down. For example, one manual shows 58.0 grains IMR-4064 as *maximum* with a 110-grain bullet in the 30-06, dropping to 55.5 grains with a 130-grain bullet, dropping again to 51.0 grains with a 150-grain bullet, and 49.5 grains with a 180-grain bullet. This does not mean that conicals are dangerous in muzzleloaders. They are not. It simply means—*follow the rules*. Never exceed the manufacturer's maximum loads, paying attention not only to powder type and charge, *but also recommended bullets*.

Proofing

Proofing is the process of securing a firearm safely and firing it remotely with heavy powder charges to see if the gun is capable of withstanding the force of the charge. While popular with gunmakers of the past, it's not what we want to do with our personal muzzleloaders and blackpowder breechloaders, which are now constructed of modern steel. It is my belief that overloads of this type, often at least double the normal maximum recommended charge, can cause unseen metal stress later resulting in failure.

The Double-Barrel Gun

Be it shotgun or double-barrel rifle, a fired barrel must never be reloaded while the unfired barrel remains capped. The loaded barrel could somehow go off with disastrous results. Al-

Consistent ramrod pressure upon the projectile produces uniformity from one shot to the next, which in turn lowers standard deviation, which in turn promotes accuracy. Of greater importance to safety, consistent ramrod pressure ensures proper seating of the shot charge or bullet.

ways remove the percussion cap from the loaded barrel before attempting to reload the fired barrel, and at all times direct the muzzles of both barrels well away from self and anything else that can be injured, be it person or property. While this advice concerning the black-powder shotgun was broached in Chapter 12, it bears repeating here because of its importance.

Load Shift

Recoil from shooting one barrel of a double-barrel gun can cause the load in the other barrel to move forward, creating a separated charge/projectile in either a double barrel shotgun or rifle, or for that matter a multiple barrel pistol. After firing one barrel, and before reloading that barrel, it's wise to ensure that the load is still firmly seated in any unfired barrel. This is accomplished by inserting the ramrod downbore to see how much of the rod protrudes beyond the muzzle. If an inordinate amount of the rod shows, this proves the load has shifted upbore and it must be pushed back down into the breech.

The Shotgun Wad Column

Safety-wise, the smart way to handle a wad column is to ensure it remains fully seated in the breech where it belongs. Yes, this is the short-start warning again. Furthermore, the wad system should be built of proper material, rather than leftovers found around the house, such as newspapers or rags. BPI (Ballistic Products Corporation), Dixie, CVA, Circle Fly Shotgun Wads, Thompson/Center, and several other companies offer both traditional and modern wads that work properly in the shotgun.

Restricted Wad Column

The wad column must be free to move upbore when it is smacked in the behind by expanding gases from the powder charge. A restricted wad column can raise pressures because of inertia. It takes more energy to put an object at rest into motion than to keep

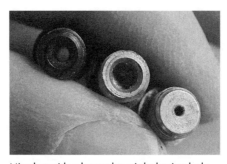

Nipples with a base plus pinhole size hole rather than a wide-open bottom seem to work best all around. Nipples with large orifices tend to increase the chance of blow-back of gases.

it going after it has gotten a start, so if that object, in this case a wad column, cannot freely get underway, it becomes a sort of bore obstruction.

Nipples

There are so few badly designed nipples on the market in this 21st century that a safety warning is all but outdated. A proper nipple has a flat base with a pinhole. Nipples with a wide open channel from cone to base can allow undue gas escape, although the law of physics (Venturi principle, I believe) tells us that gas expels in greater volume through a larger hole, in this case bore to muzzle, than a smaller hole, such as found even in the most glaring case of the large base-hole nipple. If you come across any of what I call "straight-through" nipples, discard them.

Cap Debris

Safety glasses prevent damage to the eye from cap debris. Also, for exposed hammers there is the flash cup, which helps to contain cap fragments (see Chapter 4).

The Round Ball Patch

While not a true gas-sealing gasket, the round ball patch is vital for holding the round ball down firmly upon the powder charge, among other important duties. Because of this, the patch is a safety item and must be made of properly strong material, not old rags. See Chapter 18 for more on the round ball patch.

This old-time patch cutter made round patches, but patches need not be round for good results. While patches need not be round, they should be consistent and strong. A good strong patch is more likely to retain a round bullet down in the breech where it belongs. Patches are part of safety. They must be used with round balls.

Granulations

The latest tests from the Lyman indicate a lesser degree of pressure difference from one granulation over another than most of us assumed to be the case. Regardless, kernel size, and to some degree kernel shape, does affect burn rate. For safety, the granulation recommended by the gunmaker with regard to a maximum charge should be adhered to. In other words, if the recommended load calls for FFg granulation, stick to that size.

The Capper for Safety

Cappers provide a convenient way to carry and dispense No. 10 and 11 sizes, as well as the English top hat or musket cap, and now modern primers for muzzleloaders. Cappers play a role in safety, too, keeping percussion caps and primers contained where they are unlikely to go off from an outside source. Cappers also avoid having to seat a cap or primer with bare fingers. To expand upon capper safety, remember that cappers should be kept where they will not fall into the wrong hands—the hands of curious children especially.

Blackpowder Storage and Management

Blackpowder and its substitutes should be kept in a dry location away from any source of heat, flame, or sparks, for obvious reasons—dampness can ruin the powder, and an errant source of ignition can set it off. All powder must be kept in its original container, which not only marks it carefully as to exactly what that propellant is, but also keeps it at least somewhat guarded from moisture, sparks, and other invading negatives. While not as dangerous as other products we use today, such as gasoline, blackpowder is an explosive. Accidents in manufacture persist, and a number of early day mills blew sky high from internal spark or zap of static electricity. Drying blackpowder in open trays was abandoned in the 1820s for a process using rotating wooden drums containing graphite to somewhat dissipate charges of electricity. Luckily, shooters are removed from all propellant manufacturing hazards, as noted below.

Smoking and Powder

A hot ash from a cigarette, cigar, or pipe dropped into an open can of any kind of propellant will set off the contents. The resulting fireball can constitute a very serious mishap. Immediately after dispensing powder into a horn or other proper container, the lid of any powder container must be replaced.

Let the Experts Make It

Phil Sharpe, well-known gun writer of a previous era, warned, *"Home-made black powder is extremely dangerous both to make and to use!"* He was right. Concocting blackpowder is best left to the experts. While the basics of charcoal, sulfur, and saltpeter may be available, combining these rather simple ingredients creates a product so potentially powerful that it can cause a great deal of mischief. Let the experts make it in a properly managed plant.

Lead Management

Lead fumes can be dangerous to breathe. Therefore, casting projectiles in a close area is considered poor practice. It's also unwise to cast bullets anywhere

A hunter pursuing dangerous game, such as the Cape buffalo, known as Africa's Black Death, does well to have a backup regardless of the firearm. The hunter with a single-shot muzzleloader definitely requires a backup on dangerous game.

where water may invade the molten lead, which can make it spatter widely.

Casting Bullets

Protective clothing and proper location make casting bullets a safe proposition, as the chapter on the subject concludes. Conversely, wearing sandals, slippers, and short pants is asking for trouble. See Chapter 34 for more on "running ball."

Big Game & Muzzleloaders

More than ever, muzzleloaders are super capable of dropping big game on the spot; however, these are single-shot guns, with the exception of a few doubles, and the hunter must be aware of that limitation facing a dangerous animal. Ideally, hunters of dangerous beasts of the world should have a backup standing by.

The Blackpowder Cannon

Rules for firing the blackpowder cannon are many and stringent, all for good reason. They are not toys. These days, cannonballs may be as large as

bowling balls—in fact, sometimes they are bowling balls with tremendous power and range. Cannonballs have been known to travel for a mile or more, thereby requiring safe backgrounds, as all projectiles do.

Blackpowder cannons are interesting. And cannon matches are among the most entertaining aspects of the entire sport of blackpowder shooting. Safety rules with cannons are stringent for reasons of safety with a weapon firing heavy projectiles that carry great momentum.

Muzzleloader Condition

Any broken tool embodies a potential for danger, even a screwdriver with busted bit that could slip and nick a hand. All guns, muzzleloaders included, must be in safe working order at all times. Anything less is asking for trouble. For example, a worn half-cock notch could cause the hammer to fall forward, firing the gun prematurely. Test this for yourself. If the hammer falls from thumb-pressure, the half-cock notch is worn and must be repaired before further shooting of that gun. Mainly in the past, a variety of wall-hangers found their way onto the market. They were junk then. They still are and should never be fired.

Gunsmithing

Gunsmithing is best left to the experts for any job having to do with a function that could be dangerous, such as altering the trigger or working on the lock tumbler, while worn-out guns should be scrapped or use as door stops.

Eye and Ear Protection

Your gun owner's manual includes strong warnings about eye and ear protection—shooting glasses and earplugs or muffs. Read and follow these promptings. Such warnings do not appear on bullet or powder containers, nor should they, because these are components, not part of the mechanical functioning of the gun.

Removing a load from a muzzleloader that will not fire requires extreme care. The CO2 charge remover promotes safe unloading.

It Can Happen

In the interest of helping the reader understand how a terribly unfortunate accident can occur, the following is a real life case reported in *Muzzleloader* *Magazine* for November/December 2000. The Mountain Man run is a rendezvous contest that includes moving rapidly from one challenge to the next. The match has a fire-building stage. One contestant entered the fire-making location where he was to use flint and steel to get a blaze going. He forgot to remove, or at least plug, his powder horn. No one noticed. He gathered tinder in a pile and began striking flint to steel for sparks. An errant spark found its way into his unplugged powder horn. A terrible cloud of smoke rose as the powder in the horn ignited. The horn did not explode, but it was right beneath the man's face when it erupted into flame. A witness of the accident said, "His face was burnt red and raw and not a single eyelash or eyebrow hair remained on his countenance. Part of his hair along the front of his forehead had shriveled back with the sudden heat rushing up and around his focused face." An ambulance rushed the man to the hospital. Moral of the story—always cap or plug any container that holds powder.

Eye and ear protection are obvious safety precautions. Val Forgett III wears glasses to guard his eyes and earplugs to prevent hearing loss.

Behind the firing line at all times—a common-sense safety law.

RULES OF THE ROAD
Ten Commandments of Shooting Safety
(Modified for Blackpowder Guns)

1. Always keep the muzzle pointed in a safe direction, never at anything you do not intend to shoot. Keep muzzle pointed away from self and others when loading.

2. Unload and secure guns that are not in use. Never store a charged muzzleloader.

3. Never rely on a gun's safety. Treat all guns as loaded. Make certain the half-cock notch is functioning properly.

4. Be certain of your target and what lies beyond it.

5. Never use smokeless powder in a muzzleloader that is not built for smokeless powder. Never exceed the manufacturer's maximum powder charge.

6. If a muzzleloader fails to fire, wait a few moments, continuing to maintain the muzzle safely pointed downrange. Try to fire with a new cap or fresh pan powder charge. If gun will not go off, do not pull load for several minutes.

7. Always wear eye and ear protection.

8. Be sure the barrel is clear of obstructions before firing. With a muzzleloader, also check to see that it is not already loaded, in which case two charges would be run home in one barrel.

9. Do not modify or alter a gun. If there is any question concerning the safe functioning of a firearm, have it checked by a professional gunsmith.

10. Learn the mechanical operation of your firearm. This is especially important with muzzleloaders, which require more "hands-on" attention than cartridge guns.

chapter 4

WHAT YOU WILL NEED — THE ACCOUTREMENTS

Accoutrements of old were well conceived and useful. This is an original 19th century shot pouch made of hard leather. It is as serviceable today as it was when it was made.

An older dictionary cites accoutrements as "a soldier's equipment with the exception of his weapons and clothing. A belt, blanket, and knapsack are parts of a soldier's equipment." Also, "Personal equipment. Outfit." Another vintage dictionary notes accoutrements as equipment, apparel, and dress, an old synonym being *caparison*, relating to the trappings of the knight. For our purposes, accoutrements are the tools that promote shooting blackpowder guns reliably and safely. Many of these implements never changed, and in fact have not improved appreciably over time. The modern muzzleloader movement has added a number of tools. An example of an unchanged tool that works today is the powder horn. There is no better carrying container for blackpowder. A modern plastic ready load, however, was not part of the mountain man's kit. Nor did the old-time shooter require the many new tools necessary for safe and reliable shooting of today's in-line and other modern muzzleloaders.

Accoutrements of Yesteryear

Sometimes spelled accouterments instead of accoutrements, they were the same thing—tools of the trade—indispensables required for loading, shooting, and maintaining the muzzleloader. Buckskinners, those dedicated blackpowder enthusiasts who dress 19th century and play the mountain man role, know what their heroes carried on those long trails into the Far West. These things they copy. Old-style accessories are purchased ready to go or handmade by men and women interested in teepee times. The mountain man's major goal was basic survival. His rifle was his lifeline. He counted on it to deter both two- and four-legged interlopers, as well as putting meat in camp. Though he loved

This original 19th century shot pouch was decorated with a hunting scene.

his rifle, however, harsh conditions prevented perfect maintenance. It was not unusual for a gun to fail after days, even months, of abuse. But the trailblazer did have his kit and the items he carried were put into play daily. What where these tools? Charles Hanson, in his fine book, *The Plains Rifle*, quotes Ruskin, a 19th century writer and adventurer who listed mountain man Bill Williams' 1840 outfit. Williams was a well-known trapper. His memory still lives in the northern Arizona town of Williams. Here is what this mountain man carried:

"In the shoulder-belt, which sustained his powder horn and bullet-pouch, were fastened the various instruments essential to one pursuing his mode of life. An awl [for sewing], with deer-horn handle, and the point defended by a case of cherry-wood carved by his own hand, hung at the back of the belt, side by side with a worm for cleaning the rifle; and under this was a squat and quaint-looking bullet mould, the handles guarded by strips of buckskin to save his fingers from burning when running balls, having for its companion a little bottle made from the point of an antelope's horn scraped transparent, which contained the 'medicine' used in baiting the traps."

We also know what shooters long before the mountain men carried, thanks to preserved information. Henry Kauffman, in his book *The Pennsylvania-Kentucky Rifle*, presented a document describing what was noted in the kit of certain military shooters of the 1700s. "The following letter," Kauffman writes, "from the Emmet Collection in the New York Public Library lists the accoutrements [note spelling] which were needed for a gun in the 18th century." Here is that list:

A good Fire-arm with a steel or iron Ram-Rod and a Spring to retain the same. A Worm, Priming Wire and Brush, and a Bayonet fitted to your Gun, a Scabbard and a Belt therefor, and a Cutting Sword, or a Tomahawk or a Hatchet, a pouch containing a Cartridge Belt that will hold fifteen Rounds of Cartridges [paper cartridges] at least, a hundred Buckshot, a Jack-Knife and Tow for Wadding, six Flints

and one pound of Powder, forty Leaden Bullets to your gun, a Knapsack, and Blanket, a Canteen or Wooden Bottle sufficient to hold one quart.

Back to the mountain man, his guns, pistols as well as rifles, fired *lead* balls often cast by melting lead over a fire, possible since lead melts at a comparatively low temperature. Lead (galena) was brought into the mountains at rendezvous. Of course there was also *blackpowder*, the fuel that propelled those round balls. In turn, blackpowder had to be carried in something, which turned out to be, as Ruskin reported, a *horn*. The horn could be used to prime the many flintlocks that went on the trail. But mainly it supplied fuel for the caplock plains rifle. Flintlocks needed *flints*, while percussion rifles and pistols required *percussion caps*. Although initially designed to clear the touchhole of the flintlock, another little tool was handy—the *vent* pick, nothing more than a bit of wire, but extremely important in maintaining a clear passage from the flash of powder in the pan into the waiting charge in the breech. When this same tool, essentially, was used to clear the channel in the nipple, it became a *nipple pick*. Whether flintlock or

percussion, the round ball rifle required a *cloth patch*. Some shooters carried a *charger*, which as noted below as nothing more than a simple, non-adjustable, but effective powder measure made of brass, iron, horn, antler, bone or other material.

The smith who made the rifle supplied the charger. It was his job to determine how much powder the rifle or pistol required for good shooting, and to then make a tool that held that much fuel *by volume*. The shooter simply poured powder from horn into charger and that was the correct amount. The gunsmith usually sighted the rifle for his customer, the charger supposedly gauged for an optimum amount of powder to provide power and accuracy. As for the paper cartridge, supposedly employed by the mountain men, Hanson suggests little evidence of its existence during that period. Sometimes the shooter practiced the dubious act of double charging, which was dumping two charger scoops down bore instead of one (*not* recommended). Since guns were not chronographed in the old days, shooters were not familiar with the law of diminishing returns. They concluded that more recoil and added smoke always translated into increased

The concept of a possibles bag lives on with the "possibles box" as shown here—all manner of shooting equipment in one container. A very good idea.

Recognizing the value of somewhat simple accoutrement holders from the past, Austin & Halleck offer this bag, good for ball, but also useful for many other shooting items.

power—not necessarily so. Some historians suggest pre-cut patches. Others disagree. *Patch knives* found among the gear of mountain men indicate that these men placed a hunk of material over the muzzle, followed by a ball bumped past the crown of the muzzle with the snub of the short starter. Excess patch material resting above the ball was sliced away with the patch knife, after which the patched ball was run home on top of the powder charge. However, Ned Roberts provided evidence that at least some old-time shooters used pre-cut patches.

The *worm*, a small metal corkscrew affair with a threaded shank, was run down bore with coarse cloth attached called "tow" to swab out blackpowder fouling. The worm could also be used to withdraw a stuck patch. We don't usually employ tow for cleaning today, but the mountain men were not known for the fastidious rifle maintenance that modern shooters are famous for. If a ball stuck in the bore, a *screw* could retrieve it. Picture an ordinary wood screw with head cut off and shank threaded to fit the tip of a ramrod and you have a blackpowder screw. Attached to the end of the ramrod, the screw cut into and held the stuck lead ball for retrieval. In spite of these maintenance tools, tough conditions often won out, the bore of the mountain man's rifle becoming pitted. When the bore was too eroded to shoot well, it was *freshed out* by a gunsmith, meaning bored to a larger caliber and re-rifled. The old-time kit included a *hunting bag*, also called *shooting pouch*, erroneously referred to today as a "possibles bag." The shooting bag, or pouch, normally slung over the shoulder via a strap, was a repository for vital shooting necessities, such as spare lead balls, extra flints for the flintlock, nipple wrench, vent or nipple picks, small screwdrivers, combination tools, and other devices. An exact account of the early hunting kit is impossible, varying with individuals. A *"straight starter"* might be included. This short version of the ramrod was used to start the patched ball downbore.

Not every kit had one. Today, we call it a *short starter*.

Along with the shooting bag (pouch) some historians claim there was a *"possibles bag."* In theory, the name alludes to the possibility of finding almost anything in it. Or so the tale goes. The possibles bag was probably a larger pouch in which could found a bit of tobacco, spare gunpowder, flints, patching materials, fire-steel for starting the well-known flint 'n' steel flame, and according to Hanson's *The Plains Rifle*, this kit might also have a *"fire-bag,"* which was a combination of fire-steel and tinder, sometimes carried on the mountain man's belt. In short, the possible bag was a catchall. Some students of the Far West don't buy into the possibles bag story. They think possibles simply meant an array of gear, regardless of how or where it was carried. These historians give other names for larger tote bags.

Along with the regular powder horn, which might hold about a pound of powder, the flintlock owner might have a much smaller *priming horn*. Some historians argue that the old-time shooter didn't have time to fool with a priming horn. He simply poured a little powder from his regular horn into the pan. Perhaps this is true, but there is strong evidence that priming horns were used to disperse fine-grain powder into the pan. A little *cap box* served as a container for percussion caps. There were *cappers*, too. These stored percussion caps as well as dispensing them directly onto the nipple of the firearm. The *in-line capper* held caps in a row, while the magazine capper, a larger-capacity accoutrement, held many percussion caps in a body section, gravity-feeding one at a time through a spring-loaded opening. Luckily, both styles remain available to modern shooters, including a handsome magazine capper from Tedd Cash (see Directory).

Modern Accoutrements

Most of the blackpowder shooting gear invented before the telephone and flying machine remains perfect for the modern muzzleloader. However, there are also many new devices created expressly for the high-tech firearm. The Savage Model 10ML Muzzleloader, capable of shooting smokeless as well as blackpowder, is a perfect example of an in-line front loader requiring special tools. The Savage rifle has a breech plug wrench 10-3/4 inches long, a specifically designed decapper to flick off the primer (the 10ML does not use caps), which doubles as a handle for increasing leverage on the breech plug wrench. There is also an absolutely unique module that holds a No. 209 shotgun primer. The module is inserted into the chamber of the rifle and the bolt closed down to lock the module in place as if it were a cartridge. After firing, the module is withdrawn by working the bolt to extract it from the chamber just like a spent cartridge case. The 10ML embodies ingenious design, but definitely requires the special tools supplied.

After the module is drawn free of the chamber, it's inserted into a special pocket in the decapper body to hold it in place and an extension integral to the decapper is used to force out the spent primer. The Savage rifle is loaded from the muzzle, just like any other frontloader, but with the option of blackpowder or replica propellants metered out *by volume only*, or a specific safe smokeless powder charge prepared *by exact weight only*. An example of a smokeless load is 48.0 grains *weight* Alliant Reloder 7. Because this rifle is smokeless powder capable, another tool comes into play, a bullet/powder scale to provide a specific charge weighed to the tenth of one grain. The long, heavy-duty breech plug wrench, with the decapper through the hole in the back of this tool for leverage, is used to unscrew the breech plug, thereby providing access from the breech. This allows the 10ML to be cleaned just like a modern bolt-action rifle.

It's impossible to list every specific tool supplied with each individual modern muzzleloader because of individual design. But it is clear that these new guns demanded special tools for safe and efficient operation. To that end we find that Remington's Model 700 ML muzzleloader has a rain guard that fits into the action to prevent moisture from entering the breech area. A similar device is found on the Austin & Halleck modern in-line bolt-action muzzleloader. Since breech plugs are removable for cleaning the firearm from the "back end," the modern muzzleloader is provided with a tool for the job. Markesbery has a wisely designed 4&1 Tool T-handle that screws into the rifle's ramrod for ease of loading and cleaning. This ingenious tool also contains a bullet jag, bullet starter, and nipple pick. Many modern accoutrements function like old-timer tools, but with space age design and built of contemporary materials. The list of accessories following deals with some of these accoutrements. Tools change name from time to time, and so specific titles as this is written may no longer have a place in tomorrow's catalogs. However, there will be similar replacements that do the same work, so describing them is important. Here they are:

Know Your Blackpowder Shooting Tools

For Managing Powder
The Powder Horn

Chapter 5 deals with the function of the powder horn. This section

The powder horn made perfect sense. Horn could be shaped, which was handy, but more importantly it was spark-proof and could be made waterproof as well. This horn is from October Country.

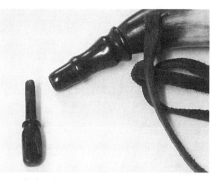

A well-fitted powder horn plug ensured a waterproof container.

talks about the horn as an object of managing powder. Essentially, it is a container for blackpowder and other proper muzzleloading propellants. It is not to be used to dispense powder directly into any blackpowder firearm. The horn remains as viable today as it was in early gun history. It proves perfect for carrying powder for at least five reasons. First, horn can be heated and shaped, ideal for bending to suit the circumstance, such as slightly wrapping into the body of the shooter who carries one. Most horns are round, but some are flat. Second, horns come in various sizes, so a shooter can elect the one just right for the task at hand. The largest horn I have seen, a 19th century example showing at the wonderful Buffalo Bill Historical Society in Cody, Wyoming, held at least two full pounds of powder. The smallest I have seen held only a couple ounces of powder and was probably used to prime the pan of a flintlock pistol or rifle. Third, horn is spark proof, as opposed to metals or other materials that might prove a source of ignition. Fourth, a powder horn can be made waterproof. Not simply moisture resistant, but capable of keeping powder dry in a rainstorm. A fifth attribute has nothing to do with function: horn can be decorated, as with scrimshaw and words. I had a custom horn inscribed with my name. A real prize, it was unfortunately stolen.

The Priming Horn

All good points attributed to the regular powder horn attend this miniature. This small horn remains useful

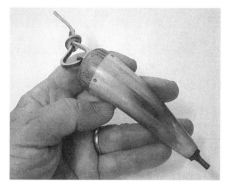

A much smaller horn was ideal for priming the pan of the flintlock rifle, shotgun, or pistol. This handsome priming horn has a spring-loaded spout. Push the nose of the spout onto the pan and a small amount of FFFFg powder is dispensed.

This is a priming tool rather than a priming horn, but it functions in the same manner. It is made of a modern synthetic material.

in carrying FFFFg blackpowder for pan priming, as well as distributing a small charge into the pan on the outside edge rather than up against the touchhole, thereby promoting a flash that stands a good chance of flying directly into the main powder charge in the breech. There were various ways of ensuring a proper small amount of powder distribution, one being a spring-loaded device that, when pushed against the base of the pan, let go a little bit of powder.

Priming Tool

Rather than horn, this device, which does the same job as the priming horn, is created as a metal flask or of modern synthetic materials.

The Charger

We know that gunmakers of the past provided (perhaps not always) chargers for their handmade firearms. The charger in its simplest form is little more than a tube with one closed end. The tube is cut to a proper length to dispense a specific charge by volume. The particular charge would be the one most useful in the specific pistol, rifle, or shotgun. Conceivably, a charger could be made to hold, just as an example,

The charger could be any implement with a fixed capacity, such as the charger shown here. This is a large charger for creating big powder charges for large projectiles, such as the 12-gauge round ball shown to the left of the charger.

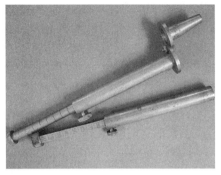

The adjustable powder measure is just that—adjustable in increments for different charge amounts. Here are two, one with a swing-out funnel, the other with an open end. Both work well.

The powder flask comes in various styles. This one from CVA is made of brass (turned black for appearance). It is, of course, non-sparking and it comes with various spouts for different charge amounts of propellant.

Chargers were and continue to be easily made and calibrated for just about any amount of propellant. The two chargers on the left are originals.

Here are two adjustable powder measures with open ends and fairly large powder charge capacity, especially the one on the right.

Here is a brass CVA powder flask, colored black, with spout removed to show interchangeability of spouts to vary powder charge amounts.

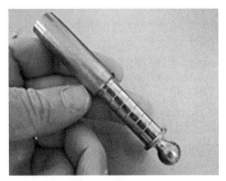

Showing a large adjustable powder measure ready to be used.

The CVA powder flask is shown here with various spouts that alter the amount of powder dispensed.

A modern powder flask from Thompson/Center is made of high-impact transparent non-sparking material.

60-grains volume FFg blackpowder for a 54-caliber hunting rifle. That would be its target load. When the hunter decided to go for bear, he could fill the charger from the powder horn, dumping that charge downbore followed by a second charge. I don't think this is what double-charging necessarily meant, because the data I normally run across explains that as the practice of loading two full charges in a rifle. We know today from chronograph studies (see Chapter 22) that such practice may have been a waste of powder with unwanted addition of recoil, smoke, and noise. Chargers were, and still are, prepared from many materials.

The Adjustable Powder Measure

While the charger, when filled to the prescribed point, normally up to the lip, threw one and only one volume of powder, the adjustable powder measure provided for many different loads. I have one that goes from 10 grains to 120 grains volume. I have another that runs from 20 grains to 150 grains in volume. Not always, but usually, adjustment is accomplished with a sliding rod within the body of the measure. The sliding rod indicates grains volume graduated

A readyloader comes in handy in the hunting field. This one has a special protrusion employed as a short starter. It holds 120-grains volume propellant.

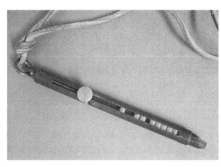

A well made in-line capper to hold No. 11 percussion caps, with leather lanyard for carrying around the neck while hunting or shooting.

This small in-line capper holds modern Small Rifle or Small Pistol primers.

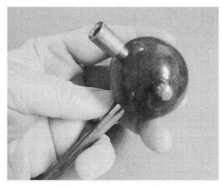

This is a typical short starter. There are many other types. Screwed in place is a special jag for protecting the nose of a pointed conical bullet.

from lowest to highest setting. Pulling the rod all the way out provides the most powder by volume. In-between charges are also possible, although impractical due to the inefficiency of blackpowder. Slight changes in powder charges for larger-bore guns show very little change in velocity. A modern-type adjustable powder measure is the T/C U-View with integral swing-out funnel and locking adjustment rod.

Powder Flasks

Flasks were provided in numerous sizes capable of presenting different powder charges commensurate with the firearm the flask was intended to feed. These were usually made of brass, since other metals might create a spark. I have also seen German silver flasks. Powder was dispensed in different ways. Spring-loaded models worked by pushing the nose of the flask against, for example, the mouth of a cap-and-ball revolver chamber. This opened the avenue for a specific powder charge to enter the chamber. Another type of flask (I have one made by CVA) has interchangeable spouts. The spouts are sized to contain a precise amount of powder by volume. I continue to carry a small powder flask in my shooting bags. These take the place of the larger powder horn. Each contains sufficient powder to reload rifle or pistol several times in concert with an adjustable powder measure. I have several compact flasks, such as the T/C Blackened Flask in solid brass and Traditions Hunter Flask & Powder Measure Set. I also have a Traditions Pyrodex Pellet Dispenser for Pyrodex Pellets and Triple Seven Pellets. It holds 18 50/50 size pellets, dispensing two at a time when the button is activated. Clear powder flasks are now available made of synthetic materials, such as polycarbonates. Keeping with the trend, they are compact and light in weight.

Thanks to the generosity of a reader, I have owned over the years an original hard leather shot flask. It holds sufficient smaller-size pellets for a considerable number of shots, and it is adjustable for 1 1/4- or 1 1/2-ounce shot charges.

There are also special powder flasks for the muzzleloading shotgun and I have two shotgun horns, one to dispense a specific charge of shot, the other to throw a specific volume of powder.

The Ready Loader

Ready loaders, also known as quick-loaders or pre-loaders, come in many designs, such as the 4-in-1 from CVA with a Lexan transparent body instantly revealing status—loaded or not loaded. It has a shirt pocket clip, a palm saver, integral bullet starter, and the powder compartment is graduated in grains volume markings. Caps on either end allow instant access to bullet or powder. There are quick-loaders designed for pellets, too, such as the Traditions Super Magnum Pellet Quick Loader. It holds three 50/50 Pyrodex Pellets on one end and a bullet compartment on the other. The covers double as cappers for one No. 11 or one musket size cap. The Pellet Packer is for shotguns. This plastic affair contains shot, wad, over-shot wad, powder, all held in place with a clip in the lid.

Cappers and Rods

Cappers

In-line cappers and magazine cappers come in brass, but there are also cappers made of contemporary materials, such as the U-View from T/C, which is designed to hold No. 209 shotgun primers. The Tedd Cash Company continues to build high-class traditional tools the old way, but in deference to modern muzzleloaders, Cash has a capper for No. 209 shotgun primers.

This short starter has a built-in muzzle protector that slides on the longer stem of the starter.

Each tool to its appointed function—the loading rod, shown here with muzzle protector at work, is ideal for the range. It is longer than the ramrod and therefore easier to use.

Shooting bags can be works of art or plain. This is a nice bag from Austin & Halleck.

The Short Starter

Used to shove the patched round ball a short distance past the muzzle, the short starter is also employed to start conicals. It normally has two protruding rods, the shorter one called the snub.

An extra nice shooting bag, custom made with embellishment.

Ramrods

The wooden ramrod matches traditional type blackpowder firearms. There are also traditional metal ramrods for various muzzleloaders, such as the Whitworth military rifled musket. My favorite pack-along shotgun has a strong brass ramrod. There are also many nearly indestructible ramrods showing in the pipes of modern muzzleloaders. These are definitely not the ramrods Dan'l Boone poked through the pipes of his long tom.

Loading Rods

Sometimes noted as wiping sticks in older literature, the loading rod is one piece of equipment that always finds its way to the range in my kit. There are many superior synthetic loading rods available. I like them better than older wooden types, although these rods have no place where tradition is the byword.

Carrying Supplies to Shooting Range or Hunting Field

A Shooting Bag for Every Gun

A bag for each blackpowder firearm is ideal. When the downwind shooter heads for the target range or hunting field, he or she simply grabs the shooting iron in question, plus appropriate pouch to match that gun, and that bag holds all essentials required for that specific firearm, not only for shooting, but for general cleanup until reaching home for a more thorough job.

The Shooting Box

A blackpowder shooting box accomplishes the same task as the shooting bag, only in a much bigger way. My shooting box is actually a standard size toolbox. Along with the usual screwdrivers, Allen wrenches, targets, hearing and eye protection, this muzzleloader box includes special tools, such

This shooting box is for the shotgun. It contains everything necessary for a full day—maybe even a week—of loading and firing the blackpowder scattergun.

as nipple wrenches and nipple picks, plus the appropriate muzzleloader powder, projectiles, patching material, and much more—a mini-warehouse of blackpowder "stuff." While there may have been a possible bag in the past full of great gear, my "possibles bag" is my shooting box. I also have a notebook and pen in my box for recording important information.

What's in Your Shooting Bag?

Here's a list from one of my shooting bags, presented only as a sample: powder measure (sometimes a charger instead), short starter, hornet nesting material, worm and screw, nipple wrench, combination tool with screwdriver, small metal box with pre-cut, pre-lubed patches, small (but ample) powder flask, priming horn, cleaning rag, solvent (in plastic eyewash bottle), ready loads (2), pipe cleaners, bristle bore brush, jag, capper, cap box (for percussion caps), extra flints (2), cleaning patches, spare nipple, small knife.

Other Stuff

Here are a few more blackpowder shooting necessaries: commercial blackpowder cleaning kit, bullet molding outfit, patch cutter, Tap-O-Cap (for making percussion caps), holsters, scabbard, gun cases, clothing (standard or buckskinning), larger knives, tomahawks, supply of cleaning patches, wiping cloths, solvents and other chemicals (including lubes), pre-cut shooting patches and patch material, extra nipples, extra ramrod, home-cast or commercial round balls, conicals, shotgun wads, shot, cleaning gear, Kap Kover, flash cup, ball bag, fusil, Kadooty, jags, nipple wrenches, and palm protector.

The Blackpowder Knife and Hawk

Not shooting instruments, but a knife, at least a jackknife, belongs in every kit. Traditions sells several, including a rendezvous-worthy trade model. Many companies offer replica knives and 'hawks pleasing to buckskinners. Carl P. Russell's *Firearms, Traps & Tools of the Mountain Man* has information on knives of that era, including trade knives, which were for trading, as the name implies, but also associated with a specific trade or line of work.

5 PUTTING THE TOOLS TO WORK

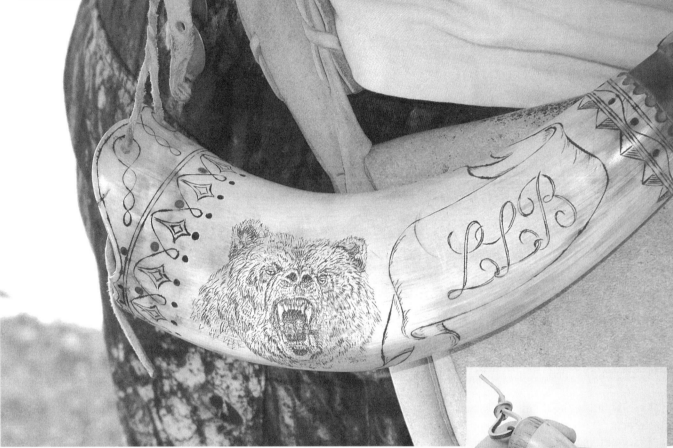

The powder horn is ultra simple to use. It remains at rest until called upon to dispense propellant and then it's simply "uncorked" for pouring from the spout.

The Powder Horn

Horn played a significant role in ancient times and it remains a useful element in the 21st century. The American bison, known familiarly as the buffalo, provided horn for powder horns and other implements, as well as decorative dress for the Plains Indian. Horn has a number of distinct properties regardless of its inauspicious origin as adornment and armament on the heads of bovines and other animals. Members of certain Indian tribes used antelope horns as decoration. Vikings never wore helmets with horns protruding from the sides. But even in that culture, horn played a role, possibly as drinking vessels and instruments or to trumpet a shrill blast into the air as announcement or warning. Shooters caught on to the many

good properties of horn very early in the game. Not to repeat all virtues, but remember that horn for powder horns can be boiled to soften, then shaped with pleasing or functional lines. The small end turns into a beautiful spout. Recall non-sparking, waterproof, and something not mentioned earlier—tough. Powder horns from ages back remain in perfect shape. You have to work at breaking one. Use is simple. Pour powder in (William Knight made a tiny funnel, also built of horn for this job) and stick the stopper in. When you need some powder, pull the stopper out and pour. *WARNING: never pour powder directly from a powder horn into the muzzle of a gun. A lingering spark from a previous firing could set off the entire cargo of the powder horn.*

To use the priming horn, push the point of the spout down upon the flintlock pan to operate the spring-loaded pre-measured reservoir and a small amount of FFFFg will flow into the pan.

Priming Horn

The smaller priming horn is equally simple to use and serves to store powder safely, in this case, pan powder. Although scholars disagree concerning past use, there is no argument that this little fellow is just right for priming the pan of any flintlock, be it rifle, pistol, or fowler (shotgun). Press the spout down on the hard surface of the flintlock pan, thus depressing the spring, which provides a trickle of priming powder, just the right amount for ignition.

Priming Tool

This little metal flask serves the same purpose as a priming horn, containing and dispensing fine-grain powder into a flintlock pan. The ones I have seen work the same as the priming horn by pushing a spring-loaded nose down to open the gate.

The Adjustable Powder Measure

As a reminder, a grain of weight is 1/7000th of a pound. In other words, there are 7000 grains weight in one pound, or 437.5 grains weight in one ounce. The name itself is somewhat unfortunate, since sometimes a single piece of powder is referred to as a grain, but is more properly a kernel or granule. Adjustable powders measures today work about the same way, usually sliding an inner rod with specific markings in grain volume either in or out, in to reduce the powder charge, out to increase the powder charge. Once the proper setting is located, the rod is locked in place. To use the adjustable powder measure, pour powder into the body from a powder horn or other proper container. Some measures have an integral funnel that rotates into place,

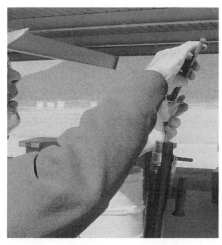

To use the adjustable powder measure—or any other measure—meter out correct amount of powder and pour the cargo straight down the muzzle.

This is a powder measure, but not an ordinary one. It is constructed of spark-proof material for metering out blackpowder. It's a handy device for the blackpowder cartridge shooter and it works like any standard powder measure.

which does two things. By swinging the funnel in line with the body of the capper, excess granules of powder are flicked off. And, of course, the funnel is also perfect for delivering the charge of powder down the bore of rifle, pistol, or shotgun, or into the chambers of the cap 'n' ball revolver. Today, there are adjustable powder measures that copy the past as well as those that would make the old mountain man blink in wonder. Original or modern, however, they do the same thing—they meter out a specific *volume* of propellant. That's the important function—volumetric charging, which is the right way to deal with black powder and its substitutes. The adjustable powder measure is perfect for black powder substitutes, such as Pyrodex and Triple Seven. Simply leave the measure at the normal setting for black powder and load by volume only.

Blackpowder Measure for Blackpowder

This is the same powder measure found on the reloading bench for smokeless powder cartridges, *but with a huge difference.* This powder measure is made of metals that are not known to

One excellent way to use the flask is in concert with a powder measure. A small flask is ideal for carrying powder in a shooting bag. Powder from the flask goes into the powder measure for a correct load.

spark. I would not include this tool here, but for the fact that it is now available, as from Hornady and Lyman. I have two friends who shoot a great deal of black powder cartridges at silhouettes. Both tell me I am wrong about half-grain loads in large bore black powder cartridges. I say prove to me that a half-grain can be detected either by chronograph or group on the target. These men, however, continue to tell me how wrong I am. Some of their charges are, as an example, 66.5-grains Swiss Fig in a 45-70 Government cartridge. Load 66.0-grains or 67.0-grains and accuracy goes from super to silly. And so these fellows meter out powder charges to near their ideal, and then they finish the charge on a powder/bullet scale to that one-half of one grain. Both have their blackpowder powder measures attached to their regular loading benches where they create ammo for their smokeless powder cartridges. And both have long drop tubes attached to these powder measures to promote the settling of the charge in the case.

The Powder/Bullet Scale

In keeping with the promise of this chapter, to explain the function of various blackpowder implements, the powder/bullet scale has found a place in blackpowder cartridge shooting and in the only muzzleloader allowed smokeless powder, the Savage 10ML. A charger in some form or another continues to see prudent use in smokeless powder charges for some guns. The Lee company offers many dippers for smokeless powder. I am, however, against the use of the adjustable black-powder measure for smokeless loads because there is no reason to do so, plus, these tools were never intended for smokeless powder in the first place. For shooters who insist that half-grain increments make their blackpowder cartridges work better, there is the powder/bullet scale. This is the very scale used to create extremely consistent loads in the modern cartridge. I use two of these. Both are electronic. The larger is from RCBS. The other is a compact scale from Lyman, which is highly accurate, but takes up very little space on the bench top. A second use I have for the powder/bullet scale is building smokeless powder loads for the Savage Model 10ML muzzleloader. My tests were with carefully scale-weighed charges of Alliant 2400 and H-4227. Several other smokeless powders are allowed in the Savage 10ML. Smokeless powder for the Savage was held to one-tenth of one-grain weight.

The Charger

The non-adjustable charger is the simplest powder measure I know of. There is nothing to making it work properly. Simply pour in the powder to the appropriate level and put the charge where it belongs. The shooter can safely make chargers because they are so simple and foolproof. Drilling out a piece of antler to a specific depth to throw a specific charge makes an interesting charger. Sometimes a cut-off cartridge case

The proper use of a ramrod or a loading rod is constant pressure to seat the bullet or shotgun wad fully upon the powder charge. A consistent pressure upon the rod load for load is recommended, while leaning body weight on the rod is definitely not recommended.

with a bit of wire wrapped around the bottom becomes an ideal charger.

The Flask

Flasks normally have some sort of metering device, or interchangeable spouts. There is nothing tricky about using the flask, other than choosing the proper one for the specific firearm in question. My original hard leather shotgun shot flask is adjustable to throw either 1-1/4 or 1-1/2 ounces of shot. All I have to do is switch to the charge that I want. My CVA flask with spouts requires only that I screw in the spout that I want for a specific powder charge. The end of the spout is blocked with a fingertip. Then the flask lever is activated, allowing powder to flow into the spout. When the lever is returned, it once again blocks powder from flowing out of the body of the flask. Flasks with screw-in spouts are adjusted for charge simply by changing the spout, longer spouts for more powder, and shorter ones for less powder. The flask that I depend upon most is the small one in my shooting bag. It allows me to leave the powder horn home.

The Readyloader

A readyloader is a handy tool for quick repeat shots. It's also good for safely containing a pre-measured volumetric powder charge in one compartment, along with a bullet in another compartment, and sometimes percussion cap(s) or primers as well. There are many different types avail-

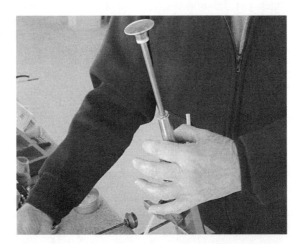

able. While not a specific readyloader, plastic 35mm film containers can be used for pre-measured shot and volumetric powder charges. The shooter simply pops the top on the powder container, squeezes the upper end to make a pouring trough, drops the charge downbore, followed by the same procedure with the shot container. Film containers are also useful for test loads with pre-measured powder charges. Since these plastic containers are non-sparking and essentially watertight, they are safe for carrying powder. With a little practice a shooter can reload his muzzleloader in a matter of seconds. Flip the top on the powder section. Pour the charge downbore. Flip the top on the bullet side of the loader. Push the bullet home on the powder charge. Undersized conicals load very rapidly. Cap and fire.

The Ramrod

The ramrod is another tool that is simple to use. After a patched round ball is put partway down the muzzle, or for that matter a conical bullet, the ramrod's job is to deliver the projectile down upon the powder charge. This is accomplished with a smooth push on the rod. The only accidents I, personally, know about with using the ramrod were caused by a very tight bullet, round or conical, virtually stuck in the bore. The shooter puts a lot of force on a wooden ramrod. It breaks and a sharp end stabs into the arm. Straight grain is imperative in the wooden ramrod to help prevent this problem. The other caution is putting far more weight on the ramrod than required to firmly seat the bullet on the powder. Smokeless powder can detonate with sufficient pressure. Blackpowder is more susceptible. I have no idea how much compression it would take to cause a black powder charge to ignite, nor do we wish to find out the hard way. So the ramrod is used judiciously to put the bullet down to the bottom of the bore, firmly. And that's it. The other caution is the same as sounded so often. The rod must be used to fully seat the bullet with no air gap—the short-start gremlin again.

Also, a ramrod can be marked for a given load. After that load is properly secured in the muzzleloader, the rod is marked where it meets the muzzle. The mark on the ramrod will appear in the same place every time that load is put downbore. If the mark on the ramrod rides up from the muzzle, there is something wrong—there is either more powder downbore than there is supposed to be or the bullet is not seated fully upon the powder. If the mark sinks out of sight, perhaps the charge was not up to snuff, or—and it happens—the shooter forgot to put powder in before seating the bullet. Loading, to be sure, is the main feature of the ramrod, but with a jag on the end it can be used as a cleaning rod. With a worm on the end, the ramrod can pull a stuck patch free. With a screw on the end, the ramrod is capable, usually, of extracting a bullet that did not seat properly, or when the firearm requires unloading without firing. I would have nothing but the proper wooden ramrod in the pipes of my original style muzzleloaders, but I appreciate the intelligent designs of ramrods for modern muzzleloaders.

The Loading/Cleaning Rod

The loading/cleaning rod is ideal on the range for firmly delivering bullets on powder charges. It serves also as a cleaning rod. Longer than a ramrod, strong, designed to hold many cleaning implements, the loading/cleaning rod is a necessary maintenance tool and many different types are available. Many different companies offer them. See the Directory. Wiping sticks are, to my mind, old-style loading/cleaning rods. They do the same work. The only main difference is that they are made of wood. And, of course, they are quite simple, being merely a wooden rod with a tip threaded female for jags, worms, screws, bore scrapers, and other implements, whereas modern loading/cleaning rods are made of space age materials.

The Muzzle Protector

The muzzle protector belongs with the ramrod and loading/cleaning rod because it is used with both types to prevent damage to the sensitive crown area of the muzzle. Even steel rods are not harmful when a muzzle protector is in place. My Navy Arms Whitworth rifle has a built-in muzzle protector. It rides on the steel rod and is put in place on the muzzle before seating a bullet. When in place, the muzzle protector ensures the rod remains centered in the bore at all times, rather than scraping the sides of the bore.

Palm Protector

Now in many different styles made of wood or high-tech materials, the palm protector does just that—it either slips over the end of the ramrod, or is part of a short starter, and it protects the hand while seating bullets.

Short Starter

The function of the short starter is just that—putting a bullet, round or conical, a short distance past the muzzle of the rifle or pistol. It is not used with the cap 'n' ball revolver or the shotgun. We're pretty sure that tightly fitted patched balls are more accurate than patched balls loose in the bore. This is where a short starter comes into play. It usually has a stub stem and a main stem, the stub, being so short, is perfect for starting the bullet, while the longer

The muzzle protector does a perfect job of centering the ramrod or loading rod in the bore to avoid the rifling at that point, thereby safeguarding the integrity of the rifling at the muzzle.

A palm protector can be a separate ball with a hole drilled into it. The end of the ramrod goes into the hole to protect the hand from the ramrod end itself. A short starter like this one has the option of inserting the end of the ramrod or loading rod into a drilled hole to serve as a palm protector.

stem drives it down far enough into the bore to allow the ramrod or loading rod to work properly. When a bullet is too high up in the bore, the ramrod and loading rod have so little length in the bore that either bends, with the wooden one likely to break.

Bullet Starters

The bullet starter is used just like a short starter and is really nothing more than a short starter with a different design. I use bullet starters on all muzzleloading rifles that do not have a recessed muzzle, because I am convinced that a conical bullet must be started square to the bore for best results, not cocked off at an angle. A bullet starter helps in getting the conical loaded correctly.

A short starter encourages a bullet into the first couple inches of the bore, although this particular bullet, a PowerBelt, normally seats perfectly into the bore by hand. Even at that, the longer stem of the short starter is required to push the bullet deeper into the bore.

This is a sophisticated nipple wrench with a ratchet system.

There are various nipple wrenches, not only with regard to size, but also type. Here are three different nipple wrenches.

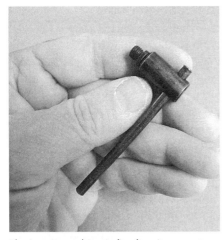

The important thing is fit when it comes to a nipple wrench. An ill-fitting wrench can damage a nipple.

The Vent Pick and Nipple Pick

Although little more than a piece of fine wire, the vent pick, also called nipple pick, is ideal for clearing fouling from the touchhole of a flintlock, as well as cap debris from the channel of a nipple. If properly sized, it can also be used to block the touchhole of a flintlock during the loading process, thereby preventing powder from packing into that area causing a "fuse" condition rather than a clear avenue from pan flame to breech. See Chapter 14 for proper flintlock loading procedures.

The Nipple Wrench and Breech Plug Wrench

There is nothing to using a nipple wrench properly, aside from making sure it fits the nipple properly. A proper breech plug wrench comes with the modern muzzleloader. Its job is simple but important—to remove the breech plug so the gun, rifle, shotgun, whatever, can be cleaned from the breech end. I find that shooters who complain they cannot pull a breech plug free with the provided wrench have failed in two ways. First, they cranked down on the breech plug wrench too forcefully. The breech plug certainly must be snugly in place. But it is has multiple fine threads and it does not require brute force to properly seat it. The other problem is failure to use anti-seize lubricant on the threads of the breech plug before screwing it back into the barrel.

Pipe Cleaners

Found at most grocery stores, pipe cleaners are intended to—of course—clean smoking pipes, but this length of wire with fuzzy fiber wrapping also makes an ideal muzzle-loading tool, acting somewhat like a nipple or vent pick, but with the ability to hold solvent. It's great for swabbing out flintlock touchholes, nipple vents, or picking up fouling from just about any hard-to-reach spot on a firearm.

Its use is self-explanatory. Just push it into the place to be cleaned or touchhole to be blocked.

The Capper

Cappers are also simple to use. In both the in-line and magazine type, a percussion cap is held in a jaw-like grip, lightly. The cap is centered on the cone of the nipple and pushed gently down, fully, to seat it on the nipple. The only trick is getting the right capper to begin with. There are different styles to match different firearms. There are also cappers for modern muzzleloaders that are specific to one and only one gun. Because of breech design, regular cappers will not function with these guns. Nowadays, there are special cappers for modern primers, large and small, as well as the big No. 208 shotgun primer and the top-hat or musket cap.

The Screw

There is nothing to using the screw properly. It is simply attached to the end of the ramrod, or better yet a loading rod (especially an unbreakable metal or synthetic one). Then the screw is centered on the round or conical bullet and screwed into the lead all the way for a good fit. Ideally, a bore protector should be used so that the screw is centered, rather than striking the rifling. The Kadooty loading tool includes a special knocker that provides extra impetus in pulling a stuck ball free. It works as a sliding hammer. This is what I use when removing a stuck bullet or if I wish to unload a loaded muzzleloader without firing it.

The Kadooty

I will leave the proper function of this device to the instruction sheet, but it does deserve special mention here because this unique loading tool serves many purposes. Along with ensuring the same pressure upon the powder charge for each shot to create uniformity, the Kadooty is also a cleaning rod, and it can be used to pull stuck bullets or sabots free. The knocker, acting as a sliding hammer, makes withdrawing these objects effortless. It's good for pistols, revolvers, and shotguns as well as rifles, and it's built to last lifetimes; comes in a handy haversack.

Jags

The jag is used by screwing it into the tip of ramrod. It works in driving a bullet fully home on the powder charge or for holding a cleaning patch to clean the bore of the gun. Jags come in various sizes and shapes, usually with concave noses to drive soft lead round balls and conicals downbore with minimal deformation. Certain breech shapes demand specific jags for proper fit. Jags that do not match the configuration of the breech section may get hung up down there.

The Worm

This is another device that is simple to use. Attach to ramrod or loading rod tip, and carefully run it downbore to snag a wayward round ball or cleaning patch. I also use the worm to loosen compacted powder downbore, especially when a load has been in the breech for a while. The bullet is pulled free with the screw, but the worm works better in breaking up that stuck powder charge.

The Fusil

Not given much mention in Chapter 4, the fusil is a confusing term. Sometimes it was used to single out a specific type of muzzleloading firearm. The fusil noted here is the one mentioned by Ned Roberts in his writings. It is a threaded metallic body that takes the place of a nipple. Instead of holding a percussion cap, it retains a modern primer. A good example of a fusil is Markesbery's 400 SRP Magnum Ignition System. It replaces the nipple of the Markesbery Outer-Line rifle, and it takes a small rifle primer rather than a percussion cap. It's fitted in place with an Allen wrench. The same wrench also fits directly into the body of the

SRP with cover removed. Fusils are not necessary for most dry weather shooting, but they can be priceless in wet conditions, making a muzzleloader fire, rather than going ftttt! Memory calls up the image of a truly huge bull elk only 12 paces away—stepped off afterwards to verify the distance. When the trigger was pulled, the sights were lined up perfectly on the neck. Only instead of a healthy boom, the rifle provided nothing more than a tiny pop as the percussion cap was struck. Damp weather did it. While there is no guarantee, odds are a fusil with primer would have ensured ignition.

Kap Kover

The Kap Kover has been around for a long time. It fits over the top of the nipple, acting as a gasket to keep water out. It's also a safety device. The firearm will not go off until the Kap Kover is removed.

The Shooting Bag

The bag is brought up here simply not to leave it out, but its use is fully understood by anyone. It holds the good stuff needed for shooting. What can be added, however, is that size is important. I have a very small shooting bag from October Country. It's called Courier and it holds ample supplies for a hunt. The Courier is only four by six, but there isn't a muzzleloader it won't serve in the game field.

Ball Bag

There is also nothing to using this item because you don't use it. It simply holds bullets. The tanned scrotum of a bull buffalo or other super-sized bovine served to contain round bullets for the old-time hunter. Now the ball bag is made, usually, of tanned leather, but it serves the same purpose.

The Flash Cup

This little gadget was also brushed over in Chapter 4. Put a flash cup on the nipple seat and then screw a nipple in place to hold it. That is it. The cup

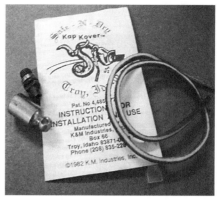

The Kap Kover helps keep out the rain and it is also a safety device.

Shooting bags can be home-crafted of the finest leather with great embellishment or practical synthetic models, like this one from Austin & Halleck.

The flash cup is attached between nipple seat and nipple to ward off flame and sparks that could otherwise damage wood in that area.

diverts flame and cap debris from wooden parts of the stock that could be burned or marred. The Tedd Cash company has excellent flash cups in different sizes. They're authentic, and if anything they add to the beauty of a rifle, rather than taking away from it.

General Cleaning Gear

The reader can figure this gear out for himself or herself. So this catch-all section simply includes the already mentioned loading/cleaning rod and other maintenance instruments, as well as patches, solvents, old toothbrushes, pipe cleaners and more, including bore brushes that are ideal for squirreling gunk out of rifling grooves or getting down into the grooves of the rifling and removing fouling. Cleaning equipment also includes everything from rags and toothbrushes to pipe cleaners.

The employment of accoutrements is not difficult. The only trick is finding the very best ones for a specific black-powder firearm. This is especially true in this day of the modern muzzleloader. But that, too, is no problem because companies have paved the way by including the right tools with their guns. While I admire the accoutrements of the past for their clever design and workings, I also have to nod approval to the equally well-designed tools that accompany modern front-loaders.

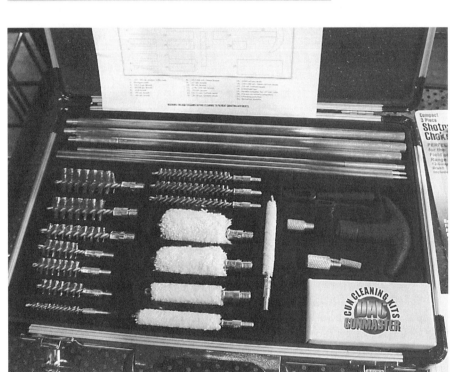

This simple ball bag was handmade of leather.

This handsome cleaning kit is but one of the useful tools in maintaining a blackpowder firearm.

chapter

6 NON-REPLICAS

The Great Plains Rifle is a crossover in the respect that it could be considered a rifle in the spirit of the 19th century. However, it stands as a non-replica because it does not replicate an original.

The Lyman Plains Pistol is very much like a caplock pistol of the 19th century that may have been carried by a mountain man. But it is not a replica, and some shooters will much prefer it over a replica, in fact.

An old Stoeger's *Shooter's Bible* showed for sale a number of blackpowder muzzleloading firearms made—I know not where—and more in tune with showing than shooting. These were non-replicas, but they were not even close to what would be found in the same fine publication decades later. The difference was function as well as appearance. The first non-replica rifles, for they were rifles, were designed to offer the shooter a strongly-made, safe, functional, long gun loaded from the muzzle with blackpowder. Rumors of the return of the Hawken flitted about hunting camps, shooting ranges, and around the "cracker barrel" of gun stores. But not to be. The name was there, but not the rifle. What was missed by those tearful over what was clearly a non-replica "Hawken" was that the vast majority of shooters would take to it like a black lab to the duck pond. I recall a lazy afternoon at my home in the foothills of a Wyo-

ming mountain range when a knock on the door announced the arrival of my friend Gene. I had been out shooting. In one corner was propped No. 47, so handsome that it would bring words of praise to the lips of all who saw it. In another corner was a non-replica of the "Hawken" persuasion. Gene eyed both, picked both up, and concluded, "This is the one I like. It feels better to me. It's shorter and lighter. And I like its looks." He was holding the non-replica rifle.

The sweeping march of the modern muzzleloader frightened non-replicas, but never sent them scurrying into darkness. The reason—exactly what my friend Gene saw—a well-made, of top-grade materials, highly manageable rifle geared for the big game hunt, mainly in calibers 50 and 54. The non-replica was, and remains, a rugged muzzleloader entirely suitable not only for big game, but also small edibles. My long-standing gripe was the rifling of

most non-replicas with the 1:48 rate of twist. I complained. Others complained. Nothing was done for a long time. This was partly because the 1:48 twist in 50- and 54-calibers works pretty well with conicals loaded up to snuff and patched round balls loaded moderately. Chapter 20 reveals why this is true. Big game hunters especially found that accuracy with Minie bullets and conicals was adequate for most hunting, especially in timber and brush. These hunters were trendsetters without, perhaps, knowing it. They chose non-replica rifles as *practical* for the blackpowder-only big game season. Cost was not high, function was good. Most of all, these hunters required a muzzleloader to take part in the fine seasons provided by game departments for "handicapped" shooters. It would come to pass that the huge surge of blackpowder popularity would be for the same reason—admission into the special "primitive" hunt.

Blackpowder Shooting Never Died Out

Blackpowder guns, muzzleloaders and their cartridge-shooting brothers, never died out. They were too interesting to perish. Well-known gunwriters such as Elmer Keith continued to shoot and pen articles on the subject of blackpowder shooting. Blackpowder itself remained available. Originals were perhaps not in plenty, but neither were they impossible to find. Even those who moved entirely away from front-loaders had a positive impact on the game. Colonel Townsend Whelen, who became known as *Mister Rifleman*, included mention of blackpowder guns in his fine book, Mr. Rifleman. He went on to note that his mentor won the 1,000 yard Wimbledon match in 1898 shooting a blackpowder cartridge, the 45-100-550 Sharps. In the background, if not foreground, blackpowder smoke continued to linger, and those who got a whiff of it very often could not help but partake of the fun.

Clubs and loosely organized shooting groups met to compare, enjoy, and shoot the firearms of yesteryear. There was the NMRLA, National Muzzle-Loading Rifle Association, dedicated to blackpowder shooters all over the U.S.A. and Canada. Gun magazines, especially *The American Rifleman*, continued to print stories about firearms long out of manufacture, many of them charcoal-burners. As noted above, catalogues from the 1940s and 1950s, such as *The Shooter's Bible*, continued to sell blackpowder guns. Two men of foresight, Turner Kirkland and Val Forgett, believed that if they pumped oxygen into the still-breathing, but not-too-lively blackpowder sport, it would resuscitate via two companies: Dixie Gun Works and Navy Arms. They were right. Replicas came first, mainly revolvers, but it took hunters and special blackpowder-only seasons to truly bring old-time guns back into the bright light of day.

21st Century Non-Replicas

Non-replica blackpowder guns exist in several categories: muzzleloading rifles, pistols, and shotguns, plus blackpowder cartridge-shooters. A ramble through the current *Gun Digest* proved to me that non-replicas have not yet been trampled into the dust by the stampede to modern charcoal-burners. It's dangerous to point out specific firearms, because blackpowder shooting is so strong today that manufacturers and importers are constantly revising their line. Nonetheless, specific rifles do lend themselves to explanation of the non-replica *type*.

Muzzleloading Non-Replica Rifles

I think it was the Thompson/Center Hawken that first alerted me to a non-replica muzzleloader style coming on the scene. To this hour, the Hawken remains an exemplary success. Thousands have been made and the ones

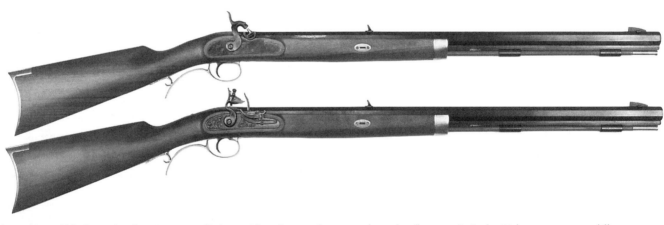

The embers of blackpowder shooting never died out. When these embers were fanned to flame again in the 20th century, many different guns were offered. This Lyman Trade Rifle is a prime example of a cross between old-time and modern. It comes in flint or percussion, but it also is available in a rate of twist rapid enough to stabilize totally modern bullets.

Two men, Turner Kirkland and Val Forgett II, are considered forerunners in bringing blackpowder guns back into general use. They both leaned toward replicas. However, rifles like this Lyman Deerstalker made a big impression on modern shooters who appreciated lighter, trimmer guns.

So interested in blending today with yesterday are modern hunters that a stainless steel version of the Lyman Deerstalker is quite popular. It retains a general old-time look, but when was there a stainless steel plains rifle in the 19th century?

Blending some old-time lines and general handling characteristics with the modern is typified in this Lyman Great Plains Hunter, a rifle designed to meet the needs of a 21st-century outdoors person who wants a modern sight on a rifle capable of shooting modern bullets.

that have been properly loaded, fired, and cared for remain in full service. There are actually more non-replica muzzleloaders available in the 21st century than were offered in the 20th. The Armsport Armoury R-140 is an example. Let's take a look. This rifle replicates nothing from the past. It has a 29-inch octagon barrel, comes in calibers 45, 50, and 54, removable breech plug (unlike the original plains rifle), and is blued, not browned. Then there is Cabela's Traditional Hawken. It is traditional of a non-replica in calibers 50 and 54 with 29-inch barrel (If there was a 29-inch barrel Hawken, I have yet to see it). This rifle comes in flint as well as percussion, but that does not make it traditional. The same company has a sporterized version of the same rifle—but with "more modern stock style and rubber recoil pad." Don't recall seeing a rubber recoil pad on a Hawken, or for that matter a Pennsylvania long rifle. The CVA St. Louis Hawken is another perfect example of the breed. The Dixie Gun Works Club Rifle is another non-replica offered in 40-caliber, "a short rifle for small game and beginning shooters," and certainly

not a replica. Traditions 50-caliber PA Pellet Flintlock is another non-replica blackpowder rifle, albeit in flintlock. So whether or not the name is traditional, these rifles resemble original rifles like Mars resembles Earth—both planets, but it ends there.

Modernized Non-Replica Muzzleloading Rifles

These rifles lie in between standard non-replicas and modern muzzleloaders, showing features of both. A prime example of this breed is the aforementioned Traditions Pellet. While it embodies non-replica features, it also has a removable breech plug and the stock is available in hardwood, in synthetic and synthetic camouflage. The modernized versions of replica muzzleloaders carry special features such as the aforementioned, including fiber-optic sights. Some of these modernized non-replica rifles also carry faster than 1:48 twist for better conical bullet stabilization. Also, we will see more of these modernized non-replicas going capable with three Pyrodex Pellets or Triple Seven Pellets

for convenient loading in the big game field. Whereas ignition for non-replicas was strictly percussion cap in the past, these modernized versions will, at least some of them, "go off" with primers or musket caps.

The Non-Replica Handgun

Not to be confused with the modern muzzleloader pistol, the non-replica handgun rests quietly in its own niche. Sometimes it resembles a side-arm of the past, as in the interesting Traditions Crockett Pistol with 10-inch blued barrel and single trigger, 32 caliber, 1:16 rate of twist. Then again, it may not look at all like an original. For example, the Traditions Pioneer Pistol

There is nothing new about micrometer-adjustable sights like this excellent Lyman model. Such sights were found on rifles in the 19th century. However, at the same time, a sight like this one was never seen on a plains rifle of old, especially with fine graduations for very percise sight changes.

This Lyman micrometer-adjustable aperture sight can now be found resting on rifle styles dating back at least a century and longer in time.

embodies classic styling, but replicates no gun of the past. CVA's Kentucky and Hawken Pistols also meet the criteria for non-replica handguns. While at first glance they look old-time, comparing either with copies of originals, such as Colt's 1860 Army, clearly proves they are not replicas. Over time there have been a number of non-replica handguns designed to serve shooters who simply want to enjoy firing side arms without concern for heritage. Lyman's Plains Pistol is one. It's not a true copy of a Hawken pistol, but it shoots fine, looks enough like the "real thing" to raise no eyebrows at rendezvous, and is very much at home in the camp or on the trail. Ruger's Old Army is another non-replica copying no handgun of the past, somewhat resembling a cross between a Remington 1858 Civil War revolver and a Ruger single-action. This well-built handgun comes in one of

four ways, all 45-caliber, but two with adjustable sights, one blued, the other stainless steel. There are also two fixed sight models, one blued, and the other stainless. One thing is certain. Non-replica handguns are not going away. We can expect more of them in the future.

The Non-Replica Shotgun

Arguably, the admired double-barrel muzzleloading shotgun found in so many catalogues today falls into the non-replica class, but it so closely embodies the spirit of yesteryear, that it falls into another category. Currently, there are very few non-replica shotguns on the market. Thompson/Center's New Englander, for example, does not appear in that company's catalogue as this is written. Other non-replica shotguns have also been dismissed. But CVA's Trapper and Gobbler shotguns do fill the bill. The Trapper is 12-gauge with a chrome-lined barrel for lead, bismuth, or steel shot. It's a 28-inch blued single-barrel gun weighing only six pounds. The hardwood stock follows the English straight grip tradition. The Gobbler is also a 12-gauge with a hardwood stock.

The Non-Replica Black Powder Cartridge Gun

Most blackpowder cartridge guns are copycats. The vast array of handguns definitely looks back to old-time

heritage. Rifles in both single-shot and lever-action repeaters, likewise.

Many More

There are many other muzzleloaders of non-replica design, such as the Kodiak Express Double Barrel Rifle as sold through Cabela's. This rifle copies no past model exactly, but comes from the world of dangerous game hunting, especially Africa, India, and Asia where wild animals lurked that could "shoot back." The Kodiak is listed with calibers 50, 54, 58, and 72; rate of twist 1:48 and weight a bit under 9-1/2 pounds. It's a percussion rifle with double hammers, and reportedly regulated to deliver bullets from each barrel into a pattern at 75 yards. October Country has a big-bore rifle that has a definite link with the past, but when all of its particulars are included, it moves into the non-replica realm, in spite of its 19th century lines. This is the Great American Sporting rifle, caliber 69, capable of handling a strong powder charge behind a big patched round ball. It can be ordered with a muzzle brake, express rear sights, three-blade, and Ashley Ghost Ring Hunting Sight Set.

Non-replicas will be around for a long time to come, but they will not occupy the status held in the past because modern muzzleoaders are moving rapidly into the number one spot. These guns will not die out, however,

Here is a combination that is seldom seen. Austin and Halleck have come up with a muzzleloader that resembles a 19th-century blackpowder cartridge lever-action rifle.

A close look at the receiver of the Austin & Halleck non-replica blackpowder rifle proves how much it resembles a 19th-century lever-action blackpowder cartridge repeater.

because they can be produced for a very reasonable market price, as CVA proves with its Bobcat Rifle at well under $125 with synthetic, only a little beyond that with walnut stock, under $140 in a special Youth Hunter model. Furthermore, the non-replica continues to fill the bill for thousands of big-game hunters who want to take advantage of the many special black-powder-only hunts offered across the country, but are not interested in shooting the guns of the old-timers.

Yes, this is the old-time 'nutcracker'-type reloading tool, and it certainly looks very much like the original, but it's better made than ever and it comes in calibers unheard of in the distant past. It has to be classified as a fine non-replica tool.

Talk about non-replica, this heavy bench gun is that. Yes, it resembles the big bench rifles of the 19th century, but it is made entirely modern—from materials to sights.

REPLICAS AND IN-THE-SPIRIT GUNS

Replicas allow shooters to relive the past, shooting the guns that America's early hunters, adventurers, explorers, frontiersmen and pioneers shot.

One dictionary definition for replica is: "any very close reproduction or copy; facsimile." That works for our purposes, but it doesn't go far enough. Replica guns can be screw-for-screw, as with certain revolvers that were so well duplicated that it took an expert to tell the difference between an original and a newly made gun. Most replicas fit the above definition, however: a close copy. Finally, there are in-the-spirit guns that function very much like the real thing, but do not reproduce it.

Replicas serve at least two important functions. They allow a shooter to relive the past, firing guns just like the old-timers carried. They're also great for collecting, where the original is either extremely difficult to locate, very expensive, or both. Serious collectors

won't want replicas in their holdings, but for the rest of us, they work just fine. In-the-spirit muzzleloaders and black-powder firearms serve only the first purpose. Study, history, shooting enjoyment, filling a niche in a collection: replicas serve all of these functions.

Who Makes Them?

Replicas are made in both the United States and abroad by many different arms manufacturers. In America, Colt has long been known for its close copies of original revolvers. The Navy Arms Co., spurred by the special interests of its president, Val Forgett, brought forth many replicas of pistols, revolvers, and rifles over the years. The guns mentioned below are currently available; however, many fine replicas no longer

featured in catalogs can be located at gun shows, newspaper classified ads, and especially in *The Gun List* and similar publications.

The Pistols

The Murdock Scottish Highlanders Pistol from Dixie Gun Works is an exact copy of an Alexander Murdock flintlock smoothbore in 52 caliber, with bright-finish steel frame and butt-shaped butt stock of ram's horn. The barrel is tapered round. Dixie also offers a Scottish Watch Pistol in 58 caliber, also a flintlock, as well as a LePage Dueling Pistol, 45 caliber, with interesting French-style vertical ribbing on the European walnut grip. Navy Arms continues to sell a reproduction of the 1805 Harpers Ferry Pistol in 58 caliber with a browned,

This Navy Arms replica of a Colt Bisley may not be a screw-for-screw copy of the original, but it is close enough to qualify as a handgun that will shoot very much like the "real thing." One change, for example, is a transfer bar to make this revolver safer than the original.

Here is a perfect example of a fine cap-and-ball replica revolver—the Whitney. It's very well made and it shoots even better than it looks.

The Colt revolver had a great impact on American history. This one is in caliber 36.

rifled barrel. Most of these pistols fired modest powder charges, but because of the caliber and bullet heft, they were quite effective up close, especially as boarding pistols when sailors from one ship swarmed upon the deck of another ship at sea. A more powerful single-shot pistol in near-replica form is Lyman's Plains Pistol, 50 or 54, with a 1:30 rate of twist. Many replica pistols are enjoyable to own, study, and shoot, while models such as the pepperbox fill gaps

in a collection when the real thing cannot be located at an acceptable price.

Cap 'n' Ball Revolvers

Soldiers on both sides of the War Between the States carried many different revolvers, including the interesting Starr, favored by some Union officers, and again available as a copy from the Navy Arms Co. The Spiller and Burr, originally produced in Atlanta, also is back. So is the Rogers and Spencer Army Model. All are very nicely manufactured for the enjoyment of today's cap 'n' ball revolver enthusiasts. Continuing in the lead, however, are the two most-used Civil War revolvers: Remington's Model of 1858 and Colt's Model 1860 Army. Colt has resurrected many of its blackpowder revolvers, including the Colt Paterson of 1842 Holster Model, gold inlaid and hand engraved. The huge Colt Walker is also in the lineup, along with many others, such as the Trapper of 1862 and the 1851 Navy. A revolver, yes, but not a sidearm, the Remington Revolving Carbine, 44 caliber with 18-inch barrel, is back. Fewer than a thousand were manufactured between 1866 and 1879.

Muskets

British soldiers brought their 18th century Brown Bess Muskets, bored 75 caliber, to America to subdue the Colonists. The same rifle in replication is offered to today's shooter who wants to relive a piece of shooting history, or do a re-enactment of the past. Replica muskets continue in force with multiple examples from many companies. The Navy Arms Co. offers examples from both Confederate and Union sides, such as the Zouave 58 caliber (Union) and the 1841 Mississippi in both 54 and 58

(Confederate). The accurate Whitworth musket, used in 19th-century target competition and a favorite of Confederate snipers, continues to be made and serves as a rugged piece well-suited to the hunting field and target range.

Pennsylvania Long Rifle

Custom gunsmiths replicate this famous piece from the Golden Age of American firearms. Good ones are as accurate as they are handsome and historical. There are also in-the-spirit Kentuckies that follow the general lines of the original, but with no attempt to copy them. Shooting these rifles is definitely an old-time experience regardless of their overall appearance. Some shooters add a Kentucky-style pistol, making a set of two: long gun and sidearm. Distinguishing between replica and in-the-spirit Kentucky long rifles is no big trick, and the commercial models are far less expensive than the customs. Mountain State Muzzleloading Supplies Co.'s Golden Classic and Silver Classic long rifles are styled to serve the buckskinner as well as hunter/shooter interested in the Pennsylvania traditional style.

The Plains Rifles

The Ithaca Hawken was about as close to a replica as a shooter could ask. It was patterned closely after an original plains rifle that supposedly belonged to Kit Carson, as I recall. Later, Navy Arms Co. took the rifle over; however, it does not appear in the current catalog. Lyman's Great Plains Rifle is still available, however, in 50 and 54 caliber, both as a flintlock or percussion gun. Here is a rifle that fully generates the spirit of old, although it is not an exacting replica. It comes in left-hand or right-hand

The Brown Bess musket is offered from several different companies as a replica of the smoothbore the Redcoats fired upon the Colonials when America was in its infancy as a country. This one is from Dixie Gun Works.

It's not all guns. This copy of a powder horn would have gone very well with an original Kentucky longrifle found on the Eastern Seaboard of early America.

Copies of powder flasks are collectible as well as useful. This is a replica of a Colt flask.

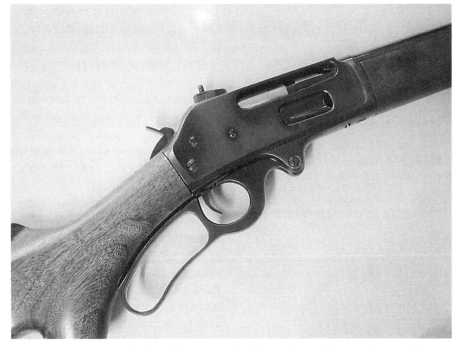

Lever-action repeaters are far from left out in replica form. This one from Marlin, actually a 336, may not truly qualify as a replica because it so closely matches the 19th century original.

One of Fadala's favorites—a replica of a Remington Rolling Block rifle, a single shot of "buffalo runner" days, this one in 38-55 Winchester.

models with a 32-inch barrel rifled a turn in 60 inches for round-ball stabilization. The Great Plains Hunter version of this rifle carries a 1:32 twist rate for conicals, giving the hunter the option of an old-style rifle that shoots popular elongated bullets. Pedersoli's Tryon Percussion Rifle, 45, 50, or 54 calibers, 32-inch barrel with 1:66 rate of twist in the 54, is a fairly close copy of the original plains rifle. Austin & Halleck's Mountain Rifle does a great job of bringing the plains rifle back to life. This 50-caliber half-stock comes in flint or percussion in 1:66 twist for ball, but with a 1:28 option for conicals. Although not historical, it is the choice of many modern downwind shooters.

Backwoods One-Man-Shop Rifles

They were called Dutch, but really they were German. The mistake came when these industrious people found their way into Pennsylvania. When asked of their origin, they said Deutch — German — but it sounded like Dutch, and that's what stuck: Pennsylvania Dutch. Among the group were fine arms makers who began to ply their

trade in the New World. Gunmaking in other parts of the country often focused on simpler and more practical rifles, because dollars were few, yet a decent rifle was still required. Sometimes called Poor Boy rifles, few are spotted these days, but there's one that's been around for a long time: Dixie Gun Works' Mountain Rifle in finished and kit choices. Percussion or flintlock, left- or right-hand, the Mountain Rifle is available in 32 as well as 50 calibers. It's a true long tom with a barrel measuring a full 41-1/4 inches. The 32 is ideal for small game and wild turkey hunting, firing a 45-grain patched round ball at more than 2,000 fps muzzle velocity with only 30 grains volume of FFFg blackpowder.

Ancients

Dixie Gun Works also offers two long guns from a distant past. The Dixie Japanese Tanegashima Matchlock is named for the Japanese island where the first matchlock came ashore in an auspicious manner via a Portuguese shipwreck. It's said that this incident brought firearms to Japan. The replica sold by Dixie is patterned after one from Kunitomo, a village near Kyoto. It's 53 inches long with a 41

One of Sam's pets is a Marlin 38-55, very much like the same Marlin of the 19th century beloved of many woodsman.

While this is not a replica of an original blackpowder shotgun shell, it fits into the spirit aspect of replicas.

1/2-inch octagonal browned barrel, 50-caliber, with only a 7-inch length of pull (distance from butt to trigger). Dixie calls for a 45-grain FFg powder charge with a .490-inch patched round ball. The other ancient rifle is also a matchlock, the English model. This predecessor of the flint-lock came to America, Dixie notes, in the 1600s to 1800s. It's 57 inches long in 72-caliber with a 44-inch Getz custom barrel. Dixie calls for 70 grains of FFg with a .715-inch patched round ball for this smoothbore rifle.

Blackpowder Cartridge Revolvers

There is no lack of blackpowder cartridge revolvers on the market today, with most of them in replica style. Cowboy Action Shooting has ignited a fire under these trustworthy handguns of yesteryear and a wealth of well-made imports copying Colts have come into the country. This includes the Bisley flat-top model (also known as the Frontier Target Model) manufactured from 1894 to 1913. It has an adjustable rear sight for windage, a spring-loaded front sight and the unique Bisley-style grip. Of course, the famous Model 1873 Peacemaker is represented in full force. Calibers are 38 Special, 44-40 Winchester and 45 Colt, also referred to as the 45 "Long" Colt, although there never really was a cartridge of that name. Navy Arms offers a reproduction of the Colt 1873 with the claim that parts will fit original Colt First and Second Generation single-action revolvers. It comes in 44-40 Winchester, 45 Colt, and also 357 Magnum. But that's not all. There's also the Smith & Wesson Schofield revolver, a break-top revolver in calibers 44-40 or 45 Colt.

Blackpowder Cartridge Single-Shot Rifles

Long before the now-popular blackpowder cartridge silhouette game played a role, there were many single-shot blackpowder cartridge rifles available, mainly in the tradition of Sharps

and Remington models. The list has grown. The Springfield Trapdoor Rifle of 1873 is on the scene, caliber 45-70 Government, along with long-range Rolling Blocks, same caliber, but also offered in 40-65, which came along to satisfy silhouette shooters who wanted to knock over metallic rams at 500 meters, but with a cartridge of modest recoil. There is even a Baby Rolling Block, 20-inch barrel, calibers 44-40 Winchester or 45 Colt. Browning's Model 1885 Single Shot in 40-65 Winchester or 45-70 Government is a copy of the famous original. The same company has a Model 1885 BPCR (Black Powder Cartridge Rifle) with Vernier tang sight for long-range shooting.

Blackpowder Cartridge Repeaters

It's as if the past has come alive. Dozens of different repeating blackpowder cartridge rifles are back in modern manufacture. They include many Winchesters, such as Oliver Winchester's Model 1866 Yellow Boy, an improvement on the Henry repeater, as well as the famous Model of 1873, noted for One of One Thousand fame with an old Jimmy Stewart feature film in its honor. Tested was a Navy Arms version of the Model 1892 Winchester, selected in 45 Colt chambering to match a Bisley Colt 45 revolver. The rifle/revolver combination proved interesting and enjoyable to shoot. For the most part, these lever-

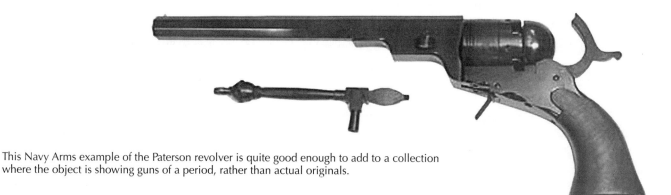

This Navy Arms example of the Paterson revolver is quite good enough to add to a collection where the object is showing guns of a period, rather than actual originals.

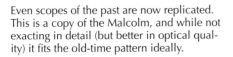

Even scopes of the past are now replicated. This is a copy of the Malcolm, and while not exacting in detail (but better in optical quality) it fits the old-time pattern ideally.

action repeaters are chambered for the 44-40 Winchester cartridge; however, as referred to above with regard to the Model 1892, the 45 Colt has also been chambered in these replicas. Not to be forgotten are Browning's modern-made replicas of past blackpowder cartridge rifles, including the Model 1886 and Model 1892. Remington Arms has come forth with a rifle that it made in the 19th century, the Rolling Block.

Remington's 21st century version from its Custom Shop is very much a copy of the original. It comes as a No. 1 Rolling Block Mid-Range Sporter or a No. 1 Rolling Block Silhouette Rifle with optional Vernier-type tang sight. An American walnut stock, satin blue metal finish, buckhorn rear sight and 30-inch round barrel of carbon steel are standard appointments. Options include a half-round, half-octagonal barrel; original Remington rear tang sight; front globe sight with spirit level; single set trigger; semi-fancy American walnut stock with steel Schnabel forend and steel buttplate; plus a case-colored receiver. The Silhouette model meets all requirements for the sport. It has a heavy 30-inch barrel chambered for the 45-70 Government cartridge, with button rifling (1:18 twist) for stabilizing long-range conicals such as Lyman's special LRHP bullets (Long Range High Performance).

Even cannons and mortars from the past are replicated today. This is a fair enough copy of an original mortar that launched a lead ball with blackpowder.

Blackpowder Shotguns

The double-barrel blackpowder shotgun of the hour is close enough in replication at least to deserve an in-the-spirit ranking. It certainly loads like and shoots like the original. It also enjoys ballistics on par with the old-time scattergun. In short, the experience is the same as if the gun were sold in a gun store of the 1800s. Flintlock fowlers have come and gone. These come closer, perhaps, in replication than single-shot and double guns. The 12-gauge, single-shot Pedersoli shotgun, Cylinder bore, is a faithful reproduction of an English smoothbore. It's billed as one of the best guns in that manufacturer's lineup, with a lock that "resembles the workings of an expensive clock." A half-stock in European walnut with a checkered wrist, this one comes as a 54-caliber rifle as well with 1:66 twist for round-ball shooting.

So Many More

Replicas abound today, in spite of a lack of Hawken design among plains rifles. There's the Harpers Ferry rifle, Springfield Musket, Enfield Musket, Smith Carbine, percussion Sharps in various models, 1766 Charleville Musket, Waadtlander Target Rifle of Swiss origin, Bristlen Morges Target Rifle, and the list goes on. A blackpowder fan interested in replicas needs only to gather up a batch of catalogs and browse to find one suitable for his wishes and requirements.

chapter
8 THE MODERN MUZZLELOADER

Lyman Product's Mustang Breakaway is the epitome of the 21st century modern muzzleloader. It is compact, medium-light weight, carries easily, has 209 ignition and it loads and cleans easily. Of special interest is the simple manner of installing the primer. In spite of the innovation, the Mustang remains a muzzleloader—one shot at a time.

The Savage Model 10MLII closely resembles its forerunner, the accurate Savage Model 110 bolt-action rifle that comes in various calibers, such as the No. 1 big-game cartridge in the world, the 30-06 Springfield.

Initial discontent with modern muzzleloaders has gone from high fever to mild flush. Those who thought the concept ran in the wrong direction have recognized that there is no stopping this train, let alone slowing it down. The newfangled gun is here to stay, so live with it. I took a dim review of modern muzzleloaders in the beginning. But not anymore—for two good reasons. First, who am I to tell people what they must shoot? Second, I grabbed a much closer look, and while it may make my dyed-in-the-buckskin friends angry with me, I became snake-fascinated with the "new" front-loader. I found most of them well made, accurate, powerful, interesting in design, and in the final analysis, not one whit more field-worthy than many originals, non-replicas, and replicas.

They were muzzleloaders pure and simple. Chapter 2 describes the down-to-earth basics of a muzzleloader as a barrel blocked on one end, open on the other, with a means of, and avenue for, ignition. True, the modern muzzleloader is a lot more than that, but it still shoots one shot at a time before requiring reloading, and the process remains about the same: drop proper powder

charge (or Pellets) down the muzzle followed by a bullet. Then install something to make the gun go *boom*, even if today that something is often a No. 209 shotgun primer, not a percussion cap, and surely not pan powder.

The Modern Muzzleloader in Profile

Mostly in rifle format, there are also pistols and shotguns that reside in the modern muzzleloader camp. They are unrecognizable, quite often, as muzzleloaders. That is, they don't copy anything from yesteryear, not the famed Pennsylvania-Kentucky long rifle of the Daniel Boone era, or the stout plains rifle of the Fur Trade when mountain men left St. Louis to catch beaver in the Far West.

Where They Fit

The modern muzzleloader fits in the hunting field. They are worthy of target shooting, of course, and a marksman can plink away with one for hours of good fun scaring beverage cans to jump into the air. But all in all, hunters buy these guns—rifles in the main—for hunting. They buy them so they can have the closest thing to a non-muzzle-

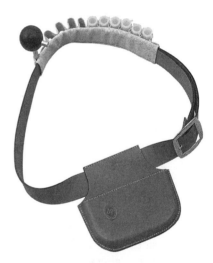

The theme of the modern muzzleloader is ease of handling. This Pedersoli shooting belt is a perfect example of that theme. It holds readyloads that can be popped down-bore quickly. Note the short starter attached to the belt.

loader as possible, while still carrying a firearm legal for the many special blackpowder-only (primitive) hunts offered by game departments everywhere. The modern muzzleloader is to blackpowder shooting what the compound bow is to archery. In archery, the beautiful recurve or longbow requires sincere practice to do well with it, shooting "instinctively" more often than not. Meanwhile, the compound bow requires less

The Modern Muzzleloader ✳ **75**

We can expect more modern muzzleloaders like this one from CVA—the company's Kodiak Pro 209 Magnum—that allows a big powder charge, is sling-ready, has clean lines, is not too long or too heavy, and is accurate. And yes, it takes the No. 209 primer.

Austin & Halleck is famous for its sleek lines in bolt-action design. The rifle resembles a fine cartridge-shooting bolt-action rifle.

This cutaway of the 45 Winchester Magnum cartridge case shows how the primed case delivers fire directly into the breech of the Ultimate muzzleloader.

alent as "its regular maximum charge." As if the Savage 10ML had not raised eyebrows, being the only front-loader to allow the use of smokeless powder, here was a rifle not intended for smokeless at all, ever, in any amount. Regardless, the Ultimate gains high potency by handling big charges of blackpowder or proper safe substitute. This powerhouse has a muzzle diameter .675-inches heavy—made to take on four Pellets as the "regular maximum" charge. Like a cartridge-shooter, the breech section is enlarged, tapering toward the muzzle. The Ultimate is built with one of two fine bolt-actions, either the Howa 1500 or Remington 40X. Trigger on the test model broke at 2 pounds 12 ounces on the Lyman electronic trigger pull gauge, crisp as a sunrise in winter Alaska.

The test rifle weighed 10 pounds in deference to the recoil developed by 200 grains volume propellant. Four Pyrodex 50/50 Pellets push a 420-grain conical bullet at 2,041 fps for a muzzle energy of 3,886 foot-pounds. My favorite ball-

hands-on practice for success due to sights, high percent relaxation making a 70-pound bow "hold back" like a 35-pound bow, plus a release for clean arrow escape. The modern muzzleloader does the same thing. It handles very much like cartridge guns of the day, with scopes, slings, relatively short barrels and light carrying weight, contemporary triggers, safeties, and many other familiar appointments.

Expect More to Come

When the Ultimate Muzzleloader arrived at my door for a wring-out, I was not surprised. The rifle followed the stream of all in-lines of the day. It had every modern feature anyone could ask for, plus a new wrinkle—a four-pellet allowance. That is, four 50/50 Pyrodex or Triple Seven Pellets equaling a full 200-grains volume FFg blackpowder equiv-

The Ultimate muzzleloader is so ultimate that it is not shipped as a blackpowder firearm. It uses regular bolt actions, both of them excellent: the Remington 40X and the Howa.

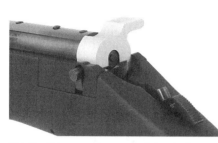

This Traditions modern muzzleloader has a rotating primer assembly that makes positioning a No. 209 primer a snap. Because it has no bolt, it is quite short for its barrel length.

Thompson/Center's Pro Hunter takes the falling block design seriously. Of course there is no falling block, since this is a muzzleloader with a breech plug. But the dropping of the assembly makes placement of the No. 209 a giveaway.

shooter in 54-caliber drives a 230-grain lead pill at 1,970 fps for a shade less than 2,000 foot-pounds. The Ultimate uses a 45 Winchester Magnum primed *cartridge case*. The manufacturer of the Ultimate says, "No Brag, Just Fact—completely burns 4 Pyrodex Pellets, documented kills at over 500 yards, advanced recoil dampening system, 55 second cleanup, fastest lock time, no blow-back, accurate, powerful, easy to load, weatherproof, safe, user-friendly, sealed breech, 50-caliber." The Ultimate also washes camp dishes and tucks the hunter in at night. Almost. Those who prefer emulation of Boone, Crockett, Kit Carson, and Jim Bridger probably won't gravitate to this prime example of where the modern muzzleloader is headed. On the other hand, the many modern muzzleloader styles presented in this chapter will warm the hearts of hunters who want to "go primitive" with a blackpowder firearm born and bred in modern times.

The Bolt-Actions

The general plan in modifying well-known bolt-action rifles such as the Remington 700 and Ruger 77 was turning the bolt into a striker. This is not true of the Savage Model 110, where the action does have lock-up value. As this is written, bolt-action style modern muzzleloaders lead the pack in sheer quantity, but other designs are also evident in healthy numbers.

This advanced marksman is competing in a blackpowder competition. He is in the process of driving a specialized bullet down the bore of a very specialized bench rest blackpowder rifle. Rifles like this were no doubt forerunners of the modern muzzleloader because they radically departed from the norm.

Falling Block Rifles

Not exactly falling blocks, but there are modern muzzleloaders today that incorporate the general concept. The Thompson/Center Omega is a current example of the drop-action family. In the company's words, "Omega's unique breech mechanism has only four moving parts. Simply pull down the trigger guard and the pivoting action drops the breechblock clear of the breech face. Slip in a 209 primer and you're primed. Pull up on the trigger guard and the pivoting action seals the breech, eliminating blowback that would foul the action. Omega is now gas-tight and

They're shorter and they're lighter. This CVA Buckhorn 209 Magnum is an example of the shorter/lighter in-line modern muzzleloader. It comes in calibers 45 or 50, both having sufficiently rapid rates of twist to stabilize longer conical bullets.

waterproof for failsafe ignition." Lofty words, but all true, I learned, by testing the rifle. The sealed breech demands no stringent clean-up, the barrel only requiring swabbing out, and with Triple Seven this chore was accomplished in a couple minutes with hot water only on a patch, followed by drying patches, and finishing up with a light touch of preserving oil.

Knight's Revolution rifle has a pivot-lock action—sure can't call it a lock—hammerless design, another weatherproof modern muzzleloader. The action is completely removable for cleaning.

The Remington Genesis Muzzleloader is not a drop-block. Rather, the block rolls out *to the side*. Remington calls it the Torch Cam breechblock. It seals the No. 209 primer from the weather when closed. "Priming takes only a split second," Remington promises. "Simply flip upward with your thumb, place the primer on the exposed breech plug and push down to lock the breech face back into place."

Break-Opens

The idea comes directly from the break-open single-barrel shotgun, for which I retain a fondness, because in my youth a neighbor loaned me a 16-gauge break-open shotgun that flew to the shoulder like a trained hawk. Seems like I couldn't miss a dove or quail with it. The latest H&R from New England Firearms takes this simple and foolproof design to a higher level. There are three muzzleloader models: Sidekick, Huntsman, and Huntsman Combo. The Sidekick is blued or stainless, high-density polymer or wood stock, 50-caliber, primed with a special patented 209 primer carrier. The Huntsman is touted as economically priced. It is 50-caliber with a polymer stock. The Combo version offers three interchangeable barrel choices: Pardner Combo, 12-gauge muzzleloader or 50-caliber bullet-shooter; Tracker II Combo with 12-gauge rifled slug barrel and 50-caliber muzzleloader; and Handi-Rifle Combo with a 243 Winchester barrel and a 50-caliber muzzleloader option.

Interestingly, this comparatively old idea offers many of the same positive features found on more current designs, such as decent water resistance, easy loading and cleaning, plus good accuracy and power in an easy-to-operate firearm. Now add multiple barrel options. Traditions entered the break-open muzzleloader market with its Pursuit in 45- or 50-caliber, plus an interchangeable 12-gauge barrel option.

They're Shorter and Lighter

Across the board, modern muzzleloaders are lighter and shorter than originals or replicas. For example, the H&R break-open muzzleloader runs 6.5-pounds with a 26-inch barrel. Due to lack of a true action, the rifle is only 42 inches long overall. The Peifer TS-93, another unique in-line frontloader in 45- or 50-caliber, has a 24-inch Douglas barrel. This nice rifle with Bell & Carlson composite stock is only a shade over 41 inches long and weighs but 7 pounds. The Traditions Pursuit runs a shade over 8 pounds. It is 44 inches long with a 28-inch barrel. This trend continues with most of the modern muzzleloaders. While the long barrels of old-time blackpowder guns did have the advantage of a longer sight radius for a clear picture, along with a welcome nose-heaviness that promoted off-hand shooting, the shorter and lighter modern muzzleloader is much more familiar to the modern marksman/hunter.

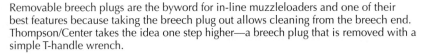

Removable breech plugs are the byword for in-line muzzleloaders and one of their best features because taking the breech plug out allows cleaning from the breech end. Thompson/Center takes the idea one step higher—a breech plug that is removed with a simple T-handle wrench.

The Thompson/Center removable breech plug works on the interrupted thread system, just like some of the old-time takedown rifles (example: Winchester Model 94 takedown). Apply a little anti-seize lubricant when the breech plug is reinstalled and shoot away knowing a twist of the wrist will take out the breech plug for after-shooting cleanup. Special tools such as the T/C T-handle are prevalent with modern muzzleloaders.

A big plus with most of today's modern muzzleloaders is weatherproof design. Rain, rain, go away—you aren't going to get into the powder charge in this T/C Pro Hunter.

The modern muzzleloader is as scope-ready as the modern smokeless powder shooting cartridge, as this Thompson/Center rifle proves. At the same time, these rifles are suitable for any other type of sight.

Because of the rate of twist, the modern muzzleloader can handle a range of conical bullets from rather short to quite long. It is also suitable for sharply pointed bullets like this Parker Productions projectile designed for longer-range shooting.

Because the modern muzzleloader has the ability to fire medium weight bullets at a good clip, special projectiles from Barnes and other bullet companies upset to impart good energy with a long wound channel—which translates into "power."

They Have Removable Breech Plugs

The majority of modern muzzleloaders have removable breech plugs. This is one of their best features for the busy sportsman who wants to shoot, go home, clean from the breech end quickly but thoroughly, and put the firearm away until the next opportunity comes along. Tip: be sure to lube breech plugs before installing after gun clean up. There are special anti-seize lubes for this job. See Chapter 30.

Special Tools

While it's impossible to study the modern muzzleloader without considerable admiration for the engineers who design them, the tools are almost as intriguing. The Markesberry rifle has a t-handle system that stores compactly, but in use turns the regular ramrod into a loading rod. Remington's Model 700ML also has specific tools that come with the rifle. Most modern muzzleloaders offer tools expressly designed to fit that specific firearm. On the other hand, some modern front-loaders require no special tools, only the accoutrements found in Chapter 4.

Safeties

Expect to find modern style safeties on most modern muzzleloaders, sometimes multiple safeties, such as cross-bolts and other styles borrowed from modern rifles. Even when there is a hammer, an additional safety may be found on a modern muzzleloader. Safeties are placed where they are easiest to put into play.

Sights

Even when sights are of the open design, modern muzzleloader sights are—modern. Fiber optic sights, both front and rear, are common. These sights truly do stand out when struck by the least amount of light. They are bright and wonderful. But they are also breakable. I prefer the type of sight from XX Sight Systems (see Directory), with Ghost Ring back and White Stripe front. These fast-action, sturdy sights are also found on my Marlin 336 38-55 rifle—because they work. Likewise my Browning 1886 Winchester copy in 45-70. However, when fiber optic sights are protected, they truly are useful. They seem to "gather" light. The other major sight type found on modern muzzleloader is the scope. Most modern muzzleloaders come from the factory drilled and tapped for scope mounts.

In-Line Ignition

Because almost all modern muzzleloaders have in-line ignition, the name itself often replaces "modern." The

Shape is important in defining the modern muzzleloader. This CVA Optima with thumbhole stock "snugs up" to the shoulder firmly for good aim and recoil management. Unlike the Kentucky rifle of long ago, drop at comb is slight with a higher comb to accommodate a scope sight.

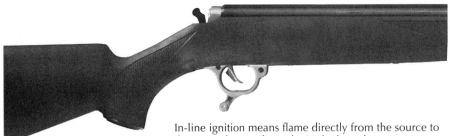

In-line ignition means flame directly from the source to the main charge of powder in the breech.

guns are simply known as "in-lines." As discussed in Chapter 2, in-line ignition means that the igniter is on the same plane as the bore of the rifle, pistol, or shotgun. It does not refer to fire from a percussion cap or primer darting directly into the powder charge in the breech. Direct ignition has been a feature of underhammer and sidehammer guns long before motorcars and flying machines. Known also as understrikers or mule ears, these guns have nipples mounted right into the barrel. There could hardly be a shorter route from flame to powder charge.

Surely, the in-line concept is new, right? About as new as the flintlock. The Paczelt flintlock embodied in-line ignition, as author Doc Carlson reported in his article, "The In-Line Muzzle Loader," appearing in the 1996 *Gun Digest*. The rifle can be seen in the Tower of London collection. The touchhole is directly in line with the powder charge. This 57-caliber fowler with 33 1/2-inch smoothbore barrel goes back to1738. Carlson also discovered that although gun maker Stanislas Paczelt's name appears on this in-line flinter, it is improbable that he invented the design because "weapons of a very similar design by other makers and of earlier dating are known" Tower of London experts explained.

The Outer-Line

Sufficiently unique to merit its own patent, the Markesbery Outer-Line rifle is, technically, not an in-line design. Colorado's game department conceded this points when, for a time, the department outlawed in-line muzzleloaders for special primitive hunts. The Markesbery rifle was brought to the attention of game managers. Sure enough, although the flame of ignition from percussion cap, Small Rifle primer, or Small Pistol primer enters the main charge in the breech in a straight line, that line is on a 45-degree angle. Therefore, it is not an in-line rifle, since in-line ignition is on the same *plane* as the powder charge.

Rate of Twist

I get a chuckle out of this one, because I complained mildly to companies that for best conical bullet stability, a somewhat faster rate of twist was desirable. My pleas fell upon deaf ears for quite some time—until gunmakers performed simple experiments. Today, faster rates of twist are the rule for modern muzzleloaders. This usually means something on the order of 1:32 or in that realm, not fast by modern bullet standards, such as the 1:10 twist found on most 30-06 rifles. See Chapter 20 for more on twist.

Bullets for Modern Muzzleloaders

The modern muzzleloader is a conical shooter by virtue of rifling twist. Chapter 20 explains why round ball rifles have slower twist, while conical-shooters have a faster rate of twist. For the most part, blackpowder bullets are still relatively short per caliber, so a truly rapid rate of twist is not required to stabilize them. Bullet choice is better than ever. The trend is to better aerodynamic shape. A rather common projectile for modern muzzleloaders is now a jacketed bullet with a sharp profile and synthetic tip in the nose. But there are many other good ones, including lead missiles capable of dropping big beasts on the spot with bone-breaking authority. The SSB from the Buffalo Bullet Company is but one such bullet. Parker Productions offers an array of lead bullets designed to deliver crushing blows, including one that expands due to hydraulic force with a compartment of oil under the nose. Choice between the high-profile projectile and blunter-nose heavy lead bullet rests with application. For antelope, where I might try a poke at 150+ yards, the spitzer shape would be my choice. For elk in timber, something on the order of Hornady's Great Plains gets the nod, especially the 425-grain number. The SSB combines both traits, good profile plus weight, and in tests only, not game, a T/C Encore 50-caliber rifle with three Pyrodex Pellets produced good groups out to 300 yards with the SSB, which was the farthest target butt at the range that day. Tip: go for bone with those big lead bullets, shots into, rather than behind, the shoulder. Big lead bullets can slip through the boiler room without telling effect, especially on deer-size game.

Modern Muzzleloader Power

As described above, even the most modern muzzleloader remains, in true effect, a barrel with one plugged end and one open end plus a means of ignition. There is no special magic here. Big power continues to mean heavy powder charges, which in turn demands a rifle designed to handle such loads. And these we have. Triple Pellets are allowed in many modern muzzleloaders with the Ultimate handling four. The rule is the same as always—*follow the maximum charge allowed by*

The modern muzzleloader pistol exhibits the same qualities as the in-line muzzleloader.

Big lead conical bullets such as these from Parker Productions shoot great from modern in-line muzzleloaders because of their faster rate of twist.

the manufacturer of the firearm. Also, watch for the law of diminishing returns There may well be a point where adding more powder increases recoil, blast, and smoke, while doing very little to promote greater bullet velocity. The modern muzzleloader is powerful and no doubt about it. On the other hand, the most powerful of the clan will not put in the shade those truly big bore guns of the past, offered again in customs or from October Country. See Chapter 37 for more. Nothing to date has supplanted a 4-bore, or for that matter, a 2-bore fire breather. When a lead bullet weighing one-fourth pound, as in the 4-bore, or one-half pound, as in the 2-bore, leaves the muzzle at velocities in the 1,500 foot-per-second range, huge force is developed, on the order of 8,745 foot-pounds for the 4-

bore and over 17,000 foot-pounds for the 2-bore. That, gentle reader, is a real dish of pasta! The deer hunter, on the other hand, does not require such potency, and so rifles such as the Gonic's Model 93 firing its special 465-grain bullet gain a muzzle energy well suited to American big game in general, being 2,650 foot-pounds. One more example of modern muzzleloader punch and we'll move on. Consider the 54-caliber Markesbery Outer-Line firing a 325-grain Markesbery Beast Buster bullet at 1,992 fps muzzle velocity with a 150-grain charge of Pyrodex. Muzzle energy runs 2,864 foot-pounds.

Shape is Important

Along with recoil pads, adjustable sights, scopes, contemporary triggers and safeties, plus slings and other appointments, the modern muzzleloader is also appreciated for its shape. Not the way these guns look, so much, because for pretty give me a Pennsylvania-Kentucky long rifle every time, but rather the familiar way they *handle* due to style. Anyone used to shooting a Remington Model 700, for example, or Ruger Model 77, or Savage Model 110, has no trouble transferring to one of these rifles in blackpowder. The same is true of every modern muzzleloader I have shot to date. They all "feel" pretty much like cartridge guns to me. This is due, in part, to stock design with less drop at comb than found on old-time muzzleloaders.

Weatherproofing

Examples of weather-resistant guns were given earlier. Most modern muzzleloaders are built to provide at least some measure of protection against moisture in the form of rain or snow, which hunters encounter often during the season. The return of the falling block has brought about excellent weatherproofing, but other styles, including the break-open and bolt-action, can also resist the type of weather that can make many an old-time blackpowder gun go *fizzle* instead of boom! Closed breeches are the major reason the modern muzzleloader thwarts the wet. And as mentioned elsewhere, the Remington Model 700 ML has a shroud to ward off inclement weather, as does Austin & Halleck's 420. While I continue to enjoy hunting with replica guns that do not possess true wet weather protection by design, I am forced to admire this trait in the modern muzzleloader—because I have lost opportunities to failed ignition due to rain mostly, and sometimes heavy snow.

Materials

Modern muzzleloaders are made of space-age materials, including high-quality steel, along with various synthetics for stocks. The Remington Model 700 MLS is a good example of this fact with its barrel of 416 stainless steel and fiberglass-reinforced synthetic stock.

Design and Manufacture

The usual modern muzzleloader sold today is well made of good materials. As an expert witness in lawsuits, I have been obliged to "blow up" several muzzleloaders. I stand amazed when I see what some shooters have been able to do inadvertently that I find difficult to accomplish on purpose. That does not mean that modern muzzleloaders can be abused. They can fail. Nor does it excuse any manufacturer who might make a less-than-ideal firearm.

The Systems Muzzleloader

The Thompson/Center Encore is a systems rifle, changing its nature in seconds from cartridge rifle, to shotgun, to muzzleloader. Cartridge choices are many, from 223 Remington to 300 Winchester Magnum, with the good old 30-06 in there along with the old but still excellent 45-70 Government. The shotgun is 20-gauge in rifled-slug barrel or smooth bore with ventilated rib. Then comes the muzzleloader: the 50-caliber 209x50 Magnum, capable of handling three 50/50 Pyrodex Pellets for a 150-grain volume charge. Markesbery's Outer-Line is a systems rifle in another way: all muzzleloader. Choices are 36-, 45-, 50-, or 54-caliber. The beauty of both of these systems guns is the fact that sights go with the barrel. For example, my own Markesbery has a 50-caliber scoped barrel for regular-season hunts when others are toting high-power repeaters, while a 54-caliber barrel with Williams aperture sight is ready for elk and other timberland animals. Other system modern muzzleloaders were noted earlier.

Modern Muzzleloader Ignition

Winchester, observing the trend in No. 209 shotgun primers for ignition, caused its engineers to come up with a No. 209 especially for muzzleloaders. This move signals the fact that the No. 209 primer is highly popular in modern muzzleloaders. This does not mean that the ordinary percussion cap is out of business. I have had, over the years, very good luck with No. 10 and No. 11 caps and continue to use them. The large top hat, or English musket cap, is also excellent.

The Modern Muzzleloading Pistol

The Thompson/Center Encore Pistol is available with many barrels chambered for a host of cartridges, along with a 15-inch 209x50 muzzleloading barrel. This 50-caliber pistol is capable of shooting a heavy bullet at good speed. It's a modern in-line muzzleloading pistol all the way. So is the Buckhunter Pro from Traditions, an in-line with adjustable folding sights, a 50-caliber pistol with exposed hammer and conical-shooting rifling twist. The good news about guns is that they last, with proper care, a very long time, and so models that are replaced can still be found in good used condition. I mention this because the discontinued T/C Scout pistol remains a favorite of mine in both 50- and 54-calibers. With the fine Encore around, we don't need the Scout, but that does not take away from this dragon slayer. The hottest load I tested in a Scout 54-caliber produced almost 1,100 fps with a 540-grain Maxi Hunter bullet for a muzzle energy over 1,400 foot-pounds. The powerful 44 Remington Magnum driving a 240-grain bullet at 1,400 fps from a 7 1/2-inch barrel develops 1,045 foot-pounds. Multiple shots out of a 44 Magnum revolver can never be discounted, but a 54-caliber 540-grain lead bullet cannot be ignored.

The Modern Muzzleloading Shotgun

Knight's 12-gauge shotgun is a defining example of this breed of in-line modern muzzleloaders. It's a single-barrel with a screw-in, Extra-Full choke intended for wild turkey hunting, but perfectly at home in the duck blind or goose pit. This one really packs a wallop with a 2-ounce maximum shot charge capable of dropping a big gobbler like a sack of wheat. The White Tominator is another prime example of a modern in-line shotgun.

The modern muzzleloader shoots no farther, has no greater accuracy or power neither potential, nor special magic over any other load-from-the-front gun. What it does offer is extreme familiarity, which is appreciated by shooters not interested in mastering the guns of yesteryear. Applying an over-used cliché, the modern muzzleloader is also *user-friendly* in that it loads easily and cleans up afterwards with a minimum of invested time and effort. These two factors—familiarity and ease of operation—have put the modern muzzleloader on the map.

9 THE CUSTOM FRONT LOADER

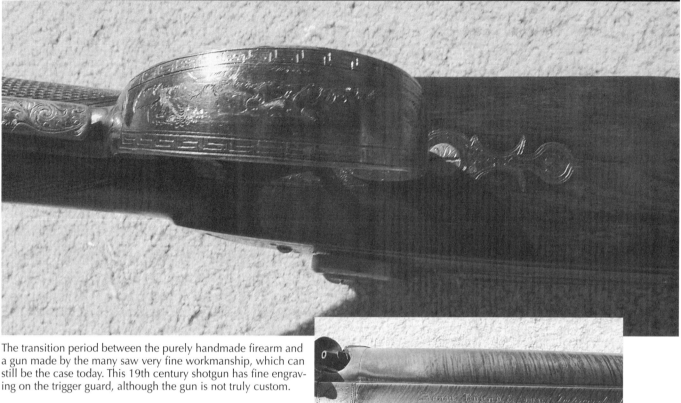

The transition period between the purely handmade firearm and a gun made by the many saw very fine workmanship, which can still be the case today. This 19th century shotgun has fine engraving on the trigger guard, although the gun is not truly custom.

The damascus barrels on this fine double barrel blackpowder percussion shotgun indicate its vintage. While "twist steel" must be considered unworthy of smokeless powder, proper blackpowder charges obviously worked fine in these barrels.

Just as there was no need to refer to "gunpowder" propellant as blackpowder in the glory days before the advent of smokeless, there was also no requirement to order a custom gun, because every rifle, pistol, and shotgun was created one at a time in a gun shop by an armsmaker, either by himself or with an apprentice at his side. Long ago in America there were locksmiths and barrelmakers that offered their individual wares for sale. A smith could, and often did, order components parts from these craftsmen.

The Industrial Revolution in England and America changed the color of that picture. Just as vehicles and other products were built in a factory, usually by assembly line, so did the gun become a product of mass production. And that was not bad, not bad at all. There remained a good bit of hands-on workmanship in over-the-counter guns, as well as continued improvement in the processes of multiple production. A friend owns a pre-64 Super Grade Model 70 Winchester that I borrow from time to time, at his insistence (he knows I really like that rifle). This factory rifle stands as a testimony to good products made in mass quantity.

Today modern technology brings us the most accurate *factory* guns ever produced. This fact covers the charcoal-burning clan as well as modern arms. Not that long ago, blackpow-der shooters were quite content with two-inch and even three-inch groups at 100 yards. Make that an inch and under now. In spite of good guns from an assembly line, there was something special about those made by hand. That is why the practice never faded away. Chapter 47 includes only a few of the modern custom gunmakers of the day who build fine smokepoles. Following the Golden Age of Firearms in America, with Pennsylvania Dutch gunsmiths (German artists in wood and metal) leading the way, there was a drop in demand for custom front-loaders. That was because factory rifles were very good and priced right. The new smokeless cartridge shooting

Factory rifles were very good and priced right following the era of handmade-only firearms in America. This 1895 Winchester rifle is definitely factory made. However, it was entirely reliable and had an action strong enough to handle the factory 30-06 Springfield loads of the day.

Not to say that factory work with high-tech computer operated machinery cannot do good work, but what is seen here is from the hand of an artist (Shelton) and so far machines have not quite caught up.

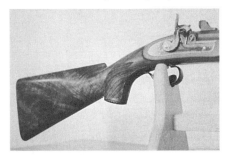

The true custom shows superior wood to metal fit (metal to wood) as seen here on a Jefroh rifle.

repeaters showed up on the late 19th century, and before that many blackpowder repeating cartridges rifles were available. Regardless, the shooting fraternity would not allow the demise of handmade blackpowder long guns and pistols, with a few scatterguns tossed in. By the era known as the Roaring Twenties in America, there were quite a few craftsmen producing a number of beautiful and functional blackpowder firearms, most of them of old-time long gun heritage.

Organization Helped

Organization helped support the work of these gifted builders of fine guns by providing a forum for informing shooters concerning who was making the guns, and how to buy one. Red Farris and his friends knew how to put things together. They were part of what became the National Muzzle-Loading Rifle Association (NMLRA). The NMLRA continues as a leading organization for blackpowder shooting. Other names rose like cream to the top during this revival. Joe Kindig wrote a fine book entitled *Thoughts on the Kentucky Rifle in its Golden Age* that spurred interest. William Large got into the game with his exceptionally fine custom barrels, winners of many shooting matches. Large lived a long life, his barrels applauded from coast to coast. He was also a help-

ful soul. After reading a piece I wrote on the subject of cleaning muzzleloaders with water, Large sent a letter. He wrote, "Never touch water to a muzzleloader barrel," going on to explain that he had made hundreds of barrels, and having lived the better part of a century at that time, figured he knew what he was talking about.

I also figured he knew what he was talking about. He said solvent was right for removing blackpowder fouling. Water was not. Of course, there was no Triple Seven powder at the time, which does use water only for a perfect aftershooting cleanup. While many great gunmakers were in the game early, they often preferred buying separate components. Hacker Martin made his from scratch. He could build all the parts himself. Along with Large and other barrelmakers, locksmiths came to the fore, perhaps the best known being Bud and Dottie Siler. While men dominated early 20th century blackpowder gunmaking, there were a few women who played a significant role as well. A lady named Mary Owensby, for example, was known for her ability to rifle a barrel the old-fashioned way: by hand with a rifling guide. While the process looks crude, it obviously produced wonderful results, as small target groups prove to this day. Read more about blackpowder 'smiths in Chapters 46 and 47.

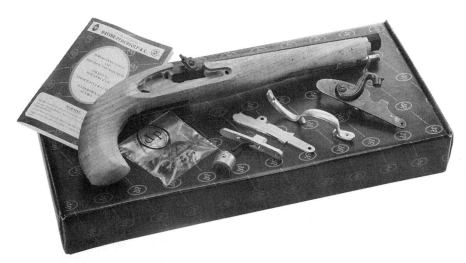

This pistol kit gives a good idea concerning the parts that go into a muzzleloader. Early gunmakers quickly figured out that it was more efficient to buy locks from a locksmith than to craft them themselves, although they usually had the skill to make a lock.

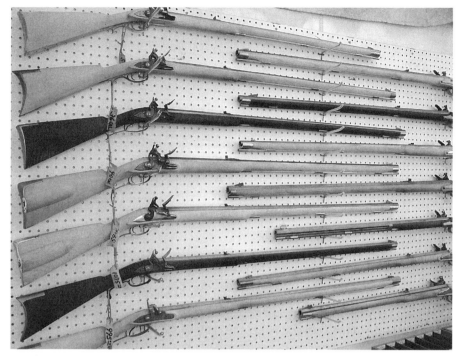

Barrel no good, gun no good—it's as simple as that. These rifles for sale at a rendezvous had to have well-made barrels or they would not please their future owners.

Will this shooter deliver his round ball to the right spot on the moving boar target? Success starts with a good barrel.

The barrel is vital to accuracy, but without a good lock that produces reliable results, the muzzleloader is not trustworthy. Good locks are available to custom gunmakers, who would choose nothing else because a poor lock would result in a poor firearm.

Makeup of the Custom Blackpowder Firearm

A true custom has no screw-for-screw clone anywhere in the world, although this is not to say that it is without relatives. The work of individual gunmakers is often easier to spot than paintings of famous artists. No heavy knowledge of art is required to tell a da Vinci from a Picasso. The same holds true for many gunmakers, whose individual style stands out as their own. Interestingly, a custom firearm is not perfect, not in the sense of machine duplication. For example, it's possible to program a computer-operated machine to engrave nearly flawless lines. The machine will not err. The lines will repeat, repeat, and repeat.

The work on a custom gun reveals the human hand. That is what makes it so desirable over the assembly-line product. In a way, the work exhibits its own kind of perfection from talented human fingers. The slight touch of imperfection makes the custom gun one of a kind; although it may take a magnifying glass to discover that all but invisible waver of a tool. The true custom shows tight wood-to-metal fit, clean lines all

around, a correct interpretation of a classic design, flawless wood and metal finish, and at least a hint of personality. If the firearm is intended to replicate an original from the past, then it should do so faithfully. Homer Dangler and other custom smiths of the 1920s were extremely good at replication, building rifles that closely duplicated originals from the past, sometimes as far back as the 1700s.

Barrels

The custom firearm has a custom barrel. That does not mean that each barrel is different. On the contrary, there should be perfection from one barrel to another so that each one that comes from the barrelmaker is identical in quality. These barrels are called custom because they are made one at a time, of course, and they are rifled with extreme care. Not to say that production barrels are no good. On a good day when the light is right on the target, I have no trouble putting three shots into an inch grouping at 100 yards with top-of-the-line production muzzleloaders wearing scope sights. Sometimes I get that lucky with iron sights, but not

Trader row at rendezvous offers a large array of stocks for making a rifle. These are good stocks worthy of producing excellent rifles, but the custom gunmaker will start from a blank and "whittle out" his own stock.

often. This is with specific loads that the rifle—we're talking about rifles now—shoot well. Temporarily scooping a few ball-shooting muzzleloaders produced superb target groupings, so it's not the conical alone that can put 'em on the mark. The custom barrel bears a rate of twist that matches bullets to be fired in the finished product.

For example, I had a custom 54-caliber rifle built to handle extreme powder charges with its heavy barrel of finest quality steel. Because the bullets (most of them home-cast) were long for their caliber (high sectional density), I wanted a rate of twist more rapid than normal for a 54, including those intended to shoot conicals. The barrel was built in Montana by Les Bauska and it proved very accurate with those long bullets.

Another blackpowder barrel of my acquaintance came from the shop of Bernie Morrison, the cheerful Cherokee Indian metallurgist who creates fine custom barrels from his shop in Hereford, Arizona. Bernie uses the cut-rifled method. I recently read the expert opinion that breaking barrels in is a myth. That is not true of cut-rifled barrels, which do require breaking in for best results. Bernie gives every new owner of one of his barrels a specific set of break-in instructions. He also breaks in some of the barrels himself. Barrelmakers advertise. As one example only, the Log Cabin Shop (see the Directory) sells custom barrels. Since I do not make guns, I rely on the gunmaker to find the right barrel.

Locks

I had a flintlock muzzleloader with a Siler lock. One time an editor from the Chicago area was visiting my home in Wyoming and we went on a cottontail rabbit hunt. Bob harbored a few doubts about repeat fire from a flintlock rifle. That day, my rifle failed to fire zero times. I credit the lock with that record. Of course, the lock was correctly wed to the rifle with the touchhole in precisely the right location in relation to the pan.

Also, the rifle was loaded specifically, as pointed out in Chapter 14. I carried the long gun tilted to keep FFFFg powder from sifting into the touchhole, thereby creating a fuze. Sure, there was the usual puff of smoke and to say that lock time (elapse from trigger pull to powder burn) was super fast would be a colorful tale and little more. But the limit of rabbits verified the fact that this flintlock "went off" on cue. And I say again that the lock, which worked like the old cliché of the "well-oiled machine," was a significant part of the success story. All of this business about locks is important to the custom front-loader story, because good locks are part of the equation in making a fine rifle, pistol, or shotgun.

Stocks

The uninitiated (myself included at one time, until I learned better) may find the cost of good wood a surprise. Parting with a thick wad of greenbacks is common for a fine piece of tree. My oft-mentioned custom 54-caliber rifle, No. 47, wears such a stock. It's curly or tiger-stripe maple with good figure, while at the same time intact of grain so that it will not readily split out at the wrist when firing full-throttle hunting loads. The custom blackpowder firearm simply must wear good wood in order to deserve the title. In fact, it would be a travesty for a gunmaker to build a custom piece with anything less than a top grade stick.

Replicating the Past

Screw-for-screw replication is not at all necessary in the building of a custom muzzleloader. Most customs do not truly replicate any firearm from the past, while many follow on the general lines of an old-time piece, but do not copy it. No. 47 is a perfect example of this. The gunmaker saw a firearm he liked in a museum. He patterned No. 47 on that basis. I wanted a plains rifle. Dennis Mulford insisted that a half-stock plains rifle of the Hawken class was about as handsome as a frog sub-

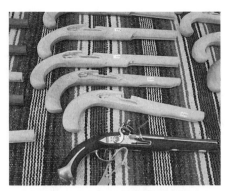

Pistols are not left out of handmade gun interest. But as with the rifle, the custom smith will create his own pistol stock from a blank.

Sam's No. 47 shows strong family resemblance to the Pennsylvania/Kentucky rifle of the East, as can be seen in the lines of the buttstock. It does not replicate any particular rifle from the past, but its building was inspired by an original seen in a museum.

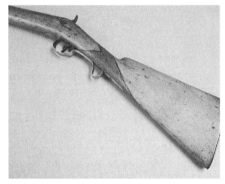

This 19th century original would fall into the general class of very plain long guns, although it is not a Poor Boy in design. It was no doubt made for work, not show.

merged in your cream of mushroom soup. If I had to have a plains rifle, then I'd best go somewhere else. I wanted Dennis to build my rifle, so I said OK to a Pennsylvania-Kentucky theme, but it must be a 54-caliber ball-shooter stout enough to safely stand up to 120 grains volume FFg blackpowder or equivalent. Mulford's museum find began life as a long gun, probably really long with a barrel that resembled a vaulting pole. But the owner had the barrel cut down and freshed out to a larger caliber and

Custom muzzleloaders often represent a particular "school" from the past, but do not necessarily duplicate a firearm from yesteryear. This Jim Gefroh rifle, shown here with an eland Jim took in Africa, does sing about old-time England, but it is a one-of-a-kind big-bore rifle.

now the barrel was only 34 inches long. The end product was handsome, and yet stout, a true custom all the way. Several who have shot it tempted me with generous offers that have so far fallen on deaf ears. An outfitter in Gunnison, Colorado shot No. 47 at a small target, off-hand, putting the round ball precisely dead-center. "Is this rifle for sale?" he asked.

Sometimes replica custom rifles are built upon simple working long guns of the past. I can think of two that I have seen not so long ago. One copied a Jaeger. It was beautiful in workmanship, but definitely not ornate. Another was a Kentucky 45-caliber ball-shooter, but absolutely plain. There are examples of what some call "poor boy" rifles. These are hardworking muzzleloaders fully capable of putting food on the table, or for that matter cutting a neat round hole in a black bullseye. However, these long guns were never pretty, nor are modern customs of the same family. To beautify a poor boy rifle would be trespassing on the goal of the replica: making a new gun that copies an old one. Frank House

built a wonderful custom long rifle to be carried by the hero in a film called *The Patriot*. House decided on replicating a John Thomas rifle featured in *Rifles of Colonial America*, another volume by the dedicated arms historian George Shumway. The resulting flintlock rifle is beyond beautiful. It is a true work of art and extraordinary talent, and a replica in the best sense of the word.

Non-Replica Customs

As hinted at earlier, most custom blackpowder guns of the day are not truly replicas of past times. They are, in fact, far too unique for that, and are true customs in the vein of "there is nothing else like this one in the whole world." As pointed out, builders' custom guns may have resemblance from one to another, but each, having been born of the human hand, varies individually.

Ordering a Custom Blackpowder Gun

Step One: the buyer must know what he or she wants in a custom rifle, and for what purpose: show, target, ren-

dezvous, hunting, and so forth. Dennis Mulford, when he was building rifles full-time, created more rifles for collecting than shooting. These were mainly for visual enjoyment, as well as sheer pride of ownership and sharing with others. Most were replicas representing a specific "school" from the past. Counties in Pennsylvania, for example, often mark these schools: Lancaster, Lehigh, and Clarion. Astute collectors and blackpowder firearm experts can put a rifle in its proper school by noting specific identifying features. I believe most custom long guns and shotguns made today, perhaps not pistols, are for hunting. There is also the option of a cartridge rifle. Andrew Fautheree (see Chapter 47) is known for blackpowder cartridge rifles as well as front-loaders.

Step Two: ask for references. A good gunmaker will be happy to share names of happy customers. Follow up on those references, being sure to ask not only how the job came out, but also how long it took.

Step Three: how much green? The sky is the limit. Rifles embellished with

Cost depends upon many factors; including prime wood that even as an unworked blank can be expensive. Embellishment also counts. Sam's No. 47 shows silver inlay here with his initials. Such touches must add to the cost of the custom piece.

This wooden sliding patch box is an extra touch that will command extra money.

The end result of a fine custom muzzleloading rifle is a lifetime of enjoyment that fully justifies the monetary investment.

a good deal of gold and silver are going to cost more than poor boys. The more ornate, the more workmanship demanded, the higher the cost. Price must be established up front.

Step Four: style—ask for what you want, but defer to the gunmaker as well. Had I stuck to my guns, so to speak, I would have owned an ordinary, albeit fine, half-stock plains rifle instead of No. 47. The gunmaker questioned my choice, rightfully so. Dig for dollars. Don't shortchange yourself. The money will be forgotten. The custom charcoal burner may be around for a hundred years or so. Borrow judiciously if you must. A true custom muzzleloader built by a qualified expert is a definite *investment*. Odds are it will appreciate in time, rather than depreciating. The master is worth his due. More goes into the building of a fine custom front-loader than meets the eye.

Step Five: the contract—get it down in writing. This is good for buyer and builder alike. Both need to know up front what is to be built and for what outlay of cash. This is especially important when it comes to wood quality and type, such as tiger-stripe maple, inlays, carvings, lock type and brand, caliber, barrel length and rifling twist, sights, finish, patch box yes or no, and all other appointments. Know what you are paying for up front. No matter how deep the well, it's wise to know how much you have to dip out and what you'll get for it.

Step Six: The smith *may* prepare a drawing of the gun's profile at a reasonable charge. The drawing is nothing more than an outline, but it's useful in providing an overall look before work is under way. What you get for your money: some gunmakers prepare their own barrels. Others buy them from specialists. Either way, a barrel must be cut to length, the muzzle crowned, dovetail slots cut for sights and underlugs fitted by the smith. The lock may require some assembly and a certain amount of tuning. The stock begins as a blank, nothing more than a hunk of wood. It must be shaped into a gunstock with filing and more filing, sanding and more sanding. Inletting is required for the barrel, lock, and other appointments. The barrel must fit perfectly into its channel, the lock into its mortise. Furniture, such as patch boxes and butt plates, is introduced into the wood with a marriage that must be perfect. Drilling the ramrod channel can be a challenge. If the hole goes astray, the stock blank becomes a candidate for knife handles or even firewood. Trigger positioning demands room for function without sloppiness. The upper-tang screw hole is drilled, the butt plate fitted, the vent hole drilled in the side of a flintlock's barrel flat. Drum and nipple may be fitted to a percussion rifle, the trigger guard installed, upper and lower tangs crafted, carving and inlays done. Metalwork may be engraved, the stock stained, metal polished, barrel browned, stock finished. From wood and metal, a firearm is born, but it is special only when created by a specialist.

Step Seven: agree on a time line for delivery. Patience may be a virtue, but waiting twice as long as promised for any work, be it a set of kitchen cabinets or a custom muzzleloading rifle, is uncalled for.

Where to Find Your Custom Gunmaker

Gun clubs and rendezvous are good places to check out custom rifles. The *Gun List* newspaper is another good lead. *Muzzle Blasts* magazine, as this is written, has a section with the names of custom artists. Custom guns have shown up in many other magazines as well, such as *Blackpowder Hunting*.

10 THE BLACKPOWDER PISTOL

Both smoothbore and rifled pistols are at home on the blackpowder gun range and at rendezvous. The pistol, due to its short barrel, is easy to load and to clean after the fun is over.

Swashbuckling pirates and equally swaggering sailors for the king clashed in many movies over time, each side brandishing not only their flashing swords, but also pistols withdrawn from waist sashes to launch a lead ball with significant smoke and flame. In fact, this scene was played often in real life, not only on the silver screen. The blackpowder pistol was, and remains, in effect a truncated shoulder arm. In flintlock or percussion, it loads just like the longer gun, and it performs many of the same uses, as noted below, from collecting to big game hunting. The pistol also has strong historical significance, playing a role in skirmishes as well as all-out battles. The blackpow-

der pistol also gained fame—or is that infamy?—as the weapon of choice in duels. Some of these pistols were not simply handsome, but beautiful in their own deadly way.

Manton was known in his time to produce high-grade pistol of a dueling nature with rainproof pans (that were not entirely watertight) and cocks (hammers) that operated smoothly on rollers. I had a chance to examine a high-grade dueling pistol as a guest of the Buffalo Bill Historical Society museum in Cody, Wyoming. The workmanship was impeccable. Allowed to carefully pull the trigger in a manner that would not harm the pistol, my well-practiced forefinger told of

a hammer release surely no heavier than three pounds and quite crisp. There were dueling pistols of 60-caliber bore dimension firing round balls that weighed in the range of about 250 grains. Probably the most famous duel in history is the deadly encounter between Alexander Hamilton and Aaron Burr. The two men had a "particular despise" for one another, the story goes, mainly because of their different political views.

Hamilton said Burr was a dangerous man not to be trusted with his post as Democratic vice president of the country. Burr took exception, demanding an apology or a duel. The apology was not forthcoming. Burr put a

British flintlock Horse Pistol is clearly for close-range defense (or offense). Check the sights out. There are no sights. It's point and fire away, but toe-to-toe with the foe, the ball from this pistol would discourage any advance. (Cody Firearms Museum).

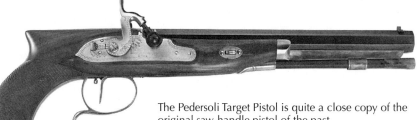

The Pedersoli Target Pistol is quite a close copy of the original saw-handle pistol of the past.

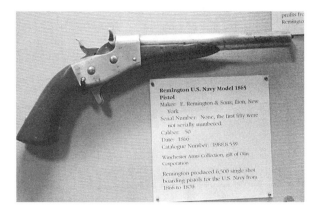

This collectible looks like a Remington Rolling Block because it is. This is the Remington U.S. Navy Model 50-caliber blackpowder pistol. Collectors can go for the "real thing" or some very nice replicas if the idea is simply for historical reference. (Cody Firearms Museum).

death-dealing ball into Hamilton. Burr was charged with murder, while when Andrew Jackson killed Charles Dickinson for ill remarks Dickinson made against Jackson's beloved wife, Jackson ended up president of the country. Dueling pistols, however, are but a small part of available models today. A multitude of pistols ranging from sincere copies to ultra-modern grace the pages of many catalogs today. There is no dearth of choice. A 21st century shooter will find everything from the smallest popgun to veritable one-hand powerhouses ready and waiting to go into action, or for that matter, hang on a wall for visual interest, or play a part in a collection.

Collecting

A major value of the blackpowder pistol is collecting, this being true due to a multitude of replicas available. Some of these are not perfect screw-for-screw copies, but they fill a historical notch all the same. For example, there is a 36-caliber Derringer patterned after percussion Derringers of the 19th century. Also: the Le Page Percussion Dueling Pistol, 44-caliber with a 10-inch barrel; the Mang Target Pistol, 38-caliber with 10 1/2-inch octagonal barrel; French-style dueling pistols, the Harper's Ferry 1806 flintlock pistol, pepperboxes (multiple barrel blackpowder pistols); the Queen Anne flintlock in 50-caliber with a

7 1/2-inch smoothbore barrel; the William Parker 50-caliber pistol, flintlock, with 10 3/8-inch barrel—and so many more.

While dueling pistols seem to collect the greater attention, other blackpowder pistols are equally collectible in both original and replica form. Duke Venturino researched the Battle of Adobe Walls, and in his fine article in *Guns* magazine, June 2005, reported the use of a 50-caliber Remington Model 1871 pistol in the fight. Of course, the "buffalo rifle" was the real reason why a couple hundred, perhaps 300, warriors could not defeat a couple dozen men armed with 50-caliber rifles. Billy Dixon, famed "buffalo runner" of the era, made a very long shot, praised as 1,538 yards. Duke V. says it never happened. The range was probably "only" a thousand yards or so.

Plinking

The most fun I have had with blackpowder pistols, with the exception of a particularly accurate T/C 45-caliber that put many cottontail rabbits in the pot, has been simple plinking. There is no defining pistol for this game. All styles, all calibers work. The only rule is—be safe—be certain of the backstop. The smallest pistol can be deadly.

Target Shooting – Informal

Related to plinking, this paper-punching activity also has no particular champion. Any pistol will do. With practice, even the no-sight flintlocks of yesteryear, a shooter can put holes in the bullseye at close range. The only rules here are as above—safety.

Target Shooting – Competition

Pistol choice here depends entirely upon the rules of the game. It is impossible to lay down one specific pistol for competition for that reason. The shooter must check the rules in order to compete with the proper pistol.

Whether plinking or shooting for score, the blackpowder pistol is one of the more enjoyable guns to load and make smoke with.

Of course it was the buffalo rifle, not a pistol that dropped so many bison on the plains. However, a brave, or rather reckless, hunter, especially among the European noblemen who came to America to kill buffalo, would ride up alongside the huge animals in order to place ball in the boiler room. After all, the Plains Indian did it with arrows.

The Mang Pistol by Pedersoli is unique in design and reputed to be a good shooter in its day. The replica is a good shooter. Plink, take small game, compete—a pistol like this one will fill the bill.

Rendezvous

The majority of rendezvous pistol-toters latch onto a pistol of the period mainly to complete an outfit. However, there are shooting games at the rendezvous for pistols. At one rendezvous I attended, there was special pistol competition that was open to any style or caliber except modern muzzleloader. Targets were both paper and inanimate objects of various types.

On the Trail

A blackpowder pistol is a worthy companion on the trail. The aforementioned 45-caliber T/C pistol with its set triggers and good sights put quite a few tasty meals in my camp as I backpack-hunted wild country. A big-bore pistol would also serve as protection against animal attack, but I think the entire area of self-defense with old-time guns is suspect, as noted below.

In Camp

A blackpowder pistol of any description is fun to have in camp. This one goes back mainly to plinking. As long as there is no threat of frightening off game, a little enjoyable practice in front of a solid dirt bank can be a nice camp pastime. The only rule is the always-safety reminder.

Small Game with a Pistol

Touched on for trail use, the pistol can put edibles in the pot, but it is also a viable tool for taking rabbits, squirrels, and any other small game as a main hunting tool. The trick is familiarity with the sights that often come on blackpowder pistols, which often amount to no true sights at all, but merely a little metal blob up front. By using front-sight-target concentration, however, which is the right method with any handgun sights, close-range small game can be put in the bag. The hunter who shoots a good deal before attempting to bag game will be the most successful. This goes back to plinking and informal target work. Small calibers are obviously the best choice, but after a period of familiarity with

a Lyman Plains Pistol in 54-caliber, I found that head shots were possible. Of course, the average from muzzle to rabbit or other small edible was on the order of about 10 to 15 yards. Rabbits, especially where I hunt in the West, do not possess college diplomas in evasive action. I have put 'em in the bag as close as a few feet away as they sat like stones waiting for me to pass by. Another pistol of personal experience is the Hopkins and Allen 36-caliber with a 1:15 rate of twist. This handy little single-shot puts a .350-inch 65-grain lead pill out at close to 1,000 fps with only 20-grains volume FFFg blackpowder or equivalent. And that's plenty for small game at close range.

Big Game with a Blackpowder Pistol

Now we're getting specialized. Whereas just about any pistol is suitable for small game, this is far from the case with deer-sized and even larger animals. There are two distinct camps here: original/replica and modern muz-

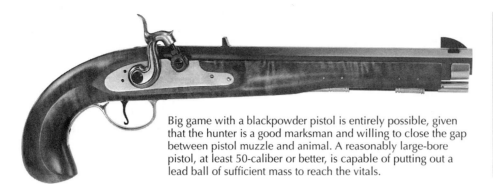

Big game with a blackpowder pistol is entirely possible, given that the hunter is a good marksman and willing to close the gap between pistol muzzle and animal. A reasonably large-bore pistol, at least 50-caliber or better, is capable of putting out a lead ball of sufficient mass to reach the vitals.

Remember that some pistols are hefty enough to handle conical bullets like these two. The 50-caliber bullet on the left is the choice for large game, while the 36-caliber bullet on the right is better suited to the smaller animals.

zleloader. There are a number of original and replica single-shot pistols that are big-game worthy.

Lyman's 54-caliber Plains Pistol drives a 225-grain round ball at 900+ fps with 50-grains volume FFg or equivalent RS or Triple Seven. Muzzle energy is below 430 foot-pounds, down to about 325 foot-pounds at 50 yards. You have to get close and put that ball right on the money for positive and humane results with this pistol, but it can be done. Another old-time style pistol of big game authority is the Harper's Ferry 1855 with a barrel a whisker shy of a foot in length. Rate of twist is 1:48, and could be faster, but I have gotten sufficient close-range accuracy with this 58-caliber pistol to know that it will do the job on deer-sized and even larger game with perfect bullet placement. That bullet, by the way, can be super-heavy. I had good luck with a 570-grain Lyman, mould No. 57730, which actually puts out a 600-grain bullet in pure lead because the mould is calibrated with an alloy.

A charge of 50-grains FFg or equivalent RS or Triple Seven puts this 600-grain slug out at less than 700 fps with an energy rating slightly below 650 foot-pounds. That's not a lot of paper power. At 50 yards, energy is down to less than 600 foot-pounds. On the other hand, this big bullet will break bone and penetrate beyond its paper figures. Then there is the modern muzzleloader pistol, a horse of a different hue, to be sure. The Scout Pistol from T/C is gone, but in its place is the Encore 209x50 Magnum. With two Pyrodex Pellets or

Triple Seven Pellets this 50-caliber pistol with its 1:28 rate of twist drives a 350-grain bullet at close to 1,500 fps for a muzzle energy in the mid-1600 foot-pounds. At 50 yards, the 350-grain bullet still carries over 1,350 foot-pounds of punch. This puts the Encore into the big-game arena.

As always, of course, there is bullet placement to consider. That's where practice comes in, not only in shooting, but dedication of the sportsman to turn himself into the 50-yard hunter, rather than trying to turn the pistol into a 150-yard big-game gun. See Chapter 42 for a couple of stalking tips. Above, a 50-caliber Remington Rolling Block pistol was mentioned, as used in the Adobe Walls conflict. A big-bore blackpowder metallic cartridge handgun like this would work on big game at close range.

Bullets for Blackpowder Pistols

As with blackpowder rifles, the two main classes of bullets for pistols include round ball and conical, the latter encompassing a wide range of styles. The smallest round ball I ever fired in a pistol ran only 22-caliber. The little custom pistol was put together mainly for plinking with tiny charges of blackpowder, although there was sufficient developed energy for small game at close range. There are a few 32-caliber pistols, but more 36s. Caliber 38 is also found now and then, the current Mang Pistol being one. This pistol, with its 1:15 rate of twist, shoots quite well with a round ball. The twist may seem fast for a .375-inch 80-grain round ball, but as clarified in Chapter 20, RPS

(revolutions per second) of a bullet is a matter of *twist rate*, but also exit velocity. The normal muzzle velocity of the Mang is around 1,000 to 1,100 fps, so the apparent rapid twist is not too rapid after all to stabilize the ball. The Hopkins & Allen Boot Pistol, Model 133, also has a 1:15 rate of twist in 36-caliber. Pistols in 45-caliber shooting round balls are many. The Rochatte Dueling Pistol in 45-caliber has a 1:18 rate of twist to stabilize its .440-inch 128-grain round ball at a nominal velocity around 950-to 1,000+ fps.

The second class of pistol bullet opens a door to many choices—conicals of just about every description. If forced to compartmentalize these bullets, "pure" lead and jacketed might be a good dividing line. Conicals were not at home on original blackpowder pistols tucked into the sashes of pirates and Navy sailors in those days of wooden ships with broad sails. The Harper's Ferry Model of 1885 is quite probably not an exception, but in the name of big power, conicals were tested in the name of big power.

Accuracy, Sights and Triggers

Sights and triggers go together as one compliments, or detracts, from the other. A pistol with wonderful sights but a trigger requiring a heavy pull is difficult to shoot well. On the other hand, the finest trigger in the land will not compensate for poor sights, or no sights at all. Taking sights first, various pistols have two major types.

The first can hardly be considered a sight at all. It's essentially a little lump of metal up front and often nothing else to line up with. At close range, and especially for informal target shooting and plinking, such sights are not only practical, but the additional challenge can add to the fun of shooting. On game, small or large, these sights demand getting close, often very close, for positive results.

The second class of sights found on pistols is best described as target quality. Oftentimes, these sights are fully adjustable. But not always. I manage some pretty fair shooting with my Lyman 54-caliber Plains Pistol with fixed rear sight. I say fixed, because it is fixed in a dovetail notch, but in fact this rear sight can be drifted left or right for horizontal bullet movement—left to bring the bullet to the left, right to move the bullet to the right on the target. The front sight, while non-adjustable, can be shortened by filing to cause a rise in bullet strike on the target, or replaced with a taller sight to bring the group down on the target.

While accurate shooting with the little lump up front on the barrel is accomplished mainly, if not only, through dedicated practice, fixed sights can be altered to bring the pattern on target, and once they are, hitting the bull's eye or other target is a matter, yes, of practice, but mainly concentrating on sight picture, always remembering front-sight-target as the key to success.

On the other end of the sight range is the fully adjustable or target sight. This sight does not have to be fancy for it to work quite well. I've had, for example, good luck with a Traditions Buckhunter Pro, caliber 50, which has a fixed front sight with a folding adjustable rear sight. Blackpowder pistol sights can also be altered or changed. Drifting the rear sight in the direction the shooter wants his or her next bul-

let to strike is a simple adjustment, as is filing down the front sight or installing a taller one to make the next bullet hit opposite of that adjustment—lower front sight to hit higher, taller front sight to hit lower. But there can be no argument that the fully adjustable rear sight is a boon to sighting in as well as making good groups on the target or delivering a projectile spot on for hunting. I'll use the T/C Encore as an example. This pistol has a fully adjustable rear sight for *both* windage and elevation. Sighting in is a rather simple matter of moving the rear sight in the direction desired for the next bullet to strike the target—up for up, down for down, unlike front sight movement. Chapter 26 deals with different sights for blackpowder guns, while 27 talks about "managing the rainbow," that is, the trajectory of bullet flight.

The Custom Blackpowder Pistol

Just as beautiful as the true custom front-loading rifle, the pistol of this class truly shines. Many contemporary gunmakers are capable of producing top-grade custom blackpowder pistols. I'm familiar with the Kennedy line, having tested both the Kennedy English Dueler and Kennedy Kentucky Pistol. Both are caliber 50. Both are flintlock. Both are replicas of past pistols. Although these guns are worthy of ownership simply to show, I fired both of them with 30-grains volume FFFg. A 1:29 rate of twist provided good accuracy, especially considering that in keeping with originality, neither pistol was dressed with adjustable sights. Through careful bench management, groups with .490-inch patched round balls fell into the two- to three-inch pattern at 25 yards. Either pistol would take small game at close range when in the hands of a practiced shooter who knows how to load and handle flintlocks.

Thompson/Center has long given the hunter a big-bore blackpowder pistol worthy of big game. The Scout, now retired from the line, came in 50 and 54. The Omega 209 Magnum is a 50-caliber muzzleloading pistol that can meet energy levels worthy of deer-sized game at 100 yards. The big T/C pistol at the lower right need not fall into the shade among the rifles.

This Lyman Plains Pistol has basic sights, but the sight picture is good and taking small game with meat-saving headshots is not too difficult. The silver bar on the side is to retain the pistol on a sash or belt.

Custom pistols are worthy choices. This set is by David Yager of Cochise Muzzleloaders, St. David, Arizona.

11 THE BLACKPOWDER REVOLVER

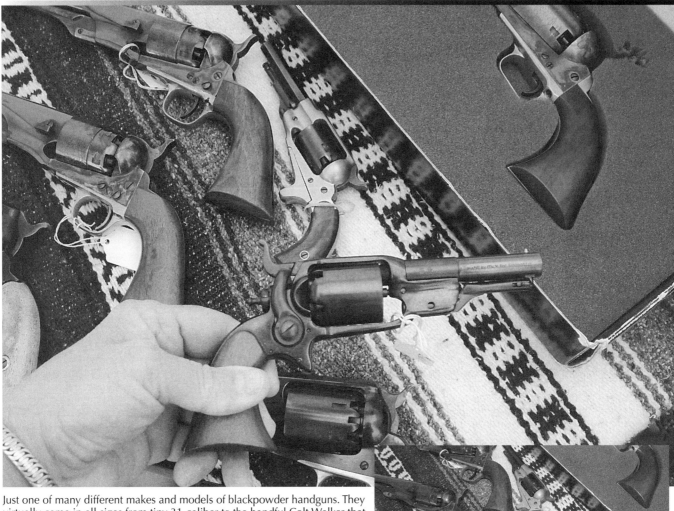

Just one of many different makes and models of blackpowder handguns. They virtually came in all sizes from tiny 31-caliber to the handful Colt Walker that was essentially carried by horse rather than a person on foot.

The blackpowder revolver comes in percussion as well as cartridge. Both are highly prominent in this early part of the 21st century, with the latter making astounding strides mainly due to the enthusiasm of Cowboy Action Shooting with meets held all over the country. These sidearms made considerable history in their day. Those involved in Indian Wars of the 19th century at first found themselves at considerable disadvantage. The intrepid native was a first-class warrior filled with bravery and resolve. He was also intelligent. It didn't take long for this fighter to recognize that while the guns of the white man were strong,

The percussion revolver evolved into many different styles. This is but one. Calibers generally ranged from about 31 to about 44.

they were also slow to shoot again once discharged. Even after the repeater saw action in the West, the rush-at-'em plan worked quite well. Knowing that the guns of their enemies had been fired, requiring reloading, the deadly Native American brave advanced at full speed. His bows were fast-loading repeaters capable of launching arrow

after arrow. This ancient tool was to be reckoned with.

Tennessee riflemen learned that back East. After delivering a terrible blow to the English at the Battle of New Orleans, these same astute marksmen had a very tough time against a band of Indians armed with bows and arrows. Now comes on the scene something

The Colt Paterson and a long line of percussion revolvers gave way to cartridge revolvers. Colt's models were well accepted. A saying came about—"God made man, but Sam Colt made them equal."

The Colt-style percussion revolver disassembled easily for cleaning, a feature appreciated by soldiers in the American Civil War. This one is ready for maintenance with a special Traditions kit designed for the task.

new—Mr. Colt's revolver from Paterson, New Jersey. Supposedly, one Indian spokesman said that now the white man could fire his single-shot rifle, but he was instantly ready to deal out more firepower, as many as the fingers on your hand. Which was right. The Paterson was a five-shot percussion or cap 'n' ball revolver. Production commenced on March of 1836, coincidentally the date marked as the fall of the Alamo. Colonel Colt patented his idea in 1835 following a sea voyage where he made his well-known wooden model to see if the idea had merit. Colt's Patent Arms Manufacturing Company produced the five-shot revolver, but sales were not brisk enough to keep the door open and it closed in 1842. This was in spite of huge victories won in part due to Colt's 36-caliber revolver, especially Plum Creek in 1840 and Enchanted Rock in 1841. A hail of bullets from the new five-shot revolver met Comanche warriors executing their typical mad run after a volley was fired from the guns of Texas Rangers. (1944 *Gun Digest*.)

Collecting

Originals are, naturally and without question, ideal for collecting. And originals are available, especially Civil War six-guns of Colt and Remington

The cap 'n' ball revolver (percussion) made a tremendous difference in the "Winning of the West." The Plains Indian rushed the rifleman after he fired. They knew it would take him a long time to reload. When the Paterson five-shot revolver came about, the story changed. "It shoots as many times as the fingers on one hand," the warriors said. This young shooter tries a Navy Arms Company replica.

manufacture. But a much less expensive means of gathering a collection for the enthusiast who simply wants to have likenesses on hand for show and tell is the replica. And replicas we have in plenty. The Colt Paterson itself is available, as from the Navy Arms Company. Several Civil War revolvers are also as close as the Internet, sold through various companies. In terms of popularity, it's probably a toss-up between the Colt 1860 Army and Remington New Model Army of 1858. Today's shooters may view the Remington as a better

Collecting blackpowder handguns is a hobby in its own right because there were so many different makes and models over time.

choice because of the topstrap design, but soldiers of the conflict did not necessarily agree. The Colt broke down faster and easier, which allowed rapid cleanup, but also the opportunity to install a fresh already-loaded cylinder. Add to these fine sidearms the interesting Spiller and Burr originally produced in Atlanta between 1862 and 1864, as well as the Rogers and Spencer Army Model made in Utica, New York, toward the end of the War Between the States. A prime example of a fine replica collectible is the Colt 1855 Sidehammer, 36-caliber percussion sidearm reputed to be Robert E. Lee's choice. Originally designed by Elisha Root with a topstrap (unlike most Colts of the era), the faithful replica comes to us through Dixie Gun Works.

The list of readily available copycats is long and exciting. To name just a few more: Colt Pocket Police 1861 Navy, 1st U.S. Model Dragoon, as well as the 2nd, 3rd Dragoons, 1851 Navy, 1862 Pocket Navy, 3rd Hartford, and of course the big Colt Walker. In blackpowder cartridge, the ever-popular Colt Peacemaker, generally offered in calibers 44 and 45, is easy to find. Sometimes this revolver is somewhat altered in style, but it always comes off being a Colt, even when the name says Beretta. A personal favorite is the Le Mat from the Navy Arms Company, a nine-shot revolver—but it didn't end there. A smooth bore under-barrel could dish out a load of shot or a fat 65-caliber lead ball. There are also conversions,

Just shooting away for sheer enjoyment is perfect with any of the blackpowder revolvers, percussion or cartridge.

Target shooting, here with a Remington cap 'n' ball revolver, is a great game with any of the blackpowder revolvers.

such as the 1851 Navy that in the late 1800s was modified from percussion to shoot the 38 Long Colt cartridge, the 1872 open top chambered for the 38 Special, and Remington's 1890 revolver in 44-40 Winchester or 45 Colt. One of my favorite blackpowder cartridge guns is the Colt Bisley, also from Navy Arms. Mine is in 45 Colt and it shoots fine. While it is more than close enough to the original to suit me, it also has a transfer bar to prevent accidental discharge if dropped. And that's a safety feature worth having.

Plinking

As with the blackpowder pistols, any blackpowder revolver is at home in the plinking arena. An afternoon of plopping bullets into a dirt bank with a cap 'n' ball six-shooter in any caliber, any style, any period, is time well spent in relaxation. Likewise blackpowder revolver handguns. Following a stint of handgun shooting training from a former SWAT team leader, for the first time in my life I was able to put bullet after bullet on target, and plenty of those bullets came from my Bisley 45, as well as a host of old-time caplock revolvers.

Target Shooting--Informal

Neighbor to plinking, this aspect of cap 'n' ball shooting or blackpowder cartridge handgun firing has no boundaries, except for the repeated advice to shoot safely with a proper backstop. Paper targets as simple as bullseyes are fine. So are various cutouts.

Target Shooting-- Competition

There are many shooting events that require a cap 'n' ball revolver. Likewise Cowboy Action Shooting for blackpowder cartridge-shooting handguns. Such events are catalogued on the Internet, as well as in *Muzzle Blasts* magazine, official publication of the National Muzzle Loading Rifle Association (NMLRA). One of the more accurate percussion sidearms often found spewing out smoke for serious target shooting is the

Ruger Old Army 45-caliber loaded with either round balls or conical bullets.

Rendezvous

Unlike pistols at rendezvous, which are often chosen to complete a period outfit as much as for shooting, the blackpowder cap 'n' ball revolver is more often a shooter. Many events are colorful, which means targets that announce hits, but there are also competitions on regular paper bullseyes. Those interested in rendezvous shooting with a blackpowder revolver must inquire of the "booshway" in charge. This person will have a list of events, including handgun shooting.

On the Trail

No surprise here, because many of the wild animal attacks on people, especially cougars near towns, are on running trails. But I was surprised to learn that coyote attacks on people have been documented. As for bears, that's a story written into many books and articles over the years concerning encounters with black bears as well as grizzlies. I don't see the ordinary cap 'n' ball revolver as right for protection on the

Rendezvous sees plenty of blackpowder percussion shooting, but Cowboy Action Shooting depends upon the blackpowder cartridge revolver. Jerry Meyer, expert blackpowder handgunner, shows a percussion revolver here.

While the blackpowder percussion revolver is most often loaded with round bullets, conicals like these (compared with a 45-caliber cartridge) are also worthy.

trail when the animal is bear-size, but a six-shot 44-caliber revolver would offer considerable comfort if a modest-sized beast decided to spoil a hiker's day. The blackpowder cartridge revolver would be even better, especially in 44-40 or 45 Colt spitting out fairly heavy bullets, even though velocity is on the low end of the spectrum.

In Camp

While not necessarily for protection, although occasions do arise when a camp gun handy to get to can save a mauling, a blackpowder cartridge handgun or cap 'n' ball percussion fits into camp life as natural as a stream running by the tent. As with the pistol, there is nothing wrong with enjoying a little shooting time in camp, provided conditions are right—no nearby neighbors to disturb or, for that matter, game. There always seems to be a safe dirt bank handy near camp.

Small Game with a Blackpowder Handgun

There is absolutely no barrier to putting small game in the bag with a blackpowder cartridge handgun or caplock revolver. The smallest caliber ordinarily encountered is 31. The Baby Dragoon Model of 1848 is 31-caliber, as is the 1849 Pocket Wells Fargo, both available in replica from several companies, such as Armsport, Cimarron and Uberti. Caliber 36, however, is more popular, as in the 1851 Navy. Most of these handguns do not have target sights. However, with practice

small game can be collected. The good news is that a 31- or 36-caliber round ball is not terribly destructive of edible meat at low speed, which is what these percussion revolvers deliver. The 1851 Navy, for example, puts out a .375-inch 80-grain round bullet at a muzzle velocity below 500 fps with a light charge of 10-grains volume Pyrodex P. In 32-20 Winchester chambering, the blackpowder cartridge revolver is a fine small game taker. Cimarron's Lightning single-action comes in 32-20, as does the same company's Model P Jr. My experience with a Colt copy from Navy Arms Company in 32-20 convinced me that at close range, and with some practice, handguns without target sights are indeed capable of putting bullets on target at close range.

Big Game with a Blackpowder Revolver

All in all, the cap 'n' ball blackpowder revolver is not on a power level normally considered big-game worthy, and much the same can be said for the blackpowder cartridge revolver. But there's an old saying I just made up that goes: "Don't judge the ability of others from your ability." My friend Ron, who was a former SWAT team leader, can put a bullet from a handgun into a small target every shot, and farther than I would ever attempt the same feat. Ron is also a good hunter capable of mounting a close stalk on big game. Give him a Ruger Old Army 45 cap 'n' ball revolver, a 44 Walker, or my 45 Colt Bisley and don't bet that a deer won't be brought into camp with one well-placed bullet. The emphasis here is "well-placed bullet." Since bullets of reasonable weight are associated with these handguns, they can penetrate quite well. Remember, too, that some of these guns have target-type sights, such as the 1858 Remington target model as well as the Ruger Old Army. Such sights promote better bullet placement.

On the face of it, though, even these comparatively strong blackpowder sidearms are no match for current big-bore

This Navy Arms Company replica of a Remington Civil War cap 'n' ball revolver is faithful with the sights, which consisted of a groove through the top strap to serve as a rear sight notch, coupled with an ordinary front sight. A practiced shooter could hit the target with such sights regularly, especially after any required adjustments were made.

big-game handguns, such as the Smith & Wesson "hand cannon" firing the 500 S&W Magnum. A strong load in the Ruger Old Army is a 40-grains volume Pyrodex P starting a .457-inch 143-grain round ball at just shy of 1,050 fps for a rating a hair under 350 foot-pounds. At 50 yards, energy is down to about 230 foot-pounds. The big Walker revolver I tested gulped 57-grains volume Pyrodex P (44.2 grains by weight) for a muzzle velocity of 1,215 fps with 462 foot-pounds of energy. Energy at 50 yards is about 300 foot-pounds. The 45 Colt in a 7th Cavalry copy with 7 1/2-inch barrel obtained the highest velocity I have tested to date with one Pyrodex 44/45 pistol Pellet, equivalent to 30 grains volume. However, the usual 37-grain charge of FFg produced more normal 45 Colt performance with a 255-grain bullet taking off at under 800 fps with 300 foot-pounds of remaining energy at 50 yards.

Bullets for Blackpowder Caplock Revolvers

Bullets for blackpowder cap 'n' ball revolvers are mainly of two breeds: round

There are conical bullets of various sizes for the blackpowder percussion revolver, caliber 36 shown here with a 22 Long Rifle cartridge for comparison.

lead ball and conical lead ball. Both shoot extremely well. A 180-grain Buffalo Bullet conical fired from an 1858 Remington Target Model cap 'n' ball revolver "put 'em on the money" at 25 yards. A light charge, only 20 grains volume, produced just shy of 600 fps, sufficient for paper-punching and small game up close. The Ruger Old Army with 7 1/2-inch barrel achieved 1,047 fps with a 143-grain .457-inch round ball and 40-grains volume Pyrodex P, with good accuracy results. The shorter-barrel Ruger Old Army at 5-1/2 inches gained 1,136 fps with the same round ball but 40-grains volume Triple Seven powder—also with fine accuracy. The Old Army also shoots a 190-grain Buffalo Bullet conical at 1,157 fps muzzle velocity burning 40-grains volume Pyrodex P. Muzzle energy is now a healthy 565 foot-pounds with this conical projectile, and an overmatch for the 38 Special, which gathers in about 300 foot-pounds with a 140-grain bullet at 1,000 fps.

Bullets for Blackpowder Cartridge Revolvers

Although it is possible to shoot round bullets in these guns, and I have done so with decent close-range accuracy in a 45 Colt six-gun, the usual projectile is a lead conical. Jacketed conicals are also a possibility, but the lead missile is more appropriate with blackpowder. The Beretta Stampede, a well-made six-gun of Colt heritage, did a fine job in 45 Colt with a heavy 250-grain lead bullet out of a Lyman #454190 mould. Velocity reached 1,117 fps with a charge of 35-grains volume GOEX

FFFg in the case. A particularly enjoyable shooting combination is one of the Colt replica revolvers in 32-20 shooting a 115-grain lead bullet out of a Lyman #311316 mould. A charge of 18-grains volume Triple Seven, which came to 18 grains by weight, developed 888 fps in this handgun. You can shoot this blackpowder cartridge revolver all morning without a hint of fatigue. The byword for large-bore blackpowder revolvers is good bullet weight. Bullets in the 250/255-grain class are commonplace in the 45 Colt. In the interesting Schofield Cavalry Revolver a 255-grain lead bullet leaves the muzzle at 916 fps with a charge of 37-grains volume Pyrodex P. Muzzle energy out to 50 yards is just short of 400 foot-pounds, but even so, the heavy bullet has a healthy impact at that distance.

Accuracy, Sights, and Triggers

As with pistols, sights and triggers are tied into accuracy, not in the sense of what the handgun can do, of course, since that is a matter of "good bullets out of good barrels," to parrot Dr. Mann's conclusion, but because good sights promote a better sight picture and good triggers allow a non-jarring release for minimal gun disturbance—in other words, maintaining the sight picture on the target without having to "yank" the trigger. These points are too obvious to belabor. Target-type sights promote improved bullet placement, as do good triggers. Inherent handgun accuracy with either the caplock or blackpowder cartridge revolver hinges on fine-tuning. Pistol-smiths do the work and do it well. A wrinkle with the cap 'n' ball revolver is chamfering the mouth of the cylinder chamber. Seating a round ball in a regular chamber normally cuts a small ring of lead from the ball. By chamfering the mouth of the chamber to make a somewhat beveled entrance, the cut-off lead ring from the round bullet is eliminated. Expert handgun shooters argue this point. One camp declares that chamfering is vital to topnotch accuracy, while the other camp says, "Prove it." My only experience with chamfering indicated a minor, and somewhat difficult to verify, improvement in accuracy. But one test does not make a statement. I'll leave this one up to the expert pistolsmith who does the chamfering job—or says no to it.

Blackpowder Handgun Cartridges

Listing a few blackpowder cartridges for handguns is especially worthwhile for this edition, because the field is growing. Due, mainly, to the Cowboy Action Shooting game, blackpowder revolvers are seeing a significant increase in interest, which in turn leads shooters to ask for, if not demand, a number of different cartridges to choose from.

32-20 Winchester

This is one of the AC/DC rounds—that is, it's at home in both rifle and handgun. While I consider the 32-20 a small-game round with turkey and small game also in the picture, it's also a wonderful cartridge for enjoyable plinking and target work. True, big game has been dropped with this little fellow. I ran across an old-timer in Wyoming who in his hunting days used nothing but a 32-20 for deer. You can bet this fellow knew how to stalk for close shots. The 32-20 was introduced in 1882 chambered in the Model 1873 Winchester lever-action rifle. Colt was soon to follow, however, with 32-20 handguns. Bullets in the 100- to 115-grain range flying from the muzzle at about the speed of sound are excellent for small game and up to javelina-size larger game. It was also used for self-defense. No surprise, since the 22 Short was originally sold as a self-defense round. But there are far better cartridges for that duty. As noted above, a 115-grain lead bullet left the muzzle at 888 fps, this from a Colt copy with a 5 1/2-inch barrel.

38-40 Winchester

Typical of cartridge nomenclature, the 38-40 is just a name. It was origi-

Taking a shot with the unique LeMat percussion revolver, designed jointly by French seafarer Colonel LeMat and Confederate General Pierre Beauregard—a nine-shot revolver with a 65-caliber under-barrel.

nally loaded with something on the order of 40 grains volume blackpowder in the old balloon-head case. But it is not a 38-caliber round. It came along in 1874 for the Winchester Model 1873 rifle, shortly chambered also in the Colt Single-Action Army six-gun. The 44-40 saw first life in 1873 along with the famous rifle. For some time, the 38-40 lay fallow because it is—yes—a 40-caliber cartridge and 40-caliber bullets were not popular. The advent of modern 40s changed that. Bullets in the 180- to 200-grain weight class take off at around 900 fps in this "necked-down 44-40" round. Hornady has a 180-

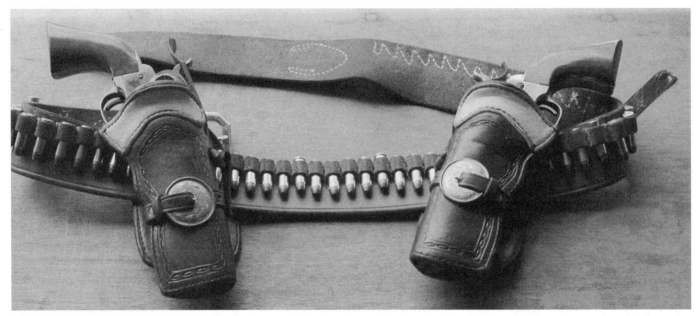

Ready for the Cowboy Action Shooting game—a double rig that would have made Deadwood Dick envious with its two matching blackpowder revolver cartridge six-shooters.

grain lead bullet for the 38-40 with a .400-inch diameter. A friend owns an original Colt in 38-40, new condition, although it was carried onto an Alaskan trail to Fairbanks at the turn of the century. The revolver shoots just fine in 38-40. Winchester's catalog of 1916 lists the 38 Winchester, not called a 38-40, with a full metal jacket or soft-point 180-grain bullet and 38-grains of powder—$24.00 per thousand rounds. The 38-40 has returned in a limited way, as in the Cimarron Model P revolver.

44-40 Winchester

Only one year older than the 38-40, this cartridge was probably the parent round. Surely, the 38-40 is but a necked-down 44-40. While it was designed originally for the Winchester '73 rifle, the cartridge soon found a home in Colt revolvers. You guessed it—just as the 38-40 is not 38-caliber, firing 40-caliber bullets instead—neither is the 44-40 44-caliber. It shoots 43-caliber bullets (bullets running .427-inch in the Hornady 205-grain lead FP Cowboy bullet. Velocity is on par with the 38-40, but bullets up to 250 grains weight are possible, giving the 44-40 a bit more power potential. Many replica

handguns, as well as rifles, are offered in this caliber. Often, there is a choice between the 44-40 or 45 Colt, as in the 38-40 Cimarron P revolver mentioned above. Colt's Single-Action Army Revolver is also available in 44-40 or 45 Colt chamberings. The list goes on. In Winchester's 1916 catalog, a shooter could buy 1,000 rounds of 44-40 ammo with 40 grains of blackpowder and a 180-grain hollowpoint bullet, for $19.00. A good round, the 44-40, but it was eventually supplanted with much larger blackpowder numbers.

44 Russian

The 44 Russian cartridge, also known as the Smith & Wesson Russian, is back in town. It arrives by demand of Cowboy Action Shooters who discovered that for various reasons, this old cartridge was considered accurate. Furthermore, it's mild and that's important when the goal is smacking a target, not with atomic force, but just hard enough to tell a hit in the Cowboy Action Shooting game. The cartridge was introduced in the S&W Model Russian single-action break-top revolver for the Russian Imperial Army, 1870. Obviously, it was a blackpowder number, as the date

shows. In 1878, Colt chambered the 44 Russian in its Bisley single-action target revolver. Bisley, incidentally, is a place—situated "on the north side of the valley of the river Frome roughly equidistant from Gloucester and Cirencester."

The charming little English community is of greater interest to us because of the NRA—not our NRA—the National Rifle Association of the United Kingdom. The Bisley range was established in 1859 for "Promoting Target Shooting throughout the United Kingdom." Hence, Colt's target model in 44 Russian carried the Bisley name to denote target capability. The 44 Russian case is almost an inch long (0.97), and it can be fired in revolvers chambered for the 44 Special and 44 Magnum, but not with great accuracy due to long bullet jump into the throat of the barrel. This round originally fired a bullet noted as 246 grains weight with 23 grains of blackpowder for around 700 to 750 fps muzzle velocity. Remember that many loads were mixed granulation. Today, you can buy a revolver chambered for the 44 Russian, as in Cimarron's 1872 Open Top as well as the Navy Arms New Model Russian Revolver. Winchester's 1916 catalog lists the 44 S&W Russian with a 246-grain lead bullet and 23 grains of blackpowder. A thousand cartridges sold for $20.00.

44 Special

The 44 Special showed up in 1907, which drops it from the ranks of true blackpowder cartridges. Smith & Wesson developed the cartridge to upgrade, at least in power, the 44 Russian. The 44 Special earns a place here because it is back in force: chambered in single-action handguns, such as the Cimarron Thunderer, EMF Hartford, and Ruger New Model Blackhawk. The real thrust of the 44 Special is not so much its place in history, but its impact on handgun power as the forerunner of the 44 Magnum. The 44 Special was listed in the 1916 Winchester catalog with a 246-grain lead bullet; undoubtedly the same loaded in the 44 Russian. The charge, however, was 26 grains of blackpowder for $22.00 per thousand. Smokeless was available with lead or "full patch" (full metal jacket) bullet at $25.00 per thousand rounds.

45 Schofield

This is a true blackpowder cartridge, and it has in recent times worked its way from the dark forest of obscurity to the bright light of Cowboy Action Shooting and other single-action games and general shooting. Here is another Smith & Wesson cartridge. Date it 1875. Put it in the ranks of the United States Army in that same year. Color it historical in the hands of General George Armstrong Custer at the Battle of the Little Bighorn. Chamber the old round in a Ruger Bisley Blackhawk and the old picture becomes a 21st-century reality. There is also the Navy Arms Schofield revolver, although I have seen this replica in 44-40 and 45 Colt only. Hornaday's 255-grain FP Cowboy bullet is just right in this cartridge. Look at 700 to 750 fps for a muzzle velocity.

45 Colt

To avoid confusion, the 45 Colt came to be the 45 *Long* Colt, although there never was a 45 Short Colt. The *Long* part does distinguish it from the 45 ACP (Automatic Colt Pistol), however. That's probably why Hornady, in one of its loading manuals, calls the cartridge the 45 Long Colt. Originally chambered for the Colt Peacemaker six-shooter, the 45 Colt has found its way into rifles in modern times. The original load was a 255-grain lead bullet and 40 grains of blackpowder in a balloon head case. Modern cartridge cases with solid heads hold a bit less powder, but are much stronger. An original 45 Colt Single-Action Army revolver got 773 fps with 37-grains volume GOEX FFg blackpowder for only 388 foot-pounds of energy at the muzzle. This belies the underlying potential of the case. When adapted to a modern Ruger Blackhawk revolver, the 45 Colt is capable of driving a 250-grain bullet at 1,400 fps and a 300-grain bullet at 1,300 fps. This puts the 45 Colt, which came along in 1973, in the 44 Magnum class; however, only in stout guns made to withstand higher pressures, not old-style single-actions. The Winchester catalog of 1916 listed ammo with a 255-grain lead bullet and 38-grains of blackpowder at $22.00 per thousand. Handloaders paid $7.00 for 1,000 255-grain bullets, or $10.50 for 1,000 primed cases. Smokeless ran $24.50 per thousand with lead bullet.

Smokeless Sometimes

Since many of the replica blackpowder *cartridge* revolvers are of modern manufacture, smokeless powder is allowed in these handguns. In many cases, however, the shooter must observe a very important fact—*the design of the gun may still say 19th century.* Therefore, cooking up "hot" smokeless powder loads can bring trouble. The only way to sensibly load with smokeless is strict consultation with a respected manual, such as Hornady's *Handbook of Cartridge Reloading.* For example, this book shows 38-40 in a Ruger Blackhawk. A top load with the 180-grain lead bullet is shown as 7.0 grains of VHT N340 for 900 fps. Many Cowboy Action Shooters prefer blackpowder, or a proper substitute for the historical smoke.

In a sense, the blackpowder cap 'n' ball, as well as blackpowder cartridge handguns, will never go obsolete because these guns are already obsolete, and yet they thrive. How can you kill a living ghost?

12 THE SMOKEPOLE SCATTERGUN

Unlikely is the word for finding Sam in a faraway camp without his short-barreled 12-gauge blackpowder shotgun. "The little gun has fed the camp often," he says.

There is good reason to believe the mountain man of the Far West fired a string of shot into the air now and then. We know that Manuel Lisa included a Brown Bess musket in his kit when he traveled up the Missouri River in 1807. While there is no solid evidence that he used this smoothbore as a shotgun, he and others carrying similar smoothbores may have. Include the "trade gun" in this discussion and the certainty of shot fired now and again escalates a couple levels. Trade guns were prominent with both mountain men and Indians in the 19th century. Call them a *fusil* or *fusee*, it doesn't matter—they were smoothbores for sure and quite capable of buzzing a beehive of little lead missiles into the air. A two-legged recipient of that load would surely retreat, if capable, while winged and furred meals were assured. These little facts

are important to modern blackpowder scattergun enthusiasts because nothing has changed. Pioneers counted on their blackpowder shotguns for game and protection. Protection, no, but I'd not give up my smokepole scattergun to provide game for my evening campfire.

If challenged to live "off the land" for an extended period of time, and I could take but one firearm, it well might be my short double-barreled percussion blackpowder shotgun spewing out a full 1-1/2 ounces of shot encouraged by 100 grains of FFg or equivalent. I might have along a few round balls as well. Realistically, the blackpowder shotgun cannot match the potency of today's shotshell because 20th and 21st century advances are but a cat whisker under amazing. In testing a batch of new turkey loads from Winchester, Remington, and Federal, I learned that

12-gauge 3-inch magnum patterns and energy delivery were better at 60 yards while older 12-gauge ammo I had on hand were better limited to 40 yards. The new 3 1/2-inch 12-gauge shotshell boasts a cargo of shot heavier than my old 10-gauge goose gun. Nonetheless, the blackpowder shotgun can be a powerhouse, and when properly fed will in turn feed its owner.

While my little backpack 12-gauge double propels its shot charge at only 1,000 fps, if I get close enough (25 yards is about ideal) it puts supper in the pot every time. Furthermore, my Knight TK-2000™ 12-gauge blackpowder shotgun truly "packs the mail" with 120-grains volume FFg blackpowder , RS, or Triple Seven behind a 2 1/2-ounce shot charge contained in a 2 1/2-ounce shot cup. Its screw-in chokes (called "advanced jug-choked") rival today's shotshell loads in

The modern muzzleloading shotgun, such as the Knight 12-gauge, is capable of launching a formidable cloud of shot through a screw-in Full choke driven by a strong powder charge. It is worthy of any goose pit, duck blind, or gobbler hunt.

If the flintlock shotgun is a fowler, then by definition if not total ancestry, this Pedersoli flintlock shotgun is of the fowler family.

pattern. Improved Cylinder and Modified chokes increase the usefulness of this blackpowder shotgun. With the Full choke screwed into the muzzle, a 2 1/2-ounce charge of No. 4 shot (338 pellets) produced a 97 percent pattern at 25 yards with 330 pellets landing in a 30-inch circle. At 30 yards, 328 pellets poked holes in the pattern paper's 30-inch circle for 96 percent. At 40 yards, 289 pellets clustered inside a 30-inch circle for an 85 percent pattern. That, according to the upcoming chart, is Extra Full choke.

The Fowler

While the fowler, which I consider a flintlock blackpowder shotgun, was highly regarded in its day, and is still viable in the hands of a good wingshooter, let's get it "out of the way" early in this chapter. The fowler does not take any longer to charge than a percussion blackpowder shotgun; but it definitely has a slower lock time, that is the elapsed time from the tripping of the trigger to the burning of the powder charge. Leading the target is vital with modern shotguns firing the most advanced ammunition; add a slower flintlock lock time and the increased challenge is obvious. In the name of learning, I fired somewhat extensively a 12-gauge fowler at clay pigeons. Had these been live birds, most would have returned to the roost that afternoon. The puff of smoke just in front of my face and the *fttttt-booom* threw me off. Be that as it may, more power to the shotgunner who can master this truly old-time blackpowder scattergun.

The Percussion Blackpowder Shotgun

Even though the above-mentioned Knight modern in-line 12-gauge shotgun does not use the old-time percussion cap, typical of so many modern muzzleloaders today that employ No. 209 shotshell primers or musket caps, it remains a percussion shotgun. And as such, represents the blackpowder shotgun ignition type of the day. This in-line shotgun is single-barrel. There are also single-barrel sidelock muzzleloading shotguns. But the double-barrel percussion blackpowder shotgun pretty much steals the show in terms of numbers. I have a Navy Arms double-barrel percussion 12-gauge that not only handles 1-1/2 ounces of shot, with 1 1/3-ounce loads from time to time, but is also built to handle steel shot. Add Full choke and this double-gun proves itself on waterfowl, including Canada geese. Rabbits, wild turkey, grouse, pheasants, sage hens—you name it. My two-barrel smokepole scattergun can handle them all. It will even take a deer and larger big game with a single 494-grain lead

Yes, this is a percussion shotgun, but with a difference. It's a double-barrel custom sidehammer.

round ball. What it is not suited for, in my opinion, is home protection. While pioneers no doubt guarded home and hearth with the blackpowder shotgun, going modern for that purpose makes more sense. Incidentally, because of its smooth bore, as well as the advent of Triple Seven powder, I can spiff up any blackpowder shotgun after a shooting session in a matter of minutes with plain water and a couple of cleaning patches.

Practical Applications for the Blackpowder Shotgun

Whether in the super-power single-barrel modern muzzleloader or replica-style the blackpowder shotgun is capable of performing at many levels—Skeet, trap, dove, and quail, even big game. It is at home not only in the field filling the game bag, but also at rendezvous, where buckskinners vie for top honors busting clay pigeons and other flying targets. If the old-time shotgun has a drawback it is loading procedure. You don't slip in another cargo of shells and bang away. Reloading requires care and deliberation, and does take some time. So let your partners with modern shotguns go their way while you enjoy making smoke on your hunt—and I promise this: it is fun. Recently, I put three sage hens in the bag with a double-barrel 12-gauge muzzleloader. I'm not sure why, but adding smoke to the scene added measurably to the experience. Let's take a look at bore sizes before marching farther on the blackpowder scattergun trail.

The blackpowder shotgun is entirely capable of taking on any game normally hunted with a modern shotgun—provided the pattern is dense and well distributed. When the shotgun is Cylinder bore (no choke) getting closer solves pattern problems—and tighter patterns can be obtained with one-piece plastic wads.

One practical application for the blackpowder shotgun is competition. Some of the shotguns seen at these competitions are custom made.

Bore Sizes

Adding to our blackpowder knowledge, it's good to know what bore size meant in days of yore because little has changed on that score. Today's 12-gauge, for example, is still in the 0.729-inch domain. *Shooting on the Wing*, an 1873 publication by "An Old Gamekeeper," actual author's name not provided, contains a rundown of shotgun bore sizes in the 19th century. Gauge/caliber relationships, according to the Old Gamekeeper, went this way:

Shotgun	Bore Sizes
Gauge	Caliber in Inches
1-gauge	1.669
4-gauge	1.052
8-gauge	0.835
10-gauge	0.775
11-gauge	0.751
12-gauge	0.729
13-gauge	0.710
16-gauge	0.662
20-gauge	0.615
24-gauge	0.579
28-gauge	0.550
32-gauge	0.526
36-gauge	0.506

Getting ready to shoot a string of shot into the sky chasing a clay pigeon, you can bet this blackpowder shotgunner has a 12-gauge. The 12 is by far the most popular bore size in today's blackpowder shotgun.

Sometimes blackpowder rifles were designated by gauge, so 10-gauge is 78-caliber; 12-gauge is 73-caliber; 16-gauge is 67-caliber; 20-gauge is 62-caliber; 28-gauge is 55-caliber.

Blackpowder Shotgun Gauge

Certain modern 12-gauge blackpowder shotguns are actually 13-gauge. Some 10-gauge muzzleloaders are truly 11-gauge. There's a good reason for this. A 13-gauge blackpowder shotgun handles loading components normally intended for a 12-gauge shotgun *shell*, while an 11-gauge frontloader handles components sized for a 10-gauge shot-

shell. Since the wad column fits *inside* the shotshell, wads are smaller than the inside diameter of the modern shotgun bore. Meanwhile, the blackpowder shotgun has no shell, so dimensioning the bore to accept components intended for the modern shotgun shell makes a perfect fit. It's vital to test components to ensure they are sized correctly for a given blackpowder shotgun. Forcing too-large wads downbore can be dangerous because pressures rise when a load cannot get smoothly underway once pushed on by gases from the burning powder charge. Wads that are too large, but forced downbore anyway, can create this situation. If a wad of any type will not run home without undue force, it is wrong for that gun.

What They Burn

In the old days, there was no choice. The blackpowder shotgun burned—blackpowder, which was called gunpowder because there was no "white" or smokeless on the scene to contrast with. That has changed. While there are powders I consider inferior and do not write about, we also have excellent blackpowder, such as the latest GOEX propellants, as well as Swiss, Elephant, and other fine products. Pyrodex has long been an excellent blackpowder substitute ideal in RS granulation (Ri-

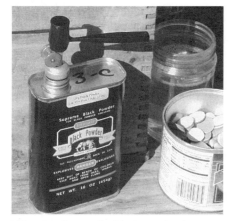

What they burn—the blackpowder shotgun burns all of the different brands of blackpowder as well as the substitutes. This competitor is loading his shotgun with Brazil's Elephant Brand.

The original blackpowder double barrel shotgun with damascus barrels was most often loaded with Fg or FFg granulation. The trend continues today.

fle/Shotgun) for the shotgun. Now we have Triple Seven, which is discussed in Chapter 25. Triple Seven's great advantage is superior power-per-grain performance while offering near smokeless powder cleaning ease. I have successfully used both Pyrodex Pellets and Triple Seven Pellets in my side-by-side muzzleloading shotguns. But the Hodgdon Powder Company does *not* recommend either for this application, stating that pelletized powder is intended for in-line muzzleloaders only, such as the aforementioned Knight shotgun. (And, of course, *any type* of smokeless powder is forbidden in any amount.)

Granulations

Finer granulations are not recommended in the shotgun. This includes Pyrodex P and FFFg blackpowder. This is a good rule, but the original reason so often stated is false. "Don't use FFFg because the high velocity it causes blown patterns." Not true. Part of my responsibility as a writer on the subject of blackpowder is judicious testing. I tested FFFg and Pyrodex P under safe conditions. Conclusion: it is possible for these finer-grain propellants to burn out a cardboard over-powder wad. And if a wad does burn out, patterns go south. On the other hand, the real reason to avoid finer granulations in blackpowder shotguns is that larger kernels are ideal in these big-bore guns

with copious volume for gas distribution. I like Fg in the 10-gauge, but find FFg workable in all gauges, along with Pyrodex RS and the large granulation Triple Seven (see Chapter 25 for more on Triple Seven).

Blackpowder Shotgun Pressures

Due to bore size, burning volume for expanding gases is large, as noted above, and therefore pressures are comparatively low in all shotguns. That is why modern or old-time shotgun barrel walls are thin by comparison to rifle barrels. Regardless, there are maximum pressures to deal with in all shooting and manufacturer/importer recommended charges are not to be exceeded. Larger granulation powders create good velocity with low pressures, always a desirable condi-

Blackpowder shotgun pressures are low because of the large bore's copious volume for powder gases to expand in. A good dose of GOEX blackpowder will be followed by an equal volume of shot, both made with the same measure, as seen resting in the shot container.

tion. Lyman's laboratory tests show 3 3/4-drams (102-grains volume) GOEX FFg developing only 2,500 psi (pounds per square inch) in a 12-gauge shotgun pushing a 1-ounce of shot charge. As mass in front of that powder charge increases, pressures rise. Keeping everything the same, powder charge and wad column, 1 1/8-ounces of shot raises pressures to 4,600 psi (3,600 psi for Pyrodex RS) and 5,000 psi with 1 1/2-ounces of shot. There is no clear ratio between pressure and shot charge here, except that more mass up front does increase pressure. By way of comparison, a pressure test of 1 1/2-ounces of No. 2 steel shot in a 12-gauge developed 4,600 psi in a 12-gauge muzzleloader with 102-grains volume, while 100-grains volume FFg blackpowder in a 50-caliber rifle gained 15,000 psi firing a 335-grain Lyman bullet with sabot. Can pressure ever skyrocket in a blackpowder shotgun? Absolutely. The wad column, especially, can cause this to happen, especially if it is so lodged in the breech that it will not readily start upbore when expanding powder gases push on it. The short-start, as often hit upon in this book, is another possible problem. When there is a gap between the powder charge and the wad column/shot cargo ahead of the charge, a bulged or even blown barrel can result. Also, a bore obstruction (such as mud stuck in the bore ahead of the charge) can break the thin walls of a shotgun barrel.

The Powder Charge – Volume for Volume

This loading method is so simple and foolproof that it amazes me as a courtroom expert witness to discover that someone got it wrong. But it happens. Volume for volume means just that. Never weigh by weight. A single measure is used, such as an adjustable measure registered in ounces of shot: 1, 1-1/4, 1-1/2, for example. Supposing a 1 1/4-ounce shot charge is desired. The measure is adjusted to that setting (obviously). That very same measure is *left at that same setting for the powder charge.* Since the shotgun will not fire if shot or wad is put down the bore first, the powder charge must be installed first (obviously), per volume, into the shotgun measure with its setting remaining, in this instance, at 1-1/4 ounces. Now the wad column is run downbore with a loading rod or ramrod, snugly upon the powder charge, followed by the shot charge, still maintaining the 1 1/4-ounce setting, with an over-shot wad to retain the shot in the breech. One shooter decided to put down a full 1-1/4 ounces of powder to match his 1 1/4-ounce shot charge. He got hurt. And no wonder. His powder charge ran well over 500 grains. But that's not all. Considering that the balance between powder and shot was now off, he added more shot. The result was a load that filled a full one-third of his barrel. Kaboom!

The blackpowder shotgun can be loaded volume for volume using one measuring device only, as seen here with the metal dipper. This does not preclude loading less powder or less shot than volume for volume.

The screw-in choke for blackpowder shotguns has made all the difference in longer-range effective patterns.

More Shot, Less Powder

While never exceeding the maximum allowable powder or shot charge, it is reasonable to *reduce* the powder charge while retaining the shot charge. In this case, the volume for volume measure is not used as it was above. A separate powder measure is employed instead. As an example only, consider a powder measure set at 80 grains volume while dropping down 1 1/4-ounces of shot. Why do this? Because of variations in wad columns and other factors that may produce a better pattern with less powder than the volume for volume method.

Same Powder Charge, Less Shot

It stands to reason that if an increase in the mass in front of the powder charge increases pressure, then reducing the shot charge while retaining the same powder charge in the blackpowder shotgun is safe. The result is higher velocity—not desirable if the pattern is blown, however. Keeping with our 1 1/4-ounce volume for volume load, in this case, the powder charge would be dropped downbore with the adjustable measure set on 1-1/4, but the measure would be reduced to 1 1/8-ounce or 1-ounce rather than leaving it at 1 1/4-ounce for the shot charge.

Choke

If ever I put the slightest dent in blackpowder shooting, it may be in the area of shotgun choke. I don't know how many letters I wrote or calls I made. "Please," I asked, "Give us choke." This is not to say that Cylinder bore is useless. My pack-along 12-gauge that provides great campfire meals on the trail is Cylinder bore. With a one-piece plastic wad it produces killing patterns at 25 yards. But it sure isn't a goose gun. For jump-shooting quail or popping a running cottontail, this no-choke scattergun is all right. It pokes out a good pattern with small pellets, but even then, there are holes. Today, thankfully, choked blackpowder shotguns are common as ants at a picnic. My Navy Arms T&T (Turkey & Trap) shotgun carries Full and Full bores, and the aforementioned Knight modern muzzleloader shotgun even has an Extra Full choke option. The latter is a screw-in choke system, which is also found on other blackpowder shotguns offering immediate pattern alteration by inserting different tubes. Choke tubes may be installed in some blackpowder shotguns that did not come with them. But there must be sufficient barrel wall thickness to accept the screw-in tubes. As a general rule, a 10-gauge with an outside barrel diameter of 0.900-inch and an inside bore diameter of 0.781-inch, leaving a wall thickness in the muzzle region of 0.0595-inch, is sufficient for installing choke tubes, according to one gunsmith. The key, of course, is not outside

This fine CVA Optima Pro 209 Shotgun exhibits the traits shooters have come to expect from a modern muzzleloader. It is easy to load, easy to clean (especially with FFg Triple Seven powder), very powerful, and it has full choke capability for any game normally hunted with a modern shotgun.

barrel diameter or inside bore diameter, but rather resulting thickness of metal at the muzzle. A12-gauge with a minimum outside diameter at the muzzle of 0.825-inch and a maximum bore diameter of 0.736-inch results in a barrel wall 0.089-inch thick divided by two, leaving 0.0445-inch thickness before the screw-in choke can be satisfactorily installed. A 20-gauge barrel with an outside minimum diameter of 0.700-inch plus a maximum bore diameter in the muzzle region of 0.626-inch leaves a barrel wall thickness of 0.037-inch, which is considered sufficient for screw-in choke tube installation.

The Jug Choke

Jug chokes, also known as *recessed chokes*, were cut from the 19th into the 20th century. The great blackpowder gunsmith, V.M. Starr, installed recessed chokes with 0.021-inch for Full, 0.015-inch for Modified, and 0.010 for Skeet choke, these predicated upon the use of cardboard wads. The standard system of choking is the opposite. Rather than recesses near the muzzle, there are constrictions. The 10-gauge shotgun with a 0.775-inch bore diameter is choked (constricted) 0.035-inch for Full choke, 0.017-inch for Modified and 0.007-inch for Improved Cylinder. The 12-gauge with a 0.729-inch bore diameter is choked 0.035-inch for Full, 0.019-inch for Modified and 0.009-inch for Improved Cylinder. The 20-gauge with a bore diameter of .617-inches calls for a constriction of 0.025-inch for Full, 0.014-inch for Modified and 0.006-inch for Improved Cylinder. Variations exist. Compare these figures with the Old Gamekeeper's data and the 20-guage goes 0.615-inches, not .0617-inches.

Art Belding, a dedicated blackpowder shotgun enthusiast, reported that the jug choke did wonders for his 12-gauge shotgun. Joe Ehlinger of Addison, Michigan accomplished the work. The gun patterned about 45 percent before the jug choke job. Afterwards, using #5 copper-plated shot with a pel-

let count of 185, and 90 grains volume GOEX FFg blackpowder with the V.M. Star wad method described below, here is what happened: Eight shots on the pattern board delivered 88, 92, 82, 91, 87, 81, 77, and 83 percent patterns. That's an average of 85 percent, or Extra-Full choke. If a blackpowder shotgun does not have sufficient "meat" at the muzzle to be fitted with choke tubes, a jug-choke may be possible.

Wad Columns

One-Piece Plastic Wad Columns

In my 12-inch barrel caplock shotgun (yes, it is a legal gun) I use one-piece plastic wads to tighten patterns, which can cause residual plastic fouling removable with a special solvent I buy from Brownell's. Other products that work are mentioned in Chapter 30, such as Butch's Bore Shine. A shotgun, modern or old-style, is no better than its pattern and the wad column can make all the difference between "holes" and density. Choking the gun is the best way to go, while plastic wads in Cylinder bore guns can help, not only by tightening patterns, but also dispersing shot more evenly. The use of a one-piece plastic wad system acts, in a way, like a choke, helping to create a denser pattern. Unfortunately, one-piece plastic wads do not always correct bad patterns. A one-piece plastic wad can hang onto a shot charge, delivering it as a mass of pellets, not a pattern. That is where the pattern board comes in, as explained below, to check out such problems *before* going into the field. Remember, too, that one-piece *standard* plastic wads work in blackpowder shotguns where a 10 is actually 11, and 12 is really 13. That's because these wads were sized to fit *inside of* the shotgun shell and are therefore not matched to the diameter of the modern shotgun bore.

Original Style Columns

Along with one-piece plastic wads, numerous other wad types can be used with the blackpowder shotgun. The simple cardboard wad, associated with the late V.M. Starr, has worked since

While the one-piece plastic wad is useful in the blackpowder shotgun, the Skeet shooter will normally stay with a standard wad column.

Original style wads are widely available today for the blackpowder shotgun. These from Austin & Halleck are cushion wads and over-shot wads.

Felt wads are useful in some blackpowder shotgun wad columns for their ability to compress and serve as a buffer. One wad column of dozens possible goes: cushion wad, felt, shot and over-shot wad.

the beginning of shotgunning, and still does. Heavy-grade cardboard wads 3/32-inch thick may be cut from display signs with a punch. These heavy wads are used over the powder charge, two of them. The shot charge goes down next with a thin cardboard wad on top to hold the shot firmly in place. That's all there is to this particular cardboard wad column. As Starr pointed out, "You can put in more wads on the powder if you wish, or if you enjoy cutting them, but my experience tells me that you are just wasting your time." Starr did not use felt wads. He did, however, win several shotgun matches against good shooters firing modern shotguns, suggesting that his simple cardboard wad system had to be effective. But do

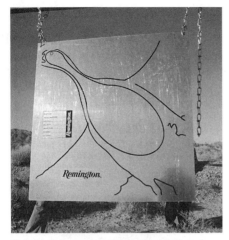

Shot varies greatly not only in size but also of course material—such as lead, bismuth, steel, and so forth. New shot is always being sought. Remington has been working on a "heavy" shot that delivers greater than normal penetration. This metal plate with goose image is used in testing penetration.

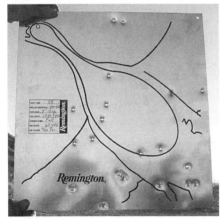

Remington engineers prove the new shot they are working on does penetrate well on a metal plate set up at ranges not normally fired at during hunting.

remember that he was a blackpowder shotgun gunsmith and his guns were properly choked. Larger granulation powders do not tend to destroy wads, which is part of the reason for these simple cardboard cutouts holding up in the old-style scattergun. Meanwhile, thick cushion fiber wads over the powder, followed by the shot charge and one thin over-powder wad make a practical setup, as does cork and other materials. See Circle Fly, Dixie, and Ballistic Products, Inc. (BPI) in the Directory for commercial wads that really work.

Choke and Pattern Density

Standardization remains elusive. However, the following choked designations with pattern percentages provide a reasonable guide. Other sources present different figures, but not so far off the board as to create a problem. Application of various chokes is guided by common sense and field experience. Common sense dictates that tighter choke is necessary to concentrate more shot on a tough target like a wild turkey or a Canada goose, while more open shot patterns are right for smaller birds on the wing, difficult to hit with fist-tight patterns, not to mention ruination of edible meat with overly tight patterns. On a pheasant hunt in Nebraska I was advised to use the tightest choke because "these birds take off at quite a distance." That distance is known as the scare radius and the advice was accurate. The birds were wild and my Full choke shotgun was right for the job.

Patterning

If I have to trade pellet velocity for pattern, velocity will be sacrificed every time. Pellet velocity and energy are important, but I have experienced high-grade results with shot traveling under the speed of sound. While no right-thinking deer hunter would take to the woods with an unsighted rifle, it's amazing how many of us ignore shotgun patterns. The blackpowder shotgun requires patterning just like its modern counterpart if the shooter is to know for certain, and with confidence, what his gun provides in shot distribution. The

process is not difficult. Pin up a large sheet of paper, such as butcher paper, at 40 yards. Fire the shotgun dead center into that large sheet of paper. Using a cardboard cutout 30 inches in diameter, draw a circle around the *concentration* of shot on the paper. Count the holes within that 30-inch circle. Divide the resulting number by the number of pellets in the load. If the shotgun load contains 100 pellets and fifty of them are in that 30-inch circle, the pattern is 50 percent or Improved Cylinder.

Also important is *the way* shot is distributed on the paper. Although the above shotgun put half of its charge within the 30-inch circle, were there large holes in the pattern, or were the pellets well distributed? A few trials are required to tell the story. The serious shooter should pattern his shotgun several times until he has a clear picture of the average pattern his or her gun develops. It's not unusual for a shotgun to pattern 75 percent, but with gaps (holes.) If this situation occurs, juggling load components is recommended. A simple change in shot size may do the trick. For example, if #8 shot produces what is called a "blown pattern," one with holes, #6 shot may cure the problem, or vice versa. Another trick is altering the balance (ratio) of shot to powder, as described above. This may not always provide a denser pattern, but quite often holes disappear. Never juggle components haphazardly. Nor must the shotgun be loaded with either more shot or powder than allowed by the shotgun manufacturer.

Choke Values

Extra-Full	80 percent or tighter
Full Choke	70 to 79 percent
Improved Modified	65 to 69 percent
Modified	55 to 64 percent
Improved Cylinder I	50 to 54 percent
Improved Cylinder II	45 to 49 percent
Cylinder	under 45 percent

The number of pellets in a shot charge must be known before pattern density can be measured. Consult the chart below. Only by knowing the number of pellets in the load can the shooter determine the percentage that landed inside the standardized 30-inch circle, using the choke values provided above. Recall that the Knight 12-gauge delivered an Extra Full choke pattern, which was determined by first knowing how many pellets were in the load.

Shot for Blackpowder Muzzleloading Shotguns

Lead

Consider that *ye olde* mountain man, as well as the leatherstocking Eastern Seaboard adventurer, and pioneers to follow, had no handy gun store where nice round lead pellets were sold. That is where cubed and swan shot came into play. For cubed shot, a sheet of lead was literally chopped into small cubes, sized as desired by the shooter. Talk about fliers! However, while these little cubes of lead were anything but aerodynamic, they apparently worked to some degree, as reported by old-timers who relied on cubed shot to gather their supper. At close range on small edibles, such as quail and cottontails, the cubes buzzed their way through with considerable effect. Since these and similar game are usually harvested at under twenty paces, cubed lead

sufficed. Swan shot was quite another matter and a warning precedes its manufacture: *Never attempt to make swan shot. It is a dangerous process* with the possibility of severe burns. Swan shot was created by pouring molten lead through a screen, the drops of hot lead falling into a cooling medium, such as water. The shot hardened when it hit the liquid, often with a tiny tail on each pellet, remindful of the south end of a swan flying north. Historically interesting, swan shot has been totally outstripped by modern shot and there is no need for it today. Proper lead shot is widely available and fairly priced. There is even reclaimed shot for sale from time to time, this being pellets gathered up at skeet and trap club ranges.

Lead Shot Disadvantage

Literature shows that lead pellets can kill ducks, especially bottom-feeders that pick up spent pellets, ingesting them, the result being lead poisoning.

Lead Shot Advantages

Lead is a heavy element. Therefore, lead pellets retain energy well, promoting penetration and dealing out game-taking authority downrange. Lead shot is also easy on the bore.

Steel

Steel shot is created from soft steel wire, formed into pellets, annealed (heating followed by slow cooling), and finally coated. The process is not unlike the manufacture of steel ball bearings.

Initially, shooters had a difficult time with steel shot, often reporting poor patterns and less than spectacular results on game. Much of this has been corrected by learning how to manage steel shot, especially with regard to shotgun choke. Furthermore, current steel shot is much better than the original product.

Steel Shot Disadvantages

Steel shot, being about 30 percent lighter than lead pellet for pellet, loses velocity faster than lead pellets. Larger pellets are relied on to carry more energy downrange. Meanwhile, larger pellets mean fewer per shot charge. So there is less energy per pellet in a load, as well as fewer pellets. Steel can also score a bore because of its hardness. Furthermore, tighter patterns require more precise shooting.

Steel Shot Advantages

While steel shot incorporates negatives, it also enjoys good properties. Soft lead shot deforms in the bore, creating pellets that look like miniature flying saucers. These are called fliers, and they soon depart the pattern. Steel shot does

Shot is but one variation in the possible blackpowder shotgun load. This shooter is prepared with different wads for different patterns. Also take note of the solution in the open jar to moisten a cardboard wad for easier seating, but which also acts as a cleaner.

Number of Pellets in a Shot Charge		
Shot Size	Diameter in Inches	No. of Pellets per Ounce
No. 12	.05	2,385
No. 9	.08	588
No. 8	.09	410
No. 7-1/2	.095	350
No. 6	.11	225
No. 5	.12	170
No. 4	.13	135
No. 2	.15	90
BB	.18	50

Shot is rather easily tested for penetration with a ballistic gelatin block like this one. It is a simple matter of backing off a specific distance and firing into the block, which tests not only the penetration ability of specific shot (such as steel, bismuth, lead, etc.) but also the arrival energy of the pellets.

not deform into fliers. Also, while lead pellets can be quite round, steel pellets are generally more uniform in shape for better flight than an egg-shaped pellet. Steel creates more uniform pellets for little size difference within a given number. A bag of No. 5s, for example, consists of pellets that uniformly run 0.120-inch diameter. A short shot string means pellets are bunched up in a "cloud" rather than strung out, although all shot flies in somewhat of a string. Lead pellets may form a string several feet long at 40-yards. Steel pellets provide a shorter shot string.

Shooting Steel Shot in Muzzleloaders

Although steel shot can score a barrel that is not built to withstand the harder metal, several companies now offer muzzleloading shotguns with steel-shooting capability, such as a Navy Arms Company 10-gauge double-gun that I happen to have. Along with requiring a barrel intended to shoot steel shot without bore damage, the blackpowder shooter must choose the right shot size. Pellets larger than necessary result in thin patterns. For example, #6 steel shot (0.110-inch diameter) and

#5 steel shot (0.120-inch diameter) provide results similar to lead #5 shot. BBB steel (.190-inch diameter) is appropriate for large birds, such as geese. BB steel (0.180-inch) is chosen when a higher pellet count is desired. Even large ducks can be dropped with #1 steel (0.160-inch diameter). Less choke can also help. Whereas Full choke was ideal with lead shot, Modified usually provides better patterns with steel shot.

Bismuth

One dictionary calls it "A lustrous, reddish, white metallic element (symbol Bi)," going on to say that it is used in medicine and cosmetics. It's the "Bis" in Pepto-Bismol. Pure bismuth is on the brittle side, but making it into an alloy with 3 percent tin improves integrity. It is also harder than lead, except for very hard lead alloys, which are on par with bismuth.

Bismuth Disadvantages

Bismuth is expensive.

Bismuth Advantages

Bismuth is a legal non-toxic shot that is heavier than steel, and almost as dense as lead. Whereas a steel pellet may be 27 percent lighter than a lead pellet of the same size, the difference with bismuth is closer to 8 percent. It is softer than steel and therefore can be shot in standard barrels. It "carries up" well, retaining good velocity/energy. BPI offers a guide to shooting bismuth.

Tungsten-Iron

Tungsten is "a steel gray, brittle, heavy metallic element of the chromium group." Its symbol is W.

Tungsten Disadvantages

As with bismuth, tungsten is not cheap. It is also very hard. On the Brinell hardness scale, lead's number is 12 to 14, while bismuth is 18, quite close. Steel goes 118. Tungsten runs 240. Tungsten is therefore unsuited to before-steel barrels, scoring the bores. Even with steel-capable barrels, manufacturers use thick plastic shop cups to protect bores. While this thick cup restricts payloads in shotshells, the blackpowder muzzleloader, of course, has no

shell to worry about. (This condition has been alleviated somewhat in shotgun shells with thinner but tougher plastic cups.)

Tungsten Advantages

Tungsten is almost as dense as lead, so pellet for pellet weight is quite similar. It retains shape well and shows excellent penetration on test gelatin blocks. Tungsten pellets penetrate extremely well. They also retain shape for good patter distribution.

Tungsten-Polymers

In an attempt to improve upon tungsten shot, T-P came along. It has similar density to lead, which means it performs quite the same as lead. On the Brinell hardness scale, T-P runs 20, compared to 12 to 14 for lead. This means it can be used in shotguns that do not have steel-proof bores. T-P continues to pattern well without fliers. While T-P and bismuth outperform steel shot, it is only fair to point out that steel has improved considerably since its introduction.

Others

As this is written, experimentation continues with heavy-lead alloys and other possibilities in a world of shotgun shooting where non-toxic pellets are the law.

Blackpowder Shotgun Ballistics

Chapter 21 deals with blackpowder ballistics. Let it suffice here to say that the blackpowder shotgun is not a world behind the modern shell-shucker. Velocity cannot be matched, but dense patterns are a reality, and that's the thrust behind the muzzleloader shotgun. When a shotgun produces 80 percent patterns at 40 yards, it has to be considered effective, and using the BP-12 plastic shot cup from BPI in a 12-gauge modern muzzleloader with Extra Full choke makes that pattern possible. Furthermore, the blackpowder shotgun is capable of a large shot payload and the potency of a huge shot charge cannot be denied. A 12-gauge shotgun with 1-1/2 ounces of shot (when that much shot is allowed by the gunmaker) and 100 grains *volume* blackpowder or safe substitute produces a muzzle velocity around 1,100 fps. A 1 1/4-ounce shot charge in front of 100 volume of the proper fuel may go as high as 1,300 fps, as occurred in one test gun, but that's on the high side. Now let's take a look at the sizes of shot available for the front-loading scattergun, followed by some energy figures.

Shot Sizes

Shot sizes have never been fully standardized, but the following numbers are useful for comparison. They are not, however, the only diameters assigned to pellet numbers, especially when comparing European shot to Canadian and American shot. Steel shot is included.

Lead Shot

Size	Diameter	No./Oz.
#12	0.05	2385
#9	0.08	585
#8	0.09	410
#7-1/2	.0095	350
#6	0.11	225
#5	0.12	170
#4	0.13	135
#2	0.15	90
BB	0.18	50

Steel Shot

Size	Diameter	No./Oz.
#6	0.11	315
#4	0.13	192
#3	0.14	158
#2	0.15	125
#1	0.16	103
BB	0.18	72
T	0.20	52
F	0.22	40

Shot Energy

Lead vs. Steel Shot at 40 Yards with the Same Muzzle Velocity

Lead #6 = 2.3 foot-pounds
Steel #4 = 2.5 foot-pounds
Lead #4 = 4.4 foot-pounds
Steel #2 = 4.4 foot-pounds
Lead #2 = 7.5 foot-pounds
Steel BB = 9.0 foot-pounds
Lead BB = 15.0 foot-pounds
Steel T = 20 foot-pounds
Steel F = 24 foot-pounds

Steel shot sizes show well energy-wise because of larger diameters. For example, the lead BB is 0.18-inch diameter, while the steel T is 0.20-inch diameter, the steel F 0.22-inch. Steel shot in larger sizes carries reasonable energy. Remember, however, that when loaded properly with a volumetric measure, the weight of the steel charge is less than an equal volume of lead shot.

The Shotgun Readyload

There are many ways to carry shot, powder, and wads for the scattergun. The old-time flask worked fine and still does. Powder and shot horns are good. So are readyloads, which can be prepared in many ways. Plastic 35mm film containers are useful with pre-measured *powder* charges in one group, pre-measured *shot* charges in another. Wads can be carried in the hunting coat pocket. Working with readyloads is self-explanatory. The gunner pops a top, drops a charge, runs a wad home on top

of the powder, drops a shot charge from another plastic canister, tops off with an over-shot wad and the gun is ready to shoot after capping.

Blackpowder Shotgun Recoil

Although blackpowder burns beautifully in the scattergun with good patterns, its relative inefficiency translates into heavy charges, as in the Knight 12-gauge burning 120 grains volume. Since the weight of the powder charge is part of the recoil formula, the blackpowder shotgun does come back to say hello when fired, especially with big shot charges. The shooter concentrating on that flying target or strutting tom turkey ignores the comeback of the gun. But there is no getting around the fact that the soot-burner can "kick." A recoil pad helps. Most modern muzzle-loaders come with one.

The Versatile Blackpowder Shotgun

Successful blackpowder shotgunning is a matter of choosing the right gun for the use intended (quail, wild turkey, geese?), while loading correctly for best pattern with shot type, size, and charge. Sometimes the shotgun becomes a rifle. That is, it can be loaded with a single lead ball of considerable dimension. A .690-inch round ball weighs 494 grains in pure lead, and while a muzzle velocity of only 1,000 fps is the rule, its close-range authori-

Blackpowder shotgun ballistics were always strong. After all, the punt gun, correctly made illegal, was nothing more than a huge blackpowder shotgun usually attached to a boat and sometimes taking a whole pound of powder. Market hunters collected piles of waterfowl with the punt gun. Today, powerful blackpowder shotguns are available, such as the 12-gauge Austin & Halleck 520.

ty, especially on deer-size game, cannot be denied. Buck 'n' ball is also possible. While some literature shows this as a round ball with pellets loaded on top of it, I don't care for that concept, especially considering the extra mass of the added pellets on top of that round ball. However, a round ball in one barrel and buckshot in the other makes sense. Remember, however, that even 00 Buck weighs only 54 grains per pellet, lighter than a .350-inch round ball for a squirrel rifle and not nearly as fast out of the bore. I see Buck fired first in the buck 'n' ball load as a slow-down, followed by that chunky lead round ball to put the period on the end of the sentence.

SPECIAL BLACKPOWDER SHOTGUN SAFETY REMINDERS

Although Chapter 3 deals with general blackpowder shooting safety, a few special tips pertaining to the soot-burning scattergun are worth setting down and adhering to.

1. After firing one barrel, be certain the load in the other barrel has remained in place, especially when the one barrel has been shot a few times, the other not at all. A load may creep upbore in the unfired barrel, leaving a space between powder charge and shot charge that is tantamount to a short-start.

2. Do not use a powder horn to pour powder directly into the shotgun bore, lest a remaining spark down in "the hold" sets that powder off. Readyloads, as with plastic 35mm film containers, or a proper flask system, prove safer.

3. Uncap a loaded barrel before attempting to load a fired barrel. The danger of loading a fired barrel with the other barrel capped is glaringly evident.

4. Be certain that your shotgun bore is clear of plastic fouling if you use modern one-piece wads.

5. Use proper wad column materials only. Don't stuff newspaper, rag-cloth, or other foreign bodies down-bore in lieu of correct wads.

6. Be certain to cover and/or remove any powder container from the area before shooting. This goes for all muzzleloaders. A spark can fly into a container, be it can or horn, causing a blowup.

7. Watch out for the old ones. There are original muzzleloading shotguns that look to be in good shape, but looks can be deceiving. An original gun must be inspected by a blackpowder gunsmith before firing. Testing remotely is never a mistake, setting the gun up safely and firing with a pull cord.

8. Use only blackpowder or a safe substitute in the blackpowder shotgun. Never smokeless.

9. Load by volume only, never by weight. Steel shot weighs less per volume charge, but this is as it should be. Do not load steel, or any other shot, by weight. Do not load powder by weight.

10. No load of powder or shot is safe in a gun that is not in perfect repair. Never shoot any gun that is not sound in all respects, no matter how new it is.

13 SQUIRREL RIFLES

In days of old two small-bore calibers reigned supreme, the 40-caliber is not considered here as a true small bore. These were the 32 and the 36, the first shooting a 45-grain round ball, the second a 65-grain round ball. On the left, the 32-caliber ball is followed by a 36-caliber ball and a 54-caliber ball for contrast.

The smallbore, or squirrel rifle, as the breed came to be known, is without question the most enjoyable muzzleloader of the breed. Perhaps not the most useful, because, after all, the vast majority of front-loaders are purchased by hunters aiming for those special "primitive hunts." But a day in the thicket after cottontail rabbits, or forest for tree squirrels, or for that matter just roaming around to see what varmint roams the area, is a day well spent in relaxation and memorable enjoyment.

The Smallbore Clan

According to Captain Dillin, in his fine book, *The Kentucky Rifle*, the two most popular smallbores of the Golden Age of shooting in Early America carried either 110 or 150 round balls to the pound. The first translates to 36-caliber (.350-inch lead sphere), while the second comes up 32- caliber (.310-inch pill). Ned Roberts, in his book *The Muzzle-Loading Cap Lock Rifle*, said, "The 100 to 220 to the pound gauge - 36 [about] to 28 calibers - were called 'squirrel rifles.'" Compare at 24 balls to

the pound at .588-inch diameter; 25 balls to the pound—.585-inch diameter, 26 balls to the pound at .575-inch diameter. On the far end of the spectrum, a 4-bore carries four round ball to the pound each one weighing 1,750-grains, while 2-bore balls go a half-pound each, or 3,500-grains weight. The two most popular smallbore calibers today are 32 and 36. Smaller-than-32-caliber rifles can be custom ordered, while calibers 38 and 40 are included in this family because they are too small to be considered large-bore and they need to fit in somewhere.

Devotees of Little Lead Pills

George W. Sears comes to mind. His many readers knew him as Nessmuk, for he penned many a piece in his time. He was a minimalist, creating featherweight canoes, and living off the land with what he could comfortably carry on his back. Nessmuk lived into the era of repeating cartridge rifles, but he preferred a muzzleloader, caliber 42. "My rifle was a neat, hair-triggered Billinghurst, carrying 60

balls to the pound, a muzzle-loader, of course, and a nail-driver." On a 10-day trek in wilderness woods, Nessmuk shot but three times, but "each shot stood for a plump young deer in the 'short blue.'" Wasteful it may seem to us, and Sears apologized for using so little of the meat for himself, but this was the 19th century, and George saw a "cervine army" of deer in numbers he could not even count. What was left behind, wolves, "who never failed to take possession before I was out of sight," consumed the rest. Nessmuk got by with his smallbore firing a lead ball of about 104 grains weight because he was a superior hunter. "In hunting, 'silence is golden,'" he said, "Go quietly, slowly, and silently." Many other old-timers liked the sub-bores as well, including Ned Roberts and Captain Dillin.

Game Departments Make a Choice

When blackpowder shooting left the shadows to emerge into bright sunlight again, game departments had to

The squirrel rifle is small on power compared with the big bores, but it is big on economy. Here is a typical small-bore load laid out—one No. 11 cap, 10-grains Triple Seven FFFg powder (by volume—not even 10 grains by weight), plus one little round ball.

decide on a minimum caliber for big game. Not knowing much about the subject, many chose 40-caliber. Being used to 30-caliber as a "big bore," 40 must have seemed large. A 40-caliber conical can be heavy, limited only by rate of twist to stabilize its length. But a 40-caliber ball at .395-inch diameter runs only 93-grains weight. That is why it is included as the largest number in the smallbore clan. Knowing that much big game had been taken with a 40, I gave it a try on antelope, having a non-buck tag to fill. My partner also had a tag. We got two mature dry does, but the experience taught me the folly of a sub-bore on larger game. In late afternoon, I stalked to within 30 paces of an old doe, making a neck shot. A 50-caliber ball would have gone through like a freight train in a tunnel. The little 40-caliber ball dropped the antelope, but it was halted in its journey by a single broken vertebra. My friend made chest shot at longer range with better results, but never again did I try a 40-caliber ball on big game.

Where Squirrel Rifles Shine
Small Game

The cottontail rabbit is the No. 1 small game animal in North America. I call its kind the "whole earth game animal," because rabbits and hares exist almost everywhere. A 32-caliber squirrel rifle properly handled will dispatch a rabbit with one shot every

time with decent ball placement. I have many times filled my limit, not only when my state held it to five rabbits, but even after the 10-limit came about. Admittedly, my western rabbits are not schooled in the art of evasive action, and shots are normally quite close. Nevertheless, I can do as well with a smallbore front-loader as I can manage with a 22-rimfire rifle. The No. 2 small game animal is the tree squirrel, "tree" to distinguish it from the varmint ground squirrel band. I rank hunting bushytails with a sub-bore as a privilege. Where I hunt, you go on foot through the forest, running (in a safe manner) after Mr. Chatterbox, who then scurries up a tree. I carry a compact Bushnell binocular to separate squirrel from limb. Take careful aim. Fire. Collect your prize.

Wild Turkey

Where I hunt wild turkey, rifles are still legal. I am grateful for that. While the shotgun is a fine gobbler gun, my squirrel rifle will outdistance it by 50 yards. I especially like to hunt a particular mountain range where the birds use trails. By carefully moving along these trails, a flock is eventually sighted. Stalk for the best shot. Aim and fire, delivering one 32- or 36-caliber, ideally, where wing joins body. Flop, flop, flop. You have your bird—every time. I recall turkey hunting in Kentucky with wise old gobblers called in to about 60 yards, too far for this child to try, even with a

stout load in a blackpowder shotgun. I sat in camouflage wishing for a 32- or 36-caliber round ball rifle.

Smaller Big Game

The javelina of the Southwest and Mexico fits this niche. The largest one I ever got went 46 pounds field-dressed, but 25 to 35 pounds is closer to an average. Sixty pounds on the hoof is a big one. Arizona, where I hunt these "wild pigs," which are really musk hogs, allows the 22 Rimfire Magnum cartridge. At close range, either the 32- or 36-caliber round ball, properly loaded, provides just as much potency. Small they are, but these peccaries are pretty tough. And so headshots with these small balls are the rule.

Little Kings of Economy

A 32-caliber squirrel rifle can be fired for fewer pennies per pop than a 22-rimfire if the shooter casts his own round balls (from scrap lead) and makes his own percussion caps (using the Forster Tap-O-Cap tool). The little 32-caliber patched ball achieves 22 Long Rifle muzzle velocity with only 10 grains of FFFg blackpowder, providing 700 shots for one pound of FFFg blackpowder. The larger 36-caliber smallbore is less thrifty, but still inexpensive with home-cast round balls at 65 grains each instead of 45 grains. But it only takes 15 grains of FFFg blackpowder or Pyrodex P to achieve 22 Long Rifle muzzle velocity. That is still well over 450 shots per pound.

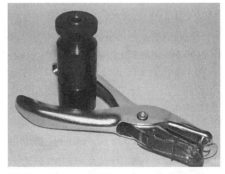

Making the small bore even more economical to shoot is the Tap-O-Cap from Forster. Add a home-cast 32-caliber or 36-caliber round ball and the small-bore costs no more to shoot, and even less, than the 22 Long Rifle.

Here is the Tap-O-Cap with rammer pulled free for a good look at the way this little tool works. Good "toy caps" are required to make viable percussion caps with this little outfit.

Rendezvous Shooting

While sub-bores are sometimes seen at rendezvous, they are not the best for some games, especially splitting a round ball on the blade edge of an axe, a popular and fun game. The larger ball has a much greater chance of striking the axe edge to become two missiles that in turn pop a balloon on either side. The same is true of the stake-buster game, where a stake is cut in half with bullets. The larger ball simply takes out a greater chunk per shot. I have, however, seen competitive shooting at rendezvous on certain targets with 40-caliber rifles.

Competition

Serious competitive shooting at any level, local to national to international, is not the best place to ply the sub-bores. Basic ballistics is part of the reason. Check out wind drift results below to see how the zephyrs attack little round balls.

Basic Target Shooting

Smallbores are as accurate as the barrels that shoot them. Sub-caliber smokepoles in 32- and 36-caliber produce five-shot groups under an inch center to center at 50 yards regularly, and that's with iron sights. One reason they cluster so closely is ease of shooting. While there's no reason to jerk the trigger regardless of the gun—it will not reduce recoil—the squirrel rifle is a neat little pea-shooter that promotes a steady hand and smooth trigger pull. But as stated above, sub-bores are not ideal on the target range, especially for

serious longer-range competition. The bigger bullet has a better chance of cutting the black.

Plinking and Practice

Here, the little round ball is king. Economy is but one reason. Mild report, minimal smoke, and nil felt recoil add to the fun. This sort of practice is practical, transferring to small game hunting, big game as well. It does not have to be all close range. Any safe backstop at any reasonable distance is acceptable. Self-challenging is the way to go, especially with shots that are at the extreme edge of practical distance for small bullets. Targets that "do something" when hit are always interesting—falling over, flying in the air, or, in the case of water-filled cans, splitting open. Ranges up to 200 yards are possible with squirrel rifles, unless the wind is strong. At the same time, shooting in the wind teaches quite a bit about all bullet drift. Once a shooter "gets the range," he or she can "dope out" Arkansas elevation and Kentucky Windage (bullet drop and bullet drift).

Children and Smaller Shooters

We know that the muzzleloader is prone to recoil due to the inefficiency of the powder charge, which in turn demands more propellant than smokeless requires to get projectile moving at reasonable velocity. In turn, the powder charge is part of the recoil formula. Squirrel rifles achieve good velocity with mild powder charges. The bullets don't weigh much either; therefore, felt recoil is minimal. Noise pollution is no problem either, because of these light loads. Even full-throttle 32- or 36-caliber squirrel rifle loads are comparatively quiet. This trait is positive not only for the shooter, but also landowners who don't cotton to the bellow of a cannon on the back forty. Smallbores prove the adage "bigger isn't always better." You don't need a baseball bat to swat a gnat. Because of its mild nature, the squirrel rifle is ideal for young marksmen on the road to blackpowder shooting. I like a muzzleloader for training newcomers because

The small bore is ideal for cheap target practice with a muzzleloader, but it is also ideal for small game. Where Sam hunts squirrels in the Rocky Mountains, a good way to bag a bushytail is hiking until one is found working the forest floor—like this tassel-eared squirrel standing in the shadow of a pine tree with just enough sun to give him away.

The squirrel is alerted. He has a tree right here, but he doesn't climb it.

Off he goes on a squirrel run to find a proper tree.

Up he climbs. The hunter with a squirrel rifle now has to locate Mr. Squirrel in the tree for a shot.

"hands on" loading clearly shows how guns work—powder, bullet, and ignition—knowledge later transferred to cartridge guns.

Smallbore Bullet Uniformity

We might think of small round balls, especially, suffering lack of uniformity. After all, the larger the ball, the less sensitive it is to a small variation in weight one to the next. Reversing that, the smaller the ball is, the more sensitive it is to variation in weight. A 400-grain bullet of any style being one grain off is only 0.0025 percent. A 45-grain bullet, as in the 32-caliber round ball, one grain off is 0.02 percent astray. Not to worry. Uniformity for commercial lead round balls is excellent. Likewise home-cast missiles. This fact is clearly proved by simple weighing of a sampling on a powder-bullet scale. A few examples prove the point. The following is from 10 round balls plucked at random from a box of 100 .310-inch diameter Hornady brand. The 10 weighed as follows: 44.7-grains, 44.6, 44.7, 44.7, 44.7, 44.7, 44.7, 44.6, 44.9, 44.6-grains weight. The extreme spread from highest to lowest weight is only 0.3 grain, three-tenths of one-grain weight—not bad when it takes 7,000-grains weight to make one pound. The average weight for this sampling is 44.69-grains weight, rounded off to 44.7 grains. A perfect .310-inch round ball in absolutely pure lead would run 44.8 grains weight. A cast .350-inch ball for a 36-caliber squirrel rifle ran: 63.5-grains weight, 63.4, 63.4, 63.4, 63.3, 63 .6, 63.7, 63.6, and 63.7 grains weight for 10 randomly picked samples. This shows an extreme spread of only 0.4 grains weight with an average ball weight of 63.5 grains weight. A .350-inch round ball of 100 percent lead content would run 64.5 grains.

Ballistics for Smallbores

Squirrel rifle ballistics are essentially perfect for many applications, as noted above. But it is worthwhile to know what each caliber can do. While conical bullets are definitely at home in smallbores, the following data are for round balls only because the vast majority of squirrel rifle shooting is with the lead sphere.

32-caliber Ball

The following results are from a 32-caliber Thompson/Center Cherokee rifle with a 25-inch barrel compared with a 32-caliber Dixie Squirrel rifle with a 41.5-inch barrel for velocity difference per barrel length. The law of diminishing returns is clearly seen in the T/C Cherokee rifle. After 30-grains volume FFFg, velocity increase is minimal. In short, burning another 10 grains volume is not worth the additional fuel consumption. Tests with the Dixie Squirrel rifle were ceased at 30 grains, although Dixie allowed considerably more powder. At 30-grains volume FFFg, the 45-grain ball is already going over 2,000 fps. Considering the application of the rifle, that's sufficient muzzle velocity. In keeping with the pledge to compare cartridges where applicable, the 22 Long Rifle rimfire with 40-grain bullet at 1,300 fps, which is a fair average muzzle velocity for most brands, has a muzzle energy of 150 foot-pounds,

To emphasize the power potential difference between small round bullets and big round bullets, here is a 32-caliber ball and a 12-bore ball—the first going 45 grains weight, the second (not a .690-inch) running right at 500 grains weight

There is simply no way that a little 32-caliber lead pill can compete power-wise with a big bullet. This is graphically shown with the 32-caliber round ball posed with a 375-grain Buffalo Bullet Company SSB conical. But a long barrel can achieve good velocity. Sam's 39-inch barrel 32-caliber squirrel rifle can do 2,000 fps with 30-grains FFFg volume.

while the 22 Winchester Magnum Rimfire with a 40-grain bullet at 1,900 fps registers 321 foot-pounds at the muzzle. Caliber 32 round balls tested for both rifles weighed 45-grains.

32-caliber Thompson/Center Cherokee Rifle

10-grains FFFg	1,120 fps 125 foot-pounds muzzle energy @100 yards: 538 fps 29 foot-pounds energy
20-grains FFFg	1,649 fps 271 foot-pounds muzzle energy @100 yards: 775 fps 60 foot-pounds energy
30-grains FFFg	1,871 fps 350 foot-pounds muzzle energy @100 yards: 879 fps 77 foot-pounds energy
40-grains FFFg	1,919 fps 368 foot-pounds muzzle energy @100 yards: 940 fps 88 foot-pounds energy

32-caliber Dixie Squirrel Rifle

10-grains FFFg	1,263 fps 170 foot-pounds muzzle energy @100 yards: 720 fps 55 foot-pounds energy
20-grains FFFg	1,776 fps 336 foot-pounds muzzle energy @100 yards: 852 fps 77 foot-pounds energy
30-grains FFFg	2,081 fps 462 foot-pounds muzzle energy @100 yards: 936 fps 93 foot-pounds energy

36-Caliber Ball

One rifle in 36-caliber was selected to demonstrate ballistics. Naturally, rifles with different barrel lengths will render different results. But the following gives a good picture of what can be done with this round ball size. A barrel length of 25 inches was selected to match up with the 32 Cherokee above, which also has a 25-inch barrel. The rifle fired .350-inch 65-grain round balls.

Although the law of diminishing returns did not attack the 36-caliber rifle at 30-grains FFFg volume, the advantage for 50-grains volume FFFg was relatively small. A shooter would do well to consider 40-grains FFFg optimum. (Chapter 15 for more on optimum VS maximum charge.)

38-Caliber Ball

Although the 38-caliber rifle is seen hardly at all these days, it insists upon mention because like the mountain climbed solely since it exists, so does this caliber exist. Fortunately, I have chronographed a 38-caliber rifle with FFFg blackpowder. The particular rifle carried a 37-inch barrel, so this factor must be taken into account for comparison with other 38-caliber rifles. The figures are for a 38-caliber .375-inch round ball weighing 80-grains.

40-caliber Ball

Although the 40-caliber rifle lies in between the worlds of smallbore vs. big-bore shooting, in point of fact, it is a favorite among those who like a mild-shooting rifle for target shooting. As a hunting number, it has its problems. Having taken turkeys with 32s and 36s, the 40, and for that matter, the 38, are truly not necessary. On the other hand, the 40 would be decidedly better than the rest of the smallbore family on javelina-size game.

And Now for the Winner

This is not truly a contest between squirrel rifle calibers, because all of them have merits and demerits. Howev-

36-caliber CVA Squirrel Rifle

20-grains FFFg	1,400 fps 283 foot-pounds muzzle energy @100 yards: 756 fps 83 foot-pounds energy
30-grains FFFg	1,651 fps 394 foot-pounds muzzle energy @100 yards: 827 fps 99 foot-pounds energy
40-grains FFFg	1,808 fps 472 foot-pounds muzzle energy @100 yards: 904 fps 118 foot-pounds energy
50-grains FFFg	1,982 fps 567 foot-pounds muzzle energy @100 yards: 932 fps 125 foot-pounds energy

Richland Arms 38-caliber Plainsman Rifle

20-grains FFFg	1,418 fps 357 foot-pounds muzzle energy @100 yards: 851 fps 129 foot-pounds energy
30-grains FFFg	1,686 fps 505 foot-pounds muzzle energy @100 yards: 944 fps 158 foot-pounds energy
40-grains FFFg	1,876 fps 625 foot-pounds muzzle energy @100 yards: 1,013 fps 182 foot-pounds energy
50-grains FFFg	1,930 fps 662 foot-pounds muzzle energy @100 yards: 1,051 fps 196 foot-pounds energy

Ozark Mountain 40-caliber Muskrat Rifle

20-grains FFFg	1,477 fps 315 foot-pounds muzzle energy @100 yards: 798 fps 92 foot-pounds energy
30-grains FFFg	1,721 fps 428 foot-pounds muzzle energy @100 yards: 878 fps 111 foot-pounds energy
40-grains FFFg	2,015 fps 586 foot-pounds muzzle energy @100 yards: 949 fps 129 foot-pounds energy

er, singling out one from the four leaves the little 32-caliber wearing the championship belt. It has plenty of energy for small game and wild turkey hunting, and a crack shot willing to stalk close can take javelina-size game, especially with the head shot. At the same time, one of the most enjoyable rifles I ever had the privilege of shooting was 40-caliber. The final choice, of course, is with the reader.

Squirrel Rifle Fuel

Granulation is the whole story here, because all of the *good* powders I tested provided fine results as long as they were in the FFFg range, as Pyrodex P, for example. FFg works in smallbores, too; however, FFFg is a better match overall. An example of this fact is the 40-caliber Muskrat rifle (above).

A charge of 40-grains FFg provided 1,751 fps, while FFFg in the same amount threw the 93-grain bullet at 2,015 feet-per second. Going to a full 50-grains volume FFg granulation still

Fadala leans to the 32-caliber as the winner in the squirrel rifle race. This adjustable powder measure tells it all. It is set on a mere 10 grains volume. It's actually only about 7 grains weight Pyrodex P!

The small bore firearm takes exactly the same lubricants and cleaning products associated with big bores.

did not match 40-grains volume FFFg GOEX. So from 32- to 40-caliber, FFFg is the choice.

Conical Bullets

While the round ball was selected as ideal for squirrel rifles, in no way does that pronouncement throw dirt on conicals in smallbores. A brief glance here at a couple is included by way of fair play. The least expensive way to shoot the smallbore is *casting* round balls, as described earlier. I have in my supplies 36-caliber Maxi-Ball bullets that go100 grains weight. I also have Buffalo Bullet Company's 125-grain 36-caliber Buffalo bullets that tested at over 1,900 fps from a 28-inch barrel.

Accuracy

A particularly fine Hatfield squirrel rifle in 36-caliber put considerable Wyoming white-meat cottontails in the pot. This flintlock, with iron sights, was always ready to put three holes measuring 1-1/2 inches center-to-center at 50 yards, with 1-3/4 inches about the poorest showing and 1 inch about the best. I contend that I have never missed a shot with this rifle for lack of accuracy. The same holds true of all the squirrel rifles I have shot. As always, bullets closest to bore size proved most accurate. Matching patches to squirrel rifles is no problem. Select a patch that creates a snug fit to bore around that ball. I have found matches from .010-inch thick all the way to .017-inch thick for different rifles. Various lubes are good. Orange Stuff from Old Western Scrounger Company found its way rubbed into cloth patches the last time I shot a squirrel rifle, but many others are also

good. Liquid lubes are especially useful for repeat shots, as in plinking or target shooting. Supposedly, old-timers came up with the idea of lubing with a liquid because the lube on the ball patch helped to dissolve fouling as the patched ball was seated downbore. Another clue to good accuracy in smallbores is factual for all blackpowder firearms, and that's the low standard deviation (SD) created by *good* propellants While SD is not the only route to accuracy—the lowest (best) SD in the world won't make an accurate bullet out of a lousy one—this factor does count. After all, if velocity alters from shot to shot, how can bullets be expected to group in the same place on the target? And SD relates to *variance* in velocity. SDs in the 10s are common for *good* propellants

Sight-in and Trajectory

As just one example, my Hatfield 36-caliber rifle sighted in to print zero at 50 yards using the 20-grains FFFg charge for 1,470 fps with a .350-inch 65-grain round ball found the pattern grouping about an inch high at 25 yards and about 2 inches low at 75 yards. Naturally, the 40-grain charge with its higher velocity shoots flatter than this, but considering a mere departure of 1 inch from line of sight at 25 yards (high) and 2 inches at 75 yards (low) no reasonable target will be missed. Other calibers in the squirrel rifle clan also do well with the 50-yard sight-in. A problem with the small ball is wind drift. My faithful 54-caliber ball-shooting rifle is punished in the wind with a deflection of about 15 inches at 100 yards in a mere 20 mile-per-hour (mph) breeze with a good hunting load. The 40-caliber ball in the same 20 mph, also with a stout load, drifts off course by about two feet. The 32s and 36s suffer even more. Learning to "dope the wind" is important with all round ball rifles, but especially so with smallbores.

Rifling Twist

Dixie Gun Works sold a little Cub rifle in 40-caliber with a 1:48 rate of twist. While 1:48 is a compromise in 50-caliber, it suited this 40-caliber rifle quite well for the reasons laid down in Chapter 20. The Dixie Tennessee Squirrel Rifle, 32-caliber, was given a 1:56 rate of twist. And it shot the patched round ball just fine. Hatfield's 36-caliber Squirrel Rifle was given a 1:40 rate of twist. In keeping with the facts of bullet stabilization, the smaller ball requires a bit faster rotation than a larger ball of greater mass. On the other hand, round balls don't demand high RPS (revolutions per second) to keep them on track, so the comparatively slower twists in squirrel rifles is right for round bullets.

Flintlock or Percussion?

I perceive the flintlock the same as I see longbows and recurves. Practiced archers with these bows are extremely deadly. Put these bowmen in thick cover and they can shoot from any angle, not worrying about straight-up bow hold or lining up sights. Likewise the flintlock. Practiced shooters win matches, sometimes against caplock competitors. Continuing with the comparison, the compound bow is right in the hands of archers who are not interested in frequent workouts and practices. The "average" blackpowder big game hunter has spoken. He shoots a modern muzzleloader. But the squirrel rifle is a little different. The stakes, you might say, are not as high. In short, smallbore flintlocks are a lot of fun to shoot and the good ones "go off" reliably.

The squirrel rifle stands alone among muzzleloaders as the mildest of all to shoot, along with good accuracy, and plenty of performance for the work it is intended to do. It is economical to shoot, and more importantly, a lot of fun. We need more smallbores, especially for shooters who prefer modern muzzleloaders.

14 LOAD 'EM RIGHT

Pre-shooting prep includes checking out a touchhole on a flintlock to ensure that it is clear and ready to transfer fire from the pan to the waiting charge in the breech. Here is a look at a clear touchhole. The same procedure applies to all other muzzleloaders.

The goal of this vital chapter is laying down a *standard* practice for preparing each blackpowder-type gun—cartridge-shooter as well as muzzleloader—not only for the best possible shooting results, but also the safest. Inconsistency in the loading procedure can compromise accuracy, but more importantly, can lead to firearm damage and even shooter endangerment.

Pre-Loading Prep

Pre-shooting preparation is essential to loading and shooting success. Here are a few things to look for: A clogged flintlock touchhole or vent in the nipple will surely retard or totally prevent ignition. Checking for overall firearm integrity is also a worthy pre-loading plan, including the stock. I had a wrist crack on a rifle. Thinking back on it, I had seen, but ignored, a hairline crack that should have been fixed. The bore must be clean. No, the entire firearm must be clean before attempting to load up. A filthy bore can destroy all chance of a proper load, and in some cases can be dangerous, especially when the bullet fails to seat properly upon the powder charge, resulting in a short-start condition. Leftover preserving oil and grease can also thwart the flame of ignition. If heavy-duty is required, a "soak" is worthwhile. Brownell's has a full line of "Officially Licensed NRA Gun Care and Cleaning Products," such as EZ-Soak, which is advertised as a "15 minute parts cleaner." It works as the name implies—immersing parts in the liquid for 10 to 15 minutes, then wiping them dry. Great stuff. Sweetshooter Three in One from Tecrolan promises to clean, lubricate, and protect, "All in one can!"

The cannon is no different in pre-shooting prep than any other muzzleloading type firearm. Here the cannoneer readies a big swab to ensure all channels are clear for loading.

Steps for Loading the Percussion Rifle or Pistol

The muzzleloading pistol is functionally a "short muzzleloading rifle" and, therefore, it is treated here with the same loading procedures. Protecting the patch from burnout is not required for target loads, but may prove useful for heavy hunting loads in big-bore pistols allowed heavy powder charges. The patch is readily protected with two or three leaves of hornet nest material between powder charge and patched bullet. See Chapter 18.

Step 1: Clearing all Channels

The simple pipe cleaner, found in the smoking section of stores everywhere, works wonders in sopping up oil or grease from any ignition channel: the touchhole of the flintlock, vent in the nipple, or fire lane of the in-line or Outer-Line muzzleloader. After pipe cleaner probing, percussion caps may be fired on the nipple to ensure a dry passage into the breech. The same is true of No. 209 shotgun or Small Rifle/Pistol primer ignition systems. A nipple or vent pick (see Chapter 4) does the same job.

Conduct a simple test for verifying a clear channel with the muzzle of the gun pointed at a lightweight object on the ground; a bit of paper, cleaning patch, twig, small leaf—anything that

will move readily. The muzzle of the *unloaded* rifle or pistol is pointed within a couple inches of the lightweight object. Standard percussion caps, such as the No. 11, musket caps, and of course No. 209 or Small Rifle/Pistol primers all have sufficient force to push a light object away. If the leaf, patch, paper—whatever—fails to jump when the rifle or pistol is fired, this indicates a blockage in the flash channel, the bore, or both, which must be cleared.

Another trick is played by ear, listening to the sound an *unloaded* gun makes when a cap or primer is detonated. A hollow-sounding *thump* indicates a clear passage, while a sharp *crack* signifies trapped gases and a blockage. The gun must be cleared before attempting to load it. Usual procedures—pipe cleaner, cleaning patches, bristle bore brush—work. After these measures have been done, another cap is fired from the *unloaded* gun, again aimed at a light object on the ground.

The process of clearing oil or grease to get a clear fire channel from cap or primer to powder charge in the breech is a Catch-22 proposition, because exploding caps on a nipple can cause a deposit of cap fouling or debris. While most percussion caps today are non-corrosive, they still expel a certain amount of residue. Also, it is possible for tiny fragments from the body of the cap to clog the nipple vent. Sometimes

the entire top of the cap body remains fixed to the cone of the nipple. Running a pipe cleaner briefly into the vent of the nipple after firing a "clearing cap" is a good plan. Use a twisting motion to pick up cap debris. This little step can save a great deal of consternation during a shooting match or at that moment of truth when a game animal is in the sights. Residual cap deposits are more likely to occur when popping percussion caps to dry the nipple than during actual shooting. This is because the loaded rifle has minor blowback that helps to clear the nipple vent, while the unloaded rifle has no blowback.

Step 2: Dropping The Powder Charge

Now that there is a clear fire channel for ignition, the pistol or rifle is brought to half-cock if it has an exposed hammer. If no hammer, then the safety remains **on** with bolt or breechblock in the open position. Hammer guns especially demand this step, because a hammer nose down flat upon the cone of the nipple (under the pressure of the mainspring of the gun) can trap air in the bore. That air pressure can in turn force a projectile partway up the bore, creating a gap between powder and projectile—including the shotgun wad column. Here is that old devil again—the short-start load as described by Ezekiel Baker in his 1835 book: "If the ball be not rammed close on the powder, the intervening air will

The exploded cap on this nipple may have sent part of itself into the vent of the nipple. A quick swipe with a pipe cleaner will ensure that such debris is removed before loading the caplock gun.

A proper powder charge is metered out. Here, a smaller powder flask is used to deliver powder into an adjustable powder measure for loading.

The powder charge held within the adjustable powder measure is now delivered straight downbore. A few taps on the side of the barrel promotes settling of the charge in the breech section of the gun.

frequently cause the barrel to burst." Baker felt that "More accidents happen from a neglect of this precaution than can be imagined." Another wrinkle—tap the side of the barrel after dropping the powder charge to encourage all granules to join their friends down in the breech. Now a proper charge of the right powder is dropped downbore. The charge is produced *by volume* with blackpowder or a proper blackpowder substitute. But it is advisable to *weigh* smokeless powder charges for the Savage Model 110ML-II muzzleloader.

Step 3: Seating a Patched Round Ball or Conical Bullet

A round ball with a heavy hunting charge may require the aforementioned patch protector in the form of a couple sheets of hornet-nest material. This is accomplished with the off-end of the loading rod or ramrod, or with a jag. No protector is required for a sabot, most lead conicals, or a light powder charge in the ball-shooting pistol or rifle. The idea is to create a firewall between the powder charge and the cloth patch. (A proper wad of various materials may be used as a bullet protector in lieu of hornet nest material in some guns.) Prov-

ing a need for a patch buffer is simple: Pick up fired patches downrange and check for damage. Proving a patch buffer works is equally simple: Pick up fired patches downrange and check for damage. At this point, the rifle or pistol has a powder charge down in the breech.

Lubricate before seating a bullet. Some shooters prefer patch cutter and strip of cloth for the round ball. The strip of cloth, perhaps 1-1/4 to 1-1/2 inch wide and of any convenient length, is laid across the muzzle, lubed first, if only with saliva. A ball is centered on the muzzle and driven down past the crown of the muzzle. A swipe of a patch knife blade leveled across the muzzle cuts away excess cloth, leaving the ball fully covered with a perfectly shaped patch. Lubrication is vital: A pre-cut patch can also be pre-lubed. For the sabot, a small dab of paste-type lube in its base is sufficient. A similar dab on the base of a conical, base only, works. A short starter is important in driving any type of projectile a short distance beyond the muzzle. The stub end goes to work first, then the longer rod. Even with the undersized Minie, the short starter is a good idea. A conical demands centering in the bore for best accuracy.

There are tools to accomplish this, one being the Thompson/Center Tru-Starter, another is the Muzzleload Bullet Aligner from Barnes. Rifles or pistols may also have rifling removed at the muzzle into the bore a short distance. This "smoothbore" start allows a conical bullet to be seated square to the bore. At this point, the projectile is *only partially seated*. Now the loading rod or ramrod comes into play, driving the missile fully down upon the powder charge. At this point, the rifle or pistol is *loaded* with powder charge and projectile. There are more fine rods today than ever before. As one example only, there is the PowerRod from XX Sight Systems. This compact rod is built of super strong material for power-seating any bullet. It also caries "witness marks" in lieu of marking a ramrod. Incidentally, tests

In this case a slightly undersized conical bullet is introduced into the muzzle by hand. An undersized patched round ball can be started similarly.

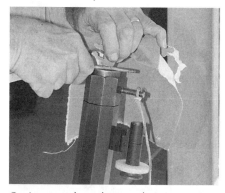

Cutting a patch on the muzzle is one way to ensure that the round ball receives full coverage. But pre-cut patches work just as well.

The ball patch is a repository for lube. With a conical bullet, lube is placed on the base section only. Here, Orange Stuff, contained in a plastic film canister for convenience, is applied into a slight hollow of a conical bullet base.

Hornet's nest is amazing stuff. While it will burn up in open air, it creates an asbestos-like buffer between the round ball patch and the powder charge, protecting the patch from burnout.

The short starter is vital for pushing the projectile partway down the bore.

Here, the stub stem of the short starter has been used to drive the bullet partway downbore.

Now the longer stem of the short starter is put into play, pushing the bullet, round or conical, farther downbore.

This ramrod has a jag with concave tip designed to deliver the bullet downbore without damaging the nose with disfiguration.

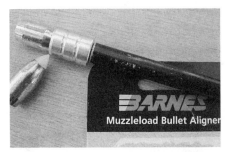

A bullet aligner helps in starting a conical projectile "square to the bore." This is an aligner from the Barnes Bullet Company.

indicate that the sprue (see glossary) of the round ball is best centered in the bore for consistency. Centering directly down is OK, but difficult to accomplish, while centering the sprue straight up is easy because the shooter can see it.

Seating the Sabot

There are two ways to install the saboted bullet downbore: sabot intact with bullet or sabot first. *Always* seat the sabot and bullet as a unit—*except* with boat-tail bullets. The danger of seating a sabot first, then a flat-based bullet is in the bullet never fully seating into the sabot. The boat-tail design on some bullets—the Buffalo Bullet Company SSB, for example—allows the sabot to be seated fully on the powder charge, followed by the boat-tail projectile. The slanted base of the boat-tail bullets provides easy entry deeply into the sabot.

One Bullet Only

It is true that there is mention of double-ball loading in some old-time literature. Please don't do it. Because I am obligated to test such things, I tried *under strict safety test conditions only* the double-round ball load. The result was lousy accuracy. The double-bullet load could also prove dangerous. Forget it.

Marking a Ramrod

Once an ideal load is found for any given rifle or pistol, the ramrod is marked to indicate proper seating depth of that load. The aforementioned PowerRod already has such witness marks. These marks can in turn be marked (as by light scratching). The process is simple. Introduce the ramrod or loading rod all the way down to touch the nose of the load in the bore—any load—not

The ramrod now goes into full play, delivering the projectile fully downbore upon the powder charge in the breech. The ramrod can be marked at the juncture of the rod and the muzzle, as with a scratch.

just rifle or pistol, but shotgun as well. Make a mark where the ramrod touches the crown of the muzzle. Forever more, that mark shows where a proper load is seated in the breech. If the witness mark rides well above the level of the muzzle crown, that indicates a problem—either a load that has worked its way back up the bore, or perhaps even a double-load, where the gun was loaded twice with a second load right on top of the first one. Not good! This factor was realized a very long time ago. Ezekiel Baker told shooters to mark their ramrods in his 1835 text. "Every rifleman should mark his rammer at the muzzle end of the barrel, when loaded, which will shew him when the ball is close down on the powder."

Bore Prep Before Firing the Shot

Ensuring the best possible consistency from one shot to the next requires similar bore condition. Dressing the bore, or firing a fouling shot is one way to prep a bore. See more in Chapter 25 on accuracy. Mopping up any excess lube from a patch or conical that may be deposited in the bore is also part of bore prep. For plinking, no need, but for target work, and even big game hunting, this step is worthwhile. It is accomplished with a cleaning patch on the end of the loading rod or ramrod *after the load is fully delivered down into the breech.* But wait a minute! Isn't this dangerous? After all, there's a loaded powder charge and projectile in the rifle or pistol. Stop and think. But a brief moment ago, you installed that same load with a ramrod or loading rod in the same manner. So this step carries no more (or less) danger than the essential bullet-seating step just performed. Naturally, the firearm is **never capped or primed** at this point. Furthermore, the muzzle is always aimed away from self, all others, and any object you do not wish to place a hole in. The clean patch mops up excess lube in the bore, giving the rifling uniformity from shot to shot. Sight in with bore clear of grease or oil. Shoot that way afterwards. Remember that an oily or greasy bore can cause a projectile to fly off-target.

Seating Pressure

As part of Step 3, whether seating a conical or a patched ball, it is important to maintain the same pressure upon the powder charge for consistency, which translates to accuracy. There are three ways to accomplish this. The first is feel. With practice, a shooter can do a pretty good job of maintaining *about* the same pressure on the powder charge. The second is using a special spring-loaded tool that fits over the end of the ramrod. The spring collapses at a specific pressure, such as 35 pounds. This is not a commercial device. The third is the Kadooty, which is designed to deliver the same pressure upon the powder charge every time. Varying pressure on the ramrod or loading rod causes a rise in standard deviation, which translates to a different velocity for each shot fired. Furthermore, blackpowder is known to burn more consistently when compacted. *Warning: Never lean body weight on a ramrod or loading rod.* Blackpowder is percussion-sensitive. For that matter, so is smokeless to a lesser degree. Any powder can detonate if put under sufficient pressure. I don't have data that reveals exact pressures required for this to happen, but why not play it safe by not leaning body weight on the ramrod or loading rod.

Sam has a special device made for him by a reader for ensuring the same pressure upon a load time after time. It is spring-loaded. When the spring collapses, which can be felt, the same pressure has been applied (35-pounds in this case) as the last load. The Kadooty is another prime way to ensure consistent pressure.

Pile-Driving (Bouncing the Ramrod) on the Seated Bullet

I am not sure how this practice got started or why, but a half-ounce of logic reveals how futile and foolish it is to *bounce the* ramrod or loading rod repeatedly upon a load already downbore. If the hammer was let down upon the cone of the nipple, blocking air escape, a load may have crept upbore—no good! But will bouncing the ramrod reseat that load? Not in a millennium. Steady force upon ramrod or loading rod is necessary to put that projectile back down firmly on the powder charge where it belongs. I've seen shooters merrily bouncing the ramrod as far out of the muzzle as possible "to make sure the load is seated properly." The only thing this has a chance of doing is damaging the nose of the bullet, which has been shown to degrade accuracy, especially with the round ball. A marked ramrod shows if a load is properly seated in the breech or not properly seated, and if not, it must be delivered to the right place, which is down in the breech with no air gap. These little "tricks" can grab a shooter. I always knew that bouncing the ramrod did nothing, but might be OK. A bit of logic and testing revealed the practice as useless. I should have read Ezekiel Baker's 1835 text, "If the ball fit air-tight, as it should do, it will require two or three pushes with the rammer [ramrod or loading rod] before the air can escape, to get it [the bullet] in its proper place. I do not recommend the ball to be bruised with the rammer, but *pushed.*" (Emphasis mine.)

Step 4: Ignition

Using a seating device—these are now available for No. 209 shotgun primers and musket caps as well as standard percussion caps—the cap or primer is set in place. A seating device is not required with all guns. For example, the Savage Model 110ML-II can be capped with a gloved hand. At this point, the rifle or pistol carries a powder charge, plus a seated missile, and is now *ready for firing.* While there is considerable talk about significant variations in muzzle velocity depending on the type of cap or primer used for ignition, extensive chronographing fails to support that theory. There can be differences in velocity with various igniters, but they are not significant. After all, the means of ignition plays a small, if any, role in transferring energy to the bullet. That's the job of the powder charge. There are also only minor velocity differences among various brands of caps or primers. (See Chapter 19.) The percussion rifle or pistol is now ready to fire. As modern muzzleloaders continue their march, means of ignition are subject to change. For example, the Ultimate Muzzleloader uses a primed 45-caliber *cartridge case* for ignition. Winchester,

Ignition! The firearm has been "capped," which nowadays may mean that a modern primer was installed, and the bullet or shot charge is on the way.

in recognizing where the trend was going, produced a special No. 209 primer with compound formulated just for ignition in muzzleloaders. Expect more ignition changes.

Steps for Loading the Flintlock Rifle and Pistol

As with the percussion muzzleloading rifle and percussion muzzleloading pistol, the flintlock pistol is also a short version of the flintlock rifle, and therefore is treated here in the same section.

Step 1: Clearing all Channels

While it's the habit of some flintlock shooters to fire off a pan of FFFFg prior to loading, the logic is questionable. Adding blackpowder fouling to the touchhole does nothing to clear it out. Otherwise, the same pre-shooting rules apply to the flintlock as prescribed above. The goals are a clean bore and a clear touchhole as an avenue for flame from the pan to the powder charge in the breech. Also an overall clean and well-serviced firearm.

Step 2: Block the Touchhole

Block the touchhole to prevent powder from the main charge from entering it. The goal is a *clear* touchhole, not one filled with powder. An unblocked touchhole may allow the invasion of powder from the main charge, sometimes filling the touchhole full. The touchhole then becomes a fuse. The flash from the pan powder must burn its way through the powder in the touchhole before it can reach the breech to set off the powder charge. This means a delay as opposed

First step in ensuring a good flintlock load is securing a good flint, or "rock," as flintlock fans like to call the little piece of stone. This flint has a nicely beveled edge and should encourage good sparks from the face of the frizzen.

The touchhole should be blocked, as with a pipe cleaner or vent pick, before dropping the powder charge. The powder charge is metered out and dropped just like the caplock rifle or pistol charge.

to the flame of ignition darting through a clear touchhole directly into the powder charge. Blocking the touchhole is simple. A pipe cleaner or nipple/vent pick does the trick. One collector of original Kentucky/Pennsylvania long rifles reported finding a feather in some shooting bags. This collector believes that some old-time shooters used the quill of the feather, which appears to be squeezed down to the size of the touchhole, to block the touchholes of their flintlock rifles.

Step 3: Clean the Frizzen Face

The frizzen supplies tiny hot curls of metal that fall into the pan, igniting the fine-grain powder therein. Friction between the flint, fondly known as the "rock," and the face of the frizzen, creates this shower of hot metal particles. However, friction-reducing grease, grime or other substance on the face of the frizzen reduces its ability to produce those hot curls of metal to ignite the fine-grain powder waiting in the pan. Solvent works great for cleaning the frizzen. Be sure to dry the frizzen after cleaning it.

Step 4: The Powder Charge

Steps 2 and 3 can be reversed of course, as long as the touchhole is blocked and the face of the frizzen is clean. The correct powder charge is up next. There is no difference between dropping a powder charge down the

muzzle of a percussion arm or a flintlock. See above.

Step 5: Priming the Pan

The touchhole block remains in place. Powder and bullet rest firmly downbore upon the powder charge. Time to remove the touchhole block and prime the pan with a fine-kernel powder. *After* priming the pan, withdraw pipe cleaner or vent/nipple pick. Advice about twisting the pipe cleaner to draw powder from the breech into the touchhole defeats the purpose of the touchhole block. Don't do it. Specific *amounts* of pan powder vary with the size of the pan, as well as the specific design of the flintlock. However, most flintlocks respond better to less, rather than more, pan powder. Half a pan, up to two-thirds, is sufficient, with care to introduce the powder to the *outside* of the pan, rather than pushed up against the touchhole. When the pan is completely full of powder, there is more tendency to "blow-out" with a big puff of smoke, but no snake-tongue flick of fire darting through the touchhole. By retaining the powder on the outside of the pan with free space between powder and touchhole, there is a greater chance for the resulting flame to find its way through the touchhole and into the breech. Good advice—carry the flintlock rifle (or fowler) tilted a little so that priming powder remains to the outside of the pan for best ignition.

One afternoon, an editor friend from Chicago visiting at my Wyoming home found himself alongside as I loaded a 36-caliber flintlock squirrel rifle in pursuit of cottontail rabbits. He asked, "Can you really get that thing to go off reliably?" The Hatfield flinter fired a couple dozen times in a row that day with no hangfire or misfire. Perhaps it would have done likewise without blocking the touchhole or cleaning the face of the frizzen or with a pan packed full of FFFFg powder, but I don't think so.

Step 6: Shooting

The flintlock is ready to fire, with hammer cocked. The shooter is prepared to squeeze the trigger with hold-steady confidence. That's what it takes with the flintlock rifle: the ability to concentrate, maintaining the sight picture beyond the puff in the pan all the way to the boom!

Touchhole Location and Touchhole Liners

Ideally, the touchhole should be installed as high on the barrel flat as practical so pan powder cannot sift into it. Also, because of the obvious invasion of flame after flame, the touchhole eventually becomes scored and essentially burned out. The fix for this is a touchhole liner, which can be installed by a gunsmith. The new liner returns the touchhole to a smooth interior surface conducive to spark travel.

Frizzen Replacement

The face of the frizzen eventually scars from multiple attacks from "the rock." When this happens, it's curtains for reliable ignition. Recall that it's the face of the frizzen, not the flint, that produces hot curls of metal to ignite the pan powder. Cure? Easy. Replace a bad frizzen with a new one.

Flint Quality

Cheap flints are too expensive. They cost missed opportunities in the game field and last place in shooting matches. *Always buy new flints for matches and special hunts* if there is any question about the condition of an existing flint. That's good economy.

Matching Flint to Frizzen

The edge of the flint must make full contact with the face of the frizzen for best results. This is easy to accomplish by first loosening the jaws of the hammer (cock in old-time literature), allowing the hammer to come forward slowly until the flint makes contact with the frizzen. Since the flint is loose in the jaws of the hammer, it can be moved so that it makes full contact with the frizzen. When it does, the jaws of the hammer are tightened to lock the flint in place. This easy method of aligning the edge of the flint with the face of the frizzen goes a long way to better spark production.

Flintlock Reliability

If flintlocks were as uncertain, unreliable, and as cantankerous as often portrayed, the early American settler would have starved to death, if not scalped before that. Beyond hunting for food and self-defense, wars were fought with flintlocks with devastating results. The Battle of New Orleans in January 1815 saw 7,000 trained British troops transported from Jamaica under General Packenham to duke it out with the Colonials. General Jackson had 5,000 men ready to meet the attack, including a handful of "Tennessee sharpshooters," as they were called. Assumptions about Americans firing from behind rocks and trees are unfounded. After all, Americans were transplanted Englishmen, many of them, and so they stood in rank and file just like the enemy, blazing away with their flintlock rifles. When the smoke cleared, literally, the British had lost 700 dead, 1,400 wounded, 500 taken prisoner. The Colonials suffered eight killed, 13 wounded. Were flintlocks in the hands of those Tennessee riflemen reliable or not? Two reasons British soldiers failed in this battle were inaccurate smoothbore muskets compared to American long rifles, and the terrific bravery of the Redcoats who continued to march forward and die rather than retreat. After all, they were among the finest soldiers in the world at the time, and they had their pride.

The flint is aligned to meet the face of the frizzen fully.

Steps for Loading the Percussion Shotgun

There are few fowlers around today, and they can be loaded the same as caplock scatterguns, with the exception of handling the idiosyncrasies of the flintlock (above). Mainly, however, it's the percussion shotgun that rules: great fun to shoot, effective on game as well as targets, easy to load, and no real trouble to clean up afterwards with its smooth bores (no rifling to catch and hold soot).

Step 1: Preliminaries

The general preliminary rules laid down above continue to apply. Start with a clean gun, fire caps to ensure a good path for ignition into the breech, use only the right powder in the right amount, and of course a safe, allowable shot charge and wad column. The gun is clean, caps are fired on nipples, and the game is afoot.

Step 2: The Powder Charge

A proper powder charge drops into the bore(s). Great caution is exercised with the double-barrel gun to ensure that each barrel receives **only one charge**. Always slip an over-powder wad into the muzzle of the charge barrel to mark it so that bore will not get a second charge.

Step 3: The Wad Column

There is no one perfect wad column. A reader wrote, "My White

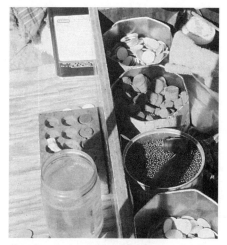

This shotgun loading box has it all—shot, wads, lubricant to douse the wad in briefly before loading, and of course powder and caps.

muzzleloading shotgun with choke tubes makes wonderful patterns with old-fashioned card wads, but not very good patterns with plastic wads." Another shooter remarked that his Navy Arms T&T 12-gauge, choked Full and Full, made fine patterns with one-piece plastic wads. (See Chapter 12.) The important maneuver is seating wads properly, whichever kind they may be. Seat them firmly upon the powder charge, but never jammed into place so movement is restricted when it comes time to shoot. **Restricted wad columns can raise** *pressures dramatically.* Wads intended for blackpowder shotguns are widely available from Ballistic Products Inc., Circle Fly, Dixie, CVA, Ox-Yoke, and other sources.

Seating the wad column is accomplished with a ramrod or loading rod with a large, flat-faced jag. Hammers are eared back into the half-cock position so air can escape through the powder charge and out the nipple vent. Hammer noses down on nipple cones block air passage, allowing air pressure in the bore to force the wads toward the muzzle, leaving a gap between the powder charge and the wad column/shot charge.

Load Shift

Warning: After firing one barrel of a double-barrel shotgun, it's OK to shoot the other barrel right away. However, if the shotgun is to be carried around, it pays to ensure the wad column/powder charge in the *unfired* barrel has remained seated.

Anyone familiar with a shotgun shell knows the loading sequence for the blackpowder shotgun—powder first, then a wad, followed by shot. The top of a shotgun shell is closed. An over-shot wad does the same thing in the muzzleloader.

Steps for Loading the Blackpowder Cap and Ball Revolver

Step 1: Preliminaries

It's the same old song: The gun must be clean with nipple vents clear and barrel entirely free of obstruction or fouling. Grease or oil in the bore, cylinder chambers, or nipple vents can cause a misfire or hang-fire. Conversely, a lack of lubrication on moving parts will cause a revolver to lock up.

Step 2: Clearing Nipple Vents

Same as ever, brush nipple channels with pipe cleaners, followed by a cap fired on each nipple of the *unloaded* gun to dry leftover metal preservers or lubes. As before, use a pipe cleaner after firing caps to remove any cap debris that may be left behind.

Step 3: Charging the Cylinder Chambers

Each cylinder chamber receives the correct amount of the right powder at this point, using a flask, charger, or adjustable powder measure. Safety notches on the Remington Model 1858 revolver serve to misalign the hammer nose with the nipples. With the hammer nose locked into a safety notch, all six chambers can be loaded. Some Colts of the period had a pin between each chamber and a notch in the hammer nose to affect the same safety condition. Many cap 'n' ball revolvers had no pins. Ideally, there is no air gap between the seated bullet and the powder in the cylinder chamber. Filling the space with an inert substance, such as cornmeal, can prevent a possible air gap.

Step 4: Seating Bullets

Seat a round or conical bullet firmly upon the powder charge using the loading rod that rests beneath the barrel. This underlever puts plenty of pressure on the bullet, making excessive force unnecessary. A dab of grease or lube is now placed on top of each fully seated bullet as it rests in the cylinder chamber. This is done to prevent chain firing—all chambers firing at once (a real wake-up call)—and to keep fouling soft.

Loading the cap 'n' ball revolver is really quite simple—a proper powder charge is installed in each cylinder chamber intended to accept a bullet. A bullet is seated on the mouth of the cylinder chamber and the loading rod is used to force the bullet down upon the powder charge, as shown here.

Using a funnel to direct the powder charge into a cylinder chamber.

Lube is placed over the nose of each bullet, round or conical, in each loaded cylinder. This step prevents chain-firing and promotes continuous shooting.

Failing to lube can cause the revolver to lock up like a vault at Fort Knox. A lubed wad can be located between bullet and powder charge to prevent chain firing, but over-bullet lube or grease remains very important to the continued functioning of the revolver. Shooting without grease or lube leads to moving parts no longer moving.

Step 5: Before Capping

Before capping the revolver, insert a nipple pick through the vent of every nipple, pushing gently forward toward the cylinder chamber to clear the passageway of powder. This prevents a fuse condition by allowing a clean avenue for percussion cap flame to enter the powder charge in each cylinder chamber.

Step 6: Capping

Use a capper to install a percussion cap on each nipple of the revolver. This is usually a No. 10 or No. 11 cap, depending upon the exact dimensions of the nipple cone. The revolver is now ready to fire and must be handled with the same care normally afforded any loaded gun. While any modern-made cartridge revolver should have a safety bar or similar mechanism to prevent discharge of the gun if it is dropped (my Navy Arms 45-caliber Colt Bisley is a fine reproduction of the original, but it does have a modern transfer bar to prevent firing if the revolver is dropped), cap 'n' ball revolvers are not necessarily privy to this feature.

Loading the Blackpowder Cartridge

As discussed in Chapter 38, the blackpowder cartridge is a law unto itself. Loading procedure includes specific lubes and careful attention to a powder charge that leaves no air gap in the case. Wads may be used, or an inert substance, such as cornmeal, to prevent the air space. The basics of blackpowder cartridge loading follow modern cartridge loading procedure—decapping to remove the fired primer; resizing the case to near original dimensions, installing a fresh primer, adding the powder charge, and seating a bullet. Although it is wise to tumble-clean a modern fired cartridge case, cleaning fouling from the blackpowder cartridge case is a must.

Loading the Blackpowder Shotgun Shell

Original blackpowder shotgun shells were far more powerful than we might imagine. A charge of powder with 1-1/4 ounces of shot might run as high as 4-1/4 drams, which comes to 116 grains for a muzzle velocity not far below 1,400 fps. Many blackpowder breechloading shotguns were choked, but from what I can gather, Full choke probably didn't produce much better than a 60 percent pattern at the nominal 40-yard pattern distance. Today, the blackpowder shotgun shell is handloaded with hulls and components liberally dispensed by several companies. I have used a shotgun shell reloading press for the job, but not for powder. I use an adjustable powder measure for that job. Blackpowder and its family are not to be used in standard reloading outfits. The same process exists as with blackpowder cartridge loading described above, from removal of spent primer to installing powder, shot, and wad system, along with a proper crimp. The Lee reloading tool is excellent for the job with its hands-on steps.

A properly loaded blackpowder handgun, revolver or pistol, can be relied upon. Sam watched this shooter fire several shots in a row without a misfire or hangfire.

15 OPTIMUM VS MAXIMUM LOADS

Here are the two basic load trains used in today's muzzleloaders. Conicals (top) are generally used in today's in-line muzzleloaders. The patched round ball (bottom) is usually found in traditional-style muzzleloaders with a slow twist. From left, the ball and patch, hornet nesting and, finally, the charge of propellant.

There is a world of difference between optimum and maximum. This chapter is designed to clarify that opening statement. An optimum load chain includes a powder charge that does not fall into the spiked pit dug by the law of diminishing returns (see below). While the powder charge is the major single ingredient in the optimum load recipe, ancillary to this point are the issues of *matched* components. This includes the bullet, but also means of ignition (minor) as well as patch or other go-between material—that is, between the powder charge and the projectile, such as a round ball patch, sabot, synthetic bullet base, wad, or other element.

There are two major goals in producing an optimum load: full power without wasted propellant and unnecessary recoil/muzzle blast/smoke, or a power range that fits the task at hand (see small-bore note below), plus accuracy. Shooting without accuracy is like h2 without the 0—it won't wash. That's why there is an entire chapter devoted to the subject of accuracy—see Chapter 25.

The Optimum Load and Accuracy

The optimum load is first cousin to consistency, which in turn is a favored relative of accuracy. As mentioned above, the optimum load is a matched load—matched to the shooting task at hand, be it big game, small game, knocking over a metal ram at 500 meters, or punching a hole in a paper target. The king of muzzle-loading rifle types is the modern style, be it in-line or one of the variations of this theme. Much has changed in loads since the Fourth Edition, let alone the past 10 years or so, rendering some old data as nearly useless. Two rifles exemplify this perfectly, although they are but two in a field of many. The Savage 10ML is allowed smokeless powder, the only front-loader of its type as this is written. The Savage uses an entirely unique system for a muzzleloader, whereby a module is locked up in the breech very much like a cartridge. Other look-alike modern muzzleloaders have bolts that are really strikers (non-locking) that engage the receiver. The Ultimate in-line modern muzzleloader currently leads a trend in heavy-load allowance. It burns not three, but four 50-grain volume-equivalent pellets for a 200-grain equivalent charge. Many of us thought that three-pellet modern muzzleloaders had reached a pinnacle as a powder charge. The Ultimate tells us otherwise. Loaded with four Pyrodex 50/50 Pellets, the Ultimate launched a 420-grain conical bullet at a chronographed 2,041 fps for 3,886 foot-pounds of muzzle energy.

Today's 30-06, which I call the "new" century-old round, develops 2,950 fps with a 180-grain bullet in Federal's High-Energy load. Out of the 26-inch barrel of my Morrison Precision 30-06, a load I found in a Barnes manual provides an average 3,006 fps with a 180-grain bullet for a cat whisker over 3,600 foot-pounds. At the muzzle, the Ultimate's top load whips the top load in the 30-06. Due to bullet design, the '06 will win the contest at 200 yards. But it is clear the Ultimate was bred to perform at a high level of power. Chapter 37 deals with even more powerful rifles, but not in the context of a modern front-loader intended for North American big game. The Ultimate would, of course, be at home where truly large beasts roam. With a professional hunter standing ready with a powerful repeater, I would not hesitate to tackle a Cape buffalo with the Ultimate. These two rifles boldly show what has happened in a comparatively short time frame. Germane to this chapter is the fact that both of these rifles do their stuff with loads that fall into the optimum category. Specifically, the Savage and Ultimate deal out big power with top-end loads adequate for moose and bears. But are these loads optimum?

The Chameleon Muzzleloader

Of course a modern rifle is capable of a wide range of loads by simply altering the cartridge. My 30-06 is a rabbit rifle with 110-grain bullets loaded way down in velocity, a wild turkey-taker with slightly stronger loads and the same bullet, a plains rifle with high-speed ammo, and in Africa—in the hands of Bob Hodgdon—my rifle knocked off a fine zebra stallion. The bullet was a 250-grain Barnes and it journeyed the full breadth of the stout zebra before coming to rest beneath the hide on the offside. Along with the many joys of shooting old-time black-powder muzzleloaders and cartridge guns, comes true versatility. The muzzleloader is ready at all times for a wide range of loads, each one put down by hand with varying amounts of different powders behind a dizzying array of bullet choices. My good friend, No. 47, shoots 54-caliber round balls at 22 Long Rifle velocity up to a measured 1,970 fps, all with a simple change in powder charge. This accurate rifle chews the X-ring out of the 25-yard offhand target with patched round balls and 60- to 70-grains volume FFg blackpowder or Pyrodex RS. In the big-game field, No. 47 digests 120-grains FFg, RS, or Triple Seven, shooting the same patched ball. Both loads are accurate in the 1:79 rate

of twist. But the lighter charge, about perfect for most target work and even small game, will never be found in No. 47 when big game is on the agenda.

Optimum vs. Maximum

There is nothing wrong with a maximum powder charge. Maximum means the top *safe* load allowed by the manufacturer of the firearm. Optimum is a different story. It's defined here as *that charge of powder that produces the best ballistic results with allowable and safe pressures*. Optimum is a carefully chosen word. While a full max load may be ideal under certain conditions, perhaps knocking over a metallic silhouette target at long range or putting a moose in the pot, an optimum load is often one of less powder for target work or deer taken from a tree stand when the range is usually 25 to 50 yards or so. The optimum load also pays attention to the *law of diminishing returns*. There are times when a maximum charge is little more than a waste of good powder, rewarding the shooter with a bigger bump on the shoulder than necessary, along with more soot in the bore and smoke in the air than necessary. This brings us to a concept that old-time shooters were seldom aware of, the law of diminishing returns. Stories of double-charging, where two times the normal

A properly placed shot, launched by an optimum charge of propellant, put this nice bull elk on the ground.

load was installed downbore, were often wasteful in powder, while delivering extra recoil with very little to no improvement in velocity.

The Law of Diminishing Returns

As promised above, there is a point where adding more powder provides very little increase in velocity. We have to be careful, because some of our modern muzzleloaders allowed great gulps of fuel do use their big cargos to advantage. But it's also easy to find examples of rifles that don't do this. Consider a 58-caliber rifle that I tested. This rifle was allowed 150-grains volume RS powder. Out of a 26-inch barrel, a 625-grain Shiloh Minie left the muzzle at 1,400 fps with 150-grains volume Pyrodex RS. Dropping all the way down to 130-grains volume RS the same bullet lost only 100 fps. While the additional 20 grains did produce a higher muzzle velocity, the increase was not worth the additional recoil. This particular rifle's optimum charge was 130-grains volume RS, not 150-grains RS, even though the rifle was allowed that charge by the manufacturer. Furthermore, and more importantly, groups with the 130-grain volume RS charge were better than groups with the 150-grain volume RS charge. And that is the real clincher. In more severe cases of this law, velocity may actually fall when more powder is added to the charge. That's because, as discussed later in Chapter 23, blackpowder and equivalents do not convert from solid to gas nearly as efficiently as smokeless powder. This means that the powder charge itself becomes part of the mass that expanding gases are trying to push out of the bore. Thereby, some of the energy from the burning powder charge is spent not on pushing the bullet, but working to drive solids left over from combustion.

The Efficient Load

Handloaders of smokeless powder cartridges read about the efficient case

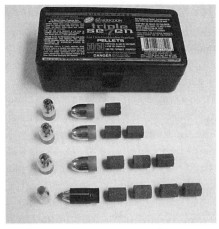

Hodgdon Triple Seven pellets make it easy to test load combinations ranging from light to heavy.

vs. the inefficient case. I am no fan of the efficient cartridge argument, believing that final results are more important than fps gained per each grain weight of powder burned. Regardless, efficiency is a reality. We see the fine 7mm/08 Remington is more efficient than the 7mm Remington Magnum. The smaller cartridge drives a 140-grain bullet at 2,900 fps. The larger cartridge pushes the same 140-grain bullet a 3,300 fps with a heavy powder charge. Efficiency steps in when the little 7mm/08 does its magic with under 50 grains of powder, while the Big 7 uses 20 grains more fuel to gain its 400 fps advantage. The 7mm/08 earned 58 fps for each grain weight of powder burned. The 7mm Magnum got 49 fps for each grain of powder consumed, a significant difference. The prize for efficiency goes to the 7mm/08, but that does not take away from the fact that the 7mm/08 load produces 2,615 foot-pounds of muzzle energy, while the 7mm Remington Magnum earns 3,386 foot-pounds. This is remindful of the good little man vs. the good big man story. In a match of strength, the good big man wins every time. When big power is demanded, the big cartridge wins and efficiency can take a walk.

A similar condition exists with the muzzleloader. For example, a particular in-line 50-caliber magnum muzzleloader allowed three 50/50 Pyrodex

Pellets for a total of 150-grains volume gained 1,459 fps with a 350-grain Buffalo Bullet. Three Pellets pushed velocity to 1,730 fps. It took a third more fuel to gain 271 fps. That is not efficient, you say. But wait a minute. Energy for two Pellets was 1,655 foot-pounds, while energy for the three Pellet load ran 2,327 foot-pounds. A hunter feeling a need for the extra punch would opt for the heavier load, in spite of it being less efficient than the lighter load. If it's a bear, the additional energy may well be worth the extra recoil. Efficiency does come to the fore, however, when adding extra powder does not produce the desired result of a flatter trajectory for the bullet with more energy downrange. Great care is especially necessary when considering the round ball and its perilous fight against the ravages of the atmosphere.

You don't see it as much today, because the voices have been silenced; however, a prominent cry from the not-too-distant past was to drop the powder charge behind the round ball, in some cases by as much as half the normal maximum load. Devotees of this argument could prove that the lighter load was more efficient because a 50-caliber ball starting at 1,974 fps reaches 100 yards doing 1,113 fps (in one actual downrange chronograph test). Meanwhile, the same ball beginning at 1,362 fps arrives at 100 yards going 858 fps. The fast ball lost 44 percent of its original energy, while the slower

Loose powder and ball fuels the traditional muzzleloader. The adjustable brass measure measures a wide range of charge levels (by volume), and the percussion cap starts the ball rolling.

ball lost only 37 percent of its energy, making the slower lead pill more efficient, especially when considering that it only took 40-grains volume FFFg to drive the slower ball at 1,362, while the faster ball required 120-grains volume FFg to start its 1,974 fps trip. The real story, however, lies in delivered energy. The faster ball arrives at 100 yards with 487 foot-pounds, while the slower one shows up packing only 289 foot-pounds. Which would you rather deliver to that buck standing a hundred yards away?

The Chronograph

The best, if not the only, means of determining when the law of diminishing returns has entered the picture is with a chronograph. Anything less is guessing. Fortunately, chronographs are now affordable. Any serious shooter can own one, including a sophisticated model such as the Oehler 35P Proof machine that provided data for this book as well as the *Gun Digest Blackpowder Loading Manual*. Data taken with the 35P was double-checked by a powder company with a professional machine costing considerably more.

Seven Steps for Building an Optimum Load

Seven simple steps uncover the law of diminishing returns gremlin, starting well below the allowable maximum and working up from that point while chronographing all results. It's an in-

Conical bullets and synthetic sabots are found in many shapes and sizes, and from a growing number of manufacturers.

teresting process. The chronograph will reveal in bold numbers when the additional powder added to the charge provided an insignificant increase in muzzle velocity, which in turn computes readily to muzzle energy.

Step One – Never exceed the manufacturer's maximum charge. Gunmakers are responsible for setting safety limits for their firearms. Many of us thought that the 150-grain charge had about peaked out. The Ultimate Muzzleloader gave the lie to that notion with its equivalent 200-grain charge. Each gun will prove a law unto itself. Although I had seen this happen for years with modern firearms, I was surprised to find a similar condition with muzzleloaders.

Step Two – As with handloading metallic cartridges, starting below maximum is always recommended, working up in five- to ten-grain increments toward the maximum allowable charge. Blackpowder and other proper muzzleloader propellants are far too inefficient to benefit from a one-grain change. That's why five- to ten-grain workups are suggested, five in caliber 45 and under, 10 in calibers over 45. One additional grain volume will not register on even the most sensitive chronograph.

Step Three – The only powders I worked with in attempting to arrive at optimum muzzleloader loads were the various offerings in blackpowder, plus Pyrodex, Triple Seven and GOEX Pinnacle. The Savage 10Ml is capable of undergoing the same load scrutiny as other muzzleloaders with either blackpowder or smokeless powder, but with the latter, loads are very much chiseled in stone and I found them to be in the optimum realm, so no further testing was done.

Step Four – Pay attention to recommended powder *granulation* when working up an optimum load. Kernel size, as clearly shown in Chapter 23, can make a significant difference in performance.

Step Five – Prepare safe bullet/powder charge test loads. For example, a particular muzzle-loading rifle may be

allowed a maximum of 120-grains FFg blackpowder or equivalent with a round ball. That's easy. The ball will always be the same. Only the powder brand and charge vary. Conicals are another matter. Individual rifles will usually "like" some conicals better than others. The Savage Model 10ML did okay with 44-caliber pistol bullets in sabots, but a particular batch of Winchester 45-caliber bullets in sabots proved more accurate in my test rifle.

Step Six – Test for accuracy. This means keeping records. It's unlikely that a shooter will remember exactly what happened with each tested load. Shooting from the bench while keeping records of groups provides solid data to work from.

Step Seven – Stick with your best loads as optimum: one powder brand, one granulation, and one bullet, all forming a chain of success. Trying other loads to see how they go is fine. However, the whole idea of building the optimum load is having something to go back to that always produces ideal results.

If the shooter adheres stringently to the maximum powder charge allowed a specific firearm, there is no need to be concerned about problems with an optimum load. Also, one gun may have several optimum loads. An in-line 54-caliber magnum muzzleloader allowed 150-grains volume FFFg blackpowder gave best accuracy with 130 grains, with minimal velocity loss as opposed to the full maximum allowable charge. That load was considered optimum for elk in the timber. However, the same rifle drove a lighter bullet accurately at higher velocity with the same powder and charge. So this rifle had at least two optimum loads both accurate. No load is worthwhile if it cannot be counted on for accuracy, and that includes big-game hunting where the most accurate load is desirable, because normal disadvantages encountered in the field already take away from accurate bullet placement, lack of a benchrest being one of those disadvantages.

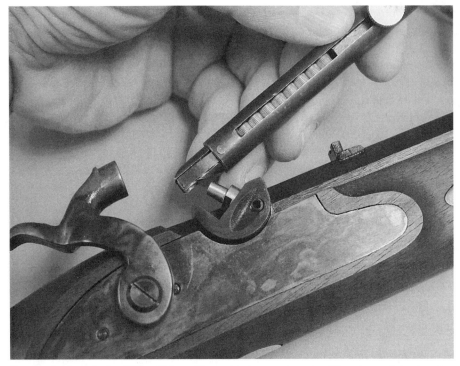

The standard cap is the #10 or #11, and is used today mostly on traditional muzzleloaders, to include revolvers, pistols and shotguns. Many in-line guns are designed for more robust igniters including rifle and shotgun primers.

Old Information

Old data can be fascinating, and some of it is spot on. Unfortunately, the latter is not always the case. A quotation from a magazine goes "To start somewhere, lay a ball on the palm of your hand and pour powder over it until it is quite covered. Set your measure for this amount. It should be within ten grains of the proper charge for that ball and rifle, *if you poured the powder over the ball with care* to just cover it." This is not a slam against the author of those words. He probably got the idea from another source, as we all have done. Anyone wishing to experiment for himself is welcome to lay a round ball in the palm of his hand, covering it with powder. Is the hand flat or cupped? A flat palm could produce a whale of a powder charge, while a ball cupped into the palm might make for a very light charge. Optimum, according to one dictionary, means "The condition or degree producing the best result." Covering a ball in the hand with powder is not the way to achieve the optimum.

New Information is Best

Who would have believed that the 21st century would find several million blackpowder shooters in the field? The number of blackpowder companies, as the Directory in this book proves, is many. Furthermore, several major gun houses have joined the muzzleloader game, including Remington, Savage, and Ruger. What was right and prudent in the past for guns of old may not stand today. So, in looking toward that optimum load, new data must be observed. Powders have changed. Into the country comes Schuetzen from Germany, Swiss from that country, and Elephant from Brazil. GOEX has Pinnacle, newly on the market as this is written. The Hodgdon Powder Company has added Triple Seven and Triple Seven Pellets to the lineup of Pyrodex and Pyrodex Pellets. See Chapter 24 for specifics on these propellants.

Optimum Loads and Igniters

The train running on the track of blackpowder shooting made an abrupt turn when it embraced means of ignition other than the standard percussion cap, normally found in sizes No. 11 and No. 10. The tophat, or English musket cap, is not new. It found its way onto various firearms a very long time ago (the Whitworth rifle, for example) because of its larger flame output. New is the fact that some modern muzzleloaders can take this larger percussion cap. Standard primers as found seated in cartridge cases were around before the telegraph. However, their use in muzzleloaders is a fairly new development. The Ultimate Muzzleloader uses a Large Rifle primer, for example, and my Markesbery rifle can employ Small Rifle primers, although I have found 100 percent ignition so far with No. 11 caps, so I don't worry about primers. How do primers figure in optimum loads? Not a lot. Optimum loads can be developed with everything from No. 11 percussion caps to No. 209 shotgun primers and all igniters in between. The only way igniters play a role in optimum loads is through surefire ignition. Some systems call for more fire than others, especially if the avenue from spark to main charge in the breech is long, circuitous, or both.

Kernel Size and Optimum Loads

This area is not as clearly defined as it once was. Tests have shown some interesting results, for example, with FFg granulation in smaller calibers. A little 32-caliber squirrel rifle with a 26-inch barrel got over 2,100 fps with a .310-inch round ball and 50-grains volume GOEX FFg blackpowder. The pressure rating with this strong load showed slightly less than 10,000 psi. The same grains volume GOEX FFFg gained a hundred fps, with 500 psi higher pressure. Obviously, the way to find the optimum powder granulation and charge in a case like this is testing for accuracy. Ballistics won't do it because both powders do a fine job. Another test, this time with a 50-caliber in-line magnum muzzle-loader allowed 150 grains volume proper propellant, including FFFg, gained 200 fps with the finer granulation over FFg. That is a significant increase in bullet speed with the finer granulation powder, which was allowed by the manufacturer as entirely safe.

Final Notes

Projectile

Twist and bore dimensions dictate the right bullet, one that proves stable and accurate while at the same time effective when big game is included in the picture. The basics of twist are always observed, as discussed in Chapter 20. That is why a 50-caliber modern muzzleloader with 1:28 rate of twist gets a conical, while a 50-caliber rifle with 1:66 rate of twist demands a round ball. Bullet choices these days are wonderfully diverse. A big 460-grain 54-caliber lead projectile from Buffalo Bullet Company was responsible for ruining my latest bullet-testing box, but I didn't mind. The show was worth the price of admission, which was repairing the blown-out sides of the box. A bullet from Parker Productions traveled the full breath of the test box, driving deeper than a particular 7mm Magnum bullet tested that day. For 200-yard shooting, Traditions T-Shock XLR flew flat and true in front of a walloping charge of Triple Seven.

Gunmakers' Suggested Loads

It's unlikely that a company will suggest shooting a bullet of another brand when that company sells its own bullets. That is why it pays to buy a few different projectiles that simply "look good," putting them to the test on the shooting range.

Accuracy First

A powerful bullet zinging right by the ear of a big-game animal is not nearly as effective as a slightly weaker missile that finds the breadbasket. Accuracy always takes precedence over power, except when accuracy can only

be gained by building a load that is too weak to do the job at hand. That is why accuracy is considered a major part of the optimum load.

Accuracy/Power Compromise

Target shooters require only that bullets reach their destination with sufficient force to punch a hole in a sheet of paper, unless the target is a silhouette that needs a good sound thumping to knock it down. Hunters have a different goal, to deliver the most impact to the most vital spot. Sometimes a compromise is ideal—good authority with accuracy. A particular 54 caliber conical shooter proved very powerful with a specific bullet, but not very accurate. Another bullet gave a little less authority, but fine accuracy. The second bullet was the first choice and the right compromise, promising proper projectile placement with enough force to get the job done.

Juggling Components Safely

The combinations are mathematically astronomical. It's all but impossible to match a bullet with every possible powder and powder charge, as well as other particulars, such as lubes and sabots. (See accuracy chapter for more on lubes and sabot choices.) While means of ignition seldom makes or breaks accuracy, small differences can occur. Then there are round ball sizes and patch choices. A lot of time can be spent at the range juggling components to make the best load. Coming up with the optimum load is actually a lot of fun as long as the shooting is accomplished safely, never exceeding maximum charges.

When asked by a newscaster where in the world all those bullets went that were manufactured in America, one spokesman said, "Most of them end up in dirt banks." How true. Testing for an optimum load means putting plenty of projectiles into dirt banks. It's both educational and enjoyable, especially when that one "pet load" emerges, that near perfect combination of all components in the load chain.

There's no substitute for good range work when it comes to evaluating different bullet and charge combinations. A solid rest, sturdy bench and the proper accessories make the load development task rewarding.

16 THE DEADLY LEAD PUMPKIN

The careful hunter with a ball-shooting rifle or big pistol must become familiar with the word "stalk." These sable antelope are a little too far for a certain poke with a lead pill. But those trees in the background may very well serve to hide a good stalk for a closer shot.

Let's pretend that we are going to make a bullet with the least bearing surface possible, that is, the projectile makes minimum contact with the bore. Our mythical bullet has a very low sectional density and C (ballistic coefficient) so that it loses about half its muzzle velocity at only 100 yards. At the same time, this bullet will be capable of dropping, with one shot, the biggest animal that walks the earth, Jumbo himself of Africa. It will conquer raging grizzlies, while at the same time, depending upon its caliber, serve to put a rabbit in the pot. Well, we don't have to pretend. This bullet has been around for a long time, and I mean round—the round ball, a simple sphere of lead. It is called round because it is, and ball because it is a bullet, a spherical bullet.

Ball also refers to conical ball, as well as military ball ammunition, referring to a jacketed projectile sanctioned by the Geneva Convention for warfare that is considered a bit more humane than a dum-dum or any other type of expanding projectile. The round ball has low sectional density. Sectional density is the ratio of a bullet expressed in pounds to the square of its diameter. The result is a number expressed in fractions of an inch. The round ball has pitiful C. Ballistics incorporates sectional density in its formula as the ratio of the bullet's sectional density to its coefficient of form. It is also expressed as a decimal number. These are true and worthy explanations, but for our sand-lot purposes, a bullet that is "long for its caliber" is high in sectional density, while a short fat one is not. And a high C bullet resembles a rocket more than a basketball. The poor, miserable round ball. Since C includes sectional density, that figure only is given for the following comparisons taken from Lyman's *Black Powder Handbook*. Remember that a high number is good. A low number is poor.

Comparing a 32-caliber round ball with a 12-bore round ball shows the significance of diameter increase not only in terms of mass, but also ballistic coefficient. Neither ball holds a candle to the 210-grain Sierra boattail included in the photo, but bigger is better where C is concerned.

For Comparison: a 180-grain 30-caliber Nosler AccuBond bullet has a C of .502
45-Caliber Round Ball (.445-inch) ~~ Ballistic Coefficient = .063
50-Caliber Round Ball (.495-inch) ~~ Ballistic Coefficient = .070
54-Caliber Round Ball (.535-inch) ~~ Ballistic Coefficient = .075
45-Caliber Minie No. 445369 ~~ Ballistic Coefficient = .151
50-Caliber Maxi No. 504617 ~~ Ballistic Coefficient = .095
54-Caliber Minie No. 533476 ~~ Ballistic Coefficient = .137

Even the conical C is nothing to write home about. Comparing against another modern bullet, this time Hornady's racy 162-grain 7mm boattail spire point, we find a C of .514. The round ball, especially, falls on its face by comparison. The gunmakers striving to build that 200-yard modern muzzleloader were faced with a problem. Regardless of how much powder these rifles (mainly) burned, the bullets did not match up. That, of course, has been taken care of with spitzer-shape blackpowder projectiles such as those mentioned in Chapter 17: bullets like the Buffalo Bullet SSB, Northern Precision jacketed missiles, and a host of projectiles with sharply pointed synthetic noses. Lyman's 40- and 45-caliber LRHP (Long Range High Performance) bullets for 40-65 Winchester and 45-70 silhouette shooters are examples of blackpowder cartridge bullets styled for longer-range shooting. Pointed bullets shoot flatter than round ball. They arrive with much more of their initial velocity and energy intact. And yet, the simple lead pumpkin continues to drop all manner of big game. And when large enough, it can do the job fairly far downrange.

Downrange

As the round ball grows in caliber, downrange effectiveness is significantly improved due to increased mass. However, even the fine 54-caliber lead pill starting out at close to 2,000 fps loses over 40 percent of its original velocity at 100 yards, while a 54-caliber 460-grain lead Buffalo Bullet sheds less that 25 percent of its starting velocity at the same distance. Woe to the smaller lead balls, such as the 36-caliber .350-inch. Fired from a 36-caliber squirrel rifle at a muzzle velocity of over 2,000 fps, this little lead pill chugs along at less than 1,000 fps at 100 yards, delivering an energy rating less than 145 foot-pounds. But wait a minute. I've put rabbits in the pot with the 22 Short rimfire with under 100 foot-pounds *at the muzzle*. Now make the round ball a

two-bore, that is, only two round bullets to the pound, or 3,500 grains weight each. The words of 19th century big-game hunter S.W. Baker come to mind. In a letter to Gibbs of Bristol, great gunmakers of the era, Baker wrote in a letter dated August 30, 1887:

To Mr. George Gibbs, Bristol

About forty-six years ago your firm made up for me the first rifle that I ever planned. This was entirely my own idea at a time when rifle shooting was but little understood. I was only twenty years of age, but having taken a peculiar interest in the subject [of guns], I was sure that a heavy charge of powder was the first necessity to procure a high velocity, and consequently a low trajectory.

Your firm made for me a rifle weighing 22 lbs. To carry a two-groove belted [round] ball of 3 ozs., with a charge of 1 oz. (16 drams) of powder. This was the first heavy rifle that ever was introduced to Ceylon, and it is referred to in my first work, 'The Rifle and Hound in Ceylon,' as a very wonderful weapon.

This little note is included here to blaze a trail to further caliber discussion, for more than once the little saying repeats: "Caliber is all to the ball." It is caliber that makes for power, especially downrange authority, with the lead sphere. Caliber is also vital to penetration. But so is velocity. Baker included a huge powder charge (437 grains) behind the ball to promote velocity.

Penetration

On paper, the lead ball has less chance for deep penetration into the vital zones of a big game animal than long life for a snowball in the Sahara Desert sun. But the more we learn about this most inefficient of missiles, the more surprises there are in store for us. Larger-caliber balls have crashed through the full breadth of the largest four-fitted animal on this continent,

the American bison. I know because I have seen this happen with a 230-grain 54-caliber lead ball. I was not surprised when a single ball from No. 47 stopped the buffalo bull's advance with a brain shot (the charge was captured on film). But when a second round ball drove, from close range, completely through the rib cage of the bull, I was amazed. On another hunt, the same rifle put a .535-inch lead ball clear to the offside of a bull elk. Several big mule deer fell to the same lead pill. The trick is getting close. Make it large enough, and the round ball will drop an elephant in its tracks with a head shot, which is exactly what big lead balls accomplished in the hands of Africa's 19th century ivory hunters. Major Shakespear (without the "e"), author of *Wild Sports in India* and mentioned again below, said of the round ball, "I have Minie bullet-moulds for my rifles, but so long as the spherical bullets go through and through large game, I do not see the use of running the risk of shaking the stock of the gun, and of extra recoil, by using heavier balls." Sounds like Samuel Baker.

Round Ball Size and Weight

Hinted at in the first paragraph, the round ball is the lightest projectile we

Penetration of the round ball can be remarkable considering its low sectional density and poor ballistic coefficient. This waterbuck at such close range would readily drop to one 54-caliber round ball in the boiler room—and odds are the ball would make it to the offside of the beast. The waterbuck is tough, but not too tough for a lead ball.

Elk-size game like this African kudu bull are best hunted with round balls of at least 54-caliber and stalked within 75 yards for good arrival velocity, energy and penetration.

have per caliber. Even the shortest conical bullet is longer. Unlike the conical, it has no shank, and therefore cannot grow heavier than its circumference allows. A .490-inch lead pill can weigh no more than 177 grains in "pure" lead, while the weight of a 50-caliber conical jumps as high as the firearm's rate of twist allows for stabilization. The oft-noted Buffalo Bullet SSB goes 375 to 435 grains weight with an actual diameter of .452-inch on my micrometer. I have on hand another true 45-caliber bullet that weighs 600 grains. Yet, a 45-caliber round ball in .440-inch diameter weighs only 128 grains. The little spitfire 32-caliber squirrel rifle, while perfectly deadly on wild turkeys and adequate for even larger quarry

with perfectly placed shots, shoots a pill running under 50 grains weight. Additionally, every round ball is smaller than the caliber of the gun that shoots it, so it will fit downbore with a patch.

Science Gets a Spanking

I promised in the beginning to compare blackpowder with modern guns. Going back to sectional density, let's compute another number, this time for a 30-caliber 150-grain bullet. The number turns out to be .226, determined by first dividing 150 grains by 7000 to convert to pounds weight, arriving at .0214285, then squaring the bullet diameter (.308-inch) for .094864, then dividing that figure into the first for .2258865, which rounds off to .226. Here's the payoff: a 500-grain 45-caliber bullet, such as fired in the 45-70 Government cartridge, squat that it may appear, runs .341 for sec-

Here is a good visual example of size vs. weight. The 54-caliber round ball on the right weighs 230 grains. The 12-bore round ball on the left weighs 500 grains (it is not a .690-ball). Twice .540-inch is 1.08 inches. So the 12-bore round ball is not nearly twice the diameter of the 54-caliber ball, but it weighs more than twice as much.

This is no contest—as big as the 12-bore ball is it will not take on the 210-grain Sierra boattail on its right. A 500-grain ball at 1,500 fps will gain a KE close to 2,500 foot-pounds. But the 210-grain 30-caliber bullet fired from a magnum cartridge at 3,000 fps will have a KE close to 4,200 foot-pounds. And that is why fans of big bullets at modest velocity don't like Newton's KE formula.

tional density. The point being—mass counts. Even the lowly round ball gathers strength as it increases its weight. Science tells us, however, using the Newtonian method of deriving kinetic energy (KE), that the weight of a hefty round ball will not make up for lower velocity. "Power" of the round ball in foot-pounds of energy, on paper, is anemic because velocity is squared in the formula. This factor is compounded downrange as the ball loses even more speed. What I call the "new" 30-06, because of a factory load that develops 2,900 fps with a 180-grain bullet (supposedly with a triple-base powder), shows that bullet to be well ahead of a heavily loaded 54-caliber ball-shooting rifle. The 30-06 180-grain bullet at 2,900 fps has a muzzle energy of 3,362 foot-pounds. A 54-caliber 230-grain lead round starting at 2,000 fps earns a shade under 2,000 foot-pounds at the muzzle. It gets worse. At 100 yards, a 30-caliber 180-grain pointed bullet possesses a ton-and-a-half foot-pounds of energy, while the 54 has dropped to under 700 foot-pounds! These are scientific facts. But science is defied as the lowly round ball continues to bring home the bacon.

Three ways to power-up the round ball:
Caliber is all to the Ball

There it is again, "the saying." One gunwriter likened the atmosphere to a swimming pool when it comes to slowing a bullet down. As a projectile approaches the speed of sound, drag dramatically increases, escalating as a bullet flies faster and faster. We know that a high C rating is excellent for fighting the ravages of drag, so the poor round ball gets knocked on the head again because it does not enjoy a high C. That's why it loses so much speed as it progresses downrange. But there is hope. Make the ball bigger. Mass, which we refer to simply as weight for our purposes, goes far in helping a ball overcome its inherently poor flight characteristics. High velocity would help, too,

Caliber is all to the ball. This heavy 12-bore round ball at 500 grains will have a hard time catching up to the 100-yard energy of the 50-caliber Maxi ball and no chance of matching the 210-grain Sierra boattail downrange. But up close, it will do the job on any game.

if it were possible with muzzleloaders, but it isn't.

The good news is that as caliber increases, weight escalates out of proportion. There's a handy formula for proving this fact. It begins with computing the volume of a sphere. First, diameter is brought to the third power. The resulting figure is multiplied by .5236. That number is then multiplied times 2873.5, the weight of a cubic inch of pure lead. Computing for a 54-caliber round ball of .530-inch diameter: diameter to the third power is .148877; times .5236 (a constant) = .077952; times 2873.5 = 223.99, which rounds to 224 grains weight, the theoretical perfect weight of a .530-inch ball in pure lead. A .535-inch round ball in pure lead runs 230 grains weight. A .350-inch round ball weighs 65 grains. Double its diameter to .700-inch and weight does not double. It goes up almost eight times to 516 grains. This formula is also valuable for testing round ball lead purity (see Chapter 34) by comparing the actual weight of the cast ball against the theoretical perfect weight of that same size ball.

Velocity and the Round ball

We know true high velocity is not possible with blackpowder, not even with the latest formulas of replica propellants. We also know that while caliber is paramount to round ball performance, bullet speed continues to play a huge role. I especially don't buy the logic espoused by some writers that since the round ball loses speed so rap-

Barrel length is important to round ball velocity and round ball velocity is important to performance—of course. This rifle is typical of the ball-shooter.

idly, why bother worrying about gaining good velocity in the first place? They also reasoned, and in this they were correct, that faster bullets shed more velocity *proportionally* than slower bullets. That's the efficiency argument again. Beyond the speed of sound, the atmosphere does play havoc with a bullet. So why not go with smaller powder charges? The problem is, you cannot end up with something without starting out with something. And terminal velocity/energy is based upon initial velocity/energy, regardless of the fact that the round ball loses more speed, proportionally, as it starts out faster. We're forced to agree with a basic law of ballistics that the faster round ball has the advantage over a slower one. It delivers more energy at all ranges. Since energy is part of the penetration story, the faster ball drives deeper into the target than a slower one. There is bullet deformity to consider here, since higher speed will flatten that lead ball much more than lower speed. But the aforementioned bison that was shot "clear through" with a round ball saw that lead sphere arriving at over 1,800 fps due to the extreme

close range of the shot. Finally, the faster ball shoots flatter, making a hit more certain downrange.

The Value of Pure Lead in the Round Ball

The word "pure" associated with lead means, in reality, "almost pure." It's nearly impossible to come off with lead that is 100 percent free of any other metal. Chapter 34 on bullet casting discusses how to render lead as pure as possible with equipment normally used by bullet casters. Pure lead is ideal for three important reasons. First, a round ball of pure lead will be at its heaviest, heavier than one containing other elements. Second, pure lead obturates in the bore better than a harder substance. While the round ball does not make direct contact with the rifling, it remains important that that ball fill out against the patch as much as possible for best guidance in the bore. Recall that a bullet at rest is predisposed, due to inertia, to remain at rest, so when it's smacked with pressure from an ignited powder charge, it tends to foreshorten slightly. Third, pure lead enjoys high molecular cohesion. In other words, it stays together rather than fragmenting, and this becomes important to penetration in a big-game animal. Because the ball hangs together rather than going to pieces, it is capable of creating long wound channels. While pure lead can be purchased and salvaged "dirty" lead cleaned up, pure lead balls are also

The value of "pure" lead for the round ball is repeated with the lead conical bullet shown here. Both the round ball (left), and the conical have retained most of their original before-shooting weight because lead has high molecular cohesion. In other words, it does not readily fragment. Sierra 210-grain boattail included in photo for perspective.

available ready to shoot, from companies such as Speer, Hornady, the Buffalo Bullet Company and others. Example: a Speer .535-inch round ball scale-weighed 230 grains—right on the nose. See Chapter 34 for proving lead purity.

Choosing the Right Ball

Matching the gun to the game has been a common sense approach since the Pilgrims waded ashore a couple hundred years ago, likewise matching bullets to the game. While larger round balls always have more energy retention than smaller ones, they are not appropriate for all shooting. Round balls in 32- and 36-caliber, for example, are wonderful for small game, wild turkeys and up to javelina-size animals: the latter only with perfect bullet placement. Furthermore, economy is much in favor of small round balls for the obvious reason of lead conservation alone. It's possible to shoot the 32-caliber squirrel rifle cheaper than the 22-rimfire, especially when caps are formed with the Forster Tap-O-Cap tool using metal from beverage cans. While the 32 and 36 (38s and 40s can also be useful) are great for the small stuff, 50s and 54s dominate for just about everything else, including rendezvous games. The larger lead pills usually have the advantage, be it a long-range game of hitting the gong or a short-range contest striking

the cutting edge of an axe to split the ball in two so it will hit double targets.

Round Ball Performance by Caliber

32-Caliber Round Ball

Weighing 45 grains in .310-inch diameter, this little pill can travel over 2,000 fps at the muzzle. Properly loaded, it will drop the biggest gobbler in the woods with one shot, while not destroying too much white meat. It will also put cottontails, squirrels, and varmints in the bag at ranges up to a hundred yards (I get a lot closer). It is cheap to shoot. Only 10 grains of FFFg blackpowder drives the little 32 round ball at 22 Long Rifle muzzle velocity.

36-Caliber Round Ball

Weighing 65 grains in .350-inch diameter, the 36 lends a tad more confidence to the wild turkey hunter, while performing a bit better on larger varmints downrange. For rabbits and squirrels, the 36 has nothing on the 32, however, and it does cost a little more to shoot. While the 32 gains 22 Long Rifle velocity with 10 grains of FFFg for 700 shots per pound of powder, it takes 15 grains of the same fuel to launch the 36 at about the same speed.

40-Caliber Round Ball

Game department personnel, having to come up with a minimum caliber for big game, often seized on the

Size and application—choosing the right size round ball for the job. The little 32-caliber lead sphere on the left is perfect for small game and wild turkey. The 54-caliber ball in the center will take up to elk and moose at closer ranges, and the 12-bore ball can turn a 12-gauge shotgun into a formidable close-range big-game taker.

40. It probably sounded pretty large to shooters who considered 30-calibers big bores. The 40-caliber ball is fine for target shooting, but it only weighs 93 grains in .395-inch diameter. This is larger than necessary for small game, but not heavy enough for big game, in spite of the tons of venison the little pill has no doubt taken over the ages. Rifles bored for the 40-caliber round ball are mild and accurate. But ballistic facts put the 40 in a middle zone, as its lacking popularity shows. A 40-caliber Muskrat rifle with 36-inch barrel fired a .395-inch 93-grain round ball at 1,993 fps with 50 grains volume FFFg blackpowder for a muzzle energy of 820 foot-pounds. At 100 yards, energy dropped to only 214 foot-pounds.

45-Caliber Round Ball

Those who have had an opportunity to study numerous original Kentucky/Pennsylvania long rifles find that 45-caliber was highly popular in the Golden Age of American Firearms. A collector in Pennsylvania showed me 300 originals. Most were 45-caliber. Today the 45-caliber round ball is leagues behind the 50 and 54 in popularity. A .445-inch round ball goes 133 grains weight. Even when pushed at 2,000 fps muzzle velocity, remaining energy at 100 yards is only a little over 300 foot-pounds.

50-Caliber Round Ball

A 50-caliber .490-inch round ball weighs 177 grains in pure lead. Kicked off at almost 2,000 fps, muzzle energy is around 1,500 foot-pounds with close to 500 foot-pounds remaining at 100

If moose meat for the winter means the difference between eating prime protein or a lot of other stuff and you're carrying a muzzleloader, the best bet is a really big round ball or a conical bullet capable of deep penetration.

yards. The 50 is perfectly adequate for deer-sized game and it has dropped many elk and even moose from the guns of hunters willing to stalk close for that one perfect shot.

54-Caliber Round Ball

A 54-caliber round ball runs 230 grains in .535-inch diameter. From my No. 47 rifle, this lead globe leaves the bore at a chronographed 1,970 feet-per-second with a good dose of Triple Seven, Swiss, Pyrodex RS or GOEX FFg blackpowder. This puts muzzle energy close to a short ton with retained energy of about 675 foot-pounds at 100 yards. The hunter willing to get close is assured of good performance on big game, including elk and moose with the 54 ball. A special trait of the 54 is good velocity with a reasonable powder charge. After caliber 54, it takes quite a bit more powder to achieve higher velocities.

58-Caliber & Up

There is no doubt that caliber 58 and larger round balls are deadly. Very large round balls put elephants down in Africa and Ceylon with regularity. Bigger is better. This point is well illustrated with a formula matching a 50-caliber ball against a 60- caliber ball. Consider the first at .500-inch diameter, the second at .600-inch diameter. Cube each to simplify the math. The 50-caliber ball, cubed, is .125. The 60-caliber ball cubed is .216. Divide .216 by .125 and the result is 1.728, rounded to 1.73. Theory holds that the 60-caliber ball has the *potential* of gaining 1.73 times the energy of a 50-caliber ball. This is not a law. It's only a game. But it does have a degree of application.

Suppose both 50- and 60-caliber balls are fired at 2,000 fps muzzle velocity. The result is 2,877 foot-pounds of energy for the 60-caliber ball, which weighs 325 grains in pure lead, and 1,670 foot-pounds for the 50-caliber ball, which weighs 188 grains in pure lead. To prove the mathematical point, multiply 1,670, the energy of the 50-caliber ball, by 1.73, which should provide the energy of the 60-caliber ball if

the latter is truly 1.73 times more potent. The actual figure is 2,889, only two foot-pounds off of the actual energy rating of 2,887 foot-pounds. This shows that the *potential* kinetic energy of the 60-caliber ball, which is only .10-inch greater in diameter than the 50-caliber, is about 1.73 times superior. But recall that it takes a lot of fuel to drive a big ball fast, so the 2,000 foot-per-second rating given both 50- and 60-caliber round balls mentioned above is more theoretical than practical. In one chronograph test, a 62-caliber round ball achieved only 1,600 fps at the muzzle with a very large powder charge.

Hunters Who Knew

Major Shakespear, Captain Forsyth and Sir Samuel Baker, three British hunters of the 19th century, knew all about big round balls. All three proved their belief on very large game. Baker, known for his exploration of the Nile and elephant hunting in Ceylon, had this to say about the round ball for pachyderms:

I strongly vote against conical balls for dangerous game; they make too neat a wound, and are very apt to glance on striking a bone. In giving an opinion against conical balls for dangerous game, I do so from practical proofs of their inferiority. I had at one time a two-groove single

rifle, weighing 21 lbs., carrying a 3 oz. belted ball, with a charge of 12 drachms powder. This was a kind of "devil stopper," and never failed in flooring a charging elephant, although, if not struck in the brain, he might recover his legs. I had a conical mould made for this rifle, the ball of which weighed 4 oz., but instead of rendering it more invincible, it entirely destroyed its efficacy, and brought me into such scrapes that I at length gave up the conical ball as useless.

Sir Samuel stood by his convictions. He hunted with the round ball, especially in 19th-century Ceylon, even for elephants and water buffalo. He was known to shoot the latter from 300 yards with the round ball. How could the lead sphere be so effective at such a distance, especially on massive animals? Ball size was the answer. Baker's rifles were truly big bores. By our standards, caliber 58 is large. Baker would consider a 58 puny. His 12-bore guns, meaning twelve round balls to make 1 pound, were his smallbores. He relied on 4-bore for bigger animals, four to the pound, each weighing 1750 grains. And he also fired some 2-bores. Today, we think of the 458 Winchester as an elephant cartridge (which it is), but this big boy normally drives a bullet of "only" 500 grains weight. The old-time

If S.W. Baker were on the scene, he would choose a big round ball over a conical bullet for elephants.

The super long 22-caliber bullet, made especially for very quick twist rifles, can depart the muzzle at 3,000+ fps, while the 12-bore round ball is lucky to take off at about half that speed. Which will buck the wind better out to 200 yards? In spite of its mass, the big ball takes a longer time to go from muzzle to 200 yards than the speedy 22-caliber bullet—bet on the little 22 bullet to drift less at that distance.

hunter of dangerous game realized the only way his blackpowder rifle was going to prevent his being squashed by a charging beast was shooting heavy projectiles. Thus, the powder charge was not ignored and the big bores of the old-timers consumed monster charges.

October Country, well known for superb blackpowder accoutrements, especially high-quality leather goods, introduced a line of rifles designed to please traditionalists. Along with a Northwest Trade Gun, flintlock 20-gauge and a J.P. Henry 54-caliber rifle (the babies of the lineup), is the Great America Sporting Rifle, caliber 69 billed as "the most powerful traditional muzzleloader rifle manufactured today." Interestingly, the rifle is built along the lines suggested by Captain James Forsyth, a Lieutenant when he authored his well-received book, *The Sporting Rifle and Its Projectiles*, in the 19th century. Rifling twist is 1:104, very slow, and strictly intended for the round ball. The barrel is 1-1/4 inches across the flats at the octagonal portion, ending round at the muzzle 1 1/8-inches across. It has a five-step adjustable rear sight and this fire-breather fires its big round ball at 1,700 fps for a muzzle energy over 3,000 foot-pounds. October Country also has a 4-bore rifle shooting a

1,750-grain lead globe, making the 69-caliber its little brother.

The Wind and the Round Ball

Bullets drift in two ways. Right-hand twist barrels drift bullets a little to the right; left-hand twist a little to the left. Wind plays a much larger role in moving a bullet off course. High C bullets slow down less rapidly than blunt-nosed bullets, which is extremely important regarding a second factor—time of flight. The round ball suffers on both counts. Its shape is hardly the best for retaining initial velocity, so it takes longer to fly from muzzle to target, which gives the wind more *time* to push on it. While bullet mass (momentum) is vital to sustaining velocity, bullet speed has a surprising effect on wind drift. Comparing a 220 Swift with a little 50-grain bullet against a 45-70 with a 500-grain bullet easily proves this. The Swift's bullet taking off at 4,000 fps muzzle velocity drifts 8-1/2 inches at 200 yards in a 20 mile-per-hour (MPH) crosswind, while the big 500-grain bullet starting at 1,300 veers off course more than two feet at 200 yards. Round balls really suffer in the wind, especially smaller ones when the wind hums at around 30 mph, as it so often does on the plains. In a 30 mph wind, a 65-grain 36-caliber round ball starting at around 1,800 fps muzzle velocity drifts by about four feet, not at 200, but at only 100 yards. Even if the crosswind dropped to a mild 10 mph, the little pill drifts over by a foot. A bigger ball is better. Using the same 1,800 fps starting speed for comparison with the 36-caliber ball, a 30 mph crosswind moves a 230-grain .535-inch round ball two feet off course at 100 yards. That mild 10 mph breeze shoves the 54 ball over about 10 inches at 100 yards. It takes a lot of practice to shoot the round ball effectively in the wind.

Brush Busting

Over the years, bullets designed to buck brush pleased hunters to no end. The only problem was the fact that they

didn't work. Flat-nosed bullets get bullied aside by brush. So do round-nose missiles. Even the hardy 458 Winchester poking a 500-grain round nose into the brush is inviting deflection. In one demonstration of firing a 270 Winchester with a 100-grain bullet and a 45-70 with a 405-grain bullet, the 270's bullets reached the target more frequently than the 45-70's. Round balls fired through the same screen of brush were a disaster. No bullet bucks the brush like a bulldozer, while round balls are especially poor.

Long Range with Round Balls

S.W. Baker was an honest man. Even if he were not, his claims for long-range hits on big game with round ball rifles stand, because he had witnesses. He hit water buffalo in Ceylon out to 300 yards, according to reports. Baker was highly practiced, shooting at more animals in a week than the average North American hunter can hope to fire at in several seasons. He also had some miserable failures at long range in spite of huge lumps of lead fired from the tunnel-like muzzles of his big-bore rifles. Shooting far with blackpowder is done all the time, especially on silhouettes that are sometimes set up at a

Choosing the right bullet for the range is important to success. The choice is clearly represented here. Willing to stalk for a close shot? The 54-caliber round ball will do the job cleanly. Want to add yards to the round ball's effective range? Go with a conical. And for far-away shooting, admit that the modern bullet will reach long range going faster with more energy than either the ball or Maxi.

thousand yards and farther. However, the hunter owes the game to make clean kills. With a muzzleloader, that means getting closer. Stalking to 100 yards, maybe 125 yards, with a round ball rifle makes sense. The mountain man, because of familiarity with his plains rifle, probably made 200-yard shots. Joe Rose was applauded for dropping a buck antelope at rendezvous at 125 paces. The archaic pace was two yards, not one. A step was one yard, and two steps equaled one pace. Mountain man Joe Rose may have dropped the buck at 200 yards. No one will ever know. What we do know is that 200 yards is too far to shoot at game with a 50- or even 54-caliber round ball.

Trajectory

I limit my shots to 125 yards with the round ball on deer-sized game, 75 yards being far enough for elk. A round 50- to 54-caliber round ball, starting at 2,000 fps and sighted in for 75 yards, drops about a half-foot low at 125 yards. A standard conical bullet (not the shapely modern missiles designed for in-line muzzleloaders) usually begins at about 1,500 fps. The conical hangs on to its starting velocity considerably better than the round ball, starting at 1,500 while the ball takes off at around 2,000 put the two on equal ground, and both drop a half-foot below line of sight at 125 yards when sighted in for 75 yards. Even when sighted dead on at 100 yards, these bullets drop a few inches at 125. Magnum muzzleloaders of the day have extended that range to 200 yards with a bullet of higher C at higher velocity.

It's a worn old story, but it fits the round ball so well that it bears retelling. The bumblebee cannot fly. Scientifically speaking, the little bugger has far too little wing surface to lift its bulky carcass into the sky. But the bumblebee does not know it can't fly, so it continues merrily buzzing all over the place. Likewise, the round ball is no good for much of anything—on paper. Its sectional density and ballistic coefficient stink. But the round ball simply doesn't know that it's no good, so it continues printing tight groups on paper, delighting shooters at rendezvous, ringing gongs 500 yards distant, and when properly centered where it belongs from modest range, the old lead sphere drops big game just as well today as when Dan'l Boone walked the forest floors of a new America.

Fadala's long-time hunting partner, the late John Doyle, called binoculars "the eye of the hunter." Binoculars can make all the difference in hunting with the round ball gun because game found before it sees the hunter is stalkable, and stalking close with the round ball is the way to bag a buck, bull or boar with one shot—every time. These big 10x50 glasses "suck up" a lot of light for that prime time of day when game animals are up and about—early morning and late afternoon.

THE EFFICIENT CONICAL

The conical, represented here by a Parker Productions 670-grain Traditional Hunter bullet, is compared with a 494-grain 12-gauge round ball. Both are to be respected on big game. Both can penetrate deeply. The elongated bullet, however, has the edge in sectional density and ballistic coefficient and therefore will retain its energy better downrange. (210-grain Sierra 30-caliber bullet included for reference.)

I suspect that astute shooters of the past, and most certainly professionals in the gunmaking business, knew very well that a conical projectile would eat the lunch of any round ball to ever emerge from a muzzleloader. But there was a big problem—no squirrelly-gigs in the bore. That is to say, no rifling to spin that bullet on its axis so that it flew point-forward instead of wobbling through space like a disoriented duck. Furthermore, as substantiated in Chapter 16, the round bullet, in spite of its inefficient shape with pitiful sectional density and ridiculous ballistic coefficient, did quite a respectable job on targets, in the game field, and on the bat-

tleground. The theory, if not so much the practice, of rifling a bore dates from around 1500 AD in eastern Germany, or perhaps in Austria. As so often is the case, gun history remains shrouded in the dark mists of the past. The term rifling may have come from an Old French word, "rifler," which meant to scratch or groove. Initially, rifling was, more or less, scratched into the bore of the firearm.

The Jaeger rifle of Germany—jaeger meant hunter—was fairly prominent sometime in the 1600s, and it was rifled, seven grooves being common according to some authorities. Ezekiel Baker's 11th edition of *Remarks on the*

Rifle, presented to "His Majesty" from a "Gun Maker," proves students of firearms in this time frame, late 1700s/early 1800s, were concerned about rifling, although by modern standards the data were not entirely scientific. Baker writes, "It has always been considered that three-fourths, or a whole turn, in the angle of a rifle in a barrel three feet in length, was the best for throwing the ball with certainty. This mode of rifling is practiced by the Germans, French, and Americans." Baker goes on to say that "several English gunmakers are firmly of the opinion, that one turn in four feet is the best angle possible. With these angles of rifle I never could fire at long range to any degree of certainty." Baker disagreed with the idea that one turn in four feet was correct. He concluded that he found "the ball to go very random" at longer ranges. Baker reduced the rate of rifling to one quarter-turn of the ball, finding that, "The experiment succeeded to my most sanguine expectation." While Baker found that a very slight beginning of the round ball was sufficient to maintain its integrity in flight, it was soon learned that what worked for the round bullet was hopeless with an elongate projectile.

By the 19th century, there was a multitude of different conical projectiles in America alone. Who could have known that in the 20th century, and into the 21st, conical bullets for muzzleloaders and blackpowder cartridge guns would have a revival? But that is what has happened. Elongated bullets are plentiful for rifles, pistols, cap 'n' ball

The Minie ball, credited to Captain Minie, may have actually been Greener's idea. Regardless, this lead bullet lasted for a very long time in the blackpowder shooting world. Under bore size, it rammed home fairly easily, its hollow base expanding to meet the rifling grooves.

Quite unlike the blackpowder conical of old, the Hornady 300-grain 45-caliber SST-ML bullet with sharp profile polycarbonate tip is shown here with a 30-caliber Sierra bullet for comparison.

revolvers, and blackpowder cartridge guns. Today's conicals are as unique as they were over a hundred years ago. But the current trend is building projectiles expressly designed for the modern muzzleloader. Invariably, these bullets are for hunting more than target shooting, although every company producing and selling them assures unerring accuracy. Whereas but a short time ago, bullets for blackpowder guns were made of lead; in these changing times, the jacketed projectile has gained great popularity today.

This is not to suggest the lead bullet is defunct. On the contrary, Sam's Bullet Box, the simple device I use to test bullets, continues to prove beyond doubt that the big lead bullet remains extremely potent as it smashes through the test media. Heavy lead missiles from the Buffalo Bullet Company, Lyman, Parker Productions, and many other manufacturers, will not only plow through test media, but they also investigate the vitals of big-game animals with terrific force and, when placed right, with superior results. While the lead bullet remains entirely effective, it is the rocket-shaped modern-style conical that makes the 200-yard muzzleloader a reality. Diameter is all to the ball, as discussed in the previous chapter. That is not the case with

The Buffalo Bullet SST, here in the 375 grain weight, has a spitzer shape that gives it a higher ballistic coefficient than old-time conicals. The author has shot targets (for experimentation only, not for hunting) out to 300 yards with satisfactory groups using the SSB bullet in front of a heavy powder charge.

The Maxi Ball operates on the engraving system—the bullet is very close to bore size. Therefore it engraves (the rifling lands cut into it) as it is seated. (See something interesting on the lower right Maxi ball? The little "dots" of lead show a failure in casting the bullet.)

the conical. Because of increased sectional density and ballistic coefficient, good mass is obtained even in smaller calibers. Bullets weighing upwards of 400 grains are entirely possible in 40-caliber, whereas a 40-caliber round ball does not reach even 100 grains. In 45-caliber, where a round ball might go 133 grains, 500-grain and heavier conicals are commonplace.

Pigeonholing Conicals

I have broken down blackpowder conicals into a few categories for easy identification. These are the Minie, named for the French Army Captain; the Maxi, better known as the Maxi-Ball associated with the Thompson/Center Company; what I call a "standard lead bullet" for lack of a better description; pistol bullet/sabot, all copper conical; high ballistic coefficient blackpowder

This is a standard lead conical bullet, but it has a concave base that functions on the Minie principal of base expansion.

bullets, long-range conicals for blackpowder cartridge guns, and modern jacketed projectiles, usually fitted into a sabot. There has been no attempt to convince the reader that one is truly better than another because all of them work well when loaded properly. Furthermore, the rifle itself dictates which shoots best, based essentially on the pattern and style of rifling.

Captain Minie's Conical

Imagine a smoky battlefield with soldiers firing their blackpowder guns at one another. Fast reloading is paramount to winning the day. Imagine further having to put patched round balls downbore. Not fast! After firing only a few times, the bore, due to the nature of blackpowder combustion, is fairly caked up. Pretty soon, the firearm is impossible to load. What to do? Create an undersized bullet, in this case a lead conical that can be pushed down a fairly dirty bore, while at the same time taking advantage of rifling to spin it accurately downrange. Several undersized conical bullets came to the fore, but the one making it most often into books on gun history is the Minie. Not only is this bullet undersized for improved ease of loading, but upon firing it engages the rifling because of the phenomenon noted several times in this book—obturation. The bullet at rest (inertia) tends to remain at rest even when bumped in the behind by a terrific force delivered by the expanding gas of the detonated powder charge. Now if that bullet had a hollow base resulting in a "skirt," the force of gases could expand that skirt to make contact with the rifling.

You have the Minie named in honor of the French Army captain who invented it. Or did he? It's not unusual, as we know from the Nobel Prize each year, for inventors, countries apart, to come up with the same idea at about the same time. Another Frenchman, Delvigne, is sometimes credited with a hollow-base bullet before Minie's came along. However, samples of Delvigne's 1828 bullet are round, not conical.

They were an undersized lead sphere that loaded in a fouled bore. A wedge-like "pin" was embedded in the nose of the Delvigne bullet. Power-stroking the ramrod drove the "pin" into the soft lead projectile, somewhat like pounding a wedge into the handle of an axe to tighten it in place. Just as the axe handle widens because of the wedge, so did the Delvigne bullet, thereby engaging the rifling. There is another problem with Minie's claim to have invented the hollow-base conical bullet. Greener, a well-known gunner of his era, claimed that he invented the bullet credited to Minie. And it may be so. The English courts were satisfied that Greener was right, awarding him damages. The English government would never have doled out the cash if Greener could not prove his case.

Thousands of Minie-type bullets were fired in the American Civil War, especially a 500-grain 58-caliber all-lead slugger that proved a terrible killer, and was at least partially responsible for 600,000 casualties on the battlefield. The history is interesting and important to understanding, but perhaps more remarkable is the fact that the hollow-base concept lives on today. The Buffalo Bullet Company offers several Minie-type bullets, including one that I have fired often, a 58-caliber 525-grain hollowpoint hollow-base bullet that expands in the bore for rifling engagement, while also expanding on the target. This hunting bullet will drop a

bull moose when properly placed. The company rightfully claims that this big slug "delivers awesome shock power." Lyman provides a number of excellent moulds for hollow-base bullets as well, with a list worth noting. There's a 425-grain 54-caliber Minie-type bullet, along with six 58-caliber hollow-base bullets, one called the Parker-Hale at 566 grains, and a 69-caliber tipping the scales at 730 grains. Hornady's Great Plains Bullet has a tapered hollow base, along with a hollow-point for expansion, and it comes in 45, 50, or 54 sizes at 285, 385, and 435 grains. Generally speaking, the Minie is about a caliber undersized for easier loading, not only in a fouled bore, but a clean one as well. The great danger in listing specific bullets is the fact that this book will outlive them as they are replaced with new ones. But the Minie category remains valid.

The Maxi-Ball

The basic concept of the Maxi-Ball is identical to the Minie—ram home a projectile that expands to meet the rifling in the bore when the gun is fired. While the Maxi-Ball functions on the same basic principle—obturation—rifling engagement is achieved in an entirely different way. The Maxi is not undersized to the bore and there is no hollow base. The base of the Maxi is solid and flat and the Maxi is quite close to bore size. It is intended to engrave as it's seated. Engraving means that the

The Hornady Great Plains bullet, here in 54-caliber, is not a Minie, and yet it uses the Minie concept of expanding powder gases to flare out the base for a better "grab" on the rifling lands.

This is a Maxi-style bullet with a Minie-type hollow base, an obvious incorporation of the two concepts.

shank of the bullet bears indentation by the lands of the rifling. The bullet is seated normally, fully upon the powder charge. The force of the powder charge first expands the base, if ever so slightly. Remember that the bullet is already fitted to the rifling. And so it rides upbore guided by the rifling. The Maxi-Ball was never intended for speedy reloading on the battlefield. While super fast reloading is not its major function, second and third bullets go downbore quite readily, so getting a second shot on game with the Maxi does not pose any particular problem, especially if the muzzle of the gun is recessed so that there is no rifling at that point. In this way, the Minie is seated "square to the bore" and with very little help from the short starter. It can be more accurate than the Minie (not always). Furthermore, today's better lubes make Maxi loading easier than ever. There are numerous Maxi-type bullets available today from different companies, including Buffalo Bullets. Thompson/Center's "Original" Maxi-Ball lineup has long been strong with pre-lubed bullets, ready to load, in calibers 45 through 58. I took the largest black bear of my hunting career with a 370-grain 50-caliber Maxi-Ball that penetrated completely in the 6-foot, 7-inch bruin. Lyman also offers Maxi moulds so the shooter can cast his own.

Standard Lead Conical Bullet

This is a very common projectile, often cast at home by shooters of firearms ranging from original muzzleloaders to the latest bolt-action big-game rifles. A

The ordinary standard lead conical bullet comes in a variety of shapes, usually with some sort of grease groove. This conical has smooth sides.

glance into Winchester's 1916 catalog reveals numerous bullets of this type, either loaded into factory cartridges, or sold for seating into homemade ammunition. The 45-90 Winchester and 50-110 were offered with a 300-grain lead bullet in the first, 312-grain lead bullet in the second, costing $36.00 per thousand for the 45-90, $48.00 per thousand rounds for the 50-110—or $9.00 for a thousand bullets of either caliber for handloading. The 45-70 Government cartridge, still going strong today, was sold loaded at $38.00 per thousand with a 500-grain lead bullet, or buy a thousand bullets for $15.00. The ever-popular 30-30 Winchester, called the 30 Winchester in 1916, also had a 117-grain lead bullet option in a special Short Range load at $30.00 per thousand. To this day, hobbyists cast thousands of standard lead bullets in home workshops with modern moulds offered by various companies. I have examples from Rapine, NEI, and RCBS; of course the Lyman Company has been known perennially for its excellent moulds in a huge variety. For example, Lyman has a Whitworth bullet mould that produces a 45-caliber, flat-nosed 475-grain bullet that mates perfectly with my Navy Arms Whitworth replica rifle. While fired mostly in blackpowder cartridge rifles today, standard conicals work in some muzzleloaders, such as the Whitworth. Most standard conicals are round-nose, some flat-nosed, but there are also spitzers such as Lyman's spitzer mould blocks in 40- or 45-calibers: the 40 available in 385 grains, the 45 in 480 grains. Longer bullets in this style "carry up" (retain original velocity). A 50-caliber standard style lead conical weighing 430 grains, starting at 1,600 fps from a muzzleloader, reached 100 yards still chugging along at 1,300 fps. That's only a loss of 19 percent of its starting speed. A number of fine standard lead bullet moulds are also available for Sharps, Remington Rolling Blocks, Ballards, and other single-shot blackpowder cartridge rifles in numerous calibers.

The pistol bullet, as it is called, has long been used in muzzleloaders by fitting it into a sabot. These bullets worked better than many expected them to as they were fired at higher-than-handgun velocities.

Pistol Bullets in Sabots

Admittedly, I was not impressed with the notion of shooting pistol bullets in a muzzleloading rifle. But I had to change my mind. My brother brought down elk with his 50-caliber muzzleloader firing Sierra jacketed pistol bullets—one shot for each elk. Lead pistol bullets will work in the muzzleloader, as will the latest jacketed example. Most pistol bullets, and perhaps they should be noted as revolver bullets as well, were originally intended for big-bore revolvers in calibers 44 and 45. Jacketed hollow-point, jacketed soft-nose, they all work in the muzzleloader *and with more authority* because they were designed to upset (mushroom) at handgun velocities. Driven at higher muzzleloader rifle speeds, these bullets deliver considerable energy to the target. For example, my own 44 Magnum drives a 240-grain bullet from the muzzle at 1,400 fps from a 7 1/2-inch barrel. Load that same bullet in a 50-caliber muzzleloader, a Knight MK-85 that I tested, for example, and 1,700 fps is readily achieved. Meanwhile, a 44-caliber bullet would rattle down the bore of a 50-caliber rifle. Adding the ancient sabot (sah-bow) cured the problem. The term originally meant peasant's shoe, as far as I can uncover. The sabot was used in many different firearms, including cannons. Essentially, the bore-size sabot is a "cup" into which the undersized bullet is fitted.

Today's sabots are better than ever. One current company, Muzzleloader Magnum Products (MMP), offers a variety of sabots designed and constructed to withstand the higher velocities obtainable in muzzleloaders. Saboted pistol bullets from Hornady, Nosler, Thompson/Center, and other companies, as well as a fine one from Winchester, come ready to load, the sabot included with the package of projectiles. They are extremely effective on big game, especially with the "boiler room" delivery. Remember that the big lead conical is often best directed *into* the shoulder region, rather than behind, where they plow through heavy muscle and even bone. The more readily expanding pistol bullet does its best work when delivered *behind* the shoulder into the heart/lung region.

Copper Conicals

The Barnes Expander-MZ Muzzleloader bullet is made of solid copper, not an alloy, no lead whatsoever. I have tested this bullet "on the real thing" (deer) with positive results. All-copper bullets are not new. Germany had such projectiles in the 1940s, if not earlier. The Barnes no-lead bullet is designed with a huge open nose (hollow-point) to ensure expansion. At the same time, the all-metal projectile retains most of its original weight to enhance penetration. The bullet is loaded in sabots. The one I tested miked out at .451-inch. As a little "test," I fired a number of these bullets in a 50-caliber Traditions in-line muzzleloader. Accuracy was gratifying. Barnes calls its Expander-MZ "The first non-lead projectile designed specifically for use in muzzleloading rifles," designed to upset (mushroom) at impact speeds from 1,900 down to 1,000 fps. Because of this wide range of bullet upset, the bullet works well on deer-sized game especially at close range, as usually is the case from stands and blinds, out to a couple hundred yards or so. Tests in Sam's Bullet Box testing device showed the Expander-MZ retaining just about all of its original 300-grains weight at an impact velocity of 1,500 fps. In keeping with the theme of bullets not entirely dependent upon lead cores alone, there is the T.C.P. bullet from the Buffalo Bullet Company—Total Copper Plated, also fitted into sabots, and advertised as follows: "The T.C.P. bullet has a thin coat of copper plating to assure maximum expansion at all muzzleloader velocities." I had good luck with this bullet, too.

High C Muzzleloader Bullets for Longer Ranges

Recall that C is an abbreviation for ballistic coefficient, a rating that "scores" a bullet's ability to buck the atmosphere. Compared against streamlined modern jacketed bullets, blackpowder conicals always had a comparatively low C rating. This is not necessarily a black mark against more standard blackpowder missiles. Hunters who stalk for close shots, or who frequent thickets and woods where chances at game at over a hundred yards are few and far between, or who do their shooting from stands and blinds, do not need "pointed bullets." Bullets with a high C rating come into play matched up with modern muzzleloaders boasting 200+ yard accuracy. Before going on, however, let's not leave out rifles, like the Whitworth, firing high sectional density bullets of modest C, but with very long-range capability. After all, the southern snipers in the War Between the States used the Whitworth effectively. Regardless, the call sounded for bullets capable of longer-range shooting. A perfect example of an answer to this call is found in several popular bullets of the hour, including the T-Shock XLR from Traditions, with a polymer tip that can poke a hole in whang leather, the handsome Barnes Spit-Fire TMZ, as well as the aerodynamic Hornady SST/ML, a takeoff on the same company's SST modern bullet which has proven highly accurate and worthy on big game. Not to be left out are the sharp-nosed blackpowder bullets of spitzer design from the Northern Pacific Company. But high C bullets are not always jacketed. The Buffalo Bullet Company's SSB (Special Saboted Bullet) proves that.

The C rating of a bullet increases with lower velocities because bullets

Copper-clad and even solid copper bullets have made quite a dent in the blackpowder bullet market. They have delivered good penetration with better-than-expected expansion.

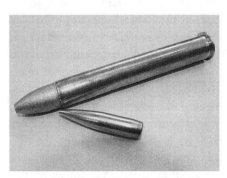
It is possible to build all-lead bullets with relatively high ballistic coefficient. This load from Tenex in the 45-120 Sharps cartridge has a high-profile bullet, especially when compared against the Minie or Maxi bullet—not to degrade either of these deadly lead projectiles.

Three contrasting bullets: far left, a 210-grain 30-caliber Sierra boattail bullet for a modern 30-caliber cartridge, long-range shooting in mind—next, a 12-bore round ball just like the ones used in Africa on big game—and on the right, a Minie-style 58-caliber bullet.

at higher velocity suffer more from the ravages of the atmosphere. Sierra, therefore, gives C data with regard to velocities. For example, the company's 300-grain 45-caliber bullet earns a ballistic coefficient of .206 for velocities of 1,900 fps and up, .211 for velocities from 1601 fps to 1,899, and .245 for velocities of 1,600 fps or lower. Muzzleloader velocities with sharp-pointed bullets weighing 300 grains and up rarely exceed 1,800 fps. When the 375-grain SSB was tested in a 50-caliber Thompson/Center 209/50 Magnum Encore muzzleloader ahead of three Pyrodex Pellets equaling 150-grains volume RS, velocity was chronographed at 1,800 fps. That bullet carries a C of .296, while its sister SSB at 435 grains goes .342. For curiosity more than application, I fired this load at a full 300 yards. While I believe in hunting "blackpowder style" with blackpowder guns, the fact is, from a steady rest these streamlined lead bullets grouped surprisingly. More realistically, sighted three inches high at 100 yards, the SSB bullets with full-throttle loads, are capable of a hold-right-on aim at 200 yards. Incidentally, the boattail base on the SSB is not necessarily a design feature for flattening trajectory. The boattail seats readily into a sabot, and the SSB is fired with a sabot. I can load a sabot down on the powder charge, after which the SSB is run home fully into the sabot. This is not true of all saboted bullets.

Long Range Conicals for Blackpowder Cartridge Rifles

Lyman came to the fore with bullets especially designed to please blackpowder cartridge silhouette shooters, who fire at metallic cutouts at terrific distances. The bullets were named LRHP, standing for Long Range High Performance, two 400-grain examples for the 40-65 Winchester and other 40-caliber blackpowder cartridges, two bullets for the 45-70 Government that will also shoot in the 45-90 Winchester, 45-120 Sharps and other 45-caliber blackpowder cartridges. The 40-caliber

400-grain Schmitzer carries a ballistic coefficient of .352, while the 40-caliber 400-grain Snover goes .435. The 45-caliber 500-grain Schmitzer is .372 and the 45-caliber 535-grain Postell is .402. The 40-caliber bullets run .409-inch diameter, while the 45-caliber bullets go .459-inch diameter. All four bullets were designed to retain sufficient ballistic force at long range to knock over the ram silhouette. With shoulder strikes, these long-range blackpowder cartridge bullets can be counted on to cleanly take big game.

The Barnes Spit-Fire bullet rides the long-range train—sharp polycarbonate tip to aid in retaining velocity and energy. This bullet can be driven at considerable velocity in muzzleloaders allowed heavy powder charges. It weighs 250 grains, is .451-inch in diameter and will be loaded into a 50-caliber sabot.

Conical Effectiveness –– A Sampling of Field Results

A survey of bullets used in harvesting big game shows:

1. Black bear: 250-grain Barnes saboted bullet, 150-grains volume Pyrodex RS powder, Knight 50-caliber rifle.
2. Elk: 300-grain Hornady saboted bullet "charged with Pyrodex," no specific amount given, Knight 50-caliber rifle.
3. Whitetail buck: 355-grain conical lead bullet, 90-grains volume Pyrodex RS, Thompson/Center 50-caliber White Mountain Carbine.
4. Pronghorn antelope: 215-grain round ball, 90-grains GOEX FFg blackpowder, long rifle, name of rifle and exact caliber not supplied.
5. Whitetail buck: 300-grain Barnes bullet, two 50/50 Pyrodex Pellets, 100-grains volume, Knight Disc 50-caliber Rifle.
6. Caribou: 240-grain jacketed pistol bullet, 110-grains volume Pyrodex RS, Knight 50-caliber rifle.
7. Elk: 300-grain Barnes bullet, 100-grains volume Pyrodex RS, Remington Model 700ML 50-caliber muzzleloader.
8. Black bear: 430-grain Maxi-Ball, 90-grains volume GOEX FFg blackpowder, Thompson/Center Fire Hawk 54-caliber rifle.
9. Whitetail buck: 300-grain Barnes bullet, two 50/50 Pyrodex Pellets for 100 grains volume, CVA FireBolt rifle.
10. Musk ox: 325-grain Barnes bullet, 110-grains volume Pyrodex RS Select, 54-caliber Knight Predator rifle.
11. Whitetail buck: 250-grain Nosler, three Pyrodex 50/50 Pellets for 150-grain volume, Thompson/Center Encore 50-caliber rifle.
12. Whitetail buck: 240-grain Sierra hollow-point bullet in sabot, two Pyrodex 50/50 Pellets (100 grains volume), Markesbery 50-caliber rifle.
13. Black bear: 435-grain T/C Maxi Hunter bullet, 80-grains volume Pyrodex RS, T/C Scout 50-caliber rifle.
14. Whitetail buck: 300-grain Barnes bullet, 120-grains GOEX FFg blackpowder, 50-caliber Markesbery 50-caliber rifle.
15. Grizzly: 325-grain Barnes bullet, 110-grains volume Pyrodex RS, Remington Model 700 ML 50-caliber rifle.
16. Black bear: 385-grain Remington lead conical, 110-grains Pyrodex RS, Remington Model 700 ML 50-caliber rifle.
17. Whitetail buck: 370-grain Maxi-Ball, 90-grains volume GOEX FFg blackpowder, T/C 50-caliber Hawken rifle.

How Far was Far?

The buffalo hunters of the 19th century were known for long-range shooting. Chances are good that these reports are accurate. They had the rifles, and conical bullets, to do the job. The rifles were mainly single-shot Sharps and Remingtons (see Chapter 31) chambered for various blackpowder cartridges. While the 45-120 Sharps is often named the favorite of these "buffalo runners," as they were called, that seems improbable since the 45-120 did not gain popularity until the end of the bison-shooting era. The standard lead bullet, according to the definition laid down in this chapter, was most likely the missile of choice among these hunters. Such bullets had pretty good C levels and were capable of deep penetration on the largest quadruped in North America. How far did the buff runners shoot at shaggies? Real far, we think, because bison are dangerous beasts, as proved by the records. Teddy Roosevelt lost a hunting partner when a big bull turned on horse and rider, lifting both into the air, a horn penetrating the hunter's thigh. A record of buffalo/human encounters in Yellowstone National Park includes death. Considering that many of these "buffalo rifles" were scoped, and that these shooters had lots of practice, a range of 300 yards and more is not far-fetched. As a side note, forget the notion that these deadly hunters with their equally deadly rifles "shot off" the bison. Sixty million bison ranged over millions of untracked wilderness. While they sure tried to wipe out the American bison (a tragedy in itself), the buffalo runners did not succeed. As in *War of the Worlds*, however, the microbe did. But that is another story.

Wind Drift Two Ways

From figures in Chapter 16, we know that the wind plays havoc with the round ball, drifting it dramatically off course. The blackpowder conical is also prone to wind drift, as are all bullets regardless of shape or starting velocity.

The conical simply must do better than the poor lead sphere, but it is surprising to learn how poorly *most* of them do in the wind. The problem, in part, is time of flight. Today, super-speed conicals with rocket-ship shape may leave the muzzle at something in the area of 2,500 fps. Most start out slower. The wind has more time to act upon a slower missile than a faster-moving bullet. Maxi-Balls and Minies do not drift as far off the path as round balls, but the difference is minimal in practical shooting. A 50-caliber .490-inch round ball starting at 2,000 fps muzzle velocity is pushed aside 18 inches at a mere 100 yards by a 20 mile-per-hour cross-wind that most of us would call a breeze.

A 50-caliber Maxi-Ball beginning its journey at 1,500 fps drifts about 16 inches at the same distance in the same wind. Higher C bullets fare much better. A 435-grain Buffalo Bullet Company SSB with a C rating of .342 drifts a third as badly in the 20 mile-per-hour crosswind as the Maxi-Ball. Lyman's 45-caliber Postell at a C of .402 moves over even less. All shooters have to learn how to "dope the wind" if they expect to put bullets in the black or the vitals on game. This means guesswork, especially in the hunting field, but with practice and experience, shooters can become proficient in figuring how far to hold off target so the bullet drifts back into the line of sight. At the shooting range, wind flags help, showing direction and to some degree speed. A flag standing directly out sideways suggests a wind in, roughly, the 30 mile-per-hour realm.

Conicals and Pressure

There's nothing tricky about figuring the maximum load for any conical blackpowder projectile. It is the maximum powder charge with that bullet allowed by the maker of the firearm. If a shooter has the least doubt about a maximum charge with a specific conical, he must contact the gun manufacturer, which is a simple matter of dialing a phone, sending a fax, or call-

ing up an email address, or checking a website. *The Gun Digest Blackpowder Loading Manual*, as well as the second edition of Lyman's blackpowder manual, includes much information on proper loads.

Powders and Conicals

Dedicated blackpowder cartridge shooters lean toward larger granulation powders. Whether it has been clearly proved that larger kernels make for better accuracy is open to question. Swiss blackpowder is offered in a 1-1/2 granulation that works well in blackpowder cartridges, while some silhouette shooters like Fg for long-range work with single-shot blackpowder rifles. Across the board, however, FFg and RS are by far the most popular in 50-caliber muzzleloaders designed to shoot conical bullets.

Does shooting conicals raise pressures compared to round balls? *Lyman's Black Powder Handbook, Second Edition*, deals with this in its numerous pressure-tested readings. For example, a 50-caliber round ball in front of 120-grains volume GOEX FFg blackpowder generates 11,500 psi pressure with a .490-inch round ball, 1:60 rate of twist, while a 50-caliber 385-grain lead conical shows a pressure of 19,700 psi from a 1:32 twist bore, same powder brand, granulation, and charge. While the conical load produced significantly more pressure, remember that the load

Big lead conical bullets like this one cast from a 570-grain Lyman Stakebuster mould (actually weighs 600 grains in "pure" lead) deliver a tremendous impact. Fadala's bullet-testing box had its sides blown out from this very bullet.

remained safe. The faster rate of twist has very little to do with the story because of added friction in the bore. Remington brought out a notice in the 21st century that went, "Using any quantity of modern smokeless powder in muzzleloading guns can result in severe injury or death to both the shooter and/or bystanders." Blackpowder or safe substitutes only in blackpowder guns firing conicals. That is the rule.

Twist and Conicals

Chapter 20 clearly reveals that round balls require very little RPS (revolutions per second) to keep them spinning on their axes, while conicals demand more RPS for stabilization. This situation is well taken care of by arms manufacturers who learned—it took a while—that the 1:48 rate of twist was not perfect for every muzzleloader in the world just because Sam and Jake Hawken made rifles that way in the 19th century. Testing for conical bullet stabilization is easy. Shoot at a paper target, preferably set up at 150 to 200 yards. Group size does not matter as long as there are some holes in the target. If all of the holes are round, the conical bullet has been stabilized. If any of the holes are elongated—the shape of a bullet striking sideways—then the conical was tumbling. Sometimes the hole will simply be irregular, rather than round, indicating yawing, which is negative stabilization. A shorter conical of less sectional density may solve the problem. If not, the rifling is probably for a round ball.

Lead revolver bullets like these shown alongside the 210-grain Sierra bullet wrought considerable havoc on the human body in days gone by. Many a bad man (and good man) fell to such bullets.

Conicals in the Revolver

Many different conical bullets are available for the cap 'n' ball revolver, especially created from bullet moulds, but also commercially, as in the Buffalo Bullet Company's 36-, 44-, and 45- caliber round-nose pre-lubed examples. The 36 at .375-inch diameter weighs 124 grains. The 44 at .451-inch diameter weighs out at 180-grains, while the 45 at .457-inch for the Ruger Old Army revolver gains 10 more grains for a 190-grain lead bullet.

The Blackpowder Slug Gun

Bullets for blackpowder slug guns are quite special and uncommon. I know of no commercial examples at this time. The super-heavy bench rifle is carefully loaded with strict uniformity. These rifles were known as a 40-rod gun, because they were counted on for tight groups at that distance—220 yards. Ned Roberts mentions the 40-rod gun in his book, *The Muzzle-Loading Cap Lock Rifle*, page 92: "In times past

many remarkably small groups have been made at 40 rods rest shooting with the most accurate muzzle-loading target rifle, equipped with false muzzle and telescopic sight, using various calibers of cylindro-conoidal bullets. Even at 60 to 100 rods [one rod equals 5.5 yards or 5.03 meters], these rifles and bullets when handled by expert rest shots would make groups that very few of our modern high-power rifles today can equal." Bullets for these bench rest slug guns were often cast in two parts fitted together with a soft base section and harder nose section.

The Sky is the Limit

After the Devel and The Bullet, I have learned to expect anything to pop up in the world of conical bullets for blackpowder guns. The Devel is, by comparison, very much like a full metal jacket bullet as found in the military and on the African safari. However, it has fins that are designed to form a shock wave that forms a good wound channel. The Bullet has a hole all the way through it from nose to base. This idea is not new. W.W. Greener, in the ninth edition of his famous book, shows exactly such a bullet developed in the 19th century. This bullet required a sabot of sorts to prevent gases from flying through the hole without pushing the bullet downbore. Likewise The Bullet. What's next? I don't have a crystal ball, but we can surely expect more conical bullets of high C ratings with sharp synthetic tips in the nose.

chapter 18

THE CLOTH PATCH (AND PAPER-PATCHED CONICAL)

The cloth patch is a vital part of the round ball load chain, in spite of the fact that it is not a gasket in terms of sealing hot expanding gases behind the spherical projectile. These patches are cut from pure Irish linen, 0.013-inch thickness, a very high grade patch material.

If you want to see a blackpowder purist turn green, suddenly speaking in tongues as if he just came down from the Tower of Babel, just tell him that his beloved cloth patch is not a gasket sealing hot gasses behind the round ball. I was at the entrance to a western rendezvous when a buckskinner on horse, who was in charge of entry, glared at me. "I know who you are," he said. "You're that self-proclaimed blackpowder expert who came up with the notion that patches aren't gaskets.

Everybody knows the round ball patch was invented to seal gasses behind the round ball!" He wasn't kidding, as verified by his carotid arteries bulging at the neck. Love of tradition is admirable when tradition means keeping the best and changing the rest. However, casting a blind eye on verified information is foolhardy. No piece of common cloth, regardless of toughness or close weave, ever created an infallible barrier against a burning powder charge. Interestingly, the super duties attending the cloth

round ball patch are overlooked. If the patch is not a gasket, then what is it good for? A heck of a lot.

The Round Ball Patch in the Beginning

Typical of shooting history in general—who invented the first envelope (jacketed bullet? How about blackpowder?)—nobody knows who came up with wrapping an undersized lead ball in some form of patch. Sometimes an American shooter gets the credit.

The round ball patch reaches back in time. These patches are round; however, square-cut patches also function as a go-between for the round ball and the walls of the bore.

John G. Dillin, author of that fine book, *The Kentucky Rifle*, published in 1924, wrote, "Here in America, balls were cast smaller than the bore and were enveloped in a 'patch' of leather or cloth to prevent contact with the barrel. The patch enabled Americans to load faster, and to fire longer without cleaning, and to outshoot all others of that time. It was the distinguishing difference between the American rifle and those of Europe." Early Americans were using patches, all right. But the idea of wrapping a piece of cloth, sometimes leather, around a lead ball to take up windage in the bore came from Europe, and it was one of man's better shooting ideas.

Dillin believed the patch was a "master stroke," as he put it, and "the last link forged in the chain of evolution which brought forth a distinctly American rifle." An interesting book titled *Espingarda Perfeyta* (The Perfect Gun) came along in 1718. The Portuguese author, J. Joav, wrote, "Others made barrels with rifling inside, some with more, and others with less rifling, all of them deep and twisted in the form of a spiral. These were loaded by putting the bullet in a little piece of leather of a thin glove, folded only once, dipped in oil, and thus it was pushed down to the bottom in such a manner that the bullet may not lose its roundness."

Simple range-shooting shows, if not perfectly, at least convincingly, that a round ball closely fit to bore size is more accurate than a greatly undersized round ball, no matter how tight the patch on the latter. A well-fit ball, I surmise, has a better chance of gaining full benefit from the rifling than one relying on the patch alone to translate rotation. The undersized bullet, round or conical, was quite likely born on the battlefield, where quick reloading was vital. Imagine the Tennessee sharpshooters at the Battle of New Orleans shooting once or twice, and then having to hammer the next ball down a fouled bore. Hunters facing a dangerous animal, such as Old Ephraim, the grizzly bear, would also welcome a fast second or even third shot. Even at the target range, repeat loading without undue force is welcome. Simply put, the undersized bullet offered a better chance for repeat shots. But for accuracy, it had to spin on its axis. The simple cloth patch took care of this. There is some obturation of a soft lead projectile caused by a slight foreshortening at the time of powder detonation. If this concept is accurate, it follows that the bullet "widens out" a little bit to better fit the bore. So the patch itself is not entirely responsible for rotation. But we know the patch does translate rotational value from rifling to bullet because picked-up bullets downrange do not bear rifling marks, and yet we know they were spinning on their way from muzzle to target. I have tested bare, but well-fitted round balls (never do this in regular shooting) to find out would happen. Naked lead balls that fit closely to the bore can achieve modest accuracy. They were used eons ago. *Warning:* There is danger in not using the patch. See why below.

William Cotton Oswell was one of the first professional ivory hunters. He liked to ride a horse hot after pachyderms. When he got close, he fired a huge round ball into the fleeing beast. More shots meant more elephants, which in turn provided more ivory, which translated to more money. William often carried a smoothbore. No rifling to gather fouling meant more shots before having to clean the gun. His method: reach into

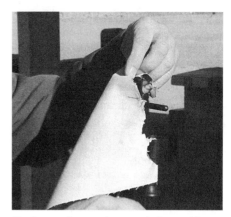

Cutting patches on the muzzle is an old practice that continues to work well. Here, a large piece of patch material is simply laid over the muzzle of the rifle in preparation for cutting.

Because this is a target rifle and a tight ball/patch marriage is desired, the ball is seated with a plastic protector and driven past the muzzle with a wooden mallet.

At this point the ball is driven past the muzzle, the patch material now firmly surrounding the lead sphere. Now the excess patch material is cut away at the muzzle with a special patch knife—or any knife.

The Cloth Patch (And Paper-Patched Conical) ✳ **151**

a pouch for a fistful of "coarse" blackpowder, drop the haphazard "charge" downbore, roll an undersized ball—literally—down the bore, provide for ignition, and blast away. Accuracy was akin to wishful thinking, but at 20 paces, Oswell's patchless lead balls found the mark regularly. This sort of sloppy loading worked for the old ivory hunter, but it is dangerous and results in lousy bullet grouping. Modern blackpowder shooters are not satisfied with groups that look like they were produced by a shotgun. The demand is close clusters on the target, which also promotes confidence in the hunting field. Today's shooters are often amazed at witnessed groups made with old-time muzzleloaders shooting patched round balls. But it happened then. And it continues to happen today.

The Amazing Properties of the Cloth Round Ball Patch

Accuracy

The patch is responsible for full rotation of the round ball because it is the go-between in the bore. Because we find no rifling marks on round lead balls dug out of the butts at the shooting range, it is safe to conclude that those balls were spinning on their axes. We know that smoothbores do not produce gilt-edged accuracy. Spinning not only keeps a ball rotating through the air on its axis,

it also averages flaws on that common axis. Well-cast round balls are not lopsided. Swaged round balls from Speer and Hornady are even more homogenous. However, it takes very little imperfection to throw a missile off course. That's why spinning is paramount to accuracy, even with the most precise round balls available.

The Cloth Patch is Not a Gasket

Accuracy with the patched ball is duly noted, but before going into other attributes of the patch, the gasket notion requires mention. Ed Yard gave the lie to the gasket theory in his *Gun Digest* article, "The Round Patched Ball and Why They Used It," in the 1980 edition. "The inherent inefficiency of the patch as a bore seal was the big factor... of the loss [in pressure]," wrote Mr. Yard. "So we find that no patch really seals," wrote the man who studied patches with a pressure gun. "Based on the test information presented here and the tabulated data appended, the major function and the practical effect of the cloth patch on a round lead ball in the American rifle is to spin a loose-fitting and easily-loaded ball to attain real accuracy. It does not really seal the bore," Yard concluded.

I put a chronograph to work on the problem, seeing what would happen to velocity if a naked round ball were fired across the screens. **This was for test**

Although the cloth patch is not a gasket, it remains extremely important in round ball shooting. Here, a patched round ball is delivered downrange with exceptional accuracy that would be impossible if the ball was not properly secured in the bore with the patch taking up windage.

purposes only. An unpatched ball can ride up the bore, creating a dangerous short-start condition. This little investigation was not a bona fide experiment. It was too imprecise for that, but it was a worthwhile demonstration. Velocity with a well-fitted ball and no patch at all was virtually the same as velocity with a patched ball. If the patch was serving as a gasket, its use would have increased velocity. Badly undersized round balls were aided in muzzle velocity by patching, but further testing convinced me that this was due to delaying the ball downbore for obturation, more than an actual gas seal.

A high-speed camera stopped the action at the rifle's muzzle. Photographically stopping the round bullet and patch as they emerged from the muzzle gave a powerful clue that the patch was not working as a gasket. The patched round ball was not first out of the muzzle. Smoke came first, followed by the patched ball. Obviously, gas had blown through the cloth patch, escaping through rifling grooves. If the patch were a true gasket, the projectile would have exited the muzzle first, perhaps with a little evidence of blow-by, but certainly not with such a definite blow of smoke

This shows the patched ball seated just beyond the muzzle, the excess patch material having been sliced away.

The ball is driven partway down the bore using a special short starter and a wooden mallet. Both short starter and mallet are special tools for this particular target rifle to ensure a very tight fit in the bore for the patched ball.

out in front of the ball. This is what we see with modern bullets coming from the muzzle—the bullet first, and then evidence of gas behind it. If a gasket, as stated in the dictionary, is: "A ring, disk, or plate of packing to make a joint or closure watertight or gastight," then the cloth patch is not a gasket, because it does not make the bore gas-tight

Safety and the Ball Patch

Warning: under no circumstances should round balls be fired without a patch. That was done only for test purposes under controlled conditions. The potential problem of the short-start requires that the topic be brought to the surface. Well, here it is again. The cloth patch wrapped around that round bullet insists that the projectile remain firmly down upon the powder charge in the bore. A properly fitted ball patch precludes the bullet from riding upbore. In a double-barrel rifle or a shotgun firing round ball, in spite of the holding power of the patch, it is wise to ensure that the unfired projectile has remained in the breech where it belongs. And odds are it has when the patch creates a tight fit around the bullet. I have tested for this with a ramrod, to see if after a full day of hiking the hills a patched ball remained snugly down in the breech. So far, the results are 100 percent positive, and that reason alone is sufficient to put a golden crown on the round ball patch. But there is more.

Consistent Pressure on the Powder Charge

If it's true, as we believe, that blackpowder functions better when reasonably compressed, then the patch serves another important function, not only retaining the round ball down in the breech for safety reasons, but maintaining a constant and specific pressure on the powder charge. The patch itself is responsible for *maintaining* this constant pressure put upon a powder charge after using the Kadooty or other method of ensuring the same pressure for every bullet seated. Standard deviation is a measure of variance that we rely on to show uniformity in a load.

Smoke precedes the exit of the patched ball, even when the fit to the bore is tight, as revealed with a high-speed camera. Regardless, the patch is vital to round ball accuracy and must never be eliminated from the round ball load chain.

Top-grade chronographs, such as the Oehler Model 35P Proof used for this work, automatically provide standard deviation figures in fps. Tests with varying ramrod pressures showed higher standard deviation figures than when ramrod pressure was consistent.

The Patch as a Go-Between

Windage is the distance in the bore on either side of an undersized bullet. The patch takes up that space. It is a go-between of rifling to projectile. We're sure that round balls do rotate in flight, and that this rotation is important to accuracy. The go-between patch, as related in accuracy notes above, does that job.

No Bore Leading

This particular attribute of the round ball patch could be challenged, because muzzleloader bullets at normal blackpowder velocities cause very little leading of the bore to begin with. However, supposing that a soft round bullet could deposit a little bit of itself in the bore when fired at higher velocities in the 2,000 fps domain, the patch surely would prevent that from happening. After all, the patched lead bullet does not come into contact with the bore at all.

Reservoir for Lube, Solvent, and Modern Chemicals

The cloth patch retains lubrication perfectly for ease of loading. It also retains various solvents, from saliva to the most advanced chemicals of the day, which in turn keep fouling soft,

thereby allowing more shots in a row before bore swabbing is necessary.

Bore Cleaning

In a way, the patch is also responsible for cleaning the bore of the firearm from shot to shot. When a lubed round ball patch is pushed downbore, it naturally cleans up some of the fouling within that bore. By using a modern patch lube that also has solvent properties, this factor becomes more prominent. The shooting patch now becomes a cleaning patch, albeit it never takes the place of proper cleaning between shooting strings.

A Few More Patch Facts

Reading Patches

Recovering patches after shooting is no problem. Usually, the spent patch is found on the ground not far in front of the muzzle of the rifle or pistol, often within 10 or 20 paces. It's a simple matter of looking for the patch, picking it up, and then reading the signs on that patch. As stated above, the patch is vital to safe and accurate round ball shooting. But it must remain somewhat intact to accomplish its intended functions. The patch has two enemies. The first is the rifling itself, specifically the lands. The second comes from the blast furnace fire of burning powder charge. The first problem results in a *cut* patch. The second problem results in a *blown patch*. The artist's conception of the perfect fired patch is just that—make-believe—you know, the patch with the black cross dead-center. That's not what we're looking for. A dark spot indicating contact with fire is the norm, but can also be avoided with hornet nest material.

The Cut Patch

The raised portion of the rifling, the lands rather than grooves, can cause a cut patch. Since the patch suffered the ravages of traveling the bore at possibly 2,000 feet per second, cutting may not always stand out clearly. Is the patch cut or burned? Here is how to find out. But first, a warning.

Warning: use only an unloaded firearm for this test.

1. Run a patched ball downbore **without a powder charge** in the firearm.

2. Do not seat the ball firmly into the breech. Use the ramrod as a gauge to determine when the patched ball is about an inch from the bottom of the bore. If a patched ball is run firmly down into the empty breech, it may get hung up there.

3. After the patched ball is seated in the empty bore, attach a screw to the end of a loading rod. *Use a muzzle protector with a screw to prevent damage to the important crown.*

4. Rotate the screw into the lead round ball to gain a good purchase on it and then withdraw that ball from the muzzle.

Study the ball. It should be free of engraving. If the ball itself is marred by the rifling, that may indicate the ball is too large for the bore and caused the patch to be cut. This condition is rare and occurs mainly with odd-sized bores. Now study the patch. It may show marks from contact with the lands, but it should not be sliced. If it is sliced, the culprit is sharp lands, since there was no exploding powder charge to harm it, nor a high-speed dash in the bore. There are two possible remedies for sharp lands. The first is lapping the bore with cleaning patches dressed with rouge or lapping compound, which can be ordered from a gun store. The second remedy is: keep on shooting. Patches flying through the bore at high speed will burnish the lands smooth in time.

The Blown Patch

This condition is indicated by holes in the patch indicating where hot gas rushed through the rifling grooves, burning the cloth patch itself. Sometimes a blown patch simply seems tattered, especially at the edges, without neat little holes. Either way, a blown patch is easily remedied. A reader in his 70s reported, many years ago, that his grandfather cured blown patches with hornet nest material. That's right, the stuff that makes up the ordinary hornet nest. The gray paper-like nesting material is a puzzle. It burns readily when touched with a match, but downbore, it works like asbestos. It's easy to use, too. After pouring the appropriate powder charge downbore, two or three thin sheets of hornet nest material follow, run home right on top of the powder charge using a ramrod or loading rod with a jag on the end. Just be sure the material does remain somewhat centered in the bore. Now the patched ball is loaded normally. The hornet nest material forms a barrier between the powder charge and the patch, yet it is so thin that it does not disrupt the work of the patch. I have yet to pick up a blown patch that was protected by hornet nest material. Rather, the patch usually retains its whiteness.

While I am a believer in patch integrity, I also recognize that torn or blown patches do not always destroy accuracy. Apparently, a partially-damaged patch can still serve its intended purposes. Also, I don't find patch problems in target loads very often, no doubt because of the powder charge being reduced, sometimes greatly, from a full-blown hunting charge of powder. However, in some cases accuracy was definitely improved by lapping a bore or shooting it smooth, to round off sharp lands, or by safeguarding the patch with hornet nest material. This seems especially true when patches are both cut and blown, which is possible. If a round ball-shooting rifle or pistol continues to shoot inaccurately after cut or blown patch problems are corrected, then obviously there is another gremlin at work, possibly a badly undersized ball, a damaged bore (especially the crown of the muzzle), and in rarer cases these days, an ill-made barrel.

Patches and Bore Wear

Lucky is the shooter who gets to the range so often that he or she wears a barrel out from firing so many patched round balls through it. We should all have that problem. There is no doubt that cloth patches do burnish the bore. How many shots are required to destroy the accuracy of the barrel is up for grabs. That would depend upon many factors, including the steel used to make the barrel in the first place, as well as lubes and patch material. There is no way to prevent bore lapping as the cloth patch rips through at two grand or so. However, it'll be a while before a rifle becomes a smoothbore. And I myself don't worry about it.

Patch Materials

The important work a patch does is clear, but it cannot accomplish its duties if made of flimsy material from the ragbag. Commercial patches are readily available and normally made from strong, close-weave cloth. Denim has been used successfully. It's sold in various thicknesses in fabric stores. But pillow or mattress ticking is more reliable. Pure Irish linen is extremely good, also located in fabric shops. It's very strong as well as reliably consistent in thickness. (I have a sheet of pure Irish linen cloth that "mikes out" at 0.013-inch thickness all over.) Commercial patches are ready to go, but Irish linen or ticking must be washed thoroughly to get rid of *sizing*, which is a starch-like substance impregnating the cloth to improve its appearance in the store. Sizing may lay down a coating in the bore of the muzzleloader. The cloth is washed normally, either by hand or in a washing machine, and then rinsed completely and allowed to dry.

A bullet is introduced to the false muzzle.

The conical projectile can only line up square to the bore with the false muzzle in place. The base of the bullet will force the two strips of paper to line up perfectly along the shank of the bullet.

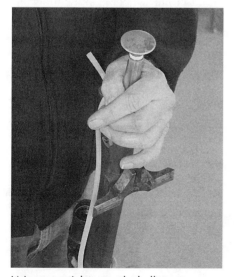

Using a special starter, the bullet, now paper-patched, is driven partially downbore.

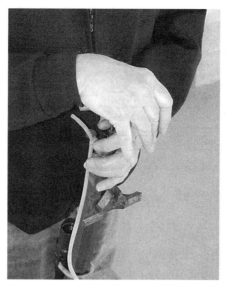

The paper-patched bullet is now fully seated upon the powder charge. The paper on the bullet serves as a go-between shank of bullet and rifling. The paper in this type of patching will fall away, unlike paper-patched bullets with paper firmly attached.

Here is a 45-caliber hexagonal bullet for the Whitworth rifled musket. It will be paper-patched.

This illustration shows how the paper was wrapped around the 45-caliber hexagonal Whitworth bullet.

Here is the 45-caliber Whitworth hexagonal bullet showing its paper-patched base, as well as two patched and one unpatched bullets, below.

Patch Configuration and Size

Patches come round just because. Square patches work just as well as round ones. Therefore, if a shooter wishes to simply cut appropriately sized square patches from washed, rinsed, and dried ticking or Irish linen, that's fine. On the other hand, round patches are the rule, just because history says so, and they do look nicer. These can also be cut by hand, especially with a template. An ideal template is the top off a bottle. Bottles come in so many sizes that there is bound to be one just right for the desired patch diameter. For example, the cap from a salad dressing bottle proved perfectly sized for a 50- or 54-caliber round ball. Removed from the bottle, the cap is placed directly on the cloth, a lead pencil used to trace around it, and there's a perfectly marked circle to cut out with sharp scissors. Pre-cut, pre-lubed patches are handy in the hunting field or on the shooting range. They keep well, clean and uncontaminated, in zip-lock sandwich bags or throat lozenge hinged metal cans. Another way to make nice patches is with a patch cutter. (See Chapter 4 for a photo of one.) This is essentially a punch with a sharp circle edge. The cloth patch material is placed on a hard wood surface, hammer blows on top of the cutter whacking out patch after patch. There are also patch cutters that use sharp rotating blades. I have purchased both types, punch and cutter, from Dixie Gun Works. As for size, a correct patch totally covers the round ball so that no part of the ball comes in contact with rifling.

Paper-Patching Conical Bullets

A shooter owned a special English rifle, but could not find the correct bullet to fit the bore, although he had located brass from which he could form proper cases. He solved the problem by patching slightly undersized jacketed bullets so that they did make full contact with the rifling. Once patched, the bullets worked perfectly in this unique rifle. Much more prominent, however, is paper-patching lead conical bullets, especially for blackpowder cartridge rifles. The paper patch serves at least three functions. It acts as a bearing surface for the rifling, very much like a cloth ball patch goes between round ball and rifling. Instead of the rifling biting into the shank of the conical lead bullet, it engraves the paper around it. The paper patch is also wrapped under the base of the bullet, which can save the important bullet base from damage. We know that damaged conical bases can harm accuracy. The paper patch also prevents bore leading, since the paper, not the bullet itself, makes contact with the rifling. Paper-patching conical bullets is not a panacea. It does not improve accuracy or function in all cases. But when it does work, it works admirably.

Various means of paper-patching bullets are available. Randolph S. Wright describes an excellent process in his information booklet, *The Paper Patched Bullet*, printed by Montana Armory. The author shows how to determine the correct length of a patch for a given projectile by wrapping the bullet with a strip of paper that rolls tightly around it three times, then cutting through all three layers with a sharp tool, such as an X-Acto knife blade. When the paper is unrolled, it has three slits. Measuring between the two farthest-apart slits, then subtracting 1/32-inch from this measurement, provides the correct length of the bullet patch, which can be adjusted later if necessary so that the patch laps around the projectile exactly twice, but no more than twice. The paper patch should be shaped like a rhomboid parallelogram. This particular shape allows the ends to match up at an angle to the bullet. The ends of the rhomboid parallelogram are cut at about a 30- to 35-degree angle. The bullet is wrapped with a double thickness of paper patching, since the patch is cut to go around the bullet almost, but not quite, two times. This means that the ends of the paper patch do not rest exactly one above the other. Naturally, the ends cannot touch, because one end is wrapped underneath, so the two ends never meet. The ends do not match up exactly, a slight space existing between them when the paper patch is cut to the correct length. This also means that the two ends of the paper patch *never overlap*, which is important. Also, the wrap of the paper patch must be in the *opposite* direction of the rifling twist. In this manner, the rotation of the projectile in the bore will not unroll the paper patch, as it might if the patch were rolled in the same direction as the rifling twist.

The process of wrapping a bullet with a paper patch is not involved, but it does take practice. The parallelogram-shaped paper patch is started with one corner located about where the bullet shank begins to taper toward the nose of the projectile. A paper thickness of .0025-inch increases a 45-caliber bullet diameter by .01-inch (one caliber), because the paper goes around the bullet twice, and that increases "both sides" of the bullet shank by .05-inch. As Wright points out, this turns a .448-inch bullet into a .458-inch diameter after paper patching. Correct paper patching material is 100 percent rag or cotton content; essentially high-grade stationery that can be purchased at an office supply house or from Montana Armory.

Well-practiced paper-patch wrappers use the dry method of wrapping. This is best because the paper falls away after it works, whereas wet-patched paper may stick to the bullet downrange, possibly compromising accuracy. Excess paper extending downward at the base of a flat-based bullet can be "tucked inward" to cover most of the projectile's base. Excess paper at the base of a hollow-base bullet can be twisted and pushed into the cavity. This is a quick look at the fascinating world of paper-patching lead bullets for use in blackpowder cartridge rifles. Those interested in more information should read carefully into Wright's manuscript, which is only nineteen pages long.

Simple that it is, the cloth patch surrounding the round ball performs many important functions. Paper-patching conical bullets can also improve performance.

FLAME OF LIFE—IGNITION

Consider the serious side of ignition. A rhino is unhappy about a hunter disturbing his afternoon nap. He decides to cause trouble. The muzzle-loader does not "go off." Not a good thing.

Just as there are blackpowder gremlins lurking about the shooting range, so are there similar monsters hiding out in the hunting field waiting to foil the best intentions of the downwind shooter. The most heinous of these creatures is Mr. Misfire. I should know. This monster causes failure of the gun to "go off," and the problem does not have to occur often to leave an indelible picture in the memory bank. I have told before of the worst misfire of my hunting career, a big elk, a royal (six-by-six) bull with bases like a weightlifter's forearms and branching tines rivaling pine tree limbs. He was but 12 paces away, called in by a man who "talks elk" fluently. I centered the German silver blade in the first step of the rear sight, set the trigger, and Ftttt! Nothing. Mr. Misfire had done his mischief, in cahoots with Colorado rain. A 235-grain round ball would have cen-

tered the neck. I know because after the hammer fell, the sights were still perfectly aligned on target. The bull stood for moment, and then ambled away. He must have known he did not have to run from a hunter whose rifle was no more effective than a broomstick. I have to admit that if I had one of the almost-not-a-muzzleloader in-line or outer-line modern rifles, that bull would have been mine. He also would have been mine had I not forgotten my rain-proofing kit back home in Wyoming.

Ignition is to the rifle what a starter is to a vehicle. No starter, no go. When a blackpowder gun, any gun from a 31-caliber pistol to a 4-bore rifle, fails to fire, the shooter has little more in his grasp than an assembly of useless parts. The loss is especially felt when that shot may have taken first place at a contest, or when a big-game animal of harvestable proportion is gone forever.

Shooters of modern firearms are not familiar with misfires and hang-fires. It's a matter of an enclosed cartridge case versus the "open" system of the typical front-loader. In that essentially watertight case rests not only the powder, but also a well-seated primer, sometimes sealed with a touch of clear nail polish. The bullet seals off the other end. Fixed ammo, as opposed to loose components loaded by hand just before the shot, can suffer from a good drowning, but the reader need ask but one question; "When was the last time a cartridge failed to fire in my Winchester Model 94 deer rifle?" The answer for most of us will be—never. I've had old 22-rimfire ammo fail, but it was fodder found in an attic, probably stored when the president of the country owned a buggy whip. Knowing of the misfire/hang-fire dilemma in blackpowder shooting, especially with regard to muzzleloaders, gun designers went to work on the problem, the solution being nearly waterproof modern muzzleloaders today. Regardless, the wise blackpowder shooter wants to know about ignition.

Early Ignition

Smoldering rope, punk, or match of some sort was the first igniter of "gunpowder." The ancient matchlock relied on this brand of fire. Before the matchlock, the firestick was touched off with heated irons, smoldering coals, slow matches, hot wires, and other sources of heat. Hot curls of metal, which are in effect nothing more than bits of fire, remained an igniter throughout snaphaunce and flintlock history. The concept of crashing a flint against something that in turn emits spark or flame was born in prehistory. Lock the flint into the jaws of a hammer; allow it to come down hard against a piece of metal with a scraping blow, and the result is—you have a flintlock. But you don't have to use flint. The wheellock (see Chapter 2) did a fine job of igniting gunpowder with pyrites. In turn, it takes no great backward leap in history to arrive at the conclusion that early shooters developed fine-grain powder for more surefire ignition. We still rely

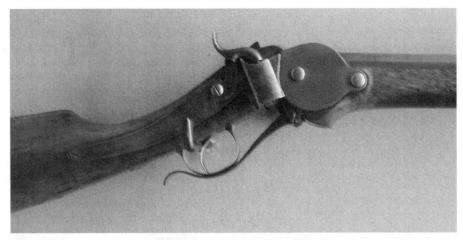

Many different sources of ignition were invented over time, including tube locks, pill locks, tape primers, and more—until the advent of the percussion cap, forerunner of the modern primer, came on the scene—and even that was not a total takeover from the flintlock.

on FFFFg (4F) as our main pan powder in flintlocks. There is also Elephant brand FFFFFg. I tried it only once in an original 42-caliber flintlock rifle loaned by the late Professor Charles Keim, Alaskan master guide who got me started on the charcoal-burning trail. And it worked fine.

The Tube Lock

The tube lock was essentially a hammer gun. It's what the hammer hit that made it interesting—a small tube filled with fulminate of mercury, an impact-sensitive explosive that made its

way into modern primers. The falling hammer crushed the tube, the resulting explosion creating a flash to ignite powder in the breech. We might suppose the tube lock to be the forerunner of the percussion cap, but gun history says not. The tube lock was patented in 1816 by one of the leading gunmakers of the era, Joseph Manton. We don't know the exact birthday of the percussion cap, but it is generally dated *before* Manton's tube lock. Reverend Alexander John Forsyth gets the credit, although it may not be deserved. The Scottish clergyman apparently played with fire, the result being a patent dated April 11 of 1807 for his invention. Melvin M. Johnson, Jr., and Charles T. Haven praise Forsyth, but these two experts, authors of *Ammunition*, claim that the clergyman worked on percussion sensitive compounds *starting* in 1807 and running through 1816. The authors also note that the percussion cap was not in military use until the period between 1840 and 1845. We do know that the flintlock was not supplanted by the percussion cap even after its wide acceptance in 1845.

The Pill Lock

The pill lock precedes both tube lock and percussion cap. The pill itself was a tiny pellet filled with what literature calls simply "detonating powder." A hammer fell upon the pill, setting it

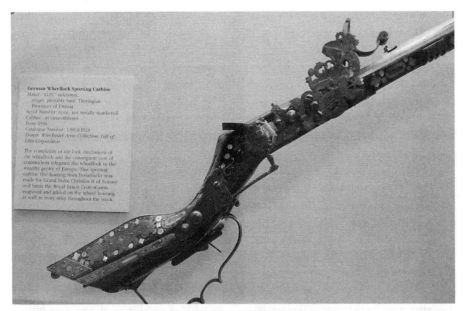

Early ignition was not entirely foolproof, but on the other hand neither was it a matter of luck. The guns "went off" quite regularly, as proved by casualty figures in early wars where guns were used.

Experimentation advanced ignition design from smoldering rope to various methods of causing sparks to ignite pan powder for a hot flash into the breech.

Down Under, so well acted by Tom Selleck, has seen a long-range Sharps in action. The Sharps also remains hot in the blackpowder silhouette game (see Chapter 31). Disc primers were tiny copper discs launched forward one at a time by the action of the hammer. Each disc contained fulminate of mercury, which exploded when struck by the hammer nose. The sparks emanating from the exploded disk flew into the breech to ignite the powder therein.

Many Others

Those interested in pursuing the history of ignition further will find plenty of information. Students will learn about the Maynard cartridge and Burnside cartridge, as well as pin-fires and rimfires and much more. But for us—on to the percussion cap!

The Percussion Cap

Patents help, but not all great inventions were so protected. As previously mentioned, Rev. Forsyth is generally credited with the percussion cap. But not everyone agrees. Captain Joshua Shaw of Philadelphia is noted in certain arms histories as father of the percussion cap, his work dating back to 1814. The claim holds water, but regardless of who came up with the cap, the concept of installing fulminate within a small metal container (cup) was ingenious. It changed shooting forever, because the modern primer is no more than an updated percussion

off, which in turn exploded fire into the powder charge in the breech. Once again, we're dealing with percussion-sensitivity. French chemists were ordered by Napoleon in the era of 1797 to 1804 to find a substitute for saltpeter in gunpowder, because the General required a lot of blackpowder for his style of artillery warfare. They failed, but in their search came up with fulminate of mercury and oxymuriate of potash (chlorate of potash). Forsyth, apparently, became interested in these compounds, using at least the first in his percussion cap. Apparently, Forsyth experimented with percussion-sensitive compounds first in the pan of the flintlock by mixing with powder. It did not go well, the powerful compounds literally blowing powder out of the pan rather than promoting better ignition.

The Tape Primer

While a clergyman gets credit for the percussion cap, the invention of the tape primer in 1845 goes to a dentist, Edward Maynard. Typical of gun history, there remain questions about exact dates. The purpose of exploring early ignition is to build our understanding of how blackpowder guns fire today. That's why we look at this outdated device. To get an idea of how the tape primer worked, envision of a roll of "toy caps." The tape primer was essentially two strips of tape with interspaced fulminate pods lodged between these strips. The tape was fed over the top of the nipple mechanically by a ratchet. Each time the hammer was eared back into battery (firing position), the tape advanced to offer a new priming pod under the hammer nose. The falling hammer in turn whacked the tape and—pop! Remaining was a means of delivering the fire from the detonation into a waiting powder charge in a breech. I have no personal knowledge of the tape primer, but have to wonder about how much fire it produced.

Disc Primers

Arms historians think the disc primer came along in 1852. While the date could be a bit off, we do know the inventor. He was Christian Sharps, whose name not only survives, but thrives today in his single-shot blackpowder falling block rifle. Anyone who has enjoyed the fine movie, *Quigley*

No one knows for certain who invented the percussion cap, but as simple as the cap is, it still required knowledge of chemical reaction harnessed into a little cup that fit upon a device to deliver a spark into the breech. These percussion caps are safeguarded in a Tedd Cash cap box.

cap. The percussion cap today remains very much like those popular in the 19th century. Certainly the concept is identical, even if body materials differ. Percussion-sensitive fulminates are the fire. The key is "percussion-sensitive," hence percussion cap. Whack the cap. The fulminate explodes, producing flame. Deliver the flame to a powder charge and you have—ignition! The nipple completed the picture. It not only retained the cap on its cone. It also incorporated a vent, which directed flame into a channel; that channel in turn leading to the breech.

Hot Caps

A good cap had to be consistent, providing similar duration of flame from one to the next, plus emitting a spark lasting long enough to reach the powder charge every time. A proper percussion cap became a precise detonator with specific repeatable and reliable properties. The big push for years was the hot cap; "hot" referring to one that threw a powerful flame. But early hot caps were not always reliable. Those testing the situation decided that a "cool" cap could be just as effective as a hot one, perhaps much more so. The ideal cap delivered just enough spark to bring about ignition. It did not explode too violently, which could actually cause it to "blow up" on the cone of the nipple, rather than shooting a flame down into the nipple vent. In a sense, the too-hot cap could all but "blow itself out." It went Crack! on the nipple, flame seeming to spatter, for lack of a better term, rather than channeling under control through the vent and into the powder charge. Also, an overly powerful cap was subject to excessive metal debris that might clog the nipple, impeding flame progress when the next cap was fired. This situation could cause a misfire, or at least a hang-fire. We now have hot caps that throw the same flame every time. They are the best the world of muzzle-loading has ever seen, providing a sustained spark, rather than a short-lived

blast. Because the term "magnum" has such appeal, CCI attached this handle to one of its caps. However, the CCI Magnum percussion cap is not to be confused with "hot" caps of the past. This cap provides consistent flame with good duration. The same is true of Remington and RWS percussion caps—they're hot enough, but the "flame' is under control.

The Non-Corrosive Cap

A non-corrosive cap with black-powder seems to make no sense. Why worry about a little soot from the cap when about half of the charge becomes fouling anyway? As this is written, there remain a few corrosive type caps on the market. They are fine for general plinking and informal target shooting. But I recommend non-corrosive caps for serious work. The non-corrosive percussion cap's main advantage comes in during the before-loading popping of caps to clean nipples of lingering oil, ensuring a clear channel all the way from cone of nipple into the breech. A corrosive cap can deposit "smudge" in the nipple vent, nipple seat, even the breech area, rather than cleaning these spots. The non-corrosive cap may also leave a bit of itself behind, even to the point of clogging the vent of the nipple. But that is easily cured with a pipe cleaner or nipple pick before putting a fresh cap on for firing.

The non-corrosive cap was created not to prevent corrosion during or even after firing, but especially in firing caps in order to clear nipples, after which the residue from a corrosive cap could cause a problem.

The Waterproof Cap

Some caps withstand moisture better than others, right down to running water over them. This is easy to test. At the range, dampen a cap and see what happens to ignition. The most waterproof cap in the world will fail when soaked, meaning we should call them "water-resistant" rather than waterproof. But these caps do tend to pop more reliably than non-waterproofed caps under the stress of high moisture. On a hunting trip especially, the so-called "lacquered" cap is worthy. How to tell? Already stated—dampen a few caps at the range and see what happens. Since torture testing is part of my work, I have been known to douse caps in the kitchen sink under running water. Wet. Shake 'em out and put them on paper toweling to dry. Give them a try. Some caps are, if not waterproof, certainly highly water-resistant. This fact, however, will not save the day when a firearm is subjected to considerable rain or wet snow.

Cap Sizes and Construction

Percussion caps are not created equally in terms of output, duration of spark, constancy, and other particulars. They also come in various sizes. The No. 11 percussion cap is a standard for most rifle, pistol, and shotgun nipples, while a No. 10 is better on some revolvers. A shooting friend

Waterproofing caps makes them water-resistant, if not entirely waterproof (as in a good soaking). Many caps today, including musket caps, do have some type of waterproofing.

The musket cap was invented to provide more spark. And it does. Musket caps are usually associated with muskets, but can also be used with nipples that replace the No. 11 with the musket cap. The reverse is equally true. There are nipples that convert muskets to No. 11.

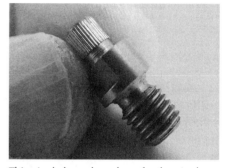

This nipple has a large base for the nipple seat but the cone of the nipple is sized to take a No. 11 percussion cap.

There is little difference between the smooth-side percussion cap and the ribbed. The ribbed design is for better fragmentation on the cone of the nipple so the spent cap will fall away more readily. However, the smooth-bodied cap usually falls away as well.

complained, "Why don't they make more No. 10 caps? No. 11s just fall off the nipple [of the revolver.]" The cure is: change nipples or look further for No. 10 caps. If a No. 11 does not fit the cone of the nipple; accuse the nipple, not the cap. Minor variations in cap sizes from brand to brand have existed over time. For example, a No. 11 cap in Brand A may be identical in size to a No. 12 cap in Brand B. But manufacturers have listened, and this situation is now corrected. Measuring with a micrometer, a regular CCI No. 11 cap went 0.1775-inch. The CCI Magnum No. 11 cap measured .01775-inch. An RWS No. 11 cap was 0.177-inch across. A Remington No. 11 cap was 0.185-inch across—all very similar in size, which has not always been the case. Another percussion cap criterion is cup construction, ribbed or smooth. Both work equally well. I contend that the ribbed cap style came about to promote easy extraction of a fired cap on the nipple. But non-ribbed fired caps come off quite easily as well. Oftentimes, the cap of either style simply falls away after firing the gun. A more important cap body difference is malleability. Brittle caps tend to fragment upon firing, while more malleable caps smash against the cone of the nipple where they either fall off of their own or are readily flicked away.

The Musket Cap

The English musket cap, nickname "tophat cap," now also called U.S. musket cap, originally served as its name implies—on muskets. And it still does. But this large cap has also come into its own for some sidelocks, even modern muzzleloaders. That's because it provides a terrific flame for ignition. It is not a "hot" cap in the negative sense of exploding on the cone of the nipple like a little bomb. Rather it puts out a long, sustained flame. Currently, these big caps are available from Germany in the RWS brand, or made in the U.S.A. by CCI. The CCI tophat cap measures 0.240-inch diameter.

Modern Primers

Conversion nipples, sometimes referred to as fusils, have been available for many years. Some muzzleloaders have fusils that replace the regular nipple. Today, however, many rifles are built expressly to use modern primers. For example, the Savage Model 10ML-II takes a No. 209 shotgun primer. Likewise Remington's unique Genesis rifle. Flip the breechblock aside. Fit a No. 209 primer directly on an exposed breech plug, lock and shoot. Fire from the hot No. 209 primer flies directly into the powder charge in a straight line. Thompson/Center's break-open Encore muzzleloader also uses No. 209

primers, not as optional, but as with the Genesis, as the firearm's means of ignition. The rifle is hinged open, revealing the back end of the removable breech plug, and a primer is installed directly into a pocket. There is even an extractor on this rifle to push out the fired primer. Meanwhile, the Markesbery Outer-Line muzzleloader has the 400 SRP unit, which screws directly into the nipple seat. While this may be considered an alternative ignition system, it's actually very much a part of the rifle's design and can be used exclusively. The 400 SRP takes Small Rifle or Small Pistol primers. While it's obvious that modern primers provide a terrific flame for ignition, it's equally true that under most conditions standard percussion caps provide total reliability. As proof of this, I have fired my own Markesbery rifle with No. 11 percussion caps only for about six years now and the rifle has enjoyed 100 percent ignition with those caps. For inclement weather, however, it might be a good idea to go with the primer-firing 400 SRP in place.

This converter unit is for the Markesbery muzzleloader. It screws into the nipple seat, but rather than taking a No. 11 percussion cap, a small pistol primer or small rifle primer is installed. The hot little primer does offer a good spark of ignition. At the same time, the author's Markesbery rifle has yet to misfire with a No. 11 percussion cap.

Working with the Percussion Cap

As already mentioned, an accepted practice of clearing the nipple of the firearm *prior to loading* is popping percussion caps on the cone of the nipple or nipples to dry things up. As also noted, bits of metal may end up within the vent (channel) of the nipple. Such debris, along with minor fouling, could prevent the clear passage of flame from the next cap, causing a misfire or hangfire. That's why running a pipe cleaner into the cone of the nipple after detonating dry-up caps is recommended to ensure that no cap debris remains behind. This step takes only a few seconds, and can prevent an ignition problem.

Cap Holders and Dispensers (Cappers)

Seating devices are now available not only for popular regular-size percussion caps, but also musket caps, No. 209 shotshell primers, and Small Pistol/Small Rifle primers. (See Chapter 4.) The Tedd Cash Company makes beautiful cappers for primers as well as percussion caps. Markesbery has a special in-line capper for Small Rifle or Small Pistol primers. This spring-loaded unit delivers one primer at a time into a loading gate, where it can then be pressed into the 400 SRP's primer seat. There are two general types of cappers: in-line spring-loaded, where caps or primers are contained in a straight line, one be-

All manner of igniters, including modern primers, have dispensers available for them such as this Tedd Cash in-line capper for musket caps. Cappers retain caps and primers in a safe and handy manner, as well as distributing the cap or primer for firing.

hind the other and gravity-fed magazine cappers. There are even special models available for individual guns, such as Ted Cash's superb magazine capper for cap 'n' ball revolvers. Cappers are considered safety devices, as well as tools providing a means of containing and dispensing caps and primers. That's because they eliminate placing caps or primers into position with the fingers. However, not all guns require cappers. The Savage Model 110ML-II and Remington Genesis are two rifles that allow installing a cap in place safely and easily, even with a gloved hand.

Evaluating Percussion Cap Performance Safely

Percussion caps can be tested and evaluated by the shooter using a screw-barrel pistol, such as the Dixie Gun Works Derringer Liegi, 44-caliber. **Keep all parts of your body clear of the pistol in this test.** Do not allow anyone else in the area when you are testing caps. The use of the pistol is entirely safe unless the shooter does something outrageously foolish. For the No. 11 size, unscrew the barrel from the pistol, exposing the breech. Place a percussion cap on the nipple. Fire in a darkened area, such as the garage at night. A flame/spark will jet from the pistol. The shooter can visually determine for himself the duration of the spark and size, as well as shape of the flame, long and slender, short and wide, or in between. Cap brands can be readily compared with this useful visual inspection method. However, if a particular cap is found worthy in shooting that is the best test of all.

Types of Nipples

Over time, a staggering number of different nipple types have emerged, considering 19th as well as 20th- and 21st-century styles. Differences in thread are several, including the 1/4-28, 6-.75 and 6-1mm metrics, 12-28s and other thread dimensions. There are also numerous design variations. There is evidence that an oversized vent (hole) in a nipple can widen the group on target. Some folks have tried to explain why. I simply say I am not sure. Blowback might be a problem, but I don't see how a little more pressure coming back out of the nipple cone can do that much to group size. On the other side of

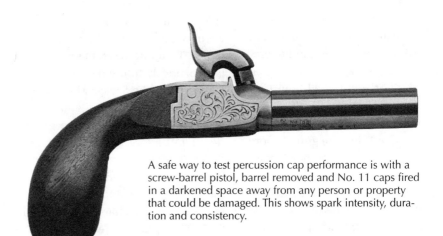

A safe way to test percussion cap performance is with a screw-barrel pistol, barrel removed and No. 11 caps fired in a darkened space away from any person or property that could be damaged. This shows spark intensity, duration and consistency.

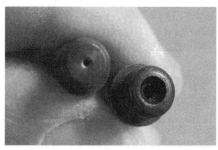

There are many different nipple configurations, including base orifices. Here are two boldly contrasted designs—a wide-open base and a flat base with a pinhole. The latter delivers a hot spark to the powder in the breech, and may also curtail blowback.

There are many different nipples available. These are a few. There are differences in thread, in length of threaded shank, in configuration of the cone, size of cone, and other features. Safety demands that the right nipple be installed into the nipple seat, not one that might cross-thread or otherwise fail to remain in the nipple seat when the gun is fired.

this stream, I've had reports from readers who claimed that accuracy with a nipple having an extremely small hole fell off and was immediately restored when a nipple of somewhat larger vent hole size was installed. Sometimes tests are foiled by the extraneous variable. We think we saw what we saw but what we really saw was caused by something we didn't see. A feeble example is Joe, who said that when he walked one route to work he always had a better day than when he took a different route. An office mate checked it out. He found that the along the "better route," Joe always had a little morning chat with a lovely lady.

The chronograph is one of the finest test tools shooters have. I put mine to work often to help solve many mysteries. When it comes to checking out

accuracy with various nipples, I learned that there is velocity loss with very large vents. However, these nipples were always what I call "straight-through." They not only had large vents, but also essentially no base. Rather, the hole went from cone to the bottom of the nipple about the same diameter all the way—big. Straight-through nipples still exist, but in very small numbers. If I come across one, I throw it away. I like some form of consistency in the world. I prefer doors to swing to the side, rather than having to enter a building with a garage-like door that goes up to get in. I like all roads in the U.S.A. to have right-hand lane only driving consistency. Fortunately, there is at least some sort of consistency in today's nipples, although it is hardly across the board. The 1/4 x 28 thread is fairly common. But there are many others. The main thing to look for in a nipple is construction of stainless steel or beryllium. The nipple should have a flat base with a pinhole for fire exit. Precise hole dimension? I cannot say. I do know there is a range that works fine, with very small and very large least desirable.

Burned-Out Nipples

The law of wear says that if it was made by man, it will eventually wear out. After all, even rocks wear down eventually. Nipples can burn out. But the good ones I have worked with over the past decade or so last for a very long time. Regardless, wisdom insists that an occasional check is smart. It takes no special tools to tell that a nipple vent (hole) has become significantly larger than it used to be. Time to change to a new one.

Burned Out or Damaged Nipple Seat

A shooter lost most of the sight in his right eye because his rifle was in poor repair, having been badly neglected over time. Part of the problem was a rusted-out nipple seat, which is the threaded hole into which the nipple fits. Of course the nipple finally blew

out as nipple seat threads provided less and less grip. We read in the journals of the 19th century mountain man about nipples blowing out. Osborne Russell, in his 19th century *Journal of a Trapper*, reported a man missing. Russell concluded that the fellow never returned because of some mishap, from a run-in with the Blackfoot, to a fallen horse, drowning, or a "bursted tube." In those days, the nipple was often referred to as a tube.

Priming Nipples

A nipple should never have to be primed by putting powder down into the cone. That is not its proper function. Such priming of the nipple could cause cap debris dispersion. The cap is the spark plug of the gun and the nipple is its guide. Nipples are designed to direct the flame of the cap right where it belongs. If this is not occurring with regularity, there is something wrong and priming the nipple is not the way to correct the problem. A different nipple may help. If the new nipple does not correct the problem, a gunsmith should check the gun for an irregularity. Furthermore, priming a proper nipple in order to shoot out a stuck ball, for example, can be impractical because a flat-base nipple with a small exit hole will trap the powder. The explosion of the cap on a primed nipple could provide less effective ignition rather than more effective.

Safety

Although Chapter 3 deals with safety, a special word is worthwhile here. Only correctly threaded nipples are safe. An incorrect nipple could blow out of the nipple seat upon firing the gun. The right size cap is also required, not one that loosely fits the cone of the nipple so that it can either fall off or blow off, nor so tight that it must be forced on the cone of the nipple, which could cause it go "go off" while being seated. Furthermore, since percussion caps are sensitive to blows—after all, that's what makes them work—never strike them with anything. Percussion caps can also be set off by heat, so they must be stored away from stoves or heaters and heater vents. And something else—percussion caps are not toys and they should not be toyed with. I heard of one fellow playing a trick on his friend by tossing a handful of percussion caps into the campfire. No one got hurt, but the caps did fly, sort of like tossing ammo into a fire, another foolish trick. While it is quite unlikely that the bullet will take flight, it being heavier than the case, a flying case in the face is not conducive to one's well-being. Caps must also be carried safely, in special cap boxes. Cash makes some nice ones. Or their original containers, or secured in cappers (in-line or magazine), or in some other sturdy holder where a blow cannot set them off. By all means, percussion caps must be stored where children cannot find them. Add a flash cup where appropriate. While a flash cup is used to prevent the burning of wood around the lock of the gun, it can also be useful in containing cap debris.

Ignition and Accuracy

While the nipple can make a difference in accuracy, today's good caps and primers are seldom the cause, directly, of poor groups. At the same time, we know from modern cartridge firearms that ignition can affect accuracy. In come cases, going to a different primer can reduce group size. So totally ignoring the source of ignition of a blackpowder gun is unwarranted. But the cap or primer is among the last I look for when a gun won't shoot well. Indirectly, ignition can make a difference. It's difficult for a marksman to make a good shot when he cannot rely on the gun going off when the trigger is pulled. Plus, hang-fires do nothing for accuracy, partly because the powder charge is not burning uniformly.

More on Ignition and Muzzle Velocity

While I do believe that nipples can make a difference in muzzle velocity, I also think this factor can be overstat-

ed. As noted above, there is a range of vent hole size that works fine, with only very small holes and very larger holes causing a potential problem. We also have such fine caps and primers today that it's quite difficult to accuse these sources of ignition when accuracy is not up to snuff. I have come to believe that as long as the powder charge is fully fired up, which is no big trick with blackpowder considering how readily it ignites, velocity will be normal. After all, it is the powder charge that creates the energy to drive bullets and shot charges, not caps or primers. In testing, there are some differences found with various igniters. I attribute these differences to normal variance, not the igniter itself. In one test, three different brands of No. 11 caps were tested by chronographing the same loads in the same gun. Total variation was 26 fps, absolutely insignificant in terms of the caps themselves.

New and Better

We are not surprised to learn that percussion caps and primers continue to undergo research and development, especially primers. Fiocchi Company USA announced a new No. 209 shotgun primer promising "improved function and safety." They worked just fine

in a modern muzzleloader. Winchester developed a No. 209 shotgun primer especially for use with Pyrodex Pellets and Triple Seven Pellets. We have to remember that different primer compounds produce different results, so claims of developing a specific primer for a specific ignition task are not blowing in the wind.

Ignition Failure

There are many different reasons for ignition failure, including bad caps, cap debris, poor firearm design, damp powder, the wrong nipple, poor touch-hole location, a badly made lock (either percussion or flint), improper loading practices, burned-out touchhole, burned-out nipple, and so forth. See Chapter 28 on troubleshooting which discusses a few problems with possible solutions. Ignition across the board is quite reliable when the firearm is in good shape with proper nipple, breech plug, percussion cap, or primer. The culprit when good guns fail to "go off" is generally moisture. Since blackpowder and replica propellants are hygroscopic (with a g), they can take on moisture from the atmosphere. Moreover, guns generally don't work well when wet. I have never tried it, but what about those movies where an actor emerges

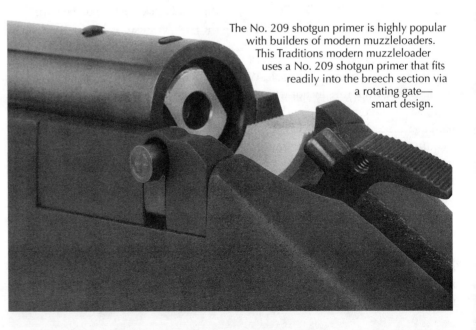

The No. 209 shotgun primer is highly popular with builders of modern muzzleloaders. This Traditions modern muzzleloader uses a No. 209 shotgun primer that fits readily into the breech section via a rotating gate—smart design.

Since the No. 209 shotgun primer has found a home in muzzleloading, companies have raced to produce a more ideal flash for front-loaders, and they have done so. Fiocchi and Winchester both came out with special No. 209 muzzleloader primers. And so has Remington, as shown here.

Waterproofing Measures

The best thing a hunter can do these days to ensure a big-game muzzleloading rifle will fire under less than ideal weather conditions, is to buy a modern muzzleloader, and I know that statement will bring color to the cheeks of my many dyed-in-the buckskin friends. They know, as well as anyone, that I admire original-style rifles the most for their historical interest, the challenge of shooting the old way with gun types that really existed "back then," and all that. But there are several modern muzzleloaders today that are, if not entirely waterproof, the next thing to it. In fact, as a little test I ran a good drip of water over a Remington Genesis and it still fired. There is another side to this issue, however. Even the flintlock can be made quite wet-resistant by simply covering the lock with plastic food wrap. I have had good luck also with the Kap Kover, which incorporates a neoprene O-ring around the nipple to prevent water invasion into the powder charge. It also has, as the name promises, a cover, that

Traditions supplies muzzle covers, like little balloons, to prevent moisture from running downbore. The kit also has percussion cap protectors that protect against rain and snow.

fits right over the top of the nipple to not only keep the percussion cap dry, but also serving as a safety barrier between hammer nose and cap until removal for firing the gun. A small toy balloon stretched over the muzzle keeps water out of the bore.

The Hang-fire

The hang-fire, also written as hang fire or hangfire, means ignition delay. The gun *does go off*, but not instantly. *Pssttt!—boom!* That's the sound of a

hang-fire. **Warning:** Continue to safely aim the firearm downrange if it does not go off when the trigger is pulled. The longest hang-fire I am personally aware of ran 1-1/2 minutes between trigger pull and firing. That is highly unusual, but it tells me that waiting for two full minutes with a hang-fire is worth the 120 seconds of "lost" time.

The Misfire

The misfire sounds like this: *Click!* The gun does not fire at all after the trigger is pulled. Once again, continue aiming in a safe direction following that click. It could be a hang-fire instead of misfire.

Flintlock Ignition

This subject was covered in Chapter 14 on loading techniques, and will not be gone over again here.

The Flash in the Pan

Many terms from the world of shooting survived to be used in today's language. Joe is a straight shooter. The idea missed the mark. Aim high! He bought the plan lock, stock, and barrel, to name but a few. An idea can be a flash in the pan—quick start, but no finish. In a flintlock rifle, a flash in the pan means the priming powder went poof!, but ignition of the powder in the breech did not follow.

Poor ignition can spoil the day. While it's not too hard to take when plinking or informal target shooting, misfires and hang-fires are downright frustrating at rendezvous, the shooting match, or in the hunting arena. Knowing the ways of percussion caps, primers, nipples, and other aspects of the ignition system, however, can prevent disappointment.

Clearly, it would be impossible to stabilize the bullets shown here with one and only one rate of twist. The two blackpowder lead conicals are relatively short for their caliber—while the bullet for the 45-120 Sharps is quite long for its caliber and obviously much more streamlined for a higher C, or ballistic coefficient rating.

As with the tall tale of the round ball patch as a gasket—not!—so goes rifling twist. I have had my share of anti-fan mail and verbal upbraiding about it. I promise, Blackpowder George, there is no such thing as one correct twist for all muzzleloader or blackpowder cartridge bullets. I said in the Introduction that comparison from old-time to modern guns paid off, and it does here. I have a 30-06 with a 1:10 rate of twist. I have a 7mm Magnum with a 1:9 rate of twist. I have a 30-30 carbine with a 1:12 rate of twist and a 32 Winchester Special carbine with a 1:16 rate of twist. The rate of twist varies with the bullet's requirement for RPS stabilization. RPS—revolutions per second—what does it take to stabilize a given bullet? The law of physics says that it is impossible for all bullets of all calibers and dimensions to stabilize at the same RPS. That is why

rate of twist varies. Tell that to the romanticist, however, and that person will stomp his feet, stammering, "I know the only right twist is 1:48 because Hawken rifles were 1:48." Maybe Sam and Jake Hawken did every barrel 1:48, but if so, it was because they either knew no better, which I doubt, or because they had one rifling machine that created that one and only rate of twist. At the same time, I agree that 1:48 is proper in certain guns, and that it does constitute a fairly good compromise in some calibers, being slow enough for the round ball and fast enough for the conical, thereby doing a fair job stabilizing both. But a turn in 48 inches is hardly correct across the board, event though it was very popular in the past.

According to Ned Roberts, author of *The Muzzle-Loading Cap Lock Rifle*, 1:48 was a standard in the late 19th

century. And no one knows why for sure. Roberts wrote, "It appears that the old-time riflesmith's 'standard' twist of rifling for round-ball rifles was one turn in 48 inches." The author went on to say that some 'smiths preferred 1:60 and even slower twists [for round ball guns]. Meanwhile, Captain James Forsyth, well-respected English shooter, understood the properties of rifling twist better than many of his peers, because he knew that no single rate of twist could possibly be correct for all calibers. His round-ball rifles carried super slow rifling twist, such as 1:112 for very large bores. Nonetheless, shooters who would laugh at the idea of rifling all modern guns with the same rate of twist buy into the idea that the smokepole somehow defies the law of science. Going back to 1895, the 25-35 Winchester had a fast 1:8 rate of twist to stabilize long 117-grain 25-caliber bullets. The 30-30, called the 30 W.C.F. (Winchester Center Fire), appeared in the same year; but it was built with a 1:12 rate of twist. Obviously, Winchester engineers knew something. There may also be different rates of twist for the same caliber. I have a 30-06 with a 1:12 twist that does fine with 110- and 150-grain bullets. I have another 30-06 with a 1:10 rate of twist that is better suited to longer, heavier, bullets.

Generally speaking, and while admittedly ignoring other factors, bullets of low sectional density (SD) and modest ballistic coefficient, known simply as C, require less RPS for stabilization in flight than bullets of higher sectional density and greater ballistic coefficient. That's why the low C round ball demands so very little spin to keep it on track, while conicals with a higher C need more RPS for stability. As caliber increases, mass must escalate, provided the larger caliber bullet also grows in length. In other words, there is a vast difference in bullet behavior between a 45 ACP 200-grain bullet and a 30-caliber 200-grain bullet. Bullets of greater mass stabilize with less RPS than "lighter" ones which demand more RPS to keep them on track. In other words, a bullet from a 32-caliber muzzleloader insists on greater RPS to keep it revolving on its axis than a bullet from a 58-caliber rifle. So there it is: *No single rate of twist can possibly be correct for all guns.*

The reason C is included in the story is due to modern streamlined blackpowder projectiles coming along, which must have more RPS than bullets of the same caliber and weight with a more blunt profile. A prime example is the SSB from the Buffalo Bullet Company. The SSBs that I have tested were 45-caliber bullet fitted into a sabot for firing in 50-caliber muzzleloaders. This bullet is long for its diameter. Moreover, it has a spitzer shape, just like so many modern jacketed bullets. Comparing another 45-caliber bullet from the same company, a 285-grain hollow-base, it's easy to see that it's much shorter for its diameter than the SSB. Because muzzleloader manufacturers finally got around to installing faster rates of twist for guns intended to shoot conicals, the SSB did all right in modern muzzleloaders. Going with an example from the modern world, there's the accurate Sierra 69-grain .224-inch diameter Match King bullet. This long-for-its-caliber bullet found its way into a 222 Remington rifle with 1:14 rate of twist. The bullet keyholed on its way to the target, hitting sideways instead of point-first. The same bullet from a Colt AR-15A2 rifle with a fast 1:7 rate of twist flew point-forward to the target, obviously stabilized.

Range of Twist per Caliber

Just as no single rate of twist is right for all bullets, at the same time, no one twist is necessary to stabilize a given projectile. There is a *range* of acceptability. The 1:24 rate of twist on my own Markesbery muzzleloader stabilizes a wide variety of bullets, from the short Buffalo Bullet Ball-et, to the aforementioned SSB Spitzer. While one rifling twist has a range of bullets it can stabilize, the same is true in reverse— one bullet can maintain its axis in flight from a range of rifling twist. The 32-caliber round ball can be stabilized with a 1:30 or a 1:50 rate of twist, depending in part upon the muzzle velocity imparted to the projectile (more on that

This is a prime example of rate of twist variation to stabilize different projectiles. The big 12-bore round ball, due not only to shape, but also mass, requires very little RPS for stabilization, while the Sierra 210-grain 30-caliber bullet demands a much faster rate of twist for stabilization.

later) because exit velocity is highly important when considering bullet stabilization and RPS.

Smoothbores by way of Comparison

Smoothbores, while more efficient and useful in the field than often credited, never produced the brand of accuracy sought after by serious marksmen, especially target shooters. There is also good reason to believe that soldiers armed with rifled guns were deadlier than those firing smoothbores. The Battle of New Orleans is a prime example of smoothbores against rifled arms. The projectile fired from a smoothbore tends to take a line of flight dictated by its distribution of mass. One reason for superb round ball accuracy from a rifled gun is equalization of discrepancies on a common axis. No lead bullet is perfect because it is not 100 percent homogenous in its molecular distribution. Even the best round bullets are microscopically lopsided. By spinning the ball, minute flaws in structure revolve around a common line or axis. So instead of one side of the ball causing it to drift off course, the sides are constantly changing position, keeping the bullet on track. The lead globe can be extremely accurate because of equalizing irregularities through spinning. Firing a round ball from a smoothbore shows this clearly. Although reasonable close-range big game accuracy can be achieved (see Chapter 36), the rifled bore produces much tighter groups.

How RPS is derived

RPS—revolutions per second—is achieved by two, and only two factors. These are *rate* of twist and *muzzle velocity*. The operative word is **rate** of twist. Barrel length is not **directly** a part of the equation. The length of the barrel, in and of itself, does *not* dictate rate of twist. Unfortunately, twist is stated as the number of turns a bullet makes as it progresses through the bore. This presents the mistaken notion that a "turn in so many inches of barrel"

The interesting Hornady Hard Ball can be fired in a sabot, as shown here. This indicates that RPS can be translated via a sabot for any projectile.

While it is somewhat difficult to see the grooves and lands at the muzzle, they are of medium depth for round ball stabilization—not shallow depth for conicals. RPS—revolutions per second—is achieved specifically by two factors: rate of twist and exit velocity. This rifle has a 1:79 rate of twist and a patched round ball leaves the muzzle at various speeds, from 1,300 fps target loads to almost 2,000 fps hunting loads—with stabilization at both slower and faster velocities.

Pistols intended to shoot the same caliber round balls as rifles have faster rates of twist. This is not because of barrel length. It is because RPS is established by both rate of twist and exit velocity. Exit velocity in the pistol will be slower than exit velocity in the longer-barreled rifle of exactly the same caliber. While it is somewhat difficult to see in a photograph of the muzzle, depth of rifling for this pistol is on the deeper side to "grab" the patched round ball.

This Ruger Model 77/50—50-caliber in-line muzzleloader—is intended for conical bullets, not round balls—and groove depth is relatively shallow with a corresponding land height, which is correct for conical stabilization.

determines how fast the bullet spins. This is not so. Again—only two factors are responsible for how fast a bullet revolves in flight: rate of twist and exit velocity. Barrel length does matter, but *not* directly! The only reason barrel length has anything to do with RPS is not because of how long the barrel is, but rather when the longer barrel generates higher velocity, one of the two factors in RPS development. For example, if we had two 50-caliber rifles with exactly the same rate of twist, one with a two-inch barrel, another with a 42-inch barrel, and if somehow both rifles could achieve the same muzzle velocity, bullets from either one would have *the same* RPS. Barrel length matters only in terms of muzzle velocity, not because of so many revolutions of the bullet in so many inches. It's too bad inches ever entered the water on this one. If the two mythical 50-caliber guns above with the same rate of twist, one with the super short barrel, the other with a longer barrel, fired the same bullet at the same velocity, there would be *no difference* in the stabilization of the projectile. Forevermore, if you must think of rate of twist as a turn in so many inches, forget inches of barrel and turn instead to inches of flight.

How about Trig and Twist?

Although it's been done on paper, and rather convincingly, missile stabilization is **not** a matter of trigonometry. Tangents of angles, graphic triangles, and little line drawings tell nothing worthwhile about rifling twist. This statement will anger readers who have believed in an explanation of rifling twist based on trigonometry. I advise

these persons to consult a scientist who understands ballistics, or to bring this chapter to that scientist, and see what he says about angles, tangents, triangles when missile stabilization and rate of twist are under discussion. Captain James Forsyth, mentioned above, worked diligently on the mathematics of rifling twist in the 19th century. While his formulas are not of much interest today, his conclusions are. Forsyth concluded, along with Major Shakespear (without the "e") and the well-known hunter, Sir Samuel Baker, that the greater the missile grows in mass, the less RPS required to stabilize it. He was right, proving his conclusions with rifles made up with very slow rates of twist to stabilize large-caliber lead spheres accurately at long range. He shot water buffalo in Ceylon at 300 yards—witnessed—with rifles of at least 12-bore and usually larger, shooting round bullets.

Stripping the Bore

Sometimes called "tripping over the rifling," stripping the bore meant that the bullet rode over the lands, rather than being guided by them. Like a train on a track, the bullet can only go where the rifling leads it. Also like a train on a track, the projectile can either stay on its "rails" or it can scoot over them and crash. When the projectile is no longer guided by the rifling, in 19th-century terminology "tripping over the rifling

While the round ball requires very little RPS for stabilization, today's black-powder conical bullets take many different shapes, including this high profile Hornady bullet in a sabot. Naturally, such a bullet demands more RPS to keep it on track than does a round ball of the same caliber, or a "blunt" conical.

Practical rifling twist is relatively easy to come by—sufficient rate of twist to stabilize specific bullets. Bullets of very high C, such as this shapely Hornady missile, demand a faster rate of twist to rotate them sufficiently for stabilization from muzzle to target. The good news is that once proper RPS is achieved, it does not fall off nearly as rapidly as forward velocity. RPS remains stable to very long ranges.

or "stripping the bore" spells disaster to accuracy. This condition can exist under various circumstances, especially with under-sized bullets that do not obturate to engage the rifling either directly or via a patch. It's also a clue about accuracy with bullets that fit well to the bore. Sometimes a round ball that is stripping the bore can be corrected with a thicker patch. Since the patched round ball does not show rifling marks, it is not profitable to collect spent examples downrange to see if they are stripping the bore.

Super Light Loads

Think first about the fact that only exit velocity and rate of twist matter in producing RPS. If this is true, then a change in exit velocity, while retaining the same rate of twist, can bring about better bullet stabilization. Consider a rifle with a comparatively fast rate of twist. A round ball fired from this rifle may prove quite inaccurate because the ball is not "grabbed" by the rifling to guide it. In short, the ball trips over the lands when loaded to a higher velocity level. That is the key: the higher velocity level. A degree of improved accuracy in this rifle can be achieved

by reducing the load, which in turn lowers the velocity of the bullet in the bore, which in turn allows the rifling a better effect on that ball. Stated another way, since RPS is a product of rate of twist and muzzle velocity, reducing muzzle velocity cuts down RPS and the lands now guide a ball that tripped over the rifling at higher velocity. Advice given that only light loads shoot accurately is wrong. In reality, when the ball was given too much speed in a rifle with a too-fast rate of twist, it stripped the rifling and flew off course. When the load was reduced, accuracy improved. This brought about the false notion that only light loads are accurate. In fact, as we know from modern bullets at super speeds, high velocity does not—*per force*—destroy accuracy. Sometimes the cause for poor accuracy with a faster bullet speed has nothing to do with RPS, but rather some other factor, such as a problem with bore or bullet.

How Deep the Grooves, How Tall the Lands

Another factor that can alter bullet behavior is depth of groove, which in turn produces the height of the land. A taller land may bite into a bullet, forcing it to spin in the bore in spite of a rate of twist normally too fast for the particular projectile. Much talk about tall lands being necessary for round ball stabilization is not necessarily chiseled in granite. Round-ball rifles with shallow grooves and modest land height shoot accurately when the rate of twist is correct. I can prove this with my own

No. 47, which is very accurate, but has rather shallow grooves and consequently modest land height. However, shallow grooves with corresponding shorter lands seem to be best for conical bullets across the board, while taller lands do little more than scarring the projectile needlessly.

Round Ball Circumference and Twist

While angles and tangents are relatively meaningless in a discussion of bullet stabilization, it is true that the circumference of a bigger ball is rotating faster than the circumference of a smaller ball. In other words, the speed of a 60-caliber lead sphere on the outside of its surface is greater than the speed of a 50-caliber lead sphere on the outside of its surface when both missiles are driven at the same velocity from a bore with the same rate of twist. Taking the 1:66 rate of twist as an example, the ball makes a single revolution per 66 inches of travel. Yes, that ball does make a half-turn in a 33-inch barrel, but this sort of thinking can muddy the waters. While the 60-caliber ball's circumference is moving faster than the 50-caliber ball's circumference, there is an equalization factor at work, because the diameter of the rifling changes in exactly the same proportion with the different calibers. So the faster surface rotation of the outside of the 60-caliber ball moves over a longer path in the 1:66 rate of twist compared against the 50-caliber ball in the same twist. It all comes out to dead equal. Do not be confused by this stuff. The importance of

The variables that affect RPS include caliber, and of course C—ballistic coefficient. Bullets of higher C require more RPS than bullets of lower C rating. This is why we find a rifle like this Sharps carrying a rate of twist in the 1:20 range—because it can shoot high sectional density bullets of relatively high C rating.

The practical side of twist comes into play as various firearms receive the rate of twist required to stabilize bullets intended for that gun. This Navy Arms 45-caliber revolver shoots rather blunt bullets, but it does fire conicals, and therefore demands a proper rate of twist to stabilize elongated missiles.

this point is that the number of turns in the bore for the 50-caliber ball and the 60-caliber ball are exactly the same in a 1:66 rate of twist barrel. And so we defer to mass when changes rate of twist as a ball caliber goes up and a 50-caliber ball-shooter may have a 1:66 rate of twist, while a 72-caliber ball has a 1:80 rate of twist.

Here is a mental model that may help produce a picture of the situation. It deals with bolts and nuts as familiar everyday items. There are two bolts and nuts in this story. One bolt is 1/4-inch in diameter. The other bolt is 1/2-inch in diameter. Both have, of course, corresponding threaded nuts. Think of the threads as rifling. Both have 20 threads to the inch, or in rifling talk, 20 turns to the inch. If *either* nut is moved down its respective bolt 1 inch, that nut will make 20 turns. That's the fact we're after in this model. In spite of the diameters of the two bolts being quite different, both are guided identically by their rate of twist. This holds true as long as the nut (or bullet) does not ride on the threads (lands), but rather is guided by them. This model is important because it reveals several facts. First, no matter if the bolt is 1/4-inch long or 2 feet long, the rate of twist imparted to the nut has to stay the same. Second, the nut can be driven that inch in one minute, one second, or one millisecond, or any

other period of time. If the nut is driven at different speeds, the revolutions per time must vary. This is important to our twist story because we can see that RPS will vary in accord with forward motion of the projectile as it is guided by the rifling.

Practical Rifling Twist

Given that RPS is developed by rate of twist and exit velocity of the missile, how many revolutions per second are required to keep an elongated bullet flying point-on? Or for that matter to maintain a round ball revolving on its axis? A projectile is like a free-moving gyroscope. In order to stabilize a gyroscope, you must spin it. Can you spin it too much? There may be a point at which the gyroscope goes crazy when it is revolved too rapidly. However, it is clearly evident that when the gyroscope slows down *below* a specific spin rate it falls over on its side. When a conical projectile is not given sufficient RPS, it may wobble in flight or keyhole (tumble). Too little RPS may also cause it to depart from its original intended line of flight. Considering two rifles, in this case real-life examples, both 54-caliber; one a ball-shooter, the other meant for conicals, the first has a rate of twist going one turn in 79 inches for the lead sphere, while the second runs 1:34. The rifle with 1:79 twist shoots a patched

ball remarkably well, as proved when a 6-24x Bausch & Lomb scope was temporarily mounted and afterwards, five-shot groups under an inch center-to-center at 100 yards from the muzzle were common. The other 54-caliber rifle with a 1:34 rate of twist will also shoot a round ball, but only if velocity of the missile is held down. Otherwise, accuracy goes to pot. However, it shoots a 460-grain Buffalo Bullet and other conicals quite well. Meanwhile, the rifle with the 1:79 rate of twist will not stabilize the conical at all, as proved by targets with elongated holes in the paper showing that the bullet tipped in flight. While a turn in 34 inches is slow for a modern cartridge shooting long bullets, it is actually on the fast side in blackpowder terms. That's because most elongated blackpowder bullets have low SD and C. On the other hand, longer blackpowder bullets, such as the Buffalo Bullet Company's SSB, shoot better with a rate of twist faster than 1:34, all other elements, such as bore quality, being equal.

Super Fast Twist

It's interesting to see what happens with truly long bullets in modern guns. This blip of information is included only to give an idea of how much RPS can be required for stabilization. A bullet known as the VLD (Very Low Drag) is

Another good example of modern muzzleloader rate of twist is this Traditions in-line 50-caliber muzzleloader. It was intended from the start to shoot conical bullets and therefore the rate of twist is closer to the 1:30 range than the 1:60 range.

Is it possible to have too rapid a rate of twist? The answer is yes, but in "real shooting" it seems to take a fairly fast rate of twist before a bullet "strips the bore," where the projectile "rides on the lands" rather than being guided by the lands. A revolver like this Ruger Old Army will shoot both round balls and short conical bullets. Rate of twist for this revolver is 1:16, which may seem fast for a round ball of only 45-caliber; however, remember that exit velocity will be lower than that from a 45-caliber rifle, so 1:16 works fine in this revolver. Bullets round or conical are not stripped in the bore.

extremely long for its caliber. The 105-grain 6mm VLD bullet keyholed from a test rifle with 1:10 rates of twist. A special barrel had to be made to stabilize these handsome projectiles. This barrel turned out to carry a 1:8 rate of twist. The 226 Barnes QT (Quick Twist) is another example of a cartridge demanding fast twist. This 22-caliber wildcat fires a 125-grain .226-inch diameter missile that runs about 1 3/8-inches in length. Experimenters found that a twist of 1:5.5 was necessary to stabilize that pencil. That's a full revolution of the bullet in only 5-1/2 inches of forward motion. A round ball would trip over that and fly wild.

Variables That Affect Twist

Numerous cause-and-effect gremlins bend the laws of linear (Newtonian) physics, seeming to make liars of the most careful ballisticians. Guns perform differently due to what are known as *extraneous variables*, those little hidden gremlins so difficult to isolate and figure out. For example, we think of a 50-caliber barrel as being a 50-caliber barrel, and it is, but all 50-caliber barrels are not the same, not even in exact bore dimensions, let alone rifling configuration. Bullet fit to the bore, therefore, varies among different firearms of the same caliber. Furthermore, once we put a rule in our "book of facts," the pages may catch fire. We know, or think we know, that accuracy is usually improved when a round bullet fits the bore fairly closely, rather than an undersized sphere requiring a thick patch to take up windage. However, it's no real surprise when a front-loader creates a good group with undersized lead pills and heavy patches. So the rules bend a little here and there.

In tests, the Savage Model 10ML definitely proved more accurate with bullets closer to bore size, .451-inch or .452-inch as opposed to .429-inch diameter. Sabots capable of withstanding higher pressures were also necessary for best results. There are also match-ups made in heaven. Sometimes we know why and sometimes we don't know why these combinations work. For example, a particular test rifle put the Buffalo Bullet Company Ball-et into tighter groups than other projectiles that *seemed* more suitable. That specific bullet shape "liked" the bore and the bore "liked" it. There is also bearing surface to consider. Bullets with long shanks have good bearing surface. Surely, more or less bearing surface has to make a difference in how a projectile "relates" to the rifling. The patched round ball, for example, has the least bearing surface of any bullet, unless a thin disc of some kind is contrived. All in all, though, one point can be taken to the bank: slow twist is better for round ball stabilization and faster is more suited to conicals.

The Practical Side of Twist Knowledge

Knowledge of rifling twist is useful in selecting an appropriate missile. The best way I know to prove which bullets are best for a given rifle is shooting. Of course, it's not bullets alone that count. The powder charge also makes an accuracy difference, not only in how that powder burns in the bore, but in how fast the charge drives the bullet, since we know that exit velocity has a lot to do with how a bullet is stabilized in

Another prime example of varying rate of twist per firearm is seen in this replica Navy Arms Remington 44-caliber revolver. Rate of twist is 1:12, which works for both round ball and short conicals. Note this is not the same rate of twist (1:16) for the Ruger Old Army, which fires only slightly larger bullets—more proof that there is a range of acceptable twist for stabilizing similar bullets.

flight. So we shoot and shoot and shoot. Which is fun. After all, that's why we came to the game, to shoot. Hopefully within a reasonable time frame, the right bullet for the rate of twist in the given rifle or pistol, not to leave out the revolver, will surface. In the meanwhile, the starting point in bullet selection is very simple. Repeat often: "Slow is for round ball, faster is for conical bullet." The modern muzzleloader is primarily a conical-shooter and smart manufacturers have avoided the old wives' tale about 1:48 being the only rate of twist in town. In fact, in the last dozen or so modern muzzleloaders I carried to the test range, here is how many had a 1:48 rate of twist: zero.

Too Much Twist?

Is it possible? Can a firearm over-stabilize a projectile? One professional barrelmaker does not think so. Les says that, "Rifling twist is like money in the bank. You can't have too much of it." I have no solid evidence of elongated bullets going wild because they were made to spin too fast. On the other hand, I have witnessed bullets keyholing down the pike because they were not given sufficient RPS to stabilize them in flight. When a conical missile makes a hole in the paper that matches the sideways profile of that bullet, I'd say the bullet was going head over heels in flight. On the other hand, over-stabilizing the round ball can mean trouble because of the aforementioned

problem of "stripping the bore." Another barrel maker had something different to say about twist. "You want just enough rotation to keep the bullet spinning on its axis, and no more. That's why we build benchrest rifles with just enough twist to rotate the bullet for stability and no more." Modern manufacturers know about rifling twist. In blackpowder guns there are three general rates of twist. The first is fast, even though in modern terms the pitch is slow, around 1:24 to 1:32. The middle-of-the-road 1:48 remains useful for short Minie bullets, as in rifled muskets, as well as for reduced round ball loads that produce low velocity. And then there is round ball twist, tortoise slow. Most 50s and 54s carry the popular 1:66 rate of twist. But my accurate Mulford No. 47 rifle has a 1:79 rate of twist.

What Happens to Bullet Spin Downrange?

Forward velocity is killed by the atmosphere. Gravity plays a role in bullet flight, but it isn't nearly as responsible as the atmosphere for slowing forward progress. Rotational velocity, on the other hand, is much better retained. This would be no more than a tidbit to file in our book of shooting knowledge, except for the fact that it does talk to us about RPS retention. We learn that once the bullet is stabilized in flight, it's going to stay flying nose-forward for quite a distance. There is a limit, of course. Eventually, like the spinning top that slows down and falls over, the bullet loses RPS to the point that it yaws in flight, sort of corkscrewing along. We also recognize by understanding rotational spin retention why the round ball continues to maintain

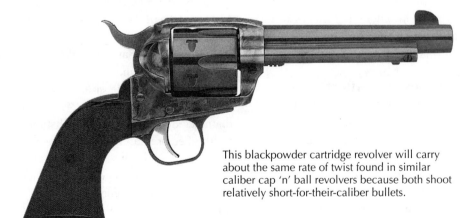

This blackpowder cartridge revolver will carry about the same rate of twist found in similar caliber cap 'n' ball revolvers because both shoot relatively short-for-their-caliber bullets.

its original attitude in flight to a reasonable distance. At the same time, see what happens to forward velocity with a round ball. Losing 50 percent of its original velocity within only 100 yards is common.

Handguns and Twist

As evidence of barrel length altering velocity and velocity being primary to RPS, handguns require faster rates of twist per caliber than rifles. This might lead some folks to believe that barrel length is, after all, an important element in rate of twist, but we know better. We know that the reason sidearms carry faster rates of twist per caliber is because of their reduced exit velocity compared to rifles. As an example, consider two 30-caliber barrels, one 30 inches long, the other 3 inches long, both with 1:10 rates of twist. Either would stabilize a 180-grain bullet perfectly if the velocity imparted by both barrels was high enough to create the proper RPS. But that won't happen. The short barrel simply won't generate sufficient velocity to provide the necessary RPS for that 180-grain 30-caliber projectile. The usual handgun barrel is not long enough to generate high velocity, so it receives a faster rate of twist to provide more RPS. For example, the Browning 45-70 single-shot rifle

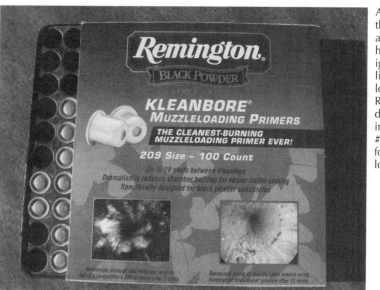

Answering the need for a specialized high-intensity igniter for in-line muzzle-loaders, Remington developed and introduced the #209 primer for muzzle-loaders.

has a 1:20 rate of twist, while the 45 Colt pistol has a 1:16 rate of twist. The rifle shoots a 45-caliber bullet in the 400- to 500-grain class, while the pistol fires a shorter bullet in the 200 to 250 grain domain. In keeping with the fact that higher mass bullets require less RPS than lighter ones, a smallbore ball-shooting rifle will have a faster rate of twist than a big-bore ball-shooting rifle. A 36-caliber squirrel rifle may have a 1:40 rate of twist, because its .350-inch ball weighs only 65-grains, demanding higher RPS to stabilize it, while a 50-caliber ball-shooting rifle carries a 1:66 rate of twist.

Blackpowder Cartridge Guns and Twist

Appropriately, blackpowder cartridge guns are built with varying rates of twist to match bullets. Just as the Whitworth muzzleloader has a 1:20 rate of twist intended for long bullets of rather high sectional density, blackpowder cartridge rifles made to shoot longer bullets also have faster rates of twist to match. On the other hand, we're not surprised to learn that blackpowder cartridge firearms shooting bullets of lesser sectional density have slower rates of twist. It's a match game—matching twist to bullets for stabilization in flight.

BLACKPOWDER BALLISTICS

Within reasonable range the blackpowder bullet is extremely reliable. A Parker Productions bullet put this buck down cleanly with one shot.

We want to know what our guns "are doing" for several reasons. Curiosity is one factor. Shooters are curious, desiring to find out what a specific firearm is capable of with a specific load. Our curiosity leads to comparison. Ballistics results provide a comparison among various firearms in several ways: energy yes, but more than that. Chapter 27, "Working with the Rainbow," deals with trajectory and how to handle trajectory. Trajectory cannot be fully understood without knowing the ballistics associated with the projectile. Along with gaining knowledge of bullet flight from muzzle to destination, ballistics relates information on the all-important energy level produced by a firearm, as well as "reverse energy," which we call recoil. Knowing how many pounds per

square inch energy a projectile earns at the muzzle as well as downrange leads to proper application. Consider a 50-caliber round ball for elk. Ballistics informs that a .490-inch round ball encouraged by 110-grains volume FFg blackpowder starts out at 1,966 from a 39-inch barrel. Energy delivered by this bullet at the muzzle is 1,507 foot-pounds. But that elk will not be standing at the muzzle.

At 100 yards downrange, the .490-inch 177-grain ball starting at 1,966 fps has slowed to 1,105 fps. Energy has now dropped to 476 foot-pounds. The elk hunter shooting a 50-caliber front-loader with a round ball should consider getting closer than 100 yards. At close range, the 50-caliber ball delivers reasonable potency. Ballistics tells this elk hunter to go to

a larger ball, or perhaps a conical, if he or she wants to shoot an elk farther than 50 to 75 yards. Ballistics applies to smallbores, too. It's good to know, for example, what a 32-caliber squirrel rifle delivers, as well as a 4-bore. Pistols and revolvers are not left out, and don't forget the shotgun. How much energy does each No. 2 pellet have at 30 yards? Enough for a clean job on a goose? Ballistics does not provide all the answers, because there is more than one criterion to consider in "killing power." But the discipline tells a highly important story about that No. 2 shotgun pellet. We learn from knowing the energy of that pellet that choke comes into play, because the goal is not a single pellet making contact with that goose, but multiple pellets for good effect.

Huge rifles like the two taken here from an old American Rifleman advertisement deliver big recoil. The 10-bore fired 10 drams Fg blackpowder. That's over 270 grains volume! And the bullet weighed 1,200 grains. The 8-bore burned 12 drams Fg (over 325 grains volume) with a 1,250-grain bullet. Both rifles weighed over 17 pounds to somewhat thwart recoil.

The U.S. Army Trapdoor Springfield fired the 45-70 Government cartridge. A 500-grain bullet at 1,200 fps was a good average velocity. Obviously, the velocity was nothing to write home about. However, the rifle proved quite effective even on big game. Why? Bullet mass.

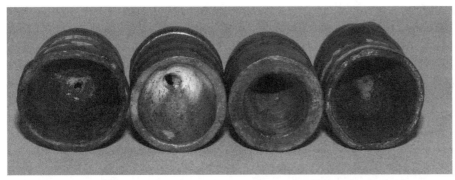

What happens to a Minie ball skirt in the bore? The story is part of interior ballistics. The skirt on the far left is rather thin. It flared. The skirt next to the right is also thin but a low powder charge did not overly flare the skirt. Next to the right is a thick skirt to withstand higher powder charges. And on the far right a skirt that flared, but flared evenly rather than egg-shaped like the one on the far left.

The round ball upsets considerably on making its wound channel in big game. The two 54-caliber round balls flanking the 180-grain 30-caliber bullet (for reference) were both taken from mule deer bucks.

Calculating power goes in favor of velocity when using Newton's formula, and yet big lead bullets like this excellent example from Parker Productions can cleanly "take" any big game in North America. That's because mass cannot be ignored, and of course, these bullets are flying well above the speed of sound.

Ballistics Inside and Outside the Barrel

Projectiles in motion—that's the name of the ballistics game in two parts—*interior ballistics*, what happens inside the bore of the gun, and *external ballistics*, how the projectile, be it round ball, modern jacketed bullet, or shot pellet, behaves from muzzle to final destination. Internal ballistics is the more elusive study of the two branches. What happens to Minie skirts in the bore, how patches truly behave in the fire of combustion, compacted powder compared against loosely packed powder charges, varying ramrod pressure vs. uniform pressure on the powder charge: these and other occurrences within the bore of the firearm fall under internal ballistics. Bullet energy at the muzzle and downrange, trajectory, wind deflection, and how projectiles perform in various media are topics under the banner of external ballistics. All data were derived with an Oehler Model 35P Proof Chronograph, nothing extrapolated, no "educated guesses." The 35P provides five pieces of information for every string of shots: highest velocity in the string, lowest velocity, average velocity, extreme spread, and standard deviation from the mean (average) velocity, all with the bush of a button. After gathering chronographed figures, energy was derived by Newton's KE formula—"energy in motion" or kinetic energy.

Calculating Power

Newton's KE (kinetic energy) formula is the only one used by ammo factories and bullet companies the world over. Final figures may be expressed differently, depending upon the country, but results interchange, be they in foot-pounds or the metric system. Foot-pound is a unit denoting the amount of energy required to lift one pound of weight one foot off the ground with earth's gravitational force. Not everyone is happy about foot-pounds of energy calculated in Newton's formula. That's because the math squares velocity. Shooters who believe that bullet weight is just as important as bullet speed balk at this. The late Elmer Keith, popular firearms author, made his fame by insisting that large-bore guns firing heavy bullets were right for big game. I sat in Elmer's Idaho living room one afternoon, along with gunmaker Frank Wells. Keith applauded Frank's fine work on my custom 7mm Remington Magnum Model 70 rifle. The old hunter allowed that the Big 7 was a pretty good deer cartridge, "as long as a heavy bullet was chosen." Certain muzzleloader fans also balk at Newton's formula favoring fast bullets, because muzzleloaders—even the hottest modern versions—do not provide high velocity, as we know it. Some may gain 2,500 fps, which is very fast for a front-loader. But not by comparison with hot smokeless powder cartridges developing 3,000 to even 4,000 fps. Regardless, Newton's KE prevails everywhere.

The formula goes like this: Square bullet velocity. Divide the resulting figure by 7,000 to reduce from pounds to grains (there are 7,000 grains weight in one pound). Divide the new number by 64.32, a constant for gravity going back to Galileo's studies. Multiply the resulting figure from these divisions by the weight of the projectile. Given a

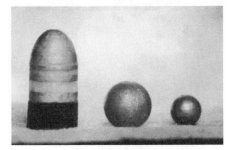

There are big bullets and then there are really big bullets. The 54-caliber round ball on the far right looks a little small compared with an 8-bore round ball and 8-bore conical.

50-caliber round ball rifle firing a 177-grain bullet at 2,000 fps muzzle velocity, square 2,000 to get 4,000,000, divide by 7,000 for 571.42857, divide again by 64.32 for 8.8841506, which is foot-pounds for *one grain weight* of bullet. Since the .490-inch round bullet weighs 177-grains, multiply by 177 for a final number, which turns out to be 1572.4946, rounded off to 1,572 foot-pounds of energy. Comparing this 177-grain round ball to a 30-06 Springfield 180-grain bullet we find the factory load doing 2,700 fps with 2,914 foot-pounds of developed energy. The round ball from the 50-caliber muzzleloader at 2,000 fps shows considerably less muzzle energy. The picture darkens even more as the lead sphere goes downrange. Is this a fair assessment? The world of physical sciences says it is.

Bullet speed is king in Newton's formula, but bullet weight is queen, and highly important to resulting energy, despite the fact that weight is not squared. The 458 Winchester with a 500-grain bullet at 2,100 fps earns almost 4,900 foot-pounds of energy in spite of its slower bullet. That's a lot of power. Furthermore, large-bore muzzleloaders also fare well with the KE formula.

William Moore's 19th century fire-breather proves this. Awesome is an overworked word these days, but if ever

Streamlined bullets like the SSB from the Buffalo Bullet Company "carry up" quite well in blackpowder rifles (and some pistols) and can be counted on for 200 yard-plus hits with regularity. These bullets should be delivered into the shoulder region. Although they are hollowpoint they are still heavy lead.

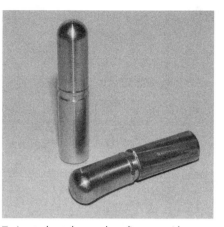

Trying to best the modern firearm with a blackpowder gun is not difficult at all—providing big bullets are fired at medium velocity. As a point of comparison this is a 220-grain Solid (bottom) taken from a Cape buffalo (30-06 used by special permission due to author's shoulder injury). It penetrated from left temple through right shoulder, ending up under the hide—over 40 inches. The point is—apply specific bullets for their intended purpose.

it applied, Moore's rifle is the place to use it. This monster 2-bore fired a round ball. Since 2-bore means two round balls to the pound, each missile weighed one-half pound, or 3,500-grains. Burning a heap of powder behind this lead bowling ball resulted in a muzzle velocity of 1,500 fps—not very fast. But wait for the energy—17,000 foot-pounds. That's more pasta at the muzzle than the 50 BMG cartridge. Working down from this huge-bore rifle, the October Country 4-bore shooting an .980-inch round bullet at 1,450 fps with 350-grains volume FFg blackpowder develops 6,794 foot-pounds of energy at the muzzle. See Chapter 37 for more on big bore power.

Outlandish Claims

Many of today's muzzleloaders allow stout powder charges with big bullets. The Savage Model 10ML-II, the only front-loader allowed smokeless powder at this time, is capable of shoving a 300-grain bullet at 2,215 fps for 3,240 foot-pounds of muzzle energy. That's more steam than a factory 30-06, except for Federal's High Energy load, which elevates the 30-06 into the 300 H&H world with a 180-grain bul-

Sam's Bullet Box is still used by the author, but he concedes that the Bullet Testtube is better.

Here is the Bullet Testtube set up for a shot. The tube will be hit from close range with a 54-caliber 348-grain PowerBelt Aerotip loaded to duplicate 200-yard arrival velocity.

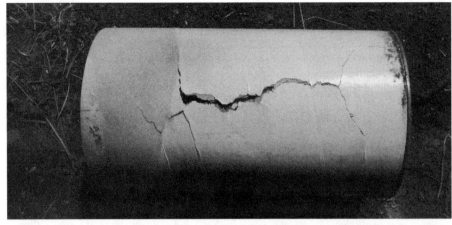

The 348-grain PowerBelt Aerotip bullet hit with sufficient impact to split open the side of the Bullet Testtube.

The impact of the 348-grain Power-Belt bullet created a dimpled-out projection in the face of the Bullet Testtube.

The Bullet Testtube cut in half reveals the wound channel of the 54-caliber 348-grain PowerBelt Aerotip bullet with a 200-yard arrival velocity. The bullet lies at the end of the wound channel.

This is the 348-grain PowerBelt 54-caliber Aerotip bullet recovered from the Bullet Testtube at a 200-yard arrival velocity.

let at over 2,900 fps. A particular 30-06 load provided in a Barnes manual chronographed 3,000 fps from a 26-inch barrel with a 180-grain bullet for darn close to 3,600 foot-pounds at the muzzle. Downrange, the high ballistic coefficient 30-caliber bullet surpasses the hottest muzzleloader in delivered energy. That is why boasting advertisements of muzzleloaders with 7mm Magnum power are simply blowing in the wind. Two-bores and 4-bores are very powerful. But those behemoths are not the norm. And even when they produce huge muzzle energies, even the largest round balls lose a lot of punch downrange. The 4-bore (above) with its muzzle energy of 6,794 foot-

pounds registers 2,783 foot-pounds at 100 yards. The super IMR-4831 30-06 Barnes load at 3,000 fps from the 26-inch barrel rifle retains 3,082 foot-pounds at 100 yards, more than the 4-bore. Meanwhile, the most popular muzzleloader today is 50-caliber, not 4-bore.

In-the-Field Reality

The above facts may seem to reduce the typical 50-caliber muzzleloader to popgun status. But field experience tells a very different story. Those of us who hunt with the round ball, let alone a heavy conical, know that if we get close enough to put, for example, a 54-caliber lead globe on the money, the camp will

have meat that night. Ballistic gelatin blocks and Sam's Bullet Box prove how deadly the muzzleloader can be. Likewise demonstrations with stacked wet newspapers and other media. My bullet box provides a high positive correlation between bullet behavior in the box and bullet behavior on big game. The box is compartmentalized, each compartment containing different material. Typically, the first compartment holds a water balloon to represent fluid. After all, isn't a living body mostly water? The second compartment contains modeling clay a couple inches thick. Consequent compartments hold newspapers wet or dry, and finally phone books to capture bullets that make it that far. One afternoon I tested a 58-claiber rifle. A 600-grain conical not only made it to the phone book level, it also blew the sides of the box out. The energy of this load, which was reduced to represent 50-yard velocity, would not match a 300 Magnum.

Regardless, heavy bullet performance came through. Tests in media do

An African wildebeest (gnu) is a tough animal, but no match for an Austin & Halleck rifle shooting a heavy bullet at good velocity.

KE is a good measure of "horsepower" in a bullet. However, it is not perfect. This is a 54-caliber round ball taken from a bull bison (American buffalo) at close range. The lead sphere traveled the entire breadth of the chest cavity in spite of somewhat modest KE compared with, for example, a 300 Winchester Magnum.

not stand as tall, however, as actual results on deer, elk, moose, bears, or other game. Range tests are static. Field experiences are dynamic. Animals of varying size at close to far distances, at rest, running, tenacious, not so tough—it all makes a difference in firearm effectiveness. But I can promise that a large-bore muzzleloader with a heavy bullet at medium velocity is very deadly.

Another Energy Theory— Pounds-Feet (P-F)

Elmer Keith, mentioned above, as well as many of his dedicated fans, came up with a formula that gave bullet weight more impetus. These big-bullet boys did not cheat velocity. They simply placed it on equal ground with bullet weight. Their theory revolved around momentum, which is the product of mass times velocity. In physics, mass is the measure of inertia for a given body, established as a quotient of the weight of the body divided by the acceleration due to gravity. On the Moon, with gravity being 1/6 that of Earth, a pound of lead weighs 1/6-pound. But the mass of the object is the same on the Moon or Earth. For present purposes, *weight* (not mass) times velocity works fine for

momentum. The fun lies in comparisons. How about a 17 Remington with 25-grain bullet at 4,100 fps muzzle velocity, a 30-06 Springfield with a 180-grain bullet at 2,700, a 230-grain 54-caliber round ball at 2,000, and a 50-caliber 375-grain Buffalo SSB Bullet at 1,800 fps? What happens in the P-F formula? The 17 Remington earns a momentum figure of 102,500, divided by 10,000 for an easier work number, which is 10.25, rounded off to 10 *pounds-feet* P-F. The 30-06 goes 49 P-F. The 54 round ball rifle shows 46, and the 50-caliber with 375-grain bullet comes up with 68 P-F. The 54-caliber round ball, *at the muzzle*, just about equals the 30-06, while the 50-caliber conical whips it by around 28 percent. Believe it? Some shooters do. Ballisticians do not.

But Keith was Right

Elmer was right, on the face of it. As caliber goes up, so does energy, and KE can be used to determine this factor. As an experiment, I had a gunsmith produce barrels chambered for a full range of cartridges built on the standard 30-06 case. Calibers ranged from the 6mm/06—a .243-inch bullet in the

necked-down 30-06 case—to the 375 Whelen, the same 30-06 case necked up to fire heavy 38-caliber bullets. Downrange ballistics, using the KE formula, proved that the 375 Whelen delivered the most energy at 200 yards. Be that as it may, modern shooters carrying cartridge big-game rifles know that the parent hundred-year-old 30-06 is more practical than the 375 Whelen, delivering high potency downrange with a relatively flat trajectory. So energy is not the only factor when considering cartridge choice, or for that matter, a load for a charcoal-burner.

KE in the Real World

While not perfect, KE is a good gauge of muzzleloader authority. The shooter gains a pretty good idea of what to expect from a muzzleloader downrange where the big-game animal is touched. Figures for a couple magnum muzzleloaders are presented below in KE terms. Pounds-feet, while showing a shred of merit, works no better, or even as well, as KE. Nor do other cooked-up formulas. In pounds-feet the little 17 Remington shows poorly with a score of only 10 P-F. Yet, that giant-killer in the hands of a good marksman can take deer-sized game cleanly with perfect bullet placement. One Montana resident has a record of seven antelope with seven shots from his 17 Remington, proving nothing, except that he's a good marksman/hunter who gets inside

The Ultimate modern muzzleloader can burn 200-grains volume FFg equivalent powder. The big powder charge is ignited with a primed 45 Winchester Magnum cartridge case, primed of course, no powder in the case.

Bullet wt. grains	P777 Pyrodex grains	V
420	200	20
325	200	23
348	200	21
195	200	26
300	250	25
300	200	23
300	150	21
300	100	19
300	50	12

:CAUTION:
For Use
Only In
BP XPRESS
500 YD
Black Powder Ri

The Ultimate modern muzzleloader has a set of ballistic notes with the rifle for powder charges up to 200-grains volume Pyrodex. Velocity with a 420-grain bullet is over 2,000 fps for a muzzle energy in the domain of 3,700 foot-pounds.

150 yards (he says) before taking a poke with the sub-caliber spitfire. Personally, I'd bet on my 54 ball-shooter every time over a 17 Remington. We must keep in mind that KE does not leave bullet mass hanging in the breeze. Nor does the formula rely solely on velocity. A good example is a 3,000-pound automobile moving only 30 miles an hour, or 44 fps. That car would deliver 91,000 foot-pounds of energy despite the slow speed.

The Magnum Muzzleloader

A new force to reckon with, the modern muzzleloader allows heavy powder charges with big bullets. No matter how energy is assessed, including the standard KE formula, these guns show well. Tests with two examples prove how powerful these rifles truly are. The Ultimate modern muzzle-

The bullet packs the mail. These heavy Parker Production lead conicals are capable of long wound channels. The Hydra-Con from Parker Productions has an oil reservoir under the nose for hydraulic bullet upset.

loader with four-Pellet allowance drives a 420-grain bullet at 2,041 fps with four Pyrodex 50/50 Pellets (200-grain volume equivalent). Muzzle energy is 3,886 foot-pounds, more fury than the standard 30-06-factory load by a good margin. This load develops 86 P-F. My Markesbery 54-caliber also safely handles heavy loads. I recently retested this rifle, chronographing with a 350-grain bullet in front of 130 grains of Swiss FFg blackpowder for close to 1,700 fps and more than a short ton of muzzle energy, or 60 P-F. Another chronograph run retesting the 54-caliber Markesbery rifle showed a 510-grain Buffalo Bullet taking off at 1,621 fps with 130 grains of Swiss FFg, 20-grains volume below maximum. Muzzle energy: pretty close to 3,000 foot-pounds, 83 P-F. P-F is included here not because ballistic science allows it, but for comparison purposes. Some game departments consider 500-foot pounds at 100 yards lethal for deer. Obviously, the Ultimate or Markesbery delivers a lot more than that. Plus, there isn't a bull moose in Moosedom that can stand up to just one well-placed bullet from either of these rifles.

The Bullet Packs the Mail

The bullet is the only deliverer of energy. Considering bullet expansion, most muzzleloader projectiles start out larger than modern bullets end up after upsetting (mushrooming) on game. Because of medium velocities, muzzleloader bullets are both manageable and a problem. They're manageable because they do not have to meet the rigors of 3,000+ fps speeds. Bullets from high-intensity cartridges fly so fast that keeping jackets and cores together, if that's the goal, becomes fairly tricky. The slower-moving muzzleloader missile is far less likely to come apart on impact. Furthermore, all-lead projectiles behave better than might be expected on big game. Molecular cohesion is the reason. In everyday language, this means that lead bullets stay together as a unit, rather than fragmenting, which in turn promotes penetration due to retained mass. A deep wound channel is the rule with big lead bullets, especially conicals. At the same time, the lead round ball upsets very well in animal tissue. The difference between how a lead conical behaves on game in contrast to how a lead round bullet behaves on game leads to important rules governing each. Heavy lead conicals with supreme penetrating power can zip right through the rib cage of deer-sized game without telling effect. On the other hand, round lead balls that expand well in a rib cage may not penetrate the shoulder bone of larger-than-deer game. Because these two bullet types differ in how they work on big game, they have different rules of placement.

Round Ball Placement

When it comes to the round ball, the best place to put this bullet is *in the chest region behind the shoulder.* That is because round balls tend to upset (mushroom) readily. My collection of round balls includes tortilla-shaped lead spheres recovered from various big-game animals up to the size of bull bison. The buffalo bull charged me, the only charge I have encountered in a long hunting career, including Cape buffalo in Africa. The first 54-caliber 230-grain round ball went completely through the head. A second shot was required when the bull, with half its brain penetrated, got up. This round ball from about five yards passed completely through the chest cavity of the big animal, ending up a flat piece of lead under the skin. That was a lot of penetration through relatively soft tissue. I think the story would have been different had that round ball met with the shoulder of the big bull.

Lead Conical Bullet Placement

A heavy conical, such as the 510-grain 54-caliber chunk of pure lead mentioned above for the Markesbery rifle, should be directed a little forward of the chest region right into the scapula or shoulder blade. Case in point—a javelina, one of the smallest of the big-game animals hunted regularly, range 20 yards, rifle a 58-caliber musket driving a 500-grain pure lead Minie with 100-grains volume FFg blackpowder. Boom! The boar looks up, moves not one inch, but instead remains planted on the spot. The hunter reloads. Boom! The boar walks in a tight circle, whirls around once, and drops. Those big lead bullets simply whistled through the target.

Handgun Bullet Placement from Muzzleloading Rifles

Handgun bullets from muzzleloading rifles behave more like round balls in big game than heavy lead conicals. Most are designed to readily open up at modest arrival velocities, and therefore do a fine job on big game with the chest strike. Case in point—a big whitetail buck, range 50 yards. Boom! A 50-caliber muzzleloader sends a Nosler 260-grain jacketed Partition bullet on its way. The buck is chest-centered. It makes one leap and plops down onto the Kentucky forest floor. Another example—elk, standing at 75 yards. Boom! A 50-caliber muzzleloader sends a 240-grain Sierra handgun bullet on target—chest strike. The elk whirls, dashes into the trees, and drops inside 25 yards.

Downrange Energy

Round balls, even big ones, lose around half of their punch at only 100-yards from the muzzle. So get close. At close range, round balls are deadly. Handgun bullets carry modest ballistic coefficient or C, but reach 100 yards with reasonable remaining steam. Blunt-nosed lead conicals shed speed faster than pointed bullets, but longer ones do quite well downrange. Spitzer-shaped conicals retain their original velocity/energy a lot better because of their higher C rating. For the majority of tree-stand hunting, racy high C bullets are of little value, round balls and blunter conicals doing the job magnificently. But for those who feel a need to have a 200-yard front-loader, shapely missiles are the ticket.

Muzzleloader Powders and Ballistics

There are many good muzzleloader and blackpowder cartridge propellants on the market today with only a few not so good in terms of energy-per-grain weight delivery and standard deviation. The good powders vary one from another in energy-per-grain yield, as well as standard deviation, but that is all right. Good is good. So while Triple Seven may deliver a bit more potency per charge than Pyrodex, that does not make Pyrodex obsolete. In fact, one shooter reported best results, overall, with Pyrodex Pellets in the Ultimate muzzleloader firing four 50/50 Pellets. It is wise to experiment with different powders to test results in specific guns. The blackpowder cartridge is a good example. Asking three prize-winning silhouette shooters what powder they preferred in their 45-70 long-range rifles, each had a different response. One said Pyrodex RS. Another liked Swiss FFg. And a third counted on GOEX Fg. Each shooter claimed experience with different powders before arriving at the one they liked best for tipping over silhouette metallic cutouts.

Beyond Velocity

Velocity is definitely a deciding factor in delivered energy; however, accuracy is also a high priority factor. Most shooters would gladly surrender a hundred fps for much improved bullet clustering, wisely so. Colonel Townsend Whelen, well-known shooter/writer of his day, said it all with his oft-quoted remark, "Only accurate rifles are interesting." Ditto for pistols and revolvers, as well as effective shotgun patterns. The fun is in the testing. It is not difficult work. The shooter heads for the range with safe components: different powders and granulations, a variety of missiles, and he or she shoots, and shoots, and shoots. Eventually, with good record keeping, the most accurate load chain surfaces. The reward is great. At the same time, bullet energy, especially where big-game hunting is the goal, must always be considered. A slightly larger group with more power is better than a slightly smaller group with a good deal less delivered energy.

Muzzleloader Bore Size and Ballistics

Smaller bores generate more pressure per powder charge than larger bores, due to volume of gas dispersion. A 32-caliber rifle firing a 45-grain round ball with 70-grains volume Elephant Brand FFg blackpowder produced 17,700 psi (pounds per square inch) pressure, while a 50-caliber rifle shooting a 177-grain round ball with the same powder and charge, Elephant FFg, 70 grains volume, generated only 6,100 psi, quite a difference. A 12-gauge muzzleloading shotgun produced 1,200 fps muzzle velocity with an ounce shot charge and 102-grains volume Elephant FFg blackpowder, psi rating only 2,200. Incidentally, the only reason a 102-grain volume charge was used rather than a 100-grain charge had nothing to do with ballistics, but rather the fact that 102-grains volume equals 3 3/4 drams equivalent.

Recoil—A Part of Ballistics

Since recoil is demonstrated in foot-pounds of energy, the factor relates to ballistics. Furthermore, recoil is extremely important in accurate shooting. A rifle that kicks you out from under your hat—and I have shot rifles that literally caused my hat to stay put while my head reared back—are more difficult for that "average" shooter to handle than mild-recoiling guns. Recoil is produced by the energy of the load. "Kick" is the price paid for power. That goes for big pistols as well as rifles. Newton's Third Law of Motion says every action has an opposite and equal reaction. The reason the

firearm doesn't fly back as fast as the missile flies forward is weight; the gun weighs a lot more than the bullet or shot charge. Newton's Third is working all the time. A person steps into a boat. He tosses a line to a partner on shore. The boat moves away from the shore in the opposite direction of the thrown rope. A rocket in space could not steer without Newton's Third. Certainly there is no air out there to "push on." When the gun goes bang! the bullet flies downrange, the firearm coming back at the shooter. Part of the recoil formula is the weight of the powder charge. Since blackpowder and its mates are not as efficient as smokeless, it takes more fuel to produce decent ballistics. Therefore, muzzleloaders generate a bit of kick (recoil), especially in big bores requiring consider-

able propellant for decent velocity. I have a 12-gauge shotgun allowed a big powder charge driving a heavy shot charge. The gun is light. It comes back and says hello on every shot.

Blackpowder Handgun Power

Ballistic performance hovers over the rifle in this chapter. Briefly, however, here's what can be expected from a blackpowder sidearm. The 44-caliber revolver produces 38 Special ballistics, while a pistol on the order of Thompson/Center's Encore in 50-caliber challenges a 30-30 rifle at close range. The blackpowder cartridge is on the mild side when loaded with blackpowder, a 45 Colt developing around 300 to 350 foot-pounds of energy. The same cartridge in a modern revolver of strong construction may be loaded

---

A few comparisons:
Rifle A: 30-06 firing 180-grain bullet in front of 55 grains weight of powder. Rifle weight, 9 pounds.
Rifle B: 54-caliber firing 230-grain ball in front of 120 grains weight of powder. Rifle weight, 9 pounds.
Rifle C: 54-caliber firing 460-grain conical in front of 150 grains of powder. Rifle weight, 10 pounds.
Free Recoil of **Rifle A** = 20 foot pounds
Free Recoil of **Rifle B** = 36 foot pounds
Free Recoil of **Rifle C** = 70 foot pounds

Formula for computing free recoil energy:
RE = recoil energy
G = gravitational constant of 32.2 ft/sec/sec.
W = weight of the gun in pounds
bw = bullet weight in grains
bv = bullet velocity in fps.
cw = weight of the powder charge in grains
C = the constant of 4700 fps, also known sometimes as the "velocity of the charge."

Muzzle velocity for the 30-06 was entered as 2,700 fps; muzzle velocity for the 54 ball-shooter was 1,975 and the initial takeoff for the 54 conical was 1,700 fps. None of these recoil figures are that hard to manage, especially when compared with a real kicker, such as the 460 Weatherby Magnum firing a 500-grain bullet with 120 grains of powder at 2,700 fps from a 10-pound rifle with a recoil energy of 116 foot pounds.

Big handgun power is possible with pistols shooting big bullets such as these 58-caliber projectiles. But it doesn't have to be 58-caliber. Heavyweight bullets can be had in smaller calibers, but not small calibers.

with smokeless powder to energy levels comparable to a 44 Magnum. A Hornady reloading manual shows the 45 Colt with a 300-grain XTP-MAG bullet at 1,300 fps muzzle velocity for over a half-ton of muzzle energy. This load is allowed only in Ruger or Thompson/ Center guns.

Muzzleloading Shotgun Ballistics

The muzzleloading shotgun gains something in the domain of a thousand fps with heavy shot charges, such as 1 1/2 ounces. A 1-ounce charge comes up with around 1,200 fps. The blackpowder shotgun cannot compete with the modern shotshell, but within range limitations, and when choked properly for a good pattern, the soot-burning scattergun fills the game bag remarkably well.

Blackpowder Shotshell Ballistics

I was surprised to learn recently that in spite of a powder charge limited by the interior dimension of the hull, the blackpowder breech-loading shotgun gained good velocity, quite on par with the muzzleloading shotgun.

Blackpowder Cartridge Rifle Ballistics

The blackpowder cartridge rifle is limited by the capacity of its metallic case. However, the big bores provide plenty of big game authority. While the 44-40 Winchester scoots a 200-grain bullet away at about 1,200 fps for a muzzle energy under 650 foot-pounds, the Sharps 45-120 cartridge loaded with 110-grains volume Fg comes in at close to 1,500 fps muzzle velocity for well over a short ton of muzzle energy.

Muzzleloader and blackpowder cartridge ballistics are an integral part of the sport, not only for discovering firearm performance, which is important on the target range and vital in the big-game hunting arena, but also for sheer enjoyment of working with interesting facts.

22 THE CHRONOGRAPH SPEAKS

Author relied on the Oehler Model 35P Proof chronograph for his tests. Comparing data with a professional chronograph at a bullet company verified measurement accuracy; the 35P gave results identical to the professional chronograph. Here the 35P is shown with light diffusers.

If I had to have just one tool for testing guns, it would be the chronograph. My Oehler 35P Proof Chronograph, a model I happen to be using currently, provides data on par with the finest "big" machines used by major bullet-making and powder companies. I know this, because data have been compared and they come out the same for my machine and the "big ones." This factor lends considerable confidence to testing. While the main task of the chronograph is ascertaining bullet velocity, the machine does so much more. The 35P I use provides five "double figures" for every shot string fired. That is, the machine reads two velocities within its three-screen span for every shot for five

criteria. That's why the 35P is called the Proof. If these two velocities vary by very much, that is a sign of trouble— something went wrong with the test and that run must be repeated. The five generated figures are highest velocity in the string (a string being anywhere from three to 10 shots), lowest velocity, extreme spread between lowest and highest, the average velocity and finally standard deviation from the mean or average velocity. The two most important figures in my work are average velocity and standard deviation. Fortunately, chronographs have dropped in price over time. A good machine can be picked up for about a hundred dollars, while more sophisticated models might

run around $400. This low price allows grassroots shooters to enjoy the many advantages of chronographing guns.

Just Nice to Know

Shooters are curious. It's just nice to know, by test, what a load produces. Since most blackpowder shooters also fire modern cartridge guns, the chronograph serves in both arenas. My friend the late Max Wilson and I were big 270 Winchester fans. Our hero was Jack O'Connor, so how could we not gravitate to Mr. 270's first choice for big game? We championed a load with H-4831 powder that supposedly got 3,200 fps with a 130-grain bullet. That load was a giant-killer! Then came the pickle-puss chronograph into our lives. Our deadly 270 load turned out to be 2,900 fps with that 130-grain bullet. Our feelings were hurt, but our rifles continued to take big game regularly. Maybe it wasn't nice to know that our hot 270s weren't so hot after all.

Debunking Old Wives' Tales

The best one I can think of offhand is the rule about building a great load by placing a round ball in the palm of the hand and covering it with powder. This romantic notion sure sounded good to me. So as a newcomer to muzzleloading, I tried it, along with a couple of friends. We soon learned that this little golden rule from yesteryear, still touted as right by some writers, had a few flaws. Depending upon how the ball settled in whose hand, the powder charge not only varied with different hands, but also in the same hands. My friends and I put this old wives' tale to the test. The chronograph showed a terrible extreme spread in velocity with horrible standard deviation (SD). The machine also proved that the way my friends and I were creating powder-over-the-ball-in-the-hand loads; most were far below safe manufacturer's maximum for our firearms. That meant very low velocity for rifles that were capable of doing a lot better.

The Cloth Ball Patch is a Gasket

I already had data from Hugh Awalt showing in a high-speed film a jet of smoke *preceding* the emergence of the round ball from the muzzle. That indicated—no, proved—that gas was getting by the patch, which meant the cloth around the lead ball was not a perfect gasket. I also knew the work of Ed Yard, who concluded that no matter how tightly a cloth patch surrounded a round ball, that patch was not a true gasket in the sense of sealing the bore against gas blow-by. Then I took the problem to the chronograph, and sure as taxes and sunshine in the southern Arizona summer, a patch did not increase round ball velocity. Under careful test conditions, I found that unpatched balls that fit the bore fairly well got the same velocity without a patch. The patch serves many extremely important functions, **including safety**. Shooting round balls without patches can be dangerous. Chapter 18 is worth a review on this subject.

Granulation Revelations

It was the chronograph that proved beyond doubt that different granulations of the same powder produced different results. I could have relied upon the good

What is that blackpowder gun really doing? The chronograph has no imagination. It simply tells the facts. A very heavy bullet in 54-caliber achieved 1,360 fps with this load. The chronograph says so. Goodbye to all old wives' tales and guesswork.

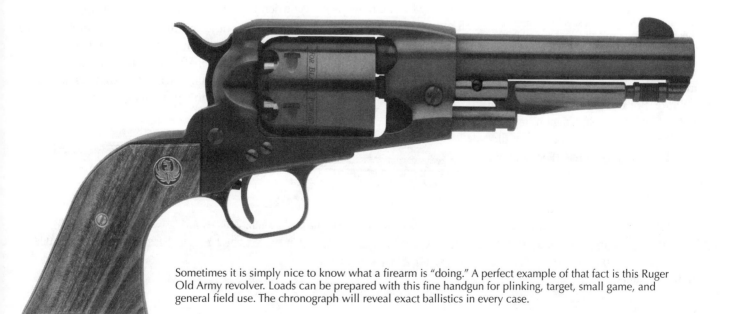

Sometimes it is simply nice to know what a firearm is "doing." A perfect example of that fact is this Ruger Old Army revolver. Loads can be prepared with this fine handgun for plinking, target, small game, and general field use. The chronograph will reveal exact ballistics in every case.

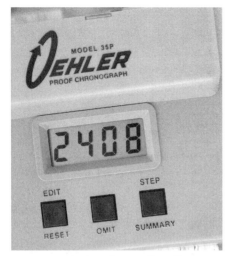

Testing powder brands as well as all aspects of loads is work for the chronograph. This modern muzzleloader allowed a big powder charge with a relatively heavy bullet achieved 2,408 fps - exactly - for that one shot only. This is not the average velocity of the load.

```
2405-01-2408
2395-02-2393
2379-03-2379
--------
03-2408  +
03-2379  -
03-0029  E
03-2393  M
03-0014  S
--------
```

The 35P renders five figures, as shown here. These are, from the top, the highest velocity in the three-shot string; the lowest velocity in the string; the extreme spread between the highest and the lowest velocity; the mean or average velocity, in this case 2,393 fps. And finally, a standard deviation figure: 14 fps here.

information provided by Lyman in that manual. But it was fun and interesting to find out for myself. The chronograph showed, in my own guns, that granulation differences were real. For example, I learned that FFg was the choice in my 54-caliber ball-shooting rifle. FFFg got higher velocity, but not enough higher for a finer-grain propellant that generated added pressure for no real gain. The chronograph also proved that FFFg was right in smallbores.

```
1959-01-1958
1929-02-1929
1910-03-1910
--------
03-1958  +
03-1910  -
03-0048  E
03-1932  M
03-0024  S
--------
```

Blackpowder and substitutes, due to their nature, normally provide very low standard deviations with respect to their quality. There have been blackpowder substitutes that do not render good low figures. The standard deviation shown here, 24 fps, is acceptable, but not to be considered excellent. Standard deviations as low as a few fps are often recorded.

Powder Brands Vary in Performance

How do we know this? The chronograph proves it. I had a chance to test a new powder that one writer claimed was the answer to all our prayers—a perfect fuel in every way. I was impressed with the talk. But became unimpressed after running loads by the Oehler 35P chronograph. Unfortunately for the new miracle powder, I had on hand a can of Swiss FFg. Load for load, charge for charge, Swiss simply destroyed the new amazing powder for velocity. It wasn't even a contest. So, you say, velocity isn't everything,

and you're right. So I took a look at SD between Swiss FFg and the new propellant. Swiss SD was very low, indicating very little variance from shot to shot, which is what we desire. The new powder had a high SD, indicating greater velocity difference from one shot to the next. While Swiss came out with about 10 fps variance from the average velocity, the new powder fell on its face with SDs in the hundred-plus range.

The Chronograph and Standard Deviation

Because the SD concept arose primarily in the fields of education and psychology, some shooters question its use in shooting. I say that SD is definitely useful in shooting, regardless of its origin. It shows the variance in a specific load in a specific gun. And that can be important to accuracy. Consider a modern rifle firing a 150-grain bullet. SD is high, in the 100+ range. The best accuracy will not prevail. Taking this to an extreme, we have a 30-06 rifle on the bench with an array of ammo, including 110-grain bullets at over 3,500 fps, 150-grain bullets at 2,900, 180-grain bullets at 2,700 and 220-grain bullets at 2,400 fps. Bullet shape (ballistic coefficient) not withstanding, these bullets will never group into the same close cluster at 200 yards. My first chronograph did not have SD capability. I had to figure data "by hand" and it was cumbersome. My 35P provides standard deviation as part of the five figures it turns out on a printed tape.

The chronograph also reveals the law of diminishing returns, where adding more powder does not provide a worthwhile increase in velocity. The well-made Ruger Model 77/50 rifle is capable of excellent power. The chronograph, however, shows when the powder charge has reached an optimum level.

By setting up a chronograph and getting accurate readings of muzzle velocity, a firearm can be sighted in properly because knowing the velocity is necessary to figure trajectory.

Due to the large and forgiving screen setup with Oehler Skyscreens, the author has been able to gather accurate downrange velocity figures.

The Law of Diminishing Returns

Understandable those old-timers who wanted to boost power sometimes went to "double-loading." I'm convinced that double loading meant doubling a standard charge for the given muzzleloading rifle, rather than putting down two heavy charges. Regard-

This little glassy eye is the key to the chronograph. It "reads" the passing of the projectile. This is a view directly down into a Skyscreen.

less, the result of pouring down all that extra powder was more noise, smoke, and recoil, but not always a significant increase in velocity. Since the bullet is the only deliverer of energy, it can only work as hard as its velocity allows it, no matter if Newton's formula or some other measurement is applied (see Chapter 21). The chronogaph immediately identifies the law of diminishing returns so that the shooter can adjust properly. A good example of this law from "real life" was a Whitworth 45-caliber rifled musket I was "wringing out" with a 490-grain cast bullet. The chronograph showed 1,306 fps with 90-grains volume FFg blackpowder. A 100-grain charge of the same powder, same bullet, provided 1,322 fps. It's clear that a mere gain of 16 fps was not worth the addition of 10-grains volume FFg. The law of diminishing returns for this rifle with the particular test bullet was 90-grains volume FFg, added fuel being a waste.

The Chronograph Helps Build Good Loads

Combine the last two factors, SD and the law of diminishing returns, and the chronograph is an excellent tool for

coming up with good loads—proper powder by brand, granulation, and charge. I use the chronograph whenever it is time to create a load for a new rifle. By doing a little shooting through the screens of the chronograph, I am able to discover what that rifle "likes" best. I recall one rifle allowed 150 grains volume blackpowder with a heavy bullet. I soon found that 130 grains provided all the velocity and power I desired, while adding more powder did not raise velocity enough to merit the extra fuel spent—more fire, noise, smoke, and recoil. Darn little added bullet speed. Furthermore, the chronograph proved that a particular powder brand in FFg granulation was ideal for power and accuracy, a nice combination. Rifles are not the only guns to benefit from building loads with a chronograph. All guns I can think of are.

Giving the Lie to the Pet Blackpowder Load

I didn't think that Pet Loads with half-grain blackpowder charges made sense. The chronograph proved the point once and for all. This was an easy test. I used the very rifle that was claimed to do its best with, if I recall, something like 60.5 grains of powder. The chronograph proved that no velocity or SD difference existed between 60.0, 60.5, and 61 grains of powder. Blackpowder is not sufficiently efficient to show differences between miniscule charges. Nor are blackpowder substitutes. This does not take away from careful load-building. Not at all. It simply shows that half-grain blackpowder charge variances are insignificant. This is quite untrue of smokeless powder. Also, as bore size diminishes, small changes in powder charge have more meaning. Regardless of this fact, muzzleloaders in bore sizes 32-caliber to 2-bore show no value in varying tiny increments of powder charge. I also have no faith that half-grain blackpowder increments do anything in the blackpowder cartridge. The chronograph proves it.

Proper management of the chronograph assures data reliability. This is a look at the ports on the Oehler 35P chronograph.

Proper management begins by taking care of the chronograph unit and the screens. The wires will be laid out so that projectiles are not fired over them.

Building Your Best Target Load

This is a neighbor to simply building a best load, but with a difference. The difference is nil concern for velocity, whereas building the best blackpowder load usually means going for power as well as accuracy, especially in the hunting muzzleloader that dominates today. But only accuracy counts in building the target load. The shooter works with different powder brands, granulations, bullets, patches—even ignition choices—until SD is very low. Then comes the actual shooting. SD cannot, by itself, guarantee accuracy, although it is a good start. The reason SD cannot, all by itself, prove the most accurate load lies mainly in the bullet. The lowest SD on the planet means nothing if the bullet is not precise. It's back to good old Dr. Mann and his conclusion that accuracy is mainly a matter of good bullets out of good barrels. There's a lot more to

accuracy than that, but the bullet can never be left out of the equation. A good bullet is so precise that it stands up to a spinner without failure. That is, it spins true, rather than wobbling. Combine a good bullet with a low SD and you're on your way to accuracy—provided the barrel of the gun is good.

The Chronograph and Sight-In

I would never begin a sight-in session for a rifle, especially a hunting rifle, without chronographing first. The reason is simple. While a bullet does not travel in a perfect parabola, that term comes close enough for our purposes, and so we rely on it. A parabola is a curve. A bullet travels not in a straight line, but in a curve, rising up from the muzzle, falling back into the line of sight, and then dropping below the line of sight downrange. Not knowing bullet velocity, sighting in becomes

a guessing game. Conversely, knowing bullet velocity, along with the C or ballistic coefficient of that bullet, gives a good starting point. In Chapter 27, various sight-in possibilities are reviewed. Every one of these is based on bullet velocity and C.

The Chronograph and Downrange Velocity/Energy

I discovered a wonderful thing with the large Skyscreens of my Oheler chronograph. Firing from the bench, very carefully, I could put a bullet from a rifle through the screens for readings downrange. This meant hiking a little bit, but not a problem. Set the screens up at 100 yards, 200, farther if the shooter has confidence that he can put a bullet through, not into, the screens at long range. Place the reading unit off to the side. Shoot three times. That's enough. Walk up to the chronograph. Hit the key and run off the data on the paper tape. And there it is—actual downrange velocity. OK, I admit it—I have blown up screens. And something else. I learned that computing downrange ballistics with math instead of actual chronographing was quite accurate. The major difference I found was higher velocity than mathematically derived data, probably due to higher altitude where I live and shoot. I also found out that C is a very significant factor in velocity retention. Bullets with higher C retained initial velocity considerably better than bullets of lower C. I don't want to mislead here. A big blunt bullet at reasonable blackpowder range does the job very well. But for those who want to shoot farther, the high C bullet is the way to go.

Sam's Bullet Box and the Chronograph

Sam's bullet box, as mentioned in Chapter 21, provides a positive correlation between how a bullet behaves in the box and how that same bullet performs in the game field. Since game is not shot at the muzzle, the only way to properly

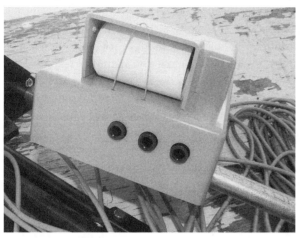

The 35P offers a paper readout, which comes in very handy. The shooter can either write on the paper the exact firearm and load, or prepare an envelope ahead of time with that data, and then insert tape results into the envelope so data is not confused.

Here the Skyscreens are properly set up with all wires leaving the screens on one side and laid out so that projectiles will not be fired over the wires. The diffusers are in place over the "eyes" that will read the flight of the projectile. Diffusers help in avoiding errant readings.

This is a view from the shooting bench to the Skyscreens. The screens are all level and matched. The distance from the muzzle to the start screen can be varied, but of course the reading will change by a few fps in accord to that distance. The author likes to set up so that the mid-screen is 12 feet from the muzzle of the gun.

test a bullet in the bullet box is by either getting away from it or—chronographing. Stepping off 100 or 200 yards—or any other yardage—from the bullet box and firing into it is workable, but not as convenient or reliable as using the chronograph. It is not as convenient because the shooter must walk back and forth between firearm and box. It is not as reliable because from a distance the bullet might not place in the center of the box where it is best tested. For reliability, we want bullets to strike the same spot (center) in the box every time so that one bullet does not have an advantage or disadvantage compared with another. The remedy is simple. Provide a load that matches downrange velocity and shoot into the box from only a few feet away. Consider a Whitworth rifled musket. Muzzle velocity with a 90-grain FFg powder charge is 1,306 fps with a 490-grain Lyman #457121 cast bullet. Tests with the Whitworth and the 490-grain bullet show 1,161

fps at 100 yards. So instead of dropping 90-grains FFg for the bullet box test, 70 grains are used. The velocity with 70 grains is close enough to the 100-yard velocity to allow firing into the box from only a few feet, but with realistic 100-yard results. The chronograph makes this possible.

Find out for Yourself

I think the data found in gun magazines is better than ever. That's because writers have chronographs. On the other hand, I have run across figures, especially from the past, which were too good to be true because they weren't true. This has not been so much in blackpowder, although some smokepole figures have proved fanciful, but glaringly off the wall for certain wildcat cartridges. The reason for such false information lies in two troughs. First, some of the older testing was done by a sort of extrapolation. There was no test machinery involved. Figures were worked up with some formula or another. Second, a few wildcatters from yesteryear were a little too excited about coming up with super figures. One fellow was known to use a chronograph. But he forgot about averages. He might shoot 10 times with very hot loads, then pick out the highest velocity from the 10 shots and call that his final figure, even though it may have been registered in a gun barrel you could cook an egg on. I like finding out for myself concerning printed data, not because distrust—because *most* of today's printed information is reliable. I guess the operative word here is "most." Furthermore, guns differ. I want to know what *my specific gun does.* And that means chronographing that gun specifically.

Settling Friendly Disputes

Once upon a time, it was called cracker barrel talk, where the boys—no women allowed—gathered at the gun shop and laid out their pearls of wisdom upon each other. Some beliefs were, to be kind, pre-science in nature. I can think of two that came my way some time ago. One shooter from a by-gone era insisted that his rifle needed to "pick up speed." That is, the bullet had to gain velocity as it went downrange. He concluded this upon having bad luck on game shot very close, much better results on game shot farther from the muzzle. I suspect the bullet. Up close, higher speed caused bullet failure. "Out yonder," the bullet had slowed down to the point where it did not "blow up" on the surface. Just a guess. Another fellow said his brother had a rifle that "shot harder" than this hunter's own rifle. The only problem was, the two rifles were identical shooting the same loads—not one jot difference in powder or bullet out of exactly the same barrel length. I'm guessing again, but could it be that the guy's brother was a better shot, his bullets placed more appropriately on game? The chronograph settles stories like these for good. The data cannot be denied.

Figuring Power

This value of the chronogaph is so obvious that it comes at the tail-end of the chapter. Of course we must know bullet velocity before we can know energy. By chronographing, computing downrange figures, or taking data from a prepared chart, as in a loading manual, two important points of power became clear to me. First, I found out about the percentage of velocity loss for a given bullet. Second, by knowing downrange velocity, energy could be assigned to a given bullet at a distance. In one test, a 50-caliber Barnes Expander-MZ 300-grain bullet starting at 1,600 fps reached 100 yards doing 1,323 fps for a velocity loss of about 17 percent and a retained energy of 1,166 foot-pounds. I also learned that an entire family of modern muzzleloader bullets fit into a similar energy retention category, losing about the same percentage of velocity per distance. While we think of muzzle as well as downrange energy mostly in rifles, all guns can be included. I tested a load in a 12-gauge black-powder shotgun to see what would happen with a 1 1/4-ounce charge of shot and 80-, 90-, and 100-grains volume FFg blackpowder. The 80-grain volume charge got 1,012 fps. The 90-grain volume charge put the shot out at 1,110 fps. And the 100-grain volume load developed 1,113 fps. For upland game, I settled for the 80-grain volume charge in this shotgun—milder to shoot and an effective pattern. The chronograph had come through again.

Data Reliability

Of course data must repeat if the figures are to be considered reliable. However, while this is true, we have to be careful about accusing information as false just because we cannot repeat it *exactly*. In fact, exact repeatability is usually a fluke. This is because there are too many variables—or frogs in the soup if you wish. The test site itself can make a difference, since altitude plays a role in bullet velocity. Plus, no two guns are absolutely identical, not even if they came off the same assembly line on the same day. Data collected at an indoor range may vary from data collected in the outdoors with the possibility of wind, cloud, and especially temperature differences where velocities may be a bit higher on hot days than cold days.

Chronograph Management

The chronograph is a marvelous machine, but it must be used correctly. Shooting across the wires is not the best idea. Insisting on perfect data in very cold conditions may also be asking for too much, although my 35P does have a special cold weather internal package to help thwart frigid weather. The screens should "see" well, rather than "looking" up at tree branches. Something as seemingly insignificant as a bee buzzing through the screens can result in faulty data. There is also the glint to consider, a form of light from some source that tries to fool the screen. Chronographs come with information. It's best to digest and follow that information for the most reliable results.

23 BLACKPOWDER CHARACTERISTICS

Chances are these riflemen of the 19th century, shown in a Cody Firearms Museum collection, agreed—and perhaps disagreed—on powder choices for their rifles. After all, there were a great many brands to choose from.

Being the oldest propellant in the world, as far as we know, it would seem the properties of blackpowder would be readily understood, with nothing further to learn about this ancient mixture of only three common ingredients. But that is not the case. Even in this 21st century, the pyrotechnics of blackpowder—precisely how this "fuel" works—are not *completely* understood. Professor F.A. Williams, physicist in propellants and fuels, declared that blackpowder's "burning mechanics remain poorly understood because of their complexity." Can you imagine? Complexity? Blackpowder is basically nothing more than

a mechanical mixture, not even a compound, of saltpeter, charcoal and sulfur. Can it be true that the scalpel edge of modern research tools is too dull to penetrate the depths of blackpowder characteristics? On the other side of the road, we do understand major traits, and that is the thrust of this chapter—a waltz through the fascinating world of the first propellant to drive missiles with telling force.

When and Where

No one on the planet knows for sure when, where, or by whom blackpowder was invented. For centuries it

Inefficient? Of course, blackpowder is not nearly as efficient as smokeless. On the other hand, it served well in many different firearms and in cannons as well, the latter with devastating effect.

was known simply as "gunpowder" for there was no smokeless or "white powder" for contrast. Perhaps it was first used in Greece. China is a possibility, along with India. Initially, blackpowder may have been ignited on the battlefield to strike fear into the hearts of the enemy, not to send a projectile downrange. However, we know from the Gentoo Code of warfare, dating before Christianity, that soon enough blackpowder became a dreaded propellant considered the work of the devil. The Gentoo Code:

The magistrate shall not make war with any deceitful machine, or with poisoned weapons, or with cannons or guns, or any kind of fire-arms, nor shall he slay in war any person born a eunuch, nor any person who, putting his arms together, supplicates for quarter, nor any person who has no means of escape.

Cannons, guns, and "fire-arms" indicate explosive force. Quintus Curtius suggests in another ancient writing that Alexander the Great encountered "fire-weapons" in India. Many ancient Chinese and Indian terms refer to fire generated by some sort of substance.

Blackpowder remains less than perfectly understood in burning characteristics. While it has been for ages nothing more than an intimate mixture of three major ingredients, blackpowder varies considerably brand to brand. Swiss, for example, is quite different from Schuetzen.

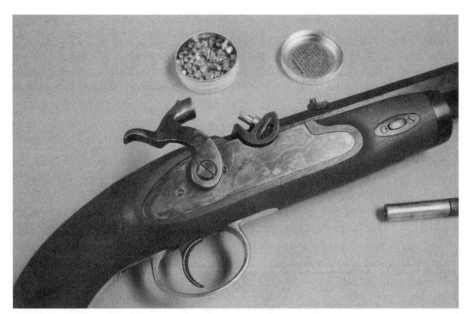

The ancients learned that blackpowder ignited easily, which was a great plus especially on the battlefield where ignition could mean winning or losing a battle, but also in the game field. The percussion cap and nipple made ignition even more reliable.

English writer Henry Wilkinson theorized that blackpowder was discovered when a cooking fire was built upon ground impregnated with niter. The ancient chef preparing his culinary coals suddenly found himself in the midst of a mild explosion. In 275 A.D. Roman Julius Africanus mentions "shooting powder" in his memoirs. There are many ancient records of an explosive. Chapter II, "The Invention of Gunpowder," in *The Gun and Its Development* by W.W. Greener, Ninth Edition, is packed with information concerning the advent of gunpowder, including the story of Berthold Schwarz, German monk of Friburg who supposedly experimented with blackpowder based upon the writings of Roger Bacon, the famous English scientist of the late 1200s. Schwarz is sometimes credited with true gunpowder by improving upon Bacon's data. We know this much: when blackpowder gained prominence, it was made in many countries in varying degrees of performance. We also know that there were many opinions concerning the propellant. Greener taught: "The shape of the grain [kernel] affects materially the combustion of the powder, the sharper diamond-shaped grains

[kernels] burning more rapidly than the rounded ones."

Greener's illustrations show blackpowder diversity, with a very fine kernel French powder, a coarser American example, and a very coarse German powder. He also mentioned Hall's mixed-grain powder. A small sampling of different brands includes Hazard's Kentucky Rifle & Sea Shooting powder, Lafflin & Rand's Orange Extra, Lightning, Ducking, Du Pont Diamond Grain, Eagle Sporting, Eagle Duck, Eagle Rifle, Oriental in America, Curtis & Harvey Diamond Grain, Col. Hawker's Duck Powder, Pigoo, Wilks and Laurence's from England. There were many others. Although all of these powders contained the same essential ingredients, they differed by exact burn rate and other properties. The manufacturing process itself promoted differences from brand to brand, and while these propellants were made up of saltpeter, charcoal, and sulfur, their performance varied.

Composition

While there have been other ingredients added to blackpowder over time––along with various methods of production—saltpeter, charcoal, and sulfur remain to this day, as they were in ancient times, the mixture that we know as blackpowder. A common, but not universal, proportion is 75/15/10—75 percent saltpeter, 15 percent charcoal, and 10 percent sulfur by weight. This mechanical, intimate, mixture can be altered while continuing to function as an explosive. Records show a formula that goes 72 parts saltpeter, 6.5 parts sulfur, 21 parts charcoal. To complete the mixture, add 0.5 and up to 2 parts "Turkey Brown Oil," believed to retard combustion. Another old-time formula is 60 pounds sodium nitrate (not potassium nitrate), 10 pounds sulfur, 17.9 pounds charcoal. Add 10 pounds ammonium nitrate, 1.2 pounds calcium carbonate and a pound of urea. Sound fanciful? This formula carried U.S. Patent No. 2,030,096. Another formula: 74 percent potassium nitrate, 15.6 percent charcoal, 10.4 percent sulfur—really little more than a massaging of the 75/15/10 mixture. Or how about 1,500 pounds either potassium nitrate or sodium nitrate, 200 pounds charcoal, 20 pounds graphite? A 1350 English formula ran 66.6/22.3/11.1

Saltpeter

Saltpeter is potassium nitrate, KNO_3, the oxidizing energy-maker of blackpowder. Oxygen content has been rated at 40 percent. (Sodium nitrate was also used as an oxidizer.) KNO_3 has a melting point of 334 degrees Centigrade, but the ignition point of blackpowder is noted as 300 to 350 degrees Centigrade. Its original sources were many, including earth containing decayed vegetation and animal tissue, decayed building foundations, and cave floors covered with bat excrement. Bat droppings produce potassium salts. Bird excrement produces sodium salts. Combine manure and urine with water in a large cement tank with a drain valve. Cover with a lid for about a year. Filter the liquid through ashes and into trays. Allow liquid to evaporate. The sediment left behind is potassium nitrate crystals. In time, saltpeter could be purchased from a druggist; much more convenient. Pyrotechnic and explosive behavior are governed primarily by a tendency for each element in a fuel to gain or lose electrons during the chemical reaction. KNO_3 answers this requirement with low cost, modest hygroscopicitiy (does not take on moisture excessively), good ignition, low melting point (334 degrees C), and considerable energy yield. By itself, KNO_3 does not make viable gunpowder. While sodium nitrate sometimes replaced potassium nitrate in blackpowder, KNO_3 was/is normally favored.

Charcoal

Charcoal acts as carbon to form the "body" of blackpowder. It provides the element C. Different charcoals affect burn rate and combustion properties, which would not be the case if charcoal were simply a medium to contain saltpeter and sulfur. Softer woods are best because hardwoods leave too much ash. Willow is often credited as making the finest charcoal for blackpowder. Cottonwood, chinaberry, redwood, some pines, cedar, and alder have also been used successfully. Charcoal was prepared by placing wood chips in a metal container, such as a drum with a small vent hole. Fire beneath the drum brought the wood to a smoldering temperature without sufficient oxygen to cause flame. When the chips smoked heavily, a match dropped through the vent hole ignited the wood briefly to complete the oxidation cycle. This method is of historical interest only. There is no need today to make charcoal, and blackpowder manufacture is extremely hazardous.

Sulfur

Sulfur function is the least understood of the three basic ingredients. It is considered a binding agent for saltpeter and charcoal, serving to maintain the integrity of the powder. However, alteration in sulfur content does change the *performance level* of blackpowder, indicating that it is more than a binder. Sulfur is not an active part of the explosion itself. It does nor provide "power." An inferior blackpowder can be made with-

This British cordite powder is included here as an example of powder differences over time—it is in great contrast with blackpowder—and at the same time cordite is in great contrast with other smokeless powders.

Smokeless powder (center) followed the trend set for blackpowder—which was different kernel sizes and composition. Blackpowder was only saltpeter, charcoal, and sulfur, but varying these basic ingredients in granulation, ratio of components, choice of charcoal, and other features was the rule.

What we may tend to forget is the fact that though blackpowder is far less potent than smokeless, it still produces sufficient energy to drive big bullets at medium velocity. This leopard was taken with a Jim Gefroh custom muzzleloader that had sufficient potency to do the job with one shot.

Blackpowder Power

One gram of blackpowder yields 718 calories of heat, 270 cubic centimeters of permanent gas, and roughly a half-gram of solid residues, proving that transformation is inefficient compared to smokeless powder. In one test, 82 grains weight FFg blackpowder left 42 grains of solids after combustion. The factor of remaining solids is related not only to powder efficiency, but also muzzleloader cleanup. Since about half of the blackpowder charge remains as solids after combustion, no wonder the bore cakes up.

Blackpowder Pressure Potential

Pressure is often a negative term in shooting because excessive pressure causes broken guns and sometimes damage to person and property. But without pressure, the bullet would remain at rest in the bore and a gun would be no more useful than a club. We know that the old wives' tale about blackpowder generating no more than 25,000 psi (pounds per square inch pressure) is bunk. Likewise the idea that an excessive powder charge simply blows harmlessly from the bore. We also know that pressures in the 100,000 psi realm were produced in the laboratory with blackpowder, as verified by U.S. Navy tests conducted between 1874 and 1878. While the blackpowder cartridge is self-limiting because of finite powder capacity, a muzzleloader bore can be crammed "plumb full" of fuel. Muzzle-

out sulfur. Sulfur may also be important in providing consistency. Furthermore, it appears that sulfur enhances the long-range integrity of blackpowder. It also lowers ignition temperature, enhancing that highly important aspect—in other words, encouraging the powder to "go off" when flame or spark makes contact. Because of these traits, sulfur remains an important part of the blackpowder formula.

Water

Water content, which can be measured, is another ingredient in blackpowder, although not noted in formulas. Since blackpowder is organic because charcoal was derived from plant life, there is a chance that it could harbor "little animals." Microbes, in other words. These creatures might in turn cause decomposition of the propellant, especially in high humidity areas because a damp medium supports microbe life. Perhaps blackpowder makers of the past understood this because we do note formulas that include isopropyl alcohol as well as whisky. These were infused into the powder-making process as part of the liquid in corning. Perhaps the alcohol and whisky helped sterilize the water by killing microbes. On the other hand, the whisky may have been internalized more by those making the powder than the powder itself. Distilled water or an ammonia additive would have served better in discouraging those little bugs. I, personally, have never seen a microbe in blackpowder.

Blackpowder pressure potential proved to be quite high—as high as 100,000 PSI—but that pressure was developed in a "closed bomb," not in a gun. The pressures generated in firearms was controllable and safe when the proper propellant was used in the proper amount—and that fact continues to exist in today's blackpowder guns. This Traditions rifle, for example, develops considerable bullet velocity with safe pressure.

loaders, therefore, are given maximum safe charges that must be followed.

After Combustion

Understanding what happens to blackpowder during and after combustion explains why we have to maintain bore integrity for best shooting results. Many compounds are formed at various stages of combustion, including a host of salts. These salts can attract moisture, the result being our old friend ferric oxide, otherwise known as rust. These ionic salts dissolve best in polar solvents, such as—water. Plain water. A few of these salts are potassium carbonate, potassium sulfate, potassium sulfide, potassium thiosulfate, potassium thiocynate, and ammonium carbonate. Along with salts, there are of course the leftover carbon and sulfur solids. Permanent gases remaining after combustion are carbon dioxide, carbon monoxide, and nitrogen, as well as hydrogen sulfide, hydrogen, and methane. Hydrogen sulfide is responsible for the rotten egg smell.

Granulation

Granulation determines how blackpowder behaves during combustion. Blackpowder is surface-burning. Particle size and shape are in part responsible for rate of combustion. The kernels are polyhedral (many-sided or many-faced). The shape of the powder charge is always cylindrical in the muzzleloader's breech when the

By regulating granulation along with other characteristics, such as charcoal choice, blackpowder has the ability to gain fairly good velocity with certain bullets like this sharp-nosed projectile from Parker Productions.

A wonderful feature of blackpowder was the fact that it could be carried in a powder horn, as Carl Constantino is doing here, and then metered out volumetrically in the field with a charger or adjustable powder measure.

charge is properly loaded (no air space between powder and bullet). When seated correctly downbore, load density is always 100 percent because there is no air space between powder and projectile, only between kernels. Both of these factors, the shape of the powder charge and load density, occur also in the blackpowder cartridge when the charge takes up all case space. Kernel dimensions also relate to generated pressure in the gun, with finer kernels yielding somewhat higher pressure per charge compared with kernels of larger dimensions. This is logical based on the fact that blackpowder is surface-burning and that kernel size alters that burning surface. Because of this, FFg blackpowder is normally recommended over finer granulations in big-bore muzzleloaders, while finer granulations are more at home in smaller-bored guns, with FFFFg considered pan powder for flintlocks.

Positive Features of Blackpowder

Blackpowder yields less "power" than smokeless. This is good because it allows function in what is essentially an "open system." That is, there is a hole in

Another positive trait of blackpowder is its ease of loading in a blackpowder cartridge such as the old Army 50-70 Government. A dipper for measuring the powder would work just fine. Blackpowder cartridges were reloaded easily in the field by the buffalo runners of the 19th century.

the end of the barrel, but oftentimes a little hole in the back of the gun in the nipple vent and flintlock touchhole, plus the vent (hole) in the breech plug that transfers flame from source of ignition to main powder charge. Blackpowder is also readily ignited, which contributes to reliable firing of the gun. Because blackpowder is not nearly as efficient as smokeless, it can be loaded by volume quite successfully. As little as a few grains weight of some double-base smokeless powders (nitrocellulose and nitroglycerine) constitute a full load in some cartridges. This means that a tiny variation can make a big difference, not only in velocity, but more importantly, pressure. Smile when someone tells you that his or her pet blackpowder load is exactly 72.5-grains FFg in a 50-caliber muzzleloader.

The finest chronograph in the world will not detect the difference between 72.5-grains FFg in that rifle compared with 72.0-grains. Try it. You may have a hard time getting a truly significant velocity change from 70.0 to 75.0 grains volume in that 50-caliber rifle. And so very accurate blackpowder loads are built by volume because that slight variation between charges does not appreciably affect velocity, which in turn means consistent bullet speed for consistent

results (very low standard deviations). Load blackpowder guns by volume. It is the right thing to do. Blackpowder was so good that some shooters stayed with it well after smokeless came along. E.N. Woodcock, dedicated hunter of his era, said in *Fifty Years a Hunter and Trapper*, "But if you should ask me what kind of gun I use, I would not hesitate to say that I prefer the 38-40 and blackpowder. This gun shoots plenty strong." Woodcock also preferred the economy of blackpowder in 1913, being about half the cost of smokeless ammo.

Finally, blackpowder is long lasting when properly stored. I have successfully fired powders that were over a hundred years old. Even when subjected to fairly high or quite cold temperatures, blackpowder does not readily deteriorate.

Negative Features of Blackpowder

If you desire to launch bullets at 3,000 fps, forget blackpowder. It won't work. If cleaning after shooting is a dreaded chore, don't give up. Buy Triple Seven and be happy. (See Chapter 24). Shooting blackpowder will foul the bore, and a fouled bore could lead to a short-start as well as inferior accuracy. Also,

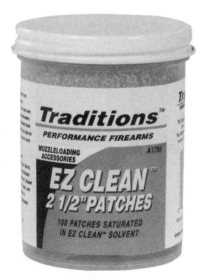

Blackpowder leaves a lot of itself behind upon combustion, but at the same time it has the good property of being very easy to remove, especially with the latest cleaning products, such as these patches from Traditions.

Among the negatives of blackpowder, recoil ranks high. Even in what amounts to a modest blackpowder cartridge (compared with something like the 50-140 Sharps) "kick" is there because it takes a large dose of blackpowder to gain reasonable velocity, as in this original Martini-Henry British Army rifle.

big-bore guns requiring heavy charges deal out strong recoil (see below). If the aroma of hydrogen sulfide offends your nostrils, shun blackpowder because after firing a shot the air around you—and perhaps your clothes as well—will stink. While blackpowder is not, of *itself*, highly corrosive, the fact that it attracts moisture, especially following combustion with those left-behind salts, can cause damage to the bore. That is why leaving a fired gun uncleaned for a long time, especially in high humidity, can bring on pitting. And there will be a cloud of smoke in the air after shooting. I like it. Some shooters may not. Other than these negatives, fire away and have a great time with the oldest propellant we know of.

Granulation

Granulation, or more accurately, kernel configuration, is important to smokeless powder combustion with extruded, flake, ball, spherical, and even spaghetti-like English cordite shapes. Granulation is also a prime consideration in blackpowder pyrotechnics. Granulation promotes a more consistent burn rate, also offering the advantage of greater powder integrity, even though kernels are of somewhat irregular size. Keep in mind that there is no standardization. William Knight of Reading, Pennsylvania is a fiend for studying blackpowder. Bill broke down 250 original 19th century blackpowder cartridges to find what granulations were used. He discovered

that only five contained granulations familiar to us today. Cartridges from 32- through 38-caliber showed an FFFg/FFFFg mix. The 45-70 Government was loaded with equal amounts of Fg and FFg.

Some of the larger Sharps rounds also carried an Fg /FFg mix. Only the big 50 Sharps was found loaded with straight Fg powder. Furthermore, old-time canister powders were quite often a mix of FFg and FFFg. The upshot of granulation is that different sizes create a different package either in the breech of the muzzleloader or the cartridge, partly because of space between various granulation sizes, which in turn determines air distribution. Also, granulation thwarts moisture better than a dust-like powder, partly because granulated kernels can be coated. All blackpowder is hygroscopic—with a "g," meaning that it tends to attract moisture. A hardened kernel absorbs less moisture than a broken-down mass of powder with flour-like consistency. Also, granulated powder is easier to transport, especially important on yesteryear's battlefield.

I am entirely satisfied with the results I get from using one and only one granulation in my own blackpowder firearms. However, a magnified view of any specific granulation reveals that there is a mix of sizes, because granulating blackpowder is not precise to begin with.

Corning

Corning was an important step in the development of a consistent blackpowder because it led to a much safer means of granulation. Corned powder was prepared wet and then turned into granules (kernels), unlike previous "serpentine" powder, which was ground dry.

The Blackpowder Burning Curve

Watching blackpowder burn in open air causes a misimpression of how blackpowder burns in the bore of a firearm. An ignited mound on the ground goes whoosh! But a blackpowder charge does no such thing in a gun barrel. The typical burning curve shows a sharp spike at ignition followed by a smooth curve. Such instant ignition may be part of the short-start problem, because the powder charge is no longer formed into a column with 100 percent loading density, but lies loose in a trough along the bottom of the bore.

Blackpowder Fouling

Noted above as a negative, suffice that modern chemicals do a lot toward reducing bore fouling, which in turn promotes more shots between bore swabbing and easier after-shooting maintenance.

Ramrod Pressure and Black Powder

The chronograph indicates that consistency in pressure upon the powder charge in the breech of the muzzleloader tends to provide lower (better) standard deviations. I have a device built for me by a reader that provides consistent 35 pounds pressure. The Kadooty also creates uniform pressure on the powder charge.

Bore Obstructions and Black Powder

Bore obstructions of any kind can destroy any barrel. The blackpowder firearm is no exception, and with a muzzleloader the situation may be compounded because the powder charge is not converted from solid to gas efficiently and a fouled bore may prevent proper seating of the load in the breech.

Spikes

A spike is an upsurge of pressure along a normal burning curve. The huge smoke ball from battleship guns was caused by smokeless charges detonated by a kick of blackpowder, which was used because blackpowder ignites so readily. But there is a difference between the original spike at ignition and spikes that occur downbore. Such a condition, should it exist, would be classified as an SEE—secondary explosion effect.

Blackpowder and Ambient Temperatures

A smokeless powder cartridge that shows no sign of adverse pressure on a cold day can indicate high pressure on a hot day, while very cold weather may rob its potency. Blackpowder remains vigorous in varying temperatures.

Blackpowder Pressures and Bore Size

A 19th-century naval report on blackpowder translated from the French notes that "In similar guns charged with the same powder, the maximum pressure is proportional to the caliber." We see this in our blackpowder loads in three ways: velocity per powder charge, velocity per bore diameter, and pressure per bore diameter. A 40-grain charge of GOEX FFg blackpowder in a 32-caliber rifle firing a 45-grain round ball delivers 1,900 fps muzzle velocity with 8,000 psi (pounds per square inch) pressure. A 50-caliber rifle firing a 177-grain round ball in front of 80-grains FFg gains 1,573 fps at 6,000 psi. In spite of burning twice as much powder, the larger bore registered 25 percent less pressure than the smaller bore.

Blackpowder at Work

There is a certain limit in the work that any fuel can perform, including blackpowder, with power representing the gas produced minus the energy consumed in pushing solids (and the bullet) through the bore, also minus heat loss. A firearm can be studied as a heat engine. Roger Ford notes in The World's Great Rifles (1998) that only a minute part of the energy developed in a cartridge actually goes toward pushing the bullet. Depending upon the specific firearm and load, the barrel alone may absorb 25 percent of the heat generated from the powder charge. This represents lost "power" in terms of work applied to a projectile. Cooling of the big barrel walls of the muzzleloader is greatest when the weight of the powder charge bears a small ratio to the interior surface of the bore, such as a modest powder charge in a big bore allowing faster barrel wall cooling than a heavy charge in a smaller bore size (less volume and also reduced bore wall surface).

Obturation

Inertia—in this case an object at rest tending to remain at rest—detains initial bullet movement in the bore. This condition can be overstated, but bullet obturation is a reality, meaning the powerful gases striking the base of the projectile cause it to slightly widen out.

The blackpowder story is quite clear in the 21st century—blackpowder continues to work well in advanced design muzzleloaders like this one—with accuracy and power, never mind how ancient the fuel may be.

It is this principle that allows accuracy with the under-bore-size Maxi-ball. Even though the Maxi-ball has a solid base, it is slightly enlarged in the bore due to obturation. If this did not occur, contact between the bullet's shank and rifling would be limited. Pressures with blackpowder are quickly raised. In one test, 2,200 psi was reached in less than 0.1 (one-tenth) of one millisecond after powder charge ignition, showing that there was instantaneous force on the projectile. Hot flame may also cause partial destruction of a conical's base, especially the skirt of a Minie. The same hot gases can also eat up a round ball patch. The first condition requires reducing the powder charge or getting a mould with a thicker skirt. The second calls for protecting the patch with a couple layers of hornet nesting material to prevent burnout. Of course, round ball obturation helps the missile gain a purchase on the lands of the rifling in spite of patch deterioration.

Patch Destruction

Blackpowder can cause *blown* patches (burned out holes) as opposed to *cut* patches, which are sliced by the rifling, not harmed by burning powder flame. See Chapter 18 for how to check patch damage.

Smoke

We love it, all that smoke generated by blackpowder. But this smoke sends a message: "Clean the gun!" Failure to do so can ruin a firearm. Lighter charges of FFFg for target shooting allow more shots before bore swabbing is necessary.

Blackpowder and Recoil

Listed as a black mark above, recoil can be a problem with heavy blackpowder charges because the weight of the charge is part of the recoil formula. Compare a 30-30 cartridge and 50-caliber muzzleloader, the first gaining 2,000 fps with less than 30 grains of powder, the second demanding about 110 grains of powder to achieve the same muzzle velocity. Since blackpowder big bores require a lot of powder for hunting loads, heavier recoil is the result. But it's manageable. Lightweight 12- and 10-gauge shotguns with heavy shot and powder charges, however, do say hello.

Storing Blackpowder

While blackpowder remains powerful over time, it must be kept cool. Heat is its major enemy. Safety-wise, it's also a good idea to place blackpowder away from any source of possible exterior ignition. Potassium sulfide rapidly heated or brought into contact with powerful oxidizers may explode. Also, potassium sulfite, when heated to a point of decomposition, emits sulfur dioxide, which can corrode metals, such as gun barrels and locks. Furthermore, the purity of potassium nitrate is suspect as powder deteriorates. Potassium nitrate and sulfur may convert to potassium sulfide, sulfite, and sulfate, which may reduce power or etch metal. "Keep your powder dry" always was, and still is,

good advice. Place a little blackpowder on the ground. Pour water over it. The powder is destroyed. Oxygen is no friend of blackpowder either. Hence the warning about well-sealed containers. As blackpowder breaks down, it becomes more hygroscopic, attracting more moisture than usual, partly because of degraded kernel integrity.

Impact Sensitive

There is a play on words here. Impact or percussion sensitive? Which is right? Suffice that blackpowder is impact sensitive. It may detonate if struck by a hard object, which would be an act of foolishness in the first place. Moreover, super pressure on a ramrod or loading rod is unwise. Such pressure is entirely uncalled for, doing no good, and possibly causing something bad to happen—ignition. Putting full body weight on the loading rod or ramrod is hereby listed as dangerous. Why some shooters get a kick out of whacking the ramrod downbore on either powder or seated bullet escapes me. This does nothing except possibly deforming the nose of a projectile.

F Sizes

The smallest shooting granulation I have come across is Elephant Brand FFFFFg (5F) blackpowder, smaller than FFFFg (4F) pan powder used in the flintlock. FFFg (3F) is an ideal kernel size for smallbore rifles and pistols as well as cap 'n' ball revolvers—plus light target/plinking loads in any muzzleloading rifle. FFg (2F) is the workhorse for big-game power in 45-caliber and larger rifles, as well as shotguns. It's also appropriate for big-bore pistols. Fg (1F) works in 12-gauge shotguns, especially the 10-bore, and is excellent in large-bore blackpowder cartridges. Fg does not yield good velocity in muzzleloaders of 45- to 58-caliber. German Wano, along with the standard F numbers, also has 4FA and 7FA unglazed powders. Swiss offers a 1-1/2 Fg powder. Cannon grade and other granulations are not included here, since they are not normally employed in blackpowder shooting.

Square Mesh Screen

It's impossible to provide one set of "go" and "no go" mesh sizes for all companies, since kernel size differs with powder companies. Therefore, the following is for general reference only.

Glazing

Glazing meant tumbling the powder, usually with graphite, in the final phase of manufacture, a process possibly dating back to the 1500s. Powder so treated was supposed to be more spark-resistant, although all manufacturers did not embrace the process.

Propellants and Explosives

In general, there are three major classes of propellant/explosives. Certain substances have the property of "going off" on their own. They are, in other words, explosive by nature. We know that magnesium and water react chemically, for example, while Greener notes picric acid and its alkaline salts as explosive, along with fulminates of silver and mercury. Fulminates made percussion caps a reality as an "explosive salt of fulminic acid containing the monovalent negative radical CNO." Fulminic acid in turn is "an unstable isomer of cyanic acid, known chiefly in the form of a highly explosive, shock-sensitive salts used as detonators." The only germane part, for our purposes, of this science talk rests in the words "shock sensitive." This stuff goes off when whacked. Install a little bit inside a tiny metal cup; slip the cup over the cone of a nipple; strike the cup with a blow, as from a gun's hammer, and the fulminate erupts into flame, that flame directed to a main charge of powder in a breech—boom! The gun fires. So that's the first class of explosive/propellant substance. The second class includes substances that do not "go off" on their own, but when joined in combination, produce considerable energy through combustion. This class includes chlorate of potassium plus sugar, or how about saltpeter and sulfur mixed in with charcoal? The third class is composed of chemical compounds such as nitroglycerine and nitrocellulose. All three classes pertain to shooting: the first with percussion caps and primers, the second blackpowder itself, and the third smokeless powder.

Smokeless Powders

Remington recently warned boldly to never use smokeless powder in a firearm intended for blackpowder only. I was not surprised to see this stated again. It is so important that it can never be said or written too often. Unfortunately, not everyone is listening. Possibly—we hope not—on this very day someone will use smokeless powder in a muzzleloader with devastating results. Please don't. The Savage Model 10ML is an entirely different system that safely handles a smokeless propellant. It includes locking lugs on the bolt of the rifle, along with a module of super-strength steel that is inserted into the chamber just like a cartridge.

Many Powders from the Past

It's important to recognize a few propellants that have come along over the years, not only from the aspect of historical interest, but to generate this warning: **Never use any of these older powders in a muzzleloader.**

Brown Powder

Under-oxidized wood, rather than full charcoal, made up brown powder with sulfur content of only three percent. That's why it turned out brown instead of black. Certain records de-

---

Square Mesh Screen Granulation Sizes

Granulation Go	Granulation No-Go	
Fg	.0689-inch	.0582-inch
FFg	.0582-inch	.0376-inch
FFFg	.0376-inch	.0170-inch
FFFFg	.017-inch	.0111-inch

Mesh screen is a fast way to sort out various kernel sizes. If powder gets "hung" up in a .0376-inch mesh, it classifies as FFg. There's a runover because the high end of FFFg is also .0376-inch size. So it's not precise, but the square mesh screen gives a general idea of kernel dimensions.

pict brown powder just as powerful as early smokeless. Odds of locating brown powder are small, thankfully, for it is entirely inappropriate in any firearm today.

Schultze Powder

Composed of "light fibrous woods similar to those used for making black gunpowder charcoal," according to W.W. Greener, this powder surfaced around 1867 and has no place in muzzleloaders or any other type of firearm. It's mentioned for historical interest only.

King's Semi-Smokeless

Patent papers prove that King's Semi-Smokeless was a modified black-powder. It achieved identical velocities as GOEX FFg in a test rifle *under strict test conditions*. Should King's Semi-Smokeless be encountered today, it should be avoided entirely. It's very old and could be contaminated or deteriorated, thereby causing damage to firearm and/or shooter.

Dense Powder

Gun Week newspaper, December 22, 1978, cited Dense Powder as "a modern smokeless powder, frequently combined with nitroglycerine, which gives ballistic results identical to those obtained with blackpowder." Dense Powder must be avoided under any and all conditions. It could blow a muzzleloader to smithereens.

Ballistite Powder

The same issue of *Gun Week* newspaper stated "Ballistite powder, also known as Nobel powder, was the first of the modern smokeless powders. First made in 1887, it consists of 40 percent nitroglycerine and 60 percent nitrocellulose." This stuff will blow your muzzleloader beyond smithereens.

Bulk Powder

Once again, *Gun Week* gets the credit for Bulk Powder, noted as obsolete smokeless powder with a nitrocellulose base. This powder could turn a muzzleloader into shrapnel.

Du Pont Bulk Smokeless

To this day, some older shooters continue to advise using this powder mixed with blackpowder to reduce fouling and improve velocity. Under strict test conditions, I mixed Du Pont Bulk Smokeless at 10 percent and 15 percent with 100 grains volume FFg. It neither produced increased velocity nor did it make after-shooting cleaning easier. **It must never be used in a muzzleloader.** Du Pont Bulk Powder was marketed from 1893 into the 1960s. Here is a warning that came with the powder: "Warning: While it [Bulk Smokeless] is intended for volumetric loading by drams it is not suitable for use as a replacement for blackpowder in the older guns." *This powder was never intended for use in a muzzleloader.*

Amberite, Axite, Cannonite, Chilworth, Coopall's Powder, Cordite and Empire

These are all old-time smokeless powders containing nitrocellulose. They've been gone for a long time, with the exception of British Cordite, which is unique in that it comes as solid *strings* of powder, looking like angel hair spaghetti. Any of these powders could destroy a muzzleloader as well as injuring the shooter.

24 PYRODEX AND TRIPLE SEVEN

Nowhere on a container of Pyrodex does it say that Pyrodex is non-corrosive. It is clean burning and it has the advantage of continuous shooting (reasonable) without cleaning between shots. Also good energy and 30 percent more shots to the pound. But after shooting with Pyrodex—clean the gun.

The search for a truly non-corrosive substitute for blackpowder has been ongoing for decades. Quite a number of shooters stayed with blackpowder after smokeless was widely available. I think of George W. Sears, Nessmuk to his readers and admirers, as well as that old trapper, E.N. Woodcock. But these and so many others did not hang onto the older propellant because they loved cleaning guns. They liked the blackpowder rifles they already owned. These hunters had great success with those guns, mainly muzzleloaders and blackpowder cartridge rifles, and saw no reason to switch to smokeless. Today's shooters are different. They were excited to hear about non-corrosive

blackpowder substitutes coming out. The only trouble was, these powders were not non-corrosive, although they cleaned up readily. Some were advertised as "no sulfur corrosion." Well, I guess not. They didn't contain sulfur. But a shooter had to swab the bore, as well as other parts, just as if blackpowder had been fired.

Then along came Pyrodex. It had specific advantages over regular blackpowder, but the Hodgdon Powder Company never said it was non-corrosive. In more recent history, there is Triple Seven. It too has excellent properties, but again, Hodgdon Powder Company did not false-claim that Triple Seven was non-corrosive. A true non-corrosive

powder is easy to detect. Shoot. Put the gun away for a week, two weeks, longer, and the bore does not deteriorate. Try that with blackpowder and trouble may follow, depending of course on humidity and other factors. Blackpowder, of itself, is not terribly corrosive. I have placed blackpowder on various pieces of metal left for weeks without undue etching of the plates. But blackpowder is hygroscopic (with a g), and this means it attracts moisture. In turn moisture produces ferric oxide, better known as rust. Rust works on metal to form pitting, which are nasty little craters in the metal. At some point, pitting in the bore renders the firearm inaccurate. Safety may also be compromised with a pitted bore that creates a great deal of drag, retarding bullet escape, and also possibly preventing full seating of the projectile downbore.

Pyrodex

What is It?

Pyrodex is called replica blackpowder. But it is more—a unique propellant in its own right. Advantages of Pyrodex over standard blackpowder are mainly three. First, cleaning between shots with Pyrodex is not necessary for a *reasonable* number of shots. This does not imply in any way that Pyrodex can be loaded and fired indefinitely without swabbing. After all, even smokeless eventually cakes up the bore. Second, Pyrodex provides more shots per pound than blackpowder because it is less dense. A powder measure set at 100 delivers close to 100-grains weight FFg blackpowder. Leave the same measure at 100 and the Pyrodex RS charge is 71.0-grains weight. That figure may vary slightly with different lots (runs) of the powder. But it holds well across the board. Because of this factor, a can of Pyrodex weighing a pound (7,000 grains) provides more shots per 100-grain charge than a can of black powder—70 shots for blackpowder, 99 for Pyrodex. Third, Pyrodex RS provides FFg blackpowder energy per volumetric load, while Pyrodex P yields similar energy to FFFg blackpowder per volumetric load. So while getting more shots out of a can, those shots remain at full velocity.

What is it? For shooting purposes and practical knowledge, all we need to know is that Pyrodex is a substitute for black powder and that it comes in RS, P, and Select granulations for specific applications.

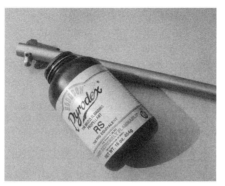

While Hodgdon Powder Company does not claim Pyrodex to be non-corrosive, neither is it overly corrosive. This barrel has fired pounds of Pyrodex over several years' time and it remains in perfect condition with only average (sometimes less than average) maintenance.

Pyrodex and Corrosion

I conducted a corrosion test that ran a full six months, ending with the barrels split longitudinally to reveal damage. I also had the metal tested with more sophisticated means than visual observation. End result: Pyrodex does not damage bores. Cleaning was accomplished in various ways with different time lapses between shooting and attending to test barrels. Blackpowder did not eat up the barrels either, in spite of less than perfect maintenance after shooting. I also learned that both blackpowder and Pyrodex, when stored properly, did not lose potency. This was not true of another propellant I had on hand undergoing "shelf life" tests. In time, this powder apparently took on enough moisture to reduce its energy output. Pyrodex is classified as a flammable Class B solid *propellant*. Blackpowder is listed as a Class A *explosive*. This is not to suggest that blackpowder cannot be shipped via certain common carriers as this is written. I received a few cans recently, albeit not through the U.S. Postal Service. While Pyrodex is entirely suitable for muzzleloaders, it is also excellent in blackpowder cartridges. As with any propellant, getting the most from Pyrodex results from understanding its nature, specific properties, and how it behaves in blackpowder guns.

RS stands for rifle/shotgun, while P is for pistol. These two granulations of Pyrodex vary in energy output per volume charge. P is for handguns and smallbore rifles, but it is also useful in mild target and plinking loads in larger-bore rifles.

Formulations

Pyrodex has not remained exactly the same from inception to present, as proved by the awarding of several U.S. patents for different formulations. Because the Hodgdon Powder Company continued research on Pyrodex over the years, today's formula is the best ever. Early Pyrodex did have ignition problems in flintlocks. I used to load a small amount of blackpowder into my flintlock guns before delivering the main charge of Pyrodex. Today's Pyrodex ignites more readily than earlier samples. Tests show this to be the case not only with standard Pyrodex in RS and P, but also with the Pyrodex Pellet when it is employed as intended in firearms with direct ignition, as found on most in-line muzzleloaders and the Markesbery Outer-Line®, as well as many others, including the Remington Genesis and similar falling or rotating breech designs.

Prepping the Bore

Also called dressing or fouling the bore, the concept runs far back in time. The goal is maintaining a bore in stable a condition. Prepping the bore requires only one shot with Pyrodex. I used to believe that it took three and even four shots, but further experience taught otherwise. Precisely identical results at the target cannot be expected when

RS and Select are not the same powders. Shooters may wish to experiment with both to see which one serves best in a specific firearm. On the left is Select, a bit darker in color than RS.

On the right is FFg blackpowder. On the left is Pyrodex RS. Granulation size is similar and so is energy output per volume, but RS at 71.0 grains by weight is equal to FFg at 100 grains by weight.

Pyrodex loads by volume just like blackpowder. This 70-grains volume charger will throw a proper amount of Pyrodex by volume. So if a load calls for 70-grains FFg, a charger like this is right for Pyrodex—by volume.

the bore differs between first and consequent shots. Therefore, while cleaning between shots for a reasonable number of firings is not necessary with Pyrodex, and can actually raise standard deviations (precise velocities from one shot to the next), dressing the bore is wise *for a target match*. It is unnecessary for hunting, where minor group size enlargement is not as vital to success. The hunter need only dry the bore of the gun completely before loading. After continued firing with Pyrodex, the bore should be swabbed clean with one more fouling shot fired before any attempt to create a tight group on a target. A single prep shot is also useful in clearing lingering oil, grease, or lube. It is impossible to set down a given number of shots with Pyrodex before the bore requires cleaning because of many variables, including the size of the powder charge. Light target loads are not going to foul the bore as rapidly as heavy hunting loads. Reminder: ensure that after firing a shot to dress the bore that the nipple vent is clear of cap debris. This is easily accomplished by poking with nipple pick or pipe cleaner.

RS, RS Select, and P

Just as blackpowder comes in granulation sizes, normally designated by Fg numbers, such as FFg, Pyrodex also has different kernels sizes. The company dropped CTG, which stood for Cartridge. In spite of its popularity with blackpowder cartridge shooters, CTG was not a big seller. Its kernel size was larger than RS and advertised as an Fg replacement. Furthermore, Hodgdon ran tests that showed RS working just fine in blackpowder cartridges. RS stand for Rifle/Shotgun. It's the workhorse of the line, considered a substitute for FFg granulation in blackpowder, and excellent in all bore sizes from 32- to over 60-caliber. It also works admirably in blackpowder shotguns of all gauges, as well as blackpowder cartridges of all sizes. RS Select Premium Muzzleloading Propellant is billed as "Specially Processed and Tested." Select is repre-

sented as a special RS offering superb kernel size uniformity. It was originally intended for target shooting, where ultimate groups were important. But Select earned its way into the hunting field as well. Today, RS and RS Select are the largest kernel sizes. Pyrodex. P stands for Pistol. It's considered a substitute for FFFg blackpowder and is employed the same way. As the finest granulation of Pyrodex, it works well in cap 'n' ball revolvers and small-bore pistols. P is also useful in small-bore rifles, such as the 32 or 36, where it develops good velocity with modest charges. It's also workable in larger-bore rifles and pistols for light practice or plinking loads.

Volumetric Loading

Pyrodex is loaded by volume, *not* weight, just like blackpowder. The latter part of the muzzleloader bore is the breech of the gun. This section of the barrel can be thought of as performing the same job as a cartridge case as the reservoir for the powder charge. After seating a projectile fully upon a volumetric charge of Pyrodex that has been delivered fully down into the breech of the muzzleloader, there is no air space left between bullet and charge. This means 100 percent load density. The same situation exists with blackpowder cartridges when loaded with a full case of Pyrodex. We know that 100 percent load density in the muzzleloader—zero air space between missile and charge—is the safe way—no air gap to create a short-start. Pyrodex in blackpowder cartridge guns also has 100 percent load density, no air space in the case. Where lighter loads are desired, air space in the blackpowder case is taken up with fillers or wads. The beauty of proper volumetric loading with Pyrodex is simplicity. A charger works fine, as does an adjustable powder measure. Range tests with Pyrodex weighed on a powder/bullet scale to a tenth-of-a-grain (weighing 71.0 grains exactly for a 100-grains volume load) provided zero improvement in groups. Nor did scale-weighed loads improve standard deviation figures (see Chapter 22). The same adjustable powder measure or charger used for blackpowder is therefore the proper tool for throwing charges with Pyrodex.

Energy Yield

While Pyrodex is about 30 percent less dense than blackpowder—71.0 grains RS with powder measure set at 100-grains volume—energy yield is on par with blackpowder. Chronographing loads comparing Pyrodex with blackpowder verify this fact. A 32-caliber squirrel rifle with 26-inch barrel achieved 2,072 fps with 40-grains volume GOEX FFFg blackpowder. The same rifle firing the same 45-grain round ball developed 2,039 fps with 40-grains volume Pyrodex P, virtually identical results. Going to a 50-caliber test rifle with conical projectiles, a 350-grain Buffalo Bullet in front of 100-grains volume GOEX FFg showed a muzzle velocity of 1,440 fps, while Pyrodex RS got 1,480 fps. Here is one more—caliber 54 with a 430-grain Thompson/Center Maxi bullet. A 100-grain volume charge of GOEX FFg produced 1,390 fps. The same volumetric charge of RS (71.0 grains weight) fired the 430-grain bullet at 1,384 fps, statistically the same performance considering normal variables.

Pressure generated by Pyrodex and Triple Seven are quite similar per volume charge. This powder measure was set at 100. It yielded 71.0-grains weight Pyrodex RS and 76.0-grains weight Triple Seven.

Pressures

As with blackpowder, overloads with Pyrodex can be dangerous. Maximum charges dictated by the gun manufacturer must be adhered to rigidly and without deviation. Pyrodex also obeys the Law of Diminishing Returns, where adding powder beyond a certain level produces no worthwhile increase in velocity. Also, overloads may cause incipient damage in a firearm that do not appear immediately, but could show up later.

After Shooting

After shooting a gun with Pyrodex, muzzleloader or blackpowder cartridge, cleaning follows the same general pattern demanded by blackpowder. I have found Pyrodex fouling relatively easy to remove from the bore and other parts of the firearm. Don't forget cartridge cases flushed with soapy water and followed by a good run in a tumbler or vibrating cartridge case cleaner using media.

Flintlocks

Today's formulation of Pyrodex works better in flintlocks than older examples. But most shooters of the old-time spark-maker prefer staying with standard blackpowder, employing FFFFg for ignition. Flintlock shooters interested in shooting Pyrodex are invited to test their personal firearms at the range.

Ignition

The No. 11 percussion cap remains highly popular with muzzleloader shooters because it works extremely

Energy yield of Pyrodex is excellent. A proper charge of FFg in this Lyman Plains Pistol is matched by the same Pyrodex RS charge by volume and not by weight. If the measure for FFg is at 50, for example, the measure is left at 50 for RS, even though by weight the RS charge will be less than the FFg charge.

Ignition with Pyrodex is good. Likewise Triple Seven.

well. However, muzzleloader ignition today is not what it used to be. The tophat or musket cap has a strong flame, but the No. 209 Shotgun primer has all but taken over with modern muzzleloaders. The Winchester Company, recognizing the trend, developed a special No. 209 primer for Pyrodex Pellet and Triple Seven Pellet ignition.

Pyrodex Lube

Pyrodex is compatible with standard lubrications on the market, as well as solvents. However, the Hodgdon Powder Company has developed a special product called, appropriately, Pyrodex Lube. It is billed as a "patch or bullet lube & cleaner all natural, biodegradable, environmentally safe." The back of the can bears instructions for use. There is also the Pyrodex Patch containing this special lube.

The Pyrodex Pellet

The package arrived in good shape. I kept my promise, tucking it away in the gun safe for future reference. Some time later, Dean Barrett, vice president with the Hodgdon Powder Company, showed up at my Wyoming home. We sat at the dining room table, the mysterious unopened package resting between us. "Go ahead and open it,"

The Pyrodex Pellet has become so popular that in some deer hunting lodges out of 20 blackpowder shooters perhaps as few as two or three will be shooting "loose powder." This trend is continuing with the Triple Seven Pellet.

Dean said. I did. And there they were, Pyrodex Pellets. While they had been laboratory tested extensively, no one had fired them in everyday rifles under everyday conditions. For the next three days, Mr. Barrett and I did just that. At the conclusion of the visit, I had but one thing to tell the visiting inventor: "You have a winner." The Pellet originally came as a 50/50, 50-caliber muzzleloader, each pellet valued at 50-grains *volume equivalent* Pyrodex RS. Shooters soon demanded a 54-caliber Pellet, the 54/60, which came along as 60-grain volumetric equivalent charge per Pellet, 54-caliber, 60-rains volume equivalent Pyro-

dex RS. A 50/30 followed, 50-caliber, 30-grains volume equivalent Pyrodex RS, ideal for juggling. For example, an 80-grain volumetric charge could be gained with one 50/50 Pellet and one 50/30 Pellet. Pellets for the cap 'n' ball revolver also became available. The line has grown since.

Triple Seven
What it Is

Thanks to the genius of Dean Barrett, Triple Seven, in the 777th formula became a viable reality. Triple Seven enjoys the same positive properties as Pyrodex, with one more advantage—easy cleanup.

Triple Seven has two superb properties—it cleans up readily with water only and a practiced blackpowder shooter can clean a gun fired with Triple Seven in just about the same time a smokeless powder firearm can be cleaned. The other strong point is strength—Triple Seven produces good velocity per volume charge.

Triple Seven Properties

Blackpowder fouling can be, and has been for ages, attacked with water. But there is a big difference with Triple Seven. One wet patch followed by a couple dry patches thoroughly cleans the bore. I cannot assign that sort of water cleanup to blackpowder. I can clean a muzzleloader fired with Triple Seven as fast as my 30-06 rifle, faster if the '06 bore is copper-fouled because getting rid of copper fouling takes time. Triple Seven is loaded safely by volume, the same as Pyrodex or blackpowder. It comes in FFg and FFFg granulations and it is less dense than blackpowder, but more dense than Pyrodex. A mea-

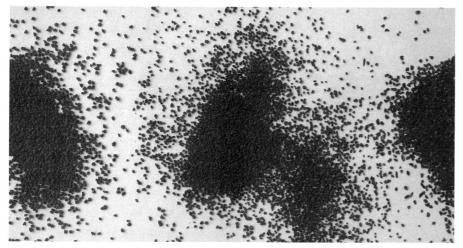

With an adjustable powder measure set at 100, here is the result of RS on the far left, Triple Seven FFg in the center, and FFg to the right. Similarity in kernel size is obvious. Furthermore, the three propellants can all be used at the same volume charge—that is, the powder measure is left at the same number for each powder.

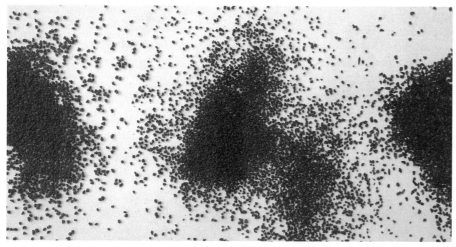

Here are three powders laid out with P on the far left, Triple Seven FFFg in the center, and FFFg blackpowder on the right. The granulation sizes show similar again and obviously smaller than RS, Triple Seven FFg or FFg blackpowder.

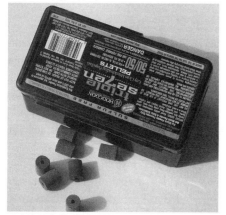

The Triple Seven Pellet had to happen. The success of the Pyrodex Pellet made it impossible to ignore a Triple Seven Pellet. However, the shooter, as always, is invited to try both in his or her particular blackpowder firearm for possible performance differences.

Triple Seven Pellets are smaller in size for the 50/50 pellet (50-caliber/50-grains volume) than 50/50 size Pyrodex Pellets because Triple Seven Pellets yield more energy than Pyrodex Pellets.

sure set at 100 gives 100 grains of GOEX FFg, 71.0 grains of Pyrodex RS, and 76.0 grains of Triple Seven. Triple Seven yields good power. A 100-grain volume charge of Triple Seven pushed a 240-grain pistol bullet at 2.006 fps from a 26-inch barrel. Ignition in my tests has so far been 100 percent. As for flintlocks, Triple Seven was never intended for the spark-maker, nor have I tried it in mine. I find zero corrosion problems when cleaning the bore with water only. Pressure is on par, per volume, with other good propellants. And one shot is sufficient for bore prepping at the target range.

Triple Seven Pellets

All of the good points associated with the Pyrodex Pellet fit the Triple Seven Pellet. I have tried the 45/50 (45-caliber, 50-grains volume), the 50/30 (50-caliber, 30-grains volume) and the 50/50 (50-caliber, 50-grains volume).

Pyrodex and Triple Seven are two extremely good blackpowder substitutes. They do not replace blackpowder. They simply offer alternatives to the older propellant.

25 BLACKPOWDER ACCURACY

Heavy bench guns were capable of fine bullet grouping in the past and the same type of accuracy exists today with these blackpowder muzzleloaders.

When blackpowder shooting regained national prominence, accuracy expectation was low. We had forgotten that both muzzleloader and blackpowder cartridge rifle produced fine accuracy in the past with grouping possible at 1,000 yards with rifled muskets as well as blackpowder cartridge longarms. This rifleman is aiming at a distant silhouette target.

F.W. Mann, a physician by calling, studied bullet flight religiously for a number of years. At the conclusion of his safari for truth, Mann summarized his findings in only a few words. He said that accuracy was mainly a matter of good bullets fired from good barrels. That truth cannot be denied. However, there is more to the story, much more. The following points are presented in random order.

Expectations False

Blackpowder shooting never died in America or Canada, as proved by continuous articles on the subject in periodicals, especially *The American Rifleman* magazine. However, replicas brought forth by Turner Kirkland of Dixie Gun Works and a little later by Val Forgett of Navy Arms, ignited smoldering coals into flame. No longer did a shooter have to look for an original to enjoy "making smoke." Revolvers, pistols, rifles, and shotguns were readily available. Special blackpowder-only big game seasons gave reason for thousands of hunters to buy front-loaders, and they did. It's safe to say that a majority of today's shooters either have a blackpowder gun of some sort or have at least fired one. Initially, there was a problem with accuracy expectation. It was lizard-crawling low. I recall elation at the range when a smokepole shooter finally got three shots to group into a Stetson cowboy hat at only 100 yards. In the 19th century and earlier, such groups were considered woefully inadequate. But we modern shooters didn't know any better, so we settled for patterns that would have been laughed at (or cried over) had they been made with a modern cartridge-firing rifle. Thankfully, that sad state of affairs changed in two ways: shooters demanded greater accuracy, and gunmakers and importers saw that they got it.

Expectations True

Initially, I was a member of that happy group of downwind shooters who were entranced and delighted with a big bellow and spew of smoke filling the air. But the aura soon faded. When Colonel Townsend Whelen, known as Mr. Rifleman in his day, said that only accurate rifles are interesting, he was right, and that applies to handguns as well. Modern shooters needed to study old-time accuracy. There were slug guns in days of yore that printed stingy groups at long range. These were not hunting rifles. They were huge, heavy, rifles that Paul Bunyan could not carry

in the field. Hunting guns of the 19th century were also capable of fine accuracy. I learned my lesson about blackpowder accuracy potential after receiving my 54-caliber round ball shooter, No. 47, from custom gunmaker Dennis Mulford. Off the bench, even with its iron sights, No. 47 could keep all of its round bullets in a half-fist-sized group at 100 yards. A local gunsmith who owned a couple accurate rifles drilled and tapped the barrels for mounts for a Bushnell 6-24X scope. With iron sights group ranged from under two inches to three inches at 100 yards. Once the rifles were scoped, groups shrank to slightly under one-inch center-to-center at 100 yards.

Consistency or Nothing at All

Mann was right about good bullets from good barrels resulting in fine accuracy, but the finest barrel in the world launching near perfect missiles will fail to group if consistency in all departments is not maintained.

Powder Charge Consistency

Blackpowder or any approved substitute, the only right way to load is by volume (not weight) with a charger or adjustable powder measure. Consistency here means establishing and

following a routine. There are various ways to establish this pattern. Here is one that works: fill charger or adjustable measure to slightly overfull, tap barrel of charger or measure a specific number of times, such as six, eight, or ten; if using a measure with a swing-out funnel, swing the funnel back in place to swipe off the few kernels of powder resting above the barrel of the measure. The charger can be leveled a little, too, as with a Popsicle stick. This sort of routine establishes consistency. Blackpowder cartridges can be treated in a similar manner using a charge or adjustable powder measure. However, we now have special mechanical blackpowder measures, such as Lyman's 55 Classic Black Powder Measure that can be used with blackpowder cartridges. **Warning:** *Never meter out blackpowder loads in a standard mechanical measure. The friction and/or static electricity normally associated with these measures could cause the powder to explode.* Lyman's 55 Classic Black Powder Measure is designed especially for blackpowder, although it will also throw smokeless powder charges safely. The internal metering bars rotate in a non-sparking brass sleeve. The powder reservoir, which holds a pound, is made of non-static aluminum.

Ramrod Pressure and Powder Charge Consistency

We believe that a mildly compressed powder charge is conducive to best burning characteristics. It follows that consistent ramrod pressure promises consistent bullet pressure upon that powder charge. A reader presented me with a neat device for maintaining consistent ramrod pressure upon the bullet/ powder charge in the breech of pistol, rifle, or shotgun. Mr. French's ramrod pressure tool had an aluminum body with a ramrod size hole in its center. Inside was a spring with a metal button on the end. The tool was fitted over the end of the ramrod via the hole. Pushing down on the tool in turn pushed down on the ramrod, the spring collapsing at

Accuracy is not limited only to blackpowder rifles. There are many blackpowder handguns that produce sufficiently tight grouping to allow target shooting as illustrated here.

40 pounds pressure. Since, I have others going 30 and 35. A commercial device that does the same job is the Kadooty, delivering the same pressure upon the bullet/powder charge for every load. For fieldwork, plinking, informal target shooting, and general hunting, applying the same pressure upon the load "by feel" is acceptable. But when testing a rifle for accuracy, a tool such as the Kadooty is more reliable. Test results shooting rifles with varying pressure on the ramrod and consistent pressure on the ramrod show that standard deviation is lower (better) with consistent ramrod pressure.

The Round Ball Patch

Chapter 18 discusses the many important functions of the cloth ball patch. In order for the patch to do this vital work, two things are paramount. First, the patch must be of good quality, not only because it must withstand its ride through the bore, but also for consistent thickness from one spot to another. Second, the patch must be of proper thickness. A tough patch material of uniform thickness is best, such as pure Irish linen cloth (sold at fabric stores) as well as commercial patches. Chapter 18 discusses picking up fired patches downrange. The fired patch should be intact, small holes notwithstanding. Blown patches can be cured with hornet nest material, a couple thin sheets between patch and powder charge downbore.

Bore Condition

The crown of the muzzle—the last contact point before the bullet leaves the firearm to take its journey, is important to accuracy. Damage here can send a bullet astray. Rifling in general must be intact and clean for best accuracy. The bore changes with each shot to some degree, especially since blackpowder does not turn from solid to gas nearly as efficiently as smokeless. At the same time, a squeaky-clean bore can be a problem.

Cleaning Between Shots

Pyrodex RS has an especially good trait—several shots can be fired before cleaning is necessary. In fact, best accuracy is usually obtained by firing one shot before attempting to create best target groups, followed by a string of shots, perhaps five, without further bore cleaning. Powders vary as to clean-burning quality, however, and the shooter is urged to provide a clean bore for powders that leave considerable fouling left behind after firing. This is easy to test. Fire three shots at 100 yards on the target cleaning between shots and not cleaning between shots to see if there is a difference in group size.

The Fouling Shot

With Pyrodex RS, I now fire one shot before attempting to create a "best group" from a rifle, or for that matter, even a pistol. I once felt that two or more fouling shots were necessary, but further experience has shown otherwise. The fouling shot preps the bore. It also helps to remove any traces of oil that can send that first bullet astray.

Accuracy with Volumetric Loads

Because blackpowder and approved substitutes are not nearly as efficient as smokeless powder, loading by volume creates excellent accuracy. Consider as a matter of comparison, the quick 17 Remington cartridge with its rather small powder capacity and tiny bore with minimal volume for powder gas dispersion. A charge of 21.0-grains AA 2520 smokeless powder drives a 25-grain bullet at 3,600 fps. By adding only one-half grain, that 21.5-grain charge of AA 2520 develops an additional 100 fps—for only one-half grain. A similar picture is painted with Bullseye smokeless powder in the 38 Special when 2.8-grains drives a 158-grain bullet at 650 fps from the test revolver, while 3.7 grains, which is considered a maximum load, achieves 800 fps. Now check out a 50-caliber muzzleloader

and you will find that 95.0-grains volume FFg and 100-grains volume FFg with various bullets will scarcely show a difference on the finest chronograph. Since blackpowder and its approved substitutes are not nearly as efficient as smokeless, it follows that a small difference in the charge will not affect muzzle velocity, which in turn means that velocity will be consistent from one shot to the next, ensuring the same placement (group) on the target each time. This does not condone sloppy powder loading practices. See notes on powder consistency (above). Anyone can test accuracy with volumetric loads vs. scale-weighed charges. It's as simple as shooting sample groups from the bench with both types.

Standard Deviation

The Oehler 35P Proof Chronograph used for all tests in this book provides five figures for each shot fired— (see Chapter 22). One of those figures is standard deviation, which is a test of variance from one shot to the next. I have found that standard deviation does not change between scale-weighed blackpowder loads and volumetric blackpowder loads. A standard deviation of 12 fps, for example, with a scale-weighed charge produces essentially the same standard deviation with charger

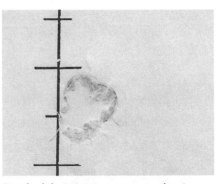

Standard deviation is a measure of variance. A high standard deviation, which can be caused by using an inferior powder as only one example, translates to a high variance in muzzle velocity, which in turn delivers bullets to different locations on the target. Obviously, this target, produced with a Parker Production bullet, enjoyed a low standard deviation from the mean (average) velocity.

Already noted was accuracy by volumetric loads. Taking that concept to another level, how about accuracy with a charger as opposed to an adjustable powder measure. It is there, including chargers made of hollowed-out antler and other materials.

or measure. Velocity also remains the same for volumetric or scale weighed loads. Others will disagree, sometimes vehemently, praising their "pet loads," such as 60.5-grains weight vs. 60- or 61-grain volume loads. I challenge that shooter to a chronograph/target duel—pet loads vs. my standard loads.

Accuracy with Volumetric Charger

Recall that a charger is a simple metal tube, cut-off piece of antler, or other device that provides one and only one volumetric charge, while the adjustable powder measure is capable of throwing various volumetric charges of powder. Here is what happened with an adjustable powder measure: Ten charges of GOEX FFG carefully thrown with a powder measure set at 100 showed a low of 99.2 grains and a high of 101.7 grains. Compared with the accuracy provided by a powder/bullet scale, that seems crude. However, because of the efficiency issue (above), the variation from 99.2 grains volume to 101.7 grains volume in the 50-caliber test rifle proved insignificant.

Powder Brand/Granulation, Charge, Bore Dimension, Rifling Twist

These factors are linked for several reasons. Muzzleloader propellants vary from brand to brand. Going strictly by how much velocity a specific powder provides in a certain gun compared against another brand of

powder is faulty. The higher velocity does not necessarily determine how good one powder is over another. Other factors, such as kernel uniformity, apply. Furthermore, there is a matter of velocity per pressure. One powder may provide a little less velocity than another, load for load, but with a good velocity/pressure ratio. Finally, minor firearm variations may favor one propellant over another. This seems to hold true for the larger blackpowder cartridges, where larger kernel propellants shows a little accuracy improvement over smaller kernel.

Bore size determines pressure, as we know from pressure gun readings. For example, a 36-caliber squirrel rifle firing a 65-grain round ball in front of 50-grains volume GOEX FFg blackpowder showed a psi rating of 11,200, while the same GOEX FFg charge in a 50-caliber rifle pushing a 177-grain round ball generated only 2,900 psi. Granulations also make a difference in pressure. Example: 50-caliber rifle, 177-grain round ball, 70-grains volume FFg Elephant Black Powder, 6,100 psi, 70-grains FFFg Elephant Black Powder, 8,300. So what does pressure have to do with accuracy? Consider bullet obturation or upset in the bore. If a charge fails to provide sufficient

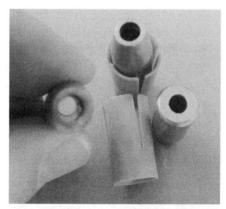

Pick your bullet, but then choose the right powder for it. This projectile is called The Bullet. It has a hole running completely through its center. Of course The Bullet requires a sabot to seal gases at the base. Fadala tried various powders with The Bullet, finding in the particular test rifle that Swiss FFFg with a mild charge produced excellent groups at 100 yards.

pressure to force the projectile into the lands for guidance, accuracy suffers. This is why shooters report poor groups with very light powder charges in *some* guns. On the other end of the spectrum, super heavy charges may "blow" a group wide open, sometimes because of actual damage to the base of a conical, which hampers its "steering" ability.

Rifling twist also plays an integrated role along with the other three criteria above. The bullet, round or conical, must be stabilized for proper flight from muzzle to target. The unstable round ball, failing to rotate on its axis, does not equalize minor discrepancies in its construction, and therefore cannot fly as true as a round ball that is spinning properly. A conical that fails to spin on its axis is in worse shape, because it will tumble in flight, doing what's called key holing, and likely to strike the target sideways instead of point on. Since it is up to rifling to provide RPS (revolutions per second) of a projectile, then twist is very much linked with accuracy. Rapid twist does nothing for the lead sphere, as proved by the fine rifles coming from October Country with super slow twist in big bores. This is the way it should be, for as the round ball grows in mass, it requires less RPS to keep it on track. That's why a little 32-caliber squirrel rifle may have a 1:40 rate of twist for a round ball, while an 8-bore goes with a turn in over a hundred inches. The conical-shooter, on the other hand, must provide a sufficient rate of twist to rotate the elongated bullet on its axis for accuracy. More on twist in Chapter 20.

Overstablization?

Can a bullet be overstabilized? My opinion, which is naught but opinion at this point, is that a bullet can be overstabilized. Consider a toy top. It remains spinning over a span of rotational velocity. Finally, when spin is too slow for stabilization, the top falls over. My guess is that the top, *if perfect*, would

Can a bullet be over-stabilized? Most likely it is not a matter of over-stabilizing a projectile, but rather the bullet being guided by the rifling—or not guided by the rifling. These round balls can "strip the rifling" or "ride over the rifling," two terms from the past to indicate a patched round ball not guided by the rifling, but rather "stripping the bore," another term meaning the same thing.

spin properly at any rate. But if imperfect, too-rapid spin could cause that imperfection to take effect, sending the top into a wobble. Since there are no absolutely perfect bullets, round or conical, perhaps over-spinning could upset flight. What does the reader think?

Altering Powder Charge

Altering the powder charge can produce a specific effect. After all, changing the powder charge varies velocity either up or down, which in turn changes RPS in a rifled firearm, which in turn may affect bullet stabilization. This is why we work within the safe range of powder allowance for a given firearm for best accuracy. Although a matter of pattern, not accuracy, it's worthwhile to note that powder charge variation changes shotgun performance as well, not only because of possible damage to a wad column, but also in how the shot charge is propelled.

Bullet Precision

We're back to the beginning with Dr. Mann and his good bullets out of good barrels argument. This point is too obvious to belabor. There are two tests for bullet precision: spinning and weighing. Spinning reveals concentricity—bullets that wobble badly when spun are not to be trusted for accuracy. Obviously, rotation on its axis overcomes *some* of the problem. Weighing

discovers too-light or too-heavy missiles. Such discrepancy kills uniformity. Bullets of varying weight cannot fly perfectly into one group. Going with an exemplar modern cartridge, consider a 30-06 shooting bullet weights of 110, 150, 180, and 220 grains at 200 yards. Unlikely that all will land in the same group. Bullet quality is not as crucial to big-game hunters as it is to benchrest shooters. But smart hunters do demand accuracy. Luckily, blackpowder shooting is loaded with fine bullets, from hand-crafted cast lead to fine swaged round balls from Hornady, Speer, and others, to a vast array of modern style projectiles, most of them fired with sabots. As only one example of swaged round bullet perfection consider 10 .535-inch Hornady round balls randomly selected from a box of 100. The average weight was 231.6 grains, the heaviest 231.9, the lightest 231.2. The variance is only 0.7-grain. Seven-tenths of one grain is a tiny percent of the ball's weight. A perfect lead .535-inch ball should go 230 grains weight. With Hornady it does, because the Hornady 54-caliber lead sphere mikes out a little over .535-inch diameter. Cast projectiles can be remarkably precise. Lyman-moulded .395-inch round balls, cast with pure lead (see Chapter 34), varied only 0.8-grain—that is only eight-tenths of one grain weight from lightest to heaviest,

Dr. Mann said accuracy was a matter of good bullets fired from good barrels. Basic, but true. Good bullets like these are concentric (by test) and if they do not shoot into a good group, the shooter must look for another cause of inaccuracy. It is not the bullet.

while a run of .520-inch cast round balls showed an extreme spread of only 0.5-grain—one-half of one grain—not a lot when it takes 7,000 grains to make one pound.

Conicals and Base Lube

I am not alone in considering that lubing the base (only) of a conical projectile is better accuracy-wise than smearing lubrication on the shank or shank and base. Dean Barrett, inventor of Triple Seven, stated that he believed the same. I base my conclusion on considerable shooting with base-lubricated conical bullets vs. all other methods. Groups seem best when the base of the bullet only is treated. Observe I can, but prove the point, I cannot.

Lube, Sabots, and Accuracy

A dab of lube on the base of the sabot (and no other part) promotes repeat shooting by helping to keep fouling a bit softer. As for greatly improved accuracy by base-lubing sabots, I have no solid evidence to offer.

Fadala's demonstrations, not to be confused with real tests, indicate that lubing the base of a conical projectile enhances accuracy more than plastering lube on the shank of the conical bullet.

The sabot turns out to be the medium that in fact guides the projectile. It must fit the bore or it will not be engaged by the rifling for rotation.

Lead Conical Alignment in the Bore

This point stands up to scrutiny. My tests show cockeyed-seated conicals going astray. The good news is that due to shape, seating a conical bullet slanted to the bore is not very likely, but it can happen. I am convinced that best conical accuracy comes from a conical projectile seated perpendicular to the bore—base-square, not titled off to the horizon. There are devices that square up the elongated bullet to the muzzle for proper seating. They are good. Also good is having the first inch or so of the muzzle recessed smooth. A competent gunsmith can bore out initial rifling at the muzzle. It this harms accuracy, I have yet to see it. In fact, it may promote long-lived accuracy because the final rifling bearing on the bullet is always protected from damage.

Lead and Copper Fouling

The ball-shooting firearm is exempt from either of these potential accuracy problems. I find no leading problem shooting conicals either, due to comparatively low velocity of these bullets. However, there are jacketed bullets that do make contact with the bore and may—emphasis on *may* leave a bit of copper fouling in the bore. We know from modern high-velocity rifles that copper fouling can make a gun go sour. Some of our blackpowder cartridge rifles are capable of smokeless powder loads. My oft-used Marlin 336 Cowboy rifle in 38-55 Winchester is a prime example. This rifle is capable of firing jacketed bullets at double the speed of sound. About once a year, this rifle is treated to a light copper fouling removal program. See Chapter 30 for discussion of shooting chemicals.

Breaking in a New Gun

Some, and most certainly not all, blackpowder firearms do better with a break-in period before asking them to provide top accuracy. My main break-in method is shooting, especially with the patched round ball. But the bore

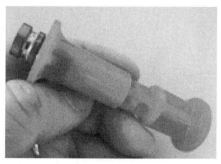

Bullet fit includes proper alignment to the bore for the conical projectile. The bullet base must be "square to the bore," not angled, for best flight.

can also be lapped to reduce sharp land edges. Shooting is more fun.

Bullet Fit

This one is for sure—best accuracy occurs when a bullet fits, rather than having a lot of windage—that is—space between the projectile and the walls of the bore. This goes for round as well as conical projectiles. Maxi-balls, especially, do best with proper bore fit because they actually engrave as they are seated and a loose Maxi cannot engrave since it doesn't make proper contact with the lands. A test with the Savage 10ML showed that 45-caliber bullets in sabots provided better accuracy than 44-caliber bullets in sabots—in the test rifle.

Rifling Depth and Accuracy

The idea that a super-tall land is imperative for accurate round ball shooting was disproved with my own 54-caliber rifle, which does not have the usual 0.10-inch or deeper groove depth. At the same time, I have other ball-shooting rifles with very deep grooves that also shoot fine. All in all, a rule of thumb that seems to work is deeper groove depth (taller land) for round ball, more shallow depth of groove for conical.

Normal Bore Wear

Shooting creates bore wear, of course. If we adhere to a decent after-shooting maintenance program, long blackpowder gun life is certain. Meanwhile, lucky is the person who "shoots out" a barrel. It takes a great deal of

shooting to accomplish that. The patch doubtless causes more bore wear than lead bullet or sabot. When a round ball rifle (or pistol) begins to throw a fatter group, going to a larger ball can help, at least for a while, and usually quite a while. Starting with a .490-inch round ball in a given rifle, for example, means going to a .495-inch ball when groups open up. A thicker patch can also help, but bullet fit to bore is more important. In severe cases, a special mould can be obtained to create an even wider bullet, perhaps .498-inch diameter for a 50-caliber rifle. When all else fails, there is rebarreling—throwing the old barrel away and fitting a new one. There are outfits that can accomplish this task perfectly, such as Morrison Precision (see Directory), maker of super-accurate barrels.

Sabots and Accuracy

The interesting Savage Model 10ML, the only muzzleloader in the world as this is written that is safe with smokeless powder, taught a lesson about sabots. Regular sabots, hit hard by smokeless powder gases, often failed. The problem was cured when Muzzleload Magnum Products brought out its High Pressure "Semi-Hemi" sabots (see Directory). Sabots have a big job to do, containing the projectile in its mad dash up-bore without burning out or breaking up. Just as it can pay off to pick up a few spent ball patches downrange, the same goes for sabots. Accuracy may improve dramatically if a sabot is found failing and is replaced with a tougher one.

Component Consistency

Murphy's Law says that if a fine product comes out, one that works perfectly, it will be removed from manufacture as soon as the company finds out how much you like it. Components do change in time, mostly for the better. Nevertheless, the shooter must keep a weather eye out for component changes that in turn alter consistency. Maybe that's why one shooter returned to the fabric shop and bought up a lifetime supply of pure Irish linen that miked out .013-inch thickness no matter which part of the cloth was tested. Yes, that was Yr. Obt. Svt., Sam.

Slippery Bores and Accuracy

Slippery bores can make bullets do bad things. For serious bullet grouping, a quick swipe of the bore after loading prevents the problem. Yes, the gun is loaded. It was also loaded when you seated the bullet on the powder charge with the same ramrod or loading rod. I run only one clean patch down after loading. That is sufficient to remove excess lube.

Accuracy and Damaged Bullets

Range tests indicate that round balls with frontal damage tend to fly off the mark, while conicals similarly affected do better. On the other hand, the base of the conical seems to do the most "steering," for when it's hurt, bullets fly wide of the mark. These statements are generalizations. However, one thing is certain—damaged bullets do not promote accuracy. All projectiles should be safeguarded from harm.

Consistent Ignition

Inconsistent ignition can attack accuracy, but a poor igniter is seldom the cause. CCI, RWS, Winchester, Federal, Remington and others produce "uniform fire" from percussion cap or modern primer. Accuse the firearm for igni-

Round balls that suffer damage from neglect, as these have, or from damage, especially nose damage, cannot be expected to deliver premium accuracy.

The firearm can only produce groups allowed by the sight picture. The fiber optic sight shown here has "light-gathering" ability and therefore shows well on the target, not to say that other sight types do not.

tion accuracy problems and you will be correct most of the time. A circuitous route from igniter to main charge of powder in the breech-through design means trouble. Or there may be an obstruction in the route from flame or spark to powder charge. A mechanical failure is also a possibility, such as a weak mainspring unable to deliver the proper hammer blow to consistently detonate the igniter. Flintlock ignition problems include: failure to follow proper loading procedure, low quality or chipped-edge flint, dirty or worn frizzen, plus touchhole burnout. An improper nipple can also cause ignition inconsistency, which in turn can affect group size. In relatively recent times, manufacturers of modern muzzleloaders have gone to the No. 209 shotgun primers. Recognizing this trend, Winchester made changes in its No. 209 shotgun primer to make it more "blackpowder compatible" with a special TripleSe7en Muzzleloading Primer to provide ideal ignition not only for Triple Seven, but also Pyrodex Pellets. Review Chapter 19 for more on ignition.

Accuracy and Sights

The high-magnification B&L scope mounted on the two muzzleloaders mentioned earlier proved the basic truth that "You can't hit what you can't see." Certain special muzzleloader-only hunts forbid scopes, and so it is up to the shooter to get the best iron sights on his hunting rifle and learn how to use them. Longer barrels found on old-time rifles aided sight picture clarity because of greater distance between front and rear sight. But even with shorter barrels, ordinary open sights, including "fixed" versions, are entirely adequate for good shooting, especially on big game. The open iron sights on No. 47, once on target, ensure meat in the pot. An oft-carried 54-caliber Markesbery Outer-Line muzzleloader increased its deadly nature with a Ghost-Ring aperture rear sight matched with a White Stripe front sight from XX Sight Systems (see Directory). I liked the match so much that my 38-55 Marlin rifle got a set as well. In lining up the iron sight, major concentration should be: front sight-target, front sight-target, front sight-target.

Sighting in or testing a blackpowder firearm for accuracy demands a proper target. You can only hit what you can see. The aiming point on a target must be precise and clear, as this target is.

Accuracy and Targets

Why do we expect good groups when we cannot truly pick a specific aiming point on the target? I have taken special pains to gather up good targets for my shooting. Luckily, there are many, as from Outers and Birchwood-Casey, to name only two companies. Sometimes, I make targets on the computer with specific aiming points that I favor. I have also found some good targets offered for free on the Internet.

The Eyes Have It

If groups out of that favorite front-loader have expanded over time, maybe it's not a problem with a worn bore or failing components. Get an eye check-up. It's the right thing to do.

Body Stable

Just as eyes must be keen to best see the target and produce good groups, the body general has to be in decent condition. That's why many Olympic shooters have a workout regimen.

Shooting Bench Tactics

Best groups off the benchrest are as possible as finding a hundred-dollar bill stuck to the bottom of your shoe when shooter form is askew. Plant both feet solidly on the ground with butt firmly on the bench seat. Get properly angled to see the target through the sights without making a pretzel out of the body. Use a good rest. I have a couple from Battenfeld that have made better shots out of me (see Directory). Place a skid pad under the right elbow for a right-handed shooter (more comfortable than elbow sliding on wooden bench top). Settle a shooting pad between shoulder and butt of rifle. Sitting solidly at the bench, the body takes full recoil. A shooting pad helps.

Old Information

Science wore swaddling clothes when blackpowder shooting was the only show in town. Data was often gathered by the light of the moon, stirred in a caldron with newts' toes, and sent forth as gospel. Not all old-time information was bogus. It's just that so much of it does nothing to promote *accuracy*, the present topic. Unfortunately, some of the most colorful tales survived, finding their way into the 21st century. Sophisticated shooters, who scoffed at daydream data for modern guns, soaked up blackpowder "rules of thumb" like a rag in a rainstorm. They went around placing round balls in the palms of their hands, covering them with powder to come up with an "accurate load." Gun store clerks who had never seen a muzzleloader were instant experts, handing out false doctrine at no charge. One representative of a gun company was overheard telling a shooter that he could load all the powder he wanted in a muzzleloader as long as he used a conical, but watch out for those round balls! Dangerous counsel. But why let facts get in the way of a good story? Muzzleloaders, cap 'n' ball revolvers, and blackpowder cartridge guns can be quite accurate when shooters pay attention to a few details.

26 Aiming Devices

The telescopic rifle sight is not new. It was invented long before smokeless powder became readily available, and it remains in use today on blackpowder rifles.

Ask and you shall receive, the saying goes. And blackpowder shooters, especially devotees of blackpowder cartridge rifles, did ask for more sight options. Their request was granted. Leatherwood's Wm. Malcomb (sic) Black Powder Cartridge Rifle Scope is a perfect example. It is a close replica of the Wm. Malcolm telescopic rifle sight of the mid- to late 1800s with the same 3/4-inch tube, along with external adjustment and 6X magnification. The mounts attach to the barrel via blocks, and the scope can be fitted to single-shot blackpowder rifles, such as the Winchester Model 1885 High-Wall, as well

as Sharps and Remingtons of buffalo hunting days (see Chapter 31). Leatherwood Hi-Lux Optics scope sights have high-quality lenses typical of modern technology. And so this scope exceeds the optical clarity of the original considerably. Elevation adjustment goes all the way out to 1,000 yards matched to the 45-70 Government cartridge, which remains the number one cartridge in blackpowder silhouette shooting today. Another period sight for the same type of rife is the MVA scope. It, too, is 6X with a 3/4-inch tube, parallax and focus adjustable, length 23 to 28 inches, standard reticule or Mil-Dot

Glass reticule. Not advertised as a replica of the Malcolm, it does have mounts patterned after the Malcolm design. Paging through *Shoot!* magazine each month is one way of locating more sights for blackpowder cartridge guns, as is searching the Internet.

Fixed Sights
Ancient Fixed Iron Sights

The true fixed iron sight was an early form. It was found on blackpowder rifles and pistols, and was indicative of a time when guns were not expected to be nail-drivers. Proof of this is the immobile front represented by

Although this front sight is on a 19th-century blackpowder cartridge rifle and not a muzzleloader, it still must be placed in the primitive sight category. It is non-adjustable and quite coarse.

Fixed sights on blackpowder revolvers do not indicate a problem in aiming, provided the shooter learns how to use these sights, and provided the gun is sighted for a specific range at the factory.

little more than a blob of metal. The rear sight was often little more than a slit. These "sights" were hardly worthy of the name, and yet they served an important function—providing an aiming point, be it ever so crude. In a duel, for example, often at very close range—sometimes little more than a handful of paces—the blob up front was much better than nothing at all. When there was a more pronounced notch on back, the front sight was optically fitted into this cleft. Precise aim was impossible with these sights, because the shooter could not generate a clean, repeatable sight picture. Improvement was imperative.

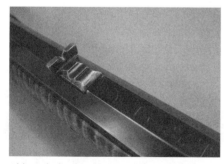

Although the fixed rear sight on the author's No. 47 custom rifle is basic, it is also highly workable. It has a double notch for closer or longer range aiming, and it is adjustable for windage in a dovetail slot.

Improved Fixed Iron Sights

These sights qualify as fixed because they have no device to move them, such as a ladder underneath the rear sight to make the rear sight go up or down. My oft-mentioned Mulford No. 47 has fixed sights. Fixed yes, but adjustable. Fixed because the rear sight

had no elevation adjustment, adjustable because the rear sight can be drifted and the front sight can be filed down or replaced with a taller one. The front sight is usually a blade dovetailed directly into the top barrel flat just behind the muzzle. The rear sight is a metal fixture with a slit or notch. It is also attached in a dovetail notch. These sights lie very low on the barrel. They come into the line of sight instantly. They also provide a clean sight picture and as such are leagues ahead of the primitive fixed sight. Drifting changed point of impact on the target (sliding with encouragement from a punch), rear sight right to hit right, left to hit left. The front sight was filed *down* to move bullet impact up, or a taller front sight was installed to *lower* bullet impact. In other words, the front sight is moved in the opposite direction of the desired point of impact on the target. Since the fixed rear sight has no elevator bar to raise or lower it, the front sight must be altered to change vertical impact. The front sight can also be adjusted for windage—that is, bullet change in impact from left to right, right to left. The front sight is drifted in its dovetail notch to the *left* to move point of im-

pact *right*, to the *right* to move point of impact to the *left*.

Fixed Iron Sights on Cap 'n' Ball Revolvers

Original-style cap 'n' ball revolvers usually have fixed sights. Two revolvers of the Civil War era are examples—the Colt Model of 1860 and Remington Model of 1858. Taking the latter, it has a barleycorn front sight integral to the front of the barrel. There is no dovetail notch to slide it in. This front sight is truly fixed in place. The only way to make the revolver hit to the right or left (horizontal adjustment) is by manipulating the front sight through bending, hopefully without breaking it off in the process. The front sight is also responsible for vertical adjustment by filing it lower for the next bullet to strike higher on the target. If the revolver is already shooting to high, metal must be added to it to make it taller. A gunsmith can usually accomplish this task. The "rear sight" on the Remington 1858 is not a sight at all, but rather a groove in the top strap of the frame. Absolutely nothing can be done to change point of impact with this groove. The 1860 Civil War Colt revolver carried the same type of front sight found on the Rem-

The buckhorn rear sight has been criticized widely, detractors saying that the "horns" cover up the target. Those who use such a rear sight successfully, including the author, consider the criticism unfounded.

A ladder type rear sight adjusts by moving the bar to raise or lower the sight. The ladder offers rapid rear sight adjustment for elevation.

ington revolver, but this time the "rear sight" was a notch cut into the hammer nose. Cocking the hammer to fire brings the hammer nose into the view of the shooter. The shooter aligns the little notch in the hammer nose with the front sight. While these fixed handgun sights are not target-shooting affairs, they work well enough for their intended purpose, which was war. A practiced shooter can do surprisingly well with these sights.

Buckhorn and Semi-Buckhorn Fixed Sights

Buckhorn and semi-buckhorn rear sights were quite popular for a long period of time. Sometimes they are adjustable, as with an elevator bar or ladder, but on many front-loaders they are not. Many modern gun writers have declared the buckhorn rear sight lousy because it supposedly covers the whole target, making precise aiming impossible. In real life, however, these sights work quite well. They have put more than one venison steak on my plate. Buckhorns and semi-buckhorns do tend to block out part of the target, but the aiming point remains as precise as that found on other rear sights. The buckhorn is simply a rear sight with "horns." When the horns curl around almost to touch, that's full buckhorn. With less curl, they're semi-buckhorns.

Overview of Fixed Sights

When set in dovetail notches, fixed sights allow windage (horizontal) adjustment by moving the rear sight left to move impact left, right to move impact right. The front sight, when it's in a dovetail notch, is drifted right to hit left, left to hit right. Elevation (vertical) adjustment is generally accomplished by filing the front sight down, installing a taller front sight, or having a gunsmith add metal to an existing fixed front sight.

Adjustable Iron Sights

The Ladder-Adjustable Open Sight

One way to accomplish iron sight adjustment is the ladder or elevator bar beneath the back sight. The ladder has graduated notches cut into it. On the shortest notch, the rear sight rests lowest on the barrel and the firearm hits lowest. On the tallest notch of the ladder, the rear sight is elevated to its highest position and the rifle hits highest. The ladder-type rear sight is normally coupled with an ordinary non-adjustable front sight. But the front sight may rest in a dovetail notch, offering lateral movement through drifting. The ladder rear sight may also ride in a dovetail notch. While elevation adjustment is accomplished with the previously described notch-in-ladder arrangement, bullet impact on the target horizontally comes by drifting the rear sight in its dovetail notch, or the front sight in its dovetail notch.

The Modern Adjustable Open Sight

The rear sights on many non-replica and modern muzzleloaders are fully adjustable in various ways. There may be elevation and windage screws, for example. When the elevation screw

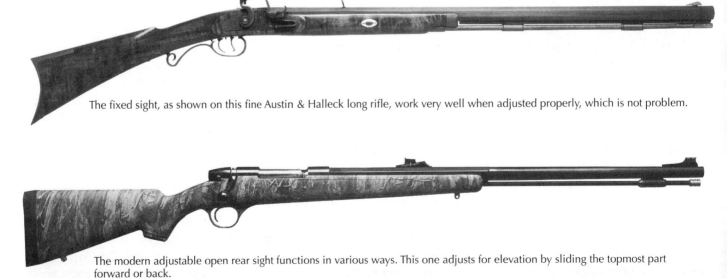

The fixed sight, as shown on this fine Austin & Halleck long rifle, work very well when adjusted properly, which is not problem.

The modern adjustable open rear sight functions in various ways. This one adjusts for elevation by sliding the topmost part forward or back.

is turned downward, the rear sight is forced upward to make the next shot striker higher on the target. There may also be a screw adjustment that moves the rear sight left or right for windage changes. Sometimes the rear sight is two-part, the notch cut into a moving plate. Two little screws hold this plate in place. Loosen the screws, move the plate up or down, tighten, and adjustment has been accomplished. There are too many variations of the adjustable iron sight to treat them all here. However, the type is easily recognized because the rear sight has adjustment capability up or down, left or right.

The Adjustable Receiver Sight

The term "receiver sight" is a misnomer on old-time style muzzleloaders because they have no receiver. They have locks instead. However, the popular modern muzzleloader has a receiver. The Ruger Model 77/50, for example, has a true receiver. Since this rifle is

The Ghost Ring receiver sight is not micrometer adjusted, but it has very fine movement and a rifle can be sighted in precisely with this sight. Here it is shown with the White Stripe front sight—an ideal combination for providing a clear sight picture.

The rear Ghost Ring sight is adjustable with a fine-thread stem on the aperture. It can be sighted in quite precisely in this manner.

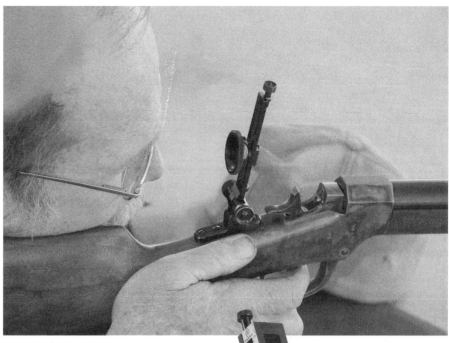

A tang sight in use.

patterned directly after the cartridge-shooter of the same bolt-action design, an adjustable receiver sight can be installed. The receiver sight may not always attach to a receiver. It may mount near the breech of a rifle, at which point it works just as well as if mounted on a true receiver. The receiver sight is also known as a peep or aperture sight. A number of blackpowder guns are drilled and tapped for receiver sights. I have a Markesbery muzzleloader with two barrels: 50- and 54-caliber. The 50 is set up for a scope, but the 54, which I use far more frequently, has an aperture sight. It is the Ghost Ring from XX Sight Systems, matched with a White Stripe front sight from the same company. The Ghost Ring with White Stripe is perfect for fast woods and thicket shooting because the object with the receiver or peep sight is to look *through*, not *at* the hole, focusing *only* the front sight on the target—very fast. More on peep sight management in Chapter 27.

The Tang Sight

This is a peep sight, but rather than mounting on the receiver, the sight is attached to the upper tang of the rifle. It's spring-loaded and can be put out of

Close view of a tang sight, so called because its base attaches to the upper tang of the rifle.

the way by collapsing down against the upper wrist of the rifle. The advantage is closeness to the eye, which optically eliminates the peep, leaving the front sight alone in clear focus, which is right. The disadvantage is closeness to the eye should recoil bring the tang sight back smartly, which has happened.

The Micrometer-Adjustable Aperture Sight

The micrometer-adjustable aperture sight provides extremely close and accurate movement, some having clicks that gauge only one-quarter minute of angle, which translates to about (not exactly) one-fourth inch at 100 yards. An example of this kind of aperture sight is Lyman's No. 57, which is offered for

The micrometer-adjustable receiver sight provides extremely close sight adjustment with precision moving parts. It is one of the best target-type metallic sights available.

A different sort of micrometer sight. The slits can be adjusted to size by rotation.

muzzleloaders. The micrometer aperture sight is one of the finest iron sights ever designed. But for hunting, receiver sights without micrometer adjustment capability are also very good. The Williams peep sight is another example of a non-micrometer peep that works well, as is the aforementioned Ghost Ring on the Markesbery 54-caliber Outer-Line rifle. The receiver or peep sight generally couples with a non-adjustable front sight, because full windage and elevation movement exists within the rear sight. The peep sight abides by the same rules as the open iron sight—move left to change bullet impact to the left, right to move bullet impact right, up for up, down for down.

This front sight can rightfully be called a globe—it is perfectly round and it rests on a pedestal.

Front Beads for Iron Sights

Choices are many. Lyman's current catalogue lists several different front sight beads with numerous height options. There is good reason for such variety—the front sight bead should match the rear sight and since there are many different rear sight styles, there must also be many front sight styles. Also, shooter preference steps in. I have a Lyman front sight with white bead on a Marlin lever-action rifle that suits me well. Simply, I like it. Among front sight options in the Lyman catalog are: No. 3 1/16-inch ivory bead, No. 3 1/16-inch gold bead, No. 28 3/32-inch ivory bead, No. 28 3/32-inch gold bead, No. 31 1/16-inch ivory bead, No. 31 1/16-inch gold bead, No. 37 3/32-inch ivory bead, No. 37 3/32-inch gold bead. No. 3 and No. 28 front sights are identical, designed to be mounted into the barrel dovetail, while No. 31 and No. 37 are for ramp mounting. Heights run from .240-inch to .500-inch. These are beautiful front sights; moreover, the various heights make it possible to alter vertical bullet placement on the target.

Bushnell's Holo Sight

Unique by design, the Bushnell Holo Sight, short for holographic, gets on target rattler-strike fast. The image perceived is of an illuminated aim point suspended in space in front of the gun. The shooter can see the sight from varying distances behind the gun. Field of view is unlimited because there is no tube with lenses. Weaver-style mounts are used to attach the Holo Sight to firearms.

Fiber Optic Sights

Fiber optic sights are remarkably clear in low light, although of course some light must strike them in order to

This is a rear fiber optic sight. Two round glowing beads are for alignment. This is a good model in that the fiber optic elements are quite protected by metal.

The front fiber optic sight works as advertised. It "picks up" light, offering a clear aiming point in woods and brush conditions as well as wide open country. The only negative is breakage. A hunter should be careful not to bang this front sight on a hard object.

show up brightly. An example of a fiber optic sight for muzzleloaders is the Traditions Tru-Glo, which comes as a set. The front sight is ramp style with fixed blade. The rear sight is fully adjustable for windage and elevation. The sight picture shows as two green dots (rear sight) and a red front sight. While the Tru-Glo is quite rugged, no optic fiber sight is as strong as a metal sight, which is its only major fault. That fault, however, can be corrected with protective ears for the front sight, as seen on some military rifles. The rear sight is less likely to strike something, so a little care prevents breakage.

The Tube Sight

The tube sight looks like a scope as it rests above the rifle barrel, but it has no glass in it. It is simply a long metal tube mounted full-length atop the rifle barrel. Far more than a simple metal tube, the tube sight was, and is, adjustable, with some sort of aiming device contained within. Tube sights were effective because they isolated the view of the shooter for concentration on the target. They also blocked out superflu-

There can be no argument that the most precise aiming instrument is the telescopic sight, shown here in use on a Remington Genesis modern muzzleloader.

ous light, such as glints from the sun's rays. A particular tube sight I studied incorporated an eyecup with a tiny hole, a peep or aperture, if you will. Mounted in the other end of the tube was a globe front sight, simply a round chunk of metal, hence "globe." The peep and globe reside in the shade, providing a clean and effective sight picture. Since the tube sight contained no optical lenses, it is classified as an iron sight.

The Scope Sight

A telescope of some sort was around in 1600, give or take a few years. The brilliant Italian scientist, Galileo Galilei, is often credited with its invention. The only problem is that he didn't. But he made a workable telescope of his own and was observing the skies as early as 1609 with 20X magnification. We know this because it is recorded that he showed his telescope to Italian officials in that year, and he also reported finding three of Jupiter's moons in 1610. Why it took so long for a workable telescope to finds its way atop a rifle is mildly puzzling. Even into the middle 20th century scope sights were not fully trusted. Dr. C.E. Hagie, in his 1946 book, *The American Rifle for Hunting and Target Shooting*, said that big-game hunters would bag more game if they "left the telescopes at home." Scopes, he said, were only for hunters who "like to put on their favorite rifles all the fancy gadgets that can be procured." Long before Hagie's time, however, a few buffalo hunters did mount scopes on their long-range rifles, sometimes 20X scopes from Germany.

The advent and proliferation of the modern muzzleloader naturally brought with it a desire to equip the 200-yard-plus front-loader with a 200-yard-plus sight. The scope sight was the only answer. Some states rule it out for special blackpowder-only hunts and some states don't. The con argument is that scopes don't match the reason for primitive-type hunts to begin with—the handicap clause. The pro argument says that rifles fitted with scopes are actually more sporting than iron sights because of more reliable bullet placement, which in turn leads to cleaner kills. A possible answer is appropriateness. Topping off a long rifle from the 1700s with a scope is not appropriate, while scoping a modern muzzleloader is, since these guns reside in their own niche anyway, between old-time front-loaders and cartridge-shooting firearms. Another criterion is individual need. Some hunters need scopes even for closer-range shooting, while others do not.

What won't wash is a shooter insisting scope sights are inventions of modern times—they are not. We know the terrestrial telescope was around in the early 1600s. Riflescopes were born of terrestrial telescopes. Continuing the historical journey that began in this scope sight section, credit Johann Lipperhey of Middleburg, Holland, a spectacle maker, with the first working model in 1608, crude and of little practical value until Galileo made it into a viable instrument. Much later we find mountain man Jim Bridger packing a telescope during the fur trade era. The riflescope appears much later. Englishman William Ellis Metford had a practical telescopic rifle sight by 1824.

This is a special scope from Bushnell specifically designed for blackpowder rifles. It offers extra light gathering, and it is built to withstand strong recoil. It's named the DDB for Dusk and Dawn Brightness.

What power? Low power is ideal in brush and woods due to a wide field of view, while high power is the way to go for best target definition, as verified by the fact that benchrest shooters interested in the best bullet groups choose high power scopes.

There is no denying the precision of the scope sight. This Bushnell DDB offers click adjustments in 1/4-inch increments. One click is valued at one-fourth of one inch at 100 yards.

The mount is just as important as the scope because if the mount fails, the scope is useless. These Durasight mounts are designed and built to retain the scope sight solidly.

He claimed that mounting one of his scopes on a rifle improved the chance of making a bull's eye, and he was willing to prove it to doubters. It took leaders of the 20th-century hunting community using scope sights to convince shooters. Jack O'Connor extolled the virtues of the scope sight, stating that it was ideal for hunters who wanted to put bullets right where they belonged on big game. Elmer Keith wrote the same, as did Colonel Townsend Whelen, Paul Curtis, Stewart Edward White, and other respected shooters of the day. From distrust, the scope sight moved into the ranks of faithful use. It's no wonder that modern American shooters look to the glass sight even for their charcoal-burners.

Which Scope?

Seeing a special need, Bushnell came up with a Banner Low Light Riflescope. The variable Dusk and Dawn line includes 11 models as this is written, each one with special DDB (Dusk and Dawn Brightness) lenses for seeing better in low light conditions. "Great for muzzleloaders," says the company. But all riflescopes work on muzzleloaders as they do on modern big-game cartridge rifles. They offer high optical resolution, providing a good clear sight picture. It is just as important to see well through a scope mounted on a front loader as it is to clearly see the target when shooting a cartridge gun. Optical resolution especially pays off when the target is in the brush or dense timber because the shooter can better make out where to aim. The blackpowder scope must be ruggedly constructed to take blackpowder recoil, especially in this day of three and even four Pellet allowance. The most popular reticle is the duplex with its heavy easy-to-see crosswire coupled with the thinner center wire for precise aiming.

What Power?

The brush and timber hunter is well equipped with a 2.5x scope, or even less magnification. Conversely, the target shooter whose goal is tight clusters is better off with high magnifica-

tion. No serious modern benchrest match in the world was won with a low-power scope because benchrest shooters know that a super-magnified target allows greatest precision of aim. If all hunting takes place in thickets for close-range whitetail deer, a low-power scope is perfectly fine. For greater precision of bullet grouping, more magnification is called for, especially with modern muzzleloaders that are now truly capable of delivering 200-plus yards big-game power. A fixed power scope is fine. A variable is better.

The Variable

Today's variable is so good that it's the best all-around choice for big-game hunting with modern cartridge gun, muzzleloader, or blackpowder breechloader. The once-upon-a-time negative features of variables are long cured. Today's variable is optically excellent, has superb reticles, and is capable of precise adjustment. I'm open-minded on most matters of guns and shooting, but find arguments in favor of fixed-power scopes weak. "I don't like big scopes." Variables may have been oversized at one time, but not now. Many are no larger than fixed-power scopes. "I prefer 6x over any other magnification." That makes no sense. Have your variable on 6x if you insist, but is 6x ideal for close-range, fast-action shooting? Is 6x is better than higher magnification for exacting bullet placement at longer ranges? The variable does it all. I say learn how to use it and be happy. Carry on low power for that jump-up-close opportunity. Rack the variable to high power for the long shot on a sedentary animal.

Scope Mounts

Modern muzzleloaders come drilled and tapped for scope mounts. It's a simple matter of buying the correct mounts to match the firearm. The scope mount should be of high quality, however, for it's responsible for retaining the glass sight firmly locked in place. A scope mount that allows movement of the sight is no bargain at any price.

27 Working With the Rainbow

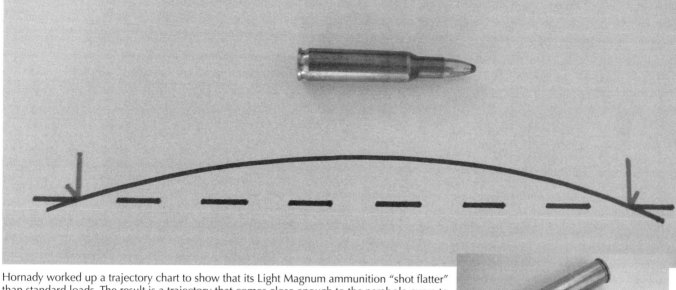

Hornady worked up a trajectory chart to show that its Light Magnum ammunition "shot flatter" than standard loads. The result is a trajectory that comes close enough to the parabola curve to allow that term's use when "working with the rainbow."

The bullet takes a rainbow flight from muzzle to final destination. While this curve may not be a perfect parabola in the science of geometry, parabola fits pretty well. One dictionary says, "a plane curve formed by the intersection of a conical surface with a plane parallel to a side of the cone." That sure doesn't sound like bullet flight to me. In order to clarify the definition, the dictionary went on to say, "*When we throw a ball, it rises for a while and then begins to fall downward; the curve it follows is called a parabola.*" That's more like it. So even though the scientific purist may balk, for our purposes bullet flight will follow the rainbow curve of the parabola. On the horizontal, throw that ball faster and it describes a flatter curve. The faster a bullet flies, the flatter the curve to the horizontal. The blackpowder firearm has never achieved true high velocity. Shooters in the old days had it really bad. S.W. Baker shot rifles in Ceylon with round balls that began their journey at around 1,500 fps. Although these lead globes resembled mandarin oranges, they dropped like meteors from the sky. And yet Baker made hits as far

out as 300 yards, witnessed. Even if the witnesses were not perfect surveyors of distance, we can bet that the shots were far. Baker managed this because he knew the parabola those big lead balls described. Knowing a bullet's arc from muzzle to target is highly valuable, and a definite part of this chapter, but not the only part.

Trajectory

Even the 220 Swift does not "shoot flat," not even to a mere 100 yards. The Swift, loaded with a 50-grain Hornady V-Max bullet, can be sighted dead on at 300 yards. So sighted, this speedy missile rises less than 2.5 inches at 100 yards. At 200 yards it is still rising, but it strikes only three inches high. At 300 yards the little V-Max is right on the money. At 400, drop is eight inches below line of sight (see below). There's a lot to be learned through comparisons. A 30-06 rifle with the hot Barnes load (heavy charge of IMR-4831 powder) puts a 180-grain boattail high-profile bullet away at a flat 3,000 fps as chronographed from a 26-inch barrel. Sighted so the bullet strikes three inches high at

Not even the 4,000 fps 220 Swift "shoots flat." It takes the curve we're calling a parabola, and that means the bullet rises above the line of sight, and then falls below the line of sight downrange. Here, two 220 Swift cartridges are shown with a 45-90 Winchester cartridge. The Swift will shoot flatter than the 45-90 and its little bullet will also drift less at hunting ranges.

100 yards, it's four inches high at 200, three inches low at 300—and at 400 yards it falls nine inches below line of sight, almost the same as the super-fast Swift. The C (ballistic coefficient) of this bullet is .452. The C of the 50-grain 22-caliber bullet is .242. Maybe there is something to this C business after all.

Bullet Speed and C First

The chronograph is a good place to start when building a new load. To sight in properly, we must know muzzle velocity. By knowing exact muzzle velocity for the specific firearm, we can

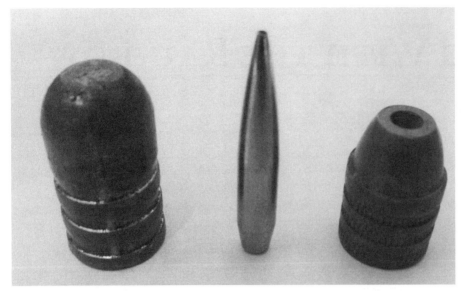

It stands to reason that bullets of very high C (ballistic coefficient) will describe a flatter trajectory curve from muzzle to target than bullets of lower C. The bullet in the center is only 22-caliber, but extremely long for its diameter. It will "carry up" quite well. The two large lead bullets, especially the blunter bullet on the far left, will have a more pronounced trajectory from muzzle to target, which means—management is necessary to score a hit—working smart with the "rainbow."

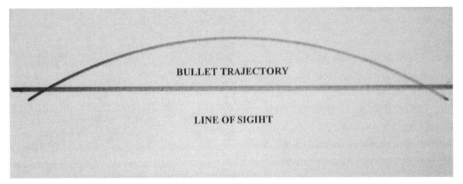

BULLET TRAJECTORY

LINE OF SIGIHT

This simple diagram clearly demonstrates line of sight, which is an imaginary flat line from eye to target. The curved line represents the rainbow—the path taken by a bullet from muzzle to target.

find out how much drop the bullet has over a given range—provided we know something else about that projectile—it's C rating. As in the example above, where the 30-06 bullet comes close to matching the 400-yard drop of the much faster Swift, everything from the smallest round balls to the biggest conicals are also subject to this thing we call C. The round ball is really in trouble. A 32-caliber lead pill has a C of only .043 noted in Lyman's second edition *Black Powder Handbook & Loading Manual*. The 36-caliber ball has a C of only .049. Ouch! A 50-caliber ball goes .070 C, while a 54-caliber runs .075. C improves with conicals. A 54-caliber 385-grain Lyman sabot bullet runs .274. High-profile blackpowder conicals have a higher C in comparison to round balls and big fat short conicals. These are the bullets relied on in the 200-yard muzzleloader.

Line of Sight

Bullet flight follows the rainbow, but when we say "above or below line of sight," what is that? Line of sight is produced by vision. The eye makes an absolutely straight "line" to the target. In the game field, line of sight continues to remain straight, but not necessarily on the horizontal, because the game may be uphill or downhill. On a target range, line of sight is horizontal to the ground if the range is correctly

prepared—flat, in other words. A model of line of sight has a *baseline* representing a horizontally flat line from muzzle to target. The line the bullet takes from muzzle to target is anything but flat. It runs along the rainbow. The bullet takes off "nose up," aiming above the line of sight. This is called the *line of departure* where the projectile leaves the baseline on its journey to the target. It crosses the line of sight twice, once fairly close to the muzzle, again at the zero point. That path is known as the bullet's *trajectory*, with zero being the exact location of sight-in. So the base line is flat, but the path of the bullet is curved. Specifically, a round ball from a well-loaded 50-caliber blackpowder rifle crosses the line of sight the first time at about 13 yards, and then again at around 75 to 80 yards, falling *below* the line of sight afterwards. Sighting a gun includes both line of sight and parabola. Knowing the path a bullet takes along the line of sight, above it and below it, allows appropriate holds for close-range targets as well as those on the outer limit of the firearm's ballistic potential.

Extreme Range

Managing the muzzleloader's rainbow includes understanding extreme range—the ultimate limit a given projectile flies. I know of no study showing how far a muzzleloader can shoot when the muzzle is elevated to 45 degrees. Clearly, bullets of higher C will shoot farther than those of blunt profile. One thing is certain—no muzzleloader normally fired today launches its missile as far as cartridges in the big-game class, which is a distance of about three miles. Until careful testing has been published, suffice that extreme range for a muzzleloader is considerably less than extreme range for modern high-intensity cartridges. Regardless, every downwind shooter must be aware that his or her guns will deliver a bullet quite some distance, certainly over a mile and more likely two miles.

Extreme range knowledge and watchfulness is vital to safety. A bullet from a high-power rifle can travel, depending of course upon the cartridge and load, as far as three miles. The tree line in this photo is well within three miles and within the reach of a high C-profile bullet fired from a top load in a muzzleloader.

Long-Range Shooting

Long-range *target* blackpowder shooting is in the bargain, emphasis on target. A piece of paper, metallic silhouette, gong, or any other inanimate object cannot be wounded, so if the shooter wishes to fire away at a thousand yards, why not? In fact, thousand-yard matches are nothing new in the smokepole business, going back at least to the 19th century and continuing to this day. Rifled muskets were often employed to put bullets downrange to a thousand yards-plus with acceptable accuracy. The Whitworth rifled musket is a perfect example of a muzzleloader capable of far-away accuracy. That's why the Confederate snipers used them in the American Civil War. A long-range shooting game practiced today by dedicated blackpowder shooters is the *silueta*, Mexican name for the sport. It means firing at metallic cutouts at

long range with single-shot blackpowder cartridge rifles (see Chapter 38). A marksman shooting an original Sharps 45-120 put on a show for *Ripley's Believe it or Not*. He hit a small metal plate repeatedly at over 1,300 yards. Far shooting on game is another story, even with the latest magnum muzzleloader. It's true that 19th-century buffalo runners shot far. But they hunted every day. We don't.

Sighting In for a Single Distance

For target shooting, a firearm can be sighted specifically for long range, even a thousand yards. Midrange trajectory (how high a bullet rises between the muzzle and the bull's eye of the target) is of no consequence until the shooter wishes to fire on a closer target, at which time specific *hold-under* is necessary to compensate for bul-

Sighting in for one and only one distance is often the case with old-time blackpowder pistols as well as original-style revolvers. The sight shown here is not readily adjustable. It is "fixed" in place. The pistol can still be sighted in very well and this sight will do fine for all closer range shooting.

A "fixed" rear sight may be movable, while a front sight can be filed down to lower it, or replaced with a taller sight. This rear sight is drifted in its dovetail notch to move bullet placement left or right. The tool in use is not a drift punch, but it is excellent for the job.

let rise. A target shooter sights his musket for a thousand yards. In order to hit the target at that range, the blackpowder bullet must rise well above the line of sight. Not a problem. But for hunting, sighting in for a practical distance is imperative. Having to figure how far to hold *under* a game animal at medium to close range for a blackpowder rifle sighted in for extreme range is difficult. The result might be a clean miss, which is all right, or wounding, which is not all right.

Sight Adjustment—Windage and Elevation

A bullet takes only two directions as it follows the rainbow—up/down and left/right of line of sight. Bullet movement left or right is called windage. Up and down is elevation. Chapter 26 talked about how to adjust sights for windage and elevation. Working with the rainbow is more than up/down bullet path. It includes left or right of line of sight. A simple rule for iron sights is: adjust rear sight in the same direction of bullet flight—move the rear sight up, the next bullet strikes higher. Move the rear sight down, the next shot hits lower. Move the rear sight left and the next bullet hits left, right to strike right. The front sight is the opposite. Lower the front sight to hit higher, raise it to hit lower. Move it left to hit right, right to hit left. The scope sight is adjusted in one of two ways. The adjustment may be in the mount. The Malcolm mount touched on in Chapter 26 has external adjustment. Most scope sights today have internal adjustment. Unscrew the cap from a turret and move the dial in the direction of the arrow, up/down, left/right. That's all there is to it. Graduations vary. "Click" adjustment is common, each click representing a specific movement, such as 1/4-inch.

Minutes of Angle

A scope sight, as well as certain micrometer-adjustable receiver sights, may be calibrated in minutes of angle. A minute of angle, sometimes written as MOA, is 1/60th of one degree. A circle has 360 degrees, or 21,600 minutes. Specifically, a minute of angle subtends (is valued at) 1.047-inch at 100 yards. For our purpose, which is practical shooting, a minute of angle is considered 1 inch at 100 yards, 2 inches at 200 yards, 3 inches at 300 yards, and so forth. So, in shooting, a quarter-minute of angle is only 1/4-inch at 100 yards, a very fine adjustment found on quite a number of riflescopes.

Sight Radius

Sight radius applies only to iron sights. Scope sights have a flat field, which totally eliminates the concept of sight radius. While sight radius is simply the distance between back sight and front sight, it's important in shooting because it has a lot to do with *sight picture*. The longer the barrel, the longer the sight radius can be. However, sight radius is determined by *where* the sights are located. A rear sight can be mounted well forward of the breech, which improves clarity for older eyes that have trouble focusing on closer objects. Iron-sight shooters ordering a custom muzzleloader have the option of leaving the back sight off at delivery. The idea is: Go to the range. Lay a flat-based sight on the top barrel flat (most customs have octagonal barrels). Move the sight up and down the barrel to determine the sharpest sight picture. Mark the spot. Have a gunsmith cut a dovetail and install a rear sight. On one long-barreled 42-caliber flintlock rifle of my acquaintance, the distance between front and rear sight was exactly 28 inches. The rear sight on this rifle was a full 9 inches forward of the base of the breech, about 14 inches from the eye.

Sight radius is simply the distance between the front and rear sights. But it can make a difference when working with the rainbow, because a greater distance between sights generally delivers a bit sharper sight picture, which is good when trying to hold "off target" for a hit.

How We See Sights

Moving the rear sight more forward of the eye can sharpen the image. This is good, but it does not suggest that the rear sight is primary to working with the rainbow, because it is not. The rear sight is vital. But front sight-target is the concentration required for consistent bullseyes with iron sights. The rear sight is employed to align the front sight properly, but it is the front sight that visually "touches" the target, be that target paper or game animal. The rear sight can be somewhat a blur provided it has done its job of alignment with the front sight. I was a terrible handgun shot. I never will be very good with the one-hand gun, probably because my major interest is rifles. However, after a training period with a former SWAT team leader, especially with his teaching me the front sight-target method, I went from having trouble hitting a cantaloupe-size target at 20 paces to winning an informal handgun competition against a fellow who had previously won serious pistol matches. Front sight-target did it.

Rear Sight Management

The aperture or peep sight, once adjusted, is all but forgotten. Look *through it*. Do not look *at it*. Use front sight-target only. Concentrating on the aperture is death to good rear sight management. For hunting, a slightly larger aperture is preferred. Ghost Ring sights on three of my rifles are set up with large apertures: Markesbery 54-caliber muzzleloader, Marlin 336 Cowboy 38-55, and Browning 1886 45-70. The Ghost Ring is easy to see through, plenty accurate; fast to put into play, and the somewhat larger orifice affords a nice bright sight picture. With open iron sights, frame of reference is important. If the front sight optically fills the rear sight notch, a precise aim-point cannot be repeated time after time. There should be a little light showing on both sides of the front sight as it rests in the notch of the rear sight. In this way, a frame of reference is created. The shooter can tell when his or her sights are truly *lined up*. Some shooters prefer the Patridge front sight, named for E.E. Patridge, one-time president of the U.S. Revolver Association. The front sight optically presents parallel sides, appearing as a rectangle that fits into a rectangular or square notch in the rear sight. Shooters can readily line up the Patridge because light clearly shows on both sides of the front sight nestled optically in the rear sight notch. Plus, it is easy to align the top of the front sight across the top of the rear sight notch, thus affording a very clear sight picture.

A Special Open Rear Sight

My 54-caliber ball-shooting rifle has a special rear sight—call it two-stage. There are two notches cut into this rear sight. The front sight is lined up with the appropriate notch for shooting closer or farther. Simple, but highly effective.

Sight Picture

The six-o'clock sight picture is often used with the Patridge sight, which means resting the target optically on top of the post-like front sight, like a pumpkin sitting on the edge of a square-topped board. The target is not covered up by the sights, which further clarifies the aim-point. The gun is sighted to print its bullet upward from the topmost of the front sight, so the bullet strikes the bullseye. An option is the "hunting" sight picture, where the front sight optically rests directly on the target. Any type of iron sight can be sighted in for this sort of picture, including the Patridge. The globe front sight, which got its name many years ago, being a small metal ball resembling a globe, remains in use, often hooded to protect from breaking. The globe usually takes the hunting sight picture rather than six-o'clock hold.

This Ghost Ring aperture sight is ideal for hunting. The shooter, however, must remember to look "through" the peep, and not "at" it. The aperture sight is good for holding off the target to compensate for wind drift or bullet drop because only the front sight is dealt with; the rear sight "automatically" centers the shooter's vision.

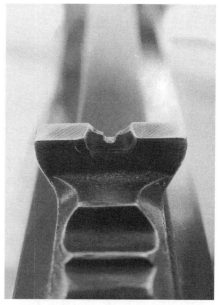

Fadala calls this rear sight "two-stage" because of the double notch. The upper wider notch is used for short to medium ranges, while the smaller U-notch below is used for longer shots—"coarse bead/fine bead" holds.

Big Game Rifle Accuracy

Hunters who hunt only tight thickets and black timber get by with rifles capable of no better than three shots into a six-inch circle at 100 yards. The rest of us are dead in the water with such rifles. I'll be after antelope this season with a front-loader capable of inch and better center-to-center groups at 100 yards. Why is that important to longer-range shooting? Because that inch grows significantly in the field. Add breathing, heartbeat, natural body tremor, and the lack of a benchrest, and the inch group at the range grows. Start with a fat group that gets fatter and your best hold may not be good enough to register a hit. I take a rest whenever possible. I also have an abiding reverence for the binocular. My binocular collection includes two that go where I go—an interesting Fujinon 10x50 that looks too big to carry, but actually causes me no grief with a shortened strap, and a Bushnell 12x50 reverse porro prism. Why are binoculars so important to me? When I see the game before it sees me, I stalk, setup, and shoot once.

Projectiles in Flight

Understanding a little bit about projectiles in flight is part of working with the rainbow. Here are a few points.

Bullet Drift

Bullet drift is the normal horizontal departure of a bullet from the line of sight in the direction of rifling twist. Right-hand twist makes bullets rotate right. These bullets, in turn, drift a little to the right in the direction of spin. Left-hand rifling twist encourages bullets to drift left. This is a minor factor.

Wind Drift

Unlike bullet drift, wind drift is vital to accurate shooting. Also known as wind *deflection*, this is the condition of the bullet drifting left or right of the line of sight due to the power of the wind. Time of flight is important in wind drift. The longer it takes a bullet to go from

This represents a "hunting" hold on game where the front sight is settled into the rear sight notch and then front sight concentration constitutes the point of aim. A six o'clock hold is where the bullet is sighted in to strike slightly above the front sight picture, rather than striking more to the location of the front sight on the target.

muzzle to target, the more time wind has to act upon it. But time of flight is not the only criterion in wind drift. C is also important. The following figures are rounded off for easy reference.

36-caliber round ball (65 grains)
– 2,000 fps muzzle velocity
Wind velocity: 20 mph
Bullet drift at 100 yards = 28 inches
Bullet drift at 200 yards = 113 inches
50-caliber round ball (182 grains)
– 2,000 fps muzzle velocity
Wind velocity: 20 mph
Bullet drift at 100 yards = 18.5 inches
Bullet drift at 200 yards = 80 inches

By comparison, a 370-grain 50-caliber Maxi-Ball starting at 1,500 fps drifts 16 inches at 100 yards in a 20 mph wind, while a 54-caliber 400-grain conical starting at 1,500 drifts 11 inches off course at 100 yards, same breeze. Good marksmen know how to "dope the wind."

Kentucky Windage and Arkansas Elevation

The "good shot" applies both Kentucky windage and Arkansas elevation to overcome wind deflection and bullet drop. Both are learned through experience. Kentucky windage is horizontal hold-off on the target. Arkansas elevation is compensation for bullet drop. Nobody can guess the exact velocity of the wind under field conditions, or the precise distance from muzzle to target, but practiced shooters do a pretty good job.

Good Targets

If you can't see it, you can't hit it, and if you cannot delineate the aim-point on your target clearly, sighting-in will be a problem. And if sighting in is a problem, working with the rainbow will be, too. Fortunately, target makers caught on and we have many good ones to choose from. We also make our own. I like a simple black square attached to a

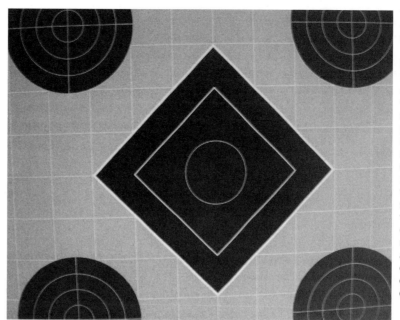

This target from Caldwell is good because it has contrast with clear aiming points. The diamond shape is especially useful with scope sights when the crosswire meets at all four corners of the diamond.

larger piece of white paper for iron sights. A much finer aiming point for scopes.

Sight-In Guide––Round Balls Starting at 1,900 to 2,000 fps

Small-Bore Round Ball
A sight-in of 50 yards works for calibers 32 and 36. Good for up to 75 yards on most small game.

Medium Round Ball
Calibers 38 to 40 also sight dead on at 50 yards, which puts these lead bullets on at about 75 yards, two or three inches low at 100.

Big-Bore Round Ball
Calibers 45 through 58—begin at 13 yards. Sight right on. Balls will be on target again at about 75 to 80 yards, a half-foot low at 125 yards, which is far enough for most big game with 45- through 58-caliber round balls.

Modern Big-Bore Conicals
The 50-caliber Ultimate Muzzleloader shoots a 300-grain Hornady SST ML bullet just shy of 2,500 fps with four Pyrodex 50/50 Pellets. Sighted to strike 3.5 inches high at 100 yards, bullets of this C rating are on again at 200.

Big-Bore Heavy Lead Bullets
Big lead bullets, like the deadly Hydra-Con by Parker Productions, shoot flat enough to ensure 200-yard strikes. These heavy lead projectiles are sighted in for 150 yards when driven by large (safe) powder charges with minimal 200-yard drop.

The Breechloader

Considering the 45-70 Government cartridge with a 500-grain round-nose bullet at 1,200 fps, sighting in to print the group three inches high at 50 yards gives a 100-yard zero, the bullet falling about six inches below line of sight at 125 yards, nine inches low at 150 yards. High ballistic coefficient bullets, such as the 535-grain 45-caliber Postell with a .402 C can be sighted in for 125-yards with an initial sight-in three inches high at 100 yards.

The Blackpowder Handgun

The cap 'n' ball revolver, as well as most muzzle-loading pistols—sight-in one inch high at 25 yards to put the bullet on target at 50 yards. Likewise blackpowder pistol.

Remember Protection

Eye and ear protection always, but when sighting in big bores with heavy hunting charges, use a pad, such as the Battenfeld Mag Shield. Working with the rainbow begins with proper sighting-in. Mule kicks on the shoulder are not conducive to best results at the bench. *Never use a sandbag between shoulder and the buttplate.* This may cause the stock to break.

Snapshooting Isn't

As a young man, I knew two miners who lived outside of Patagonia, Arizona, on the Mexican border. They were superior marksmen with their 30-30 carbines, often willing to put on a little show for me. They both assured me that they never looked at their sights—they simply "snapshot." Forget it. These men were highly practiced and they owned only one rifle each. They shot fast with accuracy, but they were using their sights. A bullet can only go where the sights are aiming.

Snapshooting, when it means firing a rifle without using the sights, is mainly a myth. A bullet must take a route in the direction that the sights indicate. This is why shooters are urged to take careful aim using good sights—and a rest doesn't hurt, either.

SIGHTING-IN TIPS

1. Insist on good iron sights. For scopes, make certain that mounts are correct and secure.

2. Tighten all screws, including sight screws. Loose screws make consistency impossible.

3. An inaccurate load cannot be expected to print consistently on the target. Work up an accurate load before sighting-in.

4. Use a benchrest with forend plus toe of stock secure on the bench top. Get comfortable, both feet flat on the ground spread a little for stability. Shooter may grip the forestock, but if recoil is not a problem, rest left hand flat on bench for right-handed shooter.

5. High-recoil rifles may skid your elbow across the surface of the bench. Pad arm to avoid elbow abrasion.

6. Use targets with well-defined aim-points.

7. Start close to get on the paper, 10 to 15 yards. Adjust sights to hit dead-center, then move targets farther out.

8. Know your trajectory before sight-in to work successfully with the rainbow.

TROUBLESHOOTING THE CHARCOAL BURNER

A basic way to ensure repeated ignition is simple—choose a good percussion cap. The day of the corrosive "cheap" cap has about run its course, but some still exist. A good No. 11 cap, such as one of these three brands, ensures ignition in a properly designed percussion firearm. Author has fired his Markesbery rifle many hundreds of times with good No. 11 caps and has yet to experience a misfire.

Sometimes the trouble with a muzzleloader that fires a few times and then won't shoot again is simply fouling in the bore that has invaded the ignition system. A good cleaning can help. Here is a kit for the job. Also, try an "all-day" lube during shooting.

Murphy's Law says that if something can go wrong, it will, and at the worst possible time. Since guns are mechanical, they are prey to failure. Today's muzzleloaders and accoutrements are well designed and are manufactured of the finest materials. Competition allows nothing else. Modern muzzleloaders fit this niche perfectly—great designs, superb materials.

Warning: the following are intended only for minor mishaps. Major problems must be brought to the attention of a competent gunsmith.

Muzzleloader Fires Once Or Twice, Then Is Difficult To Load Again

Load once OK. Load twice OK. Try to push another bullet downbore and it's no-go. The bore is fouling quickly and excessively. Overly deep grooves intended for gripping the round ball are not necessary, and yet they exist on some rifles. These little canyons catch and hold gunk. The situation improves as rifling lands wear from repeated shooting, patches polishing the bore. In the meantime, lubricate the ball patch

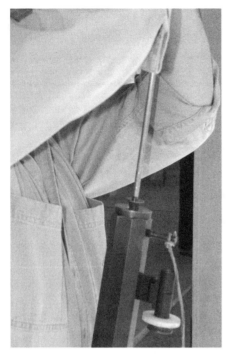

Yet another means of ensuring repeat ignition is fully ramming the ball down upon the powder charge with reasonable pressure upon the ramrod or loading rod. This not only compresses the powder charge, which promotes combustion performance, but also pushes the powder charge into position for ignition in the breech.

A lock failing to stay on half-cock is a threat to safety. It must be corrected by a competent gunsmith. This goes for any type of "lock," even when it is not a true lock. If there is a half-cock notch, that notch must be operable at all times. The Markesbery has a good system of a very secure half-cock notch while retaining a good trigger pull.

thoroughly with a liquid. The wet ball patch serves to clean. Damp does it. Total saturation is unnecessary. If the gun is a conical-shooter, put a glob of paste or cream lube on the base or in the hollow base cavity only.

Pyrodex or Triple Seven may help. Both promote continued shooting. Swiss blackpowder is another clean-burner. Proper shooting of Pyrodex includes firing a reasonable number of times *without* cleaning between shots. See Chapter 24 for more on Pyrodex. A Markesbery 54-caliber Outer-Line rifle (under range conditions) fired several times with heavy hunting charges of Swiss Black Powder and a Parker Productions lead bullet before cleaning the bore was necessary. Load down for target shooting and plinking. Lighter loads mean reduced bore fouling. Sometimes a change in bullets can turn the trick. Bullet behavior in the bore differs because bullet designs differ.

Lock Will Not Stay on Half-Cock

This problem constitutes a dangerous condition that must be corrected. Take the rifle to a gunsmith before firing one more shot. Explain the problem. The half-cock notch could be worn or the lock mortise may have swelled, binding the proper workings of the lock. A gunsmith can fix both problems.

Scoped Rifle Won't Stay Sighted-In

Check the scope mount first, both rings and base. If screws are loose, the mount itself may be the cause of the trouble. Tighten loose screws and go back to the range. Hopefully, the problem will be cured. Be certain the screwdriver or Allen wrench fit properly. Ill-fitting tools can damage screw heads. If a rifle continues to "shoot loose," meaning screws loosen again, consider a touch of Loctite on threads. There is a milder formulation of Loctite that works well on scope mounts.

Powerful blackpowder hunting rifles can produce considerable recoil, partly because of the inefficiency of blackpowder-type propellants. Reasonable velocity demands heavy powder charges. Since the *weight* of the powder charge is part of the recoil formula, muzzleloaders can "kick" pretty hard. Many modern muzzleloaders are allowed three Pyrodex or Triple Seven Pellets—that's 150 grains volume. Even the monster case of the 460 Weatherby Magnum does not take that much fuel. Heavy recoil may cause reticule wander. The cost-effective remedy is to scrap the scope and buy a one built to take more recoil. I once torture-tested a Bushnell Elite 4200 2.5-10X x 50mm. I liked the scope for its good optical resolution. But would it hold up to heavy recoil? Dozens of firings with a special 54-caliber muzzleloader allowed big charges of powder behind a 600-grain bullet and did not faze this scope. The rifle remained sighted in. To check a scope reticule, secure the scope. Place the crosswire on a target. Without moving the scope, manipulate the dials. The crosswire should respond with precise movement.

Formerly Accurate Muzzleloader Goes Sour

This problem exists more with modern cartridge guns than front-loaders. But an accurate blackpowder gun can begin shooting fatter groups. Modern arms are treated to a good bore cleaning to get rid of copper fouling. Oftentimes, this is all that is required to regain former accuracy. Bore-cleaning muzzleloaders can also restore accuracy not from copper fouling, but from stubborn powder or plastic fouling in rifling grooves. In severe cases, a gunsmith can remove the breech plug from the firearm so the bore can be attacked with a stout cleaning rod and series of bristle brush scrubbings. Modern muzzleloaders with removable breech plugs can be worked on in the home shop. I have a gun cradle from Brownells that holds the rifle for a strong cleaning. Another problem, along with loose scope mounts, is loose anything. When the gun is reassembled after cleaning,

If a brand new firearm will not shoot safely "out of the box" it is close to 100 percent certain that a better load needs to be found. Today's muzzleloaders are, due to intense competition from one company to the next, quite foolproof as they come from the factory.

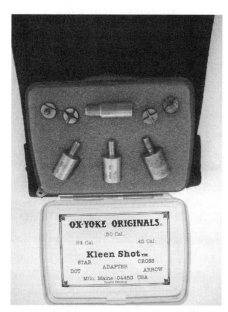

An accurate rifle may go sour. There can be many causes. One that may be overlooked is a change in bullet and/or powder charge without ensuring the new bullet is protected if it is fired in a sabot. A sabot must be strong enough to withstand the fast ride up the bore. Sabots are easily checked for integrity—just go downrange and pick up fired ones to see how they fared.

A perfect way to ensure that a lead bullet, round or conical, receives zero nose damage during the seating process is with a kit like this one from Ox-Yoke Originals. Each cutter fits onto a ramrod or loading rod. When the lead bullet is seated, the cutter engraves the nose of that bullet. There can be no deformation.

everything must be tight. This does not mean applying torque that breaks screws or bolts, but tight enough to hold everything in place where it belongs. Remember Loctite.

If a good gun goes bad and cleaning does not correct the problem, look for crown damage. If rifling in this sensitive region is damaged, accuracy can be lost, because the crown of the muzzle is the last guidance that the rifling has on a projectile. If the crown is damaged, a gunsmith can recrown the barrel. Another worthwhile investigation, especially if the muzzle crown is found to be in perfect shape, is looking into bore wear, especially with a round ball gun. A cloth patch will not burnish a bore quickly, but in time, it can have an effect. An informal bore inspection can be accomplished with a bore light. Removable breech plugs makes this operation easy. If the bore is "shot out," the firearm cannot be expected to shoot accurately. I prefer a new barrel to recutting rifling in an old barrel—except for customs and originals.

Gun Won't Shoot Accurately out of the Box

Contact the gun company. Some shooters wondered why they were not getting super accuracy with the Savage Model 10ML-II. The reason was simple. Sabots were failing. Changing to a stronger sabot did the trick. Sometimes gaining best accuracy means finding the right combination of powder and bullet. This is not work. It's fun. You got into this game to shoot, right? So go to the range and shoot—a lot—with various combinations of powder/bullet. Heaven knows there is no shortage

of each these days. Be sure to observe maximum powder charges. The right combination will eventually turn up, and if not—well—there may still be some front-loaders out there that aren't terribly accurate.

Round Ball Inaccuracy

Remember good old Dr. Mann? He was the physician who spent a good part of his life testing bullet flight, his conclusion being that in the main, accuracy was a matter of *good bullets* from good barrels. Check round balls for precision with a bullet-powder scale. Weigh a batch. The spread should be minimal because good round balls, either home-cast or from bullet companies, show well. The next little trick is rolling round balls on a flat surface. They should go straight. Wobbly lead pills are no good, suggesting perhaps a problem with lead homogeneity. If lead for the round ball is not "pure" that might be OK, provided the impurities are well distributed in the bullet. If they are not, then the ball is off-balance and cannot be expected to shoot straight. Round balls should be round, not egg-shaped. Rolling singles out the bad ones. Damage is another killer of round ball accuracy. A slightly out-of-round ball may fly pretty straight due to equalization of abnormalities on a common axis (spinning caused by rifling). Nose damage, especially, seems to throw the sphere off course, while any damage can rob accuracy.

Conical Inaccuracy

Minor aberrations are not serious, but damage to the conical, as with the round ball, can destroy accuracy. It's a good idea to protect all bullets from

The base of the conical bullet is vital to accuracy. Here, the bullet is marked with a line to indicate the exact location to install it in the blackpowder cartridge case, but at the same time the bullet is also inspected for flaws, especially a dent caused when it was released from the mould and dropped onto the holding tray.

In days of old, a leather covering, especially for a flintlock, was called a "cow's knee." Any leather protector—and it need not be made for the job as long as it will cover the lock area—will serve to ward off rain and snow. Just be sure it can be quickly removed for a shot.

A muzzleloader can be made quite rainproof even though its system is on the open side, but nothing beats weatherproofing inherent in the design, which is the case here with this Traditions break-open rifle.

dents and flat spots. The original box is acceptable for regular storage. For travel to range or hunting field, consider a metal box. Protect bullets in the box with cloth or paper towel, especially softer lead missiles that can crash into each other en route to the shooting site. Seal the box with a layer of plastic wrap if bullets are going to be stored for a while. Conicals, by my tests, suffer more from base damage than nose damage, which is opposite of what I found with round balls. If conical base or skirt is damaged, chances of best accuracy are slim.

Group Hits Left, Right, High or Low

An oily bore can cause this problem. Troubleshooting means wiping the bore free of excessive lube with a single cleaning patch after the gun is loaded. See Chapter 14 for more on this topic.

Percussion Muzzleloader Fails to go off in Damp or Rainy Weather

Take it from a fellow who knows. I told the story elsewhere about my guide, Steve Pike, who called a big six-by-six bull elk to within 12 paces. I paced the distance afterwards so I could kick myself. It had been raining, and in my haste to leave town, I forgot waterproofing materials. Worst of all, I know I would have gotten that bull, because when the rifle misfired, the sights remained lined up perfectly after the click. Here are some ideas:

Waterproofing and Foul-Proofing the Lock

Saturate a thin piece of paper, such as onionskin writing paper, with gun grease. An alternative is pre-greased protection paper that comes with new firearms, a possible source being the local gun shop. Remove the lock from its mortise in the stock and use the mortise as a pattern, cutting the greased paper to fit with a slight overlap. The paper forms a gasket between lock exterior and interior to prevent moisture from passing from the stock surface

Flintlock ignition is dependent upon several factors, beginning with location of the touchhole in relation to the pan. There are far more good locks today than poor ones, but it doesn't hurt to check touchhole location to ensure that it is fairly high on the barrel flat so that it does not become readily clogged with pan powder to cause a fuse condition.

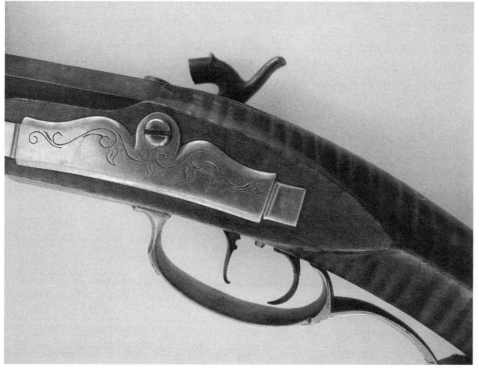

Original muzzleloaders with brass furniture should probably be allowed to go patina—that is, to color naturally. A contemporary firearm can go the same route—or brightwork can be kept bright with a brass polish.

into the important tumbler area. The greased paper gasket also discourages blackpowder fouling from attacking inner lock workings. One thin piece of greased paper will do. Excess paper might get caught up in the workings of the lock.

Serious Rain-proofing

The muzzle of the firearm is a very small area; however, rain pouring down or snow falling from a tree might gain entry, invading the powder charge. A small rubber balloon stretched over the muzzle seals the bore. There are also commercial products that do the same thing. The touchhole of the flintlock and vent of the nipple, as well as nipple seat, are real problem areas for the trespass of moisture. The vast majority of failures on rainy days come from these, not the lock or water getting wet through the muzzle. The flintlock can wear a boot, sometimes referred to as a "cow's knee." This boot covering is not entirely handy, but it beats a wet lock. Nipple and nipple seat can be waterproofed with specific devices, one being the Kap Kover. If I had my Kap Kover on No. 47, the big bull elk would have been mine. Search catalogs or Internet for other devices.

Modern Muzzleloader

Another way to foil rain and snow is with a modern muzzleloader designed to be, if not waterproof, then at least highly moisture resistant. While the rifle may not survive a submersion in a stream, it will not succumb to rain or snow.

Bad Powder

Keep your powder dry was more than a parting farewell in the old days. Damp powder is no friend to ignition.

Flintlock Fails to Go Off
Poor Spark

Historically, the bevel of the flint is supposed to face downward, but I have seen flinters go off like fireworks with reversed bevels. One thing is certain, however. The edge of the flint must mate squarely with the face of the frizzen for uniform contact. Lining up flint and frizzen was covered in Chapter 14. Flint damage is another culprit. If the flint is jagged, it's time for a new

one—or re-knapping the current one. Sometimes allowing a brand new flint to drop against the frizzen a few times helps mate the edge of the flint with the face of the frizzen. An old flint can also be re-angled in the jaws of the hammer, where it may re-knap itself with a few meetings of flint and frizzen. Sometimes moving the flint sideways slightly or a bit forward in the jaws of the hammer also presents a new contact point to the frizzen. And yes, the flint can be turned upside down (forget the rules) to facilitate a change in mating with the frizzen. Important, yet sometimes overlooked, is the condition of flint and frizzen. Both must be clean and dry, not oily. If the flintlock firearm continues to throw poor sparks with a new well-mated flint that is clean and dry and a proper frizzen, it's time to check the hammer throw. A spring may have gone weak, failing to provide a good whack of flint against frizzen. The frizzen itself can eventually wear out, too. Another problem is setting the flint back in the jaws too far. It should stick out far enough to ensure good contact with the frizzen.

Flash in the Pan

A damp or oily pan can defy proper ignition. Pan powder still goes off, but the flame does not enjoy full power. A clogged touchhole is also a possible culprit, whether invaded by a foreign object or packed full of powder. While blackpowder ignites readily, when it is

packed into a small channel such as a touchhole, a fuze may be created, slowing ignition or even causing a flash in the pan. See Chapter 14.

Percussion Cap Fails Under Dry (no rain or snow) Conditions

Modern caps are reliable. I tested RWS caps by randomly selecting 20 from the box and placing them in a high-humidity environment—a closet—on an open piece of paper. After 48 hours of running a humidifier, the caps were tested in a Dixie Screwbarrel Pistol, barrel removed. All twenty went off. Nonetheless, caps can be ruined with moisture. By firing a cap or two on the nipple prior to loading, damaged caps can be detected. If a cap does not give a good bang on the nipple during the clearing process, the shooter should expect ignition trouble. Cap debris can also cause a misfire. A damaged nipple can be a problem. The wrong nipple may also cause trouble. See Chapter 19 for more on ignition.

Brass Furniture Gets Dull

Many shooters prefer the tarnished patina look to the bright appearance. Oxidation won't hurt brass furniture, but for those who prefer the bright look, slow the oxidation process by applying a coat of beeswax to brass furniture: nose caps, patch boxes, buttplates, toe plates and other metalwork. Birchwood Casey Gun Stock Wax is good. The wax coating forms a modest, but helpful, barrier between metal and the atmosphere, keeping tarnishing to a minimum. Dull brass can also be polished with—brass polisher.

Lead Bullets Look Powdery or Moldy

Perhaps powdery and moldy are the wrong terms, but lead bullets can exhibit a whitish coating that can sometimes rubs off as a powder. Although minor surface coating may not harm accuracy

Lead balls and bullets will oxidize over time. The powdery coating doesn't affect performance, and appearance can be restored by spraying the balls with lubricant, gently rubbing to coat. Prevent oxidation by spraying when the balls and bullets are new.

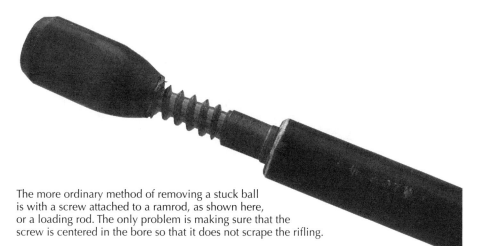

The more ordinary method of removing a stuck ball is with a screw attached to a ramrod, as shown here, or a loading rod. The only problem is making sure that the screw is centered in the bore so that it does not scrape the rifling.

(especially with a round ball wrapped in a patch), bullets can be restored to their former color. A light spray of lube does the trick, such as Rusty Duck Protective Gun Lubricant. Give it a quick jet of spray, and then gently rotate the box to treat all of the bullets to a little of the chemical. Spray beforehand to prevent discolored lead bullets.

Ramrod Problems
Ramrod Stuck Downbore

A stuck ramrod sometimes occurs during the cleaning process. A ramrod can also hang up when seating a bullet. This condition demands very careful attention. *At all times, ensure that the muzzle of the gun is pointed in a safe direction away from any person or property.* If a rod should get stuck in the bore, especially in the field where professional help is far away, consider a leather thong. It goes like this: tie the thong in a clove hitch around the extended ramrod shaft. Secure the end of the thong to a stationary object, such as a tree. Pull carefully and slowly, but steadily and strongly, on the rifle. If a stuck cleaning patch will not come free, run liquid lube down the bore and try again, always maintaining the muzzle in a safe direction. After the rod is pulled free, the bore should be thoroughly swabbed before the next load because a dirty bore probably caused the problem to begin with.

Wooden Ramrods Can Break

Modern muzzleloaders have modern ramrods. Breaking is unlikely. But wooden ramrods on traditional frontloaders can break. It is helpful to soak the ramrod in coal oil, kerosene or neat's-foot oil to render it supple, yet not so pliable that a patched ball can't be rammed home. A piece of tubing can be corked on one end, the ramrod placed inside and the tube filled with one of the liquids mentioned above. Ramrods can also be treated with boiled linseed oil to prevent drying and cracking. Don't forget to use a short-starter to move the bullet downbore a distance before using the ramrod.

Stuck Ball Downbore

Before attempting to remove a stuck ball, the gun must be uncapped or pan powder removed. The Thompson/Center CO2 Magnum Silent Ball Discharger will literally blow a stuck ball free. Lacking this device, a stuck ball can usually be removed the old-fashioned way, with a screw (not a worm). The screw should

be used with a muzzle protector. The protector centers the screw in the bore, preventing contact with bore walls and also delivering the screw to the center of the stuck ball where it belongs. A cleaning rod with a knocker, such as the Kadooty, is excellent for removing a stuck ball. If the rod does not have a knocker, the thong method noted above for freeing a stuck ramrod might have to be employed, with the muzzle always pointed in a safe direction.

Seated Ball, No Powder

Eventually, most of us will do it. We're thinking about that next shot and the patched ball is rammed home without a powder charge in the breech. Now what? The stuck ball method is the best way to get the patched ball back up the bore, using either the CO2 device or the screw attached to the end of a metal loading rod fitted with a muzzle protector. The ball may be safely shot free with a small powder charge, but if it is not driven all the way out of the bore, it should be reseated once again before trying to blow it free. If the gun has a cleanout screw, remove it. Pour a trickle of powder through the channel. Replace the cleanout screw before firing the gun. Sometimes a little powder can be trickled into the touchhole of the flintlock rifle for the same purpose. If there is no cleanout screw on the caplock firearm, the nipple can be removed and powder can be introduced through the nipple seat area. Then the nipple is returned fully to its seat before firing the ball into a safe place. The muzzle must always be pointed in a safe direction.

Some patch lube is weather-sensitive. It hardens up in colder times. Wonder Lube 1000 shows well in the winter.

The flash cup can prevent stock damage for those blackpowder firearms with an exposed nipple. Fire from the exploding cap on these guns can burn the wood beneath the nipple. The flash cup captures sparks and diverts cap debris.

Another means of protecting the nose of a bullet from deformation is choosing a bullet whose nose cannot be deformed during the seating process. This is a bullet of that nature—a Nosler Partition with jacket running up to the nose.

Stored Muzzleloader Attracts Rust

This is solved with one of the many fine rust inhibitors of the day or modern metal preservatives that thwart rust. See Chapter 30.

Patch Lube Good in Summer, But Not in Winter

There are several modern patch lubes that do not harden up in cold weather, such as Orange Stuff from Old Western Scrounger. The vast majority of lubes work well within normal temperature ranges. Arctic conditions or the Sahara may pose a different problem.

Troubleshooting the Correctly Seated Load

This one is offered elsewhere, but bears repeating. A witness mark on the ramrod or loading rod always tells the shooter when the bullet is fully seated downbore in the breech. The witness mark is made when the bullet is seated fully upon the powder charge. After ramming the bullet home, the ramrod or loading rod is left in place. A mark is made with indelible ink or a scratch on the rod where it meets the crown of the muzzle. Suppose a patched ball or conical gets stuck off of the powder charge. The marked ramrod instantly indicates the problem, the line on the rod riding *above* the muzzle.

Misses Caused by a Moved Sight

After a gun is sighted in, a tiny witness mark can be scratched from sights to barrel. Should a sight become bumped out of place, the witness mark will no longer match up between sight and barrel.

Stock Gets Burned from Ignition

The best prevention is a flash cup for percussion firearms. A flash cup diverts sparks away from the wood. A bit of masking tape around the nipple or lock area of the flintlock also prevents burned wood.

Round Ball or Conical is Nose-Damaged when Seated

The nub end of some short starters can put a deep dimple in the round or conical bullet. There are commercial short starters and jags designed to prevent bullet nose damage, such as those from Parker Productions, Buffalo Bullet Company, Barnes, T/C, Traditions and others.

These are a few tricks to keep the muzzleloader making smoke.

chapter 29

TAKING CARE OF YOUR FRIEND—MAINTENANCE

Cleaning during a shooting session not only promotes accuracy (provided the bore is prepped again for best groups), but it also makes for easier cleaning after the fun is over.

The only element preventing some shooters from joining the happy ranks of smokepole lovers is, "I would, but I don't want to clean the guns." Rumors of a truly non-corrosive propellant for muzzleloaders and blackpowder cartridge guns are blowing in the wind. No such powder exists—yet. We do have clean-burning powders that attack fouling like an alligator goes for a duck. These jewels from the laboratory have destroyed the cleanup excuse, but they are not non-corrosive. Modern chemistry has also come to the rescue with an all-out attack on fouling. This rosy chemicals picture includes blackpowder cartridges firing jacketed bullets, where

eventually a bit of copper wash may be "grace" the bore. Today's chemicals also demolish plastic wash from sabots, especially important with higher-velocity modern muzzleloaders that drive sabots through the bore at up to 2,500+ feet-per-second. Those who merrily trod the blackpowder trail come to consider their guns friends. This chapter is about taking care of those friends.

How Corrosive?

The problem with blackpowder and substitutes is that they tend to play the role of the common kitchen sink sponge—that is, they like to suck up moisture. That old salutation "keep

Maintenance is easier than ever with all blackpowder guns. Modern chemistry has come to the rescue with good cleaning products. And Triple Seven is now available in both powder form and pellet, shown here with Winchester No. 209 primers especially dedicated to Triple Seven powder. While Triple Seven is not advertised as non-corrosive, it cleans up with water only and in about the same time required for a smokeless powder cartridge firearm.

Not only do blackpowder shooters now have the best chemistry ever for maintenance, along with excellent powders such as GOEX, Swiss, Triple Seven, and others, but the modern guns are also dedicated to easier cleanup.

your powder dry" was more than empty words. Damp powder either failed to go off or reduced velocity to cork gun potency. It's easy to keep powder dry in its moisture-proof container. Most propellants last all but indefinitely when retained in their original canisters. There have been exceptions. Shelf life of these exceptions is compromised by the nature of the powder itself. I have tested these propellants with negative results. Even left in their original containers, energy-per-grain weight is reduced in time. Not to worry, however, because the majority of propellants, including regular blackpowder, do fine as long as they are not subjected to long periods of high humidity. The late Bruce Hodgdon sent me a small sample of a blackpowder he knew to be a century old. He suggested I test it, and I did. It produced full velocity. Stored blackpowder is not the problem. Potential problems occur after combustion. Chapter 23 discusses the properties of blackpowder combustion.

Easier-to-Clean Guns

Some blackpowder firearms are easier to clean than others due to barrel length, depth of grooves, removable breech plugs, and smooth bores. A muzzleloader with a 24-inch barrel is a little easier to clean than a rifle with a 34-inch barrel—less bore surface. Shorter barrels also fit better in the kitchen sink or laundry room tub for cleaning. Deep-groove rifling collects and holds more fouling than shallow-groove rifling, with, of course, smoothbores being the easiest to clean—no rifling at all. Deep-groove rifling? No problem. A bristle brush reaches into the deepest grooves. Round ball guns generally have deeper

grooves than conical-shooters. Sometimes this is unnecessarily exaggerated. Removable breech plugs make after-shooting maintenance a snap. Likewise blackpowder cartridge guns with breechblocks that expose the entire bore. The Savage Model 10M-II does well with blackpowder, but is of course easier to clean with smokeless. Meanwhile, no other muzzleloader offered as this is written can take advantage of the easier smokeless powder cleanup.

Clean While You Shoot

Cleaning while you shoot means using modern lubes. Many commercial products, liquids, pastes, and creams attack blackpowder fouling. See Chapter 30. While the all-day shooting promise can be overdone, modern blackpowder lubes pay off with easier after-shooting maintenance. The old-timer did not have this luxury. I have fired many shots with whale oil, vegetable oil, bear fat, and other substances from the pantry and under the kitchen sink. I attest to the fact that none of these worked nearly as well as modern lubes applied to ball patches, in the base of sabots and on the base of conicals.

How Clean is Clean?

In the past, I was happy when a stored muzzleloader taken from the gun safe showed only a trace of darkness on a white patch. Today, the white patch emerges white, or very close to it, especially for any of those guns that allow cleaning from the breech because these are easier to scrub out than closed breech guns. Regardless, all blackpowder guns clean up well with the methods described in this chapter.

The Evils of Poor After-Shooting Maintenance

So what happens when guns are not properly cleaned? I have studied blackpowder guns that were essentially destroyed due to poor after-shooting maintenance. These were abused firearms, left for overly long periods of time in high humidity without cleaning. One of these guns blew a nipple right out of the nipple seat. And no wonder. The nipple seat was so corroded that threads were no more than a word. What used to be threads had degenerated to be almost invisible. This sad but true story shows what can happen when guns, in general, are not maintained. Osborne Russell, in his 19th-century mountain man journal, told of guns "bursting." I would be willing to bet poor maintenance was the culprit. Russell wrote, following the failure of one of the men to return to camp, "It was then agreed that either his gun had bursted and killed him, or his horse had fallen with him over some tremendous precipice." A poorly maintained gun can also fail in accuracy, especially when the crown (muzzle) becomes corroded or worn, the rifling at this point failing to send the bullet properly on its way. A ring can build in the bore when a gun is not cleaned efficiently. This ring is a permanent etched circle in the bore's interior, a fouled area that failed to get scrubbed clean. Poor cleaning can also cause rust and result in a pitted bore. The interior of the lock may suffer from poor maintenance, especially dangerous if the notches on the tumbler are reduced by corrosion. The firearm could go off prematurely if the nose of the sear slips out of the full-cock or half-cock notch. The nipple seat area may also deteriorate. The nipple may dislodge, as stated above. The flintlock's touchhole will eventually burn out after considerable use, but left unclean, damage comes much sooner. A nipple may also burn out, causing possible ignition problems. Finally, the wood on any blackpowder firearm can suffer from neglect.

Blackpowder Corrosiveness

Many different salts are left behind following combustion (Chapter 23). These salts are reduced (broken down) with polar solvents, such as water, as well as many commercial products. At the same time, the corrosive nature of blackpowder can be overstated. Blackpowder does not "eat up" metal on contact. Having tested original muzzleloaders left in a loaded condition perhaps for years, I have yet to find one "eaten up" by blackpowder. Where the load rested in the bore, there was evidence of damage, but if blackpowder were like a powerful acid, much more harm would have occurred. While blackpowder itself is not terribly corrosive, after combustion the fouling can be big trouble. Imagine a soda cracker left out in a high-humidity environment. Soon it's soggy. If a fired muzzleloader is left loaded in a high-humidity environment, fouling will take up moisture. And that means *rust*. A six-month test with several barrels firing blackpowder and blackpowder substitutes with two cleaning methods, water-only and solvent-only, resulted in zero damage to the test barrels. While the barrels were subjected to less than perfect cleaning as part of the test, they were not left in high humidity long enough to show bore rusting.

Disassembly Before Cleaning

For cleaning, the firearm must be disassembled, sometimes nothing more than removing a breech plug on a modern muzzleloader. Pinned stocks are seldom removed, while keyed stocks are. Pins must be driven out carefully. Con-

Disassembly to the point necessary for thorough cleaning and excellent maintenance is generally no problem. This Markesbery muzzleloader "breaks down" for cleaning in only a few minutes and with just two Allen wrenches and one breech plug wrench.

sult the gunmaker for directions, ensuring that each pin is driven out from the correct side of the stock. Sometimes pins are tapered. Forcing them out the wrong way can split the stock. Careful observation can usually detect tapered pins, one end being larger than the other. Keyed stocks are simple to "unlatch." The wedge, or key, is forced free and the barrel lifted out of the barrel channel. For hooked breeches or any firearm that "comes apart" easily, removing the barrel for cleaning makes the job easier. While the lock need not be removed after every shooting session, it must be checked from time to time. Fouling can get into the workings.

Water-Only Cleanup

Ordinary tap water is acceptable because of its nature as a universal solvent. For flushing the bore with water, a cloth should be wrapped around the muzzle. If not, water can seep between barrel and stock. Water dissolves most blackpowder residue, not only on salts, but also carbon and sulfur.

Triple Seven Powder

While any blackpowder firearm can be cleaned with plain water, Triple Seven is especially formulated for water only. Two or three wet patches breaks down fouling, followed by drying patches, followed by a light coating of metal protector.

Cleaning a gun in the kitchen sink is no problem. The bad stuff runs right down the drain. Here, a solvent-soaked pipe cleaner goes after fouling in the vent of the breech plug.

Here, a breech plug rests in one of the shooter's favorite locations for cleaning his or her guns—the kitchen sink.

Steps For Water-Only Cleanup

Although concentration in this chapter is mainly on muzzleloaders, a little alteration of the cleaning program works for rifles, handguns, and shotguns that shoot blackpowder cartridges or shells.

1. Make certain that the firearm is unloaded—no cap or primer in place. "The gun went off when he was cleaning it" may be an old story, but it has happened. See Chapter 14 for using a ramrod to check, inserting the ramrod to see if it bottoms out, or if it falls short of the bottom of the breech (unloaded) or sticks far out of the muzzle (loaded gun).

2. Disassemble firearm appropriately, removing barrel and breech plug where possible.

3. Flush bore with cool water. The theory goes: cool water will not "set" fouling in the bore. This step gets the process underway, breaking down and flushing out major fouling.

4. Flush bore with hot water. Hot water heats the barrel, which in turn aids drying the bore. It is impossible with some firearms to reach every little corner with a cleaning patch or pipe cleaner. But if the bore is hot, traces of trapped water evaporate.

5. Use a bristle brush to scrub residue from rifling grooves.

6. Remove the nipple. If the firearm has a cleanout screw, remove it now. The screw allows a flow of water through the breech section. The nipple seat also affords this passageway, but the cleanout screw opens a direct port from the breech. Flushing with the cleanout screw removed helps clear powder residue directly from the breech. Water squirts out vigorously through the cleanout screw hole when poured down the muzzle.

7. Leaving the cleanout screw hole open, work the bristle brush through the bore several times with hot water, being careful to guide the stream of water away from the lock and stock of the firearm. If dirty water invades the lock, lock mortise, or barrel channel, it can promote rust and/or wood decay, especially if the mortises and channels are not well finished.

8. Douse a toothbrush with hot water and scrub the hammer nose, snail area, and metal parts around the lock, nipple seat, nipple threads and other exposed metal parts. A toothbrush does for the outer parts of the gun what a bristle brush does for the bore.

9. Dip a pipe cleaner in hot water and swab nipple vent as well as nipple seat. Same treatment for the flintlock touchhole.

10. Sop up moisture left in the bore with cleaning patches to pick up debris loosened by the bristle brush, but not carried off by the water flush.

11. Repeat Step 10 with more dry patches. The first patches out of the bore may be quite wet. Hot water promotes fast bore drying. Continue with dry patches until one emerges white or very close to white.

12. Wipe all channels, cracks, and crevices dry with pipe cleaners.

13. Dry outer metal surfaces with clean cloth. Some moisture may have been transferred to the barrel and lock during flushing.

14. Wipe the wood dry, then rub stock with a clean cloth plus a few drops of pure boiled linseed oil.

15. Go over the entire firearm with a soft clean cloth to pick up traces of residue, solvent or linseed oil from the surface of the gun.

16. Run a cleaning patch through the bore dampened with a little metal preserver.

17. Apply a light coating of metal preserving chemical to the outside of the barrel and lock.

18. Occasionally, the lock requires special cleaning. Remove it from its mortise in the stock. Blow dirt out of the workings with canned air or air hose. Use a toothbrush to flick away stubborn dirt. Wipe all exposed parts clean. Oil lightly.

19. Bright work, such as brass fittings, may be cleaned with a little Flitz on a cloth. Follow with a clean, soft, dry cloth.

20. Remember that an oily bore can throw the first shot wild, so Step 20 is cleaning the bore before firing the gun again. Also, oil in the bore can cause a hydraulic effect with possible bore damage, the oil coming between projectile and bore walls.

Tools from the world of firearms maintenance in general work well for blackpowder guns, cartridge as well as muzzleloader. This bore bristle brush will work itself down into the grooves of any rifling to remove fouling.

The revolver will require full disassembly if several cylinders of blackpowder or Pyrodex were fired.

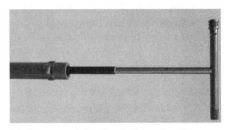

Modern muzzleloader designers' major goal is making shooting and maintenance simpler, easier, and foolproof. Here, the simple addition of a T-handle to the Markesbery ramrod turns the ramrod into a decent length range rod.

Solvent-Only Cleanup

No water whatsoever is used in this method. William Large, barrel maker for over 50 years, scolded me with the warning: "Never touch water to barrels." He went on to say that he had been shooting muzzleloaders longer than I'd been alive at the time, and he did not believe in cleaning with water, relying only on solvent to keep his barrels in perfect shooting condition. Since his barrels won literally hundreds of muzzleloader matches, I'd say Mr. Large knew what he was talking about. Nonetheless, the worn cliché "to each his own" prevails, and if a shooter feels more comfortable with an all-water cleaning. Furthermore, some shooters report that in regions of high humidity, the hot-water flush does the best job of getting gunk out, while helping the bore to dry thoroughly.

Steps For Solvent-Only Cleanup

1. Ensure that the firearm is absolutely *unloaded* before attempting disassembly or cleanup; no cap, primer, or pan powder.
2. Attach a jag to the end of a cleaning rod to hang onto the patch. Match jag/cleaning patch to avoid patch slipping off downbore (retrieve lost patch with a worm.). Soak patch with solvent and run through bore several times to loosen fouling.
3. After swabbing bore with solvent, remove nipple and cleanout screw (if the gun has one) and repeat Step 2. Waiting to remove the cleanout screw until this step promotes easy removal when solvent reaches their threads.
4. Scrub the bore with a bristle brush soaked in solvent. Depending upon how much powder was burned, anywhere from only a few passes to dozens. The brush is important to the no-water cleaning method because the bristles reach into the grooves of the rifling to scrub out fouling.

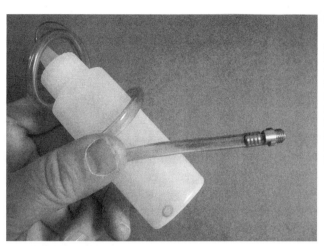

One of the handiest cleaning devices for the hunting camp or range is this little bottle with nipple seat fitting. Remove the nipple on the percussion gun, screw in the nipple seat fitting, put a tight patch on the cleaning rod, and pump solvent or water from the bottle back and forth through the bore.

Part of easy maintenance of the firearm is having a way to control the gun, especially rifle, musket, or shotgun, while the work goes on. This cleaning cradle from Brownells is ideal for that job. It is portable and it secures long guns perfectly.

5. Sop up goop in the bore with dry patches. If a lot of powder was fired, and in spite of cleaning between strings of shots, it may take a few patches to soak up all of the dark liquid in the bore after the bristle brush and solvent have gone to work.
6. Repeat Step 4 with more solvent.
7. Repeat Step 5. At this point, patches should emerge from the bore gray rather than black or dark brown.
8. Refer to Steps 12 through 19 in the water-only method, but forget the water. Use only solvent on a rag to clean exterior metal, solvent on a pipe cleaner to reach into cracks and crevices. Dry all parts well. Use pipe cleaner or toothbrush where necessary.

Good tools make the work light. These bristle brushes come in a compact holder. Fadala uses them for his smaller-bore black-powder cartridge rifles. They are always handy because of the container.

Water/Solvent Combination

This method incorporates the hot water flush, plus scrubbing the bore with a solvent-soaked bristle brush.

Steps For Water/Solvent Method

1. Be certain that gun is *unloaded* before attempting to clean it. After ensuring that it is unloaded and free of cap, primer, or pan powder, disassemble for cleaning.
2. Flush bore with cool water.
3. Flush bore with hot water.
4. Run a solvent-soaked cleaning patch through the bore several strokes.
5. Make several passes with a solvent-soaked bristle brush.
6. Remove nipple and cleanout screw (if there is a cleanout screw).
7. Run a solvent-soaked bristle brush through the bore several strokes with the nipple and cleanout screw removed.
8. Sop up all liquid from the bore with cleaning patches.
9. Clean the nipple seat and cleanout screw hole with a pipe cleaner dipped in solvent.
10. Wipe all channels with the toothbrush and pipe cleaners using only a little solvent. Over-using solvent on the toothbrush or pipe cleaner causes the solvent to run into mortises and between metal and wood parts.
11. Wipe outer portion of firearm, metal and wood, with clean rag, using a little boiled linseed oil on the stock and a little preserving oil on the metal.
12. Protect bore with a light coating of rust inhibitor or other metal preserving agent.
13. Attend to the lock if necessary, removing to clean inside with a cloth and solvent. Use pipe cleaners to get into the crevices. Lightly oil parts of lock.
14. Attend to bright work with a little Flitz on a cloth.

Markesbery Muzzleloader Cleaning Method

Although this procedure comes from a specific blackpowder company for a specific muzzleloader, the Outer-Line, it's worth looking into as an alternative.

Markesbery Method

This specific rifle is noted because of it's unique nature.

1. Ensure an unloaded unprimed firearm before proceeding.
2. Place all tools and cleaning products on bench.
3. Thread cleaning jag onto aluminum ramrod. (The Markesbery comes with a strong ramrod, plus a T-handle extension that turns the ramrod into a cleaning/wiping stick.)
4. Loosen and remove receiver/barrel lug screw (bottom of the barrel) and remove barrel from receiver.
5. Remove nipple or optional 400 SRP. Firearm is now ready for cleaning.
6. Unscrew breech plug with special tool provided.
7. Run solvent-soaked patches through bore several passes.
8. Drop the nipple into a small container of solvent or "soak." (See soak below.)
9. Wipe receiver clean with solvent cloth.
10. Run a final solvent patch through bore followed by drying patches.
11. Run a final bore patch through, lightly wet with metal preserver.
12. Reassemble rifle—important—apply anti-seize lubricant on the threads of the breech plug.

One sure way to get rid of plastic fouling in the bore of the rifle or shotgun is with a proper solvent formulated to do the job. This one is.

The sabot goes way back in history. It's an ideal go-between for bullet and rifling. If the sabot leaves behind a trace of plastic fouling, it's easy to get rid of with the proper solvent.

Modern Muzzleloaders

Modern muzzleloaders may require special cleaning methods to match specific designs. However, general cleaning methods continue to apply, the goal always being the same—return firearm to as close to unfired condition as possible.

Plastic Fouling

Plastic fouling from sabots or shotgun wads is cleared from the bore with special products, such as choke tube cleaners, which are specially formulated to attack plastic residue. Shooter's Choice, Butch's Bore Shine, Barnes CR-10, and similar chemicals also attack plastic fouling.

Copper Fouling

Copper fouling is rare in blackpowder guns that shoot jacketed bullets because of slower velocities. Should a rifle (rare in handguns) begin to shoot "fatter" groups, copper fouling could be the problem. Specialized chemicals get rid of copper fouling. Examples include Barnes CR-10, Shooters Choice X-Treme Clean (ammonia-free), Shooters Choice Copper Remover, and other similar products. Heed warnings, especially for bore cleaners with ammonia.

Shotguns, Pistols and Revolvers

Shotguns and pistols are cleaned very much like the muzzle-loading rifle. The revolver is different, a major difference being disassembly. Blackpowder fouling in the workings of the revolver can lock it up.

The pistol is very easy to maintain because of its short barrel and short overall length. The short barrel allows proper cleaning with the ramrod only, while the short length makes it a handy fit in the kitchen sink.

Cleaning a Revolver With Water

Steps For Cleaning Cap'n'ball Revolver With Water

1. Ensure the gun is unloaded and uncapped before cleaning.
2. Disassemble appropriately, including removal of all nipples from cylinder. If this is a routine cleaning after firing only a couple cylinders, the revolver may not require full disassembly.
3. Flush bore and chambers with cool water.
4. Flush bore and chambers with hot water.
5. Scrub bore with water/bristle brush.
6. Scrub cylinder and chambers with toothbrush.
7. Run cleaning wet patches through bore and chambers.
8. Dry bore and chambers with patches.
9. Use pipe cleaners and water to clean nipple vents.
10. Dry all parts. If the revolver was not fully disassembled, be certain that no water has invaded the workings of the gun. If you suspect that water has gotten into the working parts, the revolver will have to be fully stripped and all moisture removed. Parts may be dried in an oven on low heat.
11. Wipe revolver down (metal parts with an oily rag). Wooden grips wiped down with rag and a touch of linseed oil.
12. For storage, leave light trace of oil on all working parts as well as frame, barrel, and bore. Brass frames may be brought back to bright with brass cleaner.

Important: The revolver will require full disassembly if several cylinders of blackpowder or Pyrodex were fired. Be certain to observe steps carefully to avoid damage.

Soaking parts takes part of the elbow grease out of maintenance. Traditions offers a special formula and bottle for parts soaking.

Cleaning a Revolver With Solvent

Steps For Cleaning Cap 'N' Ball Revolver With Solvent

Steps are the same as water-only method, with the exception that solvent is used in place of water. Remember that the revolver demands full takedown if several cylinders are fired. Furthermore, full takedown is necessary from time to time even when the blackpowder revolver is fired only a few times.

Blackpowder Cartridge Guns

Blackpowder cartridge revolvers and rifles are maintained as modern firearms with the exception of removing blackpowder and blackpowder substitute fouling. Cartridge cases must also be cleared of fouling. Refer to soak below. Scrub of interior of case with bristle brush. Dry cases well. Run through tumbler or vibrating case cleaner for extra polish.

Parts Soak

All gun parts are subject to a parts soak, including nipples, clean-out screws, locks, removable breech plugs, cap 'n' ball revolver workings—everything. Any solvent works, as does Brownells E-Z SOAK Fifteen Minute Parts Cleaner. Use a toothbrush to loosen stubborn fouling.

Long Term

After several seasons of use, all firearms should be treated to a thorough cleaning and inspection of all parts. Blackpowder guns without removable breech plugs may require a trip to the gunsmith.

Maintenance Means Protecting

Good gun cases, especially hard ones, are wise investments, especially if the firearm goes by plane or on a horse.

Cleaning a blackpowder gun today is no big deal. It takes a little time, but the fun of blackpowder shooting is well worth the small effort required for proper maintenance.

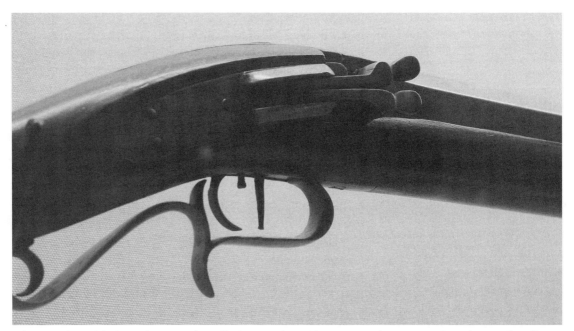

Take care of your blackpowder gun and it will take care of you. This one must have received good care. After all, it is over a century old and still showing well at the Cody Firearms museum.

chapter 30

SUBSTANCES FOR SHOOTING AND CLEANING

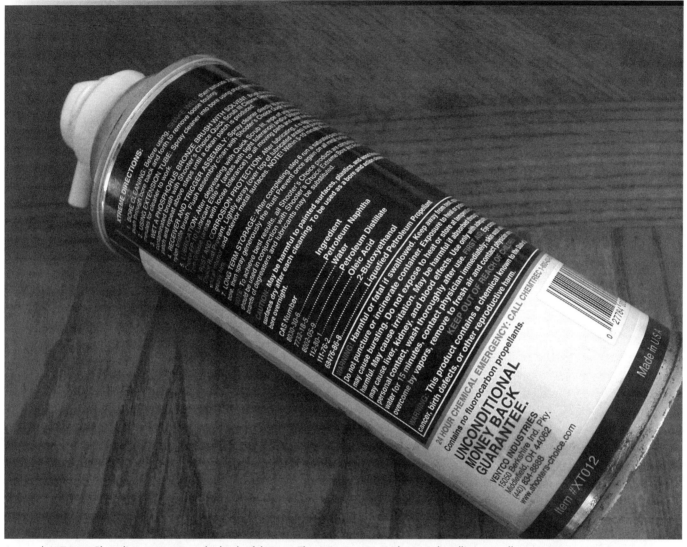

As usual, X-Treme Clean lists contents on the back of the can. This is important guidance to handling as well as storage.

The reader may not know this, but I read that whale oil was so penetrating that when the 19th century shooter filled Old Betsy from breech to muzzle with the stuff at bedtime, by morning the oil was leaking right through the pores of the metal. Bear grease was even more remarkable. It was good for curing ague, warts, lumbago, and maintaining good relations with your in-laws. And these wonderful traits were the mere beginning of bear fat's wonders. Myriad colorful patches made up the quilt of shoot-

ing in bygone days. You might think every pre-science notion on gun maintenance would have gone the way of wearing a necklace of flowers to ward off the plague, or a ring of garlic cloves to keep vampires away. But not quite. Over time, I'm sure I have had well-meaning readers mail me at least 50 under-the-sink recipes for maintaining a blackpowder firearm— muzzleloader or cartridge gun—in top working order, not to mention vast improvements in shooting, from paper-punching to dropping a big bull moose in its tracks.

Of course those old "natural" products, some of which were not so natural, were excellent for many purposes. After all, whale oil kept the lamps of America burning before Edison came up with his light bulb. And I can attest to the fact that rendered bear fat is downright useful for greasing up all manner of things. I once tried it on leather door hinges that were failing and the fat perked them right up. But yesteryear was yesteryear, and this is today, and what shooters had then and what we have now differs vastly.

Substances for Shooting and Cleaning ✳ **247**

The pioneer, as depicted in this fine painting at the Cody Firearms Museum, would have an excuse for allowing his firearm to remain less than clean on the trail, but most old guns are in pretty good shape, indicating at least reasonable care.

A treatment of current cleaning and maintenance products, company by company, would fill this chapter like Robert Frost's cup—to the brim and even above the brim. That might be all right, except that we wouldn't know the general nature of those products responsible for maintaining our important blackpowder firearms in top condition, which is always the goal. And so this chapter deals with lubes and oils and such in more general terms in an effort to clarify these after-shooting aids. But a catalog of all good brands this is not. I have named products I currently have on hand, but even this is dangerous because change in blackpowder shooting is a constant. Nonetheless, where a product is mentioned that may not be on the shelf through the duration of this edition, other similar products—I promise—will come forth to take the place of that product. Shooters dedicated to times old and honorable may be offended by a lack of respect for badger grease, possum fat, cooking oil, lard, shortening, and a multitude of old-time choices that were useful in their day, *and still work*—nobody said they didn't work—but have been outclassed by up-

New maintenance substances born of chemical science, such as this Lehigh Valley product, have outclassed old-time cleaning products.

to-date products. And by the way, many of today's maintenance products are as natural as the old stuff. I recall a fellow who sent a little can filled with "a real breakthrough in patch lubrication." I tried it and it worked. But my nose kept telling me there was something familiar about the paste. Finally, it came to me. It was lip balm. I can't imagine that this shooter bought a supply of ChapStick only to render the stuff out of tubes into little cough drop tins. But lip balm it was.

Many Ordinary Products Work

To prove I have truly do have a warm feeling for ordinary shooting products found in the kitchen cabinet, garage, under the sink, and in the storage shed, I'll honor a few here. There are many everyday liquids, pastes, creams, oils—whatever—that are entirely satisfactory in blackpowder shooting. As one example, I submit that a fine lubricant for blackpowder cartridge bullets is made up of toilet bowl ring, bee's wax, and such. There are shooters who stick a patch in their mouths to wet it because that was the only way old-timers did it, or so we've read or been told. Of course spit works because saliva is water-like and water is known as the universal solvent. Oddly enough, water is also the first choice for clearing fouling deposited by Triple Seven powder, one of the latest and best replica blackpowder propellants to come down the pike. I attest that water works as advertised with Triple Seven. I have also used ordinary drugstore isopropyl alcohol to clear bores of blackpowder fouling. If it hurt my guns, I never saw it, nor did they ever show it. And yes, lard will serve as patch lube. I have also dropped precut patches into melted Crisco, placing these lubed patches in little metal boxes that hold those "curiously strong" candies from England. Those lubed patches worked (after a fashion). If the shooter is happy with kitchen pantry and laundry room shooting products, that's OK with me.

Many ordinary cleaning products work in reducing blackpowder fouling, and that includes saliva and plain water (Triple Seven cleans up entirely with plain water). However, even if fouling is removed there is corrosion protection to consider. That's why a product such as V80 is sold.

The Spit Patch (Saliva)

Saliva has two good properties—it is always available and it costs nothing. I have no doubt that the spit patch was employed quite often in days of yore because it works far better than trying to seat a round ball wrapped in a dead dry patch. For popping beverage cans against a dirt bank, followed by a good bore cleaning, there is nothing wrong with sucking on a cloth patch and then wrapping a round ball in it for seating on the powder charge. Even for target work, why not use spit if a shooter wants to? I used to worry that saliva might bring rust into the bore. Probably not. Anyone who has spit on a rock knows that saliva dries up quickly on a warm day. And surely the inside of a fired barrel is warm. To the contrary, drying up may be a drawback in the bore, the damp patch no longer damp. I have not tried to prove this one way or the other. I found, in an attempt to see just how good the spit patch was, that the test rifle delivered round balls to the target just fine. If tradition pulls at the heart strings of the shooter, and he or

Whale oil was tremendously important in the America of old. As good as it was, however, it does not outclass the modern gun chemicals we have today.

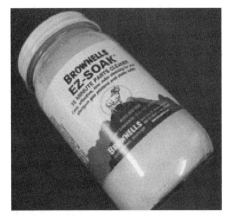

Whale oil would fail badly in competing with Brownells EZ-Soak for breaking down fouling and foreign matter on gun parts. The author relies on this and similar products to soak nipples clean.

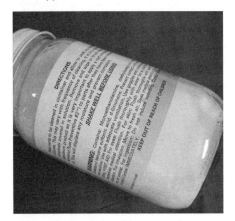

Today's chemical gun cleaning products come with clear instructions as well as a breakdown of content. EZ-Soak lists ingredients on the back of the bottle.

she simply must succumb to the palpitations, let happiness reign—and long may the spit patch survive.

Whale Oil

Praise the sperm whale. Not only was it responsible for that great novel, *Moby Dick*, but also barrels and barrels of oil brought from the sea in ships contributed greatly to the good life in early America. Aside from the many important functions of whale oil, the whale itself was responsible for a serious and important trade as whaling vessels set forth upon the sea. Ships' crews made a living at this trade, each member receiving a part of the profit, while leviathan no doubt created fortunes for ship owners. Those who survived at the dangerous business earned their daily bread and apparently a means of retirement. While whale oil lighted the homes of America in the 19th century, it was also prominent in shooting. To this hour, whale oil works as a patch lube. I attest to that fact having tried it. It does not dry out, as saliva will. I've withdrawn a patched ball served with whale oil and then purposely left downbore for a week in an unloaded rifle. The oil remained as oil. The patch continued to be soft and pliable. Whale oil does not cake up in the bore after firing, no matter how hot the blast from a heavy hunting charge in a muzzleloading rifle. There is no sludge after a shooting session. The oil deposited in the bore from shooting is completely removable with ordinary bore swabbing. I am convinced that sperm whale oil prevents rust, if by nothing more than creating a protective coating in between metal and moisture.

If my information is correct, whale oil is a polar compound that combines with surface oxide films. As such, it can also be used after the fact, that is, after rust has shown up (light rust) on a gun barrel or lock. Such application seems to help, as indicated by the reddish color of a white cleaning cloth impregnated with sperm whale oil and used to wipe down a rusty

area. Sperm whale oil tends to remain where you put it. You might say that it is sticky. Meanwhile, it is not like many animal fats, although it comes from a mammal. Rather, it is an oily wax-like substance that reminds one of jojoba. I have wiped down gunstocks with pure sperm whale oil and it seemed to both clean the wood and enhance sheen without going gummy. I have also treated leather with similar good results. Like honey, which was found edible in the ancient tombs of Egypt, sperm whale oil may have an indefinite life. I have kept a bottle of pure whale oil among my cleaning products for over 20 years and it appears to be as good as the day I bought it. Hot or cold does not affect whale oil that I know of. For a time, my cleaning supplies were temporarily stored in an outside shed as work was underway in the home. While the Wyoming summer heat was never blistering, I'm sure temperature in that shed reached into the 90s, maybe higher. The same bottle of whale oil also survived a late fall in that same shed with nighttime temperatures in the 20s. Wonderful stuff, whale oil, but hardly the alpha and omega of blackpowder shooting substances, partly because it does not break down blackpowder fouling. The bore continues to cake up regardless of how much whale oil is used on the patch. In short, I submit that modern blackpowder shooting products are better than whale oil.

Synthetic Whale Oil

Finally, whale oil became hard to get in America. The times were changing. Whaling fell into a niche similar to the buggy whip. Yankee ingenuity being what it is, someone came up with a synthetic product that mimicked most of whale oil's properties, if not all of them. I had a bottle of synthetic whale oil in my supplies for quite some time. It seemed to work like the real thing, but I finally lost track of it and never bothered to obtain any more. It's noted here simply because it existed, but not for any substantive reason.

Water Soluble Oil

While the name "moose milk" has been attached to modern products, even protected by registration, the fact is, moose milk existed not only as a name, but a specific mixture found in firearm maintenance supplies in the 19th century. The Winchester Sutler Company came up with a Moose Milk product that I found quite good, and better than the original. But for our purposes, moose milk is nothing more than water-soluble oil mixed with water. Later recipes included a dash of dish detergent. The milky color gave it its name. Where the moose part came in is anybody's guess. Water-soluble oil in water works quite well for removing blackpowder fouling. It should. After all, it is mainly water and water attacks the many salts and other solids leftover from blackpowder combustion. A big supply can be made up for nickels, too, and a bottle or two on the shooting bench is never a mistake. Just latch onto some water-soluble oil and mix it with water at a 90/10 ratio, 90 parts water, 10 parts oil. Or if you like, go as high as 25 parts oil, 75 parts water. Add a few drops of dish detergent and use the end product liberally in dousing out blackpowder fouling on the range or at home.

Shortening, Sheep Tallow, and Bear Fat

While these products serve to lubricate a patch, they have a glaring negative that is sufficient to dim my light of enthusiasm. They can all go rancid. So if a batch of patches is pre-lubed with any one of these, be it rendered from vegetable or animal, the patches might suffer a bit of natural decay in time. Another larger fault, in my book, is that none of these break down blackpowder fouling. On the good side, they melt readily and they will saturate a cloth patch fully. And, yes, I have used all three from time to time. But not anymore.

Petroleum Jelly

As a little side project, I recently made up a batch of fire starters using petroleum jelly and cotton balls. The petroleum jelly had been lying around among my gun maintenance supplies for quite some time, and I could find no other reasonable use for it. While this grease made viable fire starter, it fell far short of expectations as a patch lube. I also tried it with conicals. After all, it is grease and grease reduces friction. So patched balls impregnated with petroleum jelly slicked down the bore just fine. A dab on the base of the conical seemed to have a positive effect on keeping blackpowder fouling softer in the bore. All in all, however, it seemed to me that petroleum jelly suffered from the hot blast of burning powder in the bore, and I believe it left unwanted traces of itself in the bore. I never used it again. And I recommend the same to others.

Cooking Oils

One of the best products to come along over time is olive oil. It has a high smoking point in the frying pan, and I like it on salads, too. Wedge up some tomatoes with thin slices of onion, add olive oil, a bit of salt, and enjoy. Olive oil and salt improve artichokes and avocados. Mix with balsamic vinegar as a bread dip. But keep olive oil, along with all other cooking oils, away from your guns. These substances do not cut blackpowder fouling, and I suspect that the heat from combustion may actually burn them up in the bore. Forget 'em.

Waxes

Beeswax as a patch lube is uncalled for, as is candle wax. However, beeswax, especially in a proper combination with other ingredients, works well on wood, not as a finish, but as a wipe-down. Waxes have also been used to impregnate over-powder wads for blackpowder muzzleloading shotguns, as well as wads used over the powder charge in blackpowder cartridges.

Shortening, sheep tallow, and bear fat do nothing to remove stubborn powder residue, let alone traces of copper fouling. It takes a modern product like X-Treme Clean to do that.

Space-age gun chemicals can make firearms last longer. While most blackpowder guns do not generate sufficient velocity to cause copper deposits, more and more copper bullets are being fired in front-loaders. A product such as Barnes C-10 cures the problem.

Barnes C-10, which is used to remove copper fouling but works also to degrade other undesirable elements in the bore, comes with careful instructions because timing is important. Leaving a strong agent in the bore overly long can of itself cause damage.

Space-Age Blackpowder Chemicals

Whoever came up with "better things through chemistry" whacked that nail solidly on the head. But why spend money on these products when cheaper, natural items can be used with good effect? I believe that these space-age shooting products make the game more enjoyable by reducing cleanup time. I am also convinced that nothing I have tried from under the kitchen sink or in the cooking cupboard has given me nearly the in-between-shots bore wiping freedom afforded by the modern choices sold in gun stores. These work because they are lab-created and lab-tested by chemical engineers who know a great deal about gun care and shooting, as their most recent concoctions prove.

The Invaluable Lubricant

Everyone who drives a car knows that lubricants are absolutely essential in keeping the engine running. The fact comes home especially hard to those of us who have had an oil pump suddenly fail and—wham! The car grinds to a halt, the engine "seized up." Friction is the culprit. One surface makes strong contact with another surface and the result is heat through friction and galling—moving parts no longer moving. In a muzzleloader, friction can make seating a patched ball or conical an exercise in arm power. Lubricate the patch and the problem is squelched. The lubricant becomes a go-between creating a buffer film between two surfaces, thereby reducing the "grab" that these surfaces have for each other. I don't believe that any single good lubricant can necessarily make a blackpowder gun of any type shoot much more accurately than another good lubricant. I say this based on trying many different types. At the same time, lubrication is part of the load chain and testing different products is never a mistake. Furthermore, without some form of lubricant, accuracy can fail. I am convinced that

lubing the base of some conical bullets can improve accuracy vs. not lubing. I realize, having said this, that proving the point is difficult. But a lot of shooting leads me to believe that lubing a conical base is never a bad idea. Lubricant is vital to the workings of the gun as well as serving on patches and conical bullet bases. A dry lock can be a disaster. Dry tumbler parts may gall and seize up. Likewise a dry trigger. I learned at a seminar on gun cleaning that the best trigger lube is cigarette lighter fluid. Dousing the trigger mechanism with lighter fluid cleans contact points while leaving a fine film for lubrication, rather than an excessive coating.

Blackpowder lubes function to reduce friction, just like other lubricants, but at the same time, they should also work at reducing blackpowder fouling, especially turning "cake" into sludge.

Cake can be thought of as "baked-on" fouling, while sludge refers to fouling that's been, for lack of a better term, "softened." As cake, fouling is difficult to remove from the bore, although a bristle brush will scratch a lot of it from rifling grooves. Dry swabbing, however, is not the avenue to a squeaky clean bore—that requires turning cake to a sludge that can be cleared from the

Tetra Gun is a highly advanced lubricant that is used to facilitate the movement of all parts designed to move. While its use in semi-automatic pistols as a slide lube is well known, it is also a valuable lubricant for all types of blackpowder guns.

bore by flushing with liquids, water or solvent, or cleaning patches soaked with either. Blackpowder fouling breaks down in plain water, so for cleaning only, even between shots at the range, water is workable. But water does not perform the double-duty of a modern lubricant, lacking the ability to truly curb friction. In short, modern shooting lubricants for muzzleloaders create a slick medium between the patched ball and bore, or conical and bore, while also serving as cleaning agents. A good blackpowder lube also promotes repeat shots, while making later cleanup easier through attacking fouling right there on the range or in the field during the shooting process.

Lubricant as a Metal Protector

While a lubricant is not necessarily intended to safeguard metal from ferric oxide (otherwise known as rust) as a true metal *preserver* is formulated to do, lube does serve the important function of creating a barrier between metal and the atmosphere. It keeps moisture from reaching metal, at least to some degree, and it also acts as a shield against oxygen. Since moisture plus oxygen can attack metal, this service of the lubricant is highly valuable. Recall that one function of the cloth patch is to retain lubrication. A lubed patch is, of course, vital to reducing friction so the ball can be seated, but it also leaves a film of lubrication in the bore when that treated patch is run home on top of the powder charge. This coating remains in the bore as the firearm is carried in the field.

True Metal Preservers

The work of a true metal preserver is not to reduce friction. That is where this product differs from a lube. Nor is a metal preserver called upon to break down blackpowder fouling. Its job is precisely what the name implies—to safeguard metal from damage caused by moisture and oxygen. Fortunately, chemists have arrived at metal preservers that truly do more than sewing machine or fishing reel oils, which re-

Gun oil is far from outdated. Oil not only reduces friction, but it also creates a barrier film between metal surfaces and oxidation.

main useful in creating a thin barrier between metal and the atmosphere, but do not actually bond with that metal. Considerable experience with Accragard from the Jonad Corporation over the years provides convincing evidence that metal preservers do work. Rusty Duck Protective Gun Lube is an example of a metal preserver. It penetrates well, while remaining fluid to −50 degrees Fahrenheit. Shooter's Choice Rust Prevent is another metal preservative with lubricating qualities, and it is also noted for displacing moisture. Rusty Duck Vapor Inhibitor Protection (V.I.P.) is formulated especially for firearms that will be cased. Birchwood Casey's Barricade is sold as a rust inhibitor, but I think it also bonds to metals in a preserving fashion.

Gun Oils

Gun oils were always good; now they're even better. Hoppe's has a special No. 9 lubricating oil noted for it's water displacement qualities. Thompson/Center's No. 13 Gun Oil is noted for superior penetration. Birchwood Casey company has Synthetic Gun Oil, advertised as protecting "up to 10 times better than ordinary petroleum" with promised performance from −50 to +300 degrees Fahrenheit. Butch's Gun Oil from Lyman is another modern-day product engineered to work in conjunction with the same company's Butch's Bore Shine. Its strong point is

withstanding intense heat in the bore, plus fighting corrosion. There are many other good gun oils. Remington has one that I use often.

Anti-Seize Lubricants for Removable Breech Plugs and Nipples

This is the era of modern muzzleloaders with removable breech plugs, allowing cleaning from breech to muzzle, rather than the reverse. This is a good feature and one that I particularly appreciate. But continued shooting will quite likely cause sufficient buildup of, I suppose, minute fouling products, to lock up that breech plug. I have literally bent breech plug removal tools trying to unscrew a breech plug from one of these modern muzzleloaders. This is where anti-seize lubricants come into play. This lube is applied to the threads of the breech plug before screwing it into the breech area. Removing the breech plug after a strong shooting session is much easier with a pre-treatment of anti-seize lube. Continued firing may also cause a similar condition in the ordinary nipple due to fouling. Fouled nipple threads can lock the nipple into the nipple seat, causing difficult removal even with the best nipple wrench. A light coating of anti-seize lubricant on the nipple threads before screwing the nipple into its seat helps in preventing this problem. I've also been known to apply a trace of this stuff on screw-in shotgun chokes. Anti-seize lubricants are available at hardware stores, but there are also special products, such as Birchwood Casey Choke Tube Lube, originally intended for shotgun screw-in chokes, but also good for nipples and breech plugs. Likewise Thompson/Center's All Purpose Anti-Seize Super Lube, advertised as "A hard-working synthetic-based lube containing Teflon, which seals the threads of muzzleloading breech plugs." Rusty Duck Polymer Anti-Seizing Gun Grease is recommended for nipples and breech plugs specifically. Brownells offers a multitude of fine maintenance products, among them good anti-seize lubricants.

Shoot-All-Day Lubes

There are many products on the market today formulated for multiple shots before the bore requires swabbing. When used properly, these "all-day" lubes are excellent. The operative word is "properly." As soon as any muzzleloader bore balks at the seating of a projectile, *no matter what kind of lube is used*, it's time to swab that bore with solvent. This common sense approach, coupled with the many fine lubes on the market today, makes for safe repeat shooting. I have had good luck with a number of these lubes, including Orange Stuff from Old Western Scrounger. Thompson/Center's Bore Butter Natural Lube 1000 Plus, in original scent or fresh pine, boasts that a Thompson/Center New Englander rifle "had 1,015 shots fired through it. During that time, it never had a patch put through it. It was never cleaned; not even once!" There you have it. Coupled with the good common sense warning above, about cleaning any bore, regardless of lube, when that bore shows a need for swabbing, Bore Butter is excellent for repeat shots. Likewise Ox-Yoke's Liquid Wonder Spray Lubricant, which, as the name states, comes in a spray bottle. Pyrodex Lube is another good one, especially for breaking down Pyrodex fouling. All-day lubes work especially

Anti-seize lubricant is highly important with muzzleloaders that have removable breech plugs. A light coating of anti-seize on breech plug threads prior to installing the breech plug into the barrel will help with later removal of the breech plug.

well with target loads, less well with big hunting charges, which makes sense; the heavier charge leaving behind far more fouling to deal with.

Lubrication Types

There are four basic types of lube for blackpowder guns: liquids, greases, pastes, and creams. The last two are fairly much the same, with the exception of pastes being possibly a little thicker. Liquid patch lubes were long considered the only viable type. But that has changed. Now there are good patch lubes in all types. For example, one of the all-day lubes worked well into the patch is good. Liquids are still excellent too, such as Ol' Griz from Dixie Gun Works. Any lube compatible with the cloth patch is useful as long as it attacks the many salts left behind by blackpowder combustion. But this is not true of lubes for conicals. Liquids are no good. It takes a cream, grease, or paste to stick to the base of an elongated bullet, the base being a good place to apply a dab. Thompson/Center's Maxi Ball and Maxi-Hunter bullets are offered pre-lubed, their grease grooves neatly filled with Natural Lube 1000+ Bore Butter, which holds well in place during proper storage and loading. Liquid lubes are also no good with sabots, whereas a dab of grease, paste, or cream directly into the base of the plastic sabot works well in keeping fouling under control, also ensuring an easier job of after-shooting cleanup.

Commercial Solvents

The big difference between solvents and lubes is duty—today's commercial lubes are designed to cut fouling as well as thwart friction *during shooting*. But as good as these lubes are, they were never intended to clear the bore entirely of blackpowder fouling *after shooting*. Nor were they formulated to get rid of external film or soot that dirties the outer surfaces of our blackpowder guns, or those that invariably invade working parts. Attacking blackpowder fouling

is the work of solvents, and there are many super products today. Proving a solvent's worth is simple. Dirty guns are cleaned with A, B, and C brands. The one most liked by the individual shooter is the one that shooter should select. Or the shooter may like them all. There are so many good ones on the market today, like Rusty Duck Black Off, which gives the one-two knockout punch to dirty bores quickly. Hodgdon's Spit Patch continues to punish blackpowder fouling. So do solvents from Ox-Yoke such as Competition Bore Cleaner and Concentrated Bore Cleaner. Hoppe's No. 9 Plus solvent is formulated for blackpowder cleanup, as is T/C's No. 13 Bore Cleaner, as well as Venco's Black Powder Gel. Space prevents naming all the good solvents. Even with Triple Seven, which truly disappears with plain water cleaning patches, I have found modern solvents to work very well, especially in the field or on the shooting range.

Products that Attack Plastic Fouling

Common sense alone convinces one that a piece of plastic racing through a gun bore at up to 2,500 fps, possible with today's super magnum modern blackpowder rifles, is going to leave a little bit of itself behind in the form of fouling on lands and in grooves. I think that, from time to time at least, going after plastic wash left from sabots or shotgun wads is a worthwhile effort. I recently tested a couple solvents from Brownells that brought forth color on a cleaning patch, the same as the color of the plastic sabots I had been using. A few good solvents for plastic wash are Lyman's Butch's Bore Shine, and Venco's Shooter's Choice. The Ox-Yoke Company, recognizing the fact that plastic fouling is reality, came up with Accuracy Restorer designed especially to clear plastic residue from the bore. I would say the principals at Ox-Yoke knew that plastic wash was possible, although some shooter-writers thought otherwise and said so in print.

Bore Leading

Muzzleloaders shooting conicals seldom show bore leading because bullet speed is too low to cause a lot of that kind of trouble. More accurately, it is good bullet lube that helps to prevent leading in these guns in the first place. The high-power modern muzzleloader is currently fed jacketed bullets in sabots. So no leading problem there. On the other hand, they can handle lead bullets, too, and a trace of leading might be possible with a lead bullet at well over 2,000 fps. I have not seen this problem so far, so these are speculative words only. Nonetheless, there are products especially formulated for lead removal and they can come into play with some of our six-guns that shoot fairly fast bullets. Cowboy Action Shooting, especially, has brought on a revived love affair, not that the romance ever grew cold, with cartridge revolvers capable of shooting bullets at a pretty good clip. Hot loads are all wrong in Cowboy Action Shooting, but guess what? The ladies and gents known to frequent the game are also found now and then on the range with their guns loaded fairly hot. I still recall a severely leaded original Colt six-gun whose owner failed to become familiar with a cleaning rod. I suggested gunsmith care for that one.

Copper Fouling

Essentially non-existent in muzzleloaders and blackpowder single-shot cartridge rifles firing lead bullets, copper fouling can show up in lever-action blackpowder repeaters shooting jacketed bullets, as well as Cowboy Action revolvers shooting a lot of speedy jacketed bullets while on the regular shooting range or even out hunting. Copper fouling can cause a once-accurate barrel to produce shotgun-like groupings. Lately, I have been trying a special copper fouling removal product from Barnes called CR-10, finding it very effective. Venco

Shooter's Choice Copper Remover is another good one. The same company has a non-ammonium copper remover as well. Ammonia products are murder on copper, but its use requires following directions. Ammonia can etch metal.

The Blackpowder Cartridge

Blackpowder cartridge handguns shooting lead bullets require special lubes. But blackpowder cartridge rifles are even more demanding. There are many good ones on the market. I located some of these in Shoot!, the magazine dedicated to Cowboy Action Shooting.

The Cap 'n' Ball Revolver

There are two good reasons to lay a coating of lube on top of projectiles seated in the cylinders of cap and ball revolvers. The first is chain-fire prevention. Chain-fire is when all of the chambers fire simultaneously. I have read that this is not really a problem, that people like me more or less made up the story of chain-firing. Ask around at the gun club. Sooner or later you will find someone who has suffered a chain-fire, or who knows another shooter who has. So grease over the bullet's nose, be it round or conical, is not a bad plan. The other significant reason for lubing the blackpowder six-shooter is to allow continued firing without lockup of cylinder rotation. Lube over bullet noses helps here too, as well as grease on working parts in general. See more about this in Chapter 11.

Brand Names
May Come and Go

The little warning at the beginning of this romp through the forest trails of blackpowder maintenance products warned that brand names come and go. That's OK, because I have seen continued improvement as new and better products came along to replace others that were themselves pretty darn good.

Blue Wonder was designed to attack heavy-duty fouling in any type of fire-arm. To that end, it is acclaimed as one of the better products to do that job.

Lead bullets at lower velocity cause very little leading problem. However, as velocity increases, lead traces can accumulate on rifling lands and in rifling grooves. As with all other gun cleaning problems, there is a solution in the form of a modern chemical.

Two Great Rifles of the Buffalo Runners

chapter 31

The American bison (buffalo) is the largest animal on the North American continent, bigger than a moose, much heavier than an elk or the biggest brown or polar bear that ever lived. This bull easily weighs a ton. Bulls have been weighed right at close to 3,000 pounds.

Common sense and the smallest application of mathematics challenges the Great Buffalo Lie, as I call it, that 60 million breeding bison were "shot off" by a comparative handful of men in the latter part of the 19th century. Aaron Latham, in his book, *The Frozen Leopard*, wrote "Buffalo Bill Cody and his gang destroyed the great herds of bison." Oh, really? That a non-hunter, or even anti-hunter, could think this way is one thing, but what about hunters? What about this hunter? I, too, believed that 60 million bison roaming over millions of acres were "shot off." The American bison roamed over what are now Kansas, Texas, and Oklaho-ma—add Montana, Wyoming, Idaho, British Columbia, Saskatchewan, and Alberta and you still have only part of the bison's habitat. And you still aren't finished with the range of the bison. Helicopter gunships could not destroy 60 million bison in the time frame of the "buffalo runner" over this span of ground. It took the words of a medical doctor to put my thinking straight. Doctor Rudolph W. Koucky, pathologist, studied bison bone piles. He found that something much smaller than a bullet caused the great herds to crash—a microbe. Just as the Spanish Influenza (flu) killed more people immediately following World War I than all of the bombs and bullets in that conflict, so had the influx of infested cattle brought on the demise of the buffalo.

Their own figures condemn their thinking. From "Extinction and Depletion" we read, "In the 1800s, about 65 million bison roamed the prairies of the Great Plains. Herds were described up to 25 miles long, containing 12 million animals." J.N. Davis, buyer for the Northern Pacific Railroad, shipped 50,000 hides in 1881 and another 200,000 hides in 1882, the two peak years of the "hunt." Terrible as the figure is, the count is but a tiny percent of the estimated number of animals. There is solid evidence that part of the reason for warring on the buffalo was, as one author put it, "to starve out the American Natives." Furthermore, a representative of the Intertribal Bison Cooperative described the killing as "a calculated military strategy designed to force the Native Americans onto reservations." Another author notes that Congress, in 1870, proposed fighting the dangerous Plains Indian by wiping out his main resource of survival—the bison. Sixty million breeding bison were never exterminated by men armed with single-shot blackpowder cartridge rifles, men who got around on horseback, not motor vehicles, using mule-drawn wagons to carry out the hides. This is not to whitewash the grim facts. Heaven knows shooters tried to exterminate the bison. The slaughter is important to this chapter because it is a dark testament to the accuracy and long-range power of the single-shot blackpowder cartridge rifles touched on here.

The Shoot Was On

Bison were shot at random, not for food, nor even for hides, but to see these grand animals fall over. Here was the largest quadruped on the North American continent, bigger than a bull moose, and a single bullet could drop it. The professionals were, in their own way, proud of their job as "buffalo runners," a name they preferred being called. They even had a little song about it. It was called "The Buffalo Hunters," and it went like this: *It's all of the day long as we go trampling round In search of the buffalo that we may shoot him down: Our guns upon our shoulders; our belts of forty rounds. We send them up Salt River to some Happy Hunting Grounds.* And to the happy hunting grounds they did send them—by the thousands, albeit not millions. Any rifle that fired a projectile was, at one time or another, a "buffalo gun" in the 19th century. The mountain men of the Fur Trade did not have the deadly breechloader. And yet they were known to "make meat" of the buffalo with their lead round balls fired from muzzleloaders, especially a fat young one rather than what they called "poor cow." By the time professional hunters arrived on the scene, however, the single-shot blackpowder

The open ranges were home to millions of buffalo into the 19th century. The U.S. government wanted them gone for at least two reasons: the Plains Indian tribes depended upon the buffalo not only for food, but warm robes and many other products; also, the great herds were a problem for westward expansion.

Two Great Rifles of the Buffalo Runners ✳ **257**

The shoot was on and two blackpowder cartridge rifles dominated in the hands of the buffalo "runners," as they apparently preferred being called. One of those rifles was the Remington Rolling Block in several worthy calibers. This is an original as seen at the Cody Firearms Museum.

cartridge rifle was king, especially the two rifles that are principals in this chapter. These were the Sharps and the Remington, the first a falling block, the second a rolling block, both ingeniously designed for good accuracy with big cartridge capability.

The Great Sharps Rifle

The Gun that Shaped American Destiny. That's what Martin Rywell called the Sharps rifle in his 1979 Pioneer Press book. Rywell's title is right on the money. The Sharps rifle did help to shape American destiny, filling the hands of countless pioneers trekking westward. According to Rywell, an Indian gentleman by the name of American Horse said, "Emigrants passing up the South Platte River to Colorado between 1858 and 1865 were largely armed with Sharps military rifles." These were the forerunners of the Sharps breechload-

er. The Sharps rifle also played a role in the American Civil War where almost 100,000 rifles and carbines served Union troops. According to Rywell, Col. Hiram Berdan's Sharpshooters finally got their Sharps rifles in 1862, using them during the Seven Days Battles of June and July of that same year with devastating effect. Now we need to briefly set the scene of the Great American Buffalo Shoot, beginning with a few words about the animal itself.

The American Bison

Picture the professional buffalo hunter traveling on horse accompanied by skinners in mule-drawn wagons. In spite of the huge number of animals, herds had to be found over millions of unmapped acres with no roads. Once found, the herd had to be stalked for the kill. What has been partially forgotten is that the bison was an extremely

Only later did the western pioneers have a cabin such as this one on display at the Buffalo Bill Historical Center in Cody, Wyoming. Buffalo running was camping out affair in all weather, along with transporting hides via mule-drawn wagons.

The great Sharps rifle never truly passed into history. Today, replicas like this Pedersoli Sharps continue to chamber big blackpowder cartridges for long-range authority, mainly on metallic silhouettes, but also in the big game field.

Navy Arms Company specializes in replica rifles. This is only one of several Sharps models handled by the company. It's the Sharps No. 2 Silhouette with double-set triggers for supreme trigger control.

dangerous animal. Those who consider the beast nothing more than a milk cow have not read the appalling record of deaths and injuries in Yellowstone National Park alone, as well as other areas. Teddy Roosevelt lost a hunting partner to a bull bison that impaled the man's thigh and his horse's lungs with a single horn thrust. A Yellowstone Park warning goes, **Warning many visitors have been gored by buffalo. Buffalo can weigh 2000 pounds [actually up to 3,000 pounds] and can sprint at 30 mph, three times faster than you can run. These animals may appear tame but are wild, unpredictable, and dangerous. Do not approach buffalo.** How is it that so many could be dropped by 19th-century hunters with so few encounters? The reason was the long-range breechloader. Today, replicas of these rifles are fired in the silhouette game (see Chapter 38) at amazingly long range. A comparatively small target at 300 meters is commonplace. There are witnessed accounts of consistent groups out to 1,300 yards (the farthest distance that I know of).

The Greatness of the Sharps Rifle

In *Sharps Rifle–The Gun that Shaped American Destiny*, Rywell relates that Christian Sharps was born in Washington, New Jersey, in 1811. His early life is not well documented, but it appears that at age 19 he began working for Captain John Harris Hall at Harpers Ferry Arsenal, one of our two national armories at the time, the other being Springfield. Captain Hall was responsible for a breech-loading rifle—appropriately named the Hall Rifle. Hall was granted a government contract to produce his rifle at the Harpers Ferry Arsenal. His plan was mass production with quality. Harpers Ferry might make a thousand rifles while the Springfield arsenal produced a quarter of that number in the same time frame. Sharps was a student of firearm design. He no doubt saw the Hall Rifle as improvable. The Harpers Ferry Arsenal, opened in 1796, was shut down in 1844. Christian moved on to Ohio where he went to work on his own rifle. He was issued United States Patent No. 5763 on September 12, 1848, for a single-shot breechloader. *This rifle did not fire metallic cartridges.* A breechblock was lowered to expose an open chamber by the mere flick of a trigger guard that was also a lever. Consider the speed opposed to muzzleloading rifles, but also in comparison to Hall's Rifle. This first Sharps rifle fired a linen cartridge that was inserted into the open breech. When the breechblock was returned to battery by lifting up on the trigger guard lever, the extremely sharp edge of the breechblock itself cleanly sliced off the end of the "cartridge," exposing the powder charge to a source of ignition, which was a percussion cap. Five shots a minute was possible.

The Army liked that. The Army Ordnance Board tested the Sharps rifle, reporting on November 27, 1850, that "From the observations of the use of this rifle, the Board is of the opinion that it is superior to any of the other arms loading at the breech, and think it would be well to have further trials made, and to put some of them in the hands of troops to determine whether they are suitable to military service." By 1853, Sharps was no longer an advisor to those who were building his rifle. He opened his own firm in Philadelphia as C. Sharps & Co. The Sharps story continues with various liaisons, but for our interest, we move on to 1848 when Christian received a patent for a rifle with a vertical sliding breechblock operated by a lever. This was still not "the" rifle that would see action in the buffalo field. A compressed history of Sharps rifles shows the Model 1849 beginning production in that year, ending production

Another of the Navy Arms replica Sharps rifles is the company's Sharps Long Range Rifle with finely-adjustable tang rear sight and double-set triggers for premium trigger control. This is a rifle not unlike the one in a popular movie: *Quigley Down Under*, in which the talented actor, Tom Selleck, did the bad guys in from afar.

a year later to make way for the Model 1850. These were 44-caliber rifles. The Model 1851 came in various calibers, including 36, 44, and 52. Models continued in 52-caliber, especially, but not exclusively, until the model of 1869 in metallic calibers 44-70 and 50-70. The latter, I think, was most-used on buffalo. The famous 45-120 Sharps cartridge, or 45-120-550 when it carried 120-grains blackpowder behind a 550-grain bullet, is erroneously considered the buffalo cartridge. It was not. (See Chapter 33.)

Old Reliable and Other Sharps Rifles

This rifle was no doubt too late for the big buffalo debacle. But it was just in time for a great deal of action in the Old West. Made famous in its time, it was reborn to the general public once again (at least in a generic form) with the movie *Quigley Down Under*, starring Tom Selleck. Tom managed to blow several bad guys off their horses at amazing distances, a feat only slightly exaggerated by Hollywood because modern day Sharps shooters hit targets with reasonable consistency out to 1,000 yards and farther. The Creedmoor 1,000-yard shoot of 1877 saw the Sharps in action. One reporter said, "This never-to-be-forgotten contest has proved the Sharps improved long-range rifle to be the most perfect arm the world ever saw. The best shot of the tournament found "Bruce, the hero of the American team, who, on the last day, made the unheard-of-record, 219 out of a possible 225."

Bruce said at the close of the shoot "That Sharps Rifle made my record; I only happened to be behind it." Rigby, of the famous English Rigby gunmaking company, bought a Sharps after he saw the rifle in action. A parade of fine Sharps rifles followed, including a Mid-Range Rifle for $75 in 1878, $150 for extra fancy wood, fine finish, engraved and made to order. Mid-range was considered out to 600 yards or so. At 500 yards, one John T. Rainey of New Orleans made an off-hand showing of 70 out of 75 possible—emphasis on *off-hand*—with a Sharps rife.

Shooting the Sharps cartridge rifle remained challenging, of course. The rifle provided only one shot at a time with blackpowder demanding regular cleanup, not only of the rifle, but also cartridge cases. But the rifle was still fired much faster than a muzzleloader, and it really wasn't that difficult to maintain. After all, it cleaned from the breech. Buffalo runner Col. Frank Mayer wrote about flushing the bore with cold water, followed by urine, supposedly to introduce a touch of acidity, with a hot water rinse afterward. Also to its credit, the Sharps rifle was offered in a huge array of worthy cartridges, some of them noted in Chapter 33.

The Sharps rifle, others as well as the one that came to be called Old Reliable, were sufficiently accurate to demand precision sights. That carried over into other fine single-shot blackpowder cartridge rifles. This is not a Sharps, but it is an accurate single-shot blackpowder cartridge rifle and it does wear a fine sight.

The very early single-shot blackpowder long-range rifles became grandparents to a large number of modern single-shot cartridge rifles, some of them chambered for old-time cartridges, such as the 45-70, and others for modern cartridges like the 7mm Remington Magnum.

Because it was truly a long-range rifle, capable of winning 1,000-yard shooting matches as well as dropping buffalo at several hundred yards, it was a candidate for a telescopic rifle sight. German-made target scopes were mounted not only for target shooting, but by buffalo runners as well. Sharps cartridges were efficient due to their large calibers with heavy bullets. A catalog of the period included 40-100 through 50-100 "brass, centre fire re-loading shells" running from 1-11/16 inches through 2-1/2 inches in length and costing from $22 to $30 per thousand. Low blackpowder pressure was easy on brass and the Sharps Co. promised that "with proper care in re-loading" a cartridge case could be reloaded up to 500 times, provided that each case was cleaned after use to prevent deterioration. The Sharps was great, all right, so good that it can still get the job done today, not only at the silhouette match or ringing gongs in the distance, but also on big game. There are a number of Sharps replica rifles on the market.

One of my own testing came from the Shiloh Manufacturing Company of Big Timber, Montana, an 1874 model that was sufficiently accurate and powerful for any North American big game. The Shiloh company offers more than rifles. It is a Sharps outlet. See Directory.

The Remington Rolling Block

In spite of the fact that the Sharps was admired, greatly so, by many buffalo hunters, another rifle ranked right along with it. This rifle was even preferred by some over the Sharps. It was the Remington Rolling Block breechloader. The brilliant design of this action saw Rolling Blocks chambered for modern high-intensity cartridges in time. I had one in 7mm Mauser that proved quite accurate. It cost all of $17.95, and it came directly through the mail from Los Angeles to my home. Joseph Rider is credited with the rolling-block design built by Remington. That is why some models were called Remington-Riders. The rolling-block principle itself was hardly new, but Rider saw its full

potential. Flobert's rolling-block design came very early in gun history with its pivoting breechblock. But rather than a breech sliding up and down (the falling block), the rolling block's breech *rotated*. W.W. Greener wrote about the Remington-Rider in his revised 1910 edition of *The Gun and its Development*. He said, "The rifle was tried at Wimbledon as long ago as 1866, and attracted considerable attention at that time, in consequence of the extraordinary rapidity with which it was loaded and fired; as many as fifty-one shots were discharged within three minutes. The mechanism consists essentially of two pieces, being the breech-piece and extractor, and the other the hammer breech-bolt. This breech-piece and hammer-bolt each work upon a strong centre pin."

In function, the breechblock rolls back, a cartridge is inserted directly into the breech, and then the breechblock is rolled forward again to lock the action. The significant factor here is the hammer, which falls down into a slot within

There was argument in days of old, and the argument goes on today—which rifle is truly better? Is it the Sharps or Remington? Both have a great number of fans today, especially on the silhouette range.

the breechblock itself for a positive lockup. The Remington Rolling Block remains available to this day, just like the Sharps. Navy Arms has long championed the continuance of the design with several well-constructed replicas. Furthermore, Remington brought the rifle back briefly in two models, a No. 1 Rolling Block Mid-Range Sporter, and a No. 1 Rolling Block Silhouette rifle. I obtained a Rolling Block action from the Navy Arms Company, which became the heart of a long-range black-powder cartridge rifle put together by a friend who then built one for himself. My personal Rolling Block rifle today is a Pedersoli with round barrel. I rank

this rifle as one of my all-time favorites. Since I did not intend to shoot targets or silhouettes with the rifle, I ordered it in 38-55 Winchester for hunting. The Pedersoli Rolling Block proved quite accurate. I occupy the same camp with Dr. F.W. Mann who, after years of studying what he called "the bullet's flight," concluded that accuracy was mainly a matter of good bullets fired from good barrels. Nevertheless, there are some cartridges that prove to be more accurate than others. The 38-55 is one of those cartridges, as is the 32-40 Winchester, perhaps for reasons that are more slippery than solid. My Pedersoli 38-55 with iron sights is capable of hit-

Because the Sharps and the Remington enjoyed long-range accuracy and power, sights like this finely adjustable tang were invented, still exist, and continue to be purchased to this day. This one is from the Pedersoli Company.

The Remington Rolling Block in big blackpowder cartridge chamberings is just at home on the silhouette range as is the Sharps—and these rifles wear sights just as precise as those found on the Sharps.

One of Sam's favorite rifles is his Pedersoli Remington Rolling Block chambered for the worthy 38-55 Winchester cartridge. The rifle has a round barrel and single trigger. It carries modest weight, but is heavy enough to "hold" for the longer shots.

The Remington Rolling Block action is ingeniously simple and much stronger than one might suspect for a 19th century invention. In fact, the rifle was later chambered for the smokeless powder 7mm Mauser cartridge in a Mexican army version, as well as other smokeless cartridges.

Rolling block meant just that—the block rolled back to clear the chamber for loading, as shown here. And of course the cartridge was simply shoved in, the block pushed forward, and it was the hammer falling into the block that locked the action for shooting.

ting a fist-sized bullseye at 200 yards with a great marksman behind the sights—not me—but rather a shooter such as Ron Cox, former SWATT team commander and a fine shooter. Some of Ron's groups with the Rolling Block rival those of Hollywood.

There Were Others
The Model 1885 High Wall

Of course there were many other fine single-shot blackpowder cartridges rifles in days gone by, many of which remain available today. One is Winchester's 1885 High Wall, a fine single-shot blackpowder cartridge breech-loading rifle in replica form with all nostalgia intact. The 1885 is a worthy big-game, as well as target, rifle. The particular model of my experience is Browning's Model 1885 High Wall Single-Shot Rifle offered in modern

Fadala shoots his 38-55 Pedersoli Remington Rolling Block rifle.

calibers as well as 45-70 Government. Browning offered other single-shot blackpowder cartridge rifles over time, including the company's BPCR (Black Powder Cartridge Rifle), similar to the High Wall, except the ejector system and shell deflector have been removed. This rifle was chambered for the 40-65 as well as 45-70, and was offered in a special Creedmoor model with 34-inch barrel and windgauge sight, chambered for the 45-90. Browning also had an 1885 single-shot: the Traditional Hunter in modern calibers, plus 38-55 Winchester. While rifles come and go in manufacture, the good news is that they last indefinitely and can be found in fine used condition. So take heart when a current catalog no longer lists a rifle you wish you had bought when it was available. I also have considerable positive experience with a High Wall replica from the Navy Arms Company. Chambered in 45-70, the 1885 is worthy of truly big game, including moose.

Modern Ballards

One of the most beautiful of the 19th-century single-shot breechloaders was the Ballard. While I do not own one, I have shot one. It proved to be a memorable event. Ballard is in business again in Cody, Wyoming, just west of the Buffalo Bill Historical Center, a must-see museum holding both the Winchester and Remington collections as well as countless antique guns, paintings, artifacts, and other wonderful treasures from the past. You don't have to be a gun enthusiast to get a lot from this great museum and, yes, you will see Ballards and other single-shot blackpowder cartridge rifles. But back to Ballard. I wager that today's replicas are the finest of any era, built by talented craftsmen with materials unavailable in the 19th century. The 1885 Standard Sporting Ballard has the "thick side" action with a No. 3 contour octagon barrel. There are other models, including a special Schuetzen in the 1885 Helm style with double-set triggers. Ballard history is not as complete as Sharps. Charles H. Ballard was born in 1822 in Massachusetts, a machinist by trade. On November 5, 1861, he was granted a patent for his rifle. The Ballard name, often associated with Marlin, became a household word in its time. Today, to own a modern-made Ballard is to have one of the very best.

A Special Scope Sight

A brief aside is necessary to note a special scope sight for single-shot blackpowder cartridge rifles. It's the return of the Wm. Malcolm 6X Telescopic Rifle Sight with its 19th-century credentials intact. The scope will mount also on side-eject Winchester Model 94 rifles, for '94 owners who wish to "go back in time" a notch. It also works on muzzle-loaders, as witnessed by its attachment to an Austin & Halleck Mountain Rifle, upon which the scope looks quite fitting. While few mountain man plains rifles were outfitted with scopes, some were, and it's not a great leap in imagination to consider that more would have been scoped if such sights were readily available. The Malcolm sight came along about 150 years ago built by William Malcolm. Today, the scope is again available through Leatherwood High-Lux Optics offered by Buffalo Arms Company (see Directory). It comes with the original style external mount adjustments, which are very precise. Ballard, noted above, offers the once-popular #5 Pacific model with 28- to 32-inch barrel option, No. 4 octagon, double-set triggers—just one possible candidate for the Malcolm.

LEVER-ACTION BLACKPOWDER CARTRIDGE RIFLES

The blackpowder lever-action fan is fortunate to have excellent replica rifles available in the 21st century, such as this good one from the Cimarron Company.

Chapter 31 dealt mainly with the Sharps rifle, the Remington Rolling Block in close second place. These rifles were discussed for two reasons: historical interest and function. The blackpowder cartridge lever-action rifle also captures a significant niche in history, along with enduring field-worthiness. The lever action is primarily a North American rifle. From their beginnings, lever-guns have enjoyed great success in the U.S.A. and Canada. There are also many devotees south of the border, especially ranch hand hunters who carry their beloved *treinta & treinta* (30-30) carbines in search of venison for the table. Paco Kelly, who

wrote *An American Heritage – Lever-guns*, had it right. The lever-action rifle is our heritage. Frank Paco Kelly looked at the 1840s as "opening the door" to lever guns. Walter Hunt was awarded U.S. Patent No. 570 for what was called Rocket-ball (also Rocket Ball) ammunition. A year later, Hunt was granted another patent, this time for what he named the "Volition Repeater." The Volition had a tubular magazine—two under-levers operated the mechanism. The Volition and its ammunition are considered forerunners of Winchester lever-actions. George A. Arrowsmith, model maker and manufacturer, acquired rights to both the Hunt rifle and

Rocket-ball ammo. He had worked on the original Hunt rifle and saw in it promise of a viable repeater.

He knew the rifle could be improved, and to that end Arrowsmith hired Lewis Jennings, model maker and inventor. In late 1849, Jennings was granted a patent for his improvements on the Hunt rifle. Jennings' design eliminated the second magazine feeding lever that lay ahead of the receiver. Improved, yes, but the rifle, sometimes referred to at this stage as the Hunt-Jennings, remained plagued with flaws, so much so that many were turned into single-shots due to poor function as repeaters. Courtland C.

The lever-action rifle is mainly American. This Marlin side-eject rifle, made today and used in Cowboy Action shooting as well as hunting and many other shooting applications, carries the same basic excellent design that Marlin came up with in the 19th century. It's for the shorter cartridges, such as the 44-40.

Palmer ended up buying all Hunt's and Jennings' rights to both rifle and Rocket-ball ammunition. The rifle retained its flaws. Horace Smith apparently didn't mind, because he bought all rights to the Volition and Rocket-ball in 1855. Smith, along with Wesson, formed the new Volcanic Repeating Arms Company with 40 stockholders. Oliver Fisher Winchester was one of the stockholders, becoming director of the company. In 1857 the company failed, falling into involuntary receivership. All assets were assigned to Mr. Winchester.

Rocket-ball ammunition was caseless. Interestingly, many modern day experiments have been conducted trying to make viable caseless ammunition—simply a bullet with a hollow base holding powder; somewhat ideal, if it could work, for the military, where soldiers could carry far more caseless rounds than standard cartridges. So far, all attempts have failed to meet expectations. Rocket-ball ammo included a priming cap that held the powder inside of the bullet cavity, and of course also provided ignition. Calibers were 31 and 41. The rifle came in three barrel lengths—16, 20, and 24 inches. There was a pistol with 4-inch or 6-inch barrel lengths. A tubular magazine resided under the barrels of both rifle and pistol. The longer the barrel, the more ammo. The shorter 41-caliber pistol barrel magazine held 6 rounds, while the longer one contained a cargo of 10 Rocket-balls. The 16-inch rifle barrel held 20 rounds, the 20-inch 25 rounds, and the 24-inch 30 rounds. That was considerable firepower. The

only trouble was the second half of that word—power. There wasn't much of it. Having as many as 30 shots of essentially waterproof ammunition with little more than the quick working of a lever was good. But a figure of 56 foot-pounds of muzzle energy (barrel length not stated) proved far too low for hunting anything much larger than a rabbit, let alone producing man-stopping authority for the military.

This early lever-action, for all of its historical value as a forerunner, was in the main a failure. Misfires were noted, as well as multiple discharges of Rocket-ball ammunition in the tubular magazine. (That must have been fun.) Gas leakage around the breech was another negative. Oliver Winchester invested considerable money to keep the company afloat, but it went under all the same, going insolvent on February 18, 1857. Oliver still had a company, although it was in suspended animation until Benjamin Tyler Henry came along. Henry had Patent No. 30,446 for a rifle design and ammunition. The Henry cartridge was not worlds ahead of the Rocket-ball, but it was more reliable and slightly more powerful. The 44 Henry Flat was made with a copper case .875-inches long, and it was a rimfire (see Chapter 33). Bullets for the Henry ran 200 grains and 215-grains in lead. A charge of 26- to 28-grains blackpowder propelled these projectiles around the speed of sound, or something on the order of 1,125 feet per second. Muzzle energy was around 600 foot-pounds, which, while not high, certainly bettered the 56 foot-pounds rating of the Rocket-ball. The

Henry rifle was another rapid-shooter, holding 15 rounds in the under-barrel magazine (24-inch barrel). The Henry can be considered the first truly reliable lever-action breech-loading repeating rifle.

The Henry rifle would soon fall prey to a better one, Winchester's Model of 1866. The Cody Firearms Museum (Buffalo Bill Historical Soci-

The Winchester Model 1873 earned great fame in the 19th century because of its reliability as a repeater. While much stronger cartridges were on the horizon, the '73 and other models of the period made up in firepower for what they lacked in ballistic punch. This original is on display at the Cody Firearms Museum.

The 19th-century lever-action rifle in replica has proved to be reliable and ideal not only for the popular Cowboy Action game but for pure enjoyment, which is what is going on here with a Navy Arms Company 1873 rifle shooting blackpowder cartridges just for the experience.

Winchester knew that the Model 1866 and even the later 1873 required more potency. The company came out with an 1876 rifle, but it was the Model 1886 that truly boosted blackpowder cartridge potential with larger cartridges, such as the 45-70 government—low velocity, but big bullet. This original in the Cody Firearms Museum is chambered for the 45-70 Government.

ety) in Cody, Wyoming, has a number of important Model 1866 Winchester lever-action rifles in holding. A typical sub-model in the museum is the Winchester Model 1866 Fourth Model SRC (Saddle Ring Carbine) in 44-caliber centerfire (44-40 Winchester) with 20-inch round barrel and full magazine. The buttplate on this particular '66 has a trapdoor. The 1866 was called the Yellow Boy due to its brass receiver. The 44-40 cartridge was no thunder-maker. A 200-grain bullet at around 1,300 feet per second, depending on the load, was about it for blackpowder. My friend, the late John Kane, used a Yellow Boy in 44-40 to down a bull elk one time. This professional government hunter also shot many lions and bears with his 44-40

rifle. One shot at close range did it, but John was a professional government hunter. I would not use a 44-40 for elk or bear, having less hunting talent than Kane. Moving along, we come to the Model 1873 Winchester, also a lever-action repeater shooting center-fire ammunition. Now we have a steel frame and greater caliber choice—44-40 remained, but added were 38-40 and 32-20, both noted in Chapter 33.

Lever-action history continues to unfold with the Winchester Model 1892 and later the ultra-famous 1894, which became the most used "deer rifle" in North America for many years. But before these two rifles, Winchester had a true lever-action powerhouse in the Model of 1886. The Model 1886 had a long action capable of handling large cartridges, such as the 40-82. More powerful yet was the popular 45-70 Government, which in turn was superceded in punch by the 45-90 Winchester. There were so many sub-models and special orderings of all Winchester lever-action rifles of the 19th century that it is impossible to pin down a specific list of attributes, but one thing is certain—the Model 1886 was king for power in the era, not only with the 45-70 and 45-90, but also the 50-110 Winchester Express cartridge (not included in Chapter 33). Winchester's catalog of 1916 still offers this big boy with a 50-caliber bullet weighing 300 or 312 grains. In that year, a shooter could have 1,000 50-110 cartridges--loaded with lead hollowpoint, softpoint, or a full metal jacket bullet—for $48. The powder charge was a full 110 grains, as promised in the name of the round. The 1886 went on to carry the smokeless 33 Winchester cartridge that Ben Lilly counted on for bounty hunting cougars and bears. In keeping with development after development, the 1886 action turned into the Winchester Model 71 in 348 Winchester.

The Model 1895 lever-action came along in that time frame. This rifle marked the end of blackpowder cartridge domination in the sport-

In keeping with the trend toward more powerful lever-action blackpowder cartridge rifles, various Marlin 336-style rifles were chambered for the 45-70 cartridge, which could be fired with original 45-70 loads or even more powerful smokeless powder loads. Later, Marlin brought out its own 45-caliber cartridge—the 450 Marlin, more potent than the 45-70.

ing world. While the Model 1886 was strong enough for smokeless powder cartridges, such as the 33 Winchester, it was never offered in truly modern rounds. The Model 1895 was chambered for the 38-72 and 40-72 blackpowder cartridges to begin with, but also the 30-40 Krag (30 USA), 35 Winchester, 303 British, 405 Winchester—Teddy Roosevelt's Big Medicine—as well as the 30-03 Springfield, and soon after, the 30-06 Springfield, which was destined to become number one in the entire world for big-game hunting. It was also chambered in 7.62x54R for the Russian army. The unique box magazine of the Model 1895 allowed the use of pointed projectiles, unlike the tubular magazines of its predecessors. Having had a chance to fire an original '95, I can attest to its smooth function, although it could never compete with the bolt-action rifles to come.

Before leaving Winchester, a brief chronology of dates is in order. It goes like this, leaving out several models: 1855 (also noted as 1856), Volcanic Arms Company; 1857 New Haven Arms Company; 1860 Henry lever-action comes along; 1866 the Yellow Boy comes out—Oliver Winchester holds controlling stock in the New Haven Arms Company, which soon becomes known as the Winchester Repeating Arms Company. In 1873 the famous Winchester 1873 is introduced—including the 1 of 1,000 model that demands numer-

ous greenbacks today from collectors, when one can be found. The Model 1876 was introduced in that year. Interestingly, the single-shot Winchester came along in 1885, well after the leverguns. The 1886 more or less closes the blackpowder cartridge era as it is

This animal made the lever-action rifle famous in America—the lever-action became so well known as a deer rifle that to say, "Get your deer rifle," meant, "Get your lever-action." This was especially true of the Model 1894 which became the Model 94 Winchester, beginning as a blackpowder rifle in 1894 and turning smokeless in 1895 with the 25-35 Winchester and 30-30 Winchester.

chambered for smokeless cartridges, followed by the Model 1895.

But it was not all Winchester. John Mahlon Marlin was born in Connecticut in 1836 and became a tool and die maker. During the Civil War he worked at the Colt plant in Hartford and by 1870 he was on his own, manufacturing revolvers and derringers. Working with other ingenious gun designers, Marlin came up with the 1889 lever-action rifle with side ejection. The Model 1891 lever-action rifle followed, and later the Model 1893. Both of these were so good that neither went away. They live on today as the Model 39 Marlin and Model 336 Marlin, the oldest rifle designs still in use and as good as ever. Mr. Marlin died in 1901 at the age of 65, but his rifles lived on, the company under solid leadership. True, the company was auctioned off in 1924, but Frank Kenna was on hand to buy it—for $100—along with a $100,000 mortgage. Kenna went back to the basics, bringing out the Marlins that always worked. Of course, these rifles were chambered for popular and useful blackpowder cartridges of the time. Today, Marlin still offers rifles in good blackpowder calibers, including the never-die 45-70. A Marlin lever-action rifle in caliber 45-70 is capable of taking any North American big game as well as most wild animals across the sea. Naturally, for most power, smokeless must be considered,

Winchester decided that it could offer even more potency in a lever-action rifle and so the company developed the 405 Winchester cartridge. Old Western Scrounger came out with new 405 Winchester ammo, and of course handloaders beefed up the old round even more. The 405 was a natural progression based on big blackpowder cartridges for 19th-century lever-action rifles.

but a 500-grain bullet backed by 67.0 grains volume Swiss FFg or Pyrodex Triple Seven, as two examples only, will drop the biggest elk that ever bugled in black timber—at close range—with one shot.

I wanted a modern well-built lever-action rifle chambered for a blackpowder cartridge capable of taking deer and antelope, mainly, provided I could stalk for reasonably close shots. The choice of choices was Marlin's 336 Cowboy in 38-55 Winchester. This rifle held eight rounds in its tubular magazine resting beneath a 24-inch octagon tapered barrel. Ballard type rifling was just right for the bullets I intended

to shoot, including lead numbers running from 255 grains to 305 grains weight. Rate of twist being 1:18, bullets in all weights were well stabilized. At 7-1/2 pounds, the rifle was heavy enough to "hold steady" in the field, but no problem carrying. An overall length of 42.5-inches caused no problem in brush and wood. The rifle was fine just as it came from the factory, but a few shots later I was hooked, and so a bit of customizing was in order, if it can be called that. First, I added a sling. Remember that emulating the past was not my major goal. Big-game hunting was. This meant replacing the original forend cap with one having

an integral sling swivel eye. I bought it from Marlin and it fit perfectly. The strap, not being a true sling, was sufficiently narrow to loop over either of the two hooks on my packframe.

I modified the Camp Trails Freighter frame with a hook on either side. Why two hooks? Because if I have to carry my partner's rifle, for whatever reason, I can do so hands-free with the extra hook. I had the trigger touched up a bit by a gunsmith, but then learned of a replacement. Wild West Guns of Anchorage, Alaska, (www.wildwestguns.com) had a trigger that would break at—let's just call it extremely crisp and light. While the trigger ran around a hundred greenbacks, it was worth every penny because this rifle was going to be a companion on many hunting trails, which is exactly how it turned out. Normally, the replacement trigger would break at two to three pounds, but due to previous honing, my trigger came in a bit lighter. Since I shoot rifles with double-set triggers that break in ounces, this was no problem, although a trigger much under three pounds let-off is not recommended across the board. Wild West Guns also sent a replacement ejector, one-piece instead of two-piece. It is a lifetime ejector, not that Marlin ejectors go bad, but remember the goal—a trail rifle for any conditions, including one of my month-long excursions into the backcountry. By my own choice, I removed the cross-bolt safety. Bear in mind that doing this voids the Marlin warranty. The replacement shows as the head of a screw. I bought the replacement from Clyde Ludwig at POB 26156, Wauwatosa, WI 53226-0156

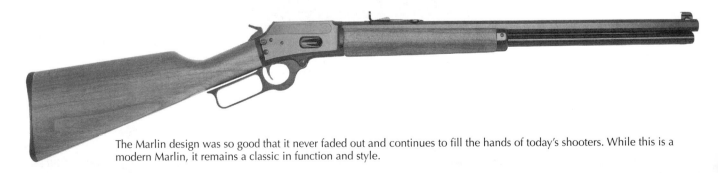

The Marlin design was so good that it never faded out and continues to fill the hands of today's shooters. While this is a modern Marlin, it remains a classic in function and style.

Fadala added a few features to his Model 336 Cowboy 38-55 rifle, one being a special trigger from Wild West Guns of Anchorage, Alaska. This is the trigger.

at about ten bucks plus three more dollars S&H.

Ron Cox, mentioned elsewhere as my expert shooting friend, quickly proved the accuracy potential of the Marlin lever-action rifle and the 38-55 cartridge by shooting, with the open iron sight that came on the rifle, groups at 50 yards that could often be covered completely with a 25-cent piece. My groups were not too far behind, but by now the rifle was quite personal and so I personalized it even further with a new set of sights. I chose the Ghost Ring rear sight from XS Sight Systems (see Directory). A blank from Brownells filled the dovetail space left by the removal of the open rear sight. A White Stripe front sight, also from XS, was added. Although I continued hunting with the spot and stalk method, using mainly one of two binoculars to find game in the distance, I also found that I could put all eight shots from the Marlin's magazine into the "kill zone" of a buck deer at 200 yards every time I used my packframe as a field rest. The hunting method with the 38-55 was simple— with either my Bushnell 12X reverse porro prism binocular or Fujinon 10X porro prism glass with individual eyepiece focus, I managed to locate game at quite a distance, both of these binoculars enjoying a high degree of optical resolution. Then the stalk was on. Especially on bedded game, the usual

shot ended up less than 100 yards. My brother, Nick Fadala, had a very short deer hunt in Wyoming—only one day allowed. He insisted on using the 38-55 and brought down a mule deer buck at about 50 yards.

Replicas abound. While my Marlin 38-55 is as original as I require for a lever-action rifle of blackpowder persuasion, there are also a number of old-timers to choose from. Navy Arms Company alone has a good listing, including the 1866 Yellow Boy in 38 Special for Cowboy Action, also 44-40 and 45 Colt. Choose a 24- or 20-inch barrel, the latter available with a saddle ring. There are several 1873 Winchesters, including the Sporting Rifle with 24-

inch barrel in calibers 357 Magnum (38 Special), 44-40, and 45 Colt, and a saddle gun carbine with 19-inch barrel. Cimarron has an 1860 Henry rifle with case-hardened frame in 44-40 or 45 Colt, as well as an 1860 Civilian Model with charcoal finish in 44-40, 44 Special, or 45 Colt. There is also an 1873 "Deluxe" Sporting Rifle with 24-inch barrel, calibers 32-20 (for mild report and recoil), 38-40 Winchester, 357 Magnum (also shoots 38 Special), 44-40, 44 Special, and 45 Colt. For those interested in Civil War history, Cimarron also has a Model 1860 Civil War Henry with military sling swivels. It even has C.G. Chapman and B. Tyler Henry inspection marks stamped into

Wild West Guns of Anchorage, Alaska, continues to use the Marlin lever-action for special big-game rifles, a testament to the 19th-century design that was so good it still serves in the 21st century.

Anyone who wants to add a big loop lever to his or her Marlin lever-action rifle has the option from Wild West Guns of Anchorage, Alaska. Here is the replacement—the Wild West Big Loop.

the barrel, plus a U.S.-marked frame. Or how about a 30-inch barrel 1873 or a 16-inch 1873 carbine? Pedersoli and other companies also offer many blackpowder lever-action copies.

Listing currently available lever-action blackpowder rifles is risky. Will the same models be around for the duration of this edition? Probably so. Cowboy Action Shooting demands it, and many marksmen have also learned that the old-time lever-action with old-time blackpowder cartridge ammunition is a joy to shoot from plinking and paper targets to game both large and small. That's probably why the president of the Pedersoli company of Italy told me he intends to continue offering

a number of lever-action blackpowder cartridge rifles. But I would like to sneak a rifle in that is not a lever-action. Since there is no other place to put it, let's consider the new version of one of the most popular rifles of the Old West—the Colt Lightning slide-action. Several companies now offer this intriguing rifle of the past, including United States Fire Arms Mfg. in Hartford—the Colt people, as well as Cimarron with a .32-20, 38-40, and 44-4. The Navy Arms Company also has not just one, but several sub-models as well. However, the one I am familiar with is the Pedersoli. It is not only beautiful and authentic, but actually more refined than the original with

nine additional safety and functional features. In 45 Colt, the Lightning will shine in the whitetail thicket with bullets in the 200- to 250-grain class.

American and Canadian shooters loved the lever-action from the beginning. They still do. Cowboy Action Shooting will demand the continuance of the older blackpowder versions, while American and Canadian hunters continue to embrace the lever-action as well. They always have. From the 1904 *Our Big Game* book by Dwight W. Huntington, we read, "A popular rifle with old and experienced woodsmen is made by Winchester Repeating Arms Company substantially as follows: It is built for nitro-powder .45-70 calibre, 22-inch round barrel, half-magazine, shot-gun stock [as opposed to crescent buttplate], fitted with Lyman ivory bead front and combination rear sight, and weighs about seven pounds." The Model 1886 Winchester! Huntington went on to praise the 45-70 Government cartridge, saying "For the nearby shooting of big game, and nearly ev-

Because open country game, such as these mule deer, often offer long-range challenges, the lever-action blackpowder cartridge rifle was supplanted first by lever-action smokeless powder rifles, and then by bolt-action long-range rifles. Today's hunters who gain great satisfaction from going for big game in open country with old-time rifles, including lever-actions, happily accept the challenge.

The lever-action rifle is big in Cowboy Action Shooting, and is especially interesting when shooting blackpowder cartridges with attending smoke, creating an old-time scene enjoyable to watch or participate in.

One of Fadala's most enjoyable hunts is going for antelope with lever-action rifles, especially his Model 336 Cowboy Marlin rifle in 38-55 Winchester.

ery shot in the woods is at close range, the initial velocity of the .45-70 leaves nothing to be desired; the trajectory is sufficiently flat and the impact of the heavier bullet is more deadly [than the new smallbore smokeless powder rounds]. Charles Hallock, in his 1879 Sportsman's Gazetteer, selects the Winchester Model 1876 as "being adapted to the heaviest game our country affords." The author narrows it down to the "1876 Central Fire, 45 cal. 350 grains of lead, 75 grains of powder, thus giving a range of power to suit the peculiarity of the game in any section of the country."

One clear Wyoming morning, with only a trace of the "gentle breeze" that normally graces the habitat of the pronghorn antelope, I found myself with a tag remaining to be filled. That particular day I had along my Fujinon 10X binocular, and with it spotted a band of "prairie goats" feeding along the edge of a sagebrush belt. The herd was easily a half-mile away. I turned the glass from the antelope to the terrain. And there it was. A long water-cut ditch that would conceal my stalk to within 50 yards of the herd. I didn't even have to bend down to sneak, the cut was so deep. Before popping my head over the edge, I picked up a piece of sagebrush to hide my face. A human face suddenly showing on the range is to antelope what opening a nighttime bedroom closet to come face to face with Dracula is to a person. The Ghost Ring aperture sight picture was clear. Crack! A 255-grain bullet from the barrel of my Marlin 336 lever-action Cowboy rifle was on its way. The antelope would have been taken with any rifle/cartridge. but the 38-55 added a touch of color to the canvas, a look back to the old times. That's what keeps the blackpowder lever-action rifle going. A look back to old times.

Starting as a blackpowder rifle in the 19th century, the Marlin lever-action rifle continues into the 21st century. The action is so good that Wild West Guns of Anchorage, Alaska, chambers special high-power big-game cartridges in the Marlin. Any shooter wishing to stay with the blackpowder theme can do so with a Marlin in 38-55 or the more powerful 45-70.

Imagine slipping into a pair of snowshoes and heading into this late fall scene with a lever-action rifle, such as Marlin's 336 38-55. In terrain like this, where shots are often close, the old blackpowder cartridge will do the job just as well as it did in the 19th century.

chapter 33
BLACKPOWDER CARTRIDGES IN REVIEW

The rimfire cartridge gave way to the centerfire, also known as central-fire, cartridge. Blackpowder continued to serve in these cartridges, such as the 38-72 and many others. The centerfires were not only reloadable; they were also more powerful than the rimfires.

The blackpowder metallic cartridge has made such an astounding recovery in the 20th and 21st centuries that a brief review of a few of these gone but never forgotten, and now back again rounds is vital to the overall theme of this Fifth Edition. Several of the cartridges entertained below are not with us today. They are included for reference only, and to add a few threads of interest to the fabric of this chapter. The advent of the metallic cartridge can be generically stated as a development closely following on the paper or linen cartridge. Early metallics were often straight-wall with a powder capacity quite like that of their predecessors in paper and cloth. Bullets were lead with velocities around the speed of sound, or roughly 1,100 to 1,200 fps, again with a few exceptions.

The Rimfires

Also noted as rimfire or rim-fire, these metallic cartridges were not only useful in the past, but also in the present. The obvious forerunner is the 22 rimfire round, beginning with the Short, which was, remarkably, created as a self-defense number, and ending with the Long Rifle, of which millions are manufactured every year the world over. In the past, larger rimfire cartridges also saw wide use. Winchester's 1896 catalog shows several larger-caliber rimfire rounds, including the 32 Short, which contained 9 grains of blackpowder pushing an 82-grain lead bullet. The 32 Long, which has been offered in modern times, carried 13 grains of blackpowder with a 90-grain lead bullet. The ballistics of the 32 Long allowed its use not only on small game, but also up to wild turkey and larger varmints. The 32 Extra Long for Ballard, Wesson, and Remington rifles, upped the powder cargo to 29 grains black, but retained the 90-grain lead projectile. There was also a 38 Short, 38 Long, and 38 Extra Long, all worthy turkey-takers, each also being capable of javelina and similar size game. The 38 Short fired a 130-grain lead bullet encouraged by 18 grains of blackpowder, the 38 Long taking a 148-grain bullet with 21 grains of blackpowder, the 38 Extra Long running a notch stronger in power with a 148-grain bullet backed by 38-grains blackpowder. Because of low velocity, these cartridges, all six here named, were not destructive of edibles, but were strong enough to satisfactorily take on the game they were intended for

Among the larger rimfires we find the 41, which was popular in its time frame in National, Williamson, Colt, Remington, Southerner, Derringer, Ballard, Forehand & Wadsworth, and Frank Wesson pistols. While not boasting much potency, the 41 rimfire remained capable of discouraging anyone bent on mischief with its 130-grain bullet and a 13-grain blackpowder charge. The 56-46 rimfire, as shown in Winchester's catalog of 1896, was adapted to Spencer sporting rifles. This case was loaded with 45 grains of blackpowder and a 330-grain bullet. One of the larger rimfire rounds of the past was the 41 Swiss, chambered in the Vetterli and other Swiss rifles and loaded with 55 grains of blackpowder behind a 310-grain bullet. This was a military cartridge in its time, and I have seen shootable Swiss rifles so chambered. The 44 Henry Flat for Henry rifles earned a huge reputation in its time because it was also chambered in the Winchester 1866 rifle, that rifle being one of the earliest successful lever-actions. I have on hand Winchester rimfire ammunition with an "H" stamped on the head. That stood for Henry, who was for many years applauded by Win-

chester for the role played by the 44 Henry Flat rifle. A bullet weighing 200 grains with 28 grains of blackpowder was nothing to write home about, but rapid fire made it deadly in numbers. A practiced rifleman could spew out a good many 200-grain bullets from his Winchester Model 1866 rifle. A warrior armed with bow and arrow had a great advantage over trails-men carrying muzzleloaders. See the plume of smoke and rush forward with arrows flying...but not against a rider with an 1866 Winchester.

The Centerfires

Rimfire metallic cartridge cases were useless after firing, just as they are today. No one goes around picking up 22 rimfire brass, except to dispose of it. The centerfire, also called central fire and center fire, was an entirely different story. As noted in Chapter 31, Sharps believed that a case could be loaded as many as 500 times, provided it was kept in good shape by cleaning thoroughly after firing to avoid deterioration through corrosion. In the

1850s, designers of cartridges did attempt to develop centerfire ammo. But very little came of those wanderings on the trail of invention until the American Civil War days as far as widespread use is concerned. Recall that Smith & Wesson enjoyed ownership of several patents, which got in the way of other cartridge designers. The Moore cartridge came along, a distinct oddity. It was more fully called the Moore Tit Cartridge because of an obvious resemblance to a certain portion of female anatomy. It was loaded from the *front end* of a revolver cylinder chamber and fired by the impact of the hammer on a "tit" filled with fulminate and protruding from the back of the round-based copper case. There was also a Thuer cartridge useful in Colt cap 'n' ball revolvers that had been converted to take metallic cartridges. This cartridge was tapered towards the rear and loaded in the front end of the cylinder chamber via the same rod used previously to seat lead round or conical bullets in the revolver. This centerfire cartridge had a replaceable primer.

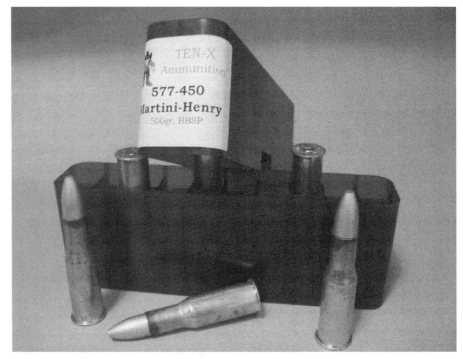

The British 577-450 Martini-Henry blackpowder cartridge was interesting not only as an example of an early centerfire, but also because it was one of the first attempts to build one cartridge from another—in this case, essentially necking-down the 577 round to hold 45-caliber bullets. Ammo built by Ten-X.

For perspective on the 577-450 blackpowder cartridge, viewing from the left: 325 WSM (Winchester Short Magnum—a very modern smokeless powder cartridge); 577-450 Martini-Henry blackpowder cartridge; 30-06 for familiar comparison; 38-72 blackpowder round (38-caliber with 72 grains of blackpowder); and the 577 Snider British blackpowder cartridge.

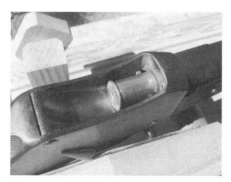

The 577-450 cartridge served in the Martini-Henry rifle, which in turn became a famous battle weapon of the Boxer Rebellion and also the Zulu Wars when the British fought the intrepid king of that tribe and its brave warriors in Africa.

Another look at the 577-450 Martin-Henry cartridge, the 577 Snider on the left, 577-450 upper, with 30-06 cartridge center for comparison.

Myriad developments ensued in a mad dash to create a better centerfire metallic cartridge. The English had its 577 Boxer Snider round for its military rifle of the same name—Snider. The Martini-Henry 577/450 Boxer cartridge followed. This cartridge, with various bullet weights, is once again available due to the discovery of a cache of old Martini-Henry rifles that are now available for sale. It must be noted that these rifles were stored for a very long time and the outlet, Atlanta Cutlery, warns against firing. Those rifles that are safe to fire, however, now have 577/450 ammo from the Ten-X company with lead bullets manufactured by the Buffalo Bullet Company. The specific 577/450 ammo I tested in a shootable Martini-Henry rifle was loaded with a 500-grain lead bullet, but plans are underway to offer a lighter bullet with a smaller powder charge in deference to shooting the old rifles more for fun than either target or hunting.

One cartridge list only for center- or central-fire cartridges available in the 1870s runs 40 items long, beginning with the 40-50 with grooved bullet and ending with the 58 Carbine. Another, which includes both sporting and military centerfire cartridges offered in the 1890s, runs over 100, including multiple loads for some. Most of these cartridges will never again see the light of manufacture. However, the ones that are back with us are high and going up all the time. Because of new developments, it is impossible to guess what blackpowder metallic cartridge from yesteryear will be resurrected, like the famed Phoenix bird, to shoot again. And so the following survey is far from complete, but useful all the same, not only because we are once again shooting these interesting and functional cartridges, but also because they made shooting history. Ten-X Ammunition (see Directory) currently offers new "old-time" ammo in numerous calibers from 25-20 to 50-90 Sharps, 45-120 Sharps, 577 Snider and many others.

The 25-20 and 32-20 blackpowder cartridges remain useful today in both blackpowder and smokeless powder loadings. From the left: 25-20, 32-20, 30-06 for comparison, then 32-20 and 25-20.

25-20 Winchester

Ammo for the 25-20 Winchester remains available and should. It is a fine little cartridge capable of doing a lot of "work" in the small-game field, especially for wild turkey where rifles are allowed by law for Ben's Bird. As the name implies, this little number was originally loaded with 20 grains of blackpowder. Charging it up today with 16 grains of FFFg or equivalent drives an 86-grain lead bullet at about 1,200 fps, depending upon barrel length. Due to low velocity, the 25-20 is easy on edible meat, but sufficiently powerful to do a good job on smaller-sized game.

32-20 Winchester

If I have ever had more fun shooting a handgun, I can't recall the time that rose above the session I had with a 32-20 Colt revolver on a shoot in West Virginia. And why? Because the 32-20 shoots a lead bullet at low velocity for plenty of power on "small stuff," plus ample accuracy on paper targets. I shot metallic silhouettes with the Navy Arms replica Colt six-gun. A 16-grain charge of FFFg in a 5 1/2-inch barrel earned 888 fps with a 115-grain lead bullet. Out of a Model 1899 rifle with 26-inch barrel the 32-20 gained 1,266 fps with 20 grains volume of Pyrodex P powder.

The 32-40 made its fame along with the 38-55 because of chambering in the Model 94 Winchester rifle, which would become one of the most famous rifles and carbines of all time. From the left: 32-40 Winchester, 38-55 Winchester, 30-06, 38-55 Winchester, and 32-40 on the far right.

The 40-65 Winchester cartridge has made a comeback in the hands of metallic silhouette shooters who find the blackpowder round strong enough to knock the ram target over, yet milder in recoil than the 45-70. From the left: 40-65, 40-82, 30-06, 40-82, and 40-65, far right.

The 40-82 is another old-time blackpowder cartridge that has caught the attention of modern shooters. Old Western Scrounger as well as Ten-X provides loaded ammunition for this cartridge.

32-40 Winchester

The Winchester 32-40 is again available as loaded ammo and can also be formed from 30-30 brass. Considered a match/target cartridge, the 32-40 was well liked by Schuetzen shooters, especially with 190- to 200-grain bullets. Although not a powerhouse, the 32-40 is capable of cleanly harvesting deer-sized game in the hands of an expert rifleman/hunter. A 165-grain bullet achieves 1,360 fps with 35 grains of FFFg blackpowder, about 100 fps less with a 190-grain bullet and 35 grains of FFg. Mild recoil joins fine accuracy in this cartridge. Its shortcoming is lack of bullet weight for silhouette shooting, where a good piece of lead is required to smack the metallic targets convincingly.

38-55 Winchester

The 38-55 fires bullets in the 255- to 300-grain class at about 1,250 to 1,300 fps with 45 grains of FFg or FFFg blackpowder. Some old-time hunters considered the 38-55 better than the 30-30 for big game. Today, the 38-55, loaded with blackpowder, is a fine target and hunting number. The round is especially worthy in brush or timber when loaded with a good lead projectile, such as the 305-grain bullet from a SAECO mold. The 38-55 is mild compared with larger-bore blackpowder cartridges that burn more powder behind heavier projectiles.

40-65 Winchester

This is a dandy cartridge that I became acquainted with while testing a prototype of a Sharps rifle, the Antietam, at the time not yet on the market. The test bullet was a 390-grain lead conical. It took off at 1,300 fps in front of 60 grains of GOEX Cartridge-grade blackpowder. The 40-65 Winchester is pleasant to shoot and has become a strong candidate for silhouette games. Forty-caliber bullets of good weight knock the ram silhouette over at long range. These same bullets are worthy of big game. Although this round is rather mild-mannered, it delivers a good-sized bullet with high penetration potential. Cases can be formed from 45-70 brass, but newly manufactured ammo is also available.

40-70 Sharps BN (Bottleneck)

Tests show no clear advantage over the 40-65 Winchester in terms of muzzle velocity, bullet for bullet, but obviously a few grains more powder push the bullet a little faster. The test rifle put a 330-grain bullet downrange at 1,350 fps with 70 grains FFg. The 40-70 delivers more punch than the 405 Winchester, Teddy Roosevelt's Big Medicine.

The 40-90s

The 40-90s are excellent blackpowder cartridges, all of them worthy of silhouette shooting, targets, and big game. Frank Mayer, the old buffalo hunter who lived into modern times, claimed that his 40-90 was more than sufficient for bison. The 40-90 cartridge group provides good power with modest recoil. Here are just a few 40s from a long list: 40-90 Bullard, 40-90 Sharps Straight, 40-90 Sharps Bottleneck, 40-90 Ideal and 40-90 Ballard (not to be confused with Bullard).

There were many larger capacity 44-caliber blackpowder cartridges available in the 19th century. However, the 44-40, despite its modest cargo of propellant, was far more popular than its big brothers. Similar cartridges were also popular. From the left: 38-40 Winchester; 44 Special (grandfather of the 44 Remington Magnum); 44-40 Winchester; 44 Russian; 30-06—44 Russian; 44-40; 44 Special; 38-40.

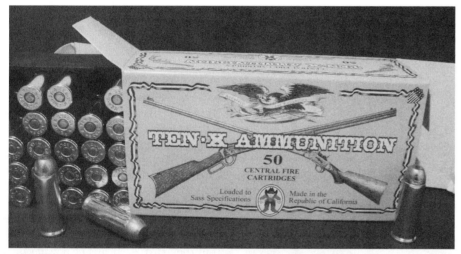

The 45 Colt is currently available from most major ammunition factories in smokeless powder. It is also big in blackpowder, as with Tex-X.

44-Caliber Blackpowder Rifle Cartridges

There is not much play on the 44-caliber blackpowder rifle cartridge. But many were available in the 19th century, and well liked. The 44-60 Sharps fired a 396-grain bullet at 1,250 fps according to *Cartridges of the World*, while the 44-70 Maynard pushed a 430-grain projectile at 1,310. There was a 44-75 Ballard Everlasting, plus a 44-77 Sharps & Remington, a 44-90 Remington, as well as a 44-90 Sharps Bottleneck, the latter driving a 520-grain bullet at 1,270 fps (*Cartridges of the World*). Other 44s include the 44-95 Peabody "What Cheer" and the 44-100 by Remington and Ballard. The former is historically interesting because it was chambered in the Remington-Hepburn, or No. 3 Long-Range Creedmoor rifle (Remington Rolling Block), so the 44-100 Remington was designed as a match round from the start.

The 45 Colt

There never was a 45 Short Colt and so there never was a 45 Long Colt for contrast, but to separate this cartridge from the 45 ACP (45 Auto), it is often listed as the 45LC, or 45 Long Colt. It is a terrific cartridge in both rifle and handgun. Out of a Beretta Stampede Colt replica, 35 grains of FFFg produced 1,117 fps with a 250-grain lead bullet from Lyman mould #454190. Not bad for a 7 1/2-inch

The 45 Colt is another old-time blackpowder cartridge that cannot be kept down. Today it is chambered in a multitude of firearms, not only revolvers, but also rifles. The replica Colt Lightning slide-action rifle offered today by Pedersoli and others can be had in 45 Colt.

The Pedersoli Colt, which is available in 44-40 or 45 Colt calibers, is offered in several styles, including this Lightning Premium Pedersoli.

The 45-70 Government has been chambered in rifles since at least 1873, beginning with the Springfield Trap Door rifle. Today, the cartridge is loaded widely, including blackpowder such as from Old Western Scrounger, this particular load with 500-grain lead bullet.

So popular is the 45-70 Government cartridge that Old Western Scrounger offers it in blackpowder loads, not only with 500-grain lead bullet, but also 405-grain lead bullet.

barrel. Higher velocity—1,344 fps—was gained with a single Pyrodex 44/45 Pellet, same barrel length. From a Marlin Model 1894 Cowboy Competition rifle the 45 Colt fired a 255-grain Hornady Cowboy at 1,115 fps with 35 grains volume of Pyrodex RS, a charge that weighed out at 25 grains. Velocity was increased by about 100 fps in a Pedersoli Colt Lightning rifle with long barrel, same load.

The 45-70 Government

There were many 45-caliber, single-shot blackpowder cartridge rifles around in the 19th century. These included, among others, the 45-75 Winchester, 45-75 Sharps Straight, 45-100 Ballard, 45-100 Remington and others. But of the 45s, the 45-70 Government retained its status, never dying out. See Chapter 37 for a little more on this amazing cartridge. As the 45-70-500, with 70 grains of blackpowder (in the old balloon-head case), 67 grains with solid-head modern case, the 500-grain bullet retains sufficient flight properties for long-range shooting and of course the same bullet is deadly on big game. Elmer Keith of big bullet fame preferred the 45-70 over many modern cartridges for elk.

The 45-90 Winchester

Essentially, a longer 45-70. It was introduced in 1886. Claims were made that the extra 20 grains of powder did great things for the 45-90 over the 45-70. More powerful, yes, but the 45-90 did not blow the 45-70 away. Nonetheless, it's a good cartridge, able to push 500-grain bullets at about the same muzzle velocity as 400-grain bullets in the 45-70.

The 45-90 2 4/10 Sharps

This 45-caliber blackpowder cartridge is commonly called a 45-90 today. The Sharps Rifle Company brought it out on June 8, 1877, as a fine long-range target round, credited with winning 1,000-yard matches as late as 1900. A target load is listed as 85 grains

Big-case 45-caliber cartridges provided good power for 19th-century blackpowder rifles. Here are two good ones, the 45-90 Winchester and 45-120 Sharps. From the left: 45-90, 45-120, 30-06, 45-120, and on the far right, 45-90.

The 50-70 Government was not only an official cartridge of the United States Army, but also popular with the buffalo runners of the 19th century. The 50-90 blackpowder cartridge provided a bit more power, but the 50-70 continued as a strong number for many years. From the left: 50-70 Government, 50-90 Winchester, 30-06, 50-90 Winchester, and on the far right, 50-70 Government.

Fg blackpowder with a 500-grain bullet at 1,226 fps.

The 45-110 Sharps

Also known as the 45-110-2 7/8 Sharps, this round is credited as being the largest 45-caliber cartridge *originally designed* for the Sharps rifle. It was chambered in the Sharps 1874 model for long-range power with a 500-grain bullet at 1,360 fps and good accuracy. For flexibility, there is a 325-grain bullet at 1,596 fps with 110 grains FFg and a 430-grain bullet is listed at 1,430 with the same charge.

The 45-120 Sharps

This fine cartridge remains well-received today, although the 45-70 Government is far more popular for silhouette. Students of the Sharps insist that Mayer and others who touted the 45-120 as an important among bison slayers were incorrect. They say—and feel they can prove—that the 45-120 was not widely in use until *after* the bison hunt. *Cartridges of the World* notes that the 45-120 was introduced in 1878-79 for the Sharps-Borchardt rifle, "though there is no documentary evidence that the Sharps factory offered rifles in this caliber." John Schoffstall, an expert on Sharps, said, "The 45-120-3 1/4 was never chambered in an original Sharps rifle." I tested a 490-grain bullet from

Lyman mould No. 457121. It weighed 480 grains in No. 2 alloy. A charge of 110 grains Fg blackpowder propelled this 480-grain bullet at 1,482 fps for a muzzle energy of 2,341 foot-pounds. Remaining velocity at 100 yards was 1,230 for 1,613 foot-pounds, strong enough for any big game on the continent. On calm days, putting five shots into a 6-inch bullseye at 200 yards from the bench posed no problem. Mayer claimed that, "At distances above 500 and up to 1,000 yards, the 45-120-550 Sharps with patched bullets is absolutely unsurpassed by any weapon known to man." Its only problem was that if the Sharps was never chambered for the 45-120, which rifle was Mayer speaking of?

The 50-70 Government

This popular 19th century cartridge saw plenty of action in the Far West. From a Sharps rifle with 32-inch barrel, a 528-grain bullet out of an RCBS #50-515 mould got 1,163 fps with 70 grains of Fg blackpowder. Noted as Government, because it was, this cartridge found its way into the Trapdoor Springfield breech-loading rifle of 1866. The Sioux made a successful raid, described later as the Fetterman Massacre, against troops led by Major Fetterman. The major and all his men died before reinforcements reached

The huge 50-140 Sharps cartridge is another long-ago round that remains available, albeit on a more limited basis than the far more popular 45-70 and similar old-timers. Old Western Scrounger offers loaded 50-140 ammo with a 635-grain lead round-nose bullet. and blackpowder.

them. Led by Chief White Cloud, the Sioux warriors were met by soldiers armed with 50-70 "britch loaders," as they called the rifles. The warriors "died in droves," thinking at first they were going up against muzzleloaders.

The 50-70-1 1/3 Sharps

This round was also known as the 50-70 Government and it apparently saw much use for hunting in the 1800s. The short cartridge delivered 1,071 fps with a 500-grain bullet and 70 grains GOEX Fg blackpowder. Not a lot of bullet speed, but almost 1,300 foot-pounds of energy. A 528-grain lead bullet left the muzzle at 1,051 fps for 1,320 foot-pounds of muzzle energy. Some students of the buffalo hunting era feel that the 50-70 was a prime cartridge for dropping the hapless shaggies.

The 50-140 Sharps

There were many 50s in the 19th century. Passing over the rest, the 50-140 commands attention. This was a truly big round and not an original Sharps chambering. The cartridge appeared circa 1884, three years after the Sharps company no longer manufactured rifles. This was also the last year

of widespread buffalo hunting. The cartridge was known as the 50-140-3 1/4, as well as the 50-140-700, the latter for a 700-grain bullet. The Big Fifty I tested drove a 638-grain NEI-cast lead projectile at 1,413 fps with 140 grains of Pyrodex CTG grade powder (no longer available) for a muzzle energy of 2,829 foot-pounds, an energy rating normally associated with modern big-game cartridges.

So Many More

Apologies to the many blackpowder cartridges left out in our survey due to space restrictions. This includes some that are back with us.

Handloading the Blackpowder Cartridge

This in-depth topic is best handled in books written for the sole purpose of loading blackpowder cartridge ammunition. For present purposes, only a few skeletal notes are provided. For in-depth information, consider *SPG Lubricants BP Cartridge Reloading Primer* by Mike Venturino and Steve Garb, a 1992 publication. This book, only 116 pages long, is packed with worthwhile information, such as Mike Venturino's

introduction, which explains the merits of single-shot blackpowder cartridge rifles. Chapter 1 provides the basics in loading technique, dealing with bullets, lead alloys, bullet sizing, custom bullet moulds, primers, powders, wads, the cartridge case, drop tubes, bullet seating, and cartridge case cleanup (with hot soapy water). Steve Garb tells about "Reloading the Match Cartridge" in one chapter. A number of loads are explained for many cartridges, beginning with the 32-40—introduced in 1884 by Ballard as a Schuetzen round. Later the 32-40 saw action in lever-action Marlins and Winchesters. Interesting information, but of more importance are all the specifications noted for the cartridge, as well as a good sample load. The 38-55 is treated to two sample loads in this text. The 38-56 has one. Particulars are interesting. The 38-56, for example, is shown with a 310-grain Hoch custom bullet, 1:30 ratio tin/lead alloy, bullet sized to .377-inch diameter, 55 grains FFg blackpowder, Federal 215 Magnum primer, and a wad made from a waxed milk carton. Velocity came out at 1,308 fps. The test rifle was a Winchester High Wall with 30-inch barrel, 1:18 rate of twist.

As a cartridge history story unto itself, here are a few cartridges to consider, both smokeless and blackpowder. From the left: the world's most popular big-game cartridge: 30-06 Springfield; the 577-450 Martini-Henry blackpowder cartridge of British military fame; the 577 Snider from whence the 577-450 sprang and a noted British military cartridge in its own right; the modern 325 WSM Winchester Short Magnum, typical of a late 20th century/early 21st century trend to "short, fat cartridges." Next to last, the 38-72 Winchester blackpowder cartridge, typical of the 19th century blackpowder cartridge era, and finally, the admittedly odd 226 Barnes wildcat, essentially a 22-caliber shooting a super long 125-grain bullet that its admirers promise will penetrate the full breadth of a bull moose.

Five Simple Notes on Blackpowder Cartridge Handloading

1. A Case Full of Powder

It is common practice to load large blackpowder cartridges such as the 45-70 Government with very small charges of smokeless powder. While it is just as difficult to prove as the short-started bullet warning sounded often in this book, the fact is, some rifles have been destroyed with light smokeless powder charges in large old-time cartridges. In one case, a shooter experienced a catastrophic failure with a Sharps replica in 45-70. While approved smokeless powder loads should cause no problem, shooting the blackpowder cartridge with a case full of blackpowder or Pyrodex leaves no air space. This 100-percent load density condition also produces good accuracy.

2. The Blackpowder Powder Measure

A regular powder measure must not be used to meter out blackpowder, or any blackpowder substitute. That's because static electricity or the simple friction of metallic working parts created in these measures (which were developed for smokeless powder, not blackpowder) could possibly result in detonation. Now there are special metering devices for blackpowder from Lyman and Hornady. The measure features a non-static reservoir and non-sparking internal parts.

3. How to Get More Blackpowder in the Case

The reason old-time powder charges for certain cartridge cases cannot readily fit into these cases is the change of design through time. The old balloon-head case actually had a greater interior powder capacity than the modern case because the head was thinner. These weaker cases were replaced with new cases having more metal in the head, therefore stronger and safer. That's why it's difficult, for example, to get 70 grains of Fg blackpowder into the 45-70 case, which was originally intended to hold that much propellant when the bullet was seated. More blackpowder or Pyrodex can, however, be settled into a case through the use of a drop-tube, an old and widespread practice. The drop tube is just that: a long tube. Powder is funneled in from the top and, by allowing the charge to slowly trickle down the tube and into the case, the charge is distributed evenly into a compact column. An example of a commercial drop tube is Lyman's 24-inch Powder Drop Tube. It ties in with the Lyman 55 Classic Black Powder Measure noted above.

4. Use Magnum Primers

Shooters who live and breathe blackpowder cartridge loading, such as Mike Venturino, taught the rest of us that magnum primers do a better job in larger blackpowder cartridges than do milder ones. I have since enjoyed success with the Federal 215 Large Rifle primer and similar magnum primers. The exact reason for this fact is slippery, since blackpowder ignites readily, with the usual No. 11 percussion cap. But magnum primers it is.

5. Paper-Patched Bullets

Paper-patched bullets show good accuracy. (So do bare lead bullets.) The blackpowder cartridge fan, however, should consider paper-patched bullets in his or her personal rifle.

RUNNING BALL—BULLET CASTING

Lead bars ready for liquefying and then moulding into projectiles, in this case for blackpowder firearms, although cast bullets are extremely useful in modern cartridge guns as well.

You do it with lead—that is, making excellent bullets for blackpowder guns, muzzleloader or cartridge. It doesn't matter. Lead is ideal for either. Lead is one of the first metals known to early man—add copper, as proved when the 3,500-year-old mummy called the Ice Man was found frozen in the Italian Alps. His axe head was made of copper. An old word for lead was *plumbum* with historical evidence of its use dating as early as 6500 B.C. in Turkey. Lead gets its scientific notation—Pb—from plumbum. Ancient alchemists associated lead as a symbol

for Saturn as they attempted to turn this base metal into gold with obvious repeated failure. Lead is found naturally only in small amounts in the free metal state. It occurs mainly as minerals, the most important of which is galena, or lead sulfide. Note that the mountain man referred to lead for his bullets as galena. Galena was the commercial source of lead that came into the Far West at rendezvous. Actual smelting of lead is noted as an early 16th-century occurrence, but I doubt it. Consider that the Ice Man's copper axe threw previous dates of copper

Lead has served as bullet material for ages. Here, two metallic cartridges are shown with appropriate lead bullets, the big 577 Snider (left) and its "little sister" 577-450 Martini-Henry, with the 30-06 in the center for comparison.

tools into a tailspin. For our purposes—making superior projectiles—we need to know that lead is a soft metal 11 times heavier than water. It melts at 327.4 degrees Centigrade. Converting to Fahrenheit like this: C x 9/5 +32, so 327.4 times 9/5 plus 32 equals 621 degrees. Both factors—weight and temperature—are of extreme importance in bullet-making.

Because lead is dense (heavy) it turns into bullets that have the mass to not only retain energy over long range, but also to penetrate animal tissue and bone. Lead has high molecular cohesion, which simply means it stays together as a unit rather than fragmenting. This is why I have recovered lead bullets, round and conical, that retained the bulk of their original weight even after passing through the entire chest cavity of a big-game animal—elk and buffalo included. That lead melts at a comparatively low temperature was very important to the mountain man and his predecessors who stuck a pot on coals to create moulded bullets. The buffalo-runner also casts bullets, sometimes recasting those found within the bison. "We used the softest lead that we could buy," said buffalo runner Hanna. The Lone Ranger of comic and film has been shown melting silver at the campfire to make his bullets. Never happened. Alchemists considered silver (Ag) a symbol for the moon. Silver melts at 1,763.2 degrees Fahrenheit with a casting temperature over 1,000 degrees Centigrade, somewhat out of reach for the ordinary campfire. Add density and melting point together and it is easy to understand why lead was the obvious choice for bullets and remains an ideal choice for making bullets today. Another great asset of lead is its ability to meld with other metals, such as tin, antimony, bismuth, and more, to create alloys, such as the popular Alloy No. 2. Some of the best blackpowder cartridge bullets are an alloy of lead and tin.

Running ball, as the old-timers sometimes called moulding bullets, is a hobby in its own right, just like handloading ammunition. There are three basic reasons for running ball today: economy, creating bullets for special guns, and the pure enjoyment casting affords. Admittedly, today's ammunition is cheaper than ever *for basic loads*. High-grade ammo can cost a few dollars per round. I found a case of 12-gauge shotgun shells for $35.00. As a young fellow, $3.50 a box was a good buy, and a dollar was worth far more than it is today. Twenty-two Long Rifle ammo ran 75 cents a box. I can buy 22-rimfire ammo in bulk today for not a lot more. Regardless, the cheapest shooting I know of is a 32-caliber squirrel rifle, especially with "scrounged" lead. I have 200 pounds given to me by a fellow who saved cable lead. Locating bullets for some guns is next to impossible. I have a 42-caliber flintlock that "likes" .425-inch round balls. I discovered a mould for it and now have an endless supply that would be difficult to come by commercially. Making lead projectiles is an enjoyable pastime, a calming enterprise combining fun with relaxation. It's a safe operation when the rules are followed. It can be dangerous when the rules are ignored. Additionally, there is a modicum of pride in casting bullets that create stingy groups on paper or put game on the table. Bullet casting is part of a shooter's testament to self-reliance, as well as his or her education. Did I already say it's also fun?

The Tools
Moulds

There are several companies offering moulds in dozens of different configurations and calibers, not only for muzzleloaders and blackpowder cartridge guns, but for modern arms as well, including slugs for shotgun shells. A glance into Lyman's catalogue shows conical moulds from 22- through 69-caliber, with round ball moulds running 36- to 75-caliber. Dixie Gun Works offers round ball moulds in a basic design, without sprue-cutters,

Original style moulds, such as this one offered by Pedersoli, were relatively simple, but at the same time entirely workable, even at the campfire, due to lead's comparatively lower melting temperature.

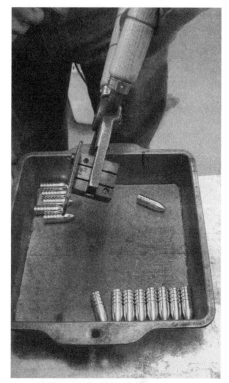

Bullets of many different styles can be turned out of moulds creating lead projectiles that serve many purposes, from plinking to elephant hunting. This Lyman bullet style is flat-point with grease grooves.

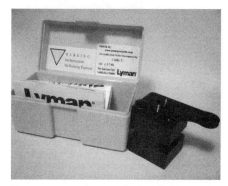

This is a currently-manufactured precision mould from Lyman. It's an iron mould, which means it takes a little time to heat up before casting a perfect bullet, but on the other hand, it continues to make many projectiles before overheating.

This Lyman mould is double cavity, so that it creates essentially twice as many bullets in almost the same time as a single cavity mould.

Looking into the double-cavity Lyman mould we see what the lead bullet will look like after casting.

There is almost no limit to the particular bullet configuration possible from a mould. Here is a hexagonal bullet for the Whitworth rifled musket.

in .310-inch to .850-inch diameters in increments of .001-inch. Dixie also has moulds for the 45-70, 50-70, and a host of projectiles from the Civil War era, such as the 52-caliber Sharps and Colt Root 56-caliber rifle. Rapine has special moulds for Cowboy Action Shooting for the 38-40 Winchester, 44-40 Winchester, and 45 Colt. RCBS has many moulds for sale. Lee Engineering also has a good list of moulds. Hoch is another source of moulds. The list goes on. (See Directory.)

These are single-cavity moulds, but double-cavity and multiple-cavity moulds are also available. Prices vary widely. Currently, Lyman sells its excellent life-long moulds for about 65 dollars—standard rifle bullets from 22- through 50-caliber. Pistol moulds go for the same with calibers running 30 to 50, the latter for the 500 S&W. A particularly interesting pistol mould is 44-caliber, hollow-point, 250-grains—#429640.

I would take on deer-sized game at closer ranges with the Colt Lightning 45 Colt shooting these cast bullets. And I would so with confidence. Whitworth and Volunteer bullet moulds run 450 and 475 grains weight. Plains bullets and Minies, as well as Maxi-balls, go 50- to 69-caliber. Some Lyman moulds are double-cavity—same price. A four-cavity mould runs more, the better part of a hundred bucks. There are more specialty moulds offered than ever, including a Whitworth that creates a 575-grain bullet, but expect to pay a lot more for it since the bullet is hexagonal at 1 3/8-inches in length. Dixie Gun Works continues to offer special moulds. The Shiloh Sharps Company has many moulds that are ideal for Sharps rifles. Meanwhile, Lee Precision Engineering has REAL moulds in several bullets and weights; Rapine also offers a long list of moulds, as does the NEI Company. I have a Lyman Parker Rifle Bullet mould that produces a 565-grain shallow cavity base Minie bullets for 58-caliber muskets with 1:48 twist. There are also moulds for high-profile bullets, such as Lyman's #410660, which makes a 40-caliber 385-grain bullet. RCBS also has a fine line of bullet moulds in various sizes.

Mould Handles

Some mould handles are integral to the mould block itself, such as the Kentucky-style brass moulds from Dixie Gun Works. The authentic scissors-style handle contains a sprue-cutter. (Remember that the sprue is the "tail" left on the bullet after casting.) Other mould blocks require separate handles, which save the bullet caster a few bucks, since the handles transfer to different blocks.

Bullet Sizing Dies

Various bullet sizing dies are available, such as those from RCBS and Lyman, which are precision-manufactured to hold a +/- .002-inch diameter variance with hand-polished interiors. Various bullet-sizing dies "true up" cast lead bullets, where necessary. The lead bullet is forced through the die, reducing its diameter slightly to conform to the exact interior dimensions of the unit.

Basic Melting Pot

The simple melting pot is ideal for smaller amounts of lead, and of course is essential at the campfire where there is no electrical plug-in for a furnace. Lyman's basic melting pot holds 10 pounds of lead. Since lead melts at 621 degrees Fahrenheit, this little pot is ideal on coals.

Basic Plug-In Melting Pot

This electric lead melting pot has no temperature control gauge. But it does offer the convenience of plugging into an outlet in a location that has good ventilation along with shelter from any form of moisture, especially rain, which can cause molten lead to spatter out of the pot.

Furnace

The Lee Production Furnace is a good example because it incorporates temperature control. The RCBS Pro-Melt Furnace is for high temperature casting. I have a Lyman electric furnace resting by a Lyman Lube Sizer situated

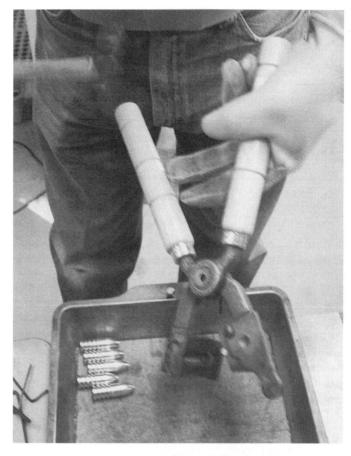

These Lyman mould handles accept various mould blocks, rather than being attached to any one mould.

After a bullet is moulded, it can be run into a sizing die for further perfection.

The full-fledged furnace is ideal for making large quantities of high-quality bullets. This one is from Lyman and it has a large capacity. This furnace has a heating platform to bring the mould to casting temperatures faster.

Some form of dipper or ladle is necessary to transport molten lead from pot or furnace to mould.

The casting thermometer takes all guesswork out of molten lead or lead alloy.

Dipper/Ladle

While the terms are sometimes interchanged, a dipper has a partially closed bowl, while a ladle is more spoon-like. The dipper also has a pouring spout. Lyman's wooden handled, cast-iron long-stem dipper holds about a half-ounce of molten lead. While this capacity is good for making extremely heavy bullets, it is has another important trait—forcing molten lead deeply into the cavity mould, which discourages air pockets.

Casting Thermometer

Lyman's casting thermometer ranges from 200 to 1,000 degrees, ideal for testing the temperature of molten lead in a pot, also useful for checking the actual temperature of molten lead in a furnace.

Ingot Mould

Sort of like a Jell-O mould, ingots accept molten lead that hardens into a specific shape for storage. Lyman's one-pound ingot mould has a 30-degree draft, so cooled lead ingots are easily removed.

Spoon

A large kitchen tablespoon is useful in skimming dross (foreign materials) from the surface of molten lead in pot or furnace. Must be used with gloves at all times.

Gloves, Eye Protection, Clothing

Gloves and goggles are obvious safety devices for casting bullets, gloves

near both Lyman and Hornady special blackpowder measures. This furnace has an industrial-grade thermostat coupled to a remote sensor on the bottom of the reservoir. It's 800 watts and holds 22 pounds of lead, which is especially handy when making tin/lead alloy blackpowder cartridge bullets. Lyman's Mag 20 Electric furnace is an-

other heavy-duty 800-watt unit with bottom-pour valve system designed for casting a great many excellent projectiles each session. Lyman also has a Magdipper Casting Furnace that uses a ladle, as well as a Mini-Mag Furnace with 10-pound capacity. These various "lead-melters" offer a variety of price levels to choose from.

to protect hands, goggles to ensure against a splash of molten lead. Less obvious are clothing—shoes, not open sandals, long pants, not shorts, shirts that cover the arms.

Moulder's Hammer

Not entirely necessary, because a hardwood dowel also does the job, a moulder's hammer has a head of nylon or other material that will not damage a mould. It's useful in knocking the hinged sprue plate aside to set the finished bullet free. A moulder's hammer may also have a pick end with a sharp point for encouraging a stuck cast bullet free. Having to use the pick end usually spoils the bullet, but it was stuck and had to be freed, so no big loss.

Bullet Casting Kit

Lyman's Master Casting Kit offers a good way to get started in bullet making. It includes the *Lyman Cast Bullet Handbook*, a title that is packed with information on bullet-making.

Bullet/Powder Scale

A bullet/powder scale is important for weighing finished cast bullets to the tenth of a grain weight for test purposes. Weighing finished bullets instantly ferrets out the light ones with air pockets.

Supplies

Blackpowder cartridge bullets require special lubes. The most comprehensive listing of lubricants for shooting that I have run across is the meticulous compilation by Ralph Schneider titled "Cast Bullet Lubricants, The Lube List," which Mr. Schneider updated recently. The Schneider list runs 32 pages. While lubes are for bullets, there are so-called "fluxing" products that help "purify" molten lead. Paraffin is one. Paraffin can be purchased at grocery stores. There are also commercial lead-purifiers formulated to separate dirt and other unwanted products from molten lead. They do not remove tin, antimony, zinc, or bismuth. But they do encourage these, along with unwanted materials, to separate from molten lead. Lead for muzzleloaders is cleaned and left as "pure." Lead for blackpowder cartridge guns is prepared as an alloy, such as lead/tin, making a harder projectile.

Lead for Bullet Casting

If scientists set out to create a near-perfect metal for muzzleloaders, blackpowder cartridge guns, as well as modern firearms (for certain applications), they would be hard pressed to come up with anything better than lead, its high points noted at the beginning of this chapter. Lead has been wedded to silver, even, for very hard silver-enriched bullets. Of course, this was not accomplished over a campfire. I saw a sliver-enriched bullet recovered from the carcass of a Cape buffalo bull, one of the toughest animals on any continent. The bullet had penetrated deeply while retaining over 85 percent of its original weight. Blackpowder cartridge bullets can be cast as alloy such as lead/tin in various ratios. One example is 30 parts lead to one part tin (1:30 ratio). Other ratios are 1:20 and 1:16. A 1:16 ratio bullet proved excellent in a 38-55 Remington Rolling Block replica rifle that I shoot often. Harder cast bullets fare well with full-throttle loads, being better suited to withstand the blast furnace of powder combustion as well as a ride through the bore faster than the speed of sound.

Purifying Lead for Bullet Casting

The process of fluxing combines various metals within the lead to form an alloy, as with tin and lead, antimony and lead, or both of these metals (and

A bullet/powder scale is used to check actual weight of the finished product. This ensures uniformity. Bullets that are significantly lighter in weight than the average have pockets of air or impurities.

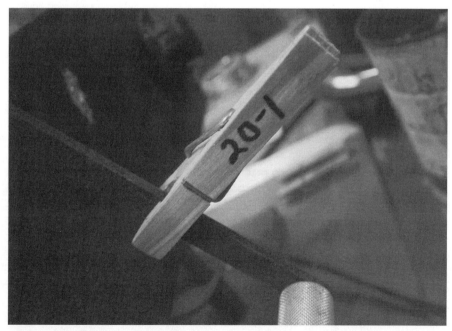

Lead can be separated out as to quality and alloy. This clothespin is used to attach to the lead intended for casting a 20:1 alloy of lead to tin.

others) added to lead. Purifying lead for the purpose of making round or conical bullets is another matter, however. The goal is taking out everything but the lead. It is impossible to have 100-percent pure lead; however, nearly pure lead can be obtained. The first step is melting the lead supply in a pot or furnace. Although lead turns from solid to liquid state at only 621 degrees Fahrenheit, lead for purifying should be heated to about 800 degrees Fahrenheit by setting the temperature gauge on the furnace or checking with a thermometer for pot-melted lead. Temperature at this level will not melt harder metals within the lead, but it will promote their release. And since these metals are lighter than lead, they naturally flow to the top of the pot or furnace, which is perfect, because on the surface they can be skimmed away using that large tablespoon. The spoon, held in a gloved hand for protection, skims off the dross (floating impurities) on the surface of the lead. Dross is set aside in a metal container for discarding. It can be very hot, and will burn a workbench top.

Add a fluxing agent, in spite of the fact that this is not truly a fluxing operation. One choice is with a small chunk of paraffin (wax) about the size of a thumbnail dropped directly into the molten lead (gloves on to protect hands). This makes considerable smoke, which can be subdued with a lighted match. Be careful as flames rise above the molten lead. Use a long-handled ladle or spoon with a long shank. The flames can also cause a burn to the face, so it's vital that the caster keep his body back from the molten lead at all times, rather than leaning over the pot or furnace. Furthermore, while casting is always conducted with plenty of ventilation, there is no reason to breathe in the fumes coming from molten lead. In place of paraffin, commercial caster's flux may be used, following the directions on the container exactly. I find this better than paraffin, especially Marvelux from Brownells. Marvelux is so effective that it's best used sparingly.

Here, Marvelux fluxing agent is added to the molten lead. A saltshaker is used because so little Marvelux is required to do the job. Note gloved hand. Gloves are essential in bullet casting.

Cleaning lead for all bullets is important, and that includes bullets that will be cast as an alloy. Impurities rise to the surface.

Here, molten lead is introduced into the mould, the ladle retained in place for a few seconds to give the lead a chance to fill the mould fully.

After a little tap on the hinge pin with a caster's hammer, the sprue plate is turned aside so the bullet can be released from the mould.

Tip: put Marvelux in a saltshaker with rice. The rice prevents Marvelux from caking up. But the rice kernels will not pass through the holes in the saltshaker. Then just shake a little bit into the molten lead for the cleaning/fluxing process. At this point, most impurities in the lead have been skimmed away with the spoon or ladle. There will be minute traces of tin, antimony, or other heavier metals within the lead, but not enough to harden the product greatly. The lead is now ready to cast muzzleloader bullets. For blackpowder cartridge bullets, the addition of tin in the proper amount is called for, fluxing this time to *combine* tin with lead into an alloy.

A round or conical bullet of pure lead is important for muzzleloaders because it upsets well in the bore—obturation once again. Even the round ball surrounded by a patch obturates to some degree, important for a better relation to the patch, the patch in turn translating the rotational value of the rifling to the ball to spin it. A Minie, or any bullet with a hollow base, obviously must expand or the shank will not engage the rifling, in which case there is no rotation. Maxi bullets also shoot best in pure lead because they engrave well when seated and they also obturate nicely. So pure lead is best for both of these muzzleloader bullets to take up some windage in the bore. Lead alloy, however, is generally right for blackpowder cartridge guns because the bullet-to-bore relationship is very different. Even so, alloys are best made by starting with pure lead. So cleaning lead for alloy bullets remains important. Mould lead into one-pound ingots to make ratios easier. Consider a 1:20 alloy: 20 one-pound ingots of lead join one pound of tin. Or a half-pound of tin joins 10 one-pound ingots of lead. For a 1:30 ratio, a half-pound of tin is fluxed into 15 one-pounds of lead ingots. Any ratio is possible, including the 1:16 some blackpowder cartridge shooters prefer. A source of tin can be found in the Yellow Pages of the phone book under metals, oftentimes sold in handy one-pound units.

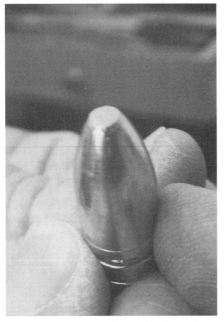

A beautiful bullet cast by the blackpowder shooter himself or herself.

Sizing a finished lead bullet.

Casting Temperatures

Experimenting with various lead temperatures is useful. Larger projectile moulds may require a little hotter temperature than smaller bullet moulds. Also, the type of mould makes a difference, aluminum blocks heating up faster than cast-iron blocks. The good news is that if a bullet comes out poorly, it can be set aside and then returned to the pot for recasting. Also, conicals may require a little higher lead temperature than round balls, especially when they have grease grooves that must be fully formed. When lead is too hot, a frosty-looking bullet is produced, rather than one with proper smooth skin. Lead that is too cold makes an incomplete or wrinkled bullet. As one example only, a lead temperature of 850 degrees formed good bullets from a Lyman mould for a 500-grain 45-caliber bullet. The goal is a fully formed bullet, free of air pockets, with a smooth shiny silver surface. The projectile must also weigh right on the money. A perfect bullet will not fall from the mould every time, but creating 50 to 100 good bullets in a session can be expected.

Turning Molten Lead Into Bullets

Purified lead brought to the right operating temperature is now ready to flow into the mould like water, quickly hardening into the shape of the mould's interior cavity. A ladle, dipper, or pour spout on a furnace introduces the molten lead into the mould. Allowing lead to fully flow into the mould cavity works best. Moulds go 'way back in time. The Ice Man's copper axe, noted earlier, had to be formed in a mould, perhaps of wood or soapstone. But soft moulds do not produce perfect missiles because cavity dimensions change as they heat up, just as telephone lines grow longer in summer and shorter in winter due to temperature variation. Furthermore, today's shooters and hunters expect a great deal from their muzzleloaders and blackpowder cartridge guns. Whereas an imperfect bullet, as long as it was sufficiently accurate to take game, may have pleased an early outdoorsman, it is not acceptable today. Fortunately, contemporary iron and aluminum moulds make projectiles of extremely close tolerances.

As with all other aspects of shooting, making bullets requires consistency, the end result being a round or conical bullet possessing great uniformity. Singly, the individual bullet must be precise. Collectively, all bullets in the run must fit into the group, varying very little from one projectile to the next. This sort of reliability is not difficult to come by when bullets are cast correctly from purified lead or proper alloy at the right temperature in good moulds. Of course, visual inspection alone won't prove the worth of a bullet, and spinners from the world of benchrest shooting are set aside as well. The bullet must be weighed to ensure gyroscopic perfection in order to spin on its axis—in other words, no lopsidedness due to air pockets. Rotation helps distribute discrepancies, but even rapid spinning on its axis will not overcome a bad bullet. It will not group if it has air pockets, or traces of heavier metals running through it haphazardly, rather than homogenously as is the case with a well-produced alloy missile.

Sources of Lead

Lead purchased from a plumbing supply house or builder's mart can be expensive. That is why blackpowder shooters spend time searching for *plumbum* in many different places. Old buildings sometimes give up lead that is associated with pipes. Telephone cable sheathing is supposed to be 98 percent pure, so it makes a great source of bullet lead when it can be found and bargained for. Tire weights are chiefly lead, but they must be melted down and purified to remove other metals. Lead seals from moneybags and other uses, such as on railroad car doors, are also almost pure. However, even if lead is purchased, bullet casting is still a bargain. A pound makes about 40 50-caliber round balls or 30 54-caliber spheres. Big bullets require more metal, of course, but even a 500-gain conical goes 14 to the pound. Smallbores are much more economical to cast. The little 32-caliber squirrel rifle shoots 45-grain bullets at 155 to the pound. That's a good return for a pound of galena.

Testing Round Ball Integrity

Collect cast round balls in a container. Set up your bullet/powder scale. Measure your round bullet with a micrometer. Consider a 50-caliber round ball "miked out" at .490-inch diameter. Cube the diameter. So .490 times .490 times .490 equals 0.117649. Multiply this by a constant—.5236, which comes out 0.6101164. Multiply again by 2,873.5, the weight of one cubic inch of pure lead, which results in 177.010520625. Forget all the numbers after the decimal and you have 177-grains weight. Now set up your bullet/powder scale and weigh each cast round ball from the run that you just finished. Here is a ball that goes 177-grains weight. Perfect. Another, and another, and another, and then one that weighs out at 168.7 grains. No good. Put it back in the pot for remelting. It's that simple to prove the proper weight of a round ball that is supposed to be cast in pure lead. You may end up slightly off the mark due to minor impurities in the lead. That's OK, as long as the bullets run the same weight one to another. For cast conical bullets you can skip any formula. Simply make your best batch of projectiles. Weigh them all. Toss out the ones that don't match up with the rest.

Be Safe

As with all aspects of shooting, there is only one way to cast bullets—the safe way. Accidents can happen. They are part of life. Also, equipment can be faulty. If a product, be it a gun or a car tire, fails through faulty design or other problem, that's not the user's fault. Casting is safer, statistically, than taking a bath, but a person can slip in the tub, and a bullet maker can burn a hole in his toe.

Safety Rules for Casting Bullets

1. Cast bullets only in good ventilation. Lead fumes can be harmful. The NRA conducted tests with a Mine Safety Appliance Company device hanging directly over molten lead to detect lead dust and fumes. Only trace amounts were discovered. However, concerning lead pollution, the NRA concluded, "A maker and user of bullets possibly can be poisoned by lead, under sufficiently extraordinary exposure. This can hardly exist for the individual casting bullets on a scale for his own use, with reasonable ventilation and sanitation." *Always cast bullets in a well-ventilated area only, never in closed quarters.*

2. Along with casting bullets in a safe environment of good ventilation, ensure that the source of heat does not produce carbon monoxide. Melting lead with a camp stove, for example, requires good ventilation. Carbon monoxide is a colorless, odorless, tasteless gas, and therefore can be very difficult to detect. Headaches, nausea, and dizziness may be signs of impending carbon monoxide poisoning.

3. Molten lead must never be exposed to water. Bullet casting on a porch is all right if there is a good roof overhead. Should it begin to rain, all bullet casting must come to a halt. Water landing in molten lead can create a tremendous rush of steam capable of blowing lead right out of the pot or furnace and into the air.

4. Bullets must be cast in a fire-safe area, preferably with a cement floor, not over wood or other combustible materials. Spilled molten lead is obviously very hot, perhaps 850 degrees Fahrenheit or hotter.

5. Only cast bullets in a private area where there is no human traffic, especially children who could run into the pot or furnace, spilling its molten contents.

6. Safety glasses are a must for all bullet casting.

7. Long pants—never shorts—are imperative when casting bullets. Hot lead may still burn a clothed leg, but having a barrier between molten metal and skin is highly important.

8. Shoes, not moccasins or sandals, are worn to protect the feet from molten lead.

9. A long-sleeved shirt, not short-sleeved, offers a little barrier between hot lead and flesh. Once again, a little protection is far better than none at all.

10. Gloves are absolutely essential at all times.

11. Casting bullets for hours on end is a mistake. Casting demands full attention and a tired person is not always fully attentive. Also, there's no point hovering over the pot or furnace. Stand back. Give it some room. The human body can take on lead through fumes, and once it does, getting rid of it can be slow. There is also a cumulative effect, as with carbon monoxide.

12. Do not touch freshly-made bullets. They are very hot.

Closing Tips

1. Competitive shooters, such as those involved in blackpowder cartridge silhouette shooting, may wish to purchase pure lead, which is available with a rating over 99 percent free of heavier metals.

2. While paraffin has been known to serve as a fluxing agent for making blackpowder bullets for competition, the shooter may wish to purchase a commercial product. Follow instructions.

3. When making alloy bullets, rely on a fairly hot product, somewhere in the 800-degree Fahrenheit range.

4. Ensure that as lead alloy is used up and the metal supply is replenished, the melting furnace receives the proper ratio of tin to lead for good blackpowder cartridge bullets.

5. Even though lead has been purified for making muzzleloader bullets, not blackpowder cartridge projectiles, skimming the surface of the molten lead from time to time during the casting process is worthwhile.

6. Iron moulds are more rugged than aluminum moulds. They take longer to heat up, but also make more bullets before getting too hot. Aluminum moulds heat up fast, good bullets showing up quickly. Aluminum moulds can also last indefinitely with proper treatment. They cool down quickly when overheated, so bullet casting can continue. Both types are worthy choices.

7. Multiple-cavity moulds create more bullets faster than single-cavity moulds, but the latter are fine for most bullet-making.

8. Moulds must be properly broken in if they are to make good bullets and last a long time. Break-in instructions come with the mould, also rules for best care.

9. Heating the mould—dip end of aluminum mould block into molten lead to warm it. Rest an iron mould on the warming plate if the furnace has one. Also run bullets to warm an iron mould.

10. Managing a dipper or ladle begins with filling it quite full of molten lead. With one continuous motion, put the spout up against the chamfered hole in the mould. Hold the spout in place firmly, and then tip the mould downward so molten lead flows freely into the mould. Hold the dipper for a second, allowing the mould cavity to fill fully. This practice reduces air pockets in the finished product.

11. If a fin appears around the base of the bullet, this indicates the sprue plate has probably warped. Lubricating the sprue plate joint can usually prevent this problem. A machinist may be able to fix a warped sprue plate, or it may have to be replaced with a new one.

12. Go gently with the moulder's hammer or hardwood dowel in knocking the sprue plate aside.

13. Drop freshly-cast bullets onto soft surfaces, such as piece of cardboard or lint-free cloth—not a metal plate.

14. Along with weighing cast bullets on a powder/bullet scale, consider checking their diameters with a micrometer to see that they are coming out the right size.

15. There are several good books on casting bullets, each one bringing the shooter closer to perfecting this hobby within a hobby.

What to Expect

Near perfection is not too much to ask in a cast bullet, round or conical, for muzzleloader or blackpowder cartridge gun. Home-cast bullets should be as good as commercial lead projectiles of the same caliber and type, absolutely uniform and accurate. If cast bullets are not top rate, the causes are probably impure lead, the wrong casting temperature or sometimes the technique, such as failing to truly fill the mould cavity with molten lead. Millions of cast bullets are prepared every year by shooters enjoying every phase of the operation, including what could be the best part, walking up to a target with a close group, or a game animal destined to grace the table that was taken with a projectile made by the blackpowder marksman/hunter himself.

There is special enjoyment in shooting bullets cast by the shooter.

RIFLED MUSKET RANGE AND POWER

They may look overly long and slightly clumsy to handle, but the barrel length produces a long sight radius for a clear sight picture, and the rifles are not overly heavy. The rifled musket, in fact, handles well.

One of the most useful long arms of any era is the musket. Muskets were generally considered smoothbore military long guns. One American dictionary calls them an "archaic smoothbore," another "a smoothbore long-barreled firearm." The Oxford English Dictionary labels the musket an "early form of hand firearm." Origin of the word comes from "fledged arrow," fledged indicating an arrow with feathers. When the musket earned rifling, it became the "rifled musket." These blackpowder muzzleloaders deliver a deadly message downrange. The Whitworth rifled musket is capable of hitting a target at 1,000 yards and pro-

ducing consistent groups. Being military-oriented, muskets have another good quality—built-in *ruggedness* to keep the rifle intact under battlefield conditions that might wreck a daintier firearm. The term also applies to the Musketeers, as in the famous fictional "Three Musketeers." The Musketeers are from the period 1622 to 1786 when they served as the French Royal Body Guard. America had its Springfield Rifled Musket, the word "rifled" added to indicate: *not* a smoothbore. Today's rifled musket is mainly a replica copying a real piece from the past. The Navy Arms Company, dedicated to replicas, has a series of muskets in the lineup,

including the famous Whitworth, but also the Parker-Hale 1853 Three-Band Enfield, Parker-Hale 1861 Musketoon, and several others. I am a fan of the Parker-Hale Volunteer .451 for its allowance of heavy powder charge for good power and range.

Rifled muskets belie their appearance. They look heavy and clumsy. They are generally neither. While not lightweights, these long guns have good balance and handling characteristics. Why hunters have not figured this out in greater numbers I do not know. The Volunteer, for example, has a 32-inch barrel, the Whitworth a 36-inch barrel. Neither is unwieldy in the field, although both represent heavier examples of the breed, running about 9-1/2 to 10-1/2 pounds depending upon exact model. The carbines are much lighter, and of course shorter. The J.P. Murray 1862-1864 Cavalry Carbine wears a 23-inch barrel and weighs only 7 pounds, 9 ounces. In 58-caliber, its ideal for hunting game such as wild boar and deer in the brush. The Murray delivers a terrific blow with 500-grain bullets. However, even this big bore does not match the punch of the Volunteer with its 130-grains volume FFg powder charge and heavy bullet at 1,500 fps. That's a muzzle energy close to 2,500 foot-pounds, more pasta than the 45-70 Government, which drives similar bullets at about 1,200 fps. The Volunteer's medium weight is a plus with heavy loads. The mass provides stability in the field, unlike flyweights that are sparrows to carry, but also flighty when it comes time to pull down on game, especially after a hunter has been hiking in the mountains and may be a little out of breath.

Caplocks and Flintlocks

Most of the currently offered rifled muskets are caplocks taking the tophat or English musket cap. (More about musket caps in Chapter 19.) There are, however, quite a number of military-type muskets in smoothbore, beginning with one of the most famous in history, the Brown Bess. The Brown Bess, the shoulder weapon Redcoats fired against the Colonials in the American Revolution, was also used in the French and Indian Wars. George Washington favored the smoothbore for its easier loading (no rifling) and faster cleaning (no rifling), which in turn meant more shots fired at the enemy. There is also a Brown Bess carbine, still 75-caliber, but with a 30-inch instead of 40-inch barrel. A real carbine, that! The 1763 Charleville musket, also a smoothbore, is "only" 69-caliber, while the 1803 Harpers Ferry of Lewis & Clark fame ran a mere 54-caliber (also smoothbore). The Marquis de Lafayette, incidentally, delivered 25,000 of the Charleville to General Washington.

Sights

Original rifled muskets had a variety of different sights, some not worthy of the name, being mere lumps of metal. The rifled musket of our main interest has *adjustable sights* with windage and elevation built in. The Whitworth I personally shoot a good deal has a hooded globe front sight. The hood is essential, because the globe, a

The percussion ignition quickly took over in the rifled musket. Caps made sense when rapid loading was crucial. Here, a shooter fixes a tophat (musket cap) on a rifled musket. It's easy to do because the nipple stands out.

little round ball, rests on a stem and the stem can be damaged in the field, rendering the rifle useless until the front sight is replaced. The front sight pedestal is drifted for windage. The back sight is open with a shallow U-shaped notch. A clear sight picture is possible, because the front globe does not optically fill the rear U-notch, leaving light on both sides for reference. The rear sight is adjusted for windage via a screw that attaches the sight plate firmly in place. Elevation adjustment is tremendous, the rear sight sliding in a rail. The body of the sight has elevator notches so that as the rear sight is moved in the rail, it makes contact with the notches in three numbered slots marked 1, 2, and 3; 1 being the lowest elevation, 3 the highest.

For super long-range shooting, the sliding bar is pulled upward, putting a second notch into position. With the rear sight flipped up, the muzzle of the rifle can be severely raised for distant

In essence, the Martini-Henry is a rifled musket and was chosen to represent sights. Here, the rear sight is relaxed. This offers a standard shallow rear sight notch to match up with a simple front sight.

The rear sight on the Martini-Henry, which was selected as a type of rifled musket for the purpose of showing sights, is here in the raised position for long-range shooting. While velocity with the rifled musket was quite low with a standard service powder charge, the heavy bullet had devastating impact at long range.

shots. In the raised position, the readings on the bar start at 5 and go up to 10. Other rifled muskets have very different sights, of course, since the Whitworth was not only a military musket, but also a target rifle. The Dixie C.S. "Richmond" musket, built originally after the Federal arsenal at Harpers Ferry was captured in April of 1861 and the equipment moved to a Confederate ordnance facility in Virginia, had a blade front sight with leaf-adjustable rear sight. The Zouave rifled musket wore a similar front sight, but the rear sight was blued steel with two flip-ups. The J.P. Murray Artillery Carbine has a brass blade front sight with a dovetailed open rear sight.

Calibers

The Whitworth and Volunteer are 45-caliber (.451-inch), while many other muskets are 58-caliber (.577-inch), such as the Zouave and Musketoon, the latter with its short 24-inch barrel. The 1853 Parker-Hale Three Band and 1858 Two Band are both 58 (.577-inch) caliber. Obviously, the thrust with these rifled muskets was large bore for big power. The Brown Bess musket is 75-caliber, firing a 12-gauge round ball. In shooting the Bess, I had on hand only .690-inch balls, but, well patched, these worked all right.

Bullets

The "regular" rifled muskets—Zouave, Musketoon, Mississippi Rifle of 1841—and many others, shoot Minie-type bullets, such as the 530-grain .577-inch Minie from Lyman mould #577611. They also handle Thompson/Center Maxi-Balls in 58-caliber. Rate of twist for these rifles is 1:48, which stabilizes the rather short missiles they shoot. (See Chapter 20 for twist information.) The Volunteer and Whitworth both carry 1:20 twist and are therefore geared for long 45-caliber bullets that carry well downrange. The Volunteer and Whitworth handle "standard lead conicals." Chapter 17 discusses this bullet type. Tests with Lyman's 490-grain

.457-inch bullet mould #457121 provided good accuracy in both rifles. While 58-caliber bullets are less streamlined with a lower ballistic coefficient (C), they pack a lot of weight with considerable penetration potential. Volunteer and Whitworth 45-caliber rifled muskets, on the other hand, shoots bullets that are as heavy as those fired in 58-caliber muskets, up to 600 grains and even more. As an example, the 58-caliber Dixie U.S. Model 1861 Springfield rifled musket (with 40-inch barrel, but only 8 pounds weight) normally shoots a Minie-type bullet that runs between 500 and 600 grains. Forty-five caliber bullets, being about the same weight as the 58-caliber bullets, are much longer per diameter, resulting in higher sectional density (SD).

The Historical Zouave Rifled Musket

Several companies, including Dixie, Navy Arms, and Pedersoli, offer rugged 58-caliber Zouave rifles. The Remington Arms Company made a good many of these rifles in the 19th century. The Zouave is bored 58-caliber. It has a blade front sight with two flip-ups. Some Zouaves have different sights. The barrel on my test rifle ran 32-1/2 inches, weight 9-1/2 pounds. Typically, the Zouave is another rugged rifled musket. A 530-grain Lyman Minie (mould #577611) left the muzzle at 1,100 fps with 80-grains volume FFg blackpowder. One company gave the 80-grain volume load as maximum, even though it produced less than 6,000 psi pressure. Pyrodex provided a surprisingly low 3,400 psi with 80-grains volume RS and a 315-grain Lyman Minie for a muzzle velocity just over 1,200 fps. Another company allowed 100-grains volume blackpowder or Pyrodex. Now the Zouave produced just shy of 1,400 fps with a pressure rating just over 5,000 psi. Don't find fault with varying pressure results. That's normal with different test conditions, and all pressures with the Zouave were low. As always, the big bullet must be taken into account. High KE energy figures are not possible with low velocity. The 100-grain volume load at 1,400 fps muzzle velocity reached only 1,371 foot-pounds with the 315-grain Minie. A 460-grain Minie with 100-grains volume GOEX FFg produced a shade less than 1,300 fps for an improved 1,727 foot-pounds. At close range, I would not hesitate to take on a moose with a 58-caliber Zouave. After all, original 30-30 ammo with a 160-grain bullet at 1,970 fps and less than 1,400 foot-pounds of muzzle energy put plenty of moose meat in camp. Coupled with the 58-caliber bullet and well over three-fourths of a short ton of muzzle energy, the Zouave is clearly big game-worthy.

The Zouave in History

The Zouaves were fighting men noted for their special uniforms as well as military ability. They wore what began as North African-style apparel, which became altered considerably over time. French fighters made up companies of Zouaves. Captain George B. McClellan, a U.S. Army observer in the Crimea, held the Zouave in great esteem. He influenced others to similar thinking and a Zouave-like soldier emerged in Eastern America. Eventually, there were several Zouave-type fighting groups in mid-19th century America. Both the North and South had Zouave units during the Civil War. To this day, the colorful outfits remain before the public as teams of

Civil War reenactors wear the Zouave uniforms. Historian Joe Bilby noted one Zouave uniform as "red fezzes with blue tassels, blue jackets trimmed in red, red shirts and sashes, blue and white pillow ticking baggy pants, blue and white horizontally striped hose and white gaiters." He also said, in his article "Zou-Zou-Zou-T I G R R R" for the Dixie Gun Works *Blackpowder Annual 1995*, that "guns carried by Zouaves did not differ from those of other volunteer regiments." Therefore, the Zouave name, generally attached to the Remington rifled musket of 1863, goes somewhat unfounded and mysterious. A 69-caliber smoothbore was more likely found among the Zouaves. "There is no evi-

The standard army load for a 58-caliber musket might be in the range of 60 grains volume. Even this load, which is on the low end, is game-worthy at close range. But the rifled musket is capable of much more. It can be loaded safely, in accordance with the maker's maximum load rule, to give a big bullet a healthy velocity of moose-taking proportion. On this shoot, everyone enjoyed firing a rifled musket—especially with the old army charge, which created only mild recoil.

dence," Bilby points out, "that any of the Zouaves were issued the colorful Remington Model 1863 or 'Zouave' rifle." So when the modern blackpowder shooter speaks of the Zouave, he means the rifle style described above, and not the soldier.

45-Caliber vs. 58-Caliber

The two major calibers for rifled muskets are different not only in size, but also configuration, and therefore sectional density (SD) and ballistic coefficient (C). SD and C have little meaning at close range. The late Val Forgett II of the Navy Arms Company managed to take all manner of African game, including elephant, with a 58-caliber rifled musket, the bullet penetrating deeply in spite of comparatively low SD and C. In timber and brush country, where shots are close on deer, wild boar, even elk and moose, the 58, by sheer virtue of bullet mass, can get the job done, especially with decent powder charges resulting in 1,400 to 1,500 fps. A 58-caliber missile makes an impressive wound channel. Many completely penetrated Sam's Bullet Box, pushing through water balloons, clay blocks, even wet newspapers and large "wish books" from Sears and J. C. Penny.

The 45-caliber rifled musket marches to a different drummer. These are generally a little more refined than their larger-bore counterparts, and are more

And one more thing—the rugged rifled musket is plenty accurate for big-game hunting and can also be called upon to hit a target downrange with regularity—which makes it enjoyable to own.

accurate for longer-range shooting. The Volunteer and Whitworth Military Target Rifle are two prime examples of 45-caliber long-range rifled muskets. Either is a magnum in its own right, with apology for that over-used word. Lyman tests of the Volunteer matched ballistics appearing in *The Gun Digest Blackpowder Loading Manual*. They allowed 130 grains volume of blackpowder behind a bullet in the 475-grain to 490-grain range for a muzzle velocity of 1,500 fps, overpowering the 45-70 Government, also the 45-90 Winchester, and for that matter, some of the more impressive Sharps cartridges.

The Whitworth Rifled Musket

The Volunteer is interesting ballistically. But the Whitworth is more intriguing historically. It's called a target rifle because it was devised as a long-range instrument. Both the Blue and the Gray used Whitworths during our own Civil War to pick each other off at great distances. (See Chapter 48.) The Whitworth also achieved fame as a 1,000-yard match rifle and the replica version can still slap bullets through the bullseye at great range. Sir Joseph Whitworth, father of the rifle, was a master toolmaker. He was born in 1803 and died in 1887, in-between creating his special shoot-far rifle. Whitworth's claim to fame was a bore of hexagonal configuration, supposedly the voodoo that made close bullet groups. Bullets were cast to match the esoteric bore style. (Lyman has a hexagonal mould today.) My belief is that Sir Joseph's oddball rifling system was not entirely responsible for the rifle's accuracy. The Whitworth clustered bullets well because the firearm was carefully made with missiles properly stabilized by a 1:20 rate of twist. Bullets of high SD and C flew point-on all the way to a thousand yards because they had enough initial spin to keep them rotating on their axes. We know that bullets lose forward velocity rapidly due to the ravages of the atmosphere, while rotational velocity holds up over long range. So once the Whitworth bullet was stabilized, there was sufficient spin to keep it rotating on its axis at long range rather than yawing (wobbling) or keyholing (flipping over and over) before reaching a distant target. Something else that made the Whitworth rifled musket shoot true: good bullets. This factor is not often mentioned in the Whitworth story. But if bullets were not well cast, accuracy would have been nothing more than wishful thinking. Rotation or spin overcomes minor bullet eccentricity. But when a missile is lopsided, or its base is at the oblique, chances of good groups fall into the "slim to none" category. Without doubt, Whitworth bullets were well-made in the 19th century, just as they are today.

Ned Roberts, one of the principals behind the 257 Roberts cartridge, was a fan of the Whitworth. He tried various bullets, including a 530-grain design that provided excellent results at the target range. My replica Whitworth test rifle with .451-inch bore and 34-inch barrel weighed in at 9-1/2 pounds. It showed good accuracy with a number of well-cast bullets ranging from 480 to 550 grains. The Volunteer also gave excellent results in both power and accuracy. In my shooting both rifles used musket caps for ignition. Mine were RWS brand from Germany. We also have excellent musket caps from CCI. Musket caps produce good fire and positive ignition. In the hunting field, Whitworth and Volunteer rifles prove their mettle. Val Forgett II took a Wyoming antelope with a Whitworth, making an impressive shot at long range. Long sight radius and refined iron sights encourage solid bullet placement on deer-sized targets beyond 200 yards, shooter ability always playing its role. Power-wise, the Whitworth and Volunteer match up well with some of the "hot" in-lines of the day. They are also field-worthy, with integral swivels for a sling.

Big Game Effectiveness

The old cliché goes, "It's not what you him 'em with; it's where you hit 'em that counts." A bullet in the brisket, in other words, is not as effective as one in the boiler room. On the other hand, ballistics cannot be left out of the picture. Having seen game dropped with 45-caliber rifled muskets, it is clear to me that big solid lead bullets are capable of tremendous penetration. On the other hand, they do not upset (mushroom) greatly due to lower velocity and solid lead construction. And so the correct placement of these long lead missiles is *into* the shoulder rather than behind it, especially on thin-skinned deer-sized animals, which drop like a sack of wheat with one hit. Logic dictates that on larger animals, such as moose, bear or elk, a heavy lead bullet of good SD is deadly. Elmer Keith, Mr. Big Bore of his time, did quite well on elk, moose, and bear with 45-caliber blackpowder cartridge bullets traveling no faster than projectiles from 45-caliber rifled muskets. If anything, the nod goes to the musket, with the exception, of course, of smokeless powder loads that produce higher velocity than blackpowder muskets are capable of. Perhaps a bullet in the shoulder instead of chest region loses a little more meat. On the other hand, the game is put down swiftly. As a guide friend put it, "Better to lose five pounds of meat than a whole animal."

Legality of the Rifled Musket

Rifled muskets are replicas of old-time guns and as such should be allowed for any blackpowder-only primitive season. A problem with 45-caliber bullets, however, arises in Colorado, where the projectile cannot be more than twice the length of its diameter. Bullets in the 400- to 500-, even 600-grain range in 45-caliber are definitely more than twice as long as their diameter. The rule is not a safety measure, because in the same territory on hunts for the same animals magnum centerfire rifles are legal. And they certainly have a longer extreme range than blackpowder muskets. Furthermore, the rifled musket is a front-loader in every regard, firing only blackpowder, Pyrodex or Triple Seven, loaded from the front one bullet at a time.

Rifled Musket Triggers

Partly due to its military heritage, the rifled musket is a single-trigger firearm. A proper multiple-lever (double-set) trigger breaks cleaner than either Whitworth or Volunteer triggers. But both of these single-stage (non-set) triggers are acceptable for hunting. One example broke at 3-1/2 pounds, with minimal creep. Other rifled musket triggers were not that good. A gunsmith can improve these triggers, but tampering by the rest of us is not recommended, because judicious filing is called for and it would be easy to overdo metal removal, creating an unsafe situation.

Loads and Accuracy with Rifled Muskets

Since manufacturers and importers are responsible for maximum allowable powder charges for the guns they make or sell, shooters must abide by their rulings. Due to large bore size and consequent volume for powder gases to work in, pressures are modest in big-bore muskets and maximum loads must be honored. Powder charges are, as always, created volumetrically with an adjustable powder measure or charger. Accuracy variation between 70-, 80-, and 90-grain powder charges were impossible to detect with the Whitworth or the Volunteer, or other rifled muskets. When I see silhouette shooters consistently tagging the metallic cutouts that look like flyspecks in the distance, I feel confident that a good rifleman with an accurate rifled musket can count on taking game beyond 200 yards. Smoothbores, on the other hand, are not going to deliver pinpoint accuracy. See the next chapter for remarks. History shows that English archers could create tighter groups with arrows than Brown Bess shooters could with gunpowder and ball.

Light vs. Heavy Powder Charges

Light powder charges are OK for plinking and informal target shooting with rifled muskets, but they do not develop a great deal of big-game potency. For example, the only load I found for the 1861 Springfield rifle was 60 grains FFg, which reduced the rifle's ballistic effectiveness to popgun status even with a 58-caliber bullet. I think going for a velocity around the speed of sound for big-game hunting with a musket makes sense. The Musketoon shot a 505-grain Buffalo Bullet at 1,226 fps with 100-grains volume Pyrodex for a muzzle energy close to 1,700 foot-pounds, and remaining energy well over a half short ton at 100 yards. This is more than sufficient for deer.

Rifled Musket Big-Game Hunting Loads

Specifications

Rifle:	Navy Arms Whitworth Rifled Musket
Caliber:	45 (.451-inch)
Barrel:	36 inches
Twist:	1:20
Bullet:	490-grain Lyman cast, #457121
Load:	90 grains volume FFg (manufacturer's maximum recommendation)
Muzzle Velocity:	1,306 fps
Muzzle Energy:	1,856 foot-pounds
100-yard Velocity:	1,112 fps
100-yard Energy:	1,346 foot-pounds

Specifications

Rifle:	Navy Arms Volunteer Rifled Musket
Caliber:	45 (.451-inch)
Barrel:	32 inches
Twist:	1:20
Bullet:	490-grain Lyman cast, #457121
Load:	130 grains volume FFg (manufacturer's maximum recommendation)
Muzzle Velocity:	1,474 fps
Muzzle Energy:	2,365 foot-pounds
100-yard Velocity:	1,254 fps
100-yard Energy:	1,711 foot-pounds
Load:	130 grains volume Pyrodex RS
Muzzle Velocity:	1,514 fps
Muzzle Energy:	2,495 foot-pounds
100-yard Velocity:	1,290 fps
100-yard Energy:	1,811 foot-pounds

Specifications

Rifle:	**Navy Arms Zouave Rifled Musket**
Caliber:	58
Barrel:	32-1/2 inches
Twist:	1:48
Bullet:	530-grain .577-inch Minie, Lyman #577611
Load:	80 grains volume FFg (manufacturer's maximum recommendation)
Muzzle Velocity:	1,095 fps
Muzzle Energy:	1,411 foot-pounds
100-yard Velocity:	953 fps
100-yard Energy:	1,069 foot-pounds

Specifications

Rifle:	**Navy Arms Model 1841 Mississippi Rifled Musket**
Caliber:	58
Barrel:	33 inches
Twist:	1:48
Bullet:	530-grain .577-inch Minie, #577611
Load:	80 grains volume FFg (manufacturer's maximum recommendation)
Muzzle Velocity:	1,102 fps
Muzzle Energy:	1,430 foot-pounds
100-yard Velocity:	959 fps
100-yard Energy:	1,083 foot-pounds

Specifications

Rifle:	**Navy Arms JP Murray Artillery Carbine Rifled Musket**
Caliber:	58
Barrel:	23-1/2 inches
Twist:	1:48
Bullet:	530-grain .577-inch Minie, Lyman #577611
Load:	70 grains volume FFg (manufacturer's maximum recommendation)
Muzzle Velocity:	980 fps
Muzzle Energy:	1,131 foot-pounds
100-yard Velocity:	882 fps
100-yard Energy:	916 foot-pounds

Specifications

Rifle:	**Navy Arms 1853 3-Band Enfield Rifled Musket**
Caliber:	58
Barrel:	39 inches
Twist:	1:48
Bullet:	505-grain Buffalo Bullet Co.
Load:	100 grains volume Pyrodex RS
Muzzle Velocity:	1,274 fps
Muzzle Energy:	1,820 foot-pounds
100-yard Velocity:	1,101 fps
100-yard Energy:	1,360 foot-pounds

Specifications

Rifle:	Navy Arms Parker-Hale Musketoon Rifled Musket
Caliber:	58
Barrel:	24 inches
Twist:	1:48
Bullet:	505-grain Buffalo Bullet Co.
Load:	100-grains volume Pyrodex RS (71.0 grains weight, manufacturer's maximum recommendation)
Muzzle Velocity:	1,226 fps
Muzzle Energy:	1,686 foot-pounds
100-yard Velocity:	1,043 fps
100-yard Energy:	1,220 foot-pounds

Specifications

Rifle:	Dixie 1861 Springfield Musket
Caliber:	58
Barrel:	40 inches
Twist:	1:48
Bullet:	505-grain .577-inch cast bullet, Lyman #575213 (Note: although mould read 505 grains, actual bullet weight was 517 grains)
Load:	60 grains volume FFg (from literature; Dixie offered no maximum recommendation)
Muzzle Velocity:	753 fps
Muzzle Energy:	651 foot-pounds
100-yard Velocity:	676 fps
100-yard Energy:	525 foot-pounds

Specifications

Rifle:	Dixie Zouave Carbine
Caliber:	58
Barrel:	26 inches
Twist:	1:56
Bullet:	460-grain Minie, Lyman #575213-OS (Old Style)
Load:	100 grains volume Pyrodex RS
Muzzle Velocity:	1,064 fps
Muzzle Energy:	1,157 foot-pounds
100-yard Velocity:	883 fps
100-yard Energy:	797 foot-pounds

Specifications (for comparison purposes only)

Rifle:	Dixie Brown Bess Musket
Caliber:	75 (actually 74-caliber bore)
Barrel:	41-3/4 inches
Twist:	Smoothbore
Bullet:	494-grain .690-inch round ball
Load:	80-grains volume FFg (from literature; Dixie offered no manufacturer's maximum recommendation)
Muzzle Velocity:	809 fps
Muzzle Energy:	718 foot-pounds
100-yard Velocity:	680 fps
100-yard Energy:	507 foot-pounds

In Parting

The rifled musket is one more viable choice for blackpowder shooters, not only for big game, but also target and enjoyable plinking on inanimate targets in front of a dirt bank. While the blackpowder silhouette game is officially restricted to breechloaders, the Whitworth would hold its own in that match, while shorter rifled muskets are workable on big game with close shots, as in hunting wild boar or whitetails in thick cover. The Volunteer rifle and Whitworth are overall winners in brush, timber, or open country with their long bullets at decent muzzle velocities. The military developed rifled muskets to be blue-collar all the way: honest, hard working, at home in briar, bramble, cat claw jungle, black timber and thickets; reliable and unlikely to fail following a minor conflict with the terrain. Muskets will never threaten the tremendous popularity of the modern muzzleloader, but for some hunters in certain environments, these rugged rifles could be just about ideal.

SHOOTING WITHOUT RIFLING—
SMOOTHBORES

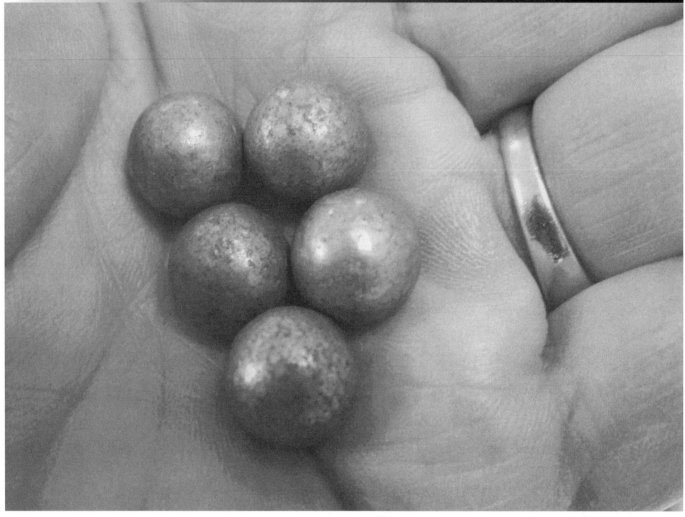

The smoothbore shoulder arm can carry multiple round balls (buckshot), a payload of birdshot, or a single round ball of significant mass. This is why the smoothbore is called the most versatile of all guns—especially as a survival firearm.

The writer said, "Probably the most functional of all guns is the smoothbore." I might not take it that far, but his point rides on high waves. "If I were forced to take just one survival gun, it would have to be the smoothbore," he continued. Probably so. The fellow reminded us that the smoothbore launches a single (large) projectile with sufficient close-range accuracy and pasta to down a moose. I agree with the next accolade the writer heaped on the smoothbore, that a blast of buckshot is good medicine in the thicket at close range. The author of the little piece concluded that the smoothbore was good for any upland game. Of course it is. Smoothbores dominated blackpowder shooting for centuries, remaining active long after rifled arms were available. That's because some shooters appreciated the fact that smoothbores were, and still are, easy to load and easy to clean, since there are no grooves to imprison fouling. Nineteenth-century ivory hunter William Cotton Oswell preferred his smoothbore for elephant hunting because it was fast to reload, especially when riding full gallop on his horse while pursuing pachyderms. Oswell was not forced to use a smoothbore; he died in 1893 in the era of rifled arms. S.W. Baker said Oswell was the first white man to show up in certain parts of South Africa. And when Oswell did show up, he was carrying his favorite "rifle," only it was a smoothbore made by Purdey.

Smoothbores for Really Big Game

Oswell's Purdey was a 10-gauge weighing 10 pounds charged with "six drachms of fine powder" according to Baker, who borrowed the piece from Oswell for an African hunt. The term *drachm* was synonymous with dram during this era, rather than the 60-grain

The smoothbore has been called the most versatile firearm ever developed: load it with shot for birds and small game, a large round ball for bigger game. This Pedersoli flintlock smoothbore is an example of the type.

apothecary weight. A drachm or dram equals 27.34 grains weight, so the load was about 164 grains of powder, give or take. Sometimes powder was simply tossed downbore as a "fistful." Baker wrote that he enjoyed great success with Oswell's smoothbore, reporting "There could not have been a better form of muzzle-loader than this No. 10 double-barrel smoothbore. It was very accurate at 50 yards. (*Big Game Shooting*, 1902.) Of course, "very accurate" must be qualified. Baker was hunting the largest four-footed animal in the world, tons and tons big, and at close-encounter range. Oswell preferred pre-patched round balls for his 10-bore, wrapping them in either "waxed kid" (leather) or linen. The "object of the smooth-bore was easy loading," said Baker. The pre-patched ball was rolled tightly in cloth or leather with any excess trimmed close with "metal scissors" so that the wrapping became part of the projectile. The powder charge was also pre-measured and carried in a paper cylinder, "the end of which could be bitten off," Baker noted. The whole package of powder, paper and all, was thrust downbore after the end was nipped off, followed by the pre-patched ball rammed home with a "powerful loading rod." Later on, Baker cursed smoothbores in print. He admired his mentor's to begin with, but found smoothbores lacking in long-range shooting compared to precision-made rifled long arms, which is what Baker carried for big-game hunting in Africa and Ceylon. In his book, *The Rifle and the Hound in Ceylon*, S.W. verbally cut the smoothbore to ribbons with an abrupt tongue-lashing: "Smooth bores I count for nothing, although I have frequently used them," said he.

Another well-known hunter of his era, J.H. Walsh, pen name "Stonehenge," also downplayed smoothbores for hunting. In his book, *Modern Sportsman's Gun & Rifle*, Walsh warned: "If, however, the six-inch circle at 50 yards could be depended on, I should be ready to admit that for large game it [a

The smoothbore musket, as used here on a Seneca run at a special blackpowder shoot, was a military weapon for a very long while and remained favored by some leaders, including George Washington, because of fast cleaning and easy loading.

Hitting a distant target was often considered mainly good luck with a smoothbore musket, but proper loading with good round balls provides more than luck. This target set up on a Seneca run is for smoothbore only—and the shooting has to be in a hurry. It will be hit.

This target group was made by a smoothbore musket on a Seneca run, which entails a time limit. The shooter must dash from one target post to the next, loading and then firing with his flintlock.

smoothbore] is a most useful weapon; and with this view I have repeatedly tested smooth-bores by various makers, but the trial has invariably ended in disappointment. Sometimes the first or second, but oftener further on in a short trial, a wild shot occurred, and of course this wild shot may be the one to cost a sportsman his life, when charged by any kind of large game." On the other hand, many military men of the past applauded the smoothbore. Our

own General George Washington often replaced rifled arms with muskets, believing the smoothbore a better tool for battle; easier to keep in repair; simpler, faster to reload for rapid fire, and it carried a fixed bayonet better than a rifle, or so the general believed.

The Brown Bess smoothbore musket remained Britain's first choice of arms for a very long time, firing a .753-inch ball (11-bore) with 70 grains of powder. General George Hanger, said to be the best shot in the British Army (he served with Hessian Jaegers during the Revolution), reported that "a soldier's musket, if not exceedingly ill-bored (as many of them are), will strike the figure of a man at eighty yards; it may even at 100," but he concluded that "firing at a man at 200 yards with a common musket, you may just as well fire at the moon." (*American Rifleman*, August 1947.) Notice that Hanger thought smoothbores were more manageable on the battlefield than rifles, but he did not consider them accurate. At the Battle of New Orleans, American rifled arms badly whipped British smoothbores. A number of American hunters continued to prefer smoothbores well into the era of rifled long arms. Many traveling in the early 1800s with Lewis and Clark into the Far West carried "fusils." A fusil was a smoothbore shoulder weapon, the word borrowed from the French meaning either steel or tinderbox. Sometimes, fusils were noted as "trade rifle quality" arms, meaning cheap guns used for bartering. They were mentioned in print as shoulder arms as far back as 1515 in French hunting ordinances, but were still in use during the 19th century in one form or another.

The Pacton Green Shoot

The historical pull of the smoothbore is magnetic. If these muskets were so worthless and inaccurate, why did they hang on for so long, even after rifled arms were widely available? Furthermore, their use continues today in modern times for a few special black-powder-only hunts where rifles are not

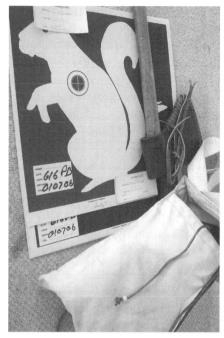

Targets for the Seneca Run with smoothbore musket are not miniscule, but they represent a practical size from real life shooting. When the hunter said, "We will be in meat with my smoothbore," he was right—if he knew how to load for accuracy.

Although shooting the smoothbore musket without a patch around the ball has been done, it's not the best idea partly because the ball could move back up the bore, causing a short-start condition. A tightly-fitted ball loaded by a shooter paying attention to the attitude of his or her muzzle might be a different story. Also, graphite-coated wads have been used successfully between round ball and powder charge in the smoothbore.

allowed. But do hunters packing the much-maligned smoothbore have a prayer of cleanly dropping a deer, even at woods ranges of only fifty or sixty yards? Even the longbow out-shot the common musket back in 1792 in a match on Pacton Green, Cumberland. The range was "over 100 yards" and the bowman placed sixteen arrows out of twenty in the target (size not given). Meanwhile, the best musketeer only hit the target twelve for twenty tries. As Karl Foster (of rifled slug fame) said in the *American Rifleman*, "Round balls in smooth barrels have lacked accuracy since guns were first made." (October 1936 issue.) In Scotland, 1803, soldiers practiced to meet Napoleon by firing their muskets. They were content when "every fifth or sixth shot is made to take place in a target of three feet diameter at the distance of 100 yards." (*American Rifleman*, August 1947.) When I presented this quotation to one of my buckskinner friends who had recently laid out a fat wad of greenbacks for a custom smoothbore, he replied, "Must have been damn poor shots." And he went on to tell me that if ever I was in need of venison steaks, just let him get within seventy-five yards of a buck and "We'll be in meat with my smoothbore." Then he added, "Of course, I stalk for close shots. You do remember stalking, don't you? That's where you get close before you shoot," he said sarcastically. Before turning to tests of my own, I continued leafing through pages in books and magazines for more information, running across a piece by Harry Root Merklee, a well-known authority on blackpowder arms. His article resided in the *Muzzle Blasts* magazine of April, 1961. Here is what Harry learned about accuracy with military smoothbore flintlock muskets:

Five men of military age assembled at a local range, each armed with a cal. 69 smooth-bore flintlock musket. These were rifles of the Napoleonic wars and were in first class condition. Except for minor details of construction, these

muskets were the same as those used during most of the flintlock period, which includes the American Revolution. The loads for these muskets varied according to their owner's preference but all used the same caliber round ball which would slide down the bore of its own weight; 'fall down' would be a better description, a rattling fit at any rate. No patch was used of any kind. Powder charges ranged from 3-1/2 to 5 drams of FFG powder. Regular shotgun wads of felt 3/8-inch thick were used over both powder and ball.

That was the shootout Mr. Merklee described. Note that no patch was used. I doubt that a patch would have made much difference with these muskets in this particular instance. A wad held the ball in place for safety, and while a patch can transfer the impetus of the rifling to the projectile, remember there was no rifling in these smoothbores. Here is what happened: Shooting from a sitting position, the above-mentioned marksmen kept most bullets within a 16-inch circle at 50 yards. Sights on these muskets were too crude to ask for much more in the first place, and trigger pull was referred to as "horrible." Powder charges ranged from 3.5 drams to 5 drams, being about 96 to 137 grains. Recoil proved bothersome with the latter from the sitting position, mainly due to the poorly designed stocks of these guns. The 69-caliber round balls would have weighed in the neighborhood of 500 grains, depending upon exact diameter. The round balls I shoot in my smoothbore 12-gauge are .690-inch in diameter and average 494 grains. A 16-inch group at 50 yards is a poor showing, but all shooting was done sitting, not from a bench. What could be accomplished under slightly more favorable circumstances? I contended, along with many others, that I could "live off the land" for a while with a smoothbore muzzleloader. But would shooting one for accuracy make me eat crow?

Working with the Shotgun

My first attempt in getting a shotgun to print a group at 50 yards was frustrating. I needed a smoothbore for a special hunt, and the only one I had at the time was a double-barrel blackpowder shotgun. My bullet was round, .695-inch in diameter, 502 grains weight, patched for a tight bore fit. I had faith in the formidable chunk of lead—if I could deliver it to the proper zone on a buck. My initial load was 80-grains volume GOEX FFg for 907 fps. Pressure with this charge, in spite of the heavy bullet, was minimal (I checked it out with Lyman). So I immediately kicked the charge up to 100-grains volume FFg for 1,190 fps from the 28-inch barrels. Muzzle energy ran 1,579 foot-pounds. Power-wise, the shotgun firing a round ball was all right. But accuracy proved dismal. The shotgun wore no sights. That was a negative, but smoothbore muskets of long ago were usually bereft of proper sights, too, and history shows some success with those old guns. My goal was not lofty. I wanted to harvest a deer along the creek bottom in heavy cover. If I could consistently land those big round bullets into a one-foot square target at 40 paces, I would be mildly confident of cleanly taking a whitetail buck in the brush. The 12-gauge round ball had been tested in Sam's Bullet Box, penetrating a couple feet of media at 50 yards for a significant "wound channel" with the 100-grain charge. But I failed to keep all bullets inside that 12-inch target at only 40 yards. I can throw rocks that well.

Lousy accuracy was not the only problem. The left barrel had a penchant for dropping projectiles into the black at 40 paces with modest regularity, while the right barrel often sent its missiles completely off target, missing everything, including the target frame. I tried the old trick of filing the muzzles to regulate the barrels (make them shoot to the same point of impact). Cutting the inside edge of the right-hand muzzle brought the ball over slightly in point of impact, but nothing close to true. I gave up after the muzzle looked like a kid with a hacksaw attacked it. I almost concluded that expecting accuracy with a smoothbore was hopeless. But wait a minute, I told myself. A precisely cast round ball has no reason *not* to fly relatively well for a short distance, even when not spinning on its axis. The round balls I was shooting were not lopsided. A crude but not altogether worthless test is rolling round balls on a flat surface. High quality lead pills do not wobble or bounce. They take a fairly straight track. These balls tracked fine. Another thought: the ball's center of mass rotated on its axis the same as a conical with imperfections in the ball itself causing projectiles to leave the bore at a different angle of departure. Because matter in motion moves in a straight line, the "heavy" part of the projectile would determine the initial line of flight of the round ball. An imperfect ball would tend to travel on a tangent from the line of the axis. In

Any blackpowder shotgun from any era is a potential smoothbore musket. Just push down a patched round ball firm on the powder charge and you have it. This custom blackpowder shotgun could be loaded with a patched ball for deer-size game and larger.

other words, static imbalance would ruin accuracy in a lopsided round ball. These round bullets spun quite well, staying in one spot as they whirled. They were not lopsided.

So the test round balls were uniform, weighing the same from one to the next, and recall that they rolled and spun fine. If static imbalance (the actual precision of the projectile in terms of mass distribution) existed in those missiles of the past, the boys would be lucky to infrequently hit a 3-foot target at 100 paces. Close range "reasonable" accuracy potential in smoothbores hinged on good lead spheres. A sphere is less sensitive to rotational stabilization than a conical—obvious. W.W. Greener said, "Rifling, therefore, is of greater importance when a conical or elongated projectile is used than when the bullet is spherical" (from *The Gun*). The principle of rotating an elongated missile for stabilization was a phenomenon proved eons ago. There are even relics of crossbow bolts with grooves *intended* to create spiral motion in flight. The big ball had mass going for it. The greater the mass, the greater the inertia. The heavier the projectile, the less rotation on its axis necessary to stabilize it. And for big-game hunting with the smoothbore muzzleloader, missiles of *at least* 1/2-inch diameter prevailed. The .690-inch ball that fit the bores of most 12-gauge shotguns, for example, weighed 494 grains. My larger round bullets weighed 502 grains. Thompson/Center's 56-caliber round ball, tried in a smoothbore later, weighed 252 grains.

Ball Mass and Accuracy

A smaller diameter ball gains greater advantage from rifling than a larger ball. Or to reverse that, the larger ball flies truer than the smaller one when neither enjoys the benefit of rifling. This is because the larger bullet is inherently more stable. Further research brought Ezekiel Baker's work to light. You remember Zeke, the court ballistician who wrote gunnery treatises for His Majesty George IV. He said in his 11th edition

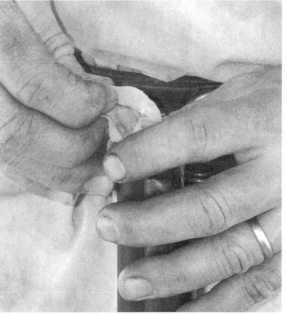

The Seneca Run is a good place to learn about smoothbore (flintlock for the one I attended) accuracy. Here, a normal patch is laid over the muzzle to be followed by a round ball, then all run home on the powder charge.

Starting the Seneca Run with a smoothbore flintlock musket—stand in the circle; set off a charge of FFFFg in the pan to prove there is no load downbore; ready, set, go—start loading up and be ready to head out to the first target.

The heavy round ball is capable of flying along a relatively straight path partly due to mass, partly due to homogeneous structure—all lead (only minor impurities) with no air pockets hiding inside. Here, Carl Constantino takes a shot at one of the targets along the run.

ball accuracy because it "averaged" the imperfections in the ball on a common axis. In other words, a slightly lopsided rotating ball traded imperfections along a common axis. Another way to say it: rifling twist equalizes lopsidedness on the axis through rotation. In my later tests, round ball projectiles were pre-sorted, which improved accuracy in the shotgun because the balls were fired in groups. In this way, round balls of the same weight flew together. But I remained unhappy. I knew there was something special about the 56-caliber round ball from Thompson/Center. I tested them for myself. They were uniform. Sorting was not necessary. The greatest variation in random sampling of 10 balls was only 0.9-grain. The heaviest in the string was 252.1 grains, the lightest 251.2. The micrometer gave an average diameter of .552-inch. If the T/C ball were pure lead, it would weigh 253 grains. Weighing proved that the T/C ball was precise, and it was not an alloy. Weighing did not prove homogeneity. But it did prove uniformity. What would happen if these good T/C round balls were fired from a well-made smoothbore like the Thompson/Center 56-caliber Renegade with adjustable rear sight? This smoothbore was created to give blackpowder hunters a reliable firearm where law or desire called for a non-rifled bore. Sights at last! Even with a good benchrest, reducing extraneous variables with shotgun bead "sights" resulted in spinning wheels. The T/C Renegade proved totally reliable, with100 percent ignition using CCI No. 11 caps. The test run included shooting 80 .550-inch T/C cast "265-grain" projectiles. (The weight written on the box.) Actually, these round balls averaged closer to .551-.552 average diameter, so nominal weight ran 252 grains.

of the work, "The Honorable Board of Ordnance being anxious to ascertain if rifling a large piece would have the same advantage over smooth barrels which rifles possess over muskets, and would be equally effective in carrying the ball, the experiment was tried at Woolrich [on May 15, 1806] with two wall-piece barrels of equal dimensions, one rifled, the other not rifled." The barrels were 4 feet, 6 inches long, each weighing 20 pounds. The projectiles were 5-gauge round balls. The advantage of the rifled piece was not nearly as pronounced as it had been with smaller round balls of 20-gauge size. What was not tried, was careful sorting of round balls in 20-gauge and smaller smoothbores. It was known that balls "created by pressure," swaged, in other words, were highly uniform. I found no old

tests in which smoothbores were fired with carefully weighed (sorted) round balls. In other words, would *balanced* spherical missiles make a difference in the smoothbore? Static stability would improve, which would in turn improve dynamic stability. So even though test round balls were uniform, what would happen if they were carefully sorted into specific groups by weight? Maybe I was onto something.

Things Get Better

Years later, Dr. F.W. Mann concluded, after thousands of experiments, that accuracy was mainly a matter of precision projectiles fired from precision barrels. The sphere, if perfect, should in theory fly true, even from a smoothbore. Of course, round ball *perfection* is not possible. Rifling vastly improved round

The Renegade with Sights

Loads came from the T/C manual, *Shooting Thompson/Center Black Powder Guns.* The load chain was: T/C cloth patch, a No. 11 cap, and Maxi-Lube. My personal tests were with three different patch types and three different lubes. The shooting patches were .005-inch, .010-inch, and .013-inch, the first two from Gunther Stifter's German supply house, the last of my own cut from pure Irish linen. The .010-patch proved best of the three, only because it loaded with comparative ease, while still providing a tight bore fit. While a patch is not a true gasket, as we know from Chapter 18, no cloth patch seals hot expanding powder gas behind the ball. But the patch remains highly valuable, as also pointed out in Chapter 18. It is normally best to have a tight ball/patch fit to detain the ball on the powder charge, and to maintain a consistent load pressure. My direct load pressure on the ramrod was 45-pounds with one tool I had on hand, later 35 pounds pressure was maintained by a special tool the late Chuck French built for me. I could detect no difference in the two pressures and have stuck with 35 pounds.

The lubes for the test were grease, cream, and liquid. All three worked equally well in terms of accuracy. Ini-

One factor in smoothbore musket shooting is the fact that sights are seldom highly refined. The front sight on this smoothbore musket is a perfect example of that fact. It is adequate for taking a reasonable sight picture, but not for pinpointing a spot on the target.

A lead sphere, if perfect, would fly fairly well along a specific path rather than wobbling off on a tangent. Subsequently, shooters began casting better round bullets. Carl Constantino rams a round ball home in preparation to fire on another target.

tially, shooting from the 50-yard bench found the balls striking the black with a 6-inch center-to-center group, good enough for deer in the thicket. Early 100-yard tests were purely blowing in the wind. Mainly, I credit the good sights on the T/C Renegade for the improvement. These sights were fine for hunting brush and timber country where closer shots are the rule. The hunter who wishes to mount a scope on his smoothbore has my blessings, as long as scopes are allowed on that special muzzleloader-only hunt. Changing powder charges, incidentally, did not affect accuracy, which remained the same with the three allowed powder charges for the Renegade: 80-, 90- and 100-grains volume FFg. In light of that fact, and with regard to gaining the highest power, only the 100-grain volume charge was retained. It developed a mere 6,000 LUP (Lead Units of Pressure) with comparatively mild recoil. Muzzle velocity averaged 1,366 fps. Thompson/Center data showed 1,300 fps on my Oehler chronograph. That is remarkably close.

Boom! A big round ball is on its way fired from the smooth bore of a flintlock musket. If the shooter can hit a reasonable size target at a typical hunting distance with the smoothbore, that certainly speaks to its usefulness in the game field.

For the nitpickers, the test site was at an altitude of 6,000 feet, temperature hovering around 85-degrees Fahrenheit. Muzzle energy of this load was 1,044 foot-pounds shooting the 252-grain ball. At 50 yards, the chronograph showed a retained velocity of 1,101 fps for the 56-caliber ball, with 50-yard energy of 678 foot-pounds. There is nothing wrong with that energy delivery, considering the size of the ball and its high penetration capability.

Trial with Buckshot

Being a former reader of comic books and admirer of the silver screen, I knew what buckshot could do. A blast from a shotgun loaded with multiple big pellets could mow down a whole row of trees in the forest, including any hapless deer in the path. To my dismay, however, I found that while the ultra-modern shotgun shell loaded with 0 and 00 was much deadlier than past

ammo, the same was not true of my side-by-side scattergun, which earned that title by scattering like casting seed in a farm field. That cowboy riding shotgun in the stagecoach would be a formidable foe up close, but if the bad guys started shooting from a distance, he'd better duck and pray. I had a little fun with this. (I can be devious at times.) A friend said my little excursions with buckshot were astray. I took a tape to our shooting site and measured my friend from armpit to armpit—19 inches. I cut a hunk of cardboard 19 by 19 square. Three shots at the square at 50 paces brought zero pellets on target. Once the range was reduced to 20 paces, however, things changed. I had to admit that the cowboy riding shotgun, if he had an opportunity that close, would repel those would-be robbers like ghost-scared kids in a haunted house. This was all I did with OO Buck, but it was enough to convince that in a tight

thicket a buck jumping 20 paces from the toe of my boot was venison.

The Upshot
of the Smoothbore Venture

Back to the single round ball, there's no doubt that it is deadly. I would not hesitate to place one behind the shoulder of a bull elk, knowing that the soft lead will flatten, but with mass continuing to ensure deep penetration. As for accuracy, it is achievable, but rifling was invented for a purpose and that purpose was spinning bullets, round or conical, to promote stabilization and downrange grouping. My smoothbore confidence falls with buckshot unless the target is quite close. Modern buckshot shells are decidedly better than ever, but stuffing big pellets into the muzzle of a smoothbore, be it shotgun, musket, whatever, makes for a short-range proposition. I tried buffers from BPI (see Directory) and results improved a little. Also bothersome is the fact that no single buckshot pellet is very powerful. The 00 buckshot I had on hand miked at 0.33-inch diameter. Taking the diameter to the third power times .5236 times 2,873.5 says that 00 buck runs 54.0 grains per pellet. In the modern shotshell pushing this pellet at 1,450 fps, energy runs 252 foot-pounds.

If several pellets strike home, that's not so bad, but if only one lands, that's not a lot of authority. And remember that even these faster-moving pellets from the modern shotgun won't be going 1,450 fps at 50 yards. Move that pellet down to perhaps 1,200 fps in the blackpowder smoothbore and energy runs only 173 foot-pounds per pellet—at the muzzle. At 50 yards, a 00 buck pellet starting at 1,200 fps is fortunate to chug along at 950, reducing delivered energy to 108 foot-pounds. In conclusion, it's safe to say that a blackpowder smoothbore throwing several 00 pellets would be deadly on deer-sized game at close range, while a single ball will drop much larger animals, but also within reasonable range. At the end of all shooting, the sighted Renegade smoothbore was keeping its round balls in an eight-inch group at 100 yards with sufficient remaining energy to drop a deer. In the meanwhile, there are steps that can be taken to improve round ball accuracy in the blackpowder smoothbore. Those steps are:

These targets were set up with smoothbore musket shooting (flintlock) in mind. If they were not reasonable to hit with a smoothbore, they would not be on the range.

Specific Accuracy Steps for Improved Round Ball Smoothbore Accuracy

Rules for Better Results

1. Sort round balls by weight, discarding those that do not fall within the norm for the batch. Round balls are capable of excellent uniformity in weight, whether commercial or home-cast.
2. Ensure a consistent powder charge by following a set procedure when using the powder measure. The smoothbore needs every break it can get in order to achieve hunting accuracy, and charge-for-charge consistency always promotes accuracy.
3. Use a buffer, such as hornet nest material, between the powder charge and the patched ball. This little step provides assurance of good patch condition, which in turn may promote accuracy in some cases.
4. Use good patches that take up the windage in the bore. Although the patch cannot translate the rotational value imparted by rifling because there is no rifling in the smoothbore, the patch is part of the load chain, and it must hold the round ball firmly on the powder charge with good pressure.
5. Be sure to wipe excess lube from the bore following loading. This step ensures the same bore condition from shot to shot, and such consistency never harms accuracy.
6. Review accuracy aspects as outlined in Chapter 23 to be certain that you've done all you can do to upgrade smoothbore accuracy.
7. Choose large calibers. Large round balls have more accuracy potential than small ones because they have more mass and tend to stay "on line" better. In short, they are more stable in flight, while smaller balls also have great accuracy potential with rifling spinning them.
8. If possible, have sights fitted to a smoothbore intended for big game hunting. No firearm can be expected to shoot well without proper sights.

Consistency is Vital

The ball-shooting smoothbore proved amply accurate for deer hunting in woods and timber with proper management. Previous shotgun clusters shrank to consistent 100-yard 8-inch groups with iron sights. A test with a scope sight mounted on the smoothbore revealed a modest increase in accuracy potential. At 50 yards, 3-inch center-to-center groups were common, but decent good groups at any range were possible only after using a careful loading process combined with precise missiles, such as those supplied for this test from Thompson/Center. Also, consistency of powder charge was maintained by over-filling the measure, tapping the barrel of the measure 10 times, then swiping off excess kernels of powder by swinging the funnel section of the measure into line with the barrel.

A buffer of hornet nest material between the patched ball and charge ensured patch integrity. Hornet nest material does not catch fire inside the bore, thus saving the patch from burnout. Moreover, a buffer between patch and charge serves to absorb excess lube that might attack the powder charge. Another step in the accuracy process was wiping the bore free of excess lube after the load was seated in the breech of the gun. Firing several groups with

Robert Rez seems satisfied with his Seneca Run performance, shooting his smoothbore flint-lock musket with round ball. Shooting the smoothbores is fun!

lander single-barrel 12-gauge shotgun with auxiliary rifled 50-caliber barrel. The smoothbore barrel was loaded with one .690-inch round patched ball using the sequence mentioned above with hornet nest buffer. This test centered on Pyrodex RS powder with a charge of 100 grains volume (70.5 grains weight for the particular lot of powder). Accuracy was more than acceptable, especially considering the shotgun bead as an aiming device instead of true sights with 6-inch center-to-center groups at 50 yards. Carefully loaded, the New Englander could be counted on to strike the chest area of a deer at close range, which was the goal all along. Also interesting was a test run with a Navy Arms Company Terry Texas Ranger 12-gauge shotgun. This little shotgun was offered with a 12-inch barrel. In the brush, it carried out of the way and came to shoulder rattlesnake-fast. Initially, one barrel was loaded with buckshot, the other a single patched .690-inch round ball. The buckshot load was disappointing, so both barrels were consequently loaded with a single patched round ball, one *only* to each bore, of course, as this is a full-weight projectile. Eighty-grains volume Fg blackpowder provided over 900 fps muzzle velocity. Not much for energy, but a good wallop at close range on deer-sized game.

There is no particular reason for a hunter to abandon his rifled muzzle-loader for a smoothbore. However, it was gratifying to learn that a smoothbore could be capable of closer-range hunting accuracy, while realistically not coming close to the accuracy provided by rifled arms. The last word: Where the law requires a smoothbore—or a blackpowder hunter, for his own reasons, chooses a smoothbore—effective close-range ball placement is totally possible on deer-sized game and larger.

the bore untouched (damp) after seating the ball and several groups with the bore wiped with a cleaning patch after seating the ball proved that the latter were always better in the particular test firearm, plus point of impact remained constant with the dry bore method of loading. Final sight-in was also accomplished with a lube-free bore.

Most interesting were follow-up tests with various smoothbore guns, including a Thompson/Center New Eng-

chapter

37 THE BIG THUMPERS

Energy transfer from high-velocity modern bullets and blackpowder bullets is not the same. However, the two blackpowder bullets shown here, flanked by streamlined 210-grain Sierra 30-caliber bullets, will provide a big "thump" on big game.

North American shooters and hunters label any cartridge of big game-taking authority a big bore, including the "deer rounds," such as the 30-30 Winchester. African hunters smile at this. A big bore on the Dark Continent is over 375-caliber, while the 375 H&H Magnum itself is generally considered a "medium." My own PH (professional hunter), Johan Wolvaardt, considers his 416 *the beginning* of the big bores. Big-bore handguns are generally thought of as 44-caliber and over, with the 50 S&W currently representing a true heavy in the revolver realm. Shotguns don't come into this picture because they are all big bore, and quite capable of taking big game, but they're classified as shotguns even when they pack a big cargo of 00 buckshot to ward off the claws of a leopard, or a heavy lead slug for big game. The bigbbore *rifle* is fuel for this campfire. But before going

there, a nod to the shotgun and pistol is required. It is commonplace in Africa to have a 12-gauge shotgun in a night-time leopard blind, the gun loaded with buckshot. And as for pistols, the larger-bores can be big thumpers, but not on the order of rifles.

Kinetic Energy

The big thumpers usually, but not always, generate considerable kinetic energy (KE). The "not always" part comes in when a rifled musket launches a 58-caliber lead bullet at about the speed of sound with a KE rating in the 1,600 foot-pounds energy range. Compare with a 375 H&H Magnum and a 270-grain bullet at 2,700 fps and the musket loses, since 375 energy for this load runs 4,372 foot-pounds. In turn, the 375 shrinks in the shadow of the 600 Nitro Express with a 900-grain bullet at 1,900

fps for 7,216 foot-pounds. But surprise of surprises, there were more powerful blackpowder ball-shooting rifles in the 19th century. One of these was built by William Moore and it tans the hide of the 600 Nitro Express. Moore's shoul-

By way of comparison, check out a 180-grain 30-caliber bullet taken from a big game animal. The bullet struck at very high velocity, which is not normally the same kind of energy transfer from a black-powder bullet.

Blackpowder guns relied upon to deliver a strong impact on the target always gravitated to big bores. This back-action lock smoothbore shot a round ball that weighed over 400 grains.

Talk about a big blackpowder thumper—how about a cannon or mortar? Only one thing provided the terrific impact that these deadly weapons possessed—huge projectiles.

der cannon was 2-bore, shoving a *half-pound* round ball from the muzzle at 1,500 fps for 17,491 foot-pounds KE. A 3,500-grain bullet, even at relatively low velocity, is a real Heller. Winchester brought out its 458 to match the ballistics of the highly-regarded 470 English rifle, which fired a 500-grain bullet (with standard loads) at about 2,150 fps. The 458 Winchester, although of smaller caliber, also pushed a 500-grain bullet at 2,150 fps in the factory load for 5,133 foot-pounds KE at the muzzle.

Smallbore Effectiveness

Good hunters who work for a sure shot chuckle at others who insist on high KE bullets for big game. An Arizona hunter of my acquaintance once had a dozen one-shot successes on deer with 12 shots. Now he has 20 in a row—all with a 22-250 Remington shooting a puny 50-grain bullet at 3,800 fps. A landowner wishing to rid his new ranch of a domestic elk herd offered the entire bunch for sale—but due to larger calibers being too loud, he said, all elk were dropped with a .22-250 rifle only. I hope they were headshots. A Montana hunter dropped several antelope in succession with a 17 Remington—a tiny 25-grain bullet starting at 4,100 fps. In spite of the high velocity of these two cartridges, both are totally outranked in KE by the big thumpers. The 22-250 develops 1,604 foot-pounds at the muzzle, while the 17 Remington earns only 933 foot-pounds! A game warden saddled with the duty of dispatching car-struck deer on the highway relies on a 220 Swift for the job. He said he never needed more than one shot. Good hunting practices and straight shooting can never be underrated. That's why smallbores are capable of doing big jobs. But they do not defy the laws of physics. Bigger bullets, even at modest velocities, throw dirt, powerwise, on small bullets, regardless of small bullet speed.

"Knockdown Power"

The term "knockdown power" has been around as long as hunters discussed guns around the pot-bellied stove at the old gun shop. Heavier bullets are generally credited with considerable knockdown ability. As an example, I had one fellow tell me he had switched to a 220-grain soft-point bullet in his 30-06, even for deer, because it had so much more knockdown power compared to 150- or 180-grain bullets. In light of the fact that the venerable gun writer, Jack O'Connor, reported shooting completely through a large grizzly bear with standard velocity factory ammo and 180-grain bullets, we must ask how much more penetration the 220-grain bullet fan wanted. Not to suggest that a 220-grain 30-caliber bullet is anything but deadly. It is, partially due to its mass, but also good sectional density (SD). By special permission, I was allowed to take a Cape buffalo in Africa with a 30-06 and I did choose a 220-grain bullet, in part for the mass, but also because it was a solid. The bullet, from 60 yards, penetrated over 40-inches of Cape buffalo bull. The bull fell dead as Pharaoh's whiskers. But it was hardly *knocked off it's* feet. Why was that? Because that does not happen even with an elephant rifle.

A big bullet, not even a 600-grain chunk of lead from a front-loader, does not knock an animal off its feet. It can look that way, and it doesn't take a 600-grain missile to create the illusion. I watched an antelope buck (through a 20X spotting scope) struck by a high-speed bullet from a 7mm Magnum. The animal flew right off its feet—at least it looked that way. But it was not knocked down. The antelope uncoiled its "springs" after being hit, launching itself into the air and over on its side in a cloud of dust. There is conjecture, and then there are the laws of physics. I'll take the latter. The law of physics says no animal is blown off its feet when struck with a bullet fired from a gun any of us would normally fire from the shoulder. This fact has been known for a long time. A book from 1903, *Mechanics for Engineers* by Maurer, Roark, and Washa, refuted the knockdown argument. Here is how the authors told it: "The forward momentum of any bullet can be no greater than the rearward momentum of the recoiling gun from which it was fired—actually it is less due to loss of forward momentum in powder gas—[so] the bullet exerts on the object it hits no greater *impulse* [italics mine] than the gun exerts on the shooter." (Page 270)

The authors of *Mechanics for Engineers* vote "No way!" when it comes to "knockdown power." A gun capable of truly tossing a big game animal through space would knock the shooter off his feet, too. The term "impulse" follows. It has a special meaning. A five-pound bucket of sand lifted one foot high represents five foot-pounds of work (energy). That same bucket can be set back down slowly or dropped to the floor with a thud. If the bucket is dropped it picks up speed (and momentum), hitting harder than if it had been returned to the ground slowly. That harder hit from dropping the bucket is called impulse. This sort of understanding is important, because blackpowder shooters need to know what their guns *cannot* do, as well as what they *can* do. Stories of taking a 58-caliber musket with 525-grain Minie ball and blowing a deer sideways through the air with "knockdown power" are totally mythical. On the other hand, there isn't a buck in the land that will remain standing for very long after that Minie bullet passes through both shoulders.

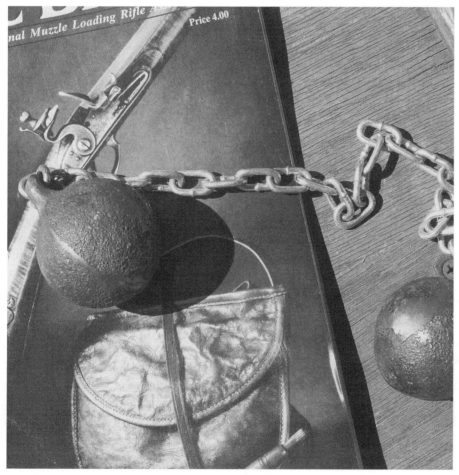

Consider this cannonball with chain; it takes very little imagination to see how much devastation it could cause in battle. The chain is bad enough, but the immense size of the projectile carried the real power.

All elk are large. All elk require a good thump to bring them down cleanly. This one was dropped with one shot from an Austin & Halleck rifle, a firearm capable of pushing a heavy bullet at good speed.

Stopping Power and Impulse

Bullets fired from anything resembling normal guns don't knock game down. But big bullets are definitely the choice for *stopping* the charge of the heaviest and toughest game in the world, from North America's coastal grizzly (brown bear) to Africa's rhino. The fellow counting on a 220 Swift to stop the charge of a Cape buffalo should have his will made out before he heads into the bush, because he's going to lose the jousting match. Better to whack the beast with a great big bullet going half the speed of the Swift, or even slower, than make it angry with a bee sting from a tiny missile blowing up on the hide. No right-thinking hunter would face a dangerous angry beast with a blackpowder single-shot rifle unless that rifle launched a big bullet (with a cool bodyguard standing by with a powerful repeater as well). The point is, big bullets, even from muzzleloaders, have their own brand of authority. They are the backbone of the big thumpers. Energy is energy is energy. But how that energy is delivered makes a difference in performance. A blow from a two-pound hammer is capable of delivering a thousand pounds of force, yet that blow only drives a nail a short distance into soft pinewood. At the same time, a 38 Special with a mere 250-pounds of force may send a bullet through several inches of the same wood. Part of the reason for this is work VS. time, or how long energy is applied. When an object is moved any distance (any object, including a bullet), time is consumed. It does not matter what the object is, or how it is moved. The hammer blow consumes only a tiny fragment of time. The 38 Special bullet applies its energy longer to the wood. This concept is all-important to energy delivery. Big bullets are capable of doing several things, including deep penetration to create long wound channels. So while big bullets don't knock animals down, their mass is formidable. So is their sheer caliber. Many blackpowder bullets start out larger in diameter than modern bullets expand to after upsetting or "mushrooming."

Mass and Power

If it works, we should be able to play a little math game with a couple of round bullets: 54-caliber and 30-caliber, sizes .540-inch diameter and .300-inch diameter. The game looks like this: .540 to the third power over .330 to the third power, .157464 divided by .027, resulting in 5.832. On the sheer size of bullet diameter alone, if the simple formula works, the .540-inch ball should be 5.832 times more potent than the .300-inch ball at *exactly the same velocity*. The weight of the .540-inch ball is 240 grains in pure lead, while the weight of the .300-inch ball is only 41 grains. The KE of the .300-inch ball at 41 grains is 364 foot-pounds. So if we multiply 364 foot-pound by 5.832 we should have the energy of the .540-inch round ball. Let's see: 364 times 5.832 results in 2,132 foot-pounds. Using the KE formula for a 240-grain bullet at 2,000 fps we get—2,132 foot-pounds. This little exercise has about as much practical value as wearing a wreath of garlic to ward off vampires. But it does tell an interesting and even useful story—the fact that mass counts for a lot when it comes to dealing out power from a firearm. Naturally, if we

Another big thumper worthy of the name—a Gefroh powerhouse built to take strong powder charges behind big bullets. Power of course comes from velocity, but with a muzzleloader the heavy bullet is what truly carries the mail because high velocity in the modern sense is not possible.

The hunting of dangerous game with a muzzleloader demands a reliable backup. Big lead bullets can do the job, however, especially on thin-skinned smaller game such as a leopard, a very dangerous customer. For truly large and dangerous animals, super-bores are the right medicine.

raise the velocity of that .300-inch ball to 3,000 fps or even 4,000 fps, KE rises significantly. At 3,000 fps the .300-inch ball turns up 820 foot-pounds. At 4,000 fps, it yields 1,457 foot-pounds. That's a lot better, but still well under the KE of the big ball at only half the velocity.

Dangerous Game Rifles—19th Century

Big-game hunters had it figured out early, even for stags in Scotland, as well as much larger beasts. Britishers did not require big-bore rifles—not in Britain. But when Queen Victoria came along in 1837, soon wed to Prince Albert, things changed. Apparently, both of them liked Scotland. Albert, being a hunter, went for "deer" in the Highlands. Since he was doing it, others wanted to hunt stag also. And they did, which required rifles larger than necessary in Jolly Olde England. Moreover, the British Empire was growing—vastly—to reach the point where "the sun never set" on held territories. English hunters were now in Ceylon, India, and of course Africa. The "deer" of Scotland were miniature com-

pared with the larger beasts of these three lands. Furthermore, many animals in these territories were dangerous. Stags in Scotland were not known to charge in an attempt to squash a hunter. Not so elephants, water buffalo, Cape buffalo, rhinos, tigers, lions, and other wild animals. A 10-bore rifle was now on the small side, with 4-bores making up the real charge-stopping artillery. Round bullets were prominent in the beginning. A number of hunters, especially Sir Samuel Baker, continued to prefer the lead sphere over the conical. But the two-groove Cape Rifle also had its following. It fired a heavy bullet wearing two fins, which fitted into two grooves in the rifle. This "winged" bullet, as it was called, did not strip the rifling. It rode in its grooves like a train on a track.

Sir Samuel's Tiger

There is much to be learned from the account of S.W. Baker in India on the trail of a tiger. Baker was riding an elephant named Moolah Bux, an animal that had tiger hunting experience. The plan included a bunch of Indian na-

tives coursing through the jungle in an attempt to harass the tiger into running toward the elephant-mounted hunter. The tiger, taking unkindly to the din created by the natives, wreaked havoc among them, but in the meantime continued to move in the desired direction. Baker finally got in a shot with a 557 double rifle which, being too early for smokeless, was charged with blackpowder. Baker yelled out, "Where is the tiger?" To which one man, in a tree by now, called out that the striped death was right below him. The tiger immediately charged toward Moolah Bux, at which point Baker let go with one barrel as Moolah Bux thrashed the foliage in front of him with his trunk. Then, to use Baker's words, "Moolah Bux stood suddenly like a rock. That gave me a splendid opportunity, and the .577 bullet rolled the enemy over like a rabbit."

Baker continued, "Almost at the same instant, having performed a summersault, the tiger disappeared, and fell struggling among the high grass and bushes about 15 paces distant." Moolah Bux moved forward and Baker shot again. The business was over, except for what Baker might have called "collateral damage." One native came along "covered with blood." Another borne by companions "completely deluged with blood." A third had been "torn to the ground with remorseless fury" as the beaters pushed the tiger. Baker said, "I began to reflect that tiger-shooting might be fun to some, but death to others, who, poor fellows, had to advance unarmed through dangerous jungle." Baker concluded that the tiger would normally run from the din created by the beaters, but a com-

The Pedersoli Double Rifle can deal out a healthy thump when loaded strongly and allows a quick follow-up shot, thereby delivering two big bullets to the target in a short time-frame.

Today's modern muzzleloaders, like this one from Thompson/Center, are built to take heavy bullets with big powder charges. They definitely qualify as big thumpers, considering they deliver sufficient energy for game the size of moose.

panion had previously wounded it. "Berry's .577 hollow Express was to produce this trumpery wound, which had enraged the animal without creating any serious injury" Baker said. He also praised the elephant that he rode as so much steadier than horses of the hunter's acquaintance.

Baker accused a lighter-than-normal bullet fired with 6 drams of powder (164 grains) as causing the bullet to "blow up" on the hide of the tiger, rather than penetrating. He said, "A comparison with the effect of my .577 with the same charge of 6 drams, but with a solid bullet of ordinary pure lead weighing 648 grains, was very instructive." We agree. We do learn much from field experience. His first bullet penetrated the right flank, coursing through lungs, and finally breaking the opposite shoulder bone. Baker concluded that, "If the bullet had been made of an admixture of tin or other alloy to produce extreme hardness, it would have passed through the body of the tiger with high velocity, but the animal would have escaped the striking energy." S.W. concludes, "It is this striking energy, the knocking-down power of a projectile, that is so necessary when hunting dangerous game." Well, Sir Samuel, not quite, but we get the idea. The bullet did not knock the tiger off its feet, but the lead projectile of large caliber and heavy weight penetrated well, doing considerable damage as it created the wound channel. Tissue damage, along with bone breaking, brought the tiger down.

Captain Forsyth's Buffalo

Captain James Forsyth, whose *Sporting Rifle* book on blackpowder big-bore rifles is studied to this day, wrote in another book, *The Highlands of Central India*, 1889, of a buffalo hunt. The water buffalo is big enough to be quite dangerous, and apparently was at times, at least in India and Ceylon, but not as belligerent as the African Cape buffalo. While sources reveal that it is the hippopotamus that causes most animal/man deaths in Africa, this is due mainly to natives traveling the waterways occupied by these territorial behemoths. In fact, knowledgeable persons insist the Cape buffalo is more dangerous in terms of direct attack on humans. Re-

gardless that the African Cape buffalo is the more dangerous animal, Captain Forsyth did encounter an ill-tempered water buffalo in India. The bull had been wounded. A farmer, who did not cotton to the destruction of his rice paddy by the bull and his girlfriend, asked for and received "help" from an official at the nearest police station. The policeman, in Forsyth's words, "contented himself with firing away all his ammunition at half a mile's distance from the top of the house, and the bull remained the monarch of all he surveyed." Now the Captain had a wounded animal to contend with.

Forsyth goes on, "We had scarcely entered the plains when the owner of the ruined rice-fields pointed out his enemy, looming out against the horizon as large as an elephant, and we at once made preparations for the attack." Forsyth and a companion were both armed with 2-ounce rifles as they marched toward the buffalo "with our very miscellaneous pack of dogs under orders to be let go at the first shot." At 60 yards, the Captain fired, being his turn to shoot first. "Crash went two ounces of lead," he reported, "propelled by eight drams [219 grains] of

Would a blackpowder hunter be confident that he or she could drop this bull elk with one shot? When the gun launches a big bullet at reasonable velocity the answer is an unqualified yes.

We think of big recoil belonging only to big-bore rifles and shotguns loaded with heavy bullets or shot in front of big powder charges, but the revolver can supply a fairly decent bounce, too.

powder, against his tough hide." This brought the bull "upon his knees." More shooting ensued, a lot more, including shots with other rifles—one firing a three-ounce bullet. "He had sixteen bullets in him," the Captain reported, "before he died, several of large calibre, and at close quarters." Interestingly, Forsyth draws a conclusion opposite that of Baker's, saying, "We were, however, shooting with bullets of plain lead, and I found that my first two-ounce ball, propelled by eight drams of powder, had flattened out on his shoulder, pulverising bones, however, and completely laming him. After this, we used hardened projectiles."

Paying the Price

There is no free lunch when playing with big thumpers. The shooter pays the price because of Newton's Third Law of Motion—Every Action Has an Opposite and Equal Reaction. We know this as recoil, pure and simple. I kept a letter from reader John E. Collier of Colorado. John is a big-bore fan. He not only likes the big thumpers. He also shoots them. A few quotations from this brave man are in order. "My first blackpowder was a 1.135-inch (barrel)

firing a 3,106-grain conical," he wrote. John let go with a charge of 100 grains, just to warm up, then 250 grains, and finally 300 grains by volume. "The last charge recoiled off my shoulder and onto my arm," Collier reported. "A video was taken and showed it (the rifle) went straight up almost and dazed me for about 15 minutes. I have since gone to Fg. This monster weighs 23 pounds." Having no intention of giving up on big thumpers, John next called upon John Shorb of October Country to build a 4-bore for him at a weight of "only" 17 pounds. Collier fired 350-grains Fg in this rifle. But he did not stop there. He bought a 2-bore to shoot a 3,500-grain round ball. The maker of that 2-bore reported that the rifle could withstand 600 grains of blackpowder.

The very thought of that much powder hurts my shoulder. Collier tried 300 grains first and then 400 grains. A Canadian friend took the challenge, upping the charge to 550 grains. The rifle received more lead in the buttstock to help control recoil, but it remained a kicker. What added to my amazement was John's remark that the "larger of the 2-bores has a steel buttplate." Steel? I would elect for a recoil pad. An

8-pound 30-06 rifle firing a 180-grain bullet at 2,900+ fps (Federal High Energy factory ammo) develops about 20 foot-pounds of free recoil. A 9.5-pound 458 Winchester with a 500-grain bullet at 2,150 fps produces about 60 foot-pounds of "thrust-back." The 577 Nitro Express rifle at 12 to 13 pounds, pushing a 750-grain bullet close to 2,100 fps comes back with close to 100 foot-pounds of recoil energy. A 16-pound 8-bore driving a 1,200-grain conical at about 1,475 fps says hello with almost 200 foot-pounds of rearward thrust. A 4-bore shooting a 1,750-grain round ball at around 1,350 fps pushes back with about 225 foot-pounds of energy. This means that some of the truly huge big thumpers, such as Moore's 2-bore, could easily develop 300 foot-pounds of free recoil, more than most hunters weigh.

Big Thumpers of Recent Times

What I thought was a classic and fine rifle came from Big Bore Express in Idaho. It was called the Cape Sporting Rifle styled closely after Alexander Henry's rifle of the mid-1800s. "We copied the dimensions from blueprints of the original gun," the maker reported. The only significant change was the addition of an "elegant half rib" that allowed the mounting of a scope—well

Here is a viable comparison between bullets. On the far left a 180-grain 30-caliber jacketed bullet of modern design (Winchester). Even the century-old 30-06 can now achieve over 2,900 fps. Two 54-caliber round balls flank one 12-bore round ball that weighs close to 500 grains. As round ball size increases, weight (mass) grows out of proportion. This is why big bores were necessary in blackpowder firearms incapable of true high velocity.

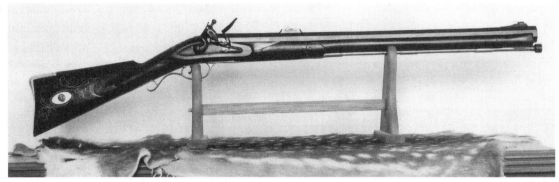

The old-time big-bore rifle for elephants and other large—really large—animals made its fame with big bullets. This Gefroh blackpowder big bore marches to exactly the same drummer. Bullets weighing up to 3,750 grains for the 2-bore delivered a heavy blow not only to game, but to the shooter as well.

forward of the shooter. The modern version of the Cape Rifle was lighter than the original due to better metals allowing trimming here and there. The match-grade barrel with a 1:20 rate of twist was for conical bullets. The Cape Rifle came in .45- and 50-calibers, the latter capable of stabilizing long bullets, which placed it in the big thumper category with strong powder charges. October Country (see Directory) continues to make extremely fine big-bore rifles. These are truly big bores. The two of my familiarity are the 8-Bore Double Rifle and 4-Bore Heavy Rifle. The 8-bore with 300-grains Fg blackpowder pushes an .820-inch 830-grain missile away at 1,435 fps. Because of velocity advantage in Newton's KE formula, this is "only" 3,796 foot-pounds. The "new" 30-06, now capable of driving a 180-grain bullet at 2,950 fps from a 24-inch barrel, even faster from a 26-inch barrel, gains close to 3,500 foot-pounds. The 2-bore Heavy Rifle shoots a .989-inch 1,445-grain bullet at 1,450 fps with 350 grains of FFg blackpowder for 6,974 foot-pound muzzle energy. Jim Craig reported a 550-pound male lion tagged with an October Country 8-bore. Craig's rifle was charged with 300 grains of FFg blackpowder. "The ball penetrated the entire length of his body," Jim reported, "and exited through his hind quarters." This is an example of momentum, and like it or not, momentum, while not allowed as acceptable in the world of ballistics, is part of the power story. Consider a 3,000-pound car at only 50 fps with 116,604 foot-pounds of energy.

Big Thumper
Blackpowder Cartridges

There were many large-bore blackpowder cartridges in the past, especially in the hands of English hunters going for the biggest big game in the world. Mainly, these cartridges ranged from 10- to 4-bore. The 8-bore was fairly popular firing a conical bullet weighing 1,250-grains. Velocity ran around 1,500 fps with a case full of blackpowder for a muzzle energy below 6,250 foot-pounds. As pointed out many times, good effect on game includes not only KE, but also sheer bullet size and weight. The idea was thumping—hence our big thumper term—a beast hard enough to discourage the continuance of a charge. Or to stop the charging animal long enough to drive another bullet home. While these cartridges qualify multiple times for the title of big thumpers, they do not out-power the old muzzleloaders for the simple fact that a cartridge has a finite capacity. You can only get in so much powder in the case and no more. Not so with muzzleloaders, and that's why we see powder charges as high as the almost ridiculous 500+ grains volume range. Sir Samuel Baker said of his 2-bore muzzleloader (not a cartridge rifle), the one he called "Baby," that it tried to whirl him around sideways upon firing. He was often left with a headache after shooting the rifle only once or twice. Sometimes Baby even gave him a nosebleed. Consider that our man Baker was a big fellow noted as "a very large and powerful man." He embarrassed a circus strong man by breaking chains around his own chest merely

Blackpowder cartridges were capable of packing a big wallop, always because of projectile mass. The 45-60 would not be placed at the top end of the blackpowder cartridge scale, but its big lead bullet penetrated deeply enough to put down considerable big game in its time, and it can still do it.

by flexing his muscles. He also demonstrated in Scotland that he could kill a "deer" [stag] with only a knife.

North America's Current Big Thumpers

Aside from October Country rifles, as well as custom-made guns in the truly big bore realm, the current big thumpers are mainly in 50- and 54-calibers, firing bullets that range up to about 675 grains weight. There are many exceptions and the last remark is a broad generalization. Part of the story resides with good bullets and good bullet placement. Principals behind the PowerBelt Bullet wanted a projectile that penetrated well, at the same time opening up reasonably—all with good accuracy. The president of Power-Belt, Mike McMichaels, has now killed everything from ground squirrels to elephant. That last animal is not mentioned for effect. Mike really did bop a big pachyderm. The bullet is remindful of the excellent BlackBelt designed by Robert "Bob" Kearns of Idaho. Kearns' idea was to bypass the sabot and attach a gas-sealing "belt" to the base of a bore-size bullet. The Power-Belt also has a gas-sealing belt on its base. There are other good bullets, far too many to enumerate here, and sincere apologies to those left out. I have had good luck with the SSB from the Buffalo Bullet Company and the heavy lead Hydra-Con from Parker Productions. The high ballistic coefficient SSB groups well downrange with considerable retained energy, while the big Hyrda-Cons, such as the 54-caliber 675-grain number that one of my rifles shoots very well, uses hydraulics to ensure "mushrooming," but due to mass, the big bullets penetrate as well as opening up an impressive wound channel. The Knight company claim its own 52-caliber inline as "Most Powerful Muzzleloader in Production Today!" with a 375-grain bullet and 3,127 foot-pounds of muzzle energy. Other muzzleloader manufacturers may challenge that claim, especially October Country with its 4-bore

rifle, as well as the Ultimate of Chapter 8 and its 200-grain volume powder charge allowance.

Handling the Big Thumpers

Three important points in handling the big thumpers: First, never shoot full-power loads unless for chronographing, sighting in, or hunting. The big-bore powerhouse can be fun to shoot with mild loads when it's not necessary to burn the fully allowed cargo of powder. Second, consider a recoil pad. I have a 54-caliber rifle going into the field shortly. That rifle is now with a gunsmith getting a new Pachmayr recoil pad. I am partial to Pachmayr pads because Pachmayr pads are partial to my shoulder. Third, at the bench I always use a shoulder pad. Mine is the Past from Battenfeld Technologies. I noticed many silhouette shooters wearing the same pad at the last contest I attended.

More to Come

We can expect more in the way of big thumpers, not so much in the old-time camp of huge bores with outrageous powder charges. But more along the line of modern rifles like the Ultimate with powder charges ranging into the 200-grains volume category behind bullets of good weight with decent ballistic properties. Meanwhile, we are doing more than all right with what we have—rifles taking on large doses of blackpowder or safe substitute propellant with bullets of good mass at medium velocity and impressive downrange energy.

A 12-gauge round ball, resting here in the midst of 50-caliber Maxi balls weighing 370-grains each, runs about 494-grains weight depending upon exact diameter in "pure" lead. Even at the lower speed delivered from a regular 12-gauge blackpowder shotgun, the big ball, from close range, will make a formidable wound channel.

One way to tame recoil delivered by a big thumper is with a good recoil pad, emphasis on good. The name Pachmayr has translated to "good recoil pad" for decades, only today with new materials and better designs it does a better job than ever.

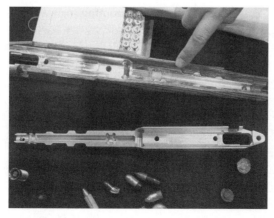

The Ultimate muzzleloader with its allowable 200-grain volume powder charge has a special barrel bedding system to promote accuracy and also to hold up to plenty of strong recoil. The Ultimate is a member of the ultra-modern muzzleloader clan devised to turn the front-loader into a big thumper.

SILUETA AND COWBOY ACTION SHOOTING

Cowboy Action Shooting has captured the imagination of thousands, not only shooters, but spectators as well. It is one of the few shooting sports that has sufficient action to keep onlookers looking on.

They differ markedly, but both games thrive in the 21st century—the long-range silhouette game and Cowboy Action Shooting. Each ranks high among the national shooting sports and are climbing in popularity in the U.S. and Canada. Well-constructed rules govern each sport, but neither is over-organized to the point of discouraging shooting *enjoyment*. Competitive, certainly; but at the same time these shooting games display considerable historical color. The long-range rifle is reminiscent of buffalo days of the 19th century, while handguns, rifles, and shotguns in the cowboy game display vignettes of the Old West. The black-powder cartridge came of age — again — with hunters desiring to find out

what it was like to pack single-shot breechloaders or lever-action repeaters shooting cartridges born before smokeless powder. But it's been the two games that brought the old-time cartridge to its present height of popularity: silhouette for the single-shot rifle, Cowboy Action Shooting for lever-action repeaters, blackpowder cartridge revolvers, and older-style shotguns. Replica guns abound for both games, along with an incredibly complete line of ammunition and loading components—plus every kind of accoutrement anyone could imagine or wish for, as well as special books on the subjects, including loading manuals. There is no end in sight. Both events continue to grow in membership.

The Blackpowder Single-Shot Silhouette Game
Informal and Local Shoots

While national, if not global, rules and regulations hover over the sport of silhouette shooting with blackpowder cartridge single-shot breech-loading rifles, clubs all over North America continue to fashion their own special blackpowder cartridge games. Rules vary with each group. For example, how about a "Buffalo Gong Shoot," in which "any single-shot breech-loading cartridge rifle or replica in the spirit of the late 1800s to early 1900s" is acceptable? Blackpowder or Pyrodex are allowed in this contest, with duplex loads (smokeless mixed with blackpowder) or smokeless powder forbidden.

Only metallic sights are admissible, no scopes. Cast lead bullets were legal projectiles, nothing else, and these had to be without gas checks. The major competition was a metal gong at 200 yards, offhand shooting only, but as it turned out, the most watched and enjoyed aspect of this particular shoot was the buffalo (American bison) metallic cutout placed at 900 yards. Boom! Wait a bit. Clang! Everybody loved it, shooter and spectator alike.

The buffalo metallic silhouette was not an offhand event. All shooters used crossed sticks. The range was opened one day ahead of the match so that shooters could visit with each other, have some fun, and practice a little before the real thing got under way. This local shootout was typical with plenty of rules, but nothing as stringent as national competition requires. The local shoot is always geared for a good time, even when prizes are offered. Oftentimes muzzleloading events are included along with the blackpowder cartridge games. While gongs and metallic silhouettes are the usual targets, the home club is not bound to regulations, types or sizes of targets, or shooting distances. They make the rules. After all, the shoot has nothing to do with national competition, which is a whole different world.

Shooting Far – Really Far

Perhaps the biggest draw in shooting single-shot blackpowder cartridge rifles is not the rifles — although they are immensely interesting, especially with regard to history — but how *far away* those targets are! Anyone who has shot long-range competition, or for that matter, informal distance gunnery, has the utmost respect for a shooter who can hit a target at *several hundred* yards with a high-power scope and super cartridge firing a high-velocity, ballistically efficient bullet. Shooters who actually go to a range where distance from muzzle to target is several hundred yards quickly learn that the shot made on that deer across the canyon that seemed to be that far wasn't — at

least most of the time. One of the greatest long-range marksmen of all time is Dave Gullo. Gullo demonstrated his ability with an original breech-loading single-shot blackpowder cartridge rifle, a piece 120 years old wearing Vernier tang sights. The target was a gong placed on a white buffalo cutout. The distance was — wait for it — 1,123 yards. That is two-thirds of a mile.

Gullo believes it took 3.5 seconds for the bullet to span the distance from muzzle to that distant target. This could be right, because he could shoot, set the rifle aside, peek in his spotting scope, and see the bullet hit the gong, where it arrives with a *clang*! and clearly visible splash of lead. Dave casts his own bullets, ensuring that none of these projectiles suffers an occlusion of any kind. An air pocket would drift the bullet off course by a wide margin. Gullo reports that in order for the projectile to hit on target at more than 1,000 yards, he must, as he put it, "aim 50 feet high." He shoots from a benchrest, right? Wrong. This marksman uses crossed sticks only, no bench. That anyone can do this with any sort of repetition lends credence to some of the old buffalo-runner tales, with claims of strikes out to several hundred yards. It also proves that single-shot blackpowder cartridge rifles of yesteryear were capable of high marks in accuracy, resulting in long-range hits on modest-sized targets. Because of the ability of both guns and shooters to hit targets time after time at long range with blackpowder cartridge

rifles, a new game was born. Actually, that's not true. Adding the single-shot, soot-burning rifle was new, but the game came to life some time ago in another country.

The Silueta Game is Born

The roots of blackpowder-cartridge silhouette shooting reach down into the rich soil of a sport that began in Mexico. It's difficult to say just when, nor do I have information on exactly who came up with the original idea for the formal silueta match. I do know that in the late 1950s and early 1960s, Victor Ruiz, a well-known marksman from Nogales, Sonora, Mexico, along with several of his shooting companions, such as Milo Martinez, another fine marksman, were firing away at metal cutouts at long range from the offhand position only. Interest grew in the sport, partly because Mexican shooters invited north-of-the-border riflemen to join them. The silueta match soon became a hands-across-the-border friendly competition, and became a fledgling international game, with literally hundreds of participants, that continues to thrive today. Of course, U.S. shooters had to organize silueta into a match with specific rules and regulations, from that point creating an organization to watch over the new sport with rule-making authority.

Modern Rifle Silhouette Shoot

The original silhouette match was built around the centerfire sporting rifle. Rules called for a rifle that a hunter would likely carry into the field for big game. The rifle was to weigh no more

The metallic silhouettes look like these, but have specific sizes for each animal.

Shooting far, really far, looks like this—little black dots in the distance that must be picked up in metallic sights, and that is just the beginning. Wind factors are extremely important, for a slow-moving blackpowder bullet, even one of high sectional density, can be moved well off course over such great distance.

than 8 pounds with scope, as I recall. In the beginning, shooters played the game with the same rifles they used for deer and other big-game hunting. As the shoot became more sophisticated, however, many rules were designed to keep the sport from deteriorating. As with every sport, special equipment was soon available, which is always the case from pole-vaulting to ping-pong. A unique scope-sighted silhouette rifle came along, most-often chambered for the 308 Winchester cartridge. Of course, there were official standards established for the size of the metallic cutouts and the distances at which they were placed.

Blackpowder Cartridge Silhouette

The formal blackpowder cartridge metallic-silhouette game is definitely an offshoot of the original smokeless-powder cartridge match. It is NRA-sponsored, with the first official shoot held near Raton, N.M., at the NRA Whittington Center in 1985. The event has been run annually ever since, with ever-increasing interest. Canada has joined in with its own national competition. Australians also shoot blackpowder

cartridge silhouette matches, although the game may be in jeopardy in that country because of firearms legislation enacted in the late 20th century.

The Rifles

The rules have changed, and may change again, so it is unwise to set anything down in concrete. The only sure way to find out exactly what is allowed currently is to contact the parent organization, which is not a problem. A cut-off date for rifle manufacture was mandated in the beginning and remains vital to the sport. After all, the competition is for 19th-century, single-shot blackpowder cartridge rifles. The year 1892 was established as a cutoff manufacturing date for legal blackpowder silhouette rifles for formal competition. Before that ruling, 1895 and 1896 were the rifle manufacturing-date limits. Official rulings exist within the parameters of the NRA Blackpowder Cartridge Rifle (BPCR) Silhouette matches. However, the organization found that inclusion or exclusion of specific rifles was not entirely simple. For example, the Stevens 44-1/2, with its falling-block ac-

tion and exposed hammer, would seem to be disallowed because the 44-1/2 dates from 1903. But the rifle followed a design matching the spirit, intention—and even mechanics of the 19th-century single-shot breech-loading blackpowder cartridge rifle, and so it was let in the door. The sport still has growing pains, and further changes in allowable rifles may be seen.

Browning, noting the great interest generated in the BPCR Silhouette sport, introduced its version of the 1885 single shot, calling it, appropriately, the Browning Model 1885 BPCR (Black Powder Cartridge Rifle). It even has a long-range metallic sight suited to the game. A few original and rebuilt Sharps rifles, especially the model of 1874, became quite popular in silhouette shooting. But it's mainly the modern replica of this rifle that dominates. Currently, the Winchester Model 1885 High Wall is also popular. Add to these a number of Remington rolling blocks, most of them modern-made replicas, with a few originals, as well as customs built on original or replica actions. There are also Hepburns and Ballards, and even Trapdoor Springfields.

The Cartridge

Since the legal rifle for the sport is a single-shot breechloader of American design, military or sporting, with an exposed hammer, it only makes sense

The modern silhouette game can be formal or informal. A local club may arrange for its own silhouette match. But most silhouette shoots are conducted under a set of agreed rules that apply everywhere.

that the cartridge must follow. The two rifles most carried by the buffalo runner of the latter part of the 19th century qualified immediately, these being the Remington Rolling Block and the Sharps, not to exclude the original Winchester single-shot breechloader, or for that matter the Trapdoor mentioned in Chapter 45. What were the cartridges for these rifles? There were many, but the rules call for only original 19th-century rounds, and they must be of American origin. For example, a great number of Remington rolling blocks were chambered for the 43 Egyptian, but that cartridge is not allowed in formal silhouette competition, at least at the time this work was under way.

While the 45-70 Government cartridge continues as number one in the game, popularity of the 40-65 Winchester is on the rise. The reason is quite simple: Many rounds are fired during a match. The 45-70 with a 400- or 500-grain bullet in front of a full package of fuel delivers a fairly strong blow to the shoulder. The 40-65 is milder, while still providing enough punch to knock over a metallic silhouette. Actually, there are dozens of rounds that qualify for this sport. The Sharps line alone includes a multitude of them. One shoot had the following cartridges: 40-70, 40-50, 45-100, and 44-100, just to mention a few. The list also included, by the way, the huge 50-140 Sharps. While the accurate and mild 38-55 Winchester cartridge has shown up at some matches, it's just a touch shy of striking power to knock down the big ram target, as is the nice little 32-40 Winchester round, which simply does not pack enough bullet weight for the task.

Sights

Only iron sights are allowed. Open sights are approved, but they would create an insurmountable handicap. The Vernier tang sight is the rule in this game because it mounts on the tang close enough to the eye to provide a long sight radius, and it is, after all, a peep sight. Furthermore, it can be ad-

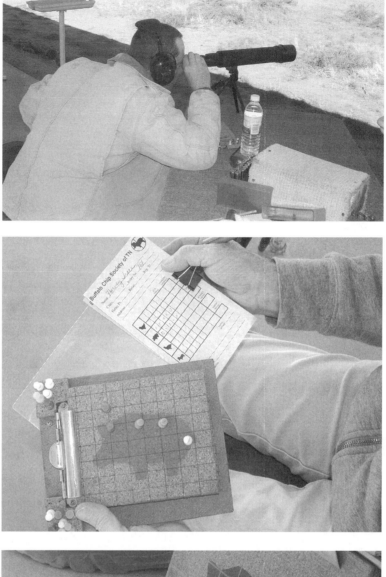

The shooter needs a spotter to tell him or her, the shooter, where the bullets are landing. A good spotter is invaluable, being able to show where bullets strike off target as well as on.

The spotter drives a tack into the board to show the shooter where his or her bullet landed—hopefully clanging on the metal target somewhere, but sometimes off target.

Time is of the essence in the silhouette game. If it were not, matches would run on and on as shooters waited for perfect wind conditions, better lighting, or simply an improved physical and mental attitude toward the target.

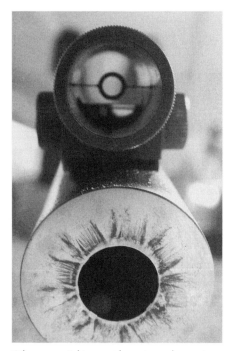

Of course, sights must be extremely precise to allow the shooter to gain visual perspective of the target and hold so that a bullet is delivered from the muzzle far downrange to the silhouette. This is looking directly into the muzzle of a rifle for a view of one particular sight type.

justed for great distances with quick and accurate sighting changes. It is not, however, the only sight used. There are other allowable designs. But no scopes.

The Targets, Distances, and Rules

The targets are the same as those used in the modern rifle silhouette match: chicken, pig, turkey, and sheep. The chicken is placed at 200 meters, the pig at 300, the turkey at 385, and the sheep at a full 500 meters. Cross-sticks (also called crossed sticks) are

This range is marked off to show which silhouette is up. This one is the javelina, Spanish word for the small peccary of South America, Mexico, and the Southwestern United States.

allowed for the pig, turkey, and sheep, but the chicken is shot offhand and is considered the toughest target to hit, even though it's the closest. The sport is amazingly difficult. Every target looks like a fly speck on a window "away out there," and remember that only iron sights are allowed so there is no magnification! Even the sheep, the largest target, is a mere 13 inches high and 32 inches long. The turkey is taller — 23 inches — but that includes the head and neck. The body itself is only 11 by 13 inches in size; picture that at 385 meters.

Shooters simply have to be highly skilled in order to have a chance at competing in this competition. While heavy rifles are allowed, and heavy rifles do sit well from offhand and rest steady on the cross-sticks, maximum legal weight is 12 pounds, 2 ounces as this is written. That is a far cry from a blackpowder bench gun, for example, that can weigh much more. Once again, contact with the parent organization is vital for the latest rules of the silhouette game.

Allowable Powder and Ballistics

Ballistics plays a strong role in the difficulty of this fascinating shooting sport. Velocities range from around 1,100 fps to about 1,300 fps. With only Pyrodex and blackpowder allowed, hopes for higher velocities are eliminated. This means delivered energies at long range are relatively low. A hit target counts for nothing. It must fall over. That's why the larger calibers are

imperative. The sheep weighs about 50 pounds, and it's a full 500 meters from the muzzle. Bullets much under 40 caliber simply don't have the remaining punch to *always* knock the sheep off its feet, so to speak. It's difficult trying to hit the target at 500 meters with iron sights and a high-trajectory firearm. But hitting it and getting no score is very discouraging. The 45-caliber bullet, weighing around 400 or 500 grains, has enough punch left, even at long range, to knock over the target when the bullet hits. Big lead bullets in the 40-caliber league also qualify.

Drop-Tube Powder Loading

Consider a hole in the ground to be filled with a bunch of rocks. Rocks can be haphazardly dumped into the hole or tossed in a few at a time. Dropping all the rocks in at once will not allow them to settle evenly, which means there will be air gaps between the rocks. Settling them in a few at a time reduces space between the rocks, creating greater uniformity. The same is true of powder. If a charge of blackpowder or Pyrodex is dumped into the case all at once, it will not settle nearly as well as trickling in a few grains at a time. The shape of the kernel, being irregular, has something to do with this. Now lengthen the fall of the kernels and a firmly packed charge is much more likely. That's where the drop tube comes in. It allows powder to enter the case from as high as 30 inches or so, but it also introduces the powder a few granules at a time. It can take several seconds to drop a powder charge into a case. For competition, and even for good hunting loads, the drop tube method comes highly recommended. There is nothing new about it. Drop tubes have been around for a very long time. It's simply an old trick that works very well in producing an evenly packed powder charge. Now there are commercial blackpowder measures offered with drop tubes available. These are safe for use with blackpowder because of their design, construction and materials.

The Primer

After packing the powder into the case via the drop-tube method, the usual condition is 100 percent load density, or very close to it. While many gun writers, including this one, recommended mild primers in the past because blackpowder ignites readily, that position had to be reversed. Today, magnum primers are recommended for blackpowder cartridges, at least the larger-capacity rounds.

The Bullet

The typical bullet for the 19th-century blackpowder cartridge did not have a rocket-like profile. Therefore, it did not possess a high ballistic coefficient. Velocities are already quite low in the blackpowder cartridge, which means a looping trajectory. Adding blunt-nosed bullets promotes even greater drop. Of course, the tubular magazine of the blackpowder lever-action rifle demanded, and still demands, the blunt-nosed bullet. But the single-shot breechloader does not. That's why serious silhouette shooters have gravitated to projectiles with a higher ballistic coefficient. Lyman even came along with spitzer-shaped bullets in both 40- and 45-caliber, especially aimed toward long-range shooting with the 40-65 Winchester and similar rounds, plus the 45-70 Government and other cartridges of that class.

Prepared Ammo

Several companies offer blackpowder cartridges, ready-loaded, for the silhouette fan. Two that come to mind are Old Western Scrounger and Ten-X. The first has been at the game for quite some time, with ammunition prepared under the guidance of the company, but not in-house. The second as newly organized in 2005 with a commitment to offer excellent ammunition for blackpowder guns in general. Both companies have expanded their line.

Wind and Sun

Both wind and sun play prominent rolls in blackpowder cartridge competitive shooting. The wind can drift bullets completely off target. Part of the reason is the time of flight, which is very long. With bullets leaving the muzzle at 1,100 to 1,300 fps, and ranges up to 500 meters and more, it takes quite a while for a bullet to go from muzzle to target. The wind has all that time to play on the projectile, so it is common for a breeze to blow a big blackpowder projectile way off the mark. A mere 10-mph zephyr can drift a bullet off course by several feet from muzzle to sheep silhouette at 500 meters. The sun also plays a role. Light striking the sights can greatly alter bullet placement. That's why covered front sights are prominent.

The Spotter

Because of severe bullet drop, the use of iron sights, wind and light problems, and a host of other gremlins, the spotter becomes a tremendous asset. He's allowed to sit by the shooter and watch through a telescope to see where the bullets hit. If he's good, he'll be able to tell the marksman where his missile landed, which prompts a sight or hold adjustment for the next shot. The ideal method is using tacks pinned onto a similitude of the silhouette target—chicken, pig, javelina, or sheep. This way, the shooter knows right where his bullets struck. If the spotter is good, he or she will be able to stick tacks off the target as well as on the target.

Minimum Accuracy

Mike Venturino, an avid blackpowder cartridge fan for years and well-known writer on the subject, concluded that a 4-inch group at 200 yards constituted minimum accuracy for competition in the silhouette game.

Triggers

Double-set triggers are common. While the rule of hold and squeeze always pertains, being able to touch off a shot at just the right moment is invaluable. The set-trigger, with a very light breaking point, allows that. It's not a trigger jerk, but a clean, controlled touch-off made possible by that set trigger.

Growing Sport

The blackpowder cartridge and single-shot rifle are back in full force. Blackpowder silhouette shooting on a formal level will probably undergo a few more changes in the future, but that's healthy. Hopefully, the usual tendency to upgrade that prevails in any sport will be carefully regulated. Those steering the sport recognize that if they allow the rules to grow lax, the game will lose a great deal of its appeal.

Cowboy Action Shooting

America has had a love affair with the cowboy since the 19th century, with dime novels making outlandish claims of fast-drawing and straight-shooting rivaled only by comics, cheap-paper books, and B-movies that showed Tim McCoy, Tom Mix, Tex Ritter, Lash LaRue, Gene Autry, Roy Rogers, and many others doing the impossible with six-guns and lever-action rifles. It's no wonder that the Cowboy Action Shooting game caught on. Although B-western films faded away some time ago, they were replaced by movies that continued to herald the American gun-toting cowboy. Anyone interested in this game should contact SASS: the Single Action Shooting Society currently reachable at (714) 694-1800 by phone, or by e-mail at sasseot@aol.com, or http://www.sassnet.com on the Internet. SASS offers a wealth of information on the sport, plus information on clubs nationwide. Members of SASS receive a permanent alias registration. That's right, the shooter gets to name himself, such as Deadeye Dick or Straight Shot Sue, and that handle is registered, almost like a trademark. There is also a permanent member number assigned to each person, the SASS star badge with that number impressed on it, SASS Marshal lapel pin, membership certificate, subscription to *The Cowboy Chronicle*, a bi-monthly

The rifle for Cowboy Action Shooting is generally a lever-action appropriate for the 19th century, although the Colt Lightning slide-action rifle certainly fits the same time frame, using blackpowder cartridges. Blackpowder puts an extra dose of nostalgia into the action.

Lady shooters are certainly welcome and they do compete well in the Cowboy Action Shooting game, their colorful outfits standing second place to their good shooting.

journal for the organization, the *SASS Shooters Handbook* or *SASS Mounted Shooters Handbook*, and a SASS membership card. Life Members receive a Gold Collector's Badge.

There is also a SASS RO Course — Range Operation Safety — given by a person known as the Territorial Governor at the home club, or at the End of Trail Winter Range, and at all SASS regional events. There's a study booklet available for the course. Safety is, of course, of main importance in all Cowboy Action Shooting events. SASS also keeps shooters abreast of legalities, such as California's passage of a bill excluding firearms capable of holding more than 10 rounds, which affects some of the lever-action rifles popular with Cowboy Action Shooters. "Legislature readily agreed that our cowboy guns were not the intended subject of this legislation," SASS News reported. "Although technically illegal, the Department of Justice wrote a letter to SASS and communicated with the Riverside County (site of END of TRAIL) District Attorney's Office and Sheriff's Office assuring us the law would not be enforced." This is the kind of service SASS is known for, along with a tight rein on rules and regulations. There is also a SASS Mercantile, where members can purchase casual wear bearing the SASS logo, collectible pocket and lapel pins, the SASS Colt Single-Action Revolver, custom orders, deluxe collectibles, log items, and much more, including a video and book collection to choose from.

How the Game is Played

Although Cowboy Action Shooting is not strictly a blackpowder sport, the spirit of the guns is definitely old-time. Furthermore, many fans do load their shootin' irons with blackpowder, which is entirely legal for the competitions. Three general firearms play a role in cowboy action shooting: revolver, rifle, and shotgun. The revolver is single-action and very much a part of the blackpowder scene. The rifle is usually the same, but the Model 1894, which origi-

As with the rifle, the blackpowder revolver cartridge must match the proper era for it to be legal in the Cowboy Action Shooting game. How about shooting off the back of a galloping horse?

nally came along in blackpowder-only cartridges, was later chambered to a number of smokeless rounds. Shotguns are generally seen in two major styles: side-by-side double barrel and the Winchester Model 1897 pump-action with exposed hammer. This great old gun continues to please a lot of shooters, including this one, mine being a refurbished '97 in 12 gauge with Modified choke. Since some of the events call for three rounds with the shotgun, the pump is a good choice. Rate of feeding three rounds into the '97 is remarkably fast, starting with an empty gun, which is the rule. John Taffin in his fine book, *Action Shooting Cowboy Style*, a 1999 Krause Publications title, runs through the range of revolvers, rifles, and shotguns mainly used in the events. Part I, the Introduction, includes photos of many legendary B-western cowboy heroes, such as Buck Jones, who proved he was truly a hero when he died in 1942 trying to rescue people from a burning building. My hero, Tim McCoy, with his big cowboy hat, is shown, along with Gordon "Wild Bill" Elliott and William Boyd, better known as Hopalong Cassidy. And, of course, Roy Rogers, the King of the Cowboys.

Taffin goes into clothing for the game, as well as the intended spirit. There are various stages for shooting, with the clock running to time contestants, but the local club has wide latitude in cooking up its own rules, as long as all safety tenets are observed. Local matches often use four or five individual shooting stages, while a dozen or more are the rule for national matches. Shooting positions may be offhand standing, sitting or prone. Targets can be paper or metal, but at one local club match, bowling pins were used. Under SASS rules, there are five shooting categories: Blackpowder, Traditional, Modern, Dualist and Frontiersman. Blackpowder includes single-action percussion revolvers or cartridge revolvers loaded with blackpowder. Fixed-sight Ruger Vaquero or Old Army handguns are allowed. Lever-action guns must also be blackpowder style. Pump-actions, such as Colt made in the 19th century, are also legal. Traditional is the most popular, according to Taffin. The guns are similar, but may be loaded with smokeless powder. It's not all blackpowder cartridges, as the 357 Magnum is allowed. Duelist is an optional category with all shooting accomplished one-handed only. Frontiersman is also an optional category. It requires two early frontier revolvers, original or replica, or the Ruger Old Army with fixed sights.

Guns and Ammo

Cap and ball revolvers are allowed, such as the Colt Model 1860 of American Civil War fame. Many others are also used. Smith & Wesson single-action revolvers are also part of the game, including the Schofield model. Remington single-action cartridge revolvers are also included. Of course, Colts in many styles, including the Bisley, are all right. Ruger revolvers also play a role. Taffin supplies a multitude of good loads for Cowboy Action Shooting in many of the handguns, including data on the popular 44-40 Winchester. This round with Winchester factory ammo will group inside an inch at 50 feet — this

distance is used because most Cowboy Action Shooting is close. The 44 Colt is back with factory loads from Black Hills Ammunition. Many other rounds are discussed, including the 32-20 Winchester and what Taffin calls turn-of-the-century cartridges, such as the 38 Special. Lever-action rifles are well represented, with the Winchester Model 1892 very popular, along with the 1894 Winchester. Of course, Models 1866 and 1873 are also in the game. So are Marlins, such as that company's 1894 Cowboy model in 44-40 Winchester. Ammo for these rifles includes many 44-40s, along with 45 Colt, but many other rounds are also legal. Shotguns, as mentioned, include double

Time is of the essence. Skill in hitting is imperative to placing, but the shooting must be accomplished within a given period of time. This shooter moves rapidly into position for his next turn.

Another shooter fires on his target as the horse races on. This requires two major skills—fast and accurate shooting, as well as excellent horsemanship.

This shooter goes with a single-shot blackpowder cartridge rifle of Winchester Single Shot persuasion.

barrel side-by-sides and the Winchester Model 97 with appropriate shells.

Typical Local Club Match

A match held in Arizona included several stages. One stage went: "Start standing at middle window of fort both hands on flag rope, one pistol holstered. Rifle with nine rounds staged at left portal and shotgun staged at middle window." At the buzzer, the shooter gets moving, shooting the different targets from the specific positions stated in the rules. At another stage, rules were entirely different for the shooting match. It went like this: "Start standing at a bar holding bottle with strong hand, rifle with six rounds and open empty shotgun staged on bar, two pistols holstered. At buzzer, drop bottle and with rifle shoot the rifle targets twice each, stage rifle with shotgun, shoot S1, S2 and S3. Mandatory: pick up bottle and move to table and set bottle on table, then sweep the pistol targets twice with pistols staging or holstering after each pistol is emptied."

Range Safety Rules

Twenty-two rules were outlined in the brochure for the above Cowboy Action Shooting local club meeting. The first was that every shooter would act as a safety officer, responsible for his own conduct, while alerting others to any possibly unsafe activity. Eye protection is mandatory for everyone, including spectators standing nearby. All firearms must be unloaded at all times except when on the course. All guns must be properly stored. No alcoholic beverages may be carried. Foul language or unsportsmanlike conduct may result in disqualification. Now that's a set of rules Gene Autry would have been proud of.

The blackpowder cartridge, not always loaded with blackpowder, is far from dead, as popular single-shot breech-loading rifle silhouette and Cowboy Action Shooting prove. Old-time blackpowder cartridge guns and loads are also growing in hunting popularity.

The shotgun is hardly left out of the match. Old-time blackpowder shotguns are allowed, one being Winchester's Model of 1897, but the double-barrel blackpowder shotgun is also allowed.

The little derringer is not left out of the Cowboy Action Shooting game.

Another lady shooter takes her turn on the Cowboy Action Shooting target range, her outfit complete and colorful.

RENDEZVOUS—A SHOOTING GAME

This is winter in the country trapped by the mountain man. Travel from the east into the mountains and onto the plains was virtually impossible, and so the rendezvous came about, where wagons from the East could enter the Far West to trade for beaver pelts.

The original rendezvous was a matter of business enterprise and Yankee Trader ingenuity, luring a gang of devil-may-care adventurers to wander the few-trails region of the Far West in search of beaver streams. With the beaver hat a hot item in the world of fashion, the wise paper-pushers back East had a perfect market. The plan was simple and effective. Let the mountain men, as they would be known, trap flat-tails, bringing the pelts to a central location in summer. Meet them there with wagons loaded with things they enjoyed once, but had no more, and mark everything up many-fold. Trade dollar

values for beaver blankets. A trapper could have a thousand, even two showing for his season's labor — good money in an era where a skilled worker might make a buck and a half a day. Whiskey at 30 cents a gallon in St. Louis was cut with water and sold for $2 a pint at rendezvous. Coffee and sugar at a dime a pound back East clipped the mountain men at two greenbacks a pound out West. But that was OK. One mountain man traded the sum value of two grand for the hand of a chief's daughter, they say. She must have been a beauty.

William Ashley was one of the principals in the plan, advertising in the

Missouri Gazette, a St. Louis newspaper, on Feb. 13, 1822. He asked for, and got, "enterprising young men." That most of these stalwart lads would never see home again was either not considered, or not an issue at all. Trapping beaver was hard work, the least damage coming from icy streams that brought on rheumatism, the worst luck running into Bugs' Boys, the Blackfoot Indian, landlord of the territory and one fine warrior whose arrows found the mark all too often. They made their mark, many places west taking their names: Jackson Hole, Wyo.; Bridger National Forest, Bridger, Mont.; Henry's Fork of the Snake River; Bonneville Pass, Laramie, Wyo., named for the slain mountain man Jacques LaRamie; and many more. Fall came and went. Winter set in. Finally, summer arrived. Off to rendezvous to see old friends and trade beaver pelts for whiskey, tobacco and pretty things to lure a young Indian maiden.

The first rendezvous was held in 1825 when Gen. Ashley gathered his trappers on what is now known as Henry's Fork of the Green River. The actual site is two miles from the present town site of Daniel, Wyo., which in turn is not far from the larger city of Pinedale, Wyo. Every year, there is a pageant held in honor of the mountain men. There also is a museum in his honor. Although the original rendezvous was a business venture, it turned out to be much more than that. Those meetings in the summer brought together white trappers and Indians in a way nothing else had ever done before. Although there were disputes, there was also comradeship. The rendezvous was a time for renewing old acquaintances and making new ones. Along with fur trading, there was story telling, knife and tomahawk throwing, swapping, new and used wares for sale, many games *and shooting matches*, the grist for this mill. Some shooting matches are as exciting as watching grass grow. Competitions set up by buckskinners, however, have flair, are often creative, fun to do and fun to watch. Some are taken from history, but many others were cooked up by modern buckskinners.

A Few Shooting Tips
Cleaning During a Match

There are generally no rules pertaining to the use of original cleaning chemicals. This means that all-day lubes, as described in Chapter 19, are OK. Also, most matches allow blackpowder substitutes. Pyrodex, as explained in Chapter 15, does not require cleaning between shots for a reasonable number, and there is still the smoke that helps to give these matches an aura of old times.

The Fouling Shot

A fresh bore may shoot slightly off the mark, even if it has been dried with a cleaning patch before and after loading. That first round ball or conical flying wide of the mark can be critical for many matches, opening up an otherwise tight group, missing the blade of the ax, or flying alongside that charcoal briquette. Firing one fouling shot before the match begins is normally allowed and it makes sense for blackpowder, Pyrodex or Clear Shot.

Leftover Lube in the Bore

We've crossed this creek before — an oily, wet, or greasy bore may throw a projectile off course. Where the accuracy of the shot is absolutely vital, it's wise to sight in with a dry bore and maintain a dry bore during a match.

The mountain man, as this depiction suggests, wore considerable Indian dress. After all, without the teaching and direct help from the Indian, more mountain man deaths would have been added to an already grim figure. He was a beaver trapper—trading the pelts at the summer rendezvous.

This is easily accomplished by running a cleaning patch downbore after loading. Dangerous? No more so than running the patched ball or conical down on the powder charge, which was necessary to load the gun. The gun must first be sighted in with a dry bore.

Altering Loads for a Match

The idea is to sight in for a match with a specific load, sticking to every aspect of that load chain for the match. A rifle sighted in with a heavy hunting load, then changing that load for the match, is not going to shoot in the same place. Powder, bullet, patch, and lube: Every detail should remain the same. My no. 47 custom 54-caliber round-ball rifle is an especially accurate rifle, and because its rear sight has two notches, no special sighting is required, not even for the 25-yard offhand match. The front sight matches up with the lower rear sight notch picture, and with a 70-grain charge of powder, the round balls chop right into the bullseye 25 yards away.

A New Flint

A modified Seneca Run was under way, with flintlocks only allowed. Fire, run, stop, aim, fire, run, stop, aim — reloading, of course, for each new target. One of the participants walked up to me during the match and said, "I read what you said about a new flint. It pays off." Naturally, if a flint is doing its job perfectly, it's not changed, but if there is any question about sure-fire sparks, the old rock has to go, replaced with a new one. That's likewise for all other aspects of flintlock fire — as noted in Chapter 39 on troubleshooting.

Consistency

It's the same song with the same words: consistency or nothing at all in every respect. While most matches do not require the kind of accuracy that demands a pressure regulator — which places the same force on the bullet, hence the powder charge, for each and every shot — it is worthwhile to seat projectiles with as close to the same force as possible for each load. Some shooters prefer slamming the ramrod down several

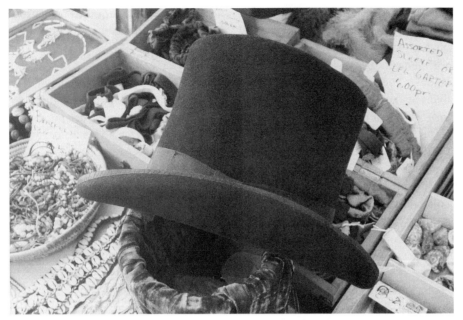
What the Fur Trade era was all about—the top hat made of beaver felt.

without knowing where his rifle, pistol, or revolver shoots. If sights are fully intact, and the blackpowder gun was sighted in for the last shoot, concern is nil to minimal. Otherwise, the shooter must repair or replace sights, while ensuring that his smokepole is sighted in before heading to the rendezvous.

The Games
Knockdown Targets

There are all kinds of targets that fall when struck. Cowboy Action Shooting, for example, has hinged metal plates that tip over from a shotgun blast. It doesn't take much at close range to smack these plates over. A shooter at one event described his handload as 7/8

strokes against the seated bullet. While this may compact the charge to some degree, it is not a necessary step. Good sustained force on the ramrod will seat a bullet fully upon the powder charge. The ramrod should be marked to show that the round ball or conical is all the way home on the powder charge for every shot. Consistency with the powder measure also makes sense, rather than haphazardly dropping powder home. A routine pays off. Sometimes it's a matter of fractions of an inch that makes the difference between a hit and a miss, a win or a loss.

Revolver Lock-Up

An improperly lubed revolver can lock up like a rusted hinge, and Murphy's Law says it will happen in the middle of a match. An all-day type of cream on top of the ball just before shooting can help keep the cylinder turning on your cap 'n' ball revolver. Also, after cleaning, a film of modern high-grade, grease-type lubricant on the interior moving parts of the revolver is helpful.

Check Sights and/or Sight In Before a Shoot

Amazingly, there are shooters who reach the rendezvous with broken or bent sights. Almost as surprising is the marksman who arrives for the shoot

Not directly related to shooting, but important to the overall theme of the rendezvous, is the tipi. Many rendezvous fans (buckskinners) are highly adept at setting up and living comfortably in this Plains Indian dwelling.

Cleaning during a match is important to continuous good grouping of bullets. This rifle is secured for cleaning during a shoot.

The fouling shot is preliminary to many rendezvous games.

ounce of No. 5 shot. Silhouettes are, of course, intended to keel over when hit. It's the only thing that counts for score. Pinging and ringing mean nothing, nor does seeing a bullet smack the silhouette through a spotting scope. The important aspect of this game is providing sufficient energy to knock a target over. For long-range shooting with round balls (some events are patched round ball only), with targets as far away as 500 yards (or farther, depending upon the game), the larger-caliber ball makes the difference. Furthermore, in spite of the fact that heavy powder charges are not as efficient as smaller charges, the round ball should be given a pretty

good start, not only for energy, but also for the trajectory pattern.

The Silhouette Shoot

The silhouette game is played nationally, and seriously, with single-shot blackpowder cartridge rifles. Chapter 38 touches on that. However, informal silhouettes not associated with the national organization that makes the rules can be rendezvous events for muzzleloaders. A shoot in Nebraska saw an entire series of metallic cutouts set up at various ranges for patched round ball only. Everyone loved the match — those watching as well as participating. Once again, the larger round ball wins out, retaining more of its initial energy

than a lighter lead pill, which is vital to knocking the metal animal profile over with one hit.

Splitting the Ball on the Ax Blade

This continues to be one of the most enjoyable matches at rendezvous for shooters and onlookers alike, and it seems to have come from out of the past. The idea is cutting a lead round ball into two pieces on the exposed blade of an ax. A double-bit ax is buried into the center of a large piece of tree stump, one sharp edge protruding outward. A good hit on the exposed blade slices the single bullet into two missiles. Balloons, clay pigeons, anything that will break, are set up alongside the ax blade. If only one breaks, that's not good. Both are supposed to get thumped as the ball divides into two parts. This is an offhand event, and as such, rifles of good weight with long sight radius help steadiness and ball placement. Also, a larger-caliber ball makes mathematical good sense. A near miss with a 40-caliber ball may have been a hit with a 50-caliber ball. It also helps to sight in for this event with horizontal grouping considered absolutely critical. The exposed ax blade affords several inches of vertical latitude, but horizontal latitude is confined to the mere *width* of the ax blade.

The Ricochet Target

Not popular, but interesting, is the ricochet match, where a chunk of heavy metal, such as boilerplate, is placed so that a ball can be skipped from its surface into a safety bank. Situated at the backstop is a breakable target, such as a balloon, clay pigeon, or other object, which is ideal for shooters and spectators. The shooter must skillfully glance the round ball off the boilerplate so that it strikes the target.

The Distant Gong

Rendezvous shooting games play on the senses. Watching a silhouette tip over is more fun for shooter and bystander than a hole in a paper target that no one can even see until the target is brought closer, or the shooter goes up-range to take a look. The sense

A fresh flint helps ensure flintlock ignition, which in all rendezvous shoots, such as the Seneca match, is vital to competing.

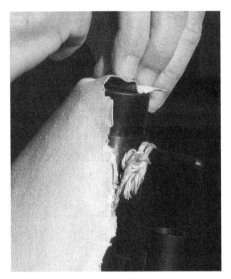

As always, premium care is necessary in loading for hunting and of course for all shooting matches.

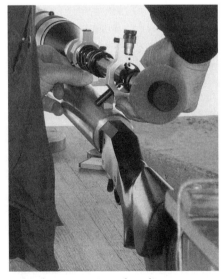

Sights that are not in perfect alignment can only spell one message—You lost the match. This is especially true when the sight, in this case telescopic, is removed after each shot and replaced before the next.

of hearing is treated to a show when the bullet cracks into something that makes a noise. Even with earplugs in place, a metal gong sends back a distinct clang when struck. These are often set up at long range, sometimes so far that the shooter has to pick out an aiming point well above the target. At one rendezvous gong event, the shooter had to aim his rifle to strike a metal gong 500 yards away. Considering the looping trajectory of a round ball, even from a large-bore rifle, it's no simple trick to guide a lead sphere out to 500 yards with accuracy. Successful shooters hit the 500-yard gong because they used a consistent aiming point far above the target — a visible white spot on the mountain in the background in this particular case. Once again, the larger round ball is better than the smaller one, not only for retained energy, but also trajectory, especially with a safe but strong powder charge behind it.

The Stakebuster Match

The stakebuster match incorporates a wooden plank usually about 6 inches wide, but any other size will work. Two shooters generally team up for this one. The idea is to cut the plank in half with rifle fire. Again, larger calibers are best for mathematical reasons. Fewer hits are required with bigger bullets. Calibers 58 and larger are ideal. Also helpful is sighting in carefully for this close-range event. It takes skill to draw a line across the wood with successive bullet strikes in order to cut the stake in two.

Swinging Charcoal Briquettes

Briquettes swinging on strings suspended from a horizontal wire make interesting targets, with a puff of smoke denoting a solid hit. A good-holding offhand rifle, preferably with a long barrel for muzzle weight and an extended sight radius, helps the shooter in this event.

Playing Cards

Playing cards set up to face the shooter edge-wise are great targets. These are normally arranged at close range, so spectators can witness bullets

hitting the cards. Many times, the bullet will make only a slice across the face of the card. It takes a direct hit to cut the card in two.

The Seneca Run

The Seneca Run can be played in different ways. Above, a run with smoothbore flintlocks only was the rule, but rifles are certainly at home in this fast-paced event, which reminds one a little of the Olympic Biathlon. The shooter must successfully accomplish a series of tasks, running from station to station. He must run the course at good speed, because he is up against the clock as well as the targets placed along the way. The marksman with the highest score in the least time is the winner. Rules can vary greatly, not only with the allowed firearm — flintlock, flintlock smoothbore, pistol, revolver — but also the tasks. In one Seneca Run, the shooter had to score on several targets arranged along a path, and after the last target, he was obliged to run back to the starting point to make a fire with tinder, flint, and steel. The tomahawk may be included as part of the run, as may the knife. Running from one target to the next requires reloading *safely*. Shooting is usually offhand, but one match allowed any stance, even prone. This is a shoot for the athletic. Good shooters who are slow on their feet do not normally claim first place. Ideally, the shooter uses a firearm he is highly familiar with so that he can not only hit the target readily, but also reload without a hitch. Since most Seneca Runs are conducted with offhand shooting, that longer-barreled, steady-holding rifle with good sight radius is right for the job. It should also hang well, meaning a little front-heavy.

The Running Boar

This match requires a special wall with a regulation size opening through which passes a boar target "running," that is, on the move from left to right, right to left. Only specific muzzleloaders are allowed. Winners know how much to lead, and you can bet that everyone who competes seriously has great follow-through—his or her rifle continuing to move even after the trigger is pulled.

The Slug Gun

Overused words such as *remarkable* and *awesome* would fit this game—if only they weren't so abused, because both words apply. These are very heavy and very special rifles shooting cast elongated bullets normally introduced "square to the bore" via a false muzzle, which is an alignment tool that fits precisely on the actual muzzle and removed after the bullet is delivered partway down the bore. The slug gun shoot is a benchrest affair, but not the same as other benchrest matches. It is exclusive unto itself strictly for the slug gun. No other is allowed, but in most cases it wouldn't matter anyway because a slug gun is pretty hard to match at a blackpowder shoot.

The Log Rest

This event simulates hunting conditions. It can be operated in many different ways. One is to have a walking path, strictly regulated. The contestant strolls along the path, encountering targets at intervals, and always at varying distances. Some are half-hidden by brush. Some are close, some far. Targets can be metallic silhouettes, paper targets with a dirt backstop, cutouts of animals, clay pigeons, and just about anything else. At each station, the shooter is provided with a log. The shooter may take the prone position, or sometimes sits and rests the forend of the rifle on the log. Although heavy-barrel rifles seem to do OK when the barrel itself is rested, as proved by many blackpowder-cartridge rifle shooters, consistency is best maintained by resting the forend of the muzzleloader over the log, rather than the barrel. Also, a heavy rifle, 9 pounds or more, rests more solidly in place than a lighter rifle, which is always the case regardless of rifle type.

Regulation Targets

There are many regulation target matches at rendezvous. They are not,

perhaps, as interesting as the novelty shoots, but they are valuable, and, in fact, show off the shooter and his equipment very well. Offhand shooting at regulation targets can be held at 25, 50, 100, 200 yards, even farther. Clearly, the more accurate the firearm the better, be it rifle, pistol, or revolver. As always, the stable firearm is at an advantage. With a rifle, that generally means the heavier model with longer barrel that has forward weight for steady holding and a long sight radius. Practice for the match should involve the same targets, as well as the same firearm and loads, to will be used at rendezvous. Learning to put bullet holes in a specific target face does not always transfer to another style target.

Knife and Hawk Tossing

Throwing knives and tomahawks is an art in itself requiring good knives and 'hawks to begin with, but also considerable practice.

Shotgun Competition

The shotgun is an obvious tool of competition at any rendezvous. Events can range from trap to Skeet and anything in between, the only limitation being the range of the shotgun and the imagination of the event designers. A look at the blackpowder shotguns used in playing this game will raise an eyebrow. Many are custom made to exacting specifications.

The Primitive Bow at Rendezvous

Mountain men were interested in bows and arrows. Osborne Russell in his *Journal of a Trapper* reports on running across a group of Snake Indians, as he called them. Editor Haines suggests that these were probably Sheepeater Indians, the only aboriginal peoples known to inhabit the Yellowstone Plateau. "They were well armed with bows and arrows with obsidian. The bows were beautifully wrought from Sheep, Buffaloe and Elk secured with Deer and Elk sinews and ornamented with porcupine quills and generally about 3 feet long," Russell reported.

Just one of many different rendezvous targets—metal pegs waiting to be struck and sent flying.

Cross-sticks serve as a rest for a prone shot at the silhouette match.

Here is an axe blade with cutting edge facing outward. The object of this match is cutting a round ball into two pieces by striking the blade edge. Then the two pieces in turn are supposed to each hit a clay pigeon, balloon, or any target that registers a hit, these being set up on either side of the blade.

Here is splitting the round ball on the blade of an axe, ready to shoot at. Success comes from striking the edge of the axe blade, thereby splitting the lead ball into two pieces, each piece striking a target placed on either side of the axe head.

The running boar match is one of the most enjoyable events at blackpowder shoots in general and at rendezvous gatherings where this demanding target is set up. This running boar event was held at a range where the event was properly run.

This Seneca Run is shooting out of the pouch only—no readyloads handy to slip downbore. The shooter much reach into his shooting bag for components—including pan powder, since this particular Run was flintlock smoothbore musket only.

The moving boar is fired upon. This takes proper lead, firing with the rifle in motion, or else the ball will zip behind the boar.

There are various types of heavy bench guns, but the goal is always the same—the best possible groups on the target.

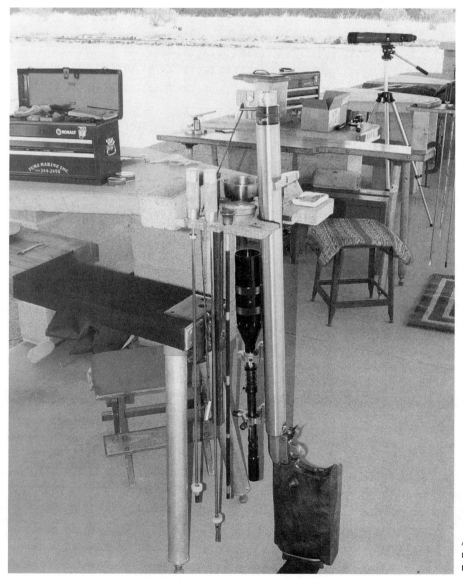

A look at a bench gun—heavy weight with massive barrel indicate that this rifle was never meant to be carried into the field.

The author also saw an Indian buffalo hunt first-hand. "At length an Indian pursued a Cow close to me running alongside of her he let slip an arrow and she fell." There would be nothing wrong with a mountain man using the bow and arrow to procure a little camp food, especially in a region where a gunshot might be heard by "the wrong people." At rendezvous, primitive type bows are definitely at home, and shooting matches may be held. The bows are made by different artisans. See Traditional Bowyers guide in *Traditional Archery*, a Stackpole Books publication from 1999 for bowmakers dealing in primitive-style archery tackle.

Anything Safe Goes

As long as it's safe, rendezvous shooting matches can range from moving targets on a taut wire — a great event, usually a boar sliding from right to left, then left to right — to multiple-skill competitions, where rifle, handgun, and even shotgun are put into play in a single match, similar to Cowboy Action Shooting. Most events have spectator interest. Something goes *clang* like a gong in the distance, or *poof*, when a charcoal briquette blows up, or *pop* as balloons are riddled with split-in-two round balls. Meanwhile, silhouettes and many other types of targets topple over when struck. This is good, because it promotes interest in the great sport of blackpowder shooting. Unlike the blackpowder-cartridge silhouette shooting and Cowboy Action Shooting, which are both nationally organized, rendezvous games are designed more for entertainment than score, with fun for shooter and spectator alike.

The rendezvous may have a number of standard target faces to fire upon with bullseyes of different sizes appropriate for the distance and the firearm used in the event.

Primitive archery is often one of the games played at rendezvous and as can be seen here, it is a shooting game. This contestant is dressed in period clothing.

The primitive bow is the only type allowed—it's made of wood, essentially, and it's basically of the longbow design.

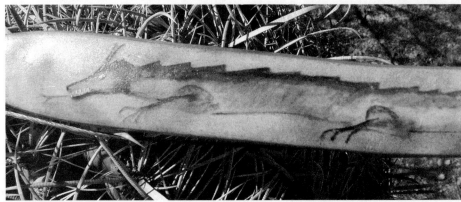

So Many More

The National Muzzle Loading Rifle Association's Western National Shoot that I visited included a number of excellent matches, many of which are named above, some which are not. There is the benchrest match, flintlock offhand match, Schuetzen, chunk gun, buffalo match, and so forth. Some are for juniors, sub-juniors, and husband-wife teams.

One of the more fascinating and colorful aspects of the rendezvous is the firing of cannon or mortar, often done at high noon and possibly again at the close of the day when the shops on trade row are closing down.

Fire-starting may not be a shooting event, but it is part of the rendezvous and expert contestants can start a flint-and-steel fire in mere seconds using only the components that are stashed in their firebugs.

40 BLACKPOWDER KNIVES AND HAWKS

Experts at both knife- and tomahawk-throwing take time out to help young people get started on the road to proficiency and safety.

Blackpowder knives and tomahawks, the latter often shortened to 'hawks, or just plain hawks, are part of the muzzleloading shooting game. There are events at rendezvous, for example, that call for knife and hawk throwing. And of course knives and hawks are also important to hunting, camping, and basic woodsmanship. A hunter may be toting an ultra-modern muzzleloader, but odds are no matter how up-to-date his knife is, the basics remain the same—a sort of wedge that parts media of one kind or another. Hawks on the trail these days are mainly hatchets or hand axes, and will be treated as such in this chapter—along with the tomahawk proper. Both knives and hawks (hatchets) have long been tools of war as well as tools of camp, trail, or competition. While our fifth edition is more dedicated to shooting than ever, knives and hawks could not be ignored.

Both kept cropping up in one way or another, especially at one particular blackpowder shoot I attended where a premier knife and hawk thrower took his time to get young people and beginners a good start in the game.

Hawks First

For no particular reason, hawks, hatchets, and hand axes demand attention first. Each year, I read again two books. These are *Witchery of Archery* by Maurice (pronounced Morris) Thompson and *Cache Lake Country* by John L. Rowlands. Borrowing from Melville's *Moby Dick*, I find that these two titles warm the winter in my soul—not figuratively, but realistically when the snow is deep outside and perhaps we are at our cabin at 8,000 feet elevation in the Rockies. The first book tells of the Thompson brothers bringing bowhunting back to America. The second is the

The hand axe is an important camp tool. Here, brush is cleared out of a deadfall to make a wind shelter for a tent.

story of Rowlands living in the back-woods alone but for two interesting neighbors, one an Indian chief. There's little of knife and hawk in the first book. I note it for reader interest only. But the second title bears a sentence that caught my eye. It went, "Your axe is the most valuable tool in the woods." Maybe so. Surely, hunters of old carried an axe, hatchet, tomahawk, or similar tool. Consider the Ice Man, frozen in the ice some 3,500 years ago, recently discovered due to the melting of a glacier in the Italian Alps. He had an axe with a copper head. That threw anthropologists' dating into a backspin, for copper was not supposed to show up for quite some time.

Long before the Ice Man, there was the stone axe. I used to have two examples, both leaning more to bopping a foe on the head than chopping firewood. Then there was the peace pipe, tomahawk and smoking instrument all in one. The frontier was loaded with axes and before that Lewis and Clark brought a batch of tomahawks over on their famous expedition into the Far West. Later, The United States Trade Office record of 1890 lists 50 pipe tomahawks from England at $100.56, plus $1.63 ship freight, 53 cents cartage over ground in America, plus a duty of $18.78—for a total of $121.50, proving that government interest in the tomahawk/hand axe had not waned. No Plains Indian warrior of merit would go without his tomahawk. Carl P. Russell in his fine book, *Firearms, Traps & Tools of the Mountain Men* wrote, "Only firearms and rum finally rivaled it [tomahawks] in importance to the Indian." The names get mixed up, but the tool stays the same. The mountain men of the 19th century carried a tomahawk but called it a "hunter's hatchet." It was shaped and sized not so differently from what we might carry today. The word "hatchet" came from various sources, one being *hachotz*, another *hatcheette*, both of these terms from the 1500s. Russell believes that Indians, soon after getting a hold of manufactured hand

Tomahawk tossing at rendezvous is a legitimate competition, with some buckskinners becoming experts at hitting a mark.

axes, called them tomahawks after the aboriginal word that it replaced.

Hand axes varied in all aspects, including the *head*, also known as the *blade* or *bit*, as well as the *eye*, the opening through which the *handle* fit, which is also known as the *helve*, and the *poll*, the blunt back end if there was such. While the shape of the bit varies greatly today, all have the same general configuration of their prehistoric precursor. The Stone Age axe, viewed from the top, is a wedge with a wider back end and

a slender forepart. Of course, the basic design of the knife is the same—a wedge that separates media, as noted earlier. U.S. government tomahawks date back in time, but so do British tomahawks. Late 18th century British soldiers of the 42nd Black Watch were equipped with hatchets. Russell's book spends 79 pages on axes of different types. And even at that, the author could not cover all examples of that one historical period alone—the Fur Trade era of the Far West. It's no wonder that the hand axe, hatchet, tomahawk—call it what you will—remains with us today in many different styles. The progression is clear. After the Fur Trade, and beyond the time of the great buffalo hunt, the axe in all its forms continued in prominence.

E.N. Woodcock, that grand old hunter and trapper, carried a hand axe. On page 97 of his book, *Fifty Years a Hunter and Trapper*, Woodcock is shown making a log set for fox, a broad-bitted hand axe hangs at his side. E. Kreps in another old *Fur-Fish-Game* publication, *Camp and Trail Methods*, divides axes into "two classes—the light belt axe or hatchet and the camp axe." That's interesting because I have a light belt axe that I carry and a camp axe. The belt axe is from Cold Steel Company (see Directory). It has a 3.5-inch primary edge of drop-forged 5150 steel and it weighs only 20 ounces. This little tomahawk has built night shelters—crisscross lat-

Buckskinners who get good at the tomahawk throw can drive the blade of the 'hawk deep into the target.

There are many fine tomahawks on the market today. These are from Cold Steel Company and are typical of the fine cutlery from that outfit. Put through tough testing, these 'hawks came through.

ticework of dead branches to support a tarp. While I harbor no such thought of defending life and limb with any type of tomahawk, many outdoorsmen of the past did just that. If a bear has a hold on the toe of your boot and you've nothing but your tomahawk, better to wield that than a series of squeals and screams. My camp axe is a Cruiser type from Gerber. Amazing how often these two hand axe/hatchet/tomahawks go into use.

A couple seasons ago I set up tent in Northern Wyoming deer country. I had done a masterful job of selecting a nice open space. While Wyoming is a windy state, that particular setting is not windy. In two decades of hunting those grounds, wind was never a problem. That night a gale force came up that threatened to make our tent airborne. In the morning I set out to check the deer situation. When I returned my wife had chopped out a deadfall, creating a wind-defying channel for our tent. She did the job with a hand axe. I'm no longer allowed to choose a campsite. The next day I got a whitetail buck in a thicket so dense that going from one place to another sometimes demanded crawling through deer passages. The buck had to be backpacked out. While of small rack, the animal was healthy of size. I made the trip in two hauls—sectioning the carcass in two pieces

with—a hand axe, of course. George W. Sears was one of the best-known and most revered woodsman of his day. His readers knew him as Nessmuk. He admired what he called a hatchet. "Before I was a dozen years old," he said, "I came to realize that a light hatchet was a sine quo non in woodcraft." We might call it the cat's pajamas instead of a sine quo non, but it means the same thing—great to have on hand, and all but indispensable.

Later still, Calvin Rutstrum, in his book *The New Way of the Wilderness* wrote, "The ax commonly used on canoe trips is the three-quarter size, often referred to as a 'boy's ax' or poleax." Poleax. We've all heard of something being poleaxed. Later still, Bernard S. Mason in *Woodcraft and Camping* refers to his "camp hatchet." Mason illustrates six types of axe useful in camping and trail hiking: Small Camp Axe by Collins, which is simply our hatchet, camp axe with 18-inch handle by the Marble Company, Hudson's Bay axe by Collins, Cruiser double-bit by Marble, Cedar Axe by Plumb, full-sized Pole Ax by Plumb, and full-bit by Knot Klipper. All but one of the names is foreign to me—being Hudson's Bay. But the idea is solid—the axe is a versatile tool that comes in many shapes and sizes. Trappers make sets with them. Hunters build camps and section big game. Campers clear tent spots, pounding in tent pegs with the poll end, wilderness backpackers build "tomahawk shelters" of interlaced branches, and of course hand axes, reasonable size tomahawks, and hatchets make little wood out of big wood for campfires. The buckskinner mainly throws his tomahawk, however, and Lynn Thompson's Special Projects Company in Ventura, California offers a course called "Fighting with a Tomahawk."

Before leaving the tomahawk to talk knife a little, here—more for fun than education—is a list of different names for the axe: tomahawk, axe, ax, hand axe, belt axe, camp axe, hatchet, camp hatchet, hunter's hatchet, poleax, pole axe, boy's axe, cruiser axe, battle axe,

Viet Nam tomahawk, pipe tomahawk, ceremonial tomahawk, frontier hawk, bad axe, rifleman's hawk, trail hawk, Norse hawk, and more. Not to be forgotten, or even moved to the back of the list of outdoor gear, *Outdoor Life* magazine, February of 2006, carried a piece on "The Old-Fashioned Tomahawk–Why You Should Add it to Your Pack." The article began with, "A thousand years ago, the Vikings brandished a weapon known as a battle-ax. Centuries later, native Americans fashioned a shorter, lighter ax called the tomahawk.

Today, sportsmen rarely think of the tomahawk as an essential gear item. Aside from traditional muzzleloader hunters, few sportsmen carry 'hawks afield.' Yet the tomahawk is more practical than a standard hatchet. The article goes on to list several facts: Indians (my Indian friends hate being called Native Americans) whacked many a pioneer over the head with a tomahawk, proving the tool's usefulness in combat. Lynn Thompson of Cold Steel has used his tomahawk to finish off wild boars, proving its worth in the game field. The tomahawk, with its narrower head, is ideal for sectioning big game precisely for packing the meat, hide, and rack out. The tomahawk produces less stress on the handler than a heavier tool. In camp the outdoorsman can use a tomahawk, according to this *Outdoor Life* piece, to pound in tent pegs, dig a latrine, trench a fire ring, chop out roots in the tent area, mash nuts for a snack, and defend himself. Lastly, "the long handle is helpful for bowhunters cutting hard-to-reach limbs for shooting lanes." There you have it.

The Muzzleloader Knife

Should probably be the outdoorsman's knife, but this book is about blackpowder. A sharp rock was probably the first "knife." The flint knife to follow was truly a knife. While the 3,500-year-old Ice Man had a copper-bladed hand axe, his knife was flint. Flint can be amazingly sharp. A doctor friend told me that tiny chips of flint are far sharper than the sharpest scalpel. In *Tools of the Old and New Stone Age* by Jacques Bordaz, the author writes, "Experiments have been shown that an animal can be skinned with a backed blade almost as rapidly as rapidly as a steel knife, by applying pressure with the index finger on the blunted edge." A backed flint knife is simply one that has one cutting edge, the other side flattened. In other words, sharp on one side of the blade only. I like knives. I have several. While I would not trade one of my modern skinning knives, such as a Benchmade that did four deer before requiring sharpening, or a Spyderco Moran Plain that remained sharp after field-dressing *and skinning* four antelope, I concur that flint can be very sharp. I have seen flint knives carried at rendezvous, when in fact the mountain man's era was well after flint went the way of the dodo bird. Nonetheless, flint is fun to fool with and yes, I had to try it—I did remove the hide from a deer with a flint knife. A Benchmade or Spyderco it was not, but it worked, and the blade didn't even break.

A patch knife is not needed for cutting patches on the muzzle of a rifle or pistol, but it sure works. Historians tell me that some kits of the mountain men had these small knives in them. I have to wonder why, since these men surely had knives at their side. I have found something interesting about the patch knife. Since I pre-cut my patches for hunting trips, I don't really have to have a patch knife handy. But I can't find a better paring knife, unless it might be a particular Cold Steel small tanto that I have, for peeling potatoes with minimal meat loss. We all know that knives are a huge business the world over. This includes many knives, handmade or commercial, specifically for blackpowder shooters. *Shoot Magazine* always carries a bundle of interesting pieces. One I particularly found interesting was "ML Knives" by Chucky, who isn't fooling me—I know this is really Mr. Andy Fink, Editor-in-Chief of the magazine. Chucky points out in this November/December 2005 issue that "When I go to a Western-action shooting event of any kind, I almost always wear a knife on my belt and occasionally one around my neck or in my boot. Mostly it is for aesthetics, however, I use these at shooting events on a regular basis."

The ML title of Chucky's article stands for ml knives copied from late 1700s and early 1800s models. Two of the knives reviewed in this issue of *Shoot! Magazine* epitomize the trend of copying period knives with accuracy. One is a belt dagger. The other is a bowie. I have a Krause Publications book in my library on the topic of *sporting knives*. Of course, the major theme centers on the modern knife—the world has never seen better. But the most fascinating knives in the book—forget utility now—were those made with damascus blades. One that

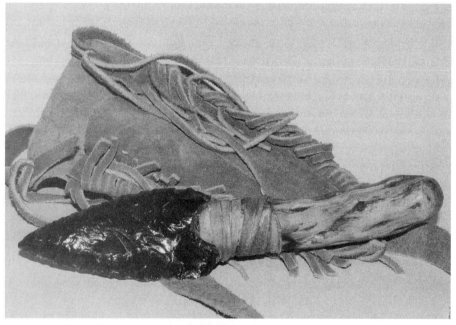

Knives as well as tomahawks were on the scene eons ago. Flint proved so useful that today tiny pieces of flint can be used in delicate surgery, since flint splinters are many times sharper than the sharpest scalpel. This flint knife was knapped by one of the author's readers.

Many different hand axe/tomahawk types came about over time and continue to come forth today. These unique models are from the McGowan Manufacturing Company. They vary according to intended use, including throwing.

A close look at the McGowan hand axe/tomahawk reveals strength of manufacture and head design.

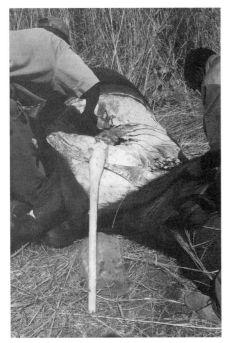

Trackers in Africa use a short-handled axe to dress author's Cape buffalo. The meat was carefully processed and delivered to a village for sharing. This particular tool is made by inserting the head into a slit in a piece of branch.

One of the more famous tomahawk embellishments from the past, still used today, is called the weeping heart.

is for keeping, not cutting, is the Boker 546 damascus with shape just like the fighting knife Colonel Rex Applegate was famous for developing for U.S. forces. "Lookin' Sharp" is another article I ran across in *Shoot! Magazine*. The byline is Hurricane, who happens to be a lot better looking than Chucky. She also looks better in her outfit. And sure as taxes and rain in Ketchikan a beautiful damascus blade knife with maple handle spans across two pages of this September/October 2005 issue. Another handsome knife is pictured. It's a guardless bowie with stag handle. One of the knives pictured in this feature article was plain-looking to the point of handsome—a bowie style with screwdriver tip and plain bone handle.

A fine little book by Harold L. Peterson, *A History of Knives*, begins with the primitive, running forward to a number of military knives. Peterson says the bowie knife "was a direct descendent of the Viking scramasax.

Bowie's name became attached to this specific knife style, which was essentially a large all-purpose knife. If you had to defend your life with a bowie, you could, as long as you weren't taking a knife to a gunfight. You might also cut your buffalo steak with the same knife or if sharp enough and you didn't mind the nicks, shave your face. According to Peterson, his brother Rezin gave Jim Bowie's first bowie to him in 1827. In 1830 Bowie had a larger knife built for him with a somewhat different design by blacksmith James Black. No one knows exactly what Bowie's knives looked like and the whole idea of a bowie knife may have faded away, but for the fame of the man who carried one. Bowie died at the Alamo in 1836, which was enough to preserve his fame. A myth grew around the man, some of the tale being more fact that fiction. Apparently, Jim's big knife was burned on his funeral pyre at the Alamo. The big knife

The Buffalo Bill Museum in Cody, Wyoming, offers this wonderful scene of a tipi on the plains. The Plains Indian did much work with his tomahawk, including trimming tipi poles as well as fighting.

is far from dead today. Atlanta Cutlery, as one example only, has a huge "1850 Bowie" that weighs in at one pound, four ounces. The blade is 12-1/2 inches long. I have a similar knife from Traditions. It will split a grouse in two with one deft stroke.

We think of the "mountain man" knife as something special. In a way it was, but not for its beauty, or even utility. It was special by being a common "butcher knife" capable of taking a pretty good beating while doing what it was meant to do—cutting anything from a chunk of leather to the hide of a buffalo. Carl P. Russell's book devotes a long chapter to "Knives of the Frontiersmen," and just as we might expect, there was no single knife of the frontiersmen. Russell writes, "Surprisingly, the design of the hunter's knife in 1800 often closely approximated the style of knives used throughout the greater part of Europe one thousand years B.C." The author refers to style, not materials. The ancient knife was often made of bronze, bronze being a broad range of copper alloys, mainly an amalgam of tin and copper, sometimes inclusive of phosphorous or aluminum. The frontiersmen's knife blade was made of steel (iron and carbon). The butcher knife, as I see it, is extremely plain in style, essentially a common trade knife. There were references in the U.S. Indian Trade Office of the late 1700s to the American Fur Company of the 1840s to a "scalping knife." This knife was not, specifically, intended to scalp anyone. It was simply a butcher knife, a cheap butcher knife at that.

"We want an article of good appearance, but cheap, to offer the U.S. Indian Office." The government got its cheap "scalping knife." One order shows 60 dozen at $10.75, or about nine cents per knife. Granted that at the time, nine cents was worth about nine pennies. Still, that was a cheap knife, even for 1840. But the government could do better. Another order came in for 200 dozen knives for $8.12, about

These tomahawks are used today for rendezvous dress, competition throwing, and many camp chores. They follow upon a 19th-century design from Indian culture.

The major difference between tomahawks of the past and today's 'hawk is today's better steel. The design, however, remains much the same.

seven cents each. What is lost in the translation, however, is the fact that the North American Indian did not have steel tools until the white man showed up. This is proved by the fact that sometimes broadheads and other tools were made from picked-up wagon wheel hoops. So the cheap butcher knife, or scalper, was not so bad after all. It cut and would last quite a long time. All in all, however, the idea was profit. The American Fur Company in New York wanted close to 100 percent profit on knives. Not a bad turnaround for a government contract, and certainly not an approach that was abandoned in the 19th century.

What it boils down to is the fact that blackpowder shooters in the 21st century require knives and tomahawks. The knives are tools found in shooting boxes or shooting bags, or worn around the waist on a belt, or tucked in a sash, or stashed in a boot. The tomahawks are equally desirable for the same duties—camp work, wearing for show, and of course, along with the knife, throwing at a target. Those who don't toss either knives or tomahawks, or wear them as part of a period costume, usually gravitate to the more modern examples of both tools.

Many different knife styles were employed in the "old days." Some were quite unique. This knife was built by one of the author's readers. It uses a pronghorn antelope horn for a handle.

For contrast, here is a Spyderco Moran knife. Is it better than old-time knives? Absolutely. The design by Moran is superb and the steel is far superior to that of old. And yet, it functions as a wedge to part material, just as the flint knife did countless ages ago.

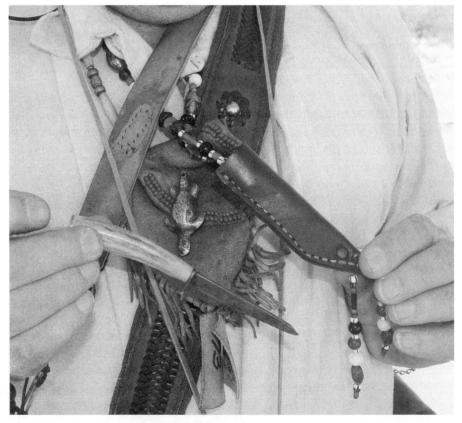

Any small knife can serve as a patch knife to slice away excess cloth from the muzzle of the ball-shooting gun.

The big knife in the foreground is of the Bowie persuasion, while the others are of different intentions, including hiding in a boot—hence "boot knife."

As a matter of stark contrast, consider the old-time butcher knife, top, with a modern knife constructed of the finest steel.

The butcher knife of the 19th century was extremely plain. It was intended to sell for very little, and yet serve relatively well. These two knives represent the general style of butcher knife that came West with the Fur Trade.

41 JUST FOR SHOW AND TELL

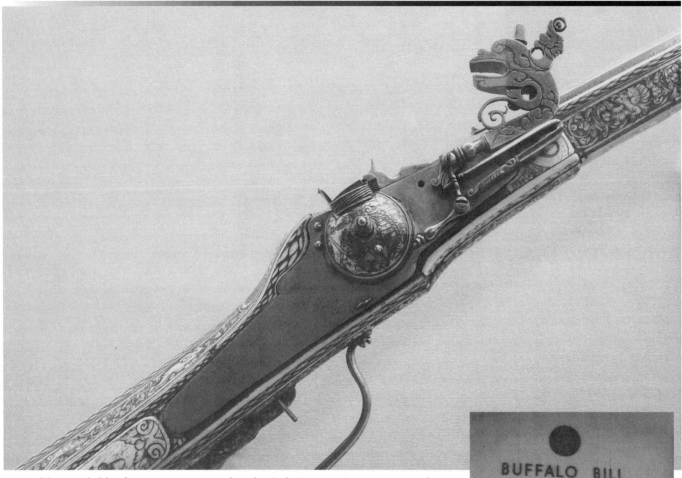

Many of the guns held in firearms museums, such as the Cody Firearms Museum, are simply irreplaceable. While only a few private collectors have a firearm like this one for "show and tell," we can all enjoy viewing guns like this at a museum.

Collecting is bigger than ever. Just about anything is collectible, from bottle caps to World War II warplanes. Some antiques, I fear, are simply "stuff" tossed into the barn or hoisted up to the attic, discarded to surface again as "treasure." This is not true of guns, or of the related software and hardware. Guns, most of them, were made to last virtually forever with decent care. They are also of terrific historical value. I marvel as a visitor to the Buffalo Bill Historical Society in Cody, Wyoming, watching and listening to people ooh and ah over guns when they, themselves, never owned a firearm in their lives. They buzz on and on about the amazing history embodied in firearms on display at this first-class museum with Winchester, Remington, Browning, Marlin and other famous collections from matchlocks to machineguns.

Originals

Because guns are built to last, originals abound from the 19th century and much earlier. In preparation for this chapter I enjoyably worked my way through a current *Gun List*. Two things became evident: you can find what you want and values have escalated since the fourth edition of this book was written. An article on the value of a Winchester single-shot pointed out a steady asking price from 1991 to 2004, around $3,750 (in excellent shape).

All persons associated with a full-scale museum have an important responsibility to the public. Two persons who do a fine job of promoting public interest and appreciation in the huge firearm collection at the Cody Firearms Museum in Cody, Wyoming are Mr. W. Warren Newman, left, and Mr. Lee Haines.

The price jumped to $6,500 in 2005. I found a Westley Richards Deluxe Droplock double-rifle, 375 flanged cartridge, new, unfired—POR—price on request. You can bet the tab resembles the sticker on a small car. A Holland and Holland, all original, pristine condition, marked as "500" caliber, had a $14,950 price tag. An original Model 1873 Winchester, caliber not noted, $2,795 in 95 percent condition. Add a Winchester 1886 in 45-90, excellent bore, $$6,495, and a Colt 1903 Pocket Model like new in original box with all papers--$1,495. How about a Jenks "Mule Ear" carbine, circa 1840s, 54-caliber sidehammer? Under $4,000 in great shape. The list goes on.

Replicas

Dedicated collectors may scoff at building a collection of replicas. However, these guns fit perfectly in history and investment is minimal compared to the "real thing." What's more, shooting replicas for a feel of days old is no problem. Value will not decrease because there is no heavy collector value to begin with. The general run of replicas is relatively complete, including rifled muskets and smoothbores, such as the Brown Bess, along with Sharps, Remington Rolling blocks, and the sought-after Colt Lightning, now built safer than ever with modern upgrades. A Winchester High Wall fetching well over $3500 is available in replica for a fraction of that price. Likewise Models 1873 and 1886 Winchesters. Modern Marlin rifles, while not necessarily replicas, are very much like Marlins of the 19th and early 20th centuries. I'm confident that my Marlin 336 Cowboy in 38-55 Winchester will shoot right along with, and perhaps better than, a similar model from the past.

What to Collect

Books

Book collecting does not have to be expensive, although there are certain titles that demand considerable greenbacks. Books are easier to find than

ever in this age of the Internet. I have my own arms library broken down into categories: gun books, hunting books, books on survival, outdoor adventure, as well as general histories, such as the Fur Trade and American Civil War. And so forth. *Gun Digest* has a long list of books pertaining to firearms collection. It is called "The Arms Library" and lists numerous titles, such as *Military Small Arms of the 20th Century, 7th Edition*, by well-known expert Ian V. Hogg. *A History of the Colt Revolver* covers that company's handguns from 1836 to 1940. *The Winchester Book* by George Madis in another good one. One of my favorites is the Marlin history by William S. Brophy. There is also a library section at the back of this book.

Cartridges

I wish I had started a cartridge collection a long time ago. But as interesting rounds came my way I passed them on, thinking I probably would not find more to make a real collection. I was naïve about collecting cartridges. My favorite search engine, Google, woke me up. I found "A Car-

tridge Collectors Glossary" reference and the IAA (International Ammunition Association, Inc.) with a Journal Cumulative Index showing 50 years of data. I also found a Collector's Corner that included hits for associations and organizations, publications; trade shows with dates, commercial listings, private collectors and more. *Cartridges of the World* from Krause Publications is a good starting place for collecting, with solid information on ammunition worldwide. Prices vary on collectible cartridges. Some are quite expensive. The 40-60 Maynard commands close to 60 dollars. A 40-70 Maynard can run $80.00. But hold on—one experimental 70-150 Winchester round may run as high as $450!

Powder horns, Flask, and Accoutrements – Blackpowder

No end to it—all sorts of blackpowder accoutrements are for sale, beginning in the Trader's Row of any rendezvous where I have found a number of treasures, most of them newly made by hand in replication of items past. This includes a long list of powder

Colt Model 1873 Single Action
Army Revolver

Maker: Colt Patent Firearms
Manufacturing Co.; Hartford, CT
Serial Number: 51193
Caliber: .44-40
Date: 1879
Catalogue Number: 1988.9.1

Gift of Lillian E. Herring

Some firearms in both public and private collections are valued in the thousands of dollars.

Collecting originals can be expensive, albeit often a good investment. For the firearms student who is satisfied with a replica of an original, these are available. Here is a fine replica from the Navy Arms Company—a close copy of the Remington Model of 1858, a revolver that saw action in the American Civil War.

Here is a well-made Gibbs DeLuxe Rifle from the Pedersoli factory in Italy. It's a shooter, but can also be held as a show and tell firearm.

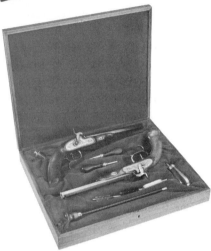

How much would a nice set of dueling pistols run—if such a set of originals could be located? A lot. These Pedersoli Dueling Pistols are handsome and representative of the dueling pistol breed at a reasonable price.

A blackpowder fan will want to see blackpowder cartridges. There are hundreds of different types from the past.

Powder flasks, horns, and many other accoutrements are collectible. Originals are fine, but a good copy such as this one from Pedersoli also round out a collection.

horns. Powder horns are highly collectible. The home page of American Powderhorns notes, "The powderhorn was the companion to every musket in early America. Carried by huntsman, soldier, and explorer alike, the powderhorn is an original American art form." Absolutely true. The American Powderhorns site is from the private collection of Rich Nard. It is not a catalog as such, but serves as a learning port of entry for anyone interested in collecting. Mark Toigo's Gallery of Powder Horns offers multiple pages of beautiful examples with an option to order a special powder horn for use or collecting. There are many other collectible accoutrements, some original, some replicated in the old tradition.

Catalogs

Old catalogs provide solid information on what used to be available and at what price. I often refer to a Winchester 1916 catalog for information on guns and ammo of that period. A Montgomery Ward & Co. catalog, Fall & Winter, 1894-1895, taught me about the Colt Hammerless Breech Loading shotgun with Damascus barrels, a 10-bore that sold for $95.00 for the engraved model—big bucks for the late 19th century when a perfectly fine Marlin side-ejector 32-20, 38-40, or 44-40 sold for $11.86. The equally excellent Marlin lever-action Model 1893 was priced at $14.18 in 32-40 or 38-55. Winchester's 1893 pump-action 12-gauge ran a shade over $16.00 in the old catalog, while the Winchester 1886 went for $21.00—from the factory—only $14.18 from Wards. The Ward catalog was complete with different sights, blackpowder gun parts, and a host of contemporary cartridges. Pin-fire paper shotgun shells were still available in 20, 16, 14, 12, and 10 gauges. Call up www.cornellpubs.com for 500-plus gun catalogs.

Old Advertisements

The Internet comes to the forefront as a shooter goes about searching for old advertisements. I have located a number of ads from the past, interesting because they embrace the times. Some would be virtually outlawed today—how about photo of a hunter posed with a defunct gorilla? Not a good ad for the 21st century!

Calendars

There are current calendars that will one day be collectible. The Winchester calendar on my desk is a prime example with the Winchester Rider on the cover along with gun and hunting scenes inside, one with a hunter on snowshoes wearing a fur cap, capote-type hooded blanket coat, Winchester lever-action rifle in hand as a large pack of wolves rounds the bend of a snow bank. The painting is titled, "Wolves with Trapper," artwork by Phillip R. Goodwin circa 1905.

Posters

A number of interesting shooting posters have surfaced over the years. I have one in my Wyoming writing office dealing with cartridges offered by the Union Metallic Company.

Advertising Tins

Original tins can be costly, but not always. I came off with a very old Remington advertising tin for a sawbuck at an auction.

Old Photographs

I have a photograph of Colonel Tim McCoy— remembered only by fans of B-western black & white films. I have another of Jimmy Stewart holding his

How about collecting various tomahawks and hand axes? And why not? There was a multitude of varying designs from the past, as well as some particularly interesting models from today's cutlery experts.

Old photographs are highly collectible. This one is of the 18th century Joanna Furnace Iron Making Complex. The photograph was taken long after the factory was defunct in 1918.

1 of 1,000 Winchester from the movie. The Internet also has Picture History, which contains a huge number of photographs of the past, including an especially interesting one of Sir S.W. Baker (see Chapter 47).

Gun Art

Gun art ranges from highly expensive bronze figures to reasonably priced works depicting all kinds of shooting. Our cabin wall in the high mountains has a wonderful print showing Plains Indians with a Sharps rifle. The warriors look mighty pleased with their find.

Where to Look

Gun Shows

Gun shows can be highly rewarding in at least three ways: entertainment, learning, and finding collectibles. I have located good gun books, powder horns, flasks, and tools of every description, along with just about any other shooting item imaginable. Finding gun shows is simple. Go on line. There is always a long list of gun show announcements in the *Gun List*.

Auctions

When the buying frenzy sets in, gun auctions are a joke. I went to one in Wyoming where police-confiscated guns were for sale. I had an eye on a few that would make good shooters for a program we run teaching kids from single parent families how to shoot safely. These were ordinary 22-rimfire rifles, used. In minutes, the bidding was *beyond* full retail. On the other hand, I have found collectible treasures at auctions, including advertising tins, old photographs, catalogs, gun books and magazines. Auctions are also on line and in gun sales publications, such as *Shotgun News* and *Gun List*.

Windfalls

Sometimes a windfall find puts excellent collectible guns and shooting accessories for sale to the public. Atlanta Cutlery/International Military Antiques acquisition of the Royal Nepalese Armory is an example with originals: P-1842 muskets, 1853 Enfield muskets, P-1864 Snyder rifles, as well as the rare "Gahendra" model Martini rifles and what I tested, the Martini-Henry variant Model P-1871 Short Lever, famous for its role in the British Army and Zulu Nation wars at the battles of Isandhlanan and Rorke's Drift. Accessories include the original Martini-Henry p-1876 Socket Bayonet, original Gahendra Martini Socket Bayonet, and the original Gurkha "Kukri" Fighting Knife made famous by the Gurkha forces in World War II. There are also a few reproduction products to go with the original guns and accessories, including a British White Buff Leather Rifle Sling, Canvas Gun Sleeve, and Martini-Henry Leather Handguard. A couple books on the general topic also—*Treasure is Where You Find It* and *Guns of the Gurkhas*.

Guns Again

Collecting by period narrows the field: guns of the Civil War, for example. I read of a collector who concentrated on Indian guns. He had among his treasures a Northwest trade musket made by Barnett dated 1866, a Model 1866 Winchester carbine with decorative tacks, a Spencer carbine, Model 1860, also adorned with tacks, flintlock military long arms, a Leman fullstock plains rifle, and many more.

Condition

The percentage value is not perfect, with the exception of 100 percent, indicating a firearm in brand new condition. However, the categories are extremely important to a collector because they represent a close approximation of condition. There are different grading systems, but first, what is a modern firearm and what is an antique?

Modern or Antique?

A modern firearm may be from a distant era. A good example is the Colt Model 1873 revolver. Antique more accurately describes firearms no longer in manufacture, *even if they have been replicated in recent times.*

Gun art comes in all forms. This little piece is not an expensive collectible, as collectibles go, but it remains a favorite of the author. It's a limited edition of "The Kiowa Scout" with his blackpowder rifle at the ready. The work is so true that it is easy to tell that the rifle is a Springfield Trap Door.

This is a contemporary tomahawk from Pedersoli, but it's easy to visualize it gracing the wall of a trophy room or shooting room of a blackpowder enthusiast.

Atlanta Cutlery/International Military Antiques found a windfall in the form of Victorian-era blackpowder cartridge rifles of the British Army. This is the Martini-Henry of that time.

Grading Systems

NIB

NIB stands for new in the box. This category pertains to manufactured arms, since custom or handmade guns never had boxes. A firearm in NIB is essentially the same as brand new with no signs of use.

Excellent

Probably no original box, but the gun is intact in all regards. It may be referred to as 100 percent factory as well, meaning no additions or deletions. An excellent firearm need not retain 100 percent original finish. Modern firearms must show 95 percent original finish, while antique guns require only 80 percent original finish to qualify. The excellent firearm is in perfect working condition, all inner parts intact and functioning. Antiques must show with clean sharp rifling, if it's a rifled arm.

Very Good

Very good condition is a high ranking. The firearm must be in prime working order with modern arms retaining at least 85 percent original finish. Antiques may retain as little as 25 percent original finish. But they must be in excellent mechanical condition with good bores and no evidence of repairs.

This Martini-Henry rifle of the Victorian era is an antique and sold as such. It's ideal for collection, and as a show-and-tell.

Poor

Inoperable firearm with collector value only. These guns must be considered dangerous to shoot. Modern arms in this category may have no original finish. Poor grade antiques rarely show any original finish with dark bores, often pitted. Guns in poor condition may show repairs and alterations with low quality workmanship.

Blackpowder Guns

Collectible blackpowder guns with important historical background are highly valuable. A prime example is the military version of the Colt Walker, the big six-gun of the 19th century meant to be carried on a horse. The Walker cap 'n' ball revolver was rare even during its days of manufacture. A military Walker in excellent condition may exceed $50,000. One in poor condition might fetch $20,000. The civilian model of the Walker, numbered from 1001 to 1100, is worth slightly less than the coveted military version, but as high as $45,000 for one ranked excellent down to around $18,000 for the same gun in poor shape.

Blackpowder guns are also valued for their special appointments, such as high-grade engraving. Certain Winchester factory lever-action rifles were

Good

A gun in good condition must be in safe for shooting. Modern firearms must retain about 60 percent original finish, while antiques in may be fairly devoid of finish. Guns in good condition may show some refinishing. Modern arms in good condition must show at least fairly good bores. Antiques rated as good may have poor bores for collecting, not shooting.

Fair

The gun must be intact and unbroken. Evidence of repair is acceptable. Modern guns must retain about 25 percent minimum finish, while antiques can be essentially devoid of original finish. Modern guns in fair condition must have shootable bores, rather than pitted ones.

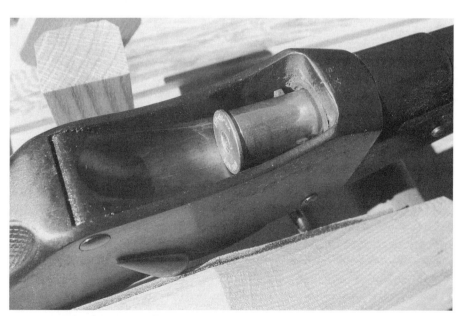

One aspect of collection goes beyond the basic historical value of a firearm to its specific operation. This antique Martini-Henry British fighting rifle is an example of a falling block action.

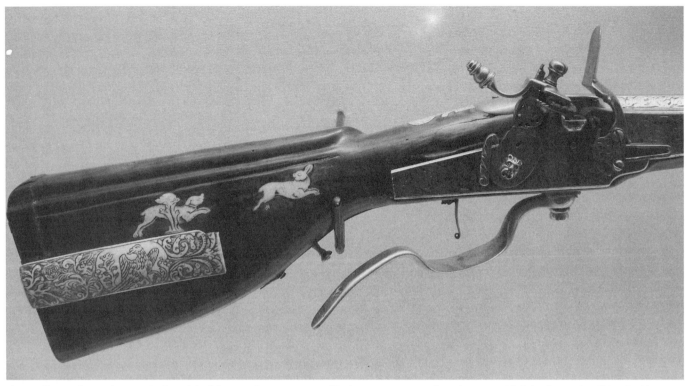

They will never be made again in the original form, and so guns created in days past command a value—provided the firearm is of historical interest.

The manufacturer makes a difference. The name "Winchester" on this 1873 declares it an original rifle that made history in its time.

highly embellished with gold and silver inlays as well as superlative engraving. Serial numbers can greatly add to the value of an old-time gun, with low numbers carrying the most weight. Matching serial numbers also count, as in a pair of cap 'n' ball revolvers with sequential numbers. Many special models were offered over the years, such as Winchester blackpowder cartridge rifles that came in various sub-models with longer or shorter barrels than ordinary, special sights, fine wood, and other features.

The Manufacturer

Firearms from better-known manufacturers noted for excellence carry bigger price tags than guns from the minor leagues. This holds true of small shops as well as large plants. An original Hawken has value based on its makers alone. A Hawken carried by Jim Bridger, Kit Carson, or some other famous mountain man is especially coveted.

Modern Custom Rifles

The guns of contemporary craftsmen can be collectible with values bound for escalation. A single example is the work of K.L. Shelton, whose custom Kentucky rifles often outrank the work of 19th century and earlier gunmakers (see Chapter 46).

Very Old

Matchlocks, wheellocks, very early flintlocks, flintlocks with in-line ignition, breech-loading flinters, all guns of the distant past hold some interest for collecting if for no other reason than vintage. Very old guns hold deep historical value, some appearing in books, such as *Guns* and *Rifles of the World* by Howard L. Blackmore and *The Flintlock: Its Origin and Development* by Torsten Link beginning with the snaphuance. *Remington, "America's Oldest Gunmaker,"* by Roy Marcot (see Chapter 45) in just one more example.

Named for a Song

The highly collectible long rifle born in Pennsylvania was named for a song about Kentucky. A Kentucky/Pennsylvania long rifle is associated with the Golden Age of American Firearms. There are numerous books on this rifle (and pistol), such as Russell Harriger's *Longrifles of Pennsylvania, Volume I, Jefferson, Clarion & Elk Counties* published by George Shumway. Col. Harriger attacked his subject in a scholarly manner, and included business records belonging to the gunsmiths themselves, showing not only the work they were commissioned to do, but also charges for their labors. *The Kentucky Rifle* by Capt. John G.W.

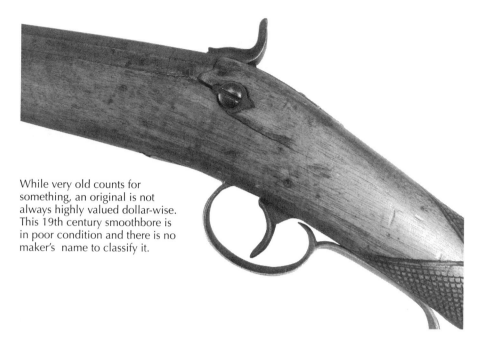

While very old counts for something, an original is not always highly valued dollar-wise. This 19th century smoothbore is in poor condition and there is no maker's name to classify it.

Dillin, printed in 1924 by The National Rifle Association, is another good book on the Kentucky rifle, as is *The Pennsylvania-Kentucky Rifle* by Henry J. Kauffman published by Stackpole Books.

Conflicts

Guns of war are also highly collectible, including wars fought with blackpowder arms. Books on war guns aid collectors with information. An example is Harold L. Peterson's *The Book of the Continental Soldier* dealing with the smoothbore musket of the period, as well as uniforms and equipment.

Guns of the Mountain Men

Serious students of the Fur Trade era know that many firearms were carried west of the Mississippi River in the early 1800s. Of course, the plains rifle captures the imagination most, the Hawken the epitome of the breed. Many books have been written on this period, such as *Firearms, Traps, & Tools of the Mountain Men* by Carl P. Russell. Russell includes knives, tomahawks, traps, and of course guns, not only Hawkens, but others as well. *The Plains Rifle* by Charles E. Hanson, Jr. includes early trade guns, Leman flintlocks, and the rifles of Sam and Jake Hawken. Books strictly on Hawkens are also available, such as John Baird's *Hawken Rifles, The Mountain Man's Choice*, The Gun Room Press, 1976. Baird also wrote *Fifteen Years in the Hawken Lode*, published in the same year by the same press.

Collecting is interesting, but also valuable. IF there were no collectors, many wonderful examples of past firearms and shooting/hunting/trapping tools would have been lost forever.

SMOKING SMALL GAME AND VARMINTS

The cottontail rabbit lives just about everywhere, and we hunters are lucky to have this little high protein game animal. Along with good food, the rabbit also provides hunting when other seasons are closed. Long live the "lowly" rabbit.

States that do it right place few restrictions on small game and varmint hunting tools, with generous seasons and bag limits, commensurate, of course, with maintaining good game populations. Blackpowder guns can lift small game and varmint hunting to an entirely new plateau. I have nothing against taking littler edibles with modern cartridge guns. I am also in favor of blipping a prairie dog, coyote, or other member of the varmint clan with a long-range rifle wearing a high-magnification scope. I do these things myself when appropriate, but they do not have

the charm, thrill or satisfaction of taking the same animals with a blackpowder gun—and that's a promise. Admittedly, if high numbers are vital, then blackpowder guns are out of the running. The rancher who wants to significantly reduce prairie dogs in his pastures looks to a shooter with a portable bench, long-range rifle, and big scope sight. The cook who must feed a big hunting camp prefers a bag limit, not two rabbits taken with a muzzleloader. That being said, my flintlock 32-caliber rifle has carried off a full bag limit of cottontail rabbits (10 where I live) in one day.

Small Game

The number one small game animal in North America, if not the entire world, is the cottontail rabbit and relatives. Powderpuff Tail lives just about everywhere from the sunny deserts of the Southwest to the frigid forests of the Northland. Wonderful to hunt, the rabbit demands no guide, no expensive license, and normally resides not too far from home. Rabbits make good food. (See *The Complete Guide to Game Care & Cookery* for handling tips and recipes for small game.) The tree squirrel is second on the small game list and, if anything, even more cherished for the extra challenge. Arizona has the most variety. There are hunters more dedicated to squirrels than to deer or ducks. Prepared correctly, this tree-dweller is also a fine dish on the table. Then there are dozens of other small edible wild things. Bullfrogs come to mind, also raccoons, opossums, porcupines, rattlesnakes, turtles, woodchucks, rockchucks, prairie dogs, muskrats, and beavers. Mainly, we shy from these creatures because we never ate 'em as a kid and won't eat 'em now. Food represents a cultural prejudice loaded with euphemisms, fancy words for stuff we wouldn't touch under its real name. Scrambled eggs are great. But scrambled embryos are nasty!

Jack the Rabbit and the Snowshoe Hare

Jack the Rabbit is classified—believe it or not—as a predator in my home state: Wyoming, while snowshoe hares are small game. But both the jackrabbit and the snowshoe are hares, not rabbits, partly because they have the split or hare lip. Many newcomers to hunting start on jacks. Mr. Long Ears is a good-sized target and when in decent numbers not too difficult to locate. They provide plenty of sport for the hunter carrying a smallbore muzzleloading rifle or any blackpowder pistol or revolver. Jacks are seldom used for human consumption, although young ones, boned, front half surrendered back to Mother Nature, are good in certain dishes. My maternal grandfather made wonderful red spaghetti sauce with boned jackrabbit back legs and backstrap (loin) meat, but he was a master chef. The snowshoe hare "eats" about the same as the jackrabbit to my taste buds. Its dark meat is OK in sauces, but not friendly to my palate fried, boiled, or baked "straight." *The Complete Guide to Game Care & Cookery* offers handling tips and recipes on hares, as well as rattlesnakes and other small fare.

Varmints and Furbearers— Which is Which?

There is considerable crossover between varmints and furbearers. The raccoon, for example, may be classified as a non-game animal, but may also be sought for its pelt or tail, and certainly the raccoon has been, and will continue to be, prepared for the supper table. Muskrats fed thousands of trappers and pioneers. But they're generally classified as furbearers and therefore non-game animals. Beavers likewise. Coyotes, foxes, and bobcats are not normally food for man, but they cross over, too, as both varmints and furbearers. Sometimes badgers fall into this dual category as well. Pelts are not always prime, therefore not too valuable on the open market. That's OK with some fishermen, who use animal hair for fly-tying.

Varmints

In keeping with political correctness, many game departments have moved away from the original and entirely accurate term "varmint" to "non-game species," so as not to offend anti-hunters and non-hunters. But everybody has a varmint. I had two neighbors who would rather starve to death than eat the meat from "one of their fellow creatures," such as squirrel or rabbit. The couple was authorized by the state game department to care for injured birds, returning many to the wilds after a stay in their "avian hospital." One day I brought them a kestrel (sparrow hawk) I found caught in a barbed wire fence. As we took the bird to its cage, I noticed something. What's that? I asked. "Oh," the lady told me, "that's our rat trap. Rats come in and eat our bird food, so we trap them." Everybody has a varmint.

For hunters who won't consider shooting anything that cannot be eaten, there are animals that go both ways. Young prairie dogs, for example, have been food for man as long as man has lived on the plains. *I strongly*

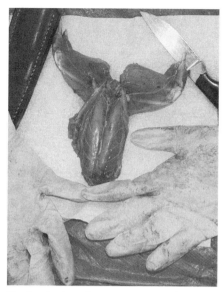
The food value of any game cannot be overlooked. The best part of the cottontail rabbit includes two big back legs and a prime back. The front half is also excellent albeit not too meaty.

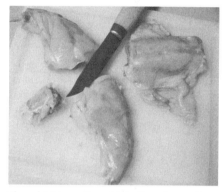
The rabbit is sectioned into five pieces, three major parts shown here: two legs and one back.

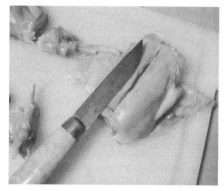
The secret to tender backstrap of rabbit is removing the tough outer tissue by slitting down the center of the spine and pulling the tissue away on both sides to be discarded.

"No hunter I know, and certainly not this one, wants to rid the world of the cunning coyote," says the author. "However," he adds, "coyotes take about 50 percent of the antelope fawns where I live, as well as pounding the sheep industry. A little control is in order."

Everybody has a varmint. The tourist in prairie dog country sees a cute animal. The rancher or farmer sees the destruction of his land. Prairie dogs are omnivorous, also cannibals, but they do devour crop plants and they make great big holes in the pasture.

recommend not touching one these days, however, since prairie dogs have been discovered with the plague in recent times. Porcupines, while not my idea of tasty fare, having tried it, are edible, while at the same time these animals destroy many valuable trees, making them varmints whether so-listed by game departments or not. I recall a privileged day on a handsome ranch where we were graciously allowed to hunt deer. The rancher bid us good luck. But he also voiced a warning. "If I find out that you ran across a porcupine and didn't shoot it, you won't be welcomed back." Trees along his stream were suffering badly and his little home on the prairie didn't have trees to spare. While porcupines are not good food, their quills are still prized for decoration on shooting bags and many other arty items. So the blackpowder hunter goes for varmints because they represent an interesting animal, sometimes providing food or pelts. There is also benefit in reducing varmint numbers. Coyotes, for example, eat many antelope fawns where I live in Wyoming. In their second year, antelope does have twins, usually a male and a female. The two little ones following behind their dame often drop to one, sometimes none, as coyotes find and eat them. Bagging coyotes means more pronghorns on the plains, a fact proved by official studies.

Some varmints are as great a challenge as big game. It takes a good to hunter to consistently bag coyotes with a smokepole, especially in areas where the 300-yard shot is commonplace for the wily wild dogs. The blackpowder hunter cannot bang away at great distance, so he must get close one way or another to make his shot count. This factor has changed somewhat with the advent of the long-range modern front-loaders, many of them fixed up with high-power scopes. Western marmots, also known as rockchucks, can be difficult to get with a muzzleloader. Woodchucks, the eastern version of the marmot, are

no pushover either. That's why long-range varmint rifles firing high-speed bullets found their way into the green fields of the rocky areas of the west. Blackpowder hunters can fire from afar with large-bore rifles, where making a hit brings certain results. But the smallbore muzzleloader has to be applied much closer, demanding a good stalk. Some of the methods described below promote that close stalk with the littler muzzleloader.

Economy of Small Game and Varmint Hunting

Small game, and some varmints as well, are often a short distance down the road, no extensive travel involved nor big outlay of cash for hunting tags or licenses. In many areas, hunting small game and varmints, after securing proper licenses, costs no more than climbing in a car and driving a few miles. Trespass fees for varmint hunters are generally unheard of on private property where deer, antelope, or other game command folding green if a hunter wants to go on deeded lands. Also, a big dollar bonus is the food. A hunter can come home with several pounds of inexpensive high-quality protein, as anyone who buys commercial rabbits in the market knows. In the case of inedibles, the reward is an interesting day in the field along with healthful exercise. Shooting economy was well established for smallbores, cast round bullets in calibers 32 and 36 setting the shooter back no more than 22 Long Rifle ammo, sometimes even less with scrap lead.

Transfer Value

Both small game and varmint hunting with a muzzleloader have tremendous transfer value to the big-game field. The hunter practices finding and stalking techniques, as well as field testing new gear from boots and coats to hats, as well as binoculars, guns, calls, and more. He also gains a great deal of field experience with loading and shooting a charcoal-burner.

The hunter can use small game and varmints as a prime excuse for getting outdoors with any type of firearm, especially a muzzleloader prior to the blackpowder-only big-game season.

Varmints and Small Game with the Muzzleloading Shotgun

Jumped game, such as rabbits, as well as squirrels doing flying trapeze acts in trees, are ripe for muzzleloading shotguns. Called-in varmints are also candidates for the scattergun. While choke-bored guns are almost imperative for wild turkeys, waterfowl, and other birds, Cylinder-bore guns are usually fine for close work on rabbits and squirrels. Loads vary in accord with game and conditions. A 12-gauge soot-burning shotgun can be loaded light for close shooting or heavy for longer range work, light for smaller game, heavy for larger varmints, such as the coyote. Any shotgun will do: flintlock or percussion, original or replica, or modern in-line. As a kid, I hunted a piece of wild entanglement fondly called "The Old Golf Course," although no one knew why it had that name. The patch of heavy brush was loaded with cotton-

tails. First attempts with a 22 rifle were fruitless. The rabbits were wild. There's one! Not any more. Jump and run, jump and run. A shotgun was brought to bear on these bunnies and Mom soon had rabbits on the table. V.M. Starr of Eden, South Dakota, the grand old man of muzzleloading shotguns, advised 1-ounce No. 5 or No. 6 shot, such as No. 6, 2 1/2-drams Fg or FFg for close-range small game. That's roughly 70 grains volume powder.

One Short Blackpowder Shotgun

A super short 12-gauge blackpowder shotgun came my way one year, a gift of Val Forgett of the Navy Arms Company, a thank-you for an antelope/deer hunt I took him on. It was the Terry Texas Ranger with 14-inch barrels—a legal length for a blackpowder shotgun. The little shotgun still goes with me on backpack trips, providing considerable campfire fare. It is deadly with 1-ounce shot and 70 grains volume FFg. Velocity chronorgraphs at only 902 fps. But small edibles are cleaning dropped at 20 to 25 yards or so (no choke) with this little fast-pointing Texas Terry Ranger, as it was called in the catalog. I carry readyloads along for this shotgun when I'm backpacking. One of my favorite loads is the 1-ounce charge above, No. 5 shot, for cottontails—seems about an ideal shot size—just as effective as No. 6, but with fewer pellets doing the job. For tighter groups (still not even up to Modified choke), a one-piece plastic wad is the choice. V.M. Starr's cardboard wads are great for closer work (see Chapter 12).

Rifles for Small Game and Varmints

For small game, the 32- or 36-caliber squirrel rifle is ideal. If forced to choose one over the other, the 32 gets the nod because it's large enough with a 45-grain round ball to get the job done and even more economical than the easy-on-the-pocketbook 36. I can't imagine requiring anything larger than

a 32 for small game. On the other hand, only headshots count for littler edibles, since food on the table is the object. I've been fortunate to enjoy several long hunts—up to a month long—in which collecting wild protein was, if not totally necessary, at least highly desirable. The small game muzzleloader is perfect on these hunts, especially since the goal is generally one and only one edible per day on the average.

Sampling of Smallbore Rifle Ballistics with Comparisons

As a quick and easy reference to small game ballistics, here are a few numbers for two small game muzzleloading rifles. For comparison, a 22 Long Rifle rimfire with a 40-grain bullet at 1,250 fps muzzle velocity gains 139 foot-pounds of muzzle energy. At 100 yards velocity is around 1,000 fps for energy of 89 foot-pounds. The smallbore rifle easily qualifies for 22 Long Rifle power, albeit the round ball loses velocity faster than the 22 Long Rifle bullet. The blackpowder smallbore is also capable of surpassing the 22 rimfire power-wise. This is especially evident with a conical, such as the 36-caliber 125-grain Buffalo Bullet. Lyman's tests showed very close to 2,000 fps muzzle velocity for this bullet with 70-grains volume FFFg blackpowder, providing a

The cottontail rabbit is generally fairly easy game to gather in for supper, especially in areas where it is not hunted, as in many parts of the Rocky Mountain chain. This rabbit was stalked to within feet before it scampered off.

muzzle energy over 1,000 foot-pounds with sufficient energy retention at 100 yards for any varmint, even mountain lion, which are, incidentally, no longer classified in that category, requiring special tags for hunting. This velocity is possible from a standard-length barrel. Regardless of the fact that the 70-grain 36-caliber conical provides greater downrange energy than a round ball of similar size, the lead globe remains ideal for small game, even larger varmints, when the range is close. For longer range shooting, the conical will, of course, win the day.

Powder Charge   Muzzle Velocity   Muzzle Energy   100-Yard Velocity   100-Yard Energy

The first figure is in grains volume, the second fps, the third foot-pounds of energy at the muzzle, the fourth fps velocity at 100-yards, the fifth figure energy in foot-pounds at 100-yards

Rifle Number One

Dixie Tennessee Squirrel Rifle, 41 1/2-inch barrel, 32-caliber, (.310-inch 45-grain round ball)

Chg./grs. vol.	Vel./fps	ME	fps/100 yds.	E/100 yds.
10 FFFg	1,263	170	720	55
20 FFFg	1,776	336	852	77
30 FFFg	2,081	462	936	93

Rifle Number Two

Hatfield Squirrel Rifle, 39 1/2-inch barrel, 36-caliber (.350-inch 65-grain round ball)

Chg./grs. vol.	Vel./fps	ME	fps/100 yds.	fpe/100 yds.
20 FFFg	1,471	312	794	91
30 FFFg	1,799	467	882	112
40 FFFg	2,023	591	956	132

Long-range shooting for varmints in terrain like this may be too challenging for the front-loader or blackpowder cartridge rifle. However, practiced marksmen can put bullets on the mark at quite long range, especially if these shooters are into the silhouette game.

Sam says, "I want a small-game rifle like this one from Austin & Halleck, but not in 50-caliber. Make it 32-caliber with a ball-shooting rate of twist. I'll load up with a modest charge of FFFg blackpowder or equivalent for economical practice and great small game/varmint hunting.

The little 32-caliber 45-grain round ball backed by only 10-grains volume FFFg is just about ideal for rabbits, squirrels, and similar small game at close range. Shorter barrels will not develop this muzzle velocity. However, cutting the barrel to only 24 inches continues to give higher than 22 Long Rifle bullet speed. Going to 20 grains volume runs muzzle velocity up to 22 Winchester Magnum Rimfire velocity and energy at close range, but the conical bullet of the 22 WMR wins the war downrange by a considerable margin. Going to a full 30-grains volume charge pushes the 32-caliber 45-grain lead pill faster than the average U.S.A. load for the 22 WMR and almost the speed of the German load from RWS with a 40-grain bullet. The 36-caliber shows a decided energy advantage over the 32, but this factor is moot when it comes to taking small game at modest range because the 32 already gives sufficient punch to do that. In the next chapter, the comparison becomes more important when the target is not rabbit or squirrel, but wild turkey.

The Small-Game Pistol

Pistol ballistics are more than ample for small game and most varmints at close range. This is true of all calibers, right down to the smallest normally available. The big question is sights. Point-at sights do not have the built-in refinement necessary for making the meat-saving headshot. But that shot can definitely be handled with good sights. It is possible to have a gunsmith mount good sights on a pistol that wears the glob, not globe, of metal up front and perhaps little more than a slit for a

back sight. Adjustability is nice, but not entirely necessary. I learned this from a Lyman Plains Pistol with fixed sights. The sights were fixed, all right, but just right for creating good groups at 25 yards, exactly where I intended to do most of my shooting. Since small game is usually a close-range proposition, fixed sights adjusted to deliver point of impact at 25 yards work well. Hold a tad under closer than 25 yards, a blip over the target beyond 25 yards, and hunt carefully for close shots that don't go beyond about 35 yards. For varmints, going to a larger bore pistol naturally extends both range and power.

The Small-Game Revolver

The smallest of the pocket revolvers will take on any small game within normal small game hunting distances. As with pistols, larger bores are more ideal for bigger varmints at greater range. As always, sights make the difference between making the animal run away from the burst of dust kicked up by the bullet, or adding food to the larder. The Ruger Old Army with adjustable sights

is a prime example of a larger-caliber revolver suitable for the biggest varmint, and with headshots, which this revolver is capable of, small game for the pot can be cleanly taken.

In the Field

There are various methods that help a blackpowder small-game hunter fill his game bag. Similar rules sand away the blackpowder handicap for varmints.

Still-Hunting

Slow-motion walking is the ticket, whether in a field for rabbits or forest for tree squirrels. Still-hunting is perhaps the most interesting way to chase small game or varmints, because it keeps a person on the move and seeing things, as well as gaining a little exercise.

Jump and Shoot

Shotgunning for cottontails is a jump-and-shoot game, not sophisticated but effective. Walk. Scare the rabbit from its lair. Shoot as it runs off. Skill requirement is fast gun mounting, a quick sight picture, and the ability to lead

There is transfer value back and forth between small game hunting and big game hunting. The hunter here uses a call for deer with hopes of putting his Knight rifle into action. However, calling varmints is done in exactly the same way.

The tree squirrel, not to be confused with the ground squirrel, is the No. 2 small game animal in North America. Hunting with a shotgun is not nearly as "sporting" as bagging a squirrel stew with a smallbore muzzle-loading rifle. But load 1-1/8 ounces of No. 7-1/2 shot in front of 80-grains volume FFg or equivalent and get the pot warmed up. Shown here is Sam's short-barrel 12-gauge percussion shotgun.

Any gun is fine for varmints in any caliber. But the squirrel rifle is right for squirrel, hence the name. Shown with a box of Hornady 32-caliber round balls is this fine Abert's squirrel, also known as the tassel-eared squirrel.

Taught by fellow writer Bob Hirsch, Sam hunts squirrels in the Rocky Mountain forests by hiking a lot in hopes of catching one feeding on the ground. Then the run is on—with an uncapped or unprimed rifle. Squirrel dashes up tree—hunter tries to spot it (binoculars help)—crack! Headshots only count.

without stopping the swing of the gun until the shot charge is away. Swinging on the target, then abruptly stopping, usually means hitting behind.

Spot and Stalk

Much like still-hunting, the difference lies in covering a little more ground a little faster, relying heavily on binoculars for spotting game in the distance and then stalking close for a perfect shot. I have had very good luck with spot-and-stalk on both small game and varmints, the binocular used to spot the animal before it sees me.

Spot-Dash-and-Tree Squirrel Hunting

This manner of squirrel hunting really works, but before going into it,

a warning: **Never run with a loaded rifle that is either primed (flintlock) or capped (percussion).** There is plenty of time to drop a little powder in a pan, or fix a cap on a nipple after the dash part of this squirrel hunting strategy. Squirrels do not live in the trees all the time. They also do not hibernate. They simply go into the den on frigid days, coming back out when the weather is more suitable. Inside, they usually have a cozy setting with a little TV and a futon. I made up the TV and futon, but comfortable these little rodents are when the weather grows damp and dismal. Squirrels work the ground considerably for food. The hunter using this method hikes a lot in prime squirrel habitat looking for a bushytail on the ground. When he spots one, he makes a mad dash straight at the little beast. The mad dash drives Chatterbox up a tree. The squirrel may head for its den, which ends the show. But usually that's not what happens. Instead, it often lies flat on a branch, difficult to spot, but there all the same. Binoculars help separate limb from Umbrella Tail. Once the squirrel is spotted, the hunter maneuvers into shooting position, rifle recently primed or capped. Now it's time for marksmanship to prevail on a tiny target amidst branches and foliage.

Calling Squirrels

Contrary to popular notion, and in spite of the squirrel's nickname of Chatterbox, squirrels are often quiet. But they have a good voice and love to use it, especially for scolding. Because squirrels like to talk, calls, such as Lohman and others work, usually provoking the squirrel from his hiding place amongst leaves or branches out onto a limb in a fighting pose. There are video and audiotapes instructive in squirrel calling. Lacking a proper call, which is best, clacking two quarters rapidly is better than no call at all. Place one quarter in the palm of one hand and with the other quarter in the other hand, rap quickly—tap, tap, tap, tap. This makes a crude, but sometimes effective, chattering sound that will bring the squirrel to attention.

Calling Varmints

Varmint calling means bringing foxes, coyotes, bobcats, and other predators into smallbore blackpowder range or close enough to drop with a heavy charge of shot from a strong muzzle-loading scattergun. There are dozens of great varmint calls these days as well as electronic devices, which may not be legal in all areas—regulations must be checked. Varmint calling basics can be learned from videos, audios, as well as books and articles. After the basics are mastered, practice makes the expert.

Decoying

Along with calling, decoying can work: calling to interest the varmint to investigate, and a stuffed rabbit, turkey, or other decoy to lure the predator closer.

Snowshoes

"Snowshoes" in this case the things worn on feet to get around in the snow, not the hare, are useful when still-hunting in winter. Snowshoeing along logging roads is enjoyable and interesting, always with an eye out for storms, of course, that can lock a hunter into the country. Tip—carry a GPS for wandering into a maze of roads or even roadless country lacking trails. No, carry the GPS no matter the road/trail situation. The miniaturized GPS of the day fits in a shirt pocket (with a button to prevent loss.) A muzzleloading rifle or shotgun adds greatly to snowshoe hunting in winter, usually one of the quietest times of the year when most folks are indoors. Carrying a daypack with essentials, like fire-starting materials, is recommended. During my residence in Fairbanks, Alaska, when the

Look hard. He's up there. The shotgun makes any of these opportunities simple. A flintlock or caplock 32-caliber squirrel rifle puts a bit more challenge into it.

The white underside of some squirrels make spotting them somewhat easier as they climb among the limbs of a tall tree.

snow piled up, my friend Kenn Oberrecht and I donned our snowshoes and took off after rabbits. Sandwiches froze into white bricks in our pockets. But we didn't let that detract from a good time. Numerous different types of snowshoes are available at sporting goods stores and through mail-order catalogues.

Reading Sign

Small game and varmint hunting can be taken as seriously as the hunter desires, right down to learning new areas by studying sign. In wintertime, it's easy to spot rabbit traffic. Trails in

the snow, especially along fence lines, give their presence away. Also, crusty snow holds droppings in stark contrasting, dark dots against the white. Varmint sign can also be studied. After all, just because its small game or varmints does not mean it isn't full-blown hunting. Many hunting skills can be honed in the small game/varmint hunt arena.

Big-game hunting is the mother lode. But small-game hunting and varminting with blackpowder guns is a vein of gold for those who take advantage of the sport.

WILD TURKEY AND OTHER BIRDS WITH THE SMOKEPOLE

The wild turkey may not have a college education among wildlife, but it is definitely one of the wariest creatures and that can make the bird a worthy challenge.

Benjamin Franklin wanted the wild turkey as our national symbol instead of the fish-eating bald eagle. That's why we sometimes call the turkey Ben's Bird. He felt the turkey was a better candidate with loftier qualities than the clawed raptor, and he apparently didn't know about the golden eagle, which is a mighty bird. Thank goodness this great statesmen lost out on this one or we couldn't hunt this fabulous avian for the challenge and outdoor enjoyment, as well as Thanksgiving and Christmas feasts. Now there's even the National Wild Turkey Federation, dedicated to this regal bird's prime continuance as a huntable species. Some states have both

Fall and Spring wild turkey seasons, as does my home, Wyoming. Along with the wild turkey, every upland bird with an open season is legal to the muzzle-loading shotgunner. Although not popular, the blackpowder breech-loading shotgun is also excellent. Blackpowder shells are once again available as factory loads, and are readily handloaded as well.

The Bird

By the early 1900s wild turkey populations were in the basement. Indiscriminate year-round hunting, avian diseases gifted to wild birds by settlers' barnyard fowl, plus lost habitat,

almost spelled doom for the wild turkey. By 1930 only twenty-one states had a grand total of around 20,000 birds. Now forty-nine states (all but Alaska) are home to our largest upland game bird with a population well over two million strong. Far-thinkers decided that one way to preserve the gobbler was transplantation. For example, a number of birds were introduced to the Rockies. Wyoming traded sage grouse to New Mexico for 15 Merriam's turkeys. About a decade later the flock grew to around a thousand. In the early 1950s, 48 turkeys, fifteen more from New Mexico plus thirty-three Wyoming residents, were turned loose in Wyoming's northeastern Black Hills region. They thrived and today that area is known as "turkey country." The Rocky Mountain chain: Arizona, New Mexico, Colorado, Montana, Idaho and other western states, now offer thousands of opportunities for turkey hunters.

Wild Turkey Hunting

Wild turkeys live different lives from area to area. A friend owns a little ranch in South Dakota. He can count on seeing wild turkeys at a given waterhole during all but the winter months. These birds must wear wristwatches, because they arrive for a drink about the same time every day, depending on the season of the year. In the Rocky Mountains, where I hunt turkeys, seasonal movement is a priceless piece of knowledge. I know which drainages to check as weather brings the birds down from higher to lower areas for feeding and roosting. Wild turkeys would be nearly impossible to locate in the vast western reaches that house them if hunters didn't know where to start looking and what to look for. Part of knowing where to look lies in the turkey's daily routine, plus roosting sites, eating habits, food preferences, watering needs, communication calls, and strutting grounds. Sign finding is highly important, since the birds do move around. The idea is simple enough—hunt where sign is fresh.

Turkey Lifestyles

I hunt the western gobbler mostly, but I have also been on the turkey trail in Kentucky. The birds I know best live a rather simple daily routine. They get up early in the morning, feed, maybe go to the watering hole, belly up to the table again for a few hours, and then possibly lay up for a short while during midday. If the mating season isn't underway they dust a little, scratch the ground here and there, feed a bit more, and finally head back to the roost in very late afternoon. They perch for the night high above any four-legged predators prowling on the ground. This daily action constitutes a lifestyle: feeding, watering, scratching, dusting, roosting, and mating (in the spring), with plenty of meandering all the while. Knowing these aspects of the wild turkey make them huntable, along with knowledge of their peculiar habits. Most of the day they are on the roam, which is fortunate for hunters. If they brushed up like whitetails, turkeys would be even more difficult to find than they already are. A band of birds may move two miles or more during a daily feeding romp. Feeding turkeys are noisy, and that's good for hunters. More than once I've cupped hands around ears to improve my all-too-human sound-sensors as I listened for gobble-gobbles. Hearing the flock swings the advantage to the hunter, who may be able to stalk the squawking and get a shot.

The wild turkey is omnivorous, eating whatever providence sets in its path, from small beasties like mice to an array of vegetable matter. Three years running I took a tom in northern Arizona because I knew of a special field filled with grasshoppers that time of the fall. Every afternoon several flocks of Merriam's turkeys stepped out of the woods and onto this grassy dinner table. I had my pick and deserve no credit for harvesting a bird, even with bow and arrow. After all, they were only twenty paces away, busily gobbling up 'hoppers. I never saw another hunter in that particular region, which is too bad. Most of those fine-eating birds fell to winter snows, coyotes, and old age instead of a swift hunter's harvest. Spiders, grubs, snails, crawdads, worms, ticks, millipedes, centipedes, beetles, salamanders, frogs, grasshoppers, and just about anything else that skitters through the grass is fair game for the wild turkey. They also eat grass, berries, and acorns, as well as leaves of many green plants and numerous cultivated crops. Wise hunters hold this image of the wild turkey: a plucky fellow, unafraid to attack anything. Fond not only of live food, but if it's green, nutty, seed-like, or just about anything else that smacks of vegetables, Ben's Bird goes for it. Turkeys gobble food down whole. They snatch it up, peck at it, pick at it,

As they feed along, wild turkeys often "talk" a lot, and that can give their location away to a stalking hunter.

The wild turkey is considered a prize trophy, and it is.

The blackpowder shotgun is ideal for wild turkey hunting, especially with Full choke capability or with a heavy charge of smaller shot from very close range, head and neck being the target.

drink. Second, turkeys live near some source of water. I have had good luck in the Black Hills of Wyoming by working trails leading to water.

Turkey Sign

Even though I never got a bird at its watering site directly, water is extremely important in turkey hunting, not only because the birds normally live near some form of liquid, but also for sign, such as tracks in mud along ponds, lakes, even streams. Therefore, the camp-out hunter is smart to park himself not to far from a source of water in turkey country. If there's a pond close by "dusting" is a good idea. This means taking a fallen branch and using it as a broom to clear away all tracks around the water's edge as best as possible. Next morning, the usual hunting plan is followed. But in the afternoon the hunter checks the waterhole to see who came to visit that day. Every track there, turkey and otherwise, will be fresh since all old sign was obliterated. If turkeys are using the watering site, hunting the immediate region makes sense with hopes of finding a flock, or if not the birds directly, then perhaps a roost. What sign to look for? A hunter does not have to be Sherlock Holmes to deduce that a fresh turkey feather lying on a trail was probably left by a turkey. And a turkey track is somewhat more impressive than a sparrow's. It will be the largest bird track in the area.

Using a one-piece plastic wad can produce a tighter pattern in blackpowder shotguns that do not have choke. This is especially important for wild turkeys and larger birds, and even then, the hunter should work for a close shot.

strip it away (such as grass seeds), clip it off, or scratch it out of the earth. Paint this picture of a *wild* turkey, rather than a barnyard vision of the bird.

The turkey is a creature of action. It can run like a racehorse, but when feeding, walking speed is around two miles an hour, except for occasional mad dashes at living things. The flock can easily cover two miles a day through its outdoor grocery store. I have found most of my western birds because of these mobile feeding habits. (Worked in Kentucky, too.) Climb to a lookout spot, especially a bluff or bank above a waterway. (Note the combination: a high spot coupled with water.) Search with the binocular, looking for the feeding flock. Listen all the while for clucks, gobbles, squawks, and sometimes what sounds like a Chihuahua lap dog lost in the woods. Find the flock. Stalk for a close shot. Shoot straight. Of course it's not that simple. But the spot-and-stalk approach works well for gobblers, especially around water. The birds don't necessarily drink every day. But a hunter may have luck hanging around a watering station for two reasons. First, a flock might just come in to

Droppings are also telltale. The female leaves amorphous blobs. J-shaped rods belong to the male bird. Dusting sites may be found along trails and often along dirt roads. One season locating a particularly handsome dusting site on an old logging road put me along that dusty artery for two evenings, resulting in locating a bachelor flock of tom birds. Scratchings also mark turkey activity. Hen scratchings are not always well defined. But toms may clear a large area under a tree with a V-shaped dugout about a foot and a half long centralized and well defined. Sometimes the V-shape loses its form, with the entire base around the tree raked away. It's not unusual to find the duff (the layer beneath ground cover) from beneath a pine tree unearthed. If deer, elk, or bear did this work, tracks will say so. If the tom bird did it, toe marks are deeply channeled into the ground by the bird's strong feet.

The Roost

The hunter who finds a "hot" roost has an excellent chance of bringing home a holiday bird. Since wild turkeys roost every evening, finding their special tree is like locating their home address. Turkeys fly well. They can lift straight up from the ground to the roosting tree. But some roosting sites are below a dirt bank or cliff. Why, no one can say, but flocks use these high places like a hang glider's take-off strip. The birds hit the tree with the grace of a hippo at a tea party, hopefully clinging to a branch that will be its night's repose. These special trees are not always easy to locate, but they are well worth looking for during scouting sessions and during the hunt itself. One afternoon my hunting partner and I located a hot roost, obvious by fresh droppings decorating the ground below. We backed off and waited. Inside of two hours there was a roaring sound as birds dived from a nearby creek bank, hitting the tree in kamikaze fashion. Filling two tags the next morning with a couple smallbore muzzleloaders was no big trick.

The small round ball, where law for turkey hunting allows rifles, is ideal for taking Ben's Bird cleanly but without undue loss of edibles. For comparison (left) is a 180-grain 30-caliber bullet, followed by two 12-gauge round balls, two 32-caliber round balls, and on the far right, two 36-caliber round balls.

Fall Calling

In the fall of the year, the call serves to locate a flock. Although a gobbler may come in to a call this time of year, such has never happened to me. However, calling remains worthwhile because the tom may respond, giving away his location. Sometimes a few blasts on a crow call will bring a "gobble-gobble" that can be followed up. An owl call has the same effect, eliciting a response. In Kentucky, every time the owl hoot echoed in the forest, a tombird replied. Once the male gives himself away, the stalk is on. Although wild turkeys are not terribly smart, they are extremely wary. So stalking means slow going with great care not to announce the approach with the crack of a twig, the human voice, or other noise. On the other hand, there is no evidence that wild turkeys sniff out the hunter as deer, elk, bear, and other game can, so watching the wind is mainly for the sake of sound transmission.

Spring Calling

Springtime calling is an entirely different matter. Amour is in the air and a tom bird can be lured into a hunter's lap, provided the hunter has talent as a caller. Those who are not expert callers should never overdo it. When a tom responds, the idea is to wait a minute, then answer briefly. Also, at least in some areas, toms won't come in to a

call after mid-morning. But they will answer a call all day, and that can be almost as good for stalking. Naturally, these are generalizations.

Strutting Grounds

In my state, only toms are legal in the spring, whereas both sexes can be hunted during the fall. So in springtime finding a strutting area is tantamount to bagging a bird. These grounds can be traditional, used from season to season, which was the situation for timbered ridges I located. These ridges lured springtime tombirds to strut for the ladies. One spring my partner and I slowly worked along one of these ridges. I had already shot a bird. But he still needed his tom. I walked slowly in front, stopping to glass ahead every few steps. The sight that presented itself in my binocu-

For choked blackpowder shotguns, this type of load works well with over-powder wad and over-shot wad.

There have actually been custom muzzleloading rifles as small as 22-caliber shooting bullets like the 22-caliber bullets shown here.

Any smaller-caliber blackpowder cartridge rifle is ideal for wild turkey hunting where rifles are allowed by law.

This is a special blackpowder metallic shotgun "shell." It's a 12-gauge and will accept a decent powder and shot charge with appropriate over-shot wad.

The metallic blackpowder shotgun "shell" accepts a No. 11 percussion cap where there would normally be a primer on a regular shotgun shell.

lars won first place in my memory that season. As I looked through the glass it was as if someone had turned a movie camera on inside my binocular. A big fan turned from side to side displaying colors no one ever got into a box of crayons. I signaled my companion and he stalked forward, coming onto several strutting toms. One well-placed shot from his 32-caliber muzzleloader and he had a prize.

Blackpowder Turkey Guns

Luckily, and I do feel fortunate, my home state continues to allow rifles for turkey hunting. Many states do not. It's a matter of personal preference, but the biggest thrills for me turkey-wise have happened with bows and muzzleloading rifles. A properly loaded 32- or 36-caliber squirrel rifle with patched round ball at about 1,800 fps will take a wild turkey in a heartbeat. The 32 normally achieves this velocity level, depending on barrel length, with about 30-grains

volume FFFg, Pyrodex P, or FFFg Triple Seven, while the 36 usually gathers this same speed with around 40 grains of the same powders (Triple Seven giving the highest velocity). In western woods, such as the Black Hills of South Dakota and Wyoming, the opportunity often comes from across a draw, not necessarily a long shot, but sometimes out of shotgun range. With a squirrel rifle, putting a bullet on target is no problem. Called-in birds can also be taken with the muzzleloading rifle. A single 32- or 36-caliber round ball cleanly drops a gobbler with little loss of meat, while at the same time carrying a little more lethality *at close range* than the 22 WMR (Winchester Magnum Rimfire). The place to aim is the pinion area where wing joins body. Another good shot is the lower back as the bird walks away. A super marksman can go for the head or neck, but these targets are very small and usually moving.

Blackpowder shotgun manufacturers and importers have seen the light, offering not only powerful guns, but also tight chokes. A powerful tightly choked blackpowder muzzleloading scattergun is a terrific turkey-taker. A 12-gauge throwing a heavy shot payload in front of a big powder charge, such as 120-grains FFg, Pyrodex RS, or Triple Seven, is a 50-yard turkey gun. Blackpowder shotguns with screw-in chokes offer Extra Eull patterns ideal for taking wild turkeys cleanly with one shot. But you don't have to have screw-in chokes necessarily. My Navy Arms T&T double-barrel caplock 12-gauge muzzleloader is choked for tight patterns. I have a 10-gauge double gun, full and Full, that is another shoo-in for the title of turkey shotgun. Chapter 12 on the blackpowder shotgun goes into detail on shot charges and patterns. As a single example, my Navy Arms T&T shotgun chronogaphed at 1,012 fps with 80-grains GOEX FFg and 1-1/4 ounces of shot. Same shot charge, same powder, but 90 grains volume gave 1,110 fps, while 100 grains volume producing only a little more pellet speed at 1,113 fps. I have used mixed shot since my teenage years, especially for dove and quail. On Ben's Bird a particularly efficient combination is a mix of No. 5s and BBs or No. 5 and No. 2 shot. The smaller pellets fill in pattern holes while the larger pellets deliver greater energy and penetration. See Chapter 12 for more on powerful blackpowder muzzleloader shotgun loads.

Not to be ignored, the little 25-20 Winchester, and especially its sister 32-20 loaded with blackpowder, are also good wild turkey-takers. The same goes for some of the defunct rimfires, such as the 32-rimfire family. I find freshly loaded 32-rimfire ammo from time to time. The 32-rimfires are good, but the 25-20 and 32-20, loaded with FFFg blackpowder, FFFg Triple Seven, or Pyrodex P, will put a bird down pronto with minimal meat loss. Neither has quite the steam associated with a 36-caliber muzzleloader pumped up with a strong powder charge behind a 125-grain lead conical. But both are adequate at close range, the 32-20 developing about 1,300 fps muzzle velocity with 20-grains volume Pyrodex P. In a lever-action old-time rifle, the 32-20 is a "fun" turkey rifle (where allowed by law).

The successful turkey hunter scouts prospective hunting areas before the season, if possible. This hunter looks for sign around streams and ponds and also tries to find a roost. The wise turkey hunter also packs a binocular, using it faithfully. This hunter covers plenty of ground, staying in the field all day, since wild turkeys, unlike lazy old whitetail bucks, eat and play by day, sleeping at night, as civilized creatures are wont to do.

Turkey Hunting Safety

The wild turkey is perfectly capable of picking out a hunter's face and form from the terrain. And so camouflage is important, especially full camo, meaning facemask and gloves. At the same time, a hunter hidden by foliage to begin with, plus being fully camouflaged, *and calling*, may convince another

hunter that the caller is a turkey. No one should ever shoot at an uncertain target. That's the basic safety rule. At the same time, the hidden caller should be on the lookout. If stalked by another hunter, it's best to make himself or herself known right away.

The Blackpowder Shotgun Shell

Everything put down above pertains also to the blackpowder shotgun *shell*, although I know of none that have the capacity of the Knight or White 12-gauge muzzleloading shotguns that are limited only by proper maximum loads and not by the capacity of a "container," which is what a shotshell is with a finite powder and shot capacity. We know that blackpowder hung on long after smokeless was available. A look at Winchester's catalog for 1916 shows Winchester's New Rival shotshell for handloading advertised as withstanding "heavy charges of blackpowder." While most shotgun ammo in this era was loaded with "dense smokeless powder," Winchester offered a "latest achievement in blackpowder shotgun ammunition," proving that in 1916 blackpowder shells were still going strong. Actually, they continued to sell into the 1940s and were available even after that by special order. In 1916 1,000 blackpowder shotgun shells, 12-gauge, averaged $25.00, while 1,000 smokeless ran more like $40.00. Remember that old-time shotguns often wore damascus (twist steel) barrels not suited for smokeless ammunition. Some of these were beautiful guns that owners did not wish to banish to a spot over the fireplace. They wanted to continue shooting these fine guns, and they did—with blackpowder shells. I use a Lee Loader for my own blackpowder 12-gauge shells.

Other Birds with Blackpowder

If hunting the wild turkey is a king's sport, which it is, then the rest of the wild birds also qualify for royal status. Here are a few flyers to consider.

Mourning and Whitewing Dove

Pass shooting is the usual way to hunt these fine dark-breasted birds. The action is fast, the target small. Near waterholes, where birds are slowing down from high-speed flight, Improved Cylinder patterns are OK. But for longer-range shooting at faster birds, a 1 1/4-ounce charge of #7 ½ or #8 shot in front of a full complement of powder, plus at least Modified if not Full choke, provides patterns necessary for success. The big trick is lead. One way to get enough in-front lead is pulling well ahead; pressing the trigger *with the gun in motion.* Leading, then stopping the swing to shoot, usually results in hitting behind, while sustained lead with trigger pulled with the gun still moving puts the shot string out in front of the bird where it belongs. Leading too much is seldom a problem on fast-flying dove. Since the shot pattern is a string, not a cloud of shot, the first part of the pattern may miss the bird, while the latter part of the string makes contact. If the first part of the string is behind the bird, where else can the remainder go but behind as well?

Quail

All kinds of quail can be hunted with the blackpowder shotgun. Bobwhites, scaled quail, Mearns, California, Gambel's—America has many different varieties. The open-choked muzzle-loading shotgun does a good job on these birds early in the season as coveys rise close to the shooter. The story changes as the birds grow wilder, increasing their "scare radius." Num-

Doves are a perfect target for the blackpowder shotgun. However, they are not easy to hit. Hunting by a waterhole provides somewhat easier shooting as the birds wave in for a drink. This dove is a native of Africa.

Ducks and geese, especially geese, demand a heavy payload of shot. Modern blackpowder shotguns allowed big shot payloads and heavy powder charges make ideal goose guns.

ber 8 shot is good early. But when the birds get wild, a heavier dose of No. 6 shot pays off. Dogs add greatly in locating birds, often holding the covey for the hunter.

Waterfowl

All waterfowl, from the smallest duck to the largest goose, is on the blackpowder shotgun list. Full choke is the way to go for pass shooting. But ducks on ponds—they call it puddle-jumping—can be taken with more open bores for wider patterns. Top loads are recommended. V.M. Starr had a duck load for his muzzleloading shotgun that went: 1 1/2-ounces of No. 4, 5, or 6 shot, depending on conditions, with 4 1/2-drams (about 120 grains volume) Fg blackpowder in his 12-gauge muzzleloader. Starr preferred No. 6 shot for a denser pattern, unless opportunities were on the long side. Then he went to 5s and 4s. Non-toxic shot is the law. Bismuth is the answer. Bismuth can be fired in most standard shotgun barrels due to softness. Read more about this excellent shot in Chapter 12.

Shorebirds

Included in this classification is the fantastic sandhill crane, a big bird standing as high as four feet off the ground. Sandhills are open season on a restricted basis with a permit system in place. Wings on this mighty bird may span 80 inches. Larger birds weigh around 12 pounds. A 12- or 10-gauge gun is called for with the strongest loads. Large bismuth shot sizes are good. Rails, on the other hand, are small. So go with smaller shot sizes.

Pheasants

Full-choke guns are the ticket for skittish birds. But Modified choke is good when hunting over dogs that hold birds for closer shots. Pheasants are fairly big birds, but not necessarily "hard-feathered," as are larger waterfowl. Some hunters prefer bigger shot sizes on pheasants, relying on a few hits with more delivered energy. However, smaller size shot, such as No. 6, is highly effective where close jumping is the rule, even No. 7 1/2 over dogs. The pheasant is a fast-flyer, and delivering the pattern up front into the head/neck region is a talent worth cultivating.

Grouse, Ptarmigan, and Partridges

The Rocky Mountain chain is home to some wonderful bird hunting, especially for members of the grouse family, such as the dusky and blue. Grouse of various sub-types are also highly regarded. Rifles, where I hunt, are allowed on mountain grouse and partridges only. These delicious birds make fine campfire fare for the hunter

The law calls for non-toxic shot on waterfowl. Bismuth is a good choice, not only for its density, but also for its allowance in blackpowder shotguns that do not have steel shot barrels.

with a smallbore muzzleloader. One well-placed 32- or 36-caliber round ball through the lung region puts them in the bag quickly. Mountain grouse can be a pushover. That's why they've been dubbed "fool hens." Sometimes they sit on a limb seeming to say, "Please take me home for supper." But once they get wild, they're plenty challenging in the high pine tree-covered mountains. I have no secret strategy for finding mountain grouse, except walking ridges. That's how I find my birds. Sage grouse are hunted with shotgun only. They are the largest grouse in America, sometimes running six pounds, the heaviest I ever heard of going eight pounds (Idaho Fish & Game report). They're big, but rather soft-feathered. I have taken a limit with as many shots using No. 6 pellets. I hunted ptarmigan in Alaska, strictly with shotgun and No. 6 shot from a Modified choke, a good combination for many upland birds.

Many Others

There are many more legal birds to hunt with a blackpowder muzzleloading shotgun or blackpowder breechloader firing blackpowder shells. In some cases, a smallbore muzzleloading rifle is legal—and practical. Local game laws prevail. Either way, adding smoke to the bird-hunting picture paints it brighter than ever.

Partridges and grouse of all kinds make perfect blackpowder shotgun fare—all great to hunt, all good to eat. This bird is a native of Africa, but America has many different grouse of its own.

Big Game with Charcoal Burners

chapter 44

The blackpowder cartridge rifle is a fine big-game piece. This is Fadala's Pedersoli Remington Rolling Block in 38-55 Winchester. It shoots a 255-grain lead bullet at sufficient velocity for big game.

Clearly, the vast majority of black-powder rifle sales go for hunting, especially special blackpowder-only or "primitive" seasons. Target shooting, Cowboy Action, and rendezvous require special guns, including replicas or originals of lever-action rifles, revolvers, and shotguns. The market share of guns for these shooting sports is strong. Nonetheless, the huge draw is big-game hunting with a front-loader. The numbers are difficult to assess, but there are easily several million shooters in the U.S. and Canada who "do black-powder." The advantages of the special blackpowder-only hunt are slightly bet-ter tag drawing odds, prime time of the year hunts (elk in rut, for example), and access to grounds not normally allowed hunters with modern guns. Initial interest in going for big game with char-coal-burners was additional challenge along with *atavism*, which when used in an everyday sense, rather than strict dictionary definition, means the joy of doing something the way our ances-tors did it, i.e. hunting with blackpow-der guns. The challenge remains, along with a love of reliving shooting history. But the strongest lure for owning a blackpowder gun is the big game primi-tive season.

The Primitive Hunt

The blackpowder-only hunt is for muzzleloaders. Blackpowder cartridge guns are included below not for the primitive hunt, but because going for big game with a single-shot or repeat-ing blackpowder cartridge firearm is exciting and rewarding. I believe that the big-game hunting adventure is elevated with any blackpowder gun. That's partially why I am excited about upcoming muzzleloader-only hunts in Texas, Ohio, and Saskatchewan. My home state, Wyoming, lacks blackpow-der-only seasons. But I still choose to use muzzleloader and blackpowder car-

What big game? Any big game with a muzzleloader or blackpowder rifle, as well as a few sidearms in the hands of hunters who are both good shots and willing to stalk for close opportunities.

tridge rifles for general seasons. I have nothing against the modern cartridge-shooter. Due to circumstances, I used a 30-06 in Africa for trophies, including a Cape buffalo by special permission. But taking big game with a muzzleloader or blackpowder cartridge gun is special.

The Rules

The rules keep changing. Colorado, for a while, excluded in-line rifles for special blackpowder-only deer and elk hunts. Then in-lines were OK. I'm told that Idaho demands a visible hammer on muzzleloaders for special big-game blackpowder only hunts. Every state differs. That is why the hunter must obtain current rules for a given state before going afield.

What Big Game?

An appropriate blackpowder firearm is right for any big game in the world. But with a warning: *Although there are blackpowder guns capable of taking even elephants, hunting wild animals that "shoot back" can be dangerous with a single-shot firearm requiring considerable reloading time. An expert marksman must back up the blackpowder hunter on dangerous game.* Only one animal has charged me in my many years of hunting. No, not the Cape buffalo of Africa. It was an American bison. I was armed with No. 47, my 54-caliber round ball rifle, while my brother Nick possessed only a camera. Photos prove the charge. A round bullet took out the right hemisphere of the brain, which stopped the bull. But the buff got back up, requiring a second ball behind the shoulder to "settle him," as the old-timers used to say. The white-tailed deer is the number one game animal hunted with blackpowder, but moose, elk, pigs—you name it—all big game is open to the charcoal-burner. The sport has blossomed not only in America and Canada, but also parts of Europe. Italy, for example, through a law placed on the books in 1991, liberalized the ownership of muzzleloaders for hunting. South Africa did the same in 2005.

Big Game Muzzleloaders

In-line muzzleloaders, most of them using No. 209 primers made especially for muzzleloaders, are dominant. But all types are viable, including rifled muskets. In fact, as far as replicas go, a rifled musket, such as the Whitworth, makes a strong big-game rifle. Consider that the 45-90 Winchester is rightfully considered a strong big-game cartridge. A well-loaded 45-caliber musket is more powerful with sometimes heavier bullets and larger powder charges. I have a Volunteer 45-caliber rifled musket allowed up to 130 grains volume of FFg or equivalent. This is essentially a 45-120-plus. An upcoming Texas hunt will find me shooting a 54-caliber Markesbery for feral hogs and javelina. Interestingly, when Colorado banned in-lines, the Markesbery was OK because ignition entered the powder charge on a 45-degree angle. Go figure. The blackpowder pistol, especially powerhouses like the Thompson/Center Scout (no longer made) or current Encore, produce big game power. Cap 'n' ball revolvers are for specialists who get close and shoot handguns very well. The list goes on, to include originals and replicas. It's a hunter's choice—within the confines of the rules.

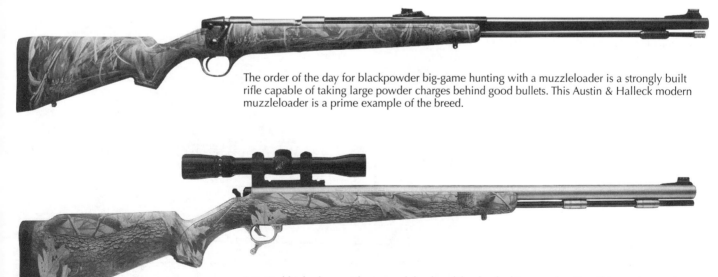

The order of the day for blackpowder big-game hunting with a muzzleloader is a strongly built rifle capable of taking large powder charges behind good bullets. This Austin & Halleck modern muzzleloader is a prime example of the breed.

A typical high-class modern muzzleloader of the day for big-game hunting, this one happening to be from Thompson/Center.

The blackpowder cartridge revolver, as in calibers 44-40 and 45 Colt, as two examples, can take big game, but only in the hands of a competent handgun marksman who is also a good hunter willing to stalk for a close shot. And of course, the hunter must be aware of legality. Not all hunts are allowed such handguns. This Stainless Steel Gunfighter from the Navy Arms Company is a well-made blackpowder cartridge handgun.

Big Game Blackpowder Cartridge Rifles and Revolvers

The world of big-bore single-shot breechloaders is ripe for big-game hunting. I have a 38-55 Pedersoli Remington Rolling Block that is deadly on big game. Lever-actions are hardly left out, not only the big boomers, but also those firing shorter, larger-bore cartridges such as the 44-40 and 45 Colt. I will employ a Pedersoli Colt Lightning 45 Colt on whitetails in the thicket this year. In a 1900 sheep hunting story by E.E. Bowles, the author said, "I have been using an old .44-caliber, blackpowder model of '73; it answers my purpose [for bighorn sheep]. Meanwhile, my Marlin 38-55 has taken several deer and antelope. Blackpowder revolvers in the hands of experts willing to stalk for close shots are strong enough to take big game—but this means perfect bullet placement with a heavy projectile. In *Still Hunting The Grizzly* 1885, Theodore Roosevelt writes that his rifle was "a 45-75 half-magazine, stocked and sighted to suit myself. At one time I had bought a double-barreled English Express, but soon threw it aside in favor of the Winchester, which, according to my experience is much the best weapon for any American game."

Sights

Regardless of the firearm, the right sights must be selected. And what are the correct sights for hunting with muzzleloader or blackpowder cartridge gun? Two things: they work for you and they are legal for the hunt in question. For example, I mounted a Bushnell Banner Dusk & Dawn, 3-9X with Circle-X reticule on a 50-caliber muzzleloader intended for stand hunting where game came in very early and very late—legal light, but not bright light. But I have a Ghost Ring "peep" sight on a 54-caliber, just right for that rifle.

Whence Comes the Power?

Same song—blackpowder power comes from heavy bullets, since true high-velocity is out of the question. Our fastest-shooting front-loaders are not in the 3,000 fps camp. Bullet weight rises with the size of the animal. This is not necessarily a caliber increase, because a 40-caliber conical bullet can weigh 400 grains, while a 40-caliber round ball goes 133 grains. I have no qualms going for whitetails with a 45 Colt Pedersoli Lightning rifle in brush country, with shots generally under 50 yards, shooting a 250-grain lead bullet. The late John Kane proved that a bullet of that general size at modest velocity could be deadly on big game in the hands of a polished hunter, which Kane was. He got close, delivering the projectile perfectly on target. The round ball, deadly as it is, loses power quickly. Therefore, the smart hunter gets close, directing the lead pill into the chest cavity. The all-lead projectile, including the round ball, remains extremely deadly with long wound channels. Then there are the big thumpers (Chapter 37) which are capable of taking any big game anywhere under the right conditions.

Bullets for Big Game

Chapter 34 on casting bullets praises lead. Lead bullets are excellent by reason of long wound channels through tissue and bone. But there are now a number of jacketed muzzleloader bullets on the market that do a terrific job on big game. While I contend that big lead bullets, especially from Parker Productions and the Buffalo Bullet Company, leave nothing to be desired with the right placement, nothing can take away from bullets like the

Today's typical big-game muzzleloader looks like this Knight rifle with scope and sling. It is powerful. It is accurate. And it will get the job done.

Whence comes the power? The power lies in big bullets at reasonable velocity. Those bullets can be round or conical. Here, a 54-caliber round ball is among a few lead conical bullets.

Blackpowder bullets for big game come in many different shapes and weights. These 54-caliber PowerBelt bullets fired accurately in a muzzleloading hunting rifle the author likes to shoot. The rifle was allowed up to 150-grains volume FFg type powder, but Sam found that 130 grains gave optimum performance.

The conical bullet cannot be denied for mass and for its ability to retain velocity better than the round ball. On the other hand, the amazing round ball seems to defy science when it comes to taking big game cleanly at closer ranges.

PowerBelt. I have earmarked the 295-grain PowerBelt Aerotip bullet for an antelope hunt. This bullet shoots relatively "flat" in the rifle I intend to carry. If I go for moose, I'll most likely load a Buffalo Bullet SSB or a big Parker Hyr-

dra-Con, both offering deep penetration. There are almost too many good bullets today, making a final choice difficult. I contend that the right bullet is the one that shoots best in the particular big-game firearm. Accuracy allows ideal bullet placement and ideal bullet placement results in quick kills. Finally, commercial or home-cast "pure" lead or alloy bullets are highly effective and cannot be left out of the lineup.

Caliber

Cartridge-shooting big-game rifles are capable of high velocity. The century-old 30-06 proves this. Today's factory load from Federal in the High Energy package puts a 180-grain bullet out at over 2,900 fps. For Africa, I handloaded a 180-grain bullet at 3,000 fps from a 26-inch barrel 30-06 using IMR-4831 powder and a load found in a Barnes manual. Forget these speeds for blackpowder guns. Go with bore size for big game. I think a 50-caliber round ball is right for deer-sized game fired on no farther than 125 yards, and preferably much closer. A 54 is good for larger game. Were I to go past 54, it would be to something on the order of a 62 or even larger round ball. Conicals do not depends entirely on bore size for weight, and therefore even a 40-caliber elongated bullet can have good mass.

Testing Big Game Bullets

Is there a way to test a big game bullet before hunting with it? Yes. We

are fortunate to have a modern commercial product—the Bullet Test Tube from Ballistic Technology. The sole purpose of this product is testing bullet expansion and wound channel. The Test Tube allows a very high positive correlation between bullet performance in the medium and on big game. The bullet is recovered from the reusable media to show not only expansion properties, but also retained weight. The best feature of the Bullet Test Tube is, I think, its ability to capture the wound channel. I want to know not only what the recovered bullet looks like and weighs, but also what it did in its progress—in other words, the wound channel that it created. The Bullet Test Tube is not designed for high-velocity big-game cartridges as it comes from the company. But it can be modified with specific Xtenders to form a single Tube to handle stronger ballistics.

Sam's Bullet Box is a homemade device also used for testing bullet performance. It is a simple wooden box, compartmentalized, with different media in the compartments. The media used do not entirely correspond with bone, body fluids, and muscle structure. However, I have found a rather high correlation between bullet action in the box and on game. Show me a bullet that "blows up" in the box and I will show you a bullet that will do the same on big game. Conversely, bullets that penetrate well in the media of the box do likewise on big game. I have settled on a some-

Testing before going hunting with a big-game bullet is never a mistake. This wound channel from a Bullet Test Tube proved that at 200 yards, the 54-caliber PowerBelt bullet arrived with considerable force.

what standard set of media for the box. The first compartment contains a water balloon to simulate the fluid content of all animals. The slabs of half-inch pine that create the compartments represent, to a degree, muscle. The second compartment holds a slab of modeling clay for a general representation of tissue. Following the clay, newspaper about an inch thick, wet or dry, is used to "torture" the bullet as bone might. Compacted newspaper also helps determine the size and shape of the wound channel. Finally, the box contains phone books. I used to use thick catalogs, but phone books serve well and with annual upgrades are widely available for free in large quantity.

The bullet box and the Bullet Test Tube reveal various levels of performance: penetration, bullet upset, also known as "mushrooming," wound channel, and retention of original weight. Comparisons between high-energy jacketed big-game bullets and missiles for muzzleloaders have proved especially interesting. Some time ago, upon testing a 58-caliber conical

This bison went down to a strong load from an Austin & Halleck rifle because the bullet created a proper wound channel that traveled through a vital region.

Blackpowder all-lead bullets in both round ball and conical configuration do a great job. Fadala took a Maine black bear that, for a while, ranked No. 1 for blackpowder in that state. The bruin fell to one shot with a 385-grain Remington conical just like the ones shown here.

The round ball never ceases to amaze as it drops big game with one well-placed shot from reasonable range. This 54-caliber round ball accounted for a mature mule deer buck with one shot delivered to the "boiler room." Note expansion.

Bullet placement on an animal the size of an American bison (buffalo) is vital for success with any rifle, including big-bore muzzleloaders. Ideally, the hunter gets close and aims to put a round ball into the lung/heart region, a heavy conical more forward into the scapula area.

weighing 625 grains and backed with a big powder charge, my bullet box was literally blown apart, the sides flattening out like birds' wings in flight. I have witnessed no such thing with cartridges up to and including 300 magnums, which is not to suggest that the 58-caliber muzzleloader is more powerful than a 300 magnum. Rather, it shows a difference in how the two bullets brought their energy to bear upon the media. **Vital:** In order to gain useful information from either the Bullet Test Tube or Sam's Bullet Box, one of two things must be carefully managed. Either the shot must be taken from a range normally associated with big-game hunting, or the load must be

reduced to match the arrival velocity of the bullet downrange.

The first is a simple matter of setting the Bullet Box or Test Tube downrange and firing a bullet into it. The problem is putting that bullet right into the middle of either device. I prefer loading down to the proper arrival velocity. Using data from *The Gun Digest Blackpowder Loading Manual* I can find the arrival velocity of a specific bullet from a particular firearm. Being exact is not important. A close approximation is good enough to discover what a bullet will do downrange. For example, if I have a 50-caliber ball-shooting rifle loaded to deliver 1,900 fps at the muzzle, I know that this round ball is doing about 1,100 fps

Knowing trajectory is vital to success for hunters who shoot out to 200+ yards on big game. How far off is this antelope buck? For a properly sighted muzzleloader firing a good bullet at good velocity, not too far. The rangefinder is the blackpowder hunters' friend in a case like this, taking guesswork out of the picture.

at 100 yards. Specifically, a 50-caliber Jonathan Browning Mountain Rifle starting at 1,974 fps found the 177-grain .490-inch round ball clocking 1,113 fps at 100 yards. Further, I know from chronograph tests that 30-grains FFg or equivalent will develop about 1,100 fps with a .490-inch 177-grain round ball. So I load the rifle with 30 grains of FFg and fire at only a few feet from the test device. Given my 45-caliber Volunteer rifled musket with a starting velocity of about 1,500 fps, I know that the 490-grain Lyman bullet will be going about 1,250 fps at 100 yards. So I load the Volunteer with only 70 instead of 130 grains of FFg and shoot into the test device at close range.

I ran tests originally run for the fourth edition again for the fifth, trying to keep things as close to the first run as possible with the exception of using the new arrangement of water balloon first, then clay, followed by newspaper packing and phone books. Results were almost identical to the first trial with all loads.

The 58-caliber 625-grain Minie bullet arriving at 1,200 fps passed through one water balloon, the clay compartment, newspaper, and phone books to completely exit the back of the bullet box. Once again, the sides of the box cratered a bit. A strong 7mm Magnum load did not penetrate as deeply, nor did it create such a large wound channel, and it certainly did not blow out the sides of my bullet box. This does not mean that a 58-caliber 625-grain Minie is more effective than a 7mm Magnum. It does show, however, that a big lead bullet possesses a semi-truck load of penetration power. The recovered 625-grain Minie weighed 512 grains (508 grains on the first test), again showing over 80 percent of its original weight and verifying the fact that lead has high molecular cohesion—the bullet staying together as a unit rather than fragmenting. While the bullet box applauded lead bullet effectiveness, it also proved that small lead round balls, as great as they are on rabbits, squirrels—even wild turkeys—are not right for big

game. I retested a .350-inch pure lead round ball for the second run. As in an earlier test, this little round ball made it only halfway through the first phone book behind the balloon and clay. A 50-caliber .490-inch round ball striking at 1,200 fps lost 40 percent of its original weight, the same as on the previous test of the same ball, and it made it through balloon, clay, one phone book, and one-half of a second phone book. A 280-grain 58-caliber round ball hitting at 1,100 fps lost only 20 percent of its original weight passing through balloon, clay, and through two phone books and almost halfway into a third, just like the first time it was tested.

The Wound Channel

The wound channel is the cavity created by a projectile. The process of creating that channel is far more complex than meets the eye. Bullet upset, or mushrooming, dispenses energy, but it also changes the shape of the wound channel. Everyone who has experience harvesting big game with modern cartridges has seen an exit hole far larger than the size of the bullet. This is extremely evident with modern high-speed mushrooming-type big game bullets. A two-inch exit hole made by a 30-06 Springfield or similar cartridge is not unusual. But did a 30-caliber bullet really expand to two-inch diameter? Of course not. Double diameter would be only six-tenths of an inch. So what happened? I watched through a 20X spotting scope as a 30-'06 bullet struck an antelope buck. The hide flew out and away from the animal as if it were a balloon. There was a two-inch exit hole, yet the bullet itself was trapped against the hide of the pronghorn. What pushed the hide out? What made the 2-inch exit hole? The bullet did, of course, but not directly. The shock wave *in front* of the projectile puffed the hide out and made the hole. Blackpowder bullets work differently. They do not possess the speed or remaining kinetic energy of the more powerful big-game cartridges. But they do create long wound channels and they can break bone like a battering ram. Unless the spine or brain is struck, however, the animal is not likely to turn toes up as it often does when a high-speed bullet hits. But delivered force can be immense.

Bullet Placement

Heavy lead bullets are not designed to open up readily. Direct them to the scapular region for best results. I once shot a javelina, big for its type, dressing almost 40-pounds, perhaps 65 pounds on the hoof. A 58 caliber conical sailed through without any sign of a hit. The hog stood there. I loaded again, fired again, the boar dropped. The bullets had zipped through the chest cavity like wind through the trees. A round ball of similar caliber in the lung region would have flattened out, delivering most of its impact to the boar, not the hill behind the animal. Tip—always check after a shot, even if it looks like a complete miss. I took a steenbok in Africa that ran after hit squarely behind the shoulder. One onlooker said, "Let's go. He missed." The leader of the safari asked me what I thought. I said I felt the shot was good. A tracker trotted out into the field and inside of two minutes held up the tiny antelope. Had we not taken time to look, a fine game animal would have fed the hyenas.

Uphill/Downhill Shooting

No one carries a slide rule on a big game hunt. Figuring exact hold-under for shots at an angle is an exercise for the desk, but totally impractical in the field. Yet we know that whether shooting at game uphill from the muzzle, or downhill, the bullet *in either case* strikes high. The best a hunter can do is take this fact into account, holding a little *under* for shots that are steeply uphill **or** downhill.

Judging the Range

I was hunting with Bob Hodgdon one afternoon in Wyoming when he put my range-guessing skill to the test. "How far is that boulder?" he asked. I guessed 175 yards. Bob put his rangefinder on the boulder. It really was about 175 yards away. "How about that one?" he asked. This boulder was steeply uphill from me. I guessed 250 yards. It turned out to be almost exactly the same distance as the first boulder. I was way off! Today we have access to rangefinders that are compact, light, and easy to carry. My Bushnell Compact weighs only 12 ounces. It's great for four purposes. It improves range estimation. Look, guess, then verify. It tells how to hold on standing game. By pre-testing various spots from a tree stand, the exact distance of an incoming animal is known. It totally annihilates "I got that deer at 450 yards!" The rangefinder proves just how far the shot really was.

Knowing Trajectory

Now that the 200-yard muzzleloader is a reality, knowing the range is more important than ever. Still preferred: stalk for the close sure shot. But with scoped front-loaders of the day, especially shooting higher ballistic coefficient bullets such as the SSB, if a hunter knows the range, he can make that 200 yard strike, but before he can do that, he must also know his bullet's trajectory. Longer-range muzzleloaders can be sighted in from the bench to strike two to three inches high at 100 yards. Then without moving the sight, the rifle is fired at a target 200 yards away. The center point of the group indicates bullet drop at 200 yards. Now the hunter knows how to hold on a big-game animal from point blank range out to 200+ yards.

In dense cover the hunter must remember that bullets of all types and weights do poorly as "brush-buckers." Round balls are especially subject to going astray in brush. The idea is to get close and shoot through a "hole" in the brush when possible—and then you might have a buck to carry back to camp.

Brush Shooting

One fine afternoon in a particularly splendid patch of Wyoming countryside I stalked a mule deer buck to only 20 yards. I used a bush to hide my approach. The bush was between us. Crack! The buck looked up, and then ambled away. I searched for sign of a hit. There was none. Finally, I hiked over the ridge. There in the view of my binocular was the very same four-by-four buck feeding in perfect health. The 54-caliber round ball had undoubtedly struck a branch, which detoured it from an 18-inch target at only 20 paces. Bullets go haywire in brush. Period. That includes heavy slugs from big bores. Even 500-grain 458 Winchester full metal jacket bullets veer off course in the brush. Best advice—get a clear shot. Forget about "brush busting." It's a myth easily tested by anyone. I ran a little demonstration at a target through brush only 50 yards away. A 243 Winchester, 458 Winchester, 54-caliber round ball, and 58-caliber conical all failed to deliver good groups on the target.

Taking the Shot on Big Game

There are several major stances for shooting big game. Offhand is one. This means standing on the hind legs and banging away. It's to be avoided whenever possible. If a shooter must go offhand and if his rifle has a carrying strap, the hasty sling method helps steady the shot. This amounts to nothing more than wrapping the left arm through the strap for a right-handed shooter. Kneeling is better than offhand, and sitting is steadier than kneeling. Prone is good when the lay of the land allows a hunter to go on his belly. I rely often on my walking stick to steady the shot, especially from offhand, but also sitting. The rules are simple: get into the steadiest possible stance; take a clean sight picture; squeeze, don't jerk, the trigger.

As part of a little test, Fadala took a blind wearing no camouflage, no UV killer, and no scent cover. Deer like this one located him instantly. Later, with camouflage, including face mask and gloves, plus UV killer, plus scent eliminator, deer like this one walked right up to the blind oblivious of the hunter.

Blackpowder Hunting Methods

The Immensely Popular Tree Stand

Take a tip from the modern whitetail bowhunter. Climb a tree. Whitetails pattern pretty well. Set up a tree stand along the right path and chances are a buck will pass by if the hunter waits long enough. Tree stand hunters take black bears, even elk and moose. I hated the tree stand at first, as well as windmill lookouts, considering them unsporting. But I was wrong. The stand was no less sporting than waiting in a duck blind or goose pit. As for boring, it was not—after I learned to enjoy the wildlife that came to call, from birds to bucks, bulls, and boars. Tree stands are great for blackpowder hunters because they generally afford close shots at slow-moving or standing animals. In the meanwhile, the world goes by. Some of the most amazing wildlife sightings occur from the stand. I once saw a golden eagle kill a mature mule deer doe as I sat perched in a windmill. Another time a coyote and badger parried about a waterhole, neither allowing the other to get a drink.

The Ground Blind

After learning to love tree stands, I tried ground blinds. Kelly Glause, a Wyoming guide stationed in Evansville,

Wyoming, set up some great ground blinds, first pits dug into the earth near waterholes, then rock corrals, finally little wooden boxes. I also had good luck with simple blinds made of cheesecloth (the material game bags are made of). The ghillie suit is a blind unto itself. A hunter outfitted in one can hide on the ground without a blind.

Lures

Especially during rut, lures work. There are several ways to use them. Two are freshening a deer scrape with lure, and lacing a trail. Tree stand hunters lay out a fine line of lure leading from brush pockets and timber to the stand. One afternoon I had four different bucks come by my stand, nose to the ground, following the scent trail I made with artificial musk.

Scents

Cover scent is important in stalking close for that one good blackpowder shot. Wildlife Research Center, Inc. has come up with superior cover scents in spray bottles. Fresh earth is a good one, also cedar, acorn, and persimmon. While still-hunting through the habitat, a little puff in the air covers human scent. Another way to go is deer or elk lure mixed with water in a spray bottle. If hunters knew how often the uncanny noses of big-game animals

Fadala had it proved to him in a big-game camp that some scent killers really work. From blinds, Sam had whitetail deer come in and "wind him" until he applied this product from Atsko on his clothing.

detected them, they would watch the wind much more carefully, also relying on cover scents.

Wind Detectors

I learned the value of a wind detector from the late Elroy French as we stalked the bushveldt in Africa. Elroy had a small bag filled with finely powdered white campfire coal dust, which he shook from time to time as we still-hunted. The little puff of smoke on the air showed not only wind direction, but how the zephyrs behaved, swirling, circling, changing. There are two major types of commercial wind detector. One is powder contained in a plastic squeeze bottle. The other is a product known as Windfloaters from AFI Outdoors Company. This stuff is like superfine lambs wool. A very tiny piece turned loose shows direction and behavior of the breeze. Dropping a little dirt in the air or a leaf is better than nothing, but compares poorly to powders and Windfloaters.

Still-Hunting

I have been a pursuit hunter all my life. Still-hunting is pursuit, not sitting still. It means moving quietly through the habitat with a specific plan. Walk a little. Look a lot. Move slowly with regard to the lay of the land, observing "field position" at all times. If you jump an animal and cannot get a shot, you were out of field position. Approach a

thicket so a deer breaks cover and you have no chance to score, you were out of field position.

Spot and Stalk

Binoculars are the key to this style of big-game hunting with a blackpowder firearm. As told before, I have two glasses that find their way into the big-game field. One is a 12x50 Bushnell reverse porro prism. The other is a Fujinon 10X with large objective lenses for light-gathering. Both glasses enjoy good optical resolution. Both have **shortened** straps for easy carrying. Spot and stalk is just what it says—find game before it finds you and plan a stalk using a wind detector to note currents that would give you away. Employ the lay of the land to hide the approach. Wear a facemask or use a bit of brush to conceal your face. Get close. Take one good shot.

The Drive

A well-devised drive is deadly on deer and can work for elk, moose, or other big game. Hunters are posted along a trail or runway while partners hike in their direction, the object being to push game. The wind detector works again, but this time to ensure that scent goes from drivers to posted hunters. Wind direction is especially vital when only one hunter is driving. Buck or bull scents the hiking hunter, and slips away. If the waiting hunter is in the right spot, a close, clean shot is his.

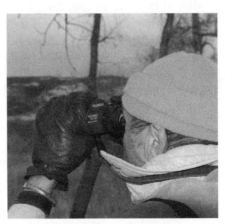

Fadala believes in strong binoculars for big game hunting in both timber and open country, sometimes even brush. Here he uses his 10x50X Fuji glass. He also likes a 12-50X Bushnell reverse porro prism, especially for the spot-and-stalk hunting style.

African hunting is guided hunting. The PH (professional hunter) runs the show. This kudu bull, taken with an Austin & Halleck muzzleloader, was part of a safari hunt in Africa. Guided hunts in North America are also prominent and filled with success.

Scouting

Big-game blackpowder hunters do well to scout an area, searching for sign of game. This sign is generally in the form of tracks and droppings. In time, a hunter learns to determine the age of such sign. By scouting an area before season, when possible, hunters don't waste time where the game is not. The topographical map helps.

The Lodge

The hunting lodge was frequented in North America a hundred years ago and is more popular than ever. The lodge normally includes guides who have either set up stands or know where game lives, both being especially helpful to blackpowder hunters. Lodges are set up on private ground with special feeding programs to ensure a healthy wild animal population.

Going Guided

Special blackpowder-only seasons are perfect going-guided opportunities. Steve Pike of Tenderfoot Outfitters, Gunnison, Colorado, is an example of a guide dedicated to bringing smokepole hunters into range of trophy elk and mule deer. Steve can talk an elk into slingshot range, let alone the reach-out of a good front-loader. Finding a guide is no big trick. Listings on the back pages of magazines pre-

Planning is always vital to success. Here, Bob Hodgdon, left, discusses a guided hunt with renowned PH Johan Wolvaardt of Mussina, South Africa. What we will go for?

A large size fanny pack holds a multitude of important gear for the big-game hunter. Here is the author's outfit, along with his ever-handy hiking staff. Note the first aid kit.

vail. State guide associations are another source. State game departments may also have a list of guides and outfitters, as my home state, Wyoming, offers. It's really that simple to get in touch with a guide.

Tracking

Having watched black trackers in Africa, I know that a man can follow an animal in the wild. I watched a fantastic tracker follow a single animal through a maze of bushveldt. I did not believe that any man could follow a single animal like that, but he proved that he could. Unfortunately, most of us are not of that caliber, but we can get better through practice. Less skilled trackers do pretty well in snow, for example, and sometimes after a good rain. Dogging steadfastly directly on the trail, however, can be a mistake. Game animals are aware of their back trails. Better to leave the direct trail from time to time, circling ahead, using a wind detector along with spray cover scent or lure.

Calling Big Game

Watching Steve Pike, the Colorado guide, call a bull elk within twelve paces was an unforgettable experience. Steve is an expert, but we can all learn to call game. I got good at calling pronghorn antelope during rut using a Lohman call. I learned from the provided audiotape. One afternoon my daughter Nicole, who had three Wyoming antelope tags (two doe, one buck), got two does down within 50 yards of each other. I

was about to go forward for the duties of field-dressing when I saw a buck in the distance. We took cover. I tuned up the Lohman antelope call and drew the buck in to a distance of 100 yards where he was cleanly taken with one shot.

Backpack Adventure

I have come to call this style "wherever I may wander" because wandering is a good way to describe it. The goal is backpacking into undisturbed territory and staying over as a means of finding that quiet spot perfect for hunting with

Calling big game works—not all the time, certainly, but sometimes very well. A grunt call can bring in whitetail bucks during the rut.

a charcoal-burner. I have gravitated to a very large fanny pack for much of my backpack hunting. But I have also not abandoned my modified Camp Trails Freighter with shelf. I carry a lightweight tent and sleeping bag and considerable gear. I thought as I became an older hunter I would lighten my load. I have, in a way, by choosing lighter, more compact tools. But especially when hunting alone, I want sufficient equipment to make it through a storm. The object is to camp with the game. In the morning, you wake up where the wild animals live, usually in a remote spot away from the beaten path. There is one thing new (for me) about this method. It is the GPS. I have two. One is the Magellan Meridian. It tells just about everything from what time it is in Beijing to the temperature in Guatemala. My other GPS is a Garmin eTrex Personal Navigator. It weighs but six ounces and runs for 22 hours on AA batteries. The GPS allows me to do two things: I can travel at will into backcountry knowing that I can find my way back out. And I can mark downed game, packing the meat out in several trips, because I can always find my way back to the carcass.

Hunting Gear

I still have not found a better waterproof garment than the lightweight parka from the Woolrich Company. I

There is no use in sighting in a muzzleloader or blackpowder cartridge rifle perfectly, only to have the rifle sight whacked out of alignment before reaching camp. That is where the hard gun case comes in. This super case is from Hardigg.

have several good boots to choose from depending upon terrain and conditions. My current sleeping bags are of two types—a big one and a backpacker. I have a bivy (one man shelter, two pounds) and a backpack tent. A comfortable hunter hunts better. Also important in backpacking is a good light. I carry two. One can be strapped on my head, keeping both hands free. The other is a Surefire, which is worth every farthing because it provides a bright beam showing the nighttime route to camp after dark.

The Big Camp

Good shelter provides good rest and a rested hunter is a safer and better outdoorsman. I have turned to a big tent. It's a Coleman Weathermaster three-room. I have also treated myself (and my wife) to two fine tent heaters—Coleman with blower and Mr. Heater. I use the tent city approach: big tent for living with satellite tents, one for gear, another

a "cook shack." Of course, this setup is for staying a while. The powerful Coleman North Star lantern that runs on non-leaded fuel provides light. I have the same lantern in the propane model for carrying around the campsite. Stay warm. Stay healthy. Hunt better from a good camp.

Protect Your Rifle

You can apply all of your knowledge of big game, scouting techniques, and hunting expertise, but the moment of truth will always be the shot. I reached camp one time with a bent front sight. Never happened again. I have gun cases that transport my firearms safely. My newest is from Hardigg (see Directory). It's a full-size Storm Case—appropriate name since it comes with press and pull latches that hold fast so the rifle inside is fully protected. It is also waterproof as long as the o-rings are not damaged or compromised with dirt. It even has a Vortex valve that adjusts air pressure automatically without letting in water. And it stands up on its own with wheels to pull it along.

The muzzleloader big game chase is the lodestone, the crown diamond, and the sun's rays of big-game hunting with a firearm. And the well-versed hunter who knows his gun and game has an excellent chance of success.

ASAT camouflage has long been considered among the best patterns for all-around hunting. Where allowed by both law and safety conditions, camouflage like this can be a real boon. Even when blaze orange must be worn, camouflage can help break up the human form while the blaze orange continues to show the hunter. Use UV killer to complete the hidden effect. UV killer from Atsko works.

Blackpowder Hunting Tips

1. Know thy rifle – or for that matter, any gun. Practice. Not only shooting, but rapid/safe loading and handling. Use the best source of ignition for your gun.
2. Sight in right – with regard to the trajectory of the given rifle (or handgun).
3. Wear two different gloves in cold weather – a thinner one on the shooting hand that does not have to be removed to make a good shot.
4. Dry the bore of oil, grease, lube—whatever—before going afield.
5. Get a stick – a staff not only helps hiking, but is also useful for shooting.
6. Same old song – seat that bullet fully in the bore. Lewis wrote in 1885 that a muzzleloader barrel could burst, not from "overcharging," but "from want of proper precaution" in fully seating a projectile (including shotgun charge).
7. Learn to use a call.
8. Consider a backup gun for long hunts.
9. Build a master hunting list so you won't forget something important.
10. Have one shooting bag for each hunting gun.
11. Make a good camp—stay warm and healthy for best hunting results.
12. Don't forget wind detector.
13. Use cover scent at the stand.
14. Deliver a round ball behind the shoulder, a heavy conical in the shoulder.
15. Hunt with getting close in mind for one sure blackpowder shot.
16. Carry blackpowder shooting essentials in your pack. Do not leave them in camp.
17. Buy and learn to use a GPS.
18. Scout the hunt area before season if possible.
19. Carry a pack with lifesaving essentials on board—bivy and tent in wilderness country.
20. Protect your guns in transit. Invest in a good gun case.

THEY MADE MUZZLELOADERS—
THE ONE-MAN SHOP
OF YESTERYEAR

chapter

45

The Buffalo Bill Historical Society locates and installs actual workrooms of various western celebrities, such as famous artists. While this is not a gunmaking room, it reveals a similar flavor to the old-time, one-man (sometimes with apprentice) gun shop.

We owe a debt of gratitude to the immigrant craftsmen of eastern America for their dedication, vision, individuality, talent, and self-sufficient attitude, persevering in a new land, laboring under a language disadvantage, and prevailing against all odds. They were from various countries—mainly Germany—but other European lands as well. And they brought with them not only their skill, but also their honest and hardworking lifestyle. They created the guns of the Golden Age of Firearms in America, arming a nation with the finest of the period. The Pennsylvania-

Kentucky long rifle chiseled a niche in the granite of American history that will never be worn away, and most likely never repeated. The beauty of these rifles has not faded with time. They remain arguably the finest-looking firearms of any period—true classics that while outstripped in range, power, and even accuracy by modern rifles, were nonetheless never surpassed for their artistic line, form and even color in both metal and wood. These rifles, as well as some pistols, were testimonies to their makers' artistic and functional craftsmanship. They were both beautiful and

serviceable the day they left the one-man shop to go forth into the hunting and target-shooting field. They remain so today.

Stewart Edward White (1873-1946), American novelist, paved a broader road in gun authorship than fiction. His *Land of Foot Prints* and other hunting titles remain, to this day, collectible works. In his book, *The Long Rifle*, White writes in *"The Grooved Barrel"* prologue, "In our country two hundred years ago shooting was the national pastime and people shot guns as today they go about golf." That was true.

This sparse room is an actual old-time gunworking location. The 'smith of old had very little to work with, but his hands were talented.

Shooting matches were commonplace, often at a "mark," which could be little more than a shingle or X carved in a tree. Some of the paper targets remain to be seen today. With open iron sights, groups were more than acceptable. The long rifle was deadly, as proved when marksmen of the American Revolution went up against what was probably the finest soldier in the world—members of the British army. Every one of these firearms came from a shop, usually a small shop with one gunmaker, with perhaps an apprentice at his side. Important to modern blackpowder shooters is the fact that the long rifle never died out, as Chapter 46 proves. The present chapter is a brief look, a mere glance, as it were, at a distant past before power tools and long before the Henry Ford concept of an assembly line came into being.

All European countries had gunmakers. Military people caught on quickly to the fact that the gun would surpass the sword. Guns in the form of cannon were to become especially effective. But the shoulder arm was not then, nor is not now, completely overtaken by tanks, mortars, RPGs, or any other instrument of warfare. Italy, France, Belgium, Austria—they all had their elite firearms craftsmen from the beginning of gunmaking history. But this all-too-

brief look at early arms-making in the small shop focuses upon the Americans and British. A large and involved book would penetrate mere inches into the depth of early gunmaking. Almost arbitrarily we look to England in a period *following* the great American long rifle. We do so because advancements in English gunmaking had a strong impact on the entire world, especially in the Victorian era when the "sun never set on the British Empire." And so to England we go with a look at only a few examples of arms manufacture. G.T. Teasdale-Buckell, editor of *Land and Water* from 1885 to 1899, authored a book entitled *Experts on Guns and Shooting*. The book was published in 1900 London. Buckell delved into an intensive study of firearms manufacture. His book begins with Joseph "Joe" Manton, who Buckell calls, "One of the little known, except

that he was the best and most unfortunate gunmaker in England."

Bucknell says, "Egg was his only rival, and if he treated sportsmen as he is reported to treat Colonel Hawker it is no wonder that his greater rival [Manton] soon outstripped him in popularity." Hawker reported that Egg was a "rascal," while Manton was apparently honest, hardworking, and straightforward. Bucknell writes, "Joseph Manton introduced a totally new era in gunmaking. So much was this the case that after his death all the men who became celebrated for their guns had been his workmen." While gunmaker Egg was definitely credited as a top gunmaker in his day, Bucknell reports that Manton had to rebore some of Colonel Hawker's guns that came from Egg's shop. Hawker, one of the best-known shooters of the era and a patron of the gunmaking art, remained close to Manton throughout Manton's career. After Manton was carried off to debtors' prison, the Colonel superintended the making of his own guns (Hawker's) at Manton's workshop, which while under bankruptcy remained in operation. Bucknell writes, "It appears that Manton's patents and law suits in their defence [sic], even in one instance against his own brother, were the ultimate cause of his ruin."

"Manton was in prison for debt in 1829, and he died in 1835 at the age of sixty-nine. From wealth, therefore, he was reduced to want, by the assistance of the lawyers and the patent laws," writes Bucknell. Hawker wrote an inscription upon a stone dedicated to Manton, saying that Manton was an "unrivaled genius," which was "established in every

Royal Highland Regiment Enlisted Man's Flintlock Pistol
Maker: Isaac Bissell; Birmingham, England

Considering the tools of the day, a fine pistol like this was possible only because the old-time gunsmith had both the talent and patience to build quality products.

A Pedersoli caplock pistol with inlays is a perfect example of what the old-time gunmaker could do in his one-man shop with only a few tools to work with. This pistol is representative of the Kentucky rifle era.

quarter of the globe, by his celebrity as the greatest artist in firearms that the world ever produced." Mighty words, but those who knew Manton and his guns agreed with Hawker's sentiment. One of Manton's firearms is explained as "A flint and percussion double gun, named on locks 'Joseph Manton,' number on guard 11028. Stub twist 14-bore 29 1/2-in. barrels, with flat top rib. The stock is well bent, 1-5/8 in. at comb and 2-1/2 in. at heel; length 14-1/2 in., and the gun weight 7-1/4 lbs. The locks have an ingenious arrangement to effect the alteration from flint to percussion or *vice versa*. The flash pans are pivoted, and carry nipples on their rear faces. They can be secured in either of their dual positions by means of small thumbscrews passing through them and engaging the pivots." Are we to believe that Manton created a firearm in both flint and percussion ignition? Yes, we are.

George Gibbs of Bristol was described as "a man who was never happy unless he was shooting." He apparently traveled in pursuit of shooting "so that Ireland as well as Cornwall and South Wales were compelled to contribute." Bucknell goes on: "Wimbledon, of course, knew him just as it knew, and Bisley knows, his son, who, we imagine, would by rifle shots be conceded the first place in the British Islands as a long-range rifle shot." Gibbs was also a hunter as well as target shooter. But his fame, be he ever so adept as a marksman, came because he was known in his time frame as a gunmaker. Many sportsmen of the time believed that "there is

no gunmaker to be found, even in London, who is his equal." T. F. Freemantle wrote much on firearms and shooting in the 19th century. He remarked that "There seems no reason to believe that it was ever equaled by any performance in America," speaking of Gibbs' 48 out of 50 strikes upon a three-foot bullseye at 1,000 yards, the target being a steel plate. Freemantle wrote, "It has had many thousands of shots fired at it at 1,000 yards, during a period now of more than thirty years, but only on this one occasion has it responded with its musical sound thirty-seven times running." Along with hitting the target 48 times out of 50, 37 times in a row, Gibbs never cleaned his rifle once.

Gibbs was reported to have "rifled every barrel of every weapon that shot

This type of metering spout is typically found on shot pouches, and allows two weights of shot to be thrown after a simple adjustment. This sort of spout can also be used to dispense black-powder, or other replica propellant.

in the English, Irish, and Scotch eights in the year 1890. This is a triumph of mechanical skill that Gibbs is not a little proud of. The reason he took personally to barrel-rifling was of a compulsory nature. His barrel-rifler declined to do some work required of him, and this difference of opinion left Gibbs with plenty of barrels, but no one to rifle them." Gibbs spent, according to his own account, three weeks doing nothing else, discovering that he could rifle a barrel better than the man he had employed earlier to do the job, a professional who had been rifling barrels all his work life. One of the best possible testimonies to Gibbs' workmanship came from our man Sir Samuel White Baker, the famed hunter/explorer of Chapter 47. Baker's letter to Gibbs began, "About forty-six years ago your firm made for me the first rifle that I ever planned." The rifle was "entirely" Baker's "idea" at a time when "rifle shooting was but little understood." He was 20 years old when he, Baker, ordered the rifle, being "sure that a heavy charge of powder was the first necessary to procure a high velocity, and consequently a low trajectory."

This may seem overly basic to the modern shooter who understands that a strong powder charge in comparison to the projectile creates high velocity. This is surely true of the fast 220 Swift, which fires bullets ranging 40 to 60 grains weight, but with smokeless powder charges running over 40 grains by weight. One 220 Swift load shows a 40-grain bullet with over 40 grains of RL-15 powder behind it. This ratio changes dramatically with big

They had to make everything, including powder horns and other accoutrements. This is the work of David Yager, Cochise Muzzleloaders, St. David, Arizona. It could be the work of a long-ago gunsmith and is a good representation of the fact.

Embellishment of handmade guns continues to this hour. This is the work of David Yager, Cochise Muzzleloaders, St. David, Arizona.

Personalizing was very much a part of the early gunsmith's work, including powder horns.

bore modern cartridges, such as the 460 Weatherby Magnum, which carries a powder charge as high as 125 grains weight behind a 500-grain bullet. But note that while the ratio is far from one to one, the charge remains strong. And so we should not look only to charge weight, but energy produced by the powder. The point is: Gibbs, from the beginning, was willing to experiment with large powder charges in big-bore guns. The rifle made for Baker in his 20th year weighed 22 pounds, two-groove rifling, firing a "belted ball of 3 ozs." with a charge Baker noted as "1 oz. (16 drams) of powder." Baker is exactly correct in that a 16-dram powder charge is a full ounce, since 16 drams equals 437.44 grains. In turn, there is 437.5-grains weight in one ounce. Baker carried the Gibbs rifle in Ceylon with great success, as reported in *The Rifle and the Hound in Ceylon*. He called it a "wonderful weapon."

The story of W. Greener and W.W. Greener runs concurrently. To this day, W.W. Greener's book, *The Gun*, is read with enthusiasm by students of firearms. W.W. Greener was the son of W. Greener (William), who was known as an experimenter in his time. W.W. followed in his father's footsteps, always experimenting with guns. *The Gun* appeared in 1835. It was heralded in its time as progressive, and in fact outdating Baker's work on firearms. Meanwhile, W. Greener "was the first to discard vent holes in the breeches, relics of the old flintlock gun. He was also instrumental in improving the hardness and quality of barrels by introducing more steel into their manufacture." W. Greener also invented the hollow-base bullet credited to Captain C.E. Minie of the French Army. To this day, we call that blackpowder projectile type the Minie ball. But in fact, W. Greener won a lawsuit proving that his hollow-base bullet came first. Buckell reported that W. Greener's "greatest achievement in gunnery was the discovery of the expanding principle for muzzle-loading rifle bullets." The English Government

American arms crafters of early days were immigrants from Germany and other countries. Meanwhile, great gun builders were at work in England and their labors influenced Americans. Here is one of the greats, G.C. Gibbs (George Gibbs).

The English gunmakers of the 19th century were a very serious lot dedicated not only to building the finest firearms of the era, but also in still competition with one another. When they sat for pictures, their formality showed.

awarded Minie 20,000 pounds for the same invention. As Bucknell put it, "Mr. Greener considered himself aggrieved of this, and the Government ultimately admitted the justice of his claim and gave him [1,000 pounds] in the Army Estimates of 1857."

The Greeners' power as gunmakers resided in genius of invention, as with most of our English armscrafters of the 19th century. W.W. Greener is credited with many patents, including the "self-acting striker" noted as "a method only superceded by the rebounding lock." More importantly was his next patent, the "famous cross bolt, produced as a single-top bolt in 1865." In 1873, W.W. had the "Treble Wedge Fast," credited as "one of the strongest breech actions ever invented." Bucknell reports that "The introduction of choke boring may be regarded as W.W. Greener's greatest achievement; his previous inventions had shown his cleverness, this one made him famous throughout the world." W.W. came up with choke boring in 1874, we're told, and of course its impact remains self-evident. Whereas a cylinder bore is quite effective at close range, choke made the shotgun a viable instrument at a much greater distance. There was controversy, however, with regard to this invention. As Bucknell stated, "We are aware that Mr. Pape, of Newcastle, considers himself the inventor of choke boring, and has been awarded a cup as such by a committee. We do not agree with that award."

A list of great gunmakers goes on, to include Beesley, Robertson, Churchill (E.J), Churchill (H.E.J), Grant, Henry Holland (of Holland and Holland fame), Froome, Lancaster, Watts, Roos, and of course James Purdey, John Rigby, and Westley Richards. But now take a sailing vessel back in time long before the English gunmakers and to another continent. Our ship lands on the shores of eastern America long before the Victorian era in Britain. We find at work gunmakers credited later with rifles bearing Swiss watch precision and Rolls Royce workmanship. Unfortunately, there is "no history we can trust," as one master gunsmith at Colonial Williamsburg put it concerning the birth and progress of the American long rifle. It is impossible to pin down the first gunmakers to land in the New World. But we are fairly safe in assuming that Jaegers (rifles built for hunting) came over with German (add the Palatine Swiss) immigration of the first decade of the 18th century, sometimes pinpointed as 1709. The French Huguenots cannot be left out of the picture. They also settled in the Lancaster Valley of Pennsylvania in Hickory Town, later renamed Gibson's Pasture, again renamed in 1729 to Lancaster. To this day, the counties of Pennsylvania are used to reference specific types of Kentucky/Pennsylvania long rifles. I give the nod to German immigrants for the famous long rifle evolved from the Jaeger brought from the Old Country.

The famous Kentucky Rifle was a product of Pennsylvania. Its name came from a song, "The Hunters of Kentucky," which went: "You gentlemen and ladies fair, who grace this famous city, Just listen if you've time to spare, whilst I rehearse a little ditty; And for an opportunity, conceive yourselves quite lucky, for tis not often here you see a hunter from Kentucky. O Kentucky, the hunters of Kentucky, O Kentucky, the hunters of Kentucky." The song was written about the Battle of New Orleans, War of 1812, where Americans armed with

Typical of old-time gunmakers was a penchant for embellishing even the lower grade firearms of the day. This very plain, original, 19th-century smoothbore is typical of the fact with its minor engraving of the trigger guard.

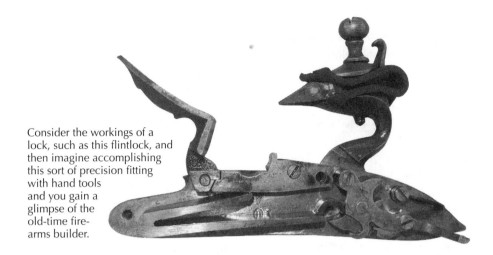

Consider the workings of a lock, such as this flintlock, and then imagine accomplishing this sort of precision fitting with hand tools and you gain a glimpse of the old-time firearms builder.

flintlock long rifles accounted for at least 2,000 British soldiers dead or wounded, plus 800 captured, while the American side lost eight dead and 13 wounded. Regardless of this historical dating, pinning down the exact birthday of the Kentucky Rifle is impossible. Joe Kindig in his *Thoughts on the Kentucky Rifle in the Golden Age* gives a very early time, well before the War of 1812. Another expert claims that the first Kentucky rifle of record was built by John Shrite in Reading, Pennsylvania, 1761. The problem is singling out the exact features that make up a Kentucky/Pennsylvania long rifle. The patch box seems to be the only truly unique American addition to an already established (in general) rifle. The Jaeger was stout, short, of big bore, but apparently small powder charge, while the Kentucky was long-barreled, graceful, smaller of bore, with sufficient powder charge to propel a round ball of about 45-caliber in the neighborhood of 2,000 fps.

We do know that German gunmakers were all over the eastern seaboard, not just in Pennsylvania. And it is clear that the long rifle was in the hands of shooters all over the east by the last quarter of the 18th century. It's also impossible to put a date on the end of the Golden Age of Firearms in America. Joe Kindig felt that the end came after the War of 1812. Daniel Boone, known to all who "do guns," certainly had a Kentucky long rifle. It was probably built by Dickert (Dechard?), who

lived in Boone's time (1735-1820). That Daniel had a Kentucky rifle in his youth, we are not certain. Dickert's gun shop was located in Lancaster County Pennsylvania, Boone's stomping grounds. I continue to credit German craftsmen of that region, because to this day we find strongholds of German people who cling to the language and the way of their forefathers who settled in Pennsylvania. I visited a friend near Brookville and he took me to visit his friends nearby. The main language in that home remained German. I'm of a mind that the Dutch name so often referred to came from *Deutch* (German) and that these gun

crafters were from *Deutchland*, Germany—*Deutch*, not Dutch. The heyday and passing of the Kentucky long rifle in America is subject for a Ph.D. dissertation, and surely far too deep for the waters of this single chapter.

But to go on, the long rifle of the Golden Age gave way to a more practical rifle. Some call it the Smoky Mountain Rifle. Others call it the Poor Boy. Its name is insignificant. What counts is the style. Embellishments by way of engraving, carving, inlays, special patch boxes, handsome furniture, and other fine appointments were set aside for a more affordable and perhaps even more serviceable rifle, especially for hunting. If it shot well, brought home the bacon, and hopefully kept interlopers at bay, it was a good rifle. Gunmaking did not wane after 1812, although it may be true that the stylish Kentucky rifle became somewhat more homely, with emphasis on *home*—a less expensive rifle for the "average" hunter/shooter of the day. Most of us have never heard of George Lanning or Samuel Salyers. On the other hand, several names remain at the forefront of old-style American gunmaking. One is Hacker Martin. Another is William Large. Hacker Martin was not full-time in the business. But

Wire inlay was one way to put art into firearms. Wire inlay is still used by today's great gunmakers.

This Pedersoli long rifle is indicative of the rifles built during the Golden Age of Firearms in America.

his rifles carried great fame and were highly desirable to own. William Large lived a very long time, and therefore a few writers of the mid-20th century and even a bit later got to know something about Bill Large.

Hacker Martin farmed some. He also ran a mill for a time. And he was known for building rifles from scratch. He made "the whole thing," including the barrel. Even many of the truly old-time riflesmiths did not make their own barrels, purchasing them from barrelmakers. But there were gunmakers of the late 19th century who created their own. There is a photograph of one Mary Owensby, noted simply as a "mountain woman" who rifled barrels. As for William Large, he was known for barrels. Not just barrels, but the best to be had in his time. I was privileged to get a letter from Bill when he was a very old man. It was a scolding, of sorts,

but with a gentle touch. He had read something I penned on cleaning a barrel. Bill admonished in his letter, "Never touch water to a barrel." He was adamant about using solvent to clear fouling from the bore of a muzzleloader. Since his barrels won literally hundreds of shooting matches, and since those barrels shot perfectly for many years, his advice had to be taken seriously. Of course, as the timeworn cliché goes, there is more than one way to skin a cat, and there is more than one way to clean the barrel of a blackpowder firearm. Luckily, men like Hacker Martin and William large remained active well into the 20th century. Martin's advice from a 1970 *Muzzle Blasts* magazine summed up my own feelings on the history of riflemaking. He said, "Anybody that tries to write a treatise on rifle-making from start to finish . . . is a candidate for an insane asylum. Several

famous authors have tried it, and who is fool enough to try to make a rifle from their written instructions?"

I am forced to end this chapter with an apology and begin the next chapter with the same. I apologize for being unable to distill the story of the men who made rifles from the beginning of what was to be the United States of America and into the latter third of the 20th century. Their names are strong, but too numerous: Eliphalet (also Eliphelet) Remington, Jr., born 1793, and the rest is history. Hatfield the gunmaker came later, and after him Royland Southgate with his numbered flintlocks. And so many others. They made muzzleloaders the world over, especially the Kentucky long rifle in America. They continued their craft into the 20th century. Without them, the wonderful talent would have perished and this book would not require the next chapter.

THEY MAKE CUSTOM MUZZLELOADERS— TODAY'S CRAFTSMEN

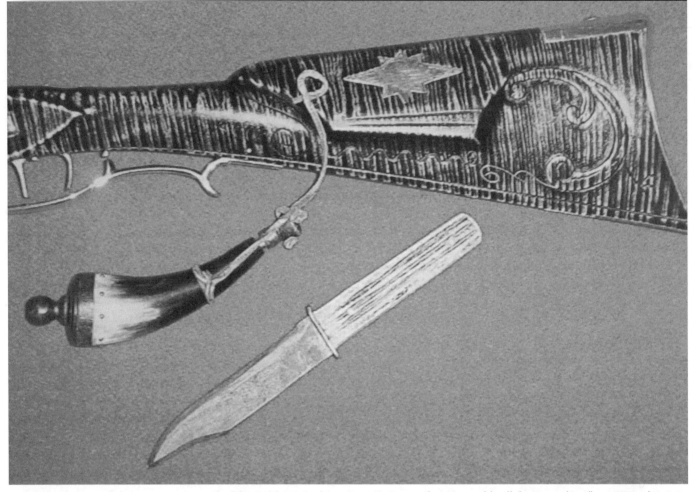

K.L. Shelton of Tucson, Arizona, creates work of the Golden Age of American Firearms, what we would call the Kentucky rifle or Pennsylvania/Kentucky rifle. Specifically, his interest lies in the Lancaster School.

Chapter 45 ended with an apology to those great names from the past, the men who were instrumental in creating fine blackpowder rifles, not only American, but European as well. This chapter begins with a similar apology to the wonderful craftsmen of the hour who are not honored here. In the Fourth Edition, a few names and addresses of contemporary builders were installed at the close of the chapter on custom blackpowder guns. But that approach falls by the wayside now. No such list is included in the present chapter because a search on the Internet is more

complete. My favorite search engine, Google, displayed many contemporary artisans by simply calling up "Custom Black Powder Gunmakers." *Muzzle Blasts* magazine has a "Contemporary Gunmakers" page where builders advertise. That such will continue is not my call. But it is certain that armscrafters interested in telling the world about themselves and their wares will always advertise. As for profiles of gunmakers, which I considered important with regard to reader understanding, chapter space ruled again. Only two modern blackpowder gunmakers are included.

Their profiles supply brief sketches of today's blackpowder gunbuilder—what he makes and perhaps even why he creates it. While I have never met either of the custom makers whose rifles are highlighted here, I am acquainted with their work. They were chosen not for similarities, but because their rifles exist in two different camps. And now we look briefly upon K.L. Shelton of Tucson, Arizona, and Jim Gefroh of Fort Collins, Colorado, the goal being to see how these two gunmakers keep alive two entirely different old-time rifle types.

Shelton's work not only rivals the artistic ability and execution of the Golden Age of American Firearms—it surpasses many prime examples of the era. His rifles are art in shooting. Apply a magnifying glass to each detail. While every feature is accomplished by hand, not a computer-assisted machine, perfection is evident. K.L. Shelton got lucky. He met Taylor Ellington outside the small village of Morehead, Kentucky, in the mid-1970s. Ellington was in his 80s at the time. He was keen about passing on his knowledge of handmaking beautiful long rifles, lest the torch of knowledge be extinguished. The beneficiary of that wish was Shelton. Not long after Ellington's tutorage, K.L. fell upon another good run of luck. He met Wayne Potts of Denver, Colorado, a man also in his 80s, also wishing to pass his knowledge on. While Ellington was a master gunbuilder, Potts was a master engraving. "It took several years before I perfected the art of stock carving, wire inlay, and engraving," K.L. said. The art demanded practice, but the basic knowledge was intact. While nothing could take the place of the education Ken received from Ellington and Potts, graduation from Murray State University in Art and Industrial Technology

Another example of Shelton's work dedicated to the Lancaster School of firearm design in Pennsylvania during the Golden Age of American Firearms.

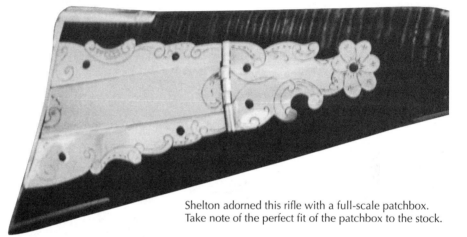

Shelton adorned this rifle with a full-scale patchbox. Take note of the perfect fit of the patchbox to the stock.

K.L. Shelton at work in his one-man shop creating beautiful Pennsylvania/Kentucky long rifles of the Golden Age era.

blended into a perfect background for a lifetime of creating fine classic muzzle-loading rifles.

Today, Ken specializes in the Lancaster School, Lancaster County, Pennsylvania, recognized by him as the birthplace of the American long rifle. This was the Kentucky rifle treated briefly in Chapter 45 and recognized as Daniel Boone's companion in his adventures. Shelton works out of a well-appointed shop, beginning each rifle by carving the stock from hard maple following the same steps adhered to by original craftsmen. Particular care is given in wood-to-metal fit, resulting in a handcrafted classic rifle born of the past, but promised to endure into the future for generations to come. The signature of the artist is impressed on the top barrel flat of each rifle. A typical example of a K.L. Shelton rifle is tiger-stripe maple with an octagon barrel ranging 36 to 42 inches, calibers 32 to 58. Siler locks are chosen in flintlock or percussion. Double-set triggers are the rule with a patchbox of brass. German

silver inlays and incised or relief carving are part of the finished product. The customer chooses caliber, barrel length, and specific component parts. He or she also has the option of personalizing the rifle with wire inlay (a beautiful touch), special carving, metal engraving, and inlays. Each rifle is a testament to authenticity to the early days of American shooting.

The rifles of Jim Gefroh are also artistically handcrafted, but with a major difference. Jim is a big-bore fan. His rifles have taken truly large game: Cape buffalo with a flintlock when Jim hunted with one of Africa's premier professionals, Johan Wolvaardt. One of Jim's customers carried a big-bore rifle of Gefroh's make into Africa for both rhino and elephant. He was a good shot, putting the big bullet where it belonged and collecting both species." I am dedicated," Jefroh says, "to keeping the big bore alive for those who wish to experience the thrill of shooting or hunting with front-loading 'stopping rifles.'" He builds rifles in both percussion and

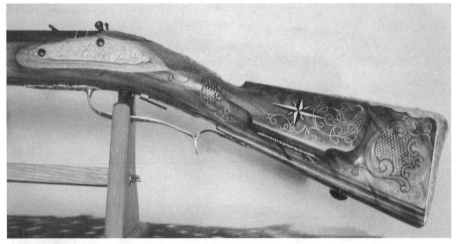

The rifles of Jim Gefroh represent an entirely different era in custom riflemaking—the true big bore capable of elephant hunting power.

Proof of power shows in this defunct rhino, one of the heaviest and toughest game animals of Africa, an animal that wears a natural suit of armor. A big-bore Gefroh rifle penetrated through that armor and into the vitals. The hunter is Kim Stuart.

Proof that a big-bore rifle can also be beautiful rests in this Jim Gefroh creation that is capable of firing a huge bullet at good velocity with a big powder charge.

flintlock. "I can build most any caliber up to and including the awesome 83-caliber (8-bore)." Jim's English rifles are made in the early Manton style with straight stock and metal pistol grip. (See Chapter 45 for Manton.) Manton's style "lends itself to the very big bores from 12 through 8," Jim says. His Rigby style is more streamlined with pistol grip reflecting the period of fine English rifles. Gefroh prefers the Rigby for his "smaller" calibers in both conical and round ball. Of course, caliber 54 is considered small when it comes to Jim's custom muzzleloading rifles.

Jefroh enjoys making full-stock German Jaeger rifles in either early European or later American transitional type. He likes the Jaeger design "with its short stout barrel ideal for those very big bores like the 8." While these guns are highly pleasing to the eye and of extremely professional manufacture, they are also rugged and dependable hunting rifles. Figured black walnut is often chosen for the stock—hooked breech—tapered barrel. All barrels are custom made to Jefroh's specifications, tapered or swamped, Forsyth rifling for shooting large round balls, but also for stabilizing very short conical bullets. (See Chapter 20.) Double-set triggers are the rule, ebony nose cap, browned furniture, right-hand or left-hand configuration. The basic custom does not include stock embellishments or relief carving. It is a true working rifle. But as such, it remains a handsome testimony to the craft of its maker. Jim offers a long list of upgrades for those who desire highly figured black English or English walnut, period relief carving, silver wirework, and inlays, including ivory-ebony hunter's star. "I can do relief sterling silver animal heads set in ivory surrounded with silver wire for a truly custom look," Jim concludes.

Chapter 45 touches on the prehistory of our modern artists in wood and metal, which of course goes back to the Old Country where firearms of the 17th century reached a high point in excellence. Europe was the starting

Another fine big-bore rifle, this one a flintlock, built by Jim Gefroh in 8-bore with wire extensive wire inlay in the buttstock.

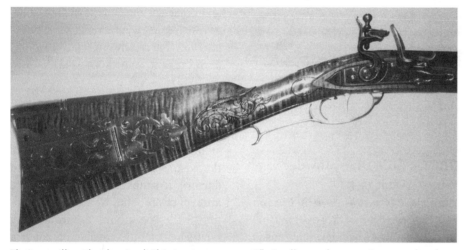

The eye will not be deceived. This is a true custom rifle in all regards—premium wood and parts, highly skilled workmanship, and overall proper lines. It will also shoot well.

Red Farris and his friends knew how to organize, which is what they did with the eventual creation of the National Muzzle-Loading Rifle Association (NMLRA). Other names rose like cream to the top during this revival. Joe Kindig wrote a fine book entitled *Thoughts on the Kentucky Rifle in its Golden Age* that spurred interest. William Large got into it through barrel-making, creating some of the finest of his time or any other date. Large lived a long life, his barrels winning matches from coast to coast. He was always willing to share information, and so his talent did not depart with him. Willingness to share knowledge led to passing on important guncrafting tips and tips that remain alive today. Specializing also came along in modern days as it had in the past. Hacker Martin made a firearm in all its separate parts. But other craftsmen preferred buying locks, barrels, and other parts ready to install. And so a whole new industry was created. Along with Bill Large and other barrel makers, locksmiths came to the fore, perhaps the best known being Bud and Dottie Siler. Today, there are separate parts crafted by different companies, as a walk along traders' row at rendezvous reveals.

No. 47

Because there continues to be interest in a particular custom rifle I have carried for a number of years, taking with it antelope, deer, elk—and the only animal charge I have ever faced, a bull bison (buffalo) a word about No. 47, my 54-caliber ball-shooting rifle, is in order. Dennis Mulford at the time lived outside of Salt Lake City, Utah. He especially enjoyed handmaking Jaeger rifles of collector quality. In fact, some of his customers bought Mulford's rifles to collect, not to shoot, and definitely never to carry into the big-game field. The story of No. 47 includes an important point of consideration for anyone interested in having a custom muzzleloader built. I wanted Dennis to make me a Hawken-type half-stock

place. But it was the Pennsylvania long rifle that kept custom muzzleloader gunmaking alive in this country. Fortunately, prime examples of original guns remained into modern times to be studied and admired. These firearms rekindled flames of interest. Could those beautiful rifles, and sometimes pistols, be created again by modern craftsmen? Fortunately, builders came along with two powerful attributes: interest and talent. They were interested in making, once again, the fine arms—as well as some of the hardworking guns not so pretty—of the past. Homer Dangler is one example. He came out of Michigan. He was soon known for building exacting copies of original rifles of the masters, his just as fine as theirs. John Newcomer was another master of the

middle era, that time between the original armsmakers and the smiths making custom blackpowder guns today. The new rifles boasted every fine appointment familiar to originals of Early America: wonderful wood carving, inlays, engraving, patchboxes, fine stock finishes, tapered barrels, swamped barrels (smaller in the middle than breech or muzzle). Some of the modern gifted craftsmen learned the trade from their fathers and grandfathers. Hacker Martin, as one example of this, picked up the fine art of building long rifles from his grandfather, who in turn learned from one of the masters in the region.

The Roaring '20s brought with it not only wild times, but also supremely fine, newly-made custom long guns of Pennsylvania heritage. Men such as

Fadala's No. 47 custom 54-caliber rifle bears a message—Live Free or Die, the New Hampshire State Motto adopted in 1945 as World War II drew to a successful close. General John Stark, Revolutionary War hero, made the full statement on July 31, 1809. It went, "Live Free or Die—Death is not the Worst of Evils."

plains rifle. He refused. And that is the point. While the customer has his or her rights, the gunmaker retains a certain degree of say in planning a project. Dennis considered the half-stock plains rifle a working gun, stout, reliable, and hunter-useful. But quite frankly plain to the point of being homely. He would not build one for me. OK, I said, but I still wanted a 54-caliber ball-shooting percussion rifle. Mulford had run across an original Kentucky rifle that had quite probably been altered for the West. The barrel had been bobbed from very long to 34 inches. The rifle may have begun life as a 50 or smaller, then freshed out to 54-caliber. It had been a flintlock, now converted by drum and nipple to percussion. No. 47 was on its way. Dennis shot an offhand group at 25 yards as a test before turning the rifle over to me. Five shots went into the bullseye. A decade later, as I hunted elk in Colorado, the outfitter asked if he could shoot my rifle. He picked a spot, fired, and put a neat round hole dead center. He made a generous offer to buy No. 47. I still own it.

The Custom Blackpowder Gun—What is It?

Handmade is not Necessarily Custom

I inspected the work of one craftsman at a gun show. His shingle said "custom gunmaker" but his work did not justify the claim. A close look at his checkering, which he proudly pointed out, looked like 20 miles of crooked road. First prerequisite for custom is, in my book, talent. Lacking that, a handmade firearm is no more than a—handmade firearm. Going forward with criteria, a true custom has no screw-for-screw clone anywhere in the world, although this is not to say that it has no cousins. The work of an individual gunmaker is often easier to spot than paintings of famous artists. Miniscule artistic knowledge is required to tell a Picasso from a Dali. The same holds true for many gunmakers whose style stands out as their own. Interestingly, a custom firearm is not perfect, not in the sense of machine duplication. For example, it's possible to program a computer-operated machine to engrave nearly flawless lines. The machine will not err. The lines will repeat, repeat, and repeat. The work on

a custom gun reveals the human hand. And that is what makes it so superior over the assembly-line product. In a way, the work exhibits its own kind of perfection from talented human fingers, but also a touch of imperfection that makes it one of a kind, although it may take a magnifying glass to discover that slight waver of the engraving tool. The true custom shows tight wood-to-metal fit, clean lines all around, correct interpretation of a classic design, super clean wood and metal finish, and a touch of personality. If the firearm is intended to replicate an original from the past, then it should do so faithfully. Homer Dangler and other custom 'smiths of the 1920s were extremely good at replication, building rifles that closely duplicated originals from the past, sometimes as far back as the 1700s.

Replicating the Past

Replica custom rifles do not always follow on the most ornate examples of the past. Sometimes they're plain and downright simple. For example, there are replicas of what we called in Chapter 45 the "poor boy," a hardworking muzzleloader fully capable of doing a day's work, which might be putting food on the table, or for that matter cutting a group into a black bullseye. These long guns were not pretty. To beautify one of that clan would be trespassing on the goal of the replica: making a new gun that copies an old one. A wonderful example is a particular long rifle built by Frank House to be carried by the hero in a film called *The Patriot*. House decided on replicating a John Thomas rifle featured in *Rifles of Colonial America*, another volume published by the dedicated arms historian George Shumway. This would not have been the common work rifle. The resulting flintlock rifle is beyond beautiful. It is a true work of art and extraordinary talent.

The Non-Replica Custom

Many custom guns of the day follow nothing from the past. But they are still custom in every sense. For example,

A true custom rifle will have no precise clone anywhere, although it may very well resemble a family of rifles that can be attributed to a given riflemaker, in this case Jim Gefroh of Fort Collins, Colorado.

the slug guns: super-heavy front-loaders fired from the bench with a single goal: to produce ultra-tight groups. These rifles are not intended as exact duplicates of any past firearm, but they are still custom-made guns. There are custom blackpowder shotguns that would be unrecognizable to shooters of the past. There are also custom guns from certain masters who prefer inventing their own styles. Therefore, an excellent custom muzzleloader need not be a replica.

The Professional Custom Blackpowder Gunmaker

The professional blackpowder gunmaker builds memorable keepsakes. Allen Martin, who was interviewed by *Muzzle Blasts* magazine's Eric Bye, pointed out that he was recognized as the leading contemporary builder of Lehigh County rifles of Allentown origin. Dixon's Gunmaker's Fair, an event held annually to honor the finest old-time traditional arms currently handmade, honored Martin with best of show overall. "It was almost covered with ribbons," Martin remarked. He began handcrafting muzzleloaders as a teen on his home farm, and by age 30 had a following of true believers, some of them returning for second, third, and fourth rifles. From a family of 13 children, Martin learned a good work ethic early on. Along with the dedication to build the best rifles he is capable of, he credits Paul Alison, Jr., for teaching him many of the basics. He relies mostly on hand tools: rasps, files, sculpturing gouges and planes, with all

A true custom rifle like this Gefroh creation will show proper fit of all parts including embellishments such as this Cape buffalo head set in ivory surrounded by silver wire inlay.

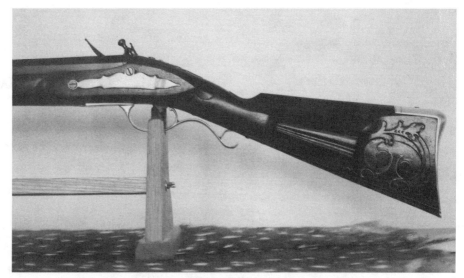

While a custom rifle may not be a replica it often comes quite close in honoring a rifle or riflemaker of the past. Gefroh's rifles do this with Jaeger and other influences.

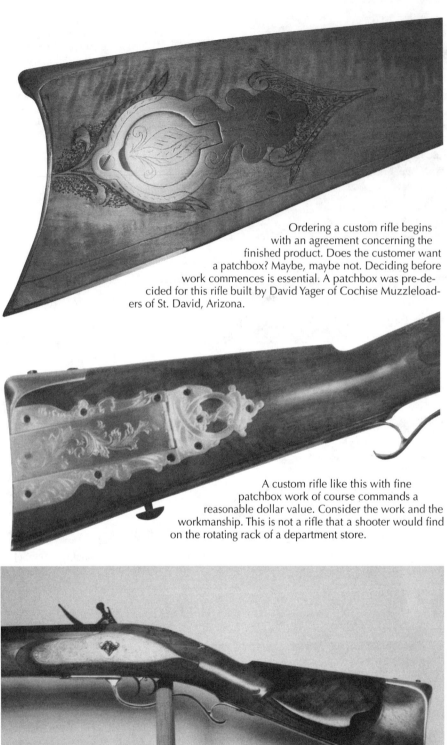

Ordering a custom rifle begins with an agreement concerning the finished product. Does the customer want a patchbox? Maybe, maybe not. Deciding before work commences is essential. A patchbox was pre-decided for this rifle built by David Yager of Cochise Muzzleloaders of St. David, Arizona.

A custom rifle like this with fine patchbox work of course commands a reasonable dollar value. Consider the work and the workmanship. This is not a rifle that a shooter would find on the rotating rack of a department store.

Cheekpiece or not? That's a call that will probably have to rest with the custom gunmaker. Gefroh added a cheekpiece to this creation because it fit the general time period of the rifle and it also added not only a fine touch, but also a help in controlling the recoil of this big-bore rifle.

metal polishing done by hand. While not a competitive target shooter, Martin admits that hunting is an important part of his life. His favorite hunting rifle is carried in the Pennsylvania flintlock-only season. He builds guns for collectors who rarely if ever shoot them. He also builds for hunters who always shoot them. He makes muzzleloaders for rendezvous as well. Of course, blackpowder custom gun builders are as individual as any artisans in the land. However, Martin's devotion to perfection and his undying interest in creating the finest firearms of old-time style are typical of the clan. And that is why he is noted here.

Ordering a Custom Blackpowder Gun

The buyer must inform the maker concerning the destination of the rifle (sometimes pistol). If it's collecting, the rifle may well be representative of one of the "schools" of the past, of which there were many. Counties in Pennsylvania often name these schools: Lancaster, Lehigh, and Clarion. If it's for hunting, then style gives way to handling, power, and range. Muzzleloader or cartridge rifle? Andrew Fautheree is known for his blackpowder cartridge rifles as well as front-loaders. He is a master at making either. Competing in contests demands the ultimate accuracy, but also fine handling qualities. Allegiance to the past may also be important, with a firearm matching a given period in time to qualify it for a certain shooting event. Once the rifle's intended purpose is established, it's time for riflemaker and future owner to get together on details. Most difficult for the buyer to understand is the builder's inertia when it comes to making a firearm that he, the builder, does not support. This was broached earlier concerning No. 47. I am glad that I listened to the gunmaker or I would not have had the rifle I have enjoyed for so many years. In an informal contest, No. 47 showed its merit. I say the rifle did. I was simply the shooter behind the trigger that day. More gifted marksmen would have done even better. But putting a round ball on target was no problem with No. 47. Targets, yes, but No. 47 was built for hunting where it shined with a .535-inch lead round ball wrapped in a .013-inch thick pure Irish-linen patch for a muzzle velocity of 1,970 fps and 1,983 foot-pounds muzzle energy.

Digging for Dollars

True custom blackpowder guns—pistol, muzzleloader, cartridge-shooter—when done properly by a real master, demand dollars. It has to be that way. There is too much time and energy involved to give these guns away. They are a great deal more than a steel barrel attached to a piece of wood. Each true custom embodies hours of intensive labor. Furthermore, talent deserves its reward and the better 'smiths of the day are extremely talented. Why should they sell their wares for pennies? Also, a custom blackpowder gun is an investment. It lasts forever, providing far more enjoyment than its price tag. Break it down by the month over many years of ownership and a top-grade rifle or pistol turns out to be a true bargain.

Where to Find
the Master Gunmaker

Internet search engines are a good starting place in locating craftsmen who create custom blackpowder guns at a professional level. Advertisements in magazines provide another source of information. *The Gun List* and *Shotgun News* are good sources for a custom gunmaker search. I have also seen work displayed in *Gun Digest*, *Shooter's Bible* and many other publications. And it does not have to be advertising. There are articles, some on shooting, others on hunting, that include information on a particular custom blackpowder firearm and its maker. An example is Jim Gefroh's piece in *Blackpowder Hunting Magazine*, Winter 2003 issue. "Nyati—200 Years Later" is Gefroh's story on "Hunting the Cape buffalo

the way it was done centuries past." Jim used a flintlock of his own creation to take the dangerous Nyati. The rifle was an 8-bore with 1:120 twist firing a short conical bullet weighing 1,360 grains, rather than the usual round ball of 860 grains. A charge of 270 grains volume FFg blackpowder drove the hardened bullet with 210 pounds of free recoil. I read with interest an article on Homer Dangler in the August 2005 issue of *Muzzle Blasts* magazine. Homer has spent 50 years creating custom muzzleloaders, to the joy of many who own and shoot his rifles. Rendezvous and competitive shoots are also worthwhile and in a way better than the Internet or ads because a prospective custom gun owner can see, first hand, the work of a particular artist. In most cases, the owner of the rifle will offer a shooting opportunity.

The Contract

Once a decision is made on a gunbuilder, it's time to draw up a contract. Normally, the 'smith requires about half of the agreed-upon price of the gun before he goes to work. Final payment is made after the firearm is finished. Also vital is agreeing on time of delivery. A six-month wait is short. A year is normal. A year and a half can be lived with. But both gunmaker and client must agree on a delivery date. There are also appointments to consider beyond the style (school) of gun. Wood prices are high. An especially fine blank now may demand what an entire rifle once cost. Along with wood choice, decisions must be made concerning patchbox, type of lock, particular barrel, inlays, carvings, sights, type of finish, trigger system, caliber, barrel length, and more. Gunsmiths have a whole list of particulars from which to choose.

What You're Paying For

No matter how deep the well, it's always nice to know what you are dipping into it for what return. Here is an

idea only, a quick look at a few of the basics required to make a custom firearm. The 'smith may prepare a drawing of the gun's profile at a reasonable charge. The drawing is nothing more than an outline. But it's useful in providing an overall look before work is under way. The parts search is easier now, with many excellent sources of everything from barrels to embellishments. A custom 'smith will have his favorite parts' houses. Some gunmakers prepare their own barrels. Others buy them from specialists. Either way, a barrel must be cut to length, the muzzle crowned, dovetail slots cut for sights and underlugs fitted by the 'smith. The lock may require some assembly and a certain amount of tuning.

The stock begins as a blank, nothing more than a hunk of wood. It must be shaped into a gunstock with filing and more filing, sanding and more sanding. Inletting is required for the barrel, lock, and other appointments. The barrel must fit perfectly into its channel, the lock into its mortise. Furniture, such as patchboxes and buttplates, is introduced into the wood with a marriage that must be perfect. Drilling the ramrod channel can be a challenge. If the hole goes astray, the stock blank becomes a candidate for knife handles or even firewood. Trigger positioning demands room for function without sloppiness. The upper-tang screw hole is drilled, the buttplate fitted, the vent hole drilled in the side of a flintlock's barrel flat. Drum and nipple may be fitted to a percussion rifle, the trigger guard installed, upper and lower tangs crafted, carving and inlays done. Metalwork may be engraved, the stock stained, metal polished, barrel browned, stock finished. From wood and metal, a firearm is born, but it is special only when created by a specialist.

The end result should be a proud gunmaker and a happy gun owner. That is the goal of each when it comes to a custom blackpowder firearm.

THEY WERE AFTER IVORY

Kim Stuart, left, shakes hands with Jim Gefroh after the taking of a bull elephant with a big-bore muzzleloading rifle built by Gefroh. Kim did it the 19th-century way, with a big bullet launched by a heavy powder charge.

The 19th-century ivory hunter, especially in Africa, but also in Ceylon and India—wherever the giant pachyderm roamed—was a businessman who made his money by collecting ivory—and what did he collect that prize with? Blackpowder guns, of course. These early hunters on the Dark Continent lived by the rifle. There is an obvious and powerful parallel between the Occidental African hunter and the mountain man of America's Far West. Both explored new territory. Both faced untold dangers. Both were in it more for adventure than riches, although the ivory hunters certainly made out better on that score than the hapless trappers who suffered hardship and even death to line the pockets of others, retaining precious little for themselves

as they were traded out of beaver plews for watered-down whisky and vastly overpriced goods brought on wagons from the East to the rendezvous meeting place in the West. It is impossible, and even wrong, to judge the elephant slayers of the distant past by modern standards. That was then. This is now. The ivory hunter believed, and he was right, that in no way could elephants be seriously reduced, regardless of the number taken, for very few hunters dotted thousands of acres, just as the American buffalo could never be "killed off" as it roamed over millions of acres in unbelievable numbers.

In their time the ivory hunters were explorers, adventurers, businessmen, and most of all, daring hunters. They shot pachyderms for ivory, and they did

it in the beginning with what they had: soot-belching, big-bore blackpowder rifles, mostly muzzleloaders. Without the guns, their story would be of little interest in this book. But throw in the firearms and their tale is told in living color. Their guns are just as interesting as those carried by the mountain man, perhaps more so because they employed them on the largest land animal in the world, not only huge, but also dangerous and intelligent. Dangerous: In an Africa bush camp a client, warned not to strike out on his own, disobeyed, taking the track of an elephant. He wanted to hunt the animal down without his guide. Instead, the elephant, apparently realizing there was a human was on his trail, circled, caught the hunter, and thrashed him against the trees. Intelligent: In Africa's Kruger Park I saw an elephant nudge a rock over to the edge of a water tank, putting a foot upon the rock to elevate himself so he could get a drink, the water being too low to reach with its trunk. This is the animal early ivory hunters were after with muzzleloading rifles.

It's been said that the English in India and the Dutch in Africa turned to big-bore, single-shot blackpowder rifles in the early 1800s. That assessment is too general in nature; however, it is true that muzzleloading 4-, 6-, and 8-bore guns were relied upon to stop the charge of the lion or bring down a fortune in ivory. Fortune? Few true fortunes were made by the time the smoke cleared, literally as well as figuratively. But this point notwithstanding, the "white" ivory hunter made his mark on the continent and in firearms history. Some say that mark was a blemish. Others realistically consider it within the context of history. Who were they, these hunters of the pachyderm? They came out of Europe, as their names imply. There was Major Shakespear (without the "e" of the famed author of Romeo and Juliet). Add S.W. Baker, Harris, Oswell, Roualeyn Gordon-Cumming, G.P. Sanderson, William Finaughty, and a host of others. They were a brave bunch. Just like the fur trappers who left their safe homes "back East" to roam among grizzlies and Blackfoot warriors out West, these men survived among animals that could smash or rip apart a human being in seconds. Add deadly snakes, as well as native peoples who were not always friendly, and a scene for dangerous adventure is set.

Only three of these hardy souls are featured here: William Cotton Oswell, Sir Samuel White Baker, better known as S.W. Baker to his readers, and Frederick Courteney Selous, who signed his name F.C. Selous (pronounced Sell-ooo). But before their brief biography, a few words about other greats of the era.

In his book, *Five Years Hunting Adventures in Africa*, covering 1843 to 1848, R. Gordon-Cumming wrote about

his guns. We learn that he used a Dickson double-barrel 12-bore that eventually "burst from too much fouling," and that he also carried a Dutch-made 6-bore, six balls to the pound, meaning that each round bullet weighed close to 1,200 grains. The 6-bore was said to be loaded with 10 to 15 drams of powder. If so, that would be about 270 to more than 400 grains of blackpowder, considering a dram as 27.34 grains weight. Even in a rifle weighing 15 pounds, free recoil was tremendous with such a large powder charge driving such a heavy bullet. Gordon-Cumming, over six feet tall and 14 stone weight, which would be 196 pounds, a British stone equaling 14 pounds, was a formidable physical figure credited with great strength. He became known as "The Lion Hunter." He also wrote *A Hunter's Life in South Africa*, an 1850 effort in two volumes. He returned to England in 1851, where he turned his rifles into pens, writing books and papers. (See the Blackpowder Library section for books on African hunting.)

Major Shakespear, from his book, *Wild Sports of India*, concerning the period from 1834 to 1859, noted that: "My own battery consists of two heavy double rifles and a double gun; the heaviest is a Westley Richards weighing twelve and a quarter pounds, length of barrel, twenty-six inches, poly-grooved, carrying bullets ten to the pound (a 10-gauge or 10-bore). It is a splendid weapon, bearing a large charge of powder without recoil; that is to say, its own bullet mould full of the strongest rifle powder." Shakespear's notes are especially interesting because of his reference to a powder charge generated from a bullet mould. In other words, it appears that he used the mould as a powder measure. But even a 10-bore mould, conical as well as round ball, would not produce a ponderous powder charge. Perhaps that is why the hunter didn't consider recoil fierce. I suspect otherwise, that his explanation of charge is not understood. Shakespear complained about a high trajectory with his 10-bore, the

Kim Stuart poses with his bull elephant taken with a big-bore blackpowder muzzleloading rifle built by Jim Gefroh. The largest land animal in the world is also one of the more dangerous beasts on the planet. But the big-bore blackpowder rifle did the job.

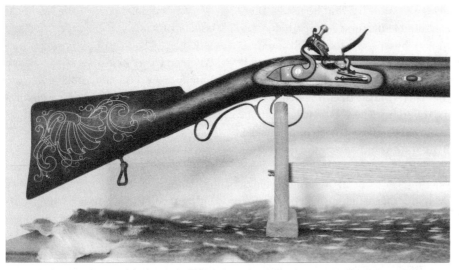

Jim Gefroh specializes in blackpowder rifles of true big bore dimension. His 8-bore fires a big bullet at sufficient velocity to ensure terrific muzzle energy. Whether with round or conical bullet, the big-bore flintlock or percussion rifle is capable of taking any of the world's big game.

bullet rising about 5 inches at 50 yards in order to strike dead on at about 100 yards. The Major's Westley Richards rifle was fitted with two rear sights, one for 150-yard shooting and the other for 250 yards. The entire story is mildly puzzling, while at the same time interesting: a looping trajectory coupled with long-range sights. Furthermore, the venerable elephant hunter considered the powder charge for his 10-bore "heavy." I say again that something was lost in the translation about Shakespear's powder charge.

William Finaughty hunted ivory in the 1860s. He carried a rifle firing a four-ounce bullet—in other words, a 4-bore, being four to the pound or 1,750 grains per each round projectile. The rifle was a smoothbore muzzleloader. In his own words, Finaughty said he loaded his 4-bore with a "handful of powder." Accuracy was not the goal because elephants were shot at very close range. Finaughty wrote of his adventures. His *The Recollection of an Elephant Hunter: 1864-1875* is a prime example of his efforts. This book was reprinted in 1916 by J.B. Lippincott, Philadelphia. Finaughty arrived in Africa in 1820 with his family, settlers in a new land. He began hunting in 1864 at the age of 21. By 1866 we find William pursuing ivory. One source notes 500 elephants

killed in five years. Finaughty hunted on horseback. As elephant herds cleverly retreated into tsetse fly country, William decided not to risk himself or his horses to the deadly fly. Read more in *The Recollections of William Finaughty: Elephant Hunter 1864-1875* from the Peter Hathaway Capstick Library of Hunting and Adventure, a St. Martin's Press book published in 1991. Finaughty had more than his share of adventure, as *Recollections* promises, including: besieged by lions, Napier's alarming accident, a terrible tragedy, a weird encounter, in a tight corner, in the midst of hostile Matabele, we lose our bearings, a double fright, their fight with a lion, chased by a buffalo, and more. He finally gave up on his smoothbore muzzleloader, turning to a breechloader, which had to be a blackpowder rifle because of the era—smokeless powder not yet widely in use.

Back to Shakespear for a moment with regard not to the hunter, but to one of his rifles. He spoke of a second 10-bore rifle with two-groove rifling instead of poly-grooved (multiple grooves). This rifle, according to the author, shot "point blank from muzzle up to ninety yards." More on point-blank below, but first, consider the sights on this rifle. They were folders built by Wilkinson of Pall Mall. The leaves of

the rear sight were set for 150, 250, and 400 yards. That in itself is intriguing. If these old-time big bores were incapable of long range, why would long-range sights be used? This 10.5-pound rifle with 30-inch barrel was a favorite of the grand old elephant hunter. But Shakespear's remarks leave a modern enthusiast wondering about actual ballistics, which is important for any study of blackpowder guns of the past. Why did Shakespear feel that his Wilkinson shot flatter than his Westley Richards? Add this to the mystery of the powder charge and bullet mould, as well as this famous hunter's remark about recoil being light in his 10-bore. At 10 balls to the pound, his 10-bore rifle fired a 700-grain projectile. And if he used the reported 8 drams of powder (close to 220 grains), velocity had to be around the speed of sound, or a bit faster, probably 1,200 fps. Shakespear noted that his rifle fired "without recoil," but in truth it had to develop around 80 foot-pounds of free recoil, while a contemporary 30-06 sporter delivers perhaps 18 foot-pounds of free recoil.

It seems wise to clear up the 19th century view of "point blank" before going on with Sanderson and Broomfield. The term did not mean that Shakespear's rifle, or any rifle, "shot flat" from muzzle to 90 yards. Point blank comes from a French term. The bullseye was a *blanc* mark, in other words, *white*. The rifle shot "point blank" when its bullet did not stray either above or below that white circle at a given range. The details of this practice are mainly lost to history. For our purpose, all we need to know is that the old-time shooter was not suggesting that his rifle "shot flat," but rather that it could be counted on to keep its projectiles within a certain vertical limit at a specific distance. Now a little about Sanderson and Broomfield before taking the path to our three major players of this chapter.

George P. Sanderson was an elephant hunter, but not in Africa. He was born in India in 1848, the son of Reverend Daniel Sanderson, a Methodist missionary to India from 1842 to 1867. The young lad was sent off to live with his father's family for schooling in Cockermouth, Cumbria. George returned to India at age 16 following his studies at the Wesley Methodist Kingswood School in Bath, where he attended from 1859 to 1863. Later, he wrote a book called *Thirteen Years Among the Wild Beasts of India*. Sanderson captured elephants as well as shooting them. Of course, these were Indian elephants. African elephants do not tame up very well at all (gross understatement). Comments on his first rifle, a 12-bore, are interesting. They go like this:" I at first killed several elephants with a No. 12 spherical ball rifle, with hard bullets and six drams of powder, but I found it insufficient for many occasions. I then had a single-barreled, center-fire No. 4 bore rifle, weighing sixteen and one-half pounds and firing ten drams [about 270-grains weight], made to order by Lang and Sons, Cockspur Street. A cartridge [meaning load] of this single barrel, however, missed fire on one occasion, and nearly brought me to grief, so I gave it up and had a center-fire No. 4 smoothbore, weighing nineteen and one-half pounds, built by W.W. Greener. This I have used ever since. I ordinarily fire twelve drams of powder [almost 330 grains weight] with it. Without something of the cannon kind, game of the ponderous class cannot be brought to fighting quarters with even a moderate degree of safety or effect."

Several points of interest are generated from Sanderson's remarks, not the least of which is the W.W. Greener smoothbore, first because it was made by that famous gunsmith and writer whose works continue as good reading to this day, and second because it was a smoothbore, which offered certain advantages: namely ease of cleaning without rifling to hold fouling, plus facility of loading for the same reason. Also, Sanderson rightly points out that an elephant hunter needed a big bore—a true big bore—to feel the slightest tinge of safety in the work of elephant hunt-

Hunters who sold ivory would take the tusks on this elephant in the 19th century. Ivory hunting could be dangerous. The African elephant is a formidable beast and in recent times has killed both native and professional hunters.

The elephant would normally be taken with a brain shot whenever possible, but in some cases a projectile delivered to the base of the tail would put the beast down until it could be dispatched. Today, hunters take elephants on a limited basis, although in some areas of Africa the pachyderm is destroying its own range due to severe overpopulation.

ing during blackpowder days. As we know from Chapter 37, big bore was not to the African or Indian hunter what it represents to us in this 21st century. A 12-gauge, for example, with its round ball under 500 grains weight, was simply too small for dangerous game. Compare with the Greener 4-bore firing a round ball weighing 1,750 grains! As an aside, consider price. A custom big-bore rifle of the 19th century could run from $750 to $1,000, so states the literature. That's a heap of wampum considering the times, a sum that could constitute the bulk of a year's wages for an ordinary workman.

William Cotton Oswell

The average modern hunter or shooter does not recognize Oswell's name. However, in his own day he was only a rock's throw from famous. Sir Samuel W. Baker, whose own brief mini-bio appears below, said of Oswell, "His name will be remembered with tears of sorrow and profound respect." Oswell was one of the first professional ivory hunters in South Africa. His name is linked with David Livingstone, and it appears that Oswell, along with a part-

William Cotton Oswell was known in England as the "Pioneer of Civilisation." He was a friend and interpreter of Dr. Livingstone, who applauded Oswell in Livingstone's "Zambest and its Tributaries." Oswell was born in 1818, died in 1893, and was remembered by S. W. Baker as a man "without a rival; and certainly without an enemy; the greatest hunter ever known in modern times."

ner named Murray, financed a Livingstone expedition that was recognized with a medal given by the French Geographical Society for the first mapping of Africa's lake systems. Oswell hunted often on horseback, and he was noted as a great rider. He took to the saddle, gave chase, and then dismounted for the shot when he was within range, "range" being something in the area of about 20 or 30 paces. Short shooting distance made Oswell's smoothbore rifle perfectly adequate. Supreme accuracy was not necessary on a target the size of an elephant's temple at such close range.

Oswell began his hunting career in Africa with a 12-bore double rifle built by Westley Richards, along with a single-barrel 8-bore that fired belted round balls weighing around 875 grains, known in everyday parlance as a "two-ounce ball." Oswell's favorite firearm, however, was a Purdey smoothbore double that, according to S.W. Baker, weighed an even 10 pounds. How did Baker know so much about Oswell's 10-bore? He borrowed the firearm from Oswell in 1861 for an expedition to the Nile. Oswell was retired at the time. Baker at first heaped great praise on the 10-gauge smoothbore, but in later writings, put smoothbores down as too inaccurate to be counted on in the field. That's understandable, because unlike Oswell, Baker took long shots. As for power, Oswell's favorite 10-bore was loaded with "six drachms of fine-grained powder," which we know meant six drams, or 164 grains. It was, of course, a muzzleloader. He wrapped his 10-gauge round balls in fine leather or linen, tightly, cutting off excess material. Then he built a paper cartridge containing both powder charge and the patched ball. To reload, this hunter nipped the end of the paper cartridge off with his teeth, dropping the powder charge, along with the paper, downbore. Then he put the pre-patched ball on the muzzle and, with a loading rod noted as "powerful," pushed the bullet firmly into the breech upon the powder charge.

Baker pointed out that Oswell's smoothbore "exhibited in an unmistakable degree the style of hunting which distinguished its determined owner. The hard walnut stock was completely eaten away for an inch of surface; the loss of wood suggested that rats had gnawed it, as there were minor traces of apparent teeth." Actually, the stock had been "chewed on" by the wait-a-bit thorn bushes common to Oswell's hunting grounds as he galloped his horse in hot pursuit of elephants. Baker reported that he returned Oswell's smoothbore in good condition, but minus the ramrod, which had been lost when one of Baker's native bearers was attacked by a group of marauders. The frightened man loaded the smoothbore just in time to save his own life, but he did not have time to withdraw the ramrod, which he fired completely through the body of one of his assailants.

Oswell hunted hard. He wrote of some of his adventures in "African Game Rifles" as part of the *Badminton Library, Big Game Shooting* published by Longmans Green & Co. of London, 1902. He said, "I spent five years in Africa. I was never ill for a single day—laid up occasionally by accident, but that was all. I had the best of companions—Murray, Vardon, Livingstone—and several capital servants, who stuck to me throughout. I never had occasion to raise a hand against a native, and my foot only once, when I found a long lazy fellow poking his paw into my sugar tin." He also noted that he "filled their stomachs," speaking of his native helpers. Baker was much more a commander than Oswell, and certainly not above dealing out punishment to people he considered inferior, since he saw himself in the superior role.

Sir Samuel White Baker

If we viewed blackpowder-shooting ivory hunters of the 19th century through the window of our own time, we would dislike most of them. Baker, we would classify as an arrogant bigot. But his time was not ours, and so we

Sir Samuel White Baker, an English knight, explored the Nile from 1861 to 1865 and was a big man at 6 feet, 6 inches tall and 250 pounds. He was born in London in 1821, married a Hungarian noblewoman when he was 41, and died in England in 1893. He authored *Ismalia* and *Eight Years Wandering in Ceylon.*

view him through a rose-colored window into the distant past. Baker was an English gentleman, knighted by the Queen herself, and so he considered natives of foreign soils beneath his station. He was known to thrash a servant who didn't do the "right thing." He also shot game at will, unlike Oswell, who spared female elephants and harvested only enough game to feed his followers. This is not a blemish on the person of Baker alone, for some American hunters disrespected wildlife just as much in the same era, especially the bison. While he hunted Africa, Baker is better known for his adventures in Ceylon, and for the book that told about those times, *The Rifle and the Hound in Ceylon*, reprinted in modern times and available as well through interlibrary loan. The book can also be purchased through the Internet. Baker was only 24 years old when he arrived in Ceylon where he hunted so heavily. Before his career ended, he also hunted the United States as well as Africa. He made two around-the-world hunting trips that included America, these taken between 1879 and 1888. His travels took him also to hunts in Asia Minor and India.

Credited with being the first English-speaking person to travel the Nile, Baker's history is easier to locate than either Cotton Oswell's life story or Selous' biography. After all, in some texts he is known as the "discoverer" of the Nile, just as Balboa is credited with "discovering" the Pacific Ocean. But our interest is in Baker's firearms and his shooting theories more than his geographical wanderings. His firearms were custom made, as money was no stumbling block for Baker. By his own claim, his first good rifle was also the first firearm to see action in Ceylon in 1845. That "good rifle" was a 4-bore muzzleloader weighing in at a trifling 21 pounds. The single-barrel rifle was two-grooved, made by Gibbs of Bristol. It was noted to shoot a "four-ounce" ball, which makes sense, as there are 16 ounces in pound, making four 4-gauge balls. Looking at it another way, each ball weighed 1,750 grains. The cannon-like rifle was loaded with 16 drams of blackpowder, or about 430 grains weight. Muzzle energy was in the neighborhood of 6,000 to 7,000 foot-pounds.

Baker was a big man. He apparently stood up to his 4-bore with impunity, for he was known to make hits with it, and other huge-bore rifles, at very long range—300 yards and farther. His backup rifle was "only" an 8-gauge single barrel, built by Blisset, with poly-grooved bore and a 2-ounce ball, which had to be a conical if it weighed two ounces in only 8-bore. It was also loaded with 16 drams of blackpowder. While in Ceylon, Baker put down a great number of elephants, along with considerable water buffalo and other game. His two single-shot rifles were not enough for him, however, so he ordered four more rifles, all 10-gauge muzzleloaders weighing about 15 pounds each. These rifles, made by Holland, became his elephant-hunting battery. He carried them in Africa as well as Ceylon, but when the British army adopted the Snider breechloader, Baker had Holland build him a double-barrel 577 that reportedly fired a 648-grain conical bullet at 1,650 fps for a muzzle energy of about 4,000 foot-pounds, well under his previous muzzleloading 4-bore. He carried this rifle to America for deer, bear, elk, and bison.

While it's difficult to say exactly how fast Baker's 4-bore round bullets were taking off at the muzzle with 16 drams of the best blackpowder, a velocity of 1,200 to 1,300 fps is not an overly generous assessment. That would be 6,000 to 7,000 foot-pounds of muzzle energy for 1,300 fps, which may be undercutting Baker's rifle considering the fact that it could have produced about 1,600 fps or a bit more. Calling it 1,400 instead of 1,300, the rifle would have generated more than 7,500 foot-pounds of muzzle energy. If 1,600 fps were achieved, the energy rating would be close to 10,000 foot-pounds, surpassing the 577 breechloader and its 648-grain bullet at 1,650 fps for 3,918 foot-pounds. The point is, Baker's breechloader was a step down from his front-loaders in ballistic force, even though it fired a conical bullet with decent retention of downrange energy.

Baker eventually gravitated to smaller firearms, owning and shooting a double-barrel 400 Holland Express rifle, which he used for deer-sized game in England and Scotland. However, when he wrote his 1891 book, *Wild Beasts and Their Ways* two years before his died, he concluded that for the largest game he would have nothing smaller than an 8-bore rifle firing a 3-ounce projectile in front of 14 drams of blackpowder (about 380 grains). Also interesting is Baker's respect for the round ball. He actually considered the lead sphere more efficient against pachyderms than even the heaviest conical. One of his reasons, and certainly not a scientific one, was explained as the "conical making too neat a wound," sort of like a rapier sliding through a bag of sawdust without imparting much energy in the target, whereas the round ball smacked hard, delivering its blow in the target instead of behind it. Some of today's round-ball fans cite Baker's work when their beloved lead spheres are downgraded. In fact, we do know that when a hunter gets close enough, round lead bullets are lethal, as promised in Chapter 16.

Frederick Courteney Selous

Selous was a gentleman we would have liked, which cannot necessarily be said of Baker. He was a man among men. Selous died a soldier, although he was not truly a professional military man. On January 4, 1917, during World War I, he was killed in action as he fought the Germans in Tanganyika as a volunteer. He was born in Regents Park, London, in 1851, making him 66 years old in 1917 when he was shot to death as he led his men against an enemy four times greater in strength. Frederick was educated mainly as a naturalist schooled in England, but finished his education in Switzerland and Germany. He was a good student and could have made a high mark in society. But he read too much of Africa and to that adventure he simply had to go. On September 4, 1871, he arrived on the Dark Continent. He was 19 years old and in possession of only 400 English pounds to launch his career as an ivory hunter. He made his way into wild territory, often straying far afield from his wagons so that he could hunt on foot undisturbed. Tracking elephants with a Hottentot native known as Cigar, F.C. lived off the land. Cigar, by the way, became a friend and partner in the chase and was far more than a "hired man." Wandering afar with only a blanket against the night and his 4-bore muzzleloader over his shoulder, Selous was a genius in the art of what we today call woodsmanship. As for his 4-bore, Selous packed along a bag filled with powder and 24, 4-ounce "round bullets," to use his words. He admitted that sometimes he did not measure his charge, simply dropping a fistful of blackpowder downbore.

Frederick Courteney Selous was a professional ivory hunter at 19 years old in 1871. He was known to grab a handful of powder in the heat of the chase and pour it downbore to reload. Born in London in 1851, he died a hero in 1917 during World War I. Selous spanned the gap between blackpowder and smokeless, going from huge, 4 bore muzzleloaders to a little 6.5mm rifle.

Anyone interested in more of the Selous story should read the man's book, *A Hunter's Wanderings in Africa*, a title still available, especially from bookstores with their quick ability to search the Internet. Luckily, J.G. Millais set down Selous's biography in a book entitled *The Life of Frederick Courtenay Selous, D.S.O.*, written in 1918 (the spelling of his middle name today is Courteney, not Courtenay). Naturalist, writer, settler, guide, explorer, even soldier, Selous' life as an ivory hunter began most interestingly when his double 12-bore Reilly rifle was stolen from a wagon on his first trip out. He ended up taking 78 elephants with a pair of Dutch-made Roer two-groove 4-bores. These were not the finest rifles of the era, but they were powerful. Selous loaded these with 16 to 18 drams of blackpowder, or 437 to 500 grains. So much powder behind the huge 1,750-grain lead ball created dreadful recoil. Selous reported: "They kicked most frightfully and in my case the punishment I received from these guns has affected my nerves to such an extent as to have materially influenced my shooting ever since, and I am heartily sorry I ever

had anything to do with them." He went on to shoot much smaller firearms, and is remembered today as the elephant hunter who used a 256-caliber rifle for big game, even elephants.

Although Selous complained that those big Dutch 4-bores harmed his shooting ability, in fact he was known as a superior marksman all his life, using the tiny 256, which is a 6.5mm rifle firing a 160-grain round-nose bullet at only 2,300 fps muzzle velocity, even for elephants. With a muzzle energy of only 1,880 foot-pounds, about like a 30-30, Selous usually downed his elephant with one perfectly placed shot. He also liked the ordinary 303 British round with a 215-grain bullet at 2,000 fps for 1,910 foot-pounds of muzzle energy. Selous loved to hunt. He hunted not only in Africa as a professional, but also in America as a sportsman. He hiked the Rocky Mountains, also ending up in Alaska with Charles Sheldon, famous naturalist of the day. He also hunted Canada for moose and other game. F.C. Selous traveled the road from muzzleloader to breechloader, and from blackpowder to smokeless. He used them all, from the most hellish big-bore blackpowder muzzleloader to the neat little Mannlicher-type, smokeless-powder smallbore.

The 19th-century elephant hunter relied on massive lead projectiles propelled by heavy hunting charges. The most powerful of these rifles, especially the 2-bores and 4-bores, remain more potent than our strongest smokeless powder rifles of the day. Consider a 2-bore firing a 3,500-grain round ball at as high as 1,500 fps. The muzzle energy of this rifle is almost 17,500 foot-pounds. To be sure, the ball lost velocity rapidly, so this immense energy was constrained to rather close range. Regardless, even when using the Newton KE formula for energy, the true big bore comes off with immense energy. The super strong 460 Weatherby Magnum with a 500-grain bullet at 2,700 fps earns only half the energy rating of the 2-bore with a heavy blackpowder charge.

SNIPERS OF THE AMERICAN CIVIL WAR

chapter 48

The Sharps rifle was beloved of Civil War snipers before it became one of the two major rifles of "buffalo days" after the Civil War. By the time of the buffalo runner, the Sharps rifle evolved into a blackpowder cartridge shooter.

Deadly riflemen were on hand for many skirmishes on American soil long before the Civil War. Being acquainted with a present-day SWAT sniper, I'm aware that the breed is still with us. Snipers were in the field for the Seven Years War, the American Revolution, the War of 1812, and, of course, long-range shooting was accomplished when the white man and Native American crossed paths in anger. Some of the stories of super-long-range shooting are just that—long-winded tales born of campfire smoke. Others are solid historical fact. Mark Twain had it right when he said, "Of course the truth is stranger than fiction. Fiction has to make sense." Certain seemingly unbelievable sniper feats that sound like fiction truly happened. Many accounts of long-range sniping by buffalo runners are probably also true. After all, these marksmen were well practiced through daily shooting. And they had accurate, long-range rifles often topped off with target-type telescopic sights of high magnification, if not the superior optics we relish in our better scopes today. Give them a clear target, even at several hundred yards, and the blackpowder boys could "dope out" wind drift and bullet drop, delivering a bullet spot-on, especially when the target was a human figure standing upright

with plenty of vertical latitude. Doubters need to attend one blackpowder cartridge silhouette match and see for themselves. The *borego* (sheep) cutout in the distance is built long-ways, much harder to hit than an upright figure, i.e., *Homo sapiens*. But smack it the shooters do, with regularity.

The First American Snipers

Shooters along the Eastern Seaboard of North America were probably the first to register long-range hits with their Kentucky/Pennsylvania rifles. British soldiers at the Battle of New Orleans felt the sting of this truth. When that little fracas was over, British soldiers lay smitten by round bullets at great distances. Later, the mountain man with his plains rifle no doubt registered hits at incredible distances, sometimes through pure chance, no doubt, but also by deliberate aim made possible by familiarity with their rifles. As with blackpowder cartridge silhouette matches, check out round ball rifle shooting with lead pills ringing gongs at 500 yards, 600 yards and farther. *Ripley's Believe it or Not* television show featured a marksman who, with an original Sharps rifle, consistently placed bullets on target at a full 1,200 yards. The American Civil War, grist for this mill, saw a good deal of sniping. Soldiers were selected because

they were gifted marksmen. After that, they were carefully *trained* to make faraway strikes on the enemy. Col. Hiram Berdan remains in living history, not as the only officer to recruit snipers for long-range shooting on the battlefield, but because he may have been the first to convince military leadership to put a *regiment* of sharpshooters together. Berdan was an amateur New York rifleman and target shooter before the war. In 1861, he organized and assembled other good marksmen to join the North as snipers.

They were called Berdan's Sharpshooters and they wreaked considerable havoc upon the enemy. Other Union sharpshooters under the command of Col. Henry A.V. Post, also a New York resident, were successful in making long-range hits on the enemy. Only those who could pass a shooting test were allowed into these two elite regiments of riflemen. The exact tests may have been lost in time. Some stories are almost preposterous, if not entirely false. One simple set of rules from the literature does seem plausible and convincing: 10 shots into a 10-inch bullseye at 200 yards from any shooting position, including prone, with apparently any rifle. That included target rifles with telescopic or any other sights. Given a good, heavy target rifle of the day with a scope, 10 shots into

Hiram Berdan remains the best-known of the sharpshooter leaders, probably because he seems to be the first man to recognize how deadly a regiment of snipers would be.

a 10-inch bull at 200 yards is entirely reasonable. Even I could do it. Considering modern silhouette contests, 200 yards is a simple poke.

The sharpshooter could shoot his own rifle, research shows, and the government reimbursed him up to $60 for its use. It's reasonable to assume that some men brought their best target-shooting guns complete with 19th-century barrel-length scope sights. The scopes noted here were not tube sights, but true telescopes, often of high magnification, albeit very limited field of view. Malcolm and Vollmer scopes were quite well known by the time of the American Civil War. Today, we see the return of the Malcolm scope in replica—but improved—form for modern blackpowder shooters to enjoy. The one I know of is 6X. Looking like tube sights, which had no glass, these metal tubes were actually precision instruments containing lenses. There is no doubt that they could turn a deadly long-range rifle into a *deadlier* long-range rifle. As we know from history, buffalo hunters later in the same

century often mounted scopes on their breechloaders that were very much like the ones used in the Civil War. Some of these scopes achieved 20X.

Claims Factual and Otherwise

An exhibition to show President Abraham Lincoln just how good the Sharpshooters were supposed to be included a hundred men firing at a man-sized target a full 600 yards. This event was said to occur in 1861. Berdan himself was among the marksmen, the report goes. Out of 100 shooters, all placed bullets in the kill zone. Berdan fired a five-shot group that ran about 10 inches in spread. While it is noted that the rifles in this shoot did wear scope sights, all 100 men hitting the target with all of their shots may seem hard to believe. But stranger things have happened. To top it off, someone asked Berdan to hit one of the targets, a figure of Jefferson Davis. Not just hit it, but to put a bullet in the eye. Berdan fired his rifle and a neat round hole appeared where once there had been a pupil—or at least very close to that spot. Maybe this happened. Maybe not. Lincoln was supposed to have remarked something about the shot being the luckiest he'd ever seen. This same story is related in a version printed in a 19th-century *Harper's* magazine article. Hitting a target the size of a human eye at 600 yards, if it happened, was probably on the order of what Honest Abe said— pure luck.

Another possibly overstated claim concerns the one-mile strike credited to a Northern sharpshooter by the name of John H. Metcalf. Supposedly, the event took place in 1864 during the Red River Campaign, specifically the battle of Pleasant Hill in Louisiana. Metcalf took aim at a Confederate general named Lainhart, the distance being over one mile according to the tale. Boom! The bullet struck home. There are many possibilities. One is that the Union sharpshooter fired and someone in the distance fell,

at which point he was credited with a one-mile hit. Perhaps the distance was over-estimated. Or the shot truly did occur (stranger things have happened). That the bullet could travel so far and remain deadly is no problem. It could have. That anyone could judge a shot at a mile is on the incredible side. But the story I ran across includes accurate measurement of the distance before the shot was fired. If the mile-away shot were made, fluke would be a good name for it. Just think about bullet drop at one mile from a 19th-century blackpowder firearm. You'd have to aim at the top of a tall house to drop a bullet on the doorstep.

Documented Claims

Then there are documented claims of long-range sniping. In *The Battle of Gettysburg*, a scholarly work by Francis Marshal printed in 1914 by the Neale Publishing Co. of New York; the death of Confederate Maj. Gen. John Sedgewick is related. Sedgewick was well known to the North as well as to the South, with his reputation as a gentleman and soldier highly regarded on both sides of the fray. In fact, it was said after his death that Sedgewick had two mourners, "friends and his foe." His soldiers of the Sixth Corps considered Sedgewick their father more than their commander. Professor Marshal related the story this way: "The numerical sacrifice of human life, however, terrible as it is, does not equal the loss to the Federal army of one life, which has issued from its ranks on its long furlough. Major-General John Sedgewick, one of its main bulwarks for years, the loved commander and father of the old reliable Sixth Corps, is among the dead. Smiling encouragement to some of his men new to battle, whom he saw dodging the bullets that whizzed past, he had just remarked, jokingly: 'Soldiers, don't dodge bullets. Why, they can't hit an elephant at this distance.' At that instant a veteran officer at his side heard the familiar thud of a bullet, and turned to remark it to Sedgewick, who at that moment gave him a smile and fell dead into his arms, shot through the head."

Whitworths and Sharps Rifles

Due to the timing of the Sedgewick episode, the best bet is that the rifle used to fell the great soldier was a Whitworth rifled musket (see Chapter 35). The Whitworth did see action in the hands of sharpshooters on both sides of the war. And why not! The rifle was accurate, firing long bullets capable of retaining velocity/energy at great distance. But while the Whitworth was without doubt worthy of the sharpshooters, the Sharps rifle seems to have caught special favor with army personnel at the time. This would be the blackpowder breech-loading Sharps. A breech-loading rifle, yes, but not a cartridge rifle. This Sharps, noted as the New Model 1859 Military Rifle, used paper or linen cartridges. Paper cartridges were nothing new at the time. The soldier nipped off the end and poured the powder downbore, followed by the bullet, or he could ram the whole cartridge, paper and all, down after exposing the powder charge. This was not, however, the case with the Sharps rifle in question. Although noted in Chapter 31, a few remarks here on this rifle are in order to fill out our sniper story.

This Sharps rifle worked quite differently from any other rifle of the exact era. Its paper or linen cartridge was inserted into the chamber, bullet forward, of course, with the rearmost of the paper or linen cartridge sticking out just a bit beyond the chamber. When the rifle was put into the battery position, the breechblock, which had a very sharp end, cut off the back of the paper or linen cartridge, thus exposing the powder charge to the flash of the percussion cap. This rifle is listed as 52-caliber with a barrel length of 30 inches and a total weight of 9 pounds. Numerous Sharps rifles in various configurations continue to thrive in 21st-century America. The Sharps New Model 1859 Military Rifle is only one of them. A Dixie Gun Works historical study shows that the First Connecticut Volunteers of Hartford first used the Sharps 1859 rifle. But it was mostly associated with the First United States (Berdan's) Sharpshooters. Two thousand were furnished to the Sharpshooters, with the U.S. Navy receiving 2,780. The balance of the 6,689 rifles built at the time was spread among various army units. Current replicas of this rifle may have a 30-inch, tapered, round barrel with six-groove rifling, 54-caliber, not 52. The rifle may also have a 1:48 rate of twist. There are simply too many Sharps replicas to single out a generic model. Shiloh Sharps alone offers several high-grade copies in various models and different calibers. Sights on these replicas are generally flip-up style with a rear elevator adjustable to 800 yards. That alone attests to the maker's belief that these rifles could do the job at very long range. The front sight is a blade. The percussion replica takes musket caps. There is also a Sharps New Model 1859 Carbine, of which approximately 115,000 were made during the Civil War. It was a favorite of cavalrymen. This could make an interesting brush rifle for whitetails and wild boar. However, it would not qualify as a muzzle-loader for blackpowder-only hunts — because, it isn't one.

The Confederate Sharpshooter

Berdan's Sharpshooters touched a nerve during their own era and the name has come to us through history. Besides, they were on the winning side, which no doubt elevated their reputation. However, the Confederate Army did have its snipers, and everything suggests that they were at least as good as their Northern brothers. Gen. Patrick Cleburne was in charge of these soldier marksmen. The South apparently put its sharpshooters to work in 1862, but not officially until 1864 did these snipers get their Whitworth rifles. In February of that year, Whitworths were issued to each man in the unit. These soldiers apparently had been armed with their own personal guns before that time. Notes show a 530-grain, 45-caliber conical bullet for the Confederate Whitworth with 2.5 drams of blackpowder, a dram, as noted often, being 27.34 grains weight. So the charge would have been 68 grains of powder, a mild target load, but the long lead bullet was known then, and still is known, to fly far point-on when the rate of twist runs on the order of 1:20.

Was Lincoln Fired Upon?

History says yes, Confederate sharpshooters fired upon Abraham Lincoln in 1864 during an attack on Washington. The Southern sharpshooters were apparently several hundred yards from the Union trenches hidden in farm buildings when a tall man in a black top hat was spotted behind the Yankee lines. The Rebel sharpshooters lost no time sighting in on the figure who was there to get a first-hand look at the battle. Ap-

Gen. Patrick Cleburne can be thought of as the counterpart of Colonel Hiram Berdan. Berdan led sharpshooters of the Union Army, while Cleburne was responsible for putting a sniper corps together for the Confederate side.

parently Honest Abe had forgotten the marksmanship of his own sharpshooters. Or did he not believe that there were any Confederate snipers in the area? Whichever, the Rebs fired a few rounds before Lincoln was dragged to cover by Gen. Wright, who was standing by. The story goes that bullets struck so close to the President that splinters actually embedded in Lincoln's clothing. But no cigar for the Rebs. They missed! Some historians wonder if the course of the war may have been altered if Lincoln was killed. I doubt it, but we'll never know for sure.

They Shot at Each Other, Too

There were apparently a number of one-on-one duels between Yankee and Rebel snipers. There is no doubt about such meetings occurring, and in some cases they may have been deliberately invoked by officers hoping to drop a sharpshooter in the other army. Some of these duels were historically recorded. One includes a Private Ide, one of Berdan's sharp-

Gen. John Sedgewick was a well-loved leader in the Confederate Army; however, he had very little respect for the long-range shooting ability of the Yankees in the distance, and for this he paid the supreme price, as history clearly records.

shooters, who engaged in a shootout with a Southern marksman in 1862. The name of the Reb sniper was not recorded or perhaps lost. The bout became a show as soldiers from both sides watched the two men fire at each other from long range. The fight ended when the unnamed Confederate marksman put a bullet through the head of the unfortunate Yankee. Another duel had Rebel sharpshooters firing on Northern soldiers who were pinned down in a ditch, just their knapsacks showing above the trench. Bullets from the Rebs chewed the knapsacks to pieces. And when one soldier exposed himself, he himself toppled over. There's also a colorful account, if there is anything colorful about wartime, of a duel between one James Ragin, a Berdan sharpshooter, and another unmarked Southern sniper. The story goes that the two men fired simultaneously. The Reb's bullet clipped Ragin in the head, creating a furrow in his hair to the scalp. The Confederate marksman did not fare so well. Ragin's bullet ended the man's shooting for that day and evermore.

Ned Roberts and His Uncle Alvaro

Ned Roberts, in his book *The Muzzle-Loading Cap Lock Rifle*, credits his uncle Alvaro (Alvaro F. Annis) with teaching him how to shoot. Roberts said that Annis was one of Berdan's Sharpshooters in the Civil War. Roberts was very proud of that, and he applauded the Sharpshooters, citing an account from *Harper's Weekly* magazine dated August 7, 1861. The item read, in part: "We illustrate herewith the exploits of Colonel Berdan and his famous sharpshooting regiment, which will shortly be heard of at the war." On Aug. 7, the colonel gave an exhibition of his skill at Weehawken, N.J., in the presence of a large crowd of spectators. The 'man target' christened Jefferson Davis was set up at a distance of a little more than 200

yards. Col. Berdan inaugurated the firing. Balancing his rifle for a moment, he fired at the head of the figure. When the smoke had cleared away, the hole made by the bullet, observed by the aid of a telescope, struck in the cheek, near the nose. The *Harper's* story went on to say that Berdan hit the target several times, calling one shot in the eye, as noted earlier, with the bullet striking "near enough to that organ to destroy its use had it been a real one." The other version of the right-eye hit is the one mentioned earlier where someone called out to hit that spot and Berdan did. This article continues that no man could enter the Sharpshooter regiment without proving that he could shoot at 600 feet (feet, not yards in this version) 10 consecutive shots "at an average of five inches from the bullseye." This seems more plausible than 600 yards, but maybe not.

But Was Uncle Alvaro Really a Berdan Sharpshooter?

Roberts mentioned his Uncle Alvaro so often that certain people decided to check the facts. On the one hand, what they learned was damaging to the story. On the other hand, there could be a reason for the discrepancy. The name Alvaro F. Annis does not appear on the roster of Berdan's Sharpshooters Regiment at all, which makes Robert's claims a problem. Nor does the War Department in Washington show Uncle Alvaro listed. What does appear is an attempt to enlist by Alvaro, which proved negative due to failing the physical exam. A year later, Alvaro Annis entered the army anyway, so the story goes, taking the place of a man who had passed the physical exam, but apparently did not relish going to war. After learning of his skilled marksmanship, the Union admitted Annis to the Sharpshooters under the name of the other soldier and Alvaro answered to that man's name. We'll never know if Uncle Alvaro made himself a Berdan Sharpshooter to impress his nephew, or if indeed he truly did take the place of another soldier whose name has floated down the stream of history, lost forever.

How Good were the Guns?

Because of the potential broadness of conflict in modern wars, we may tend to overlook just how long and bloody was the American Civil War of the 1800s. Heavy casualties were mounted in battle after battle. This is an important (and sad) testimony to the deadliness of the guns—cannons to be sure—but rifles and handguns as well. *The Battle of Gettysburg* by Francis Marshall, noted above, 1914 copyright, paints a grim picture of the depth of the fighting. Referring to this specific battle, Marshal wrote, "The decisive battle of the American Civil War has been fought to the finish—and at what cost! Out of the army of 85,674 men Meade lost 22,990 men, of whom 3,003 are killed, 2,228 die of wounds, 12,264 are wounded, and 5,435 are missing. Lee's host of 71,675 men has been reduced by the loss of 20,448 men, of whom 2,598 are killed, 1,728 die of wounds, 10,978 are wounded, and 5,150 are missing." Marshall points out that Confederate numbers in losses differs from reports because the report itself was not complete. So the grim figures do not exactly match up. Later numbers show a total of 22,100 men killed *or* wounded with a total loss of 27,525 men. Remember that these are for the Battle of Gettysburg alone. Cannons were, of course, responsible for much of the damage. But it is clear that rifles and even handguns played a huge role in this particular conflict. Consider a 58-caliber Minie striking the body just about anywhere. It would inflict terrible tissue and bone damage that medical skill and tools of the time could not cope with. And so we see after the war many men with missing limbs where a big lead bullet almost dissected an arm on its own.

They Were Great Marksmen

Regardless of overstatements and historical flaws, the American sniper was a remarkable marksman with his blackpowder rifle. Of that there is no doubt. Of course, many Americans were great shooters in the 19th century because shooting was a daily way of life at the time. And as pointed out above, the shooting prowess of our forebears lives once again with muzzleloader as well as blackpowder cartridge rifle in all manner of shooting, both games and serious matches. While a few of the feats credited to both Northern and Southern snipers may have been exaggerated, they probably were not that far-fetched, as proven by the fact that good shooters today can repeat the marksmanship with rifle types from the past, or nearly so. Perhaps the deliberate placing of a bullet in the eye at 600 yards not withstanding. Or the one-mile shot.

THE FUR TRADE AND THE MOUNTAIN MEN

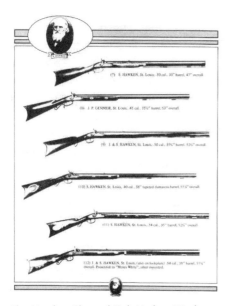

The Hawken Shop of Oak Harbor, Washington, supplied this image of some original Hawken rifles.

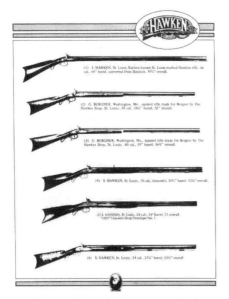

The Hawken Shop of Oak Harbor, Washington, displays another group of original Hawken rifles. The Shop has used originals to ensure the faithfulness of their rifles and kit.

The quest for the West began back East because that's where the European immigrants started life in America. They were from England in the beginning. But soon many countries contributed to the immigrant wealth that would become the melting pot called the United States of America. Early on, German craftsmen were extremely instrumental in building a unique American long rifle developed by vastly changing the Old Country German *Jaeger*, or hunting rifle. When these German immigrants arrived they were asked by residents what their country of origin was, and they replied that they were *Deutch*—German, which was mistaken as Dutch. And that is why they were called "German Dutch." The Kentucky rifle was born in Pennsylvania, its name derived, we are told, from a popular song of the day. The fantastic Kentucky/Pennsylvania long rifle was the epitome of the Golden Age of American arms. Travels by riflemen along the Eastern Seaboard into what we call the Midwest today were significant, with names such as Dan'l Boone and Davy Crockett permanently written in the pages of history. But it was another time and place that brought about the muzzleloader that influenced the blackpowder guns we shoot (mostly) today; shorter, more powerful rifles than the Pennsylvania/Kentucky long guns of the Golden Age.

It happened because of a hat. More truthfully, it was American enterprise and politics that brought explorers into what came to be known, in capital letters, as the Far West. Hot fashion called for beaver top hats, similar to the style associated with President Abraham Lincoln—a fashion statement dating to the 1400s. Western American streams were thick with beaver, and so the era known as the Fur Trade commenced in the middle 1800s, creating two developments born again in muzzleloading—the plains rifle and the rendezvous. Along with desiring beaver hides to make hats, Thomas Jefferson's political interest was an American presence in the Far West where French and English trappers, traders, and explorers were gaining a significant foothold. Jefferson commissioned Lewis and Clark to embark upon their long journey to study the environs west of the Mississippi, lay out routes for future pioneer migration, and to establish who the land truly belonged to: not foreigners, but Americans. These developments brought about the invention of the rugged plains rifle. And when blackpowder shooting boomed again, beginning in the late 1950s, it was this rifle that most pleased the modern shooter and hunter. Replica cap 'n' ball handguns actually got the ball rolling. But the trend would have leveled off on a modest plane of general interest without the rifle, because America is a nation of riflemen. So the comparatively short, stout, big-bore hunting shoulder arm fondly known as a "Hawken" became prominent in the Fur Trade era. When it appeared again in revised form, it was ready to please space-age shooters interested in big-game hunting as well as target shooting and competition, the latter often taking place during a re-enactment of the original Fur Trade gathering called the rendezvous.

But before talking about the Fur Trade, its rendezvous and rifle, let's walk to the valley for a moment to ponder a more distant past.

Roots

The greatest impact in long-range shooting and vastly improved accuracy came with the invention of rifling. After all, that is where the gun we call *rifle* got its name: from the spiral grooves within the bore. Where did they come from? Rifling (never spelled *riflings*) was another European invention, perhaps of German origin, possibly Austrian. Some sources say Gaspard Kollner of Vienna, late in the 15th century, got the idea. Others credit Augustus Kotter of Nuremberg for inventing rifling in 1520. Yet another researcher mixes the two names, coming up with a "Gaspard Koller" of Nuremberg. No matter, but it is interesting that early rifling may have had nothing to do with spinning a projectile. Originators of the no-spin theory can produce old-time guns with straight, not spiral, rifling. The idea? To aid cleaning, they say. Sounds suspicious to me. Smoothbores are much easier to clean than rifled arms, no matter how the grooves are cut. Shooters of the past figured that out, too. However, straight-groove rifling did exist. Why is open to question. Regardless of theories, the European rifle was the forerunner of the long-barreled beauty of early America called the Pennsylvania rifle. Leather-stocking lads such as Daniel Boone fought and hunted with this rifle.

British troops felt its sting on American soil. Trailblazers of the Eastern Seaboard cut many new paths into the frontier with their accurate rifles in hand. Various sources list different major calibers for the Pennsylvania long rifle. But caliber 45 prevailed. That assessment is based on three decades of studying original guns in museums, at gun shows, and in collections. A super marksman could take the little 45—45-caliber being small with a round ball—and bring home the bacon, usually in the form of Eastern white-tailed deer and wild turkeys. Of course, 45-caliber was also ample for warfare. But when the initial shove west became a push in the early 1800s, a new breed of adventurer answered the call. He relied on the long arm of the hour—at first, which was really a hodgepodge of different guns. These men were the original buckskinners and their rifles were wrong for them. While we think

The Hawken rifle today lives on in replica form, and in museums, and also in story. This is the storyteller at the Museum of the Mountain Man in Pinedale, Wyoming telling everyone about the mountain man days and ways.

of Daniel Boone softly treading the forest floors of the East, we see Jim Bridger riding his horse over the rugged Rocky Mountains, often with pack animals to tote his supplies. The lean, long, and rather lightweight Pennsylvania rifle was out of place here. It was too delicate, too small of caliber, and too darn long. Thus the plains rifle was born: shorter for horseback, larger caliber for animals much bigger than deer, as well as the dangerous grizzly bear, capable of burning heavy doses of blackpowder to gain reasonable range and power. The mother of invention, necessity, struck again. The trapper had his rifle.

Those who took trails west in search of beaver were called mountain men, and in spirit, if not replication, we most often carry their rifle today. The name "Hawken," which in reality fits only those rifles built by the Hawken brothers, became generic in modern times. And why not? In general design, it is a prime blackpowder rifle for hunting. But we can't ignore the men who carried the rifle in the 19th century. They were the most interesting explorers of American history. This is not an East/West prejudice, for the fur hunters of the Rocky Mountains were Eastern boys to begin with, a wild and crazy bunch of characters willing to risk all for a big time and free life. They thrived

in the vast unexplored territory filled with truly large game: elk, grizzlies, and the heaviest four-footed animal on the continent, the American bison or buffalo. They staked claim to the American West for Americans, winning respect with their plains rifles. A great many never returned to their eastern homes, falling prey to grizzly bears, bitter winters, rushing streams of icy water, and run-ins with "Bug's Boys," the intrepid and dangerous Blackfoot Indian.

As explained in *Powder River*, a 1938 book written by Struthers Burt, Jefferson was far-sighted, the Seward of his time, for like Seward, who saw Alaska as more than a huge ice cube, Jefferson knew that the "other half" of America, the West, was worth having. "Seward's Folly," the purchase of Alaska, haunted the man to his grave. Jefferson was more fortunate. He got the ball rolling by dispatching the great Lewis and Clark Expedition in 1804. He saw to it that the men were well supplied to carry out their duties. The surface goal was to go west to the Pacific Ocean. The underlying goal was to study the flora, fauna, and geography of the Far West while making their presence known to French and English trappers and traders. Lewis and Clark made up the head of a spear aimed at the unknown. That spear penetrated the entire breadth of

The people who lived in the Far West. Artwork at the Museum of the Mountain Man in Pinedale, Wyoming.

Western America. But along with Jefferson and Lewis and Clark, another name enters the picture. He was not a statesman, not even a major player in the expedition launched by Jefferson. He was a man born to adventure and capable of dealing with its dangers.

His name was John Colter. The L&C expedition's spirit of adventure was on the wane by August 1806. But not John Colter's. He made the acquaintance of two trappers, Forest Hancock and Joseph Dickson, on the Yellowstone River. These men had gone farther west than any American at that time, except for Lewis and Clark. Colter asked Lewis and Clark if they would honorably discharge him from their employ so he could join Hancock and Dickson in a trapping venture. He got what now seems a rather remarkable response from his commanders. The Lewis and Clark journals contain the following quote under August 14 and 15 entries: "The offer [to Colter by Hancock and Dickson] was a very advantageous one, and, as he [Colter] had always performed his duty, and his services might be dispensed with, we agreed that he might go, provided none of the rest would ask or expect a similar indulgence. To this they cheerfully answered that they wished Colter every success and would not apply for liberty to separate before we reached St. Louis." Lewis and Clark supplied Col-

ter, as well as his new partners, with gunpowder, lead, and a "variety of articles which might be useful to him, and he left us the next day." August 16, 1806, was the beginning of Colter's adventure. He spent seven years of his life, from 1803 to 1810, exploring the Far West. He discovered in 1872 what we call western Wyoming, including the land that was to become Yellowstone Park. When he later told about the Yellowstone area, with its geysers and scalding, gushing waters, he was branded a liar. People called his "imagined" land Colter's Hell.

John Colter's fascinating story is too long to relate here. But briefly, when asked by Manuel Lisa to drum up a little fur-trade business, John walked an estimated 500 miles in wintertime visiting various Indian camps in search of traders. He traveled on "webs," which we call snowshoes, carrying provisions in a backpack. Rifle in hand, Colter covered an immense territory now part of Montana and Wyoming, making it back to Manuel Lisa's trading post by spring. Obviously, the natives of the region would have killed Colter had he not been a special man. Colter explored, drew maps, and made perhaps the most exciting "run for your life" in American history. At the time of the run, John had a partner named John Potts. The two encountered a party of Blackfoot

Indians. Potts resisted and was immediately killed. Having a sense of humor, as author Burt puts it, the Indians stripped Colter of his clothing, gave him a 100-yard head start, and told him to run for it. Cactus is not confined to the low desert. And the Indians saw to it that Colter's path of escape took him through plenty of spiny plants. Feet filled with needles, John continued to run. He was fast and he stayed ahead for a long while. However, one of his pursuers was faster, catching up to the white man. Colter turned on a dime. His chaser stumbled and broke his lance. John picked it up, killing the warrior with his own weapon. He survived by reaching the Madison River, diving in, and coming up in a beaver dam, where he found both air to breathe and a hidden sanctuary in the frigid water.

The mountain man found a different world out West. The black bear of the East was represented, but so was his larger deadly cousin, the grizzly. You didn't drop a grizzly with a peashooter. You needed a stout rifle to do the job. Some camps had such a rifle, a special grizzly bear gun. I saw one in a museum. It was huge of bore, massive of barrel, capable of throwing a tremendous hunk of lead at good muzzle velocity. There were deer, too, the familiar white-tailed variety often referred to as the "common deer," along with mule deer, which were called blacktails at the time. There was an even larger deer out West—the *wapiti* or elk, as well as western moose. The mountain man also encountered vast herds of bison with herd bulls ranging as high as 3,000 pounds on the hoof. The real terror, though, was "Old Ephraim." Sometimes known as the "white bear," he was an animal that could "shoot back," often winning battles with men in spite of their firesticks. Rifles that served well in the East were not strong enough west of the Mississippi. The Pennsylvania long rifle was handsome, light in the hand, swift to the shoulder, and accurate, but no match for the bear "that walks like a man." A 45-caliber round ball of only

133 grains was a pesky fly against the flak jacket of hide and muscle worn by the grizzly.

The Plains Rifle

It is impossible to neatly categorize rifles that went west with the first explorers. There were small bores and military muskets, some noted as larger than 50-caliber in the *Journals of Lewis and Clark*. There also were smoothbores, shotguns, and various sidearms, mainly single-shot pistols. Flintlocks were prevalent. Many of these guns were inaccurate and unreliable. A new breed of rifle was needed to serve the needs of the mountain man. That new rifle was generally 50-caliber or larger, the bigger bore firing a larger round ball. The barrel was in turn heavier and wider across the flats than the Pennsylvania long arm. Greater barrel-wall thickness was necessary for strength, and the octagonal barrel of a plains rifle could be more than an inch across the flats, perhaps 1-1/8 inches. The big barrel demanded a stock to match, with a wrist thick enough to withstand the recoil of heavy powder charges. Accuracy was sufficient, although across the board probably a shade behind the eastern rifle. The sturdy, rugged plains rifle was not as handsome as the eastern long rifle. But with its shorter, heavier barrel, it carried well across the saddle and that counted for more than beauty when lives were at stake.

While barrels in the 44-inch and even longer realm were common on Pennsylvania/Kentucky rifles, the plains rifle wore a tube about 34 to 36 inches (with exceptions). Since they were made one at a time by hand, variation, not mass-production standardization, was the rule. One plains rifle could have a 33-inch barrel, another a 36-inch barrel. Along with the larger barrel and bigger stock came more weight, generally about 10 to 11 pounds, some original Hawkens tipping the scale at 15 pounds. The style was plain, although a few were embellished with carvings and inlays. The half-stock de-

The impact of the Hawken remains with us today. This Lyman Great Plains rifle is reminiscent of the original Hawken rifle, while not being a replica.

The Hawken Brothers were famous for their rifles, not their pistols, but they did make single-shot muzzleloading pistols. This CVA is not a Hawken replica, but it provides the same shooting spirit.

sign with iron furniture and no patch box lent the charm of a potato sack. Straight-grip stocks prevailed, but a few late Hawkens had pistol grips. Most wore fixed, open iron sights; a rare few sported peep sights. There were flintlock plains rifles, but most were percussion.

So here was the plains rifle: relatively short of barrel and overall length, stout, half-stock design, percussion ignition, rugged, accurate enough for big-game hunting, and very reliable. A loose stereotype is the full-stock J&S Hawken rifle pictured on page 27 of John Baird's *Hawken Rifles* book. Caliber 53 is considered average, but others were common, including 55- and even 60-caliber. Furthermore, rifles could be "freshed out," which meant rebored to a larger caliber. This occurred especially with a worn or pitted bore. But of course it also resulted in a larger-caliber rifle. A plains rifle starting out 50- or 53- caliber might end up 55- caliber or larger. The plains rifle was touted as "flat-shooting" to 150 yards, which it was not. No rifle, including the 220 Swift, shoots flat to 150 yards. However, the term was applied because the rifle could be sighted in for about 100 yards with heavy powder charges and a patched round ball and a practiced rifleman using a bit of "Arkansas elevation" could hit a target regularly at 200 yards.

The Hawken Rifle Today

Sam and Jake Hawken made superb plains rifles, so good that the name became generic. The famous name now marks an entire genre of firearms, including muzzleloaders that look as much like a Hawken as a Weatherby resembles an AK-47. Today's "Hawken" may have a barrel under 20 inches, or it might be 36 inches. It can be mass-produced or handmade. However, as this is written there are a few in-the-spirit versions, if not replicas, of the original Plains Rifle. Two I know of are beauties. These are the Mountain Rifle from Austin & Halleck and the Rocky Mountain Hawken in maple or walnut stock from Pedersoli. The latter comes in calibers 45, 50, and 54, and it so closely resembles the original that it is ideal for rendezvous shooting. For a time there was an exact copy of a Hawken offered to modern shooters. It was from the Ithaca Gun Company and it was copied, we're told, from an original reportedly owned by Kit Carson.

The Mountain Men

The mountain men were trappers. But of course due to Jefferson's plan with the Lewis and Clark Expedition, beaver trapping in the Far West was for more than pelts. It created an American presence in a land not yet entirely secured. The mountain men set up

No longer available, the Ithaca Hawken rifle was a true copy of an original, halfstock, percussion, plain iron furniture, open fixed sights, double keys.

housekeeping with permanent camps in the Rockies. They were the most outrageous, courageous, devil-may-care group to make tracks in North America. They won the West, not with a repeater, but with a plains rifle. They were sent forth by two American businessmen, William H. Ashley and Andrew Henry. Ashley was the more enterprising, while Henry was a bit more adventuresome. How would they find their trappers? What do you do when you're looking for something in America? Advertise! And so the St. Louis papers of 1822 carried this ad:

To Enterprising Young Men
The subscriber wishes to engage
ONE HUNDRED MEN, to ascend
the river Missouri to its source,
there to be employed for one, two
or three years - For particulars,
enquire of Major Andrew Henry,
near the Lead Mines, in the County
of Washington, (who will ascend
with, and command the party) or to
the subscriber at St. Louis.

Wm. H. Ashley

Free trappers, or Ashley Men, as they were called, did not receive fixed wages. They kept half of all furs in exchange for supplies and transportation to the mountains. The true mountain man was, as they put it in those days, "on his own hook." He worked for himself without wages, although there was a company in the background to supply trade goods in a summer meeting that came to be known as the rendezvous. If not fearless, the free trapper certainly acted and reacted with reckless abandon. Life was balanced like a coin on its edge. Many mistakes could be made

only once. There was no second chance. Reports filtered back to civilization concerning these wayward souls. A greenhorn at one summer rendezvous saw a card game played on the back of a dead man. The dearly departed was set up "on all fours" by his comrades, his stiff body serving as a playing surface. Life was a thread dangling among razor blades. During a skirmish, one mountain man was struck. "I'm hit," he cried out to his friends. They pretended not to hear him correctly, returning answers that offered no comfort whatsoever to the injured party.

"He says he hit one!"
"No, I said, I'm hit!'"
"Where'd you hit 'im?"
"No, it's me who's hit!"

Another time, a rabid wolf sprang into camp. The men knew the animal was crazed with hydrophobia and aware of the danger of being bitten. Instead of putting a round ball through the canine, or climbing a tree to get out of harm's way, sport ensued. "He's over here," one mountain man shouted, burying himself beneath his sleeping robes to ward off the bite of death. Shouts of "No, over here" continued. Two men were bitten. They wandered away from camp and were never seen again. It was a tough life, but just right for the fur trappers. Many of them returned to civilization only to find their old world dull. They went back to the mountains to face the dangers all over again. They were bold, foolhardy, had a pocketful of time, and no master to tell them how to spend it. Their marks in the land live to this day, scraped out trails that became highways from East to the West. Lewis and Clark, yes, but

it was individual trappers who truly mapped the Far West. Their names still grace the land: Bridger National Forest, Henry's Fork of the Snake River, Mount Fitzpatrick, Jedediah Smith Wilderness Area, Jackson, Wyo. A mountain man museum/memorial resides in Pinedale, Wyo., a tribute to the taming of the West. It is housed in a large and beautiful building displaying treasures of the era. The superb Museum of the Fur Trade in Chadron, Neb., also praises the free trapper of the West.

This is the romance of the mountain man. It is no wonder that many modern blackpowder shooters emulate him. Today, his dress, firearms, camping style, and his summer gathering time, the rendezvous, are copied by people who call themselves buckskinners. Some of these men and women live their daily lives, if not in every way, at least in spirit, as the mountain man did. The buckskinner is also a student of the fur trade, although he does not adhere to every nuance of the mountain man code. The fact is, mountain men were the same as any other group with much individual variation. Frederick Remington did more, perhaps, than any other painter to give us an image of the fur hunter; however, he was late. He painted only a reflection on the water, for the true picture had passed with the ripples of time. Bearded? Maybe, but shaving razors were found in mountain man kits. An Indian maiden was not used to facial hair and our lads were very interested in these maidens. Long hair? Probably. Indian clothes? The mountain man adopted part of the Indian costume, but not all of it. He also lived by Indian ways or he would have perished in the first Far West winter.

The Original Rendezvous

Ashley and Henry's St. Louis newspaper advertisement worked. William Ashley stayed behind attending to business details, while Maj. Andrew Henry led a party of free trappers into the West. In order to receive value for their beaver pelts, the trappers gathered at a pre-established point in summer for a rendezvous, the first taking place in 1825 when General Ashley met his free trappers on what is now known as Henry's Fork of the Green River not far from Daniel, Wyo., near Pinedale. The men trapped until freeze-up, taking refuge until spring. Now spring had come and gone, and here they were to trade their hard-earned furs for worldly goods. It was called a "shining time." Pelts went for dollar value, that is, *inflated* dollar value. The trappers needed galena (lead) for bullets, powder, butcher knives, clothing, maybe even a new rifle, precious smoking tobacco, sugar, flour. Gewgaws—trinkets the Indian ladies admired—were important. One mountain man, the story goes, gave up $2,000 worth of pelts for the hand of a chief's daughter. She must have been a knockout.

How much could a free trapper earn, plunging his hands into the frigid boreal waters of the Far West? One thousand, perhaps two in a season with rheumatism at best, a Blackfoot arrow at worst. Actually, the pay itself was not so bad, since a worker of the period made about a buck and a half a day, but the trapper really didn't get money. He traded his catch to the company store for goods, and the goods were swapped at grossly inflated prices. Whisky worth 30 cents a gallon in St. Louis was cut with water and sold for $3 a pint at rendezvous. Tobacco, coffee, and sugar at 10 cents a pound back East went for $2 a pound. Gunpowder ran the same for English Diamond Grade, while American du Pont, considered better, traded for $12 a pound. Gewgaws carried a 2,000 percent markup. A cheap Indian trade rifle worth $10 back home fetched several

times that price at rendezvous, while a fine Hawken rifle worth $40 in St. Louis commanded $80. But money was not the real issue with the mountain men. Lifestyle was. The entire season's effort evaporated in as little as one day, but the men had their goods and a fine time gambling at cards, talking with friends they had not seen for months, learning of the goings on back home, arguing, competing in shooting games, 'hawk tossin', knife-throwing, bragging, fist-fighting, and impressing the Indian women. The deal wasn't so bad. After all, there was great risk hauling loaded wagons across hostile country. The investors deserved their returns.

The Modern Rendezvous

Finally, the beaver hat slipped from fashion and the mountain men were no more. They were a presence out West, turning furs into dollars. When an era is gone, it's gone. But it can be emulated, and that's what happened. The rendezvous was born again, credit going to the NMLRA (National Muzzle Loading Rifle Association). Once again, people met on common ground to trade goods, compete in shooting, knife throwing, and fire-starting contests, and to have a big time the old way. Rendezvous sprang up both East and West, and continue to this hour. The NMLRA continues to inform about these modern shining times in its magazine, *Muzzle Blasts*, with

blackpowder clubs all over the world holding rendezvous of their own. Information concerning times and dates can be located on the Internet as well. The shooting contests are especially interesting, some off-hand at common black bullseyes, others animated. Want to have fun? Try splitting a fired round ball on the blade of an ax imbedded in a vertically oriented stump. On either side of the blade, balloons are set. If you split the ball well enough, the two pieces will break the two balloons. Or cut a wooden stake in the ground in half with bullets from your front-loader. Or ring a gong at several hundred yards (Chapter 39).

A picture of the modern rendezvous in words: In the valley, teepees stand as if painted upon the landscape, smoke rising from campfires everywhere, hovering in thin wisps on the air, catching and reflecting the natural light of day and the man-made light of fire when the sun goes down. At dark, tiny sparks from flint 'n' steel striking together play at ground level, curls of smoke rising like miniature smoke signals. Standing on a hill, an observer is mesmerized by long tongues of flame licking at the dry wood of evening campfires. He hears the people talking and laughing, as well as music on the air from dulcimers and flutes. Stew is bubbling. It's time to join friends around the campfire before resting back on a buffalo robe.

The Hawken rifle had such impact on the shooting world that the breed never died. This young shooter at rendezvous tries his hand with a Hawken-like rifle.

STARTING A NEW SHOOTER ON BLACKPOWDER

Visual respect for firearms is clearly impressed upon young minds with blackpowder firearms putting smoke and flame into the air. The noise is equally impressive, although it should be heard only through excellent hearing protection.

There are many positives in starting a new shooter on the muzzleloader/blackpowder cartridge trail. The advantages are: true understanding of firearms; understanding cartridge function; learning about shooting tools; creating loads one at a time "by hand" (including blackpowder cartridge and shotshell); respect punctuated by smoke and flame; appreciating history, making his or her own bullets; dealing with recoil; learning patience in shooting; challenges of blackpowder shooting; doing the rendezvous (if desired), Cowboy Action Shooting (if desired); the silhouette game (if desired); collecting, small-game hunting, bird hunting, big-game hunting with blackpowder guns; eligibility for special blackpowder-only hunts; understanding basic ballistics, including trajectory patterns and how to work with them; methods for improving accuracy; basic troubleshooting; and sound maintenance practices, and great sensitivity to safety.

True Understanding of Firearms

The muzzleloader, especially, produces a true understanding of firearms that will greatly benefit the new shooter. The simplicity of the muzzleloader, being essentially a barrel with a hole in the front end to dispel a bullet and a smaller hole on the other end to accept a source of ignition, clearly shows how guns work. This basic knowledge is readily transferred to cartridge guns of all types later. Additionally, because the new shooter understands how a muzzleloader works, he or she will have a great advantage when it comes to dealing with single-shot breech-loaders, bolt-actions, slide-action, and semi-automatic firearms. The parts of the firearm are also learned. See maintenance below.

Understanding Cartridge Function

There is no better way to instruct a new shooter on how a cartridge works than to teach the basic function of the muzzleloader. In effect, the shooter makes a cartridge every time he or she loads the gun. This knowledge is readily transferred to the metallic case. Where the breech of the muzzleloader contains the powder charge, now the case is a reservoir for powder; where there was a bullet in front of the powder charge in the barrel of the muzzleloader, now

Learning the tools of blackpowder shooting includes an understanding of the firearms parts. The newcomer sees here three different breech plugs. How do they differ?

there is a bullet in front of the powder charge in the fixed ammunition; whereas the muzzleloader required a source of ignition with pan powder in the flintlock or a percussion cap in the caplock, now there is a primer seated in the back end of the cartridge case.

Learning About Shooting Tools

Blackpowder shooting, with its numerous tools, gives a newcomer a sense of accessory function that becomes essential later on with modern arms. While the tools are quite different for blackpowder guns, the idea of working with accoutrements that attend shooting is well-planted. Furthermore, the tools themselves are interesting and instructional. Forevermore, the new shooter will appreciate what a powderhorn is, what a powder flask is, what a jag does, and so forth. A powder measure alone is a highly valuable shooting tool that stands as a handbook in its own right.

Creating Loads One at a Time by Hand

Perhaps one of the strongest teaching tools the newcomer has in starting with a muzzleloader is "making" his or her own ammunition one shot at a time, every time. This hands-on approach to shooting teaches a strong basic feeling of true involvement in the entire sequence. The shooter handles each component one at a time and in perfect order—powder, bullet, and ignition.

Visual Respect via Smoke and Flame

Unfortunately, our busy world does not always allow us to start a new shooter with a muzzleloader. Instead, we hand the newcomer a 22-rimfire rifle and he or she fires away. Smoke and flame are virtually nil. There can be a tendency to consider the gun a tool of relatively modest authority. The muzzleloader—be it a 50-caliber loaded down, which it must be for early training, or even a smallbore squirrel rifle—belches smoke and at times breathes fire. The fire and smoke—and we could add a report louder than the usual 22 rifle—punctuates the fact that here is a tool demanding great respect. The rules of safety come much more to light—you certainly don't want to have that muzzle pointed at anything you do not intend to shoot, because this rifle is *powerful*. I know because it breaths fire and belches smoke. We have a little shooting program going for kids from single-parent families. When possible, muzzleloaders are used although time constraints often deny that. And I can tell an immediate difference in how the young people handle a muzzleloader vs. a 22 rifle. They seem to be more interested in the muzzleloader, and they definitely show greater respect for it.

History Appreciation

While the history of modern arms development is interesting in its various aspects, especially military, America won its initial independence with smokepoles, not machine guns. There is also much to be learned about firearm

There are many advantages to starting young shooters early on the blackpowder way of shooting. Though this little girl is too young to handle a gun, she is learning respect through the actions of her father handling his Knight modern muzzleloading rifle.

A rifle like this Knight modern muzzleloader teaches cartridge function to a beginning boy or girl because the components of the cartridge exist in the muzzleloader and in proper order—starting with some form of ignition into a waiting powder charge that, in turn, propels a bullet or shot charge from the muzzle.

history from muzzleloaders, since they preceded the modern gun by centuries. The newcomer should be taught at least a few points about both histories—general events and guns—while shooting procedures are attended to. The mountain man story alone is compelling to any newcomer who has the least interest in firearms (see Chapter 49).

Making Bullets

Here is another aspect of blackpowder shooting that teaches a great deal, not only about shooting, but also about the chemistry of lead in "pure form" or alloy, plus extremely important points of safety with hot metal and

lead fumes. Newcomers to blackpowder shooting show great fascination in creating their own bullets. This is not to say that bullet casting is confined only to blackpowder guns. I just bought a Lyman mould to make bullets for 30-06 rifles because of a writing assignment that came my way. I should not have been surprised when the Lyman bullet #311041 (with gas check) made one-hole groups at 25 yards, the distance I was interested in for procuring small game and mountain grouse should a 30-06 hunter go on a long trek into the wilderness with but one rifle. Although I have cast thousands of my own bullets over time, I have yet to grow com-

placent about how accurate and useful these bullets can be. The newcomer is equally pleased and surprised when he or she fires cast bullets with great success. While not all of these shooters will go on to make their own bullets for the rest of their lives, some will. And those who will never forget having done it.

Dealing with Recoil

Recoil comes in two brands—there is "real" recoil measured as rearward thrust in foot-pounds of energy, as we did in Chapter 37 concerning the big thumpers. Then there is "felt" recoil, which breaks down into two categories: actual push on the body and infringe-

There are a number of people around today who not only know old-time history, but they also know how to live it from time to time. Jerry Meyer is that sort of person. He's a natural born teacher any beginning shooter would do well to learn from.

A young person can watch, but should not be included directly in bullet making until sufficiently mature to cast projectiles in total safety and the right conditions. In the meantime, paying attention to details such as depositing dross from lead into the proper receptacle is in itself a positive learning experience.

Dealing with recoil is a learned trait especially well taught by a lady shooter who shows that a proper load in a medium-bore muzzleloader can be handled without hurting. A beginning boy or girl watching Mom or another lady handling recoil lends confidence for later shooting.

In the concentration (I won't call it excitement) of shooting at game, felt recoil is forgotten. Felt recoil differs from "real" recoil because of *how* a firearm makes contact with the body. I cringe when I hear of a hunter, always a male, who wants to start his wife, daughter, or son with a light-kicking Model 94 Winchester carbine. The Model 94 is a wonderful rifle, but it has a comparatively narrow buttplate and, all in all, can deliver more *felt* recoil upon the shoulder and face than a more powerful cartridge in a rifle designed to come back in a straight line with more buttplate surface. Perceived recoil is broken down into the *expectation* of being "kicked" when the gun goes off, as well as the infringement on the sense of hearing. A shooter who thinks, "Boy, is this thing going to kick," has already suffered from recoil without shooting the gun. Noise can make people flinch when it comes from nothing more than a firecracker.

Learning Patience

Once again I confess that in our attempt to help new shooters we are often saddled by constraints of time, not only our own, but that of the newcomer being introduced to shooting, plus the parent who generally comes to the range with the boy or girl. And so out comes the 22-rimfire rifle. But when time permits, the muzzleloader is chosen. Among the many positive factors attending the front-loader is learning patience in shooting. There is no rat-a-tat-tat here. The loading process is slow and methodical. There is plenty of time to learn rapid reloading later on for games as well as hunting. Now the idea is taking things one step at a time, carefully and slowly. This teaches a special brand of patience that I think is important not only to better shooting, but also safety.

Blackpowder Challenge

We want our newcomer to enjoy success immediately if at all possible. That success comes in various forms, however. There is hitting the target, certainly, but also doing a proper job of loading and overall firearm management. On the other hand, when that new shooter accepts the blackpowder challenge and lives up to it, the result is special joy with faces that show it.

ment on the senses. In starting the newcomer, real recoil is no problem because any teacher who hands a new shooter a full-power load is taking the wrong track. I learned this with lady shooters who were sensitive to recoil. My sister-in-law used a rifle belonging to my wife on a hunt. She was amazed at the mild recoil and modest report of the rifle. The load was about one-third throttle. When she got her game—three deer tags she filled with three shots—she never noticed that now she was firing the "real load."

Patience in shooting is a virtue worthy of passing on to a new shooter. A muzzleloader teaches patience because it is one-load-at-a-time. Another teacher of patience is making something for blackpowder shooting or hunting—by hand. This is a turkey call made from a tip of horn and a dowel, the slate striker is in the leather pouch.

Taking a beginning shooter to a match at rendezvous or other blackpowder gathering is a great way to teach the fun of shooting the front-loader safely. The running boar match is fun to watch, especially for a beginner who might like to try it for himself or herself one day.

Silhouette shooting with blackpowder cartridge rifles is a difficult game and not ideal for the beginner who is trying to get his or her feet planted in safely and successfully handling the blackpowder firearm. However, watching shooters fire away at long-range metallics is a good way to instill interest.

Cowboy Action Shooting

As part of the program, the new shooter should go to at least one Cowboy Action Shooting game. Immediately, he or she sees the vast difference in guns, gear, and clothing compared to the rendezvous (see Chapter 38). Even if the new shooter does not want to participate in this game, he might become a fan.

Silhouette

Silhouette shooting is an advanced aspect of the blackpowder sport. Special guns and specific equipment, often quite expensive, may be required to compete, plus a lot of dedication. Nonetheless, getting a newcomer to one of these events is never a mistake. He or she instantly realizes that all of the important points learned at the basics, from consistency to safety, are in full bloom here.

Matt Wilkes is a young man who has already gained considerable experience in silhouette shooting with his Remington Rolling Block blackpowder cartridge rifle. He got started young, a good time to begin learning.

Rendezvous

Not for everyone, the rendezvous, with its 19th century dress-up, fascinating history study, plethora of interesting gear, and especially great shooting games (see Chapter 39), is a hot cup of delicious tea to some newcomers. In training a new shooter, rendezvous is always connected to the mountain man and the fur trade in the Far West story. Newcomers love going to a rendezvous. They stand all amazed at the display, not only of folks running around in capotes and other 19th century clothing, but of the guns and the shooting.

Collecting

Few of the newcomers I have seen go into collecting anything in the field of blackpowder guns and shooting. But every one of them shows interest in collections. A trip to a museum is never a mistake. A trip to a full-bore museum——such as my favorite, the Buffalo Bill Historical Center in Cody, Wyoming——is always successful.

Small Game

Small-game hunting with a smokepole is always a thrill for new shooters. While some aspects of training are imperative—such as safety and careful loading procedure—hunting is a personal choice. It is offered if possible, never pushed. The girls, if anything, get the most out of it. I don't know why. Maybe it's something inborn from the distant past, where supplying food for the family was so important, no matter how it reached the table. Many pioneer wom-

en not only learned to shoot, but also used their skills to bring important food to the family. That's how Annie Oakley got started. When she found that she could hit quail on the wing with a 22 rifle, she didn't know how special that was. But in time she found out.

Bird Hunting

Like small-game hunting, bird hunting can be a treat for a newcomer, be it shooting mountain grouse with a 32-caliber squirrel rifle or throwing shot patterns at flying targets. I don't do much with handguns or shotguns with newcomers. I consider both of these guns advanced over the rifle, especially the pistol or revolver. The shotgun, too, requires practice and learning the art of lead, swing, trigger touch-off while the gun is still in motion, and so forth. But sometimes bird hunting season is on and a new shooter may wish to give it a try.

Big Game

Big game is not for the beginner until he or she has some experience. Where I live, 14 years of age was the rule for going after big game. I hear that the rule has been challenged and 12, or even 10, is coming in. I have friends in another state who have started all of their children, boys and girls, at age 10, which is the legal minimum. They have done extremely well in the big-game field, but with intensive supervision. My friend, professional hunter Johan Wolvaardt of South Africa, started his son Ricky at age 10 on big game—really big game—not dangerous, but large. Ricky put down a massive Livingstone eland with one well-placed bullet. Since then, he has taken several other wild animals in Africa and will continue to do so.

Knowing when to start a young shooter requires a bit of observation. One of my friends insisted on turning his

An appreciation for collecting can begin with an experience in a museum, such as the Cody Firearms Museum in Cody, Wyoming. The young person starting out on the blackpowder trail can learn to appreciate a painting like this one and what it represents about the old days when all guns were blackpowder.

Starting a new blackpowder shooting in small game or bird hunting can begin by teaching an appreciation for the animals or birds to be hunted. This often means no gun, no shooting, just looking, as with this Canada goose that is not in season.

A good way to start big-game hunting when you're far too young to hunt big game is to go along with an adult—Dad or another responsible person.

Understanding Basic Ballistics

When a new shooter has created his load, putting a correct powder charge downbore after careful measurement with a proper tool, followed by the correct bullet carefully seated all the way down on the powder charge, the next lesson becomes quite simple—what have you made? The basic rules of internal and external ballistics are easily and readily taught at this point. What is going on in the bore when that gun "goes off?" What happens to the projectile as it flies downrange? The rifle becomes a classroom of its own. The student learns how the powder changes from solid to gas and in what amount, generally, that change takes place. Then how that gas pushes on a bullet; how heat is created in the bore; how the bullet does not fly flat from muzzle to target (which beginners often do not understand at all), and what happens when that missile crashes into an invisible wall called the atmosphere. Then, how the bullet carries energy downrange and how that energy is dispersed in a target. The lesson can be taught in the most basic terms that anyone old enough to handle a gun in the first place should be able to understand.

Working with Methods that Improve Accuracy

In the beginning, close-in shooting is the only way to go. It is best done at big targets, especially reactive targets. The local grocery store may have fruit and vegetables that are no longer safe for human consumption. These may go to a pig farm, but some can also be used for shooting. It is important to explain to the young shooter, especially, that this is not littering. Littering is leaving behind trash that is not biodegradable. Blowing up a spoiled tomato or cantaloupe is, instead of damaging to Mother Earth, a bonus. Every molecule will go back into the earth, sometimes after it has been eaten, and if not eaten, it still returns to nature. But it does not have to be fruit and vegetables. Cans full of water make excellent targets that explode on impact and leave no mess behind. They are picked up after

boy into a big-game hunter. The lad had about as much interest in big game as I have in wrestling alligators. As we sat on a hill one afternoon, his father and I glassing the distance for deer, I turned to see the young fellow fully engaged— not in looking for game—but in reading a book he had brought along. Furthermore, there is an age of responsibility and that age varies with individual children. If Sonny Jim cannot handle a simple chore such as taking the garbage out once a day—religiously without forgetting half the time—he is not ready to go into the field toting a deadly tool (my opinion). Conversely, there are kids who are mature at 10 years of age, and under supervision are fully capable

of hunting big game. The big trick is to leave out parental pride and look only at the facts.

Eligibility for the Special Hunt

One of the areas of preparation for young shooters who want to become big game hunters is preparing that person to be eligible to partake in the special blackpowder-only big game hunt. This means, to me, teaching all of the basics, including safety, along with small game and/or bird hunting preceding big game. However, the goal is a good one and can provide a great draw for the newcomer who wants to take part in a "primitive hunt" somewhere down the road.

shooting and properly discarded. However, as useful and important as this basic shooting strategy is, having the new shooter try his or her hand on paper targets is also important.

The concept of sighting-in is vital to the newcomer's education, and it also teaches trajectory management: why we might sight in three inches high at 100 yards to put a bullet back on target downrange. In the meantime, by studying groups on the target, the concept of improving those groups is a natural progression. The newcomer learns that groups can be improved in several ways, from selecting other bullets, for example, to altering the powder type and/or charge. Perhaps going to another sabot will make a difference, or the barrel might require special attention to remove stubborn fouling or plastic wash—even lead deposit (and more rarely copper fouling). Newcomers have no concept of the combination of events that produce accuracy, but they need to know this not only to add to their general body of shooting knowledge, but also to apply accuracy improvement strategy later on.

Basic Firearm Troubleshooting

What not to do is just as important as what to do in this part of new shooter training with a muzzleloader. I say immediately that I am not a gunsmith, let alone a blackpowder gunsmith. Therefore, I will not work on triggers or other parts of the gun, such as a tumbler in the lock, because I do not possess the knowledge and sometimes lack the tools to do this work safely. On the other hand, is it important to teach how to drift a front or rear sight that is off the mark, as well as tighten screws and other minor troubleshooting that does not walk on the road of dangerous tinkering (see Chapter 28).

Maintenance

Maintenance is more than keeping a gun in good repair when it is

When a young person is ready to hit the big-game trail, but not quite eligible yet in his home state, there is always the special ranch hunt, as in Texas. Supervision is imperative, but the young shooter who has proved himself or herself ready can take game on the ranch safely.

Fortunately there are many good people willing to help beginners take the right path in the shooting sports. These scoutmasters are busy teaching about blackpowder guns and how to make them work better, more accurately, and with safety.

taught to a newcomer to the sport of muzzleloading or shooting blackpowder cartridge guns. Of course, it is important to show how a firearm is kept in safe repair, as well as preserving it for a long life rather than allowing deterioration of either metal or wood. Maintenance is also a learning process that can foster a true understanding of firearms, especially when a rifle is "broken down" for cleaning. That process can reveal, for example, a breech plug or even the inner workings of a lock. With a breech plug removed, the new shooter can look down the barrel, actually see the rifling and better understand how the spiral lands spin a bullet.

Internalizing Safety Rules

While safety with all guns is without question the most important point that can be taught to any shooter, the blackpowder firearm provides a strong testimony to all aspects. Protecting eyes and ears is clearly understood when a gun makes smoke and a bit more noise than your average 22-rimfire training rifle. Without instilling fear, respect is taught and safe handling becomes second nature—internalized, in other words.

The greatness of blackpowder shooting becomes even more evident as a seasoned shooter takes on a newcomer to help that person, usually a young boy or girl, in learning the art and science of the sport.

chapter 51 READ ALL ABOUT IT— BLACKPOWDER BOOKS

Finding Your Books

Library, of course. Book store, naturally. But now also the Internet. Libraries, even in my tiny village in Wyoming, can do Interlibrary Loan—I have had books sent to my library from various parts of the world. Bookstores, such as Barnes & Noble, will do a free search for special blackpowder titles. And the Internet is loaded with books for sale, not only through amazon. com, but also the Google search engine and many other outlets, such as Alibris and www.thebookhauler.com, an on-line bookstore. Out-of-print books are available from all of these sources. I have also found good titles at gun shows, along with Friends of the Library sales, where discarded books are sold. The computer has made book searching fast and easy, not only at the local library or bookstore, but also from the comfort of the home office.

What to Pay

Rare books can "set you back" considerable folding green. On the other hand, facsimile editions are often available at a fraction of collector prices. I have several facsimile titles, not only of rare books, but also old-time catalogs, such as the 1944 Gun Digest and 1932 Stoeger's Shooter's Bible.

A Sampling of Titles

Action Shooting Cowboy Style, by John Taffin, Krause Publications, Iola, WI 1999. 320 pp. Slick pages with many photos to illustrate the in-depth coverage of this American shooting game by an author dedicated to the sport.

Advanced Muzzleloader's Guide, by Toby Bridges, Stoeger Publishing Co. NJ, 1985. 256 pp., illus. A guide to muzzleloading rifles, pistols, and shotguns, both flintlock and percussion.

Advanced Black Powder Hunting, by Toby Bridges, Stoeger Publishing Co. N.J. 1998. 276 pp. Guns for the muzzleloader hunter, along with tips on hunting antelope, whitetails, and other game.

The African Adventures: A Return to the Silent Places, by Peter Hathaway Capstick, St. Martin's Press, NY, 1992. 220 pp. This book brings to life four turn-of-the-century adventurers and the savage frontier they braved, including Frederick Selous.

African Hunting and Adventure, by William Charles Baldwin, Books of Zimbabwe, Bulawayo, 1981. 451 pp. Facsimile reprint of the scarce 1863 London edition. African hunting and adventure from Natal to the Zambezi.

After Big Game in Central Africa, by Edouard Foa, St. Martin's Press, NY, 1989. 400 pp. Reprint of the scarce 1899 edition. This sportsman covered 7,200 miles, mostly on foot from the Zambezi delta on the east coast to the mouth of the Congo on the west.

America's Great Gunmakers, by Wayne van Zwoll, Stoeger Publishing Co. NJ, 1992, 288 pp. This book traces in detail the evolution of guns and ammunition in America and the men who formed the companies that produced them.

The American Percussion Schuetzen Rifle, by J. Hamilton and Tom Rowe, Row Publishing Co., 295 Lake Breeze Park, Rochester, NY 14622.

American Military Shoulder Arms: Volume 1, Colonial and Revolutionary War Arms, by George D. Moller, University Press of Colorado, CO. 1993. 538 pp., illus. In-depth study of the shoulder arms of the United States. This volume covers the pre-Colonial period to the end of the American Revolution.

American Military Shoulder Arms: Volume 2, From the 1790s to the End of the Flintlock Period, by George D. Moller, University Press of Colorado,

CO. 1994. 496 pp., illus. Describes rifles, muskets, carbines, and other shoulder arms used by the armed forces of the United States from the 1790s to the end of the flintlock period in the 1840s.

Antique Guns, the Collector's Guide, 2nd Edition, edited by John Traister, Stoeger Publishing Co. NJ, 1994. 320 pp. Covers a vast spectrum of pre-1900 firearms manufactured by U.S. gunmakers as well as Canadian, French, German, Belgian, Spanish and other foreign firms.

Arms Makers of Maryland, by Daniel D. Hartzler, George Shumway Press, PA, 1975. 200 pp. A thorough study of the gunsmiths of Maryland who worked during the late 18th and early 19th centuries.

Baker's Remarks on the Rifle, by Ezekiel Baker, Standard Publications, Inc. (no date provided) Reproduction of his 1835 work, dealing with his views on blackpowder shooting.

Black Powder Cartridge Rifle Magazine, edited by John D. Baird, Spider Hill Press, 1995. Articles excerpted from Black Powder Cartridge Rifles magazine from 1980 to 1983.

Black Powder Guide, 2nd Edition, by George C. Nonte, Jr., Stoeger Publishing Co. NJ, 1991. 288 pp. How-to instructions for selection, repair, and maintenance of muzzleloaders, making your own bullets, restoring and refinishing, shooting techniques.

Blackpowder Hobby Gunsmithing, by Sam Fadala and Dale Storey, DBI Books, Inc. IL. 1994. 256 pp. A how-to-guide for gunsmithing blackpowder pistols, rifles, and shotguns.

Blackpowder Loading Manual, 3rd Edition, edited by Sam Fadala, DBI Books, Inc. IL, 1995. 368 pp. Revised and expanded edition of this landmark blackpowder loading book. Covers hundreds of loads for many blackpowder rifles, handguns and shotguns.

The Blackpowder Notebook, by Sam Fadala, Wolfe Publishing Co., AZ, 1994. 212 pp. For anyone interested in shooting muzzleloaders, this book will help improve scores and obtain accuracy and reliability.

Blue Book of Modern Black Powder Values, by Dennis Adler, Blue Book Publications, Inc., 8009 84th Avenue South, Suite 175, Minneapolis, MN 55425, 1998. A 120-page book devoted to values of blackpowder guns, including color pictures.

The Blunderbuss 1500-1900, by James D. Forman, Museum Restoration Services, Ont., Canada, 1995. About the guns employed as anti-personal weapons throughout the flintlock era.

Boarders Away, Volume II: Firearms of the Age of Fighting Sail, by William Gilkerson, Andrew Mowbray, Inc. Publishers, RI, 1993. 331 pp. Covers pistols, muskets, combustibles, and small cannons used aboard American and European fighting ships, 1626-1826.

Boss & Co. Builders of Best Guns Only, by Donald Dallas, Safari Press, CA, 1996. 336 pp. The famous London gunmaker Boss & Company is chronicled from founding by Thomas Boss (1790-1857) to the present day.

Breech-Loading Carbines of the United States Civil War Period, by Brig. Gen. John Pitman, Armory Publications, WA, 1987. The first in a series of previously unpublished manuscripts originated by the late Brigadier General John Putnam. Exploded drawings showing parts actual size following each sectioned illustration.

The Breech-Loading Single-Shot Rifle, by Major Ned H. Roberts and Kenneth L. Waters, Wolfe Publishing Co., AZ, 1995. 333 pp. A comprehensive and complete history of the evolution of the Schuetzen and single-shot rifle.

British Military Firearms 1650-1850, by Howard L. Blackmore, Stackpole Books, PA, 1994. 224 Another definitive work on British military firearms.

The British Shotgun, Volume 1, 1850-1870, by I.M. Crudington and D.J. Baker, Barrie & Jenkins, London, 1979. 256 pp. An attempt to trace, as accurately as possible, the evolution of the shotgun during its formative years in Great Britain.

The British Shotgun, Volume 2, 1871-1890, by I.M. Crudginton and D.J. Baker, Ashford Press, Southampton, 1989. 250 pp. The second volume of a definitive work on the evolution and manufacture of the British shotgun.

The British Soldier's Firearms from Smoothbore to Rifled Arms, 1850-1864, by Dr. C.H. Roads, R&R Books, Livonia, NY, 1994. 332 pp., illus. A reprint of the classic text covering the development of British military hand and shoulder firearms in the crucial years between 1850 and 1864.

Carbines of the Civil War, by John D. McAulay, Pioneer Press, Union City, TN, 1981. 123 pp. A guide for the student and collector of the colorful arms used by the Federal cavalry.

Cartridges of the World, 11th Edition, by Frank Barnes, edited by Stan Skinner, Krause Publications, Iola, WI, 552 pages. General purpose reference work for collectors, police, scientists and laymen for answers to cartridge identification questions.

Civil War Breech Loading Rifles, by John D. McAulay, Andrew Mowbray, Inc., Lincoln, RI, 1991. 144 pp., illus. Paper covers. All the major breech loading rifles of the Civil War and most, if not all, of the obscure types are detailed, illustrated and set in their historical context.

Civil War Carbines, Volume 2: The Early Years, by John D. McAulay, Andrew Mowbray, Inc., Lincoln, RI, 1991. 144 pp., illus. Paper covers. Covers the carbines made during the exciting years leading up to the outbreak of war and used by the North and South in the conflict.

Civil War Pistols, by John D. McAulay, Andrew Mowbray Inc., Lincoln, RI, 1992. 166 pp., illus. A survey of the handguns used during the American Civil War.

Collector's Illustrated Encyclopedia of the American Revolution, by George C. Neumann and Frank J. Kravic, Rebel Publishing Co., Inc., Texarkana, TX, 1989. 286 pp. A showcase of more than 2,300 artifacts made, worn, and used by those who fought in the War for Independence.

Colonial Frontier Guns, by T.M. Hamilton, Pioneer Press, Union City, TN, 1988. 176 pp., illus. Paper covers. A complete study of early flint muskets of this country.

The Colt Armory, by Ellsworth Grant, Man-at-Arms Bookshelf, Lincoln, RI, 1996. 232 pp. About the manufacturing house that built Colts.

Colt Heritage, by R.L. Wilson, Simon & Schuster, 1979. 358 pp., illus. The official history of Colt firearms 1836 to the present.

Colt Blackpowder Reproductions & Replicas, by Dennis Adler, Blue Book Publications, Inc., 8009 34th Ave. So. Suite 175, Minneapolis, MN 55425. As the title promises, a look at collector-valued Colt firearms—originals and replicas.

Colt Peacemaker British Model, by Keith Cochran, Cochran Publishing Co., Rapid City, SD, 1989. 160 pp. Covers those revolvers Colt squeezed in while completing a large order of revolvers for the U.S. Cavalry in early 1874, to those magnificent cased target revolvers used in the pistol competitions at Bisley Commons in the 1890s.

Colt Peacemaker Encyclopedia, by Keith Cochran, Keith Cochran, Rapid City, SD, 1986. 434 pp. A must-have book for the Peacemaker collector.

Colt Peacemaker Encyclopedia, Volume 2, by Keith Cochran, Cochran Publishing Co., Rapid City, SD, 1992. 416 pp. Included in this volume are extensive notes on engraved, inscribed, historical and noted revolvers, as well as those revolvers used by outlaws, lawmen, movie and television stars.

Colt Percussion Accoutrements 1834-1873, by Robin Rapley, Robin Rapley, Newport Beach, CA, 1994. 432 pp. The complete collector's guide to the identification of Colt percussion accoutrements; including Colt conversions and their values.

Colt Revolvers and the U.S. Navy 1865-1889, by C. Kenneth Moore, Dorrance and Co., Bryn Mawr, PA, 1987. 140 pp. The Navy's use of Colt handguns and other revolvers during this era of change.

Colt Rifles and Muskets from 1847-1870, by Herbert Houze, Krause Publications, Iola, WI, 1996. 192 pp. Discover previously unknown Colt models along with an extensive list of production figures for all models.

Colt's Dates of Manufacture 1837-1978, by R.L. Wilson, published by Maurie Albert, Coburg, Australia; N.A. distributor I.D.S.A. Books, Hamilton, OH, 1983. 61 pp. Valuable pocket guide to the dates of manufacture of Colt firearms up to 1978.

Colt's 100th Anniversary Firearms Manual 1836-1936: A Century of Achievement, Wolfe Publishing Co., Prescott, AZ, 1992. 100 pp. Originally published by the Colt Patent Firearms Co., this booklet covers the history, manufacturing procedures and the guns of the first 100 years of the genius of Samuel Colt.

The Colt Whitneyville-Walker Pistol, by Lt. Col. Robert D. Whittington, Brownlee Books, Hooks, TX, 1984. 96 pp., illus. Limited edition. A study of the pistol and associated characters 1846-1851.

The Complete Blackpowder Handbook, five editions, by Sam Fadala, Krause Publications, Iola WI. 1996. 416 pp. Expanded and refreshed edition of the definitive book on the subject of blackpowder.

The Complete Guide to Game Care and Cookery, by Sam Fadala, four editions, Krause Publications, WI. 1994. 320 pp. Over 500 photos illustrating the care of wild game in the field and at home with a separate recipe section providing over 400 tested recipes. A must-have for the blackpowder hunter who wants the best from his game.

Confederate Revolvers, by William A. Gary, Taylor Publishing Co., Dallas, TX, 1987. 174 pp. Comprehensive work on the rarest of Confederate weapons.

Cowboy Action Shooting, by Charley Gullett, Wolfe Publishing Co., Prescott, AZ, 1995. 400 pp. Comprehensive coverage of the guns, loads, tactics, fun and flavor of this Old West era competition.

Development of the Henry Cartridge and Self-Contained Cartridges for the Toggle-Link Winchesters, by R. Bruce McDowell, A.M.B., Metuchen, NJ, 1984. 69 pp. From powder and ball to the self-contained metallic cartridge.

Early American Waterfowling 1700's-1930, by Stephen Miller, Winchester Press, NJ, 1986. 256 pp. Two centuries of literature and art devoted to the nation's beloved hunting sport of waterfowling.

Early Indian Trade Guns: 1625-1775, by T.M. Hamilton, Museum of the Great Plains, Lawton, OK, 1968. 34 pp. Detailed descriptions of subject arms, compiled from early records and from the study of remnants found in Indian country.

East Africa and its Big Game, by Captain Sir John C. Willowghby, Wolfe Publishing Co., Prescott, AZ, 1999. 312 pp. A deluxe limited edition reprint of the scarce 1889 edition of a sporting trip narrative from Zanzibar to the borders of the Masai.

English Pistols: The Armories of H.M. Tower of London Collection, by Howard L. Blackmore, Arms and Armour Press, London, England, 1985. 64 pp. All the pistols described and pictured are from this famed collection by this expert on the subject.

European Firearms in Swedish Castles, by Kaa Wennberg, Bohuslaningens Boktryckeri AB, Uddevalla, Sweden, 1986. 156 pp. The famous collection of Count Keller, the Ettersburg Castle collection, and others. English text.

Fifteen Years in the Hawken Lode, by John D. Baird, The Gun Room Press, Highland Park, NJ, 1976. 120 pp. A collection of thoughts and observations gained from many years of intensive study of the guns from the shop of the Hawken brothers.

1851 Colt Navies, by Nathan L. Swayze, The Gun Room Press, Highland Park, NJ, 1993. 243 pp. A study of the different 1851 Colt Navy models.

Flayderman's Guide to Antique American Firearms...and Their Values, 8th Edition, by Norm Flayderman, Krause Publications, Iola, WI, 1994. 672 pp. Updated edition of this bible of the antique gun field.

Flintlock Fowlers: The First Guns Made in America, by Tom Grinslade, Scurlock Publishing Company, 1293 Myrtle Spring Road Texarkana, TX 75503. A faithful work on early American smoothbores in six categories: New England, Club-Butt, Hudson Valley, British-style, Kentucky, and Unique. A real labor of love loaded with solid information on the subject.

Frank and George Freund and the Sharps Rifle, by Gerald O. Kelver, Gerald O. Kelver, Brighton, CO, 1986. 60 pp. A guide to the Sharps rifle.

French Military Weapons, 1717-1938, by Major James E. Hicks, N. Flayderman & Co., Publishers, New Milford, CT, 1973. 281 pp. Firearms, swords, bayonets, ammunition, artillery, ordnance equipment of the French army.

The Frontier Rifleman, by H.B. LaCrosse Jr., Pioneer Press, Union City, TN, 1989. 183 pp. Dealing with the subject promised by the title, riflemen of the frontier era in America.

Game Guns & Rifles: Percussion to Hammerless Ejector in Britain, by Richard Akehurst, Trafalgar Square, N. Pomfret, VT, 1993. 192 pp. Long considered a classic, this important reprint covers the period of British gunmaking between 1830-1900.

George Schreyer, Sr. and Jr., Gunmakers of Hanover, Pennsylvania, by George Shumway, George Shumway Publishers, York, PA, 1990. 160 pp. This monograph is a detailed photographic study of almost all known surviving long rifles and smoothbore guns made by highly regarded gunsmiths George Schreyer, Sr. and Jr.

The Golden Age of Remington, by Robert W.D. Ball, Krause Publications, Iola, WI, 1995. 208 pp. For Remington collectors or firearms historians, this book provides a pictorial history of Remington through World War I. Includes value guide.

Grand Old Shotguns, by Don Zutz, Shotgun Sports Magazine, Auburn, CA, 1955. 136 pp. Don Zutz is one of the country's most recognized authorities on shotguns. This is a study of the great smoothbores, their history and how and why they were discontinued. Find out which were the most sought-after and which were the best shooters.

Great British Gunmakers: The Mantons, 1782-1878, by D.H.L. Back, Historical Firearms, Norwich, England, 1994. 218 pp. Contains detailed descriptions of all the firearms made by members of this famous family.

Great Irish Gunmakers: Messrs. Rigby, 1760-1869, by D.H.L. Back, Historical Firearms, Norwich, England, 1993. 196 pp. The history of this famous firm of Irish gunmakers illustrated with a wide selection of Rigby arms.

Great Shooters of the World, by Sam Fadala, Stoeger Publishing Co., 288-page book offers gun enthusiasts an overview of the men and women who have forged the history of firearms over the past 150 years.

A Guide to the Maynard Breechloader, by George J. Layman, Ayer, MA, 1993. 125 pp. Dedicated entirely to the Maynard family of breech-loading firearms. Coverage of the arms is given from the 1850s through the 1880s.

Gun and Camera in Southern Africa, by H. Anderson Bryden, Wolfe Publishing Co., Prescott, AZ, 1989. 201 pp. A limited edition reprint. The year was 1893 and author Bryden wandered for a year in Bechuanaland and the Kalahari Desert hunting the white rhino, lechwe, eland, and more.

The Gun and Its Development, by W.W. Greener, Bonanza Books reprint, no date. 807 pp. Greener's classic on firearms through the ages. A must have book.

Gun Collecting, by Geoffrey Boothroyd, Sportsman's Press, London, 1989. 208 pp. Comprehensive list of 19th century British gunmakers and gunsmiths.

Gun Digest, multiple annual editions, edited by Ken Ramage, Krause Publications, Iola, WI, 2001. 568 pp. Full-scale catalogue of firearms, including blackpowder guns, plus articles of interest for any shooter.

Gun Tools, Their History and Identification, by James B. Shaffer, Lee A. Rutledge, and R. Stephen Dorsey, Collector's Library, Eugene, OR, 1992. 375 pp. Written history of foreign and domestic gun tools from the flintlock period to WWII.

Gunmakers of London 1350-1850, by Howard L. Blackmore, George Shumway Publisher, York, PA, 1986. 222 pp. A listing of all the known workmen of gun making in the first 500 years, plus a history of the guilds, cutlers, armourers, founders, blacksmiths, etc. 260 gunmakers are illustrated.

Guns and Gunmaking Tools of Southern Appalachia, by John Rice Irwin, Schiffer Publishing Ltd., 1983. 118 pp. An illustrated guide to firearms from this unique American setting.

The Story of the Kentucky Rifle: Guns of the Wild West, by George Markham, Sterling Publishing Co., New York, NY, 1993. 160 pp. As the title promises, information on this great rifle of the Golden Age of American firearms.

Firearms of the American Frontier, 1849-1917: Gunsmiths of Illinois, by Curtis L. Johnson, George Shumway Publishers, York, PA, 1995. 160 pp. Genealogical information provided for nearly one thousand gunsmiths. Contains hundreds of illustrations of rifles and other guns, of handmade origin, from Illinois.

The Gunsmiths of Manhattan, 1625-1900: A Checklist of Tradesmen, by Michael H. Lewis, Museum Restoration Service, Bloomfield, Ont., Canada, 1991. 40 pp. This listing of more than 700 men in the arms trade in New York City prior to about the end of the 19th century will provide a guide for identification and further research.

The Handgun, by Geoffrey Boothroyd, David and Charles, North Pomfret, VT, 1989. 566 pp. Every chapter deals with an important period in handgun history from the 14th century to the present.

The Hawken Rifle: Its Place in History, by Charles E. Hanson, Jr., The Fur Press, Chadron, NE, 1979. 104 pp. A definitive work on this famous rifle.

Hawken Rifles, The Mountain Man's Choice, by John D. Baird, The Gun Room Press, Highland Park, NJ, 1976. 95 pp. Covers the rifles developed for the Western fur trade. Numerous specimens described and shown photographically.

Historic Pistols: The American Martial Flintlock 1760-1845, by Samuel E. Smith and Edwin W. Bitter, The Gun Room Press, Highland Park, NJ, 1986. 353 pp. Covers over 70 makers and 163 models of American martial arms.

Historical Hartford Hardware, by William W. Dalrymple, Colt Collector Press, Rapid City, SD, 1976. 42 pp. Guns of the Hartford factory.

The History and Development of Small Arms Ammunition, Volume 1, by George A. Hoyem, Armory Publications, Oceanside, CA, 1991. 230 pp. Historical treatise on ammunition, including military musket, rifle, car-

bine and primitive machinegun cartridges of the 18th and 19th centuries, together with the firearms that chambered them.

The History and Development of Small Arms Ammunition, Volume 2, by George A. Hoyem, Armory Publications, Oceanside, CA, 1991. 303 pp. Covers the blackpowder military centerfire rifle, carbine, machinegun and volley gun ammunition used in 28 nations and dominions, together with the firearms that chambered them.

The History of Winchester Firearms 1866-1992, 6th Edition, updated, expanded, and revised by Thomas Henshaw, New Win Publishing, NJ, 1993. This 280-page classic is the standard reference for all collectors and others seeking the facts about any Winchester firearm, old or new.

History of Winchester Repeating Arms Company, by Herbert G. Houze, Krause Publications, Iola, WI, 1994. 800 pp. The complete Winchester history from 1856-1981.

Hodgdon Data Manual, Hodgdon Powder Co., Shawnee Mission, KS, 1993. 797 pp. Includes Hercules, Winchester and Dupont powders; data on cartridge cases; loads; silhouette; shotshell; Pyrodex and blackpowder; conversion factors; weight equivalents, etc.

Home Gunsmithing the Colt Single Action Revolvers, by Loren W. Smith, Ray Riling Arms Books, Co., Phila., PA, 1995. 119 pp. Affords the Colt Single Action owner detailed, pertinent information on the operating and servicing of this famous and historic handgun.

How-To's for the Black Powder Cartridge Rifle Shooter, by Paul A. Matthews, Wolfe Publishing Co., Prescott, AZ, 1995. 45 pp. Covers lube recipes, good bore cleaners and over-powder wads. Tips include compressing powder charges, combating wind resistance, improving ignition and much more from a highly knowledgeable shooter.

Hunting in Many Lands, by Theodore Roosevelt and George Bird Grinnell, The Boone and Crockett Club, Dumfries, VA, 1987. 447 pp. Limited edition reprint of this 1895 classic work on hunting in Africa, India, Mongolia, etc.

Illustrations of United States Military Arms 1776-1903, and Their Inspectors' Marks, compiled by Turner Kirkland, Pioneer Press, Union City, TN. 367 pp. Reprinted from the 1949 Bannerman catalog. Valuable information for both the advanced and beginning collector.

Indian Hunts and Indian Hunters of the Old West, by Dr. Frank C. Hibben, Safari Press, Long Beach, CA, 1989. 228 pp. Tales of some of the most famous American Indian hunters of the Old West as told to the author by an old Navajo hunter.

Indian War Cartridge Pouches, Boxes and Carbine Boots, by R. Stephen Dorsey, Collector's Library, Eugene, OR, 1993. 156 pp. The key reference work to the cartridge pouches, boxes, carbine sockets and boots of the Indian War period 1865-1890.

An Introduction to the Civil War Small Arms, by Earl J. Coates and Dean S. Thomas, Thomas Publishing Co., Gettysburg, PA, 1990. 96 pp. The small arms carried by the individual soldier during the Civil War.

Jaeger Rifles, by George Shumway, George Shumway Publisher, York, PA, 1994. 108 pp. Thirty-six articles previously published in Muzzle Blasts are reproduced here. They deal with late 17th- and 18th-century rifles from Vienna, Carlsbad, Bavaria, Saxony, Brandenburg, Suhl, North-Central Germany, and the Rhine Valley.

Journals of Lewis & Clark, by Bernard DeVoto, Houghton Mifflin, Boston, MA, 1953. 506 pp. author presents the Journals intact, with studious and well-researched comments on the adventures of Lewis & Clark.

Journal of a Trapper, by Osborne Russell, edited by Aubrey L. Haines, University of Nebraska Press, Lincoln, NE, 1965. 191 pp, Haines leaves intact the fascinating report of this real life mountain man. Included: good index and notes by the author, with considerable sources listed.

The Kentucky Rifle, by Captain John G.W. Dillin, George Shumway Publisher, York, PA, 1993. Well-known book was the first attempt to tell the story of the American long rifle. This edition retains the original text and illus-

trations with supplemental footnotes provided by Dr. George Shumway.

Loading the Black Powder Rifle Cartridge, by Paul A Matthews, Wolfe Publishing Co., Prescott, AZ, 1993. 121 pp. Author Matthews brings the blackpowder cartridge shooter valuable information on the basics, including cartridge care, lubes and moulds, powder charges and developing and testing loads in his usual authoritative style.

Loading the Peacemaker, by Dave Scovill, Wolfe Publishing Co., Prescott, AZ, 1995. 227 pp. A comprehensive work about the most famous revolver ever made, including extensive load data by a trusted expert on the subject.

Longrifles of North Carolina, by John Bivens, George Shumway Publisher, York, PA, 1988. 256 pp. Covers art and evolution of the rifle, immigration and trade movements. Committee of Safety gunsmiths, characteristics of the North Carolina rifle.

Longrifles of Pennsylvania, Jefferson, Clarion & Elk Counties, by Russel H. Harringer, George Shumway Publisher, York, PA, 1984. 200 pp. Treatment in great detail of specific long rifles and gunsmiths of Pennsylvania by a dedicated student of the guns, the period, and the geographical area.

Lyman Cast Bullet Handbook, 3rd Edition, edited by C. Kenneth Ramage, Lyman Publications, Middlefield, CT, 1980. 416 pp. Information on more than 5000 tested cast bullet loads and 19 pages of trajectory and wind drift tables for cast bullets.

Lyman Black Powder Handbook, 2nd Edition, edited by Sam Fadala, Lyman Products Corporation, Middlefield, CT, 2001, 336 pp. Comprehensive load information for the modern blackpowder shooter, with hundreds of loads for a wide range of calibers.

The Manufacture of Gunflints, by Sydney B.J. Skertchly, facsimile reprint with new introduction by Seymour de Lotbiniere, Museum Restoration Service, Ontario, Canada, 1984. 90 pp. Limited edition reprinting of the very scarce London edition of 1879.

Marlin Firearms: A History of the Guns and the Company, by William S. Brophy. The Stackpole Publishing Com-

pany. From the Introduction: "This book was written to try to collect and preserver for the Marlin collector, and the historian, that information about the Marlin Firearms Company now in print, or known to exist." The author could have left out the word "try." He has done a masterful job of telling the Marlin story, beginning with the blackpowder cartridge era.

Massachusetts Military Shoulder Arms, 1784-1877, by George D. Moller, Andrew Mowbray Publisher, Lincoln, RI, 1989. 250 pp. A scholarly and heavily researched study of the military shoulder arms used by Massachusetts' shooters during the 90-year period following the Revolutionary War.

Military Bolt Action Rifles, 1841-1918, by Donald B. Webster, Museum Restoration Service, Alexander Bay, NY, 1993. 150 pp. A photographic survey of the principal rifles and carbines of the European and Asiatic powers of the last half of the 19th century and the first years of the 20th century.

Military Handguns of France, 1858-1958, by Eugene Medlin and Jean Huon, Excalibur Publications, Latham, NY, 1994. 124 pp. The first book written in English that provides students of arms with a thorough history of French military handguns.

The More Complete Cannoneer, by M.C. Switlik, Museum & Collectors Specialties Co., Monroe, MI, 1990. 199 pp. Compiled agreeably to the regulations for the U.S. War Department, 1861, and containing current observations on the use of antique cannon.

More Single Shot Rifles, by James C. Grant, The Gun Room Press, Highland Park, NJ, 1976. 324 pp. Details the guns made by Frank Wesson, Milt Farrow, Holden, Borchardt, Stevens, Remington, Winchester, Ballard and Peabody-Martini.

Mortimer, the Gunmakers, 1753-1923, by H. Lee Munson, Andrew Mowbray Inc., Lincoln, RI, 1992. 320 pp. Seen through a single, dominant, English gunmaking dynasty this fascinating study provides a window into the classical era of firearms artistry.

Muzzleloading for Deer & Turkey, by Dave Ehrig, Stackpole Books. Ehrig has done a fine job of instruction on blackpowder hunting for deer and turkey, with a good clear writing style and a genuine spirit of this special kind of hunting. The book is loaded with useful tables and data.

The Muzzle-Loading Cap Lock Rifle, by Ned H. Roberts, reprinted by Wolfe Publishing Co., Prescott, AZ, 1991. Originally published in 1940, this fascinating study of the muzzle-loading caplock rifle covers rifles on the frontier to hunting rifles, including the famous Hawken.

The Muzzle-Loading Rifle...Then and Now, by Walter M. Cline, National Muzzle Loading Rifle Association, Friendship, IN, 1991. 161 pp. This extensive compilation of the muzzleloading rifle exhibits accumulative, preserved data concerning the development of the hallowed old arms of the Southern highlands.

Naval Percussion Locks and Primers, by Lt. J.A. Dahlgren, Museum Restoration Service, Bloomfield, Canada, 1996. 140 pp. First published as an Ordnance Memoranda in 1853, this is the finest existing study of percussion locks and primers origin and development.

Ned H. Roberts and the Schuetzen Rifle, edited by Gerald O. Kelver, Brighton, CO, 1982. 99 pp. A compilation of the writings of Major Ned H. Roberts, which appeared in various gun magazines.

Old Guns and Whispering Ghosts, by Jesse L. Hardin, Shoot Magazine Corporation Publishing Company, 7154 W. State Street, No. 384, Boise, ID 83714. Fascinating stories of the Old West and the guns that attended the times, with excellent artwork and photography on the topic. A worthwhile addition to the library of any shooter interested in blackpowder rifles, shotguns, and handguns of the period. Readable and memorable.

The Paper Jacket, by Paul Matthews, Wolfe Publishing Co., Prescott, AZ, 1991. Paper covers. Up-to-date and accurate information about paper-patched bullets by an author highly regarded in the field of blackpowder cartridge shooting.

The Paper Patched Bullet, by Randolph S. Wright, C. Sharps Arms Publishers, 1985. A 19-page booklet concerning paper patches, bullets and swaging.

Patents for Inventions, Class 119 (Small Arms), 1855-1930. British Patent Office, Armory Publications, Oceanside, CA, 1993. 7 volume set. Contains 7,980 abridged patent descriptions and their sectioned line drawings, plus a 37-page alphabetical index of the patentees.

Paterson Colt Pistol Variations, by R.L. Wilson and R. Phillips, Jackson Arms Co., Dallas, TX, 1979. 250 pp. A book about the different models and barrel lengths in the Paterson Colt story.

Pennsylvania Longrifles of Note, by George Shumway, George Shumway, Publisher, York, PA, 1977. 63 pp. Illustrates and describes rifles from a number of Pennsylvania rifle-making schools.

The Pennsylvania Rifle, by Samuel E. Dyke, Sutter House, Lititz, PA, 1975. 61 pp., illus. Paper covers. $5.00. History and development, from the hunting rifle of the Germans who settled the area. Contains a full listing of all known Lancaster, PA, gunsmiths from 1729 through 1815.

The Pennsylvania-Kentucky Rifle, by Henry J. Kaufman, Stackpole Books, 1950. The development and use of the rifle in Pennsylvania in early America.

The Pitman Notes on U.S. Martial Small Arms and Ammunition, 1776-1933, Volume 2, Revolvers and Automatic Pistols, by Brig. Gen. John Pitman, Thomas Publications, Gettysburg, PA, 1990. 192 pp., illus. A most important primary source of information on United States military small arms and ammunition.

The Plains Rifle, by Charles Hanson, Gun Room Press, Highland Park, NJ, 1989. 169 pp., illus. All rifles that were made with the plainsman in mind, including pistols.

The Powder Flask Book, by Ray Riling, R&R Books, Livonia, NY, 1993. 514 pp., illus. The complete book on flasks of the 19th century. Exactly scaled pictures of 1,600 flasks are illustrated.

Purdey's, the Guns and the Family, by Richard Beaumont, David and Charles, Pomfert, VT, 1984. 248 pp., illus. Records the history of the Purdey family from 1814 to today, how the guns were and are built, and daily functioning of the factory.

The Rare and Valuable Antique Arms, by James E. Serven, Pioneer Press, Union City, TN, 1976. 106 pp., illus. Paper covers. $4.95. A guide to the collector in deciding which direction his collecting should go, investment value, historic interest, mechanical ingenuity, high art or personal preference.

The Recollections of an Elephant Hunter, 1864-1875, by William Finaughty, Books of Zimbabwe, Bulawayo, Zimbabwe, 1980. 244 pp., illus. Reprint of the scarce 1916 privately published edition. The early game hunting exploits of William Finaughty in Matabeleland and Nashonaland.

Recreating the American Longrifle, by William Buchele, et al., George Shumway, Publisher, York, PA, 1983. 175 pp., illus. Includes full-scale plans for building a Kentucky rifle.

Revolvers of the British Services 1854-1954, by W.H.J. Chamberlain and A.W.F. Taylerson, Museum Restoration Service, Ottawa, Canada, 1989. 80 pp., illus. Covers the types issued among many of the United Kingdom's naval, land or air services.

The Revolving Rifles, by Edsall James, Pioneer Press, Union City, TN, 1975. 23 pp. Valuable information on revolving cylinder rifles, from the earliest matchlock forms to the latest models of Colt and Remington.

Rhode Island Arms Makers & Gunsmiths, by William O. Archibald, Andrew Mowbray, Inc., Lincoln, RI, 1990. 108 pp., illus. A serious and informative study of an important area of American arms making.

The Rifle and the Hound in Ceylon, by S.W. Baker, Arno Press, 1967. Reprint of 19th-century work, a classic by an ivory hunter.

Sam Colt's Own Record 1847, by John Parsons, Wolfe Publishing Co., Prescott, AZ, 1992. 167 pp. Chronologically presented, the correspondence published here completes the account of the manufacture, in 1847, of the Walker Model Colt revolver.

Schuetzen Rifles, History and Loading, by Gerald O. Kelver, Gerald O. Kelver, Publisher, Brighton, CO, 1972. Reference work on these rifles, their bullets, loading, telescopic sights, accuracy, etc. A limited, numbered edition.

Scottish Firearms, by Claude Blair and Robert Woosnam-Savage, Museum Restoration Service, Bloomfield, Ont., Canada, 1995. 52 pp. Revision of the first book devoted entirely to Scottish firearms is supplemented by a register of surviving Scottish long guns.

Sharps Firearms, by Frank Seller, Frank M. Seller, Denver, CO. 1982, 358 pp. Traces the development of Sharps firearms with full range of guns made including all martial variations.

Sharps Rifle: The Gun That Shaped American Destiny, by Martin Rywell, Pioneer Press, 1979. The history, use and functioning of the Sharps rifle.

Shooting the Blackpowder Cartridge Rifle, by Paul A. Matthews, Wolfe Publishing Co., Prescott, AZ, 1994. 129 pp. A general discourse on shooting the blackpowder cartridge rifle and the procedure required to make a particular rifle perform. Written by an expert.

The Shotgun: History and Development, by Geoffrey Boothroyd, Safari Press, Huntington Beach, CA, 1995. 240 pp. The first volume in a series that traces the development of the British shotgun from the 17th century onward.

Sidelocks & Boxlocks, by Geoffrey Boothroyd, Sand Lake Press, Amity, OR, 1991. 271 pp. The story of the classic British shotgun.

Pistol Simeon North: First Official Maker of the United States, by S. North and R. North, The Gun Room Press, Highland Park, NJ, 1972. 207 pp. Reprint of the rare first edition.

Sixgun Cartridges and Loads, by Elmer Keith, The Gun Room Press, Highland Park, NJ, 1986. 151 pp. A manual covering the selection, uses and loading of the most suitable and popular revolver cartridges. Originally published in 1936. Reprint.

Spencer Firearms, by Roy Marcot, R&R Books, Livonia, NY, 1995. 237 pp. The definitive work on one of the most famous Civil War firearms.

The Sporting Rifle and Its Projectiles, by James Forsyth, Buckskin Press, 1978. This reprint of an 1863 text is a study in early ballistic data.

SPG Lubricants: BP Cartridge Reloading Primer, by Mike Venturino & Steve Garbe, SPG Lubricant, MT, 1992. 116-pages. This book is filled with topflight information on the subject of blackpowder cartridge reloading.

Springfield Shoulder Arms 1795-1865, by Claud E. Fuller, S. & S. Firearms, Glendale, NY, 1986. 76 pp. Exact reprint of the scarce 1930 edition of one of the most definitive works on Springfield flintlock and percussion muskets ever published.

Standard Catalog of Firearms, compiled by Ned Schwing, Krause Publications, Iola, WI, 2001. 1,334 pp. Huge pricing guide with 6,000 photos and 12,000 models covered. Includes a color gallery and 80,000 "real world" prices.

The Steel Canvas: Art of American Arms, by R.L. Wilson, Random House, NY, 1995. 384 pp., illus. Presented here for the first time is the breathtaking panorama of America's extraordinary engravers and embellishers of arms, from the 1700s to modern times.

The Sumptuous Flaske, by Herbert G. Houze, Andrew Mowbray, Inc., Lincoln, RI, 1989. 158 pp. Catalog of a recent show at the Buffalo Bill Historical Center bringing together some of the finest European and American powder flasks of the 16th to 19th centuries.

Tales of the Big Game Hunters, selected and introduced by Kenneth Kemp, The Sportsman's Press, London, 1986. 209 pp. Writings by some of the best-known hunters and explorers, among them: Frederick.

United States Martial Flintlocks, by Robert M. Reilly, Andrew Mowbray, Inc., Lincoln, RI, 1986. 263 pp. A comprehensive illustrated history of the flintlock in America from the Revolution to the demise of the system.

U.S. Military Arms: Dates of Manufacture from 1795, by George Madis, David Madis, Dallas, TX, 1989. 64 pp. Lists all U.S. military arms of collector interest alphabetically, covering about 250 models.

U.S. Military Small Arms 1816-1865, by Robert M. Reilly, The Gun Room Press, Highland Park, NJ, 1983. 270 pp. Covers every known type of primary and secondary martial firearms used by Federal forces.

Weapons of the Highland Regiments 1740-1780, by Anthony D. Darling, Museum Restoration Service, Bloomfield, Canada, 1996. 28 pp. This study deals with the formation and arming of the famous Highland regiments.

The Whitney Firearms, by Claud Fuller, Standard Publications, Huntington, WV, 1946. 334 pp. An authoritative history of all Whitney arms and their maker. Highly recommended. An exclusive with Ray Riling Arms Books Co.

Winchester: An American Legend, by R.L. Wilson, Random House, New York, NY, 1991. 403 pp. The official history of Winchester firearms from 1849 to the present.

The Winchester Book, by George Madis, David Madis Gun Book Distributor, Dallas, TX, 1986. 650 pp. A new, revised 25th anniversary edition of this classic book on Winchester firearms. Complete serial ranges have been added.

Winchester Dates of Manufacture 1849-1984, by George Madis, Art & Reference House, Brownsboro, TX, 1984. 59 pp. A most useful work, compiled from records of the Winchester factory.

The Winchester Era, by David Madis, Art & Reference House, Brownsville, TX, 1984. 100 pp. Story of the Winchester Company, management, employees, etc.

The Winchester Handbook, by George Madis, Art & Reference House, Lancaster, TX, 1982. 287 pp. The complete line of Winchester guns, with dates of manufacture, serial numbers, etc.

Winchester Lever Action Repeating Firearms, Volume 1, The Models of 1866, 1873 and 1876, by Arthur Pirkie, North Cape Publications, Tustin, CA, 1995. 112 pp. Complete, part-by-part description, including dimensions, finishes, markings and variations throughout the production run of these fine, collectible guns.

The Winchester Single-Shot, by John Campbell, Andrew Mowbray, Inc., Lincoln, RI, 1995. 272 pp. Covers every important aspect of this highly collectible firearm.

Periodicals of Interest to Blackpowder Shooters

American Firearms Industry
Nat'l. Assn. of Federally Licensed Firearms Dealers, 2455 E. Sunrise Blvd., Suite 916, Ft. Lauderdale, FL 33304. For firearms retailers, distributors and manufacturers. Contains reviews of blackpowder firearms and attending software and hardware.

American Gunsmith
Belvoir Publications, Inc., 75 Holly Hill Lane, Greenwich, CT 06836-2626. 03-661-6111. Technical journal of firearms repair and maintenance.

American Handgunner
Publisher's Development Corp., 12345 World Trade Drive, San Diego, CA 92128. 800-537-3006. Articles for handgun enthusiasts, competitors, police and hunters. Includes blackpowder handguns.

American Hunter
National Rifle Assn., 11250 Waples Mill Rd., Fairfax, VA 22030. Wide scope of hunting articles, including blackpowder hunts.

American Rifleman
National Rifle Assn., 11250 Waples Mill Rd., Fairfax, VA 22030 (Same address for both). Firearms articles of all kinds, blackpowder guns included.

American Survival Guide
McMullen Angus Publishing, Inc., 774 S. Placentia Ave., Placentia, CA 92670-6846. 714-572-2255; FAX: 714-572-1864. Informative information for hunters, including blackpowder hunters.

Arms Collecting
Museum Restoration Service, P.O. Box 70, Alexandria Bay, NY 13607-0070. Pertinent information on antique firearms.

The Backwoodsman Magazine
P.O. Box 627, Westcliffe, CO 81252. Subjects include muzzle-loading, woodslore, primitive survival, trapping, homesteading, blackpowder cartridge guns, 19th-century how-to.

Black Powder Cartridge News
SPG, Inc., P.O. Box 761, Livingston, MT 59047. Phone/Fax: 406-222-8416. For the blackpowder cartridge enthusiast.

Blackpowder Hunting Magazine
Intl. Blackpowder Hunting Assn., P.O. Box 1180Z, Glenrock, WY 82637. 307-436-9817. How-to and where-to features by experts on hunting; shooting; ballistics;

traditional and modern blackpowder rifles, shotguns, pistols, and cartridges.

Black Powder Times
P.O. Box 234, Lake Stevens, WA 98258. Tabloid newspaper for blackpowder activities; test reports.

Blade Magazine
Krause Publications, 700 East State St., Iola, WI 54990-0001. A magazine for all enthusiasts of handmade, factory and antique knives. Information on old-time knives.

Cartridge Journal
Robert Mellichamp, 907 Shirkmere, Houston, TX 77008. Includes blackpowder cartridges.

Deer & Deer Hunting
Krause Publications, 700 E. State St., Iola, WI 54990-0001. For the serious deer hunter. Web site: www.krause.com Good information for blackpowder deer hunters.

The Derringer Peanut
The National Association of Derringer Collectors, P.O. Box 20572, San Jose, CA 95160. A newsletter dedicated to developing the best derringer information.

Field & Stream
Time4 Media, Two Park Ave., New York, NY 10016/212-779-5000. Shooting column each issue. Articles on hunting and fishing. Occasional blackpowder hunting and shooting information.

The Fouling Shot
Official journal of the Cast Bullet Association. The Cast Bullet Association 12857 S. Road, Hoyt, KS 66440-9116. Email: cbamemdir@castbulletassoc.org. Website: www.castbulletassoc.org.

Fur-Fish-Game
A.R. Harding Pub. Co., 2878 E. Main St., Columbus, OH 43209. Practical guidance regarding trapping, fishing and hunting. Down to earth information useful to blackpowder hunters.

Gun List
700 E. State St., Iola, WI 54990. $37.98 yr. (26 issues); $66.98 2 yrs. (52 issues). Indexed market publication for firearms collectors and active shooters; guns, supplies and services. Web site: www.krause.com Every issue includes blackpowder guns for sale.

Gunmaker
ACGG, P.O. Box 812, Burlington, IA 52601-0812. The journal of custom gunmaking. Of interest to those who desire information on various aspects of custom gunmaking.

The Gunrunner
Div. of Kexco Publ. Co. Ltd., Box 565G, Lethbridge, Alb., Canada T1J 3Z4. $23.00 yr. Monthly newspaper, listing everything from antiques to artillery.

Gun Show Calendar
700 E. State St., Iola, WI 54990. Gun shows listed; chronologically and by state. Website: www.krause.com Great for the collector of any type fireararm.

Gun Week
Second Amendment Foundation, P.O. Box 488, Station C, Buffalo, NY 14209. $35.00 yr. U.S. and possessions; $45.00 yr. other countries. Tabloid paper on guns, hunting, shooting and collecting (36 issues). Includes blackpowder information.

Gun World
Y-Visionary Publishing, LP 265 South Anita Drive, Ste. 120, Orange, CA. For the hunting, reloading and shooting enthusiast. Blackpowder guns included.

Guns & Ammo
Primedia, 6420 Wilshire Blvd., Los Angeles, CA 90048/213-782-2780. Guns, shooting, and technical articles. Data on blackpowder guns.

Guns Magazine
Publishers Development Corporation, 12345 World Trade Drive, San Diego, CA 92128. 800-537-3006. In-depth articles on a wide range of guns, shooting equipment and related accessories for gun collectors, hunters and shooters. Information on all types of guns.

Handguns
Primedia, 6420 Wilshire Blvd., Los Angeles, CA 90048. 323-782-2868. $15.97 yr. For the handgunning and shooting enthusiast. Occasional information on blackpowder sidearms.

Handloader
Wolfe Publishing Co., 2626 Stearman Road, Ste. A, Prescott, AZ 86301. 520-445-7810. The journal of ammunition reloading. Solid information on blackpowder cartridge reloading and blackpowder cartridge profiles.

Journal of the Historical Breechloading Small Arms Assn.

Published annually. P.O. Box 12778, London, SE1 6XB, England. Articles for the collector plus mailings of short articles on specific arms, reprints, newsletters, etc. Blackpowder guns included.

The Marlin Collector

R.W. Paterson, 407 Lincoln Bldg., 44 Main St., Champaign, IL 61820. Information on blackpowder cartridge guns from the famous gunmaker.

Muzzle Blasts Magazine

National Muzzle Loading Rifle Assn., P.O. Box 67, Friendship, IN 47021. 812-667-5131. For the blackpowder shooter. Includes information on blackpowder shoots.

Muzzleloader Magazine

Scurlock Publishing Co., Inc., Dept. Gun, Route 5, Box 347-M, Texarkana, TX 75501.A publication for blackpowder shooters.

North American Hunter

P.O. Box 3401, Minnetonka, MN 55343. 612-936-9333. Articles on all types of North American hunting, including blackpowder guns and seasons.

Outdoor Life

Time4 Media, Two Park Ave., New York, NY 10016. Extensive coverage of hunting and shooting, including adventure articles, occasional blackpowder information.

Petersen's HUNTING Magazine

Primedia, 6420 Wilshire Blvd., Los Angeles, CA 90048. 323-782-2868. Hunting articles for all game, occasional blackpowder.

Precision Shooting

Precision Shooting, Inc., 222 McKee St., Manchester, CT 06040. U.S. Journal of the International Benchrest Shooters, and target shooting in general. Also considerable coverage of varmint shooting, as well as big bore, small bore, schuetzen, lead bullet, wildcats and precision reloading.
Web: www.precisionshooting.com.

Rifle Magazine

Wolfe Publishing Co., 2626 Stearman Road, Ste. A, Prescott, AZ 86301. 520-445-7810; Fax: 520-778-5124. The sporting firearms journal with solid information on blackpowder guns and shooting.

Safari Magazine

Safari Magazine, 4800 W. Gates Pass Rd., Tucson, AZ 85745. 602-620-1220. The journal of big game hunting, published by Safari Club International. Also publish Safari Times, a monthly newspaper, included in price of $55.00 national membership. While not dedicated to blackpowder shooting directly, Safari has pertinent information on worldwide hunting. A collectible magazine assembled by experts in the field.

Shoot! Magazine

Shoot! Magazine Corp., 1770 West State Street PMB 340, Boise ID 83702. 208-368-9920; Fax: 208-338-8428. Web site: www.shootmagazine.com Articles of interest to the cowboy action shooter, or others interested in Western-era firearms and ammunition. Handsome magazine loaded with ballistics and data on old-time guns. Collectible.

Shooting Industry

Publisher's Dev. Corp., 12345 World Trade Drive, San Diego, CA 92128. $50.00 yr. Includes information on blackpowder firearms and related items. A well-done trade publication.

Shooting Sports USA

National Rifle Assn. of America, 11250 Waples Mill Road, Fairfax, VA 22030. Annual subscriptions for NRA members are $5 for classified shooters and $10 for non-classified shooters. Covering events, techniques and personalities in competitive shooting.

Shooting Times

Primedia, 2 News Plaza, P.O. Box 1790, Peoria, IL 61656. 309-682-6626. Guns, shooting, reloading; articles on every gun activity, including occasional blackpowder.

Shotgun News

Primedia, 2 News Plaza, P.O. Box 1790, Peoria, IL 61656. 800-495-8362. Gun ads of all kinds, including many muzzle-loaders and blackpowder cartridge firearms.

The Single Shot Exhange Magazine

P.O. box 1055, York, SC 29745. Phone/Fax: 803-628-5326. Articles of interest to the blackpowder cartridge shooter and antique arms collector.

Single Shot Rifle Journal

Keith Foster, membership director. 419-393-2976. E-mail: kafos@defnet.com. Journal of the American Single Shot Rifle Assn.

Turkey Call

Natl. Wild Turkey Federation, Inc., P.O. Box 530, Edgefield, SC 29824. Information of interest for all who pursue the wild turkey, including blackpowder hunters.

Turkey & Turkey Hunting

Krause Publications, 700 E. State St., Iola, WI 54990-0001. Magazine with authoritative articles on all aspects of wild turkey behavior, biology and the successful ways to hunt better with that info. Learn the proper techniques to calling, the right equipment, and more, including blackpowder interests. Web site: www.krause.com.

The Varmint Hunter Magazine

The Varmint Hunters Assn., Box 759, Pierre, SD 57501. 800-528-4868.Valuable information for anyone interested in varmint hunting, including blackpowder hunters. Handsome magazine, well put together.

Blackpowder Associations

For the Fifth Edition, blackpowder associations will be listed only by name. Information pertaining to these associations on line is up to date, whereas listing presidents of the associations, or even what these organizations currently do is risking obsolescence. Example: as I was preparing this short list of associations (once again, go on line for a much longer list noted as *The Almost Complete List of Muzzle Loading and Buckskinner Links*) I called up "American Custom Gunmakers Guild" and was treated to full information on that blackpowder organization. State organizations are not included below. Every state has blackpowder associations, often many.

American Custom Gunmakers Guild
American Mountain Men
AmericanLongrifles.com
American Single Shot Rifle Association
American Society of Arms Collectors
Browning Collector's Association
The Cast Bullet Association Inc.
Colt Collectors Association
Contemporary Longrifle Association

Hopkins & Allen Arms & Memorabilia Society (HAAMS)
International Blackpowder Hunting Association
National Muzzle Loading Rifle Association
National Rifle Association of America
North-South Skirmish Association Inc.
Remington Society of America

Replica Percussion Revolver Association
Single Action Shooting Society
Southern California Schuetzen Society
Traditional Muzzleloader Association
U.S. Revolver Association
Winchester Arms Collectors Association

Tables

Tables of Weights & Measures

7,000 grains weight = 1 pound
437.5 grains weight = 1 ounce
15.43 grains weight = 1 gram
453.6 grams = 1 pound
25.4mm = 1 inch

Conversions

Pounds times 7,000 = grains weight
Ounces times 437.5 = grains weight
Grains times .00229 = ounces
Grams times 15.4324 = grains weight
Inches times 25.4 = millimeters
Millimeters times .03937 = inches

One meter = 39.37 inches
One yard = .914 meters
27.34 grains = 1 dram
16 drams = 1 ounce
2,000 pounds = 1 short ton
2,240 pounds = 1 long ton

Round Balls to the Pound

The following conversions are not exact, but are most useful in determining how many balls can be cast per pound of lead.

2-bore = balls to the pound
4-bore = balls to the pound
8-bore = 8 balls to the pound
10-bore = 10 balls to the pound
12-bore = 12 balls to the pound
20-bore = 20 balls to the pound
58-caliber = 25 balls to the pound
54-caliber = 30 balls to the pound
50-caliber = 40 balls to the pound
45-caliber = 53 balls to the pound
40-caliber = 75 balls to the pound
36-caliber = 108 balls to the pound
32-caliber = 155 balls to the pound

Directory of Manufacturers

ATK Ammunition and Related Products
900 Ehlen Drive
Anoka, MN 55303
Speer Bullets
2299 Snake River Avenue
Lewiston, ID 83501
208-746-2351
www.speer-bullets.com
Federal Cartridge Company with paper hulls available, Speer ammo and bullets for blackpowder guns, CCI caps, RCBS loading tools, and much more.

Atlanta Cutlery/Museum Replicas
2147 Gees Mill Road
Conyers, GA 30013
800-883-0300
www.atlantacutlery.com
Importer of antique firearms, especially Martini-Henry and similar rifles of the era, as well as accoutrements matching the guns. Also a huge lineup of knives, including Bowie designs.

A. Uberti Stoeger
Via Artigani 1, Gardone Val Trompia
Brecia, Italy 25063
011-39-030-834-1800
www.ubertireplicas.com
Long line of replica blackpowder revolvers and lever-action rifles, including the 1873 in 44-40.

Atsko/Sno-Seal, Inc.
2664 Russell Street
Orangeburg, SC 29115
800-845-2728
www.atsko.com
Important products for all hunters, but especially blackpowder hunters: includes numerous chemicals that eliminate scent, vital for close stalking and blind work. Also Sport Wash to rid clothing of human aroma. Sno-Seal for hunting boots.

Austin & Halleck, Inc.
2122 South 950 East
Provo, UT 84606-6258
801-371-0412
www.austinhalleck.com
Beautiful traditional Mountain Rifle, 50-caliber choice of 1:66 twist for ball, 1:28 for conical, percussion or flint, fancy grade available. Also a handsome and reliable modern muzzleloader, the 420 in .45 or .50 calibers. Fine workmanship. Additionally, a Model 694 American Classic lever-action reminiscent of the Model 92 Winchester in style, but 45- or 50-caliber muzzleloader. And a powerful modern muzzleloader shotgun.

Ballard Rifle, LLC
113 W. Yellowstone
Cody, WY 82414
866-997-4353
www.ballardrifles.com
Faithful high-grade reproductions of the famous Ballard rifle in various calibers. Quite probably surpasses the original in materials.

Ballistic Products, Inc. (BPI)
20015 75th Ave. North
Corcoran, MN 55340-9456
763-494-9237
www.ballisticproducts.com
Super lineup of blackpowder shotgun components, including hulls and non-toxic shot, such as Bismuth. Catalog filled with valuable shotgun information.

Ballistic Technology, Inc.
3702 Rocky Branch Road
Princeton, WV 24740
www.thebullettesttube.com
The Bullet Test Tube is designed to trap bullets in a special medium that mimics animal tissue. More than trapping a bullet, however, the Test Tube media is cut down the center to reveal the wound channel produced by the bullet.

Barnes Bullets, Inc.
750 North 2600 West
Lindon, UT 84042
801-756-4222
www.barnesbullets.com
Long list of high-grade blackpowder Expander MZ bullets as well as CR-10 solvent, the latter useful in removing copper fouling.

Battenfeld Technologies, Inc.
5885 West Van Horn Tavern Road
Columbia, MO 65203
573-445-9200
http://www.battenfeldtechnologies.com
Excellent rests for testing firearms, along with a host of high quality shooting accessories such as the Past recoil protector and Tipton rods, high-grade shooting chemicals.

Bear Creek Supply
P.O. Box 177
Waterford, CA 95386
209-874-4322
www.bearcreeksupply.com
Hard cast bullets promised not to lead the bore, including 32-20 118-grain, 38-40 180-grain, and 38-55 255-grain.

BELL Brass
See Buffalo Arms Company for the former BELL line of brass.
Cartridge cases for long line of ammunition—of special interest to shooters of old-time blackpowder cartridge guns.

Bismuth Cartridge Co.
7155 Valjean Avenue
Van Nuys, CA 91406
818-909-4742
www.bismuth-nottox.com
Blackpowder shotgunners are grateful to have bismuth shot available, especially for shotguns not especially designed for steel shot. Bismuth offers a non-toxic shot that can be fired in non-steel bores.

Black Hills Ammunition
P.O. Box 3090
Rapid City, SD 57709-3090
605-348-5150
www.black-hills.com
Excellent ammunition for blackpowder firearms, including 32-20 Winchester, 45-70, and 45 Schofield.

Brownells, Inc.
200 South Front Street
Montezuma, IA 50171
641-623-5401
www.brownells.com
Tremendous catalog of shooting accessories, including rifle cleaning cradles, numerous chemicals, and supplies of all kinds, including gunsmithing tools.

Browning
One Browning Place
Morgan, UT 84050
801-876-2711
www.browning.com
Beautiful and accurate Model 1885 Winchester replica in blackpowder cartridge calibers, along with a long line of shooting and hunting products.

Buffalo Arms Company
660 Vermeer Court
Ponderay, ID 83852
208-263-6953
www.buffaloarms.com
Headquarters for Cowboy Action Shooting clothing and supplies, long line of high-grade shooting accessories. Also cartridge cases for blackpowder rifles.

Buffalo Bullet Company
12637 Los Nietos Road
Unit A
Santa Fe Springs, CA 90670
800-423-8069
 Large list of blackpowder bullets including round balls as well as numerous conical designs such as the SSB spitzer.

Bushnell Performance Optics
9200 Cody
Overland Park, KS 66214
913-752-3400
www.bushnell.com
 Numerous telescopic rifle sights suitable for blackpowder muzzleloader and other arms along with special blackpowder scope for low light hunting. Binoculars in numerous power ranges and configurations.

Cheaper Than Dirt!
2524 NE Loop 820
Fort Worth, TX 76106-1809
817-378-5101
www.CheaperThanDirt.com
 A gold mine of bargain priced outdoor tools for the blackpowder hunter or any hunter, including clothing, tents, bivy, as well as a long lineup of military surplus items.

Cimarron Firearms Company
P.O. Box 906
Fredericksburg, TX 78624-0906
830-997-9090
www.cimarron-firearms.com
 Investment-quality historical reproduction firearms, especially Colt revolvers and lever-action blackpowder cartridge rifles. Lots of Cowboy Shooting Action guns, leather accessories.

Circle Fly Wads
3 Parlett Road
Airville, PA 17302
717-862-3600
www.circlefly.com
 Specializing in shotgun wads for blackpowder shotgun shells, including brass, as well as a long line of other wads.

Cold Steel, Inc.
3036-A Seaborg Avenue
Ventura, CA 93003
805-650-8481
www.coldsteel.com
 Extremely worthy tomahawks and many other useful cutlery implements built to withstand heavy-duty labor. Interesting lineup of knives, including cooking tools.

Dixie Gun Works
1412 West Reelfoot Ave.
Union City, TN 38281
731-885-0561
www.dixiegunworks.com
 Huge (and interesting) catalog filled with blackpowder supplies from nipple picks to firearms. A must-have catalog for the blackpowder shooter interested in any phase of the sport.

E.M.F. Company, Inc.
1900 E. Warner Ave. I-D
Santa Ana, CA 92705
949-261-6611
www.emf-company.com
 Cowboy Action Shooting reproduction guns of the Old West along with single-shot blackpowder rifles.

Forster Products, Inc.
310 E. Lanark Ave.
Lanark, IL 61046
815-493-6360
www.forsterproducts.com
 Well-made and well-designed reloading tools for the blackpowder cartridge enthusiast, including the Tap-O-Cap tool for making shooting caps for muzzleloaders.

GOEX, Inc.
P.O. Box 659
Dayline, LA 71023
318-382-9300
www.goexpowder.com
 Widely available blackpowder for muzzle-loading and blackpowder guns. Blackpowder available in different grades for different applications.

Hardigg Cases
147 North Main Street
South Deerfield, MA 01373
800-542-7344
www.stormcase.com
 The Storm Case is one of the most advanced firearm protection devices ever. Hardigg offers the case in many different sizes and shapes, as well as colors. The company claim is that nothing stands up to the power of a Storm Case. The blackpowder hunter—or any hunter—will find this statement to be true.

The Hawken Shop
P.O. Box 593
Oak Harbor, WA 98277
360-679-5657
 Original Hawken rifles and a great deal more. Fine accoutrements , locks, trade goods, knives, tomahawks (old-time beauties), collectibles, and much more. One of the more interesting modern day "old-time" shops.

Hodgdon Powder Company
P.O. Box 2932
Shawnee Mission, KS 66201
913-362-9455
www.hodgdon.com
 Hodgdon Powder Company has world famous Pyrodex and Pyrodex Pellets, but also powerful Triple Seven and Triple Seven Pellets. Triple Seven makes cleanup almost smokeless powder-simple.

Hornady Manufacturing Co.
P.O. Box 1848
Grand Island, NE 68802-1390
308-382-1390
www.hornady.com
 Excellent swaged round balls in many muzzleloader dimensions, as well as a line of pistol bullets for sabots. Also a blackpowder powder measure. And other high-quality products.

Huntington Die Specialties
601 Oro Dam Blvd.
P.O. Box 991
Oroville, CA 95965
www.huntingtons.com
 Provider of hard-to-find handloading equipment as well as reloading components.

Inhibitor – Van Patten Industries
P.O. Box 6694
Rockford, IL 61125
877-464-4248
http://www.theinhibitor.com
 The Inhibitor Rust Prevention System is scientifically formulated to protect metal surfaces from rust and corrosion. The key word is protection of all types of sporting equipment subject to rust and/or corrosion.

Kadooty Manufacturing, LLC
842 South Tamela Dr.
Lake Charles, LA 70605
318-477-7502
 Manufacturers of the Kadooty loading rod that supplies the same pressure upon the powder charge shot after shot.

Knight Rifles
P.O. Box 130
Centerville, IA 52544-2628
515-856-2626
www.knightrifles.com
 Knight is long in the business with modern muzzleloaders noted for accuracy and sure ignition with No. 209 primers. A prime example is the Knight Revolution muzzleloader, an ultramodern muzzleloader that comes with a 100-yard accuracy guarantee.

Lee Precision, Inc.
4275 Highway U
Hartford, WI 53027
262-673-3075
www.leeprecision.com

Blackpowder bullet moulds in various calibers and designs, along with some of the world's best reloading dies, also for various cartridges.

Legacy Sports International
206 South Union Street
Alexandria, VA 22314
703-548-4837
www.legacysports.com

The handsome Puma rifle Model 92 with 24-inch barrel comes in 357/38 Special and 45 Colt for Cowboy Action Shooting and hunting.

Lyman Products
475 Smith Street
Middletown, CT 06457
860-632-2020
www.lymanproducts.com

A world of useful equipment for blackpowder shooters, including superb moulds for numerous bullets, a blackpowder loading manual and a blackpowder powder measure. Also the 50-caliber Plains Pistol and Mustang Breakaway 209 Magnum Muzzleloader with magnetized primer retention system.

McGowan Manufacturing Company
4854 N. Shamrock Place, Suite 100
Tucson, AZ 85705
520-219-9759
www.mcgowanmfg.com

Numerous interesting items for the outdoor enthusiast, including the FireStone sharpener for knives. Also unique hand axes for the hunter who desires a highly compact trail-worthy tool. There is a throwing axe as well.

Michaels of Oregon Co.
P.O. Box 1690
Oregon City, OR 97045
503-655-7964
www.michaels-oregon.com

Many blackpowder shooting accessories.

Naval Ordnance Works
Route 2, Box 919
Shepherdstown, WV 25443
304-876-0998

Long line of various (sometimes rare) bullets including 4-bore and Minies for muzzleloaders.

Midway USA
5875 W. Van Horn Tavern Rd.
Columbia, MO 65203
573-445-6363
www.midwayusa.com

Mail-order house for over 12,000 shooting and reloading products from over 100 different manufacturers.

Millett Sights
16131-K Gothard St.
Huntington Beach, CA 92647
714-842-5575
www.millettsights.com

Quality scope sights for muzzleloaders along with special mounts for certain blackpowder guns.

Navy Arms Company
219 Lawn St.
Martinsburg, WV 25401
304-262-1658
www.navyarms.com

Dedicated to high-quality replica muzzleloaders and blackpowder cartridge guns, including the Whitworth 45-caliber rifled musket. Many interesting handguns, including 58-caliber pistols.

NEI Handtools, Inc.
P.O. Box 370356
El Paso, TX 79937-0356
915-772-0259
nei@columbia-center.org

Precision cast bullet moulds in a wide array of styles and calibers for muzzleloaders and blackpowder cartridge guns.

Northern Precision
329 S. James St.
Carthage, NY 13619
315-493-1711

Custom swaged bullets including a good lineup of accurate jacketed bullets for muzzleloaders.

October Country Muzzleoading, Inc.
P.O. Box 969
Hayden, ID 83835
800-735-6348
www.octobercountry.com

High-quality leather for blackpowder shooters, especially long line of shooting bags, also big bore rifles from caliber 62 all the way to 4-bore.

Oehler Research, Inc.
P.O. Box 9135
Austin, TX 78766
512-327-6900
www.oehler-research.com

Laboratory-quality chronographs at affordable prices for the shooter who wants to know "what his guns really get."

Ox-Yoke Originals
Division of Rightnour Manufacturing Co.
P.O. Box 168
Mingoville, PA 16856

Now combined with Rightnour Manufacturing Company, Ox-Yoke lubrications, cleaners, patches, wads, and myriad other items for blackpowder shooting are once again available. The same original high quality is observed in all Ox-Yoke products now manufactured at the Rightnour plant.

Old Western Scrounger, Inc.
219 Lawn Street
Martinsburg, WV 25401
304-262-9870
www.ows-ammo.com

One of the most interesting catalogs in the market with numerous blackpowder cartridges ready to shoot as well as Orange Stuff blackpowder lube. Now a part of Navy Arms.

Oregon Trail Bullet Company
P.O. Box 529
Baker City, OR 97814-0529
800-811-0548
www.laser-cast.com

Long list of hard cast (no leading) bullets ready to be fired in numerous blackpowder cartridge rifles, such as the 38-55 and 45 Colt.

Parker Productions
691 Bluegrass Dr.
Spring Creek, NV 89815
775-753-2195

The Hydra-Shock heavyweight conical bullet with internal oil reservoir for certain bullet upset. Also jacketed pistol bullets in sabots.

Pedersoli
Via Artigani 47
Gardone V.T. (BS)
Italy, 25063
011-39-0308915000
www.davide-pedersoli.com

A wealth of fine blackpowder firearms including muzzleloaders and breechloaders, especially the Rolling Block sporting rifle in 38-55 caliber as well as a reproduction of the slide-action Colt Lightning blackpowder rifle (improved with new safety features that do not take away from authenticity), plus Denali In-Line rifle with 209 ignition.

Redding Reloading Equipment
1089 Starr Rd.
Cortland, NY 13045
607-753-3331
www.redding-reloading.com

Top-quality loading equipment including dies, the SAECO lubri-sizer, lead hardness tester, and bullet moulds.

Remington Arms Co., Inc.
P.O. Box 700
Madison, NC 27025-0700
336-548-8700
www.remington.com

Remington Model 700 ML muzzleloading rifle with Model 700 bolt action, also blackpowder bullets and percussion caps. Also the Omega modern muzzleloader with unique features.

RUGER

Sturm, Ruger & Co.
200 Ruger Rd.
Prescott, AZ 86301
520-541-8820
www.ruger-firearms.com

Ruger bolt-action blackpowder rifles built along the same lines as the Ruger Model 77 cartridge rifle. Also, Ruger Old Army 45-caliber cap 'n' ball revolver with optional fully adjustable target sights. Ruger Vaquero revolver for Cowboy Action shooting in various sub-models.

Savage Arms, Inc.

118 Mountain Rd.
Suffield, CT 06078
413-568-7001
www.savagearms.com

The Savage 10 M-II bolt-action muzzleloading rifle is rugged and reliable with high velocity loading potential and 209 ignition. The only muzzleloader allowed smokeless powder at the time of the Fifth Edition.

Schuetzen Powder, LLC

7650 US Highway 287, No. 100
Arlington, TX 76001
866-809-9704
www.schuetzenpowder.com

Swiss Black Powder, plus Elephant Brand Black Powder (Brazil) and Schuetzen Black Powder (Germany), the latter produced by the Wano factory. Excellent choices for muzzleloader and blackpowder cartridge.

Shiloh Sharps Rifle Manufacturing Company

201 Centennial Drive, POB 279
Big Timber, MT 59001
406-932-4266
www.shilohrifle.com

Excellent Sharps rifles in many different models, such as the Model 1863 percussion, along with numerous 1874 models, including "The Quigley." Many cartridge choices. Top-grade workmanship.

Starline Company

1300 West Henry
Sedalia, MO 65301
800-280-6660
www.starlinebrass.com

Manufacturers of brass cartridges cases for blackpowder (and other) cartridge guns, including 50-90 Sharps, 38-55, and a number of revolver cartridges.

Thompson/Center Arms Co.

P.O. Box 5002
Rochester, NH 03867
603-332-2394
www.tcarms.com

Complete line of blackpowder products and firearms including the powerful 209x50 pistol, as well as the popular Omega and the highly advanced Pro-Hunter rifle with ultra modern features.

TDC – Tedd Cash Manufacturing Company

201 South Klein Drive, POB 130
Waunakee, WI 53597-0130
608-849-5664
www.tdcmfg.com

Super-quality, authentically manufactured blackpowder accoutrements of many kinds, including Universal Capper, Rifle Capper, capboxes, and much more.

Ten-X Ammunition

5650 Arrow Highway
Montclair, CA 91737
909-605-1617
www.TenXAmmo.com

Completely revised plant with upgraded ammunition for Cowboy Action Shooting as well as single-shot and lever-action blackpowder cartridge rifles. From 25-20 to 45-120 Sharps and larger. Many revolver calibers, including 45 Russian and 45 Schofield.

Traditions Performance Firearms

P.O. Box 776
Old Saybrook, CT 06475-0776
860-388-4656
www.traditionsfirearms.com

In-line and sidelock muzzleloading rifles, pistols, shotguns, and accessories at competitive prices in various models.

United States Firearms Mfg. Co.

445-453 Ledyard Street
Hartford, Connecticut 06114
877-227-6901
http://www.usfirearms.com

Go on line for dealer locations for these guns advertised as "Old West Firearms and Rifles Hand-made in Hartford, CT." Along with Colt handguns, such as the USFA Cowboy in 45 Colt or 38 Special, there is the Colt Lightning slide-action rifle—100 percent American Made.

White Rifles

77 North Skyline Drive (55-58)
Roosevelt, UT 84006
877-684-4867
www.whitemuzzleloading.com

White in-line muzzleloading rifles in several models, powerful 12-gauge Tominator shotgun, PowerStar SCS Self-Cleaning Saboted Bullets, plus line of accoutrements.

Wild West Guns, Inc.

7521 Old Seward Highway
Anchorage, AK 99518
907-344-4500
www.wildwestguns.com

Custom rifles, also replacement trigger and after-market parts for Marlin 336 rifles.

Winchester Ammunition

427 N. Shamrock St.
East Alton, IL 62024-1174
618-258-2000
www.winchester.com

Winchester has 38-55 brass, 209 primers for muzzleloaders, and several blackpowder cartridges ready to shoot.

Winchester Muzzleloading

5988 Peachtree Corners East
Norcross, GA 30071
770-449-4687
www.winchestermuzzleloading.com

Modern in-line style bolt-action muzzleloading rifle, plus a line of accessories.

XS Sight Systems, Inc.

2401 Ludelle
Fort Worth, TX 76105
817-536-0136
www.xssights.com

Excellent PowerRod with rotating T-handle. Also the home of the Ghost Ring sight system: Ghost Ring aperture sights coupled with White Stripe front sights.

Glossary

Accoutrement – (traditional), also accouterment (modern)—accessories pertaining to shooting, military origin, to exclude rifle and uniform.

Action – the "workings" of a firearm, lever-action, rolling block action, etc. Does not pertain to muzzleloaders.

Ampco nipple – this name applied to a special nipple made of Beryllium alloy. Although a Beryllium nipple resembles brass, it is much harder and it resists corrosion and rust. These nipples are also noted for a smaller than average flash hole to promote a more concentrated, and therefore hotter flame.

Aperture sight – also "peep sight" in everyday talk—essentially a rear sight with a hole (peep or aperture)—looking through the hole naturally centers the eye—aperture is then ignored and only front sight is aligned on target.

Back-Action Lock – sidelock muzzleloader where mainspring lies behind the hammer and tumbler rather than in front of the hammer.

Bar-Action Lock – standard sidelock muzzleloader where the hammer is located in front of the mainspring and hammer.

Ball – in modern military a full metal jacket projectile; also any bullet, such as a "round ball" or "conical ball."

Ballistic coefficient – noted as C, a number assigned to correspond to a bullet's ability to retain initial velocity—the higher the C, the better retention of bullet speed.

Ballistics – Nicolo Tartaglia, the father of ballistics, publishes his first treatise on the subject in 1537. A science of bullets in motion—interior ballistics within the bore, exterior ballistics from muzzle to projectile's final destination. Terminal ballistics—bullet's effect upon the target.

Barleycorn – A front sight style of military origin named for its resemblance to a grain of barley—presents the image of a truncated triangle, normally mounted low on the barrel, popular pre-20th century.

Barrel Pin – rather than a key holding barrel and stock together, this muzzleloader uses pins. Pins may be tapered. Therefore it is important to drive them out in the right direction to prevent splitting the stock.

Battery – may be two or more firearms, also meaning "ready to fire." A gun in battery is loaded and cocked.

Black powder – spelled as blackpowder to remove any and all reference to its color. Originally "gunpowder," a mixture of saltpeter (potassium nitrate), charcoal, and sulfur (see Chapter 23).

Bolster – the lump of metal as part of the lock that contains the nipple seat and nipple threaded into the nipple seat.

Blowback – the effect of gas from powder combustion working rearward rather than toward the muzzle to propel a projectile. The venturi principle states that the greater volume of gas from combustion will exit the larger volume escape—the muzzle of a gun rather than the touchhole or vent of a flintlock or caplock.

Bore – refers to the interior of the gun barrel, but also size of a projectile. The smaller the number the larger the bore, since reference is to "balls per pound." A 4-bore is four lead round balls to the pound, while a 2-bore is two lead round balls per pound, or twice the weight. A 4-bore round bullet goes 1,750-grains weight, while a 2-bore round bullet runs 3,500-grains weight. Sometimes referred to in "gauge."

Breech – generally the "back end" of a gun barrel, which may also contain the action. A breechloader, also breech-loader, opens at the back end to accept a cartridge, metallic, paper, linen, etc. The muzzleloader has a closed breech section—see chamber.

Breech plug – the threaded device blocking the chamber section of a barrel, removal on most modern muzzleloaders for cleaning the bore from the breech end.

Buckhorn sight – a rear sight with projections resembling horns on either side of the notch—said by some to block part of target, but in fact quite workable in shooting.

Buckshot – large pellets for smoothbore guns (shotguns) designated by numbers—the smaller the number, the larger the shot—hence, No. 4 Buck is smaller than No. 0 buck, which is smaller than No. 00 (Double aught) or No. 000 (triple-aught).

Bullet – pertaining to any single missile fired from a gun—not to be confused with shot. A bullet can be round or conical.

Caliber – the size of a single projectile, not shot, which in turn designates the size of the bore. Expressed by a number. May or may not be preceded by a decimal. Hence .50-caliber or 50-caliber. Noted in inches as well as decimals. A .50-caliber bullet is one-half inch diameter. A 7mm bullet is .284-inch diameter.

Capper – tool containing and dispensing percussion caps. See Chapters 4 and 5.

Casting (bullet casting) – the act of making bullets using molten lead poured into a mould to form a specific shape.

Centerfire – a metallic cartridge case that contains, centered in the head, a primer for ignition as opposed to a rimfire case, which holds priming mixture around the rim of the case head.

Chamber – the section of the barrel that contains the cartridge. Usually referred to as breech or breech section on a muzzleloader rather than chamber.

Charge – normally preceded by type of charge—powder charge, shot charge. But can also mean the combination of both projectile and powder. Also a "charged gun," meaning it is loaded.

Choke – a rifle can be choke-bored, meaning that the bore decreases in size, generally toward the muzzle. Shotgun: choke can be a constriction or "jug" type, the latter also known as recessed choke—both designed to encourage a shot pattern to maintain integrity downrange. The more choke, the "tighter" the pattern, as in Full choke or Extra Full choke.

Cock – archaic term for hammer.

Conical – elongated bullet to discriminate from round bullet. Cylindrical. Also cylindro-conoidal and cylindrical.

Dram – a measurement equal to 27.32 grains weight per unit. Sometimes referred to as drachm in old literature. A drachm was actually an apothecary weight of 60.0 grains. However, in shooting use drachm actually meant dram, or 27.34 grains weight. Modern shotshells still refer to "dram equivalent," such as 3 3/4-Dram Equivalent, as reference to blackpowder days when that particular shotshell was loaded with 3-1/4 drams of blackpowder. The reference is vague today, but remains in use.

Drift – in shooting there are two types of

drift—a projectile "drifting to the right or to the left" of aiming point due to rotation on its axis. A right-hand twist will encourage a projectile to drift right, and vice versa. There is also wind drift, where a projectile moves away from the aiming point in the direction of the wind.

Dross – everything floating on top of molten lead, not necessarily impurities, since dross may also contain lead, tin, and other elements that are not in themselves impure.

Escutcheon – placed where the key or wedge protrudes through the stock, the escutcheon lends strength at that point, but also prevents splitting out and is decorative as well.

Elevation – in concert with windage (below), elevation is the vertical movement of sights to cause the bullet to fly higher or lower.

Eprouvette – a powder tester. Fired by a flintlock mechanism, it was used to test the strength of blackpowder in the early days. Its use declined as blackpowder quality improved.

Fs – used to designate kernel size for blackpowder and blackpowder substitutes. The more Fs, the smaller the kernel. Fg (1F) is the largest kernel size in general shooting use, while FFFFg (4F) is considered pan powder, but there is also FFFFFg (5F).

Flash – as in "flash in the pan," a term describing pan powder ignition (flash) without ignition of the main charge in the breech. Also flash hole, the small orifice through which flame goes from primer to powder in a cartridge case.

Flask – a container made of various materials, including brass and other metals as well as leather—may contain powder or shot—powder flask, shot flask. May have interchangeable tubes to vary amount of charge. See Chapters 4 and 5.

Flint – referred to by some "buckskinners" as the "stone," because it is stone, a special stone of hardness capable of scraping hot curls of metal from a "steel" to start a fire or from the frizzen on a flintlock.

Flintlock – lock type, spring-driven, that brings a hammer or cock downward with trigger pull, the jaws of the hammer holding a flint which scrapes against a piece of metal (frizzen) to create sparks (hot curls of metal) that ignite fine-grain powder in a pan, which in turn sends a jet of flame directed to a passageway (touchhole) to the main charge in the breech for ignition of the rifle, pistol, or fowler (shotgun).

Fly – more properly a detent, but known as a "fly in the tumbler." The detent is a piece of metal that prevents the nose of the sear from falling down into the half-cock notch when the trigger is pulled.

Fouling – residue remaining after powder combustion, consisting of several chemicals. See Chapter 23.

Fowler – smoothbore shoulder arm generally thought of as a flintlock shotgun; however, also capable of firing a patched ball.

Frizzen – also noted as frizzle in some literature—the metal piece upon which the flint strikes in a flintlock firearm to cause sparks (curls of hot iron) that in turn ignite pan powder for ignition.

Fusil – mainly noted as a smoothbore flintlock firearm light in weight. May also refer to a device to accept a primer in place of a percussion cap.

Gauge – The smaller the number, the larger the bore, hence a 20-gauge is smaller in bore diameter than a 12-gauge, a 12-gauge smaller than a 10-gauge, and so forth. See "bore."

German silver – also known as electrum, bright and shiny metal, often used for front sights.

Grain – not to be confused with kernel (one piece of powder). Grain refers to weight. There are 7,000 grains weight in one pound.

Gram – metric weight measurement. One gram weighs 15.43 grains weight. There are 453.6 grams in one pound weight.

Hangfire – also hang-fire, a delay from trigger pull to ignition of powder charge, not to be confused with misfire.

Hawken – used generically to denote a specific rifle type of the first part of the 1800s associated with the mountain man—usually, but not always half-stock; usually, but not always percussion. Noted also as "plains rifle" and "mountain rifle." Specifically, rifles built by the Hawken brothers, Sam and Jake.

Ignition – various ways of "setting off" the main charge in the breech area of a gun or in a cartridge, accomplished in various ways—matchlock, flintlock, caplock, primer. Also accomplished in various mechanical ways, such as in-line ignition, underhammer, sidehammer, bolster, etc. See Chapter 19.

Kernel – also granule—one piece of powder, not to be confused with grain, which is a unit of weight.

Lock – referring to the mechanism that operates certain guns, such as sidelock muzzleloaders, but also shotguns, etc. See Chapter 2.

Mass – while often taken simply as weight in various formulas, mass is actually computed by dividing weight of the body by the acceleration of gravity (constant). Mass provides inertia. More mass, more inertia. Bullets of greater mass retain energy better than bullets of lower mass. But for shooting, weight works fine in place of mass most of the time.

Minie – name of a conical bullet with a hollow base for obturation, credited to C.E. Minie of the French army, but challenged by W. Greener of England.

Misfire – Unlike a hangfire, a misfire occurs when the trigger is pulled but the gun does not "go off" at all.

Mould – block with an interior impression of a bullet shape. Molten lead poured into the block results in a bullet of that particular shape.

Nipple – also known as a "tube" in the 19th century, the nipple is the device that retains the percussion cap in place on its cone (top) with a vent (passageway) through the nipple and into the main charge in the breech. Also called a "cone" before "nipple" became popular, although cone is better used today to indicate the very top of the nipple.

Obturation – a product of inertia. An object at rest remains at rest until acted upon by a force. A bullet remains at rest until a force (powder/gas) makes it move. The initial force on the resting bullet can cause it to very slightly "fatten out" before moving. The concept of obturation is vital to the success of the Minie bullet and all bullets with hollow bases.

Patridge sight – erroneously, "partridge." Named for E.E. Patridge, who developed the sight in the 1880s. The theme of the Patridge is "square." A square-topped front sight optically nestles into a square rear sight notch. The flattop blade front sight is often optically placed just underneath the target in the "6-o'clock hold."

Pipe – sometimes used in place of thimble, the tube through which the ramrod runs beneath the barrel. Sometimes called ferrules.

Percussion – as in percussion cap, ignition with impact sensitive chemical, normally contained in a small cup—hence percussion cap.

Powderhorn – also powder horn, actual animal horn in which the interior is used to hold powder. See Chapters 4 and 5 for merits of horn as a powder container.

Ramrod – rod of various materials, wood, metal, composites, etc., resting in the pipes or thimbles of the muzzleloader (and other guns) for the purpose of loading/cleaning, etc. Not to be confused with wiping stick.

Recoil – rearward thrust from a fired gun explained by Newton's Third Law of Motion—every action has an opposite and equal reaction.

Reticule – sometimes "reticle," but properly reticule—the aiming device within the tube of a telescopic sight, as in crosshair.

Rifling – never "riflings," grooves cut into the bore of a barrel angled so as to impart rotation to a projectile. Cutting grooves forms a raised portion referred to as lands. It is the lands that cut into the patch, sabot, or directly into the bullet.

Sabot – pronounced sah-bow from the French, originally "peasant's shoe," a "shoe" of bore size that holds a bullet of sub-bore dimension. Rifling imparts rotational value to the sabot, which in turn transfers rotational value to the bullet within the sabot. The sabot drops off downrange, usually within 20 yards or so (roughly).

Sear – a gun part that serves to engage the hammer or other device, such as a striker in some in-line muzzleloaders. When the trigger is pulled, the sear relinquishes its lock on the hammer or striker.

Sectional density – simplified as the relation to a bullet's diameter to its length, but in fact a mathematical expression usually in three-place decimal, such as .226, indicating the ratio of a bullet's mass (not weight, but mass) to its cross-sectional area. Short fat bullets have low SD, while bullets "long for their caliber" have a higher SD—mass must be included, however, to derive a specific SD.

Short-start – failure to fully seat a projectile down upon the powder charge in the breech of the gun.

Sight radius – simply the distance between the front and rear sight normally measured in inches and fraction thereof. A long sight radius may help "older eyes" in focusing from front to rear sight.

Snail – a shield that lies beneath the curve of the hammer on a muzzleloader to divert pieces of exploded percussion cap away from the shooter.

Spitzer bullet – around 1904 the Germans devised a process of making a more streamlined bullet. They called the new bullet "spitzgeschossen" for "pointed bullet." Americanized, the word became spitzer, but with the same meaning—streamlined bullet. The Buffalo Bullet Company's SSB is an example of spitzer blackpowder bullet.

Sprue – the small tail-like projection of lead left on a cast bullet after casting, removed with a sprue cutter on some moulds, but also by hand with certain moulds that do not have a sprue cutter. The place where the sprue was cut away is generally loaded facing outward from the muzzle and centered.

Standard deviation – standard deviation, SD, is a measure of variance. While the concept comes from the fields of education and psychology, mainly, it applies well to shooting. A low SD indicates greater uniformity from one shot to the next, while a higher SD indicates less uniformity from shot to shot.

Swan shot – an early shot made by pouring molten lead through a screen, which left a little "tail" on the pellet that reminded one of a swan's tail.

Tenon – a piece of metal integral to the underside of the barrel with a slot to accept a wedge or key, which in turn retains the barrel to the stock.

Thimble – sometimes referred to as a pipe, the tube through which the ramrod runs under the barrel. The first thimble near the muzzle is called the entry thimble.

Touchhole – the passageway from the pan of the flintlock into the breech where the main powder charge resides.

Trajectory – bullets do not "fly flat" from any gun, no matter starting velocity. Instead, the projectile describes an arc. While the arc is not exactly a parabola, it comes close enough.

Tube sight – not necessarily noted as forerunner to the scope sight, the tube sight was just that—a tube without lenses, but could have some form of aiming device within it. Its main function was concentration of sight picture.

Tumbler – interior part of the lock that holds the half-cock notch and full-cock notch, as well as fly (detent) if there is one. The tumbler is responsible for hammer movement when the trigger is pulled and the sear is disengaged.

Wedge – also key, the piece of metal, flat, that runs through the stock to hold the barrel and the stock together.

Windage – two meanings: windage is the space between a round bullet in the bore and the walls of the bore, that space taken up by the patch. It also refers to the horizontal (left-right) movement of sights to bring a bullet to fire to the left or the right.

Wiping stick – also wiping rod, like a ramrod only longer and therefore better suited to loading and cleaning at the shooting range.

The Ultimate Blackpowder Library

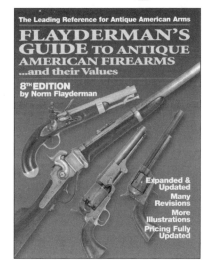
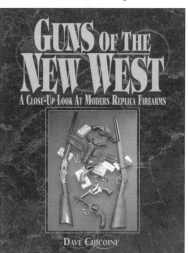

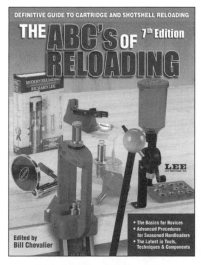
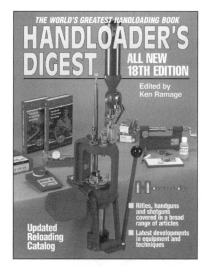

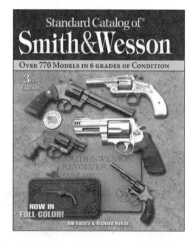
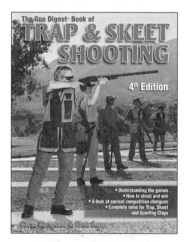